Years of Peril and Ambition

The Oxford History of the United States

David M. Kennedy, *General Editor*

YEARS OF PERIL AND AMBITION

U.S. Foreign Relations, 1776–1921

GEORGE C. HERRING

OXFORD
UNIVERSITY PRESS

OXFORD
UNIVERSITY PRESS

Oxford University Press is a department of the University of Oxford.
It furthers the University's objective of excellence in research, scholarship,
and education by publishing worldwide. Oxford is a registered trade mark of
Oxford University Press in the UK and certain other countries.

Published in the United States of America by Oxford University Press
198 Madison Avenue, New York, NY 10016, United States of America.

© Oxford University Press 2008

First published as an Oxford University Press paperback in 2011
Two-volume second edition published in 2017

Names: Herring, George C., 1936- author.
Title: From colony to superpower / George C. Herring.
Description: Second edition. | New York : Oxford University Press, 2017. |
    Revision of paperback edition published in 2011. | Includes
    bibliographical references and index.
Identifiers: LCCN 2016025664| ISBN 9780190212469 (vol. 1 : pbk.) |
    ISBN 9780190212476 (vol. 2 : pbk.)
Subjects: LCSH: United States—Foreign relations.
Classification: LCC E183.7 .H44 2017 | DDC 327.73—dc23 LC record available at
https://lccn.loc.gov/2016025664

Acknowledgments

My thanks, once again, to Susan Ferber of Oxford University Press for guiding the parent volume, *From Colony to Superpower*, to completion. Susan also developed the idea for this split edition and got the project under way. Tim Bent took it over last year, offered insightful comments on the new material, and helped get these volumes ready for publication. Alyssa O'Connell managed with admirable efficiency the acquisition of permissions for the images and took care of numerous other tasks that go with the production of a book. I enjoyed working with her, and greatly appreciate her help. Thomas Finnegan skillfully copyedited the new material, and Amy Whitmer patiently and with good humor guided this Luddite through the process of electronic editing.

As General Editor of the Oxford History of the United States series, David M. Kennedy rescued me several times during the production of *From Colony to Superpower* and these two volumes. He helped establish the framework for this split edition and pushed me on several very important features until I got them right. David has no peer as an editor.

My wife, Dottie Leathers, has continued to support my research and writing long after she might have asked whether I couldn't find something else to do. These volumes, like *From Colony to Superpower*, are dedicated to her with my love.

Contents

Years of Peril and Ambition

Introduction

In late 1776, Benjamin Franklin braved a month-long passage to Europe in cramped quarters aboard a small ship in stormy seas. Already an international celebrity for his scientific experiments, the seventy-year-old diplomat traveled to France as a supplicant, seeking the money and supplies desperately needed to sustain his infant nation's then precarious war for independence against world power Great Britain. Less than a century and a half later, in December 1918, United States president Woodrow Wilson crossed the Atlantic in nine days aboard the luxury liner SS *George Washington* convoyed by the battleship *Pennsylvania* and escorted into the French port of Brest by an armada of ten battleships and twenty-eight destroyers. The United States by this time had established itself as the world's greatest economic power. Its intervention in the Great War in 1917 tipped the scales for the Allies. Wilson came to Europe as a peacemaker with the dream not simply of negotiating a treaty formally ending the war but also of creating an enduring peace by reshaping world politics and economics according to American principles.

Years of Peril and Ambition charts the meteoric rise of the United States from a loose group of small, disparate, and quarrelsome British colonies huddled along the Atlantic coast of North America and surrounded by often hostile Indians and the possessions of unfriendly European nations into an economic giant and emerging great power at the end of World War I.

It is an epic story, of restless settlers pushing out against weak restraints, of explorers, sea captains, adventurers, merchants and missionaries carrying American ways to new lands. It analyzes countless crises, some erupting in war, others resolved peaceably through skillful diplomacy, inadvertence, or luck. Above all, *Years of Peril and Ambition* is a history of United States' expansionism, commercial and political, across the North American continent, into the Caribbean and Pacific, and beyond.

A grand cast of characters parades through these pages: statesmen like George Washington, Abraham Lincoln, and of course Wilson; diplomats of extraordinary acumen such as Franklin, the lesser known Nicholas P. Trist, who sacrificed his career by making peace with Mexico against his president's wishes, and Townsend Harris, who served with distinction in Japan before the American Civil War; rogues like William Walker, the prince of filibusters, who made himself president of Nicaragua briefly in the 1850s; and worthy adversaries such as the charismatic Tecumseh, who set out before the War of 1812 to build a confederacy of northern and southern Indian tribes to resist American expansion, as well as Emilio Aguinaldo, the leader of a Filipino insurrection at the turn of the twentieth century.

Wars set the mileposts on the U.S. road to world power.[1] Americans think of themselves as a peace-loving people, but few other nations have shouldered arms so frequently. Indeed, from 1776 through the First World War, every generation of American young men marched off to war. Armed conflict forged bonds of nationhood, nurtured national pride, and fostered myths about the nation's singular virtue and indomitability. This volume will analyze the causes, course, and consequences of the nation's wars and particularly their central role in its relentlessly aggressive expansionism.

Also contrary to popular belief, foreign policy has from the outset been central to America's national experience. The enduring idea of an isolationist United States is a myth often conveniently used to safeguard the nation's self-image as an innocent in world affairs. In fact, from 1776 until 1921, the United States was an active and influential player in world affairs. Foreign policy profoundly shaped American life.

The United States did usually act *unilaterally* through these years. Such a policy seemed eminently sensible to eighteenth- and nineteenth-century Americans who rightly feared that entanglement in Europe's wars and contamination from its politics could threaten their republican experiment. Unilateralism also derived from geography. The United States was "blessed among nations," French ambassador Jules Jusserand observed in the early 1900s, perhaps with a touch of envy. "On the north she had a weak neighbor; on the south, another weak neighbor; on the east, fish, and on the west, fish."[2] Indeed, throughout much of the nineteenth century and beyond, geography conferred upon the United States an advantage enjoyed by few nations—the absence of dire foreign threats—permitting it to avoid binding foreign commitments and to expand and prosper with minimal distraction from abroad; "free security," historian C. Vann Woodward aptly called it.[3] Unilateralism served the United States well during its first century and a half. It also bred a certain smug parochialism and indifference and even hostility toward other peoples and

1. Quoted in Geoffrey Perrett, *A Country Made by War* (New York, 1989), 562.
2. Quoted in Steven Walt, *Taming American Power: The Global Response to American Primacy* (New York, 2005), 39.
3. C. Vann Woodward, *The Future of the Past* (New York, 1989), 109.

cultures and an aversion to traditional diplomacy with its emphasis on give and take.

While focusing on the nation's official diplomacy, this volume goes further by looking more broadly at American foreign relations, including the private, unofficial, and non-state contacts that have shaped the nation's engagement with the world. It focuses, too, on the dissenting voices that have often swayed foreign policy decisions. And it places American actions in the larger context of an ever changing international system, that configuration among nations of economic, political, and military power that shapes the world at any given time, and, that the U.S. at times influenced and was influenced by.

The pages that follow examine the constitutional and institutional structures that have shaped U.S. foreign policy. The legal scholar Edward Corwin once observed that the Constitution's separation of powers between the executive and legislative branches of the U.S. government offered an "invitation to struggle for the privilege of directing American foreign policy."[4] From the bitter fight between George Washington and the Congress over ratification of the 1794 Jay Treaty to Wilson's epic battle with the Senate over the League of Nations, the two branches have engaged in often titanic struggles. Throughout U.S. history and more than in many other nations, domestic politics has exerted a powerful influence on foreign policy—and vice versa.

The United States has taken a distinctive approach toward its foreign policy and diplomacy. From the birth of the nation—and indeed when there was little basis for doing so—Americans held a boundless faith in their nation's destiny.[5] The revolutionary generation did not hesitate to use the world "empire," although its meaning to them differed sharply from the imperial practices they ascribed to Europeans. The bumptious and swaggering generation of the 1840s firmly believed that America's Manifest Destiny was to spread across the North American continent—and even beyond. The thrashing of Spain in 1898 signaled to Americans—and to others—the mature nation's emergence as a major power. Amidst the carnage of World War I, Wilson set out to realize the founders' dreams by claiming for the United States what he believed to be its rightful role as world leader.

Americans have held decidedly different views about their place in the world. On the one hand, from the start, they were drawn as though by

4. Quoted in Steven Casey, "When Congress Gets Mad: Foreign Policy Battles in the 1950s and Today," *Foreign Affairs* (January/February 2016), 76.
5. Michael H. Hunt, *Ideology and U.S. Foreign Policy* (New Haven, CT, 1987), 19–45.

magnetic force to the planet's commercial riches. From the revolution forward, the pursuit of economic self-interest ensured a high level of global involvement.

They have also seen themselves as distinctively different, a people apart—American exceptionalism, it is customarily called. The revolutionary generation rebelled not simply against Britain but also against Old World ways. They associated conventional diplomacy among nations with royalty and found it repugnant. They saw themselves as heralds of a *novus ordo seclorum*, a new world order in which enlightened diplomacy based on free trade would transform world politics and economics into a more beneficent system that would serve the broader interests of mankind rather than the narrow, selfish interest of monarchs and their courts. In the early national period, Americans flaunted their distinctiveness by rejecting the trappings of European diplomacy, even the traditional, formal dress, and by refusing to appoint ambassadors, a rank that smacked of royalty. Emerging as a world power in the late nineteenth century, the nation made its peace with conventional diplomatic practices. But Americans continued to see themselves as distinctive and as harbingers of a new order. For Wilson, the horrors of the Great War exposed more than ever the insanity of European power politics, prompting him to set forth a scheme for reforming world politics according to *American* ideals.

From Massachusetts Bay Colony founder John Winthrop's invocation of a "city upon a hill" through Wilson, Americans have also seen themselves as a chosen people with a providential mission; "God's American Israel," the Puritans called it.[6] They have prided themselves on their unique innocence and virtue. At times, they have felt a special obligation to extend the blessings of liberty to others. The ideal of a providential mission has spurred a drive to do good in the world, manifested in the work of private individuals such as merchants, missionaries, and educators. It has also undergirded the Wilsonian dream of the United States as world leader. This sense of a special destiny has also at times spawned arrogance. Disdain for native peoples and Mexicans built in part on deeply entrenched views of racial superiority fueled America's rush across the continent. Similar sentiments led to the imposition of colonial rule on Filipinos and Puerto Ricans and to the establishment of protectorates throughout the Caribbean region.[7] Beginning with an ill-fated incursion into Canada in 1775, America's sense of its grand historical mission has

---

6. Richard H. Van Alstyne, *Empire and Independence: The International History of the American Revolution* (New York, 1965), 4.

7. Hunt, *Ideology*, 46–91.

even justified spreading the blessings of liberty by force. The ironic result, in most cases, was to spark fierce nationalist resistance among the peoples invaded.

The ideological fervor and messianic streak that have stamped U.S. foreign policy have been balanced by offsetting forces. Pragmatism is basic to the American character, and in diplomacy U.S. officials have often departed from ideology to achieve important goals. Indeed, diplomats such as Franklin and Lincoln went further by developing a uniquely American brand of practical idealism, adhering to the nation's professed ideals while vigorously pursuing vital interests. U.S. policymakers have also been swayed by what Jefferson in the Declaration of Independence called a "decent respect for the opinion of mankind." Concern for their standing in the eyes of the world's peoples has at times checked their nation's more aggressive tendencies.

Despite claims to moral superiority and disdain for Old World diplomacy, the United States throughout its history has behaved more like a traditional great power than Americans have perhaps realized or might care to admit. U.S. policymakers have been shrewd analysts of world politics. They have energetically pursued and zealously protected interests deemed vital. From the founders of the eighteenth century to the end of World War I, Americans frequently played the game of world politics with impressive skill.

Americans often bemoan their nation's failures in foreign policy, but from 1776 to 1921 the United States achieved spectacular success. To be sure, like all countries, it suffered failures. At the same time, during its first century and a half, it compiled a record of achievement with little precedent in history. Amidst the turmoil of European wars, it achieved independence and put the new republic on a sound footing. It conquered a continent and established dominion over the Caribbean and western Pacific regions. Its intervention in 1917 decided the outcome of an epic world struggle. The United States emerged from the Great War the world's most powerful nation economically and potentially militarily, and was poised—however unsteadily—for global engagement in what would come to be called the American Century.

1

"To Begin the World Over Again"

Foreign Policy and the Birth of the Republic, 1776–1788

"We have every opportunity and every encouragement before us, to form the noblest, and purest constitution on the face of the earth," revolutionary pamphleteer Tom Paine wrote in late 1775. Paine's words came at a time when the American colonists in their struggle with Great Britain suffered military defeat and economic distress. They were bitterly divided between those who sought independence and those who preferred accommodation. Only thirty-seven years old when he arrived in the United States in 1774, Paine had been a corset maker and minor British government functionary. His best-selling pamphlet *Common Sense* made an impassioned appeal for independence. It was "absurd," he insisted, for a "continent to be perpetually governed by an island." A declaration of independence would gain for America assistance from England's enemies, France and Spain. It would secure for an independent America peace and prosperity. The colonists had been dragged into Europe's wars by their connection with England. Without such ties, there would be no cause for European hostility. Freed of British restrictions, commerce would "secure us the peace and friendship of all Europe because it is in the interest of all Europe to have America as a free port."[1]

Paine's call for independence makes clear the centrality of foreign policy to the birth of the American republic. His arguments hinged on estimates of the importance of the colonies in the international system of the late eighteenth century. They suggest the significant role foreign policy would assume in the achievement of independence and the adoption of a new constitution. They set forth basic principles that would shape U.S. foreign policy for years to come. They hint at the essential characteristics of what would become a distinctively American approach to foreign policy. The Revolutionary generation held to an expansive vision, a certainty of their future greatness and destiny. They believed themselves a chosen people and brought to their interactions with others a certain self-righteousness

---

1. Thomas P. Slaughter, ed., *Common Sense and Related Writings* (Boston, 2001), 89, 90, 93.

and disdain for established practice. They saw themselves as harbingers of a new world order, creating forms of governance and commerce that would appeal to peoples everywhere and change the course of world history. "We have it in our power to begin the world over again," Paine wrote. Idealistic in their vision, in their actions Americans demonstrated a pragmatism born perhaps of necessity that helped ensure the success of their revolution and the promulgation of the Constitution.[2]

I

From their foundation, the American colonies were an integral part of the British Empire and hence of an Atlantic trading community. According to the dictates of mercantilism, then the dominant school of economic thought, the colonies supplied the mother country with timber, tobacco, and other agricultural products and purchased its manufactured goods. But the Americans also broke from prescribed trade patterns. New England and New York developed an extensive illicit commerce with French Canada, even while Britain was at war with France. They also opened a lucrative commerce with Dutch and French colonies in the West Indies, selling food and other necessities and buying sugar more cheaply than it could be acquired from the British West Indies. Americans benefited in many ways from Britain's mercantilist Navigation Acts, but they staunchly resisted efforts to curb their trade with the colonies of other European nations. They became champions of free trade well before the Revolution.[3]

The American colonies were also part of a Eurocentric "international" community. Formed at the Peace of Westphalia in 1648, this new system sought to end years of bloody religious strife by enlarging the stature and role of the nation-state. Based in part on concepts developed by Hugo Grotius, the Dutch political theorist and father of international law, Westphalia established principles such as the sovereign equality of states, the territorial integrity of the state, non-interference by one state in the domestic affairs of others, peaceful resolution of disputes, and the obligation to abide by international agreements. After Westphalia, diplomacy and war came under the purview of civil rather than religious authority. A corps of professional diplomats emerged to handle interstate relations. A code was produced to guide their conduct. François de Callières's

2. Ibid., 113; Felix Gilbert, *The Beginnings of American Foreign Policy: To the Farewell Address* (New York, 1965), 37–43. See also David W. Fitzsimons, "Thomas Paine's New World Order: Idealistic Internationalism in the Ideology of Early American Foreign Policy," *Diplomatic History* 19 (Fall 1995), 574–78.
3. Max Savelle, *The Origins of American Diplomacy: The International History of Anglo-America* (New York, 1967), 540–44.

classic manual of the eighteenth-century diplomatic art affirmed that negotiations should be conducted in good faith, honorably, and without
deceit—"a lie always leaves a drop of poison behind." On the other hand,
spies were essential for information gathering, and bribes—although that
word was not used—were encouraged. Negotiation required keen powers
of observation, concentration on the task at hand, sound judgment, and
presence of mind, de Callières explained. But a "gift presented in the
right spirit, at the right moment, by the right person, may act with tenfold
power upon him who receives it." It was also important to cultivate the
ladies of the court, for "the greatest events have sometimes followed the
toss of a fan or the nod of a head."[4]

Far from eliminating war, the new system simply changed the reasons
for fighting and the means of combat. Issues of war and peace were decided on the basis of national interest as defined by the monarch and his
court. Nation-states acted on the basis of realpolitik rather than religious
considerations, changing sides in alliances when it suited their foreign
policy goals.[5] Rulers deliberately restricted the means and ends of combat. They had seen the costs and dangers of unleashing the passions of
their people. They had made substantial investments in their armies,
needed them for domestic order, and were loath to risk them in battle.
Once involved in war, they sought to avoid major battles, employed professional armies in cautious strategies of attrition, used tactics emphasizing maneuver and fortification, and held to unwritten rules protecting
civilian lives and property. The aim was to sustain the balance of power
rather than destroy the enemy. War was to be conducted with minimal
intrusion into the lives of the people. Indeed, that master practitioner of
limited war, Prussia's Frederick the Great, once observed that war was not
a success if most people knew it was going on.

In the international system of the eighteenth century, Spain, the
Netherlands, and Sweden, the great powers of an earlier era, were in decline, while France, Great Britain, Austria, Prussia, and Russia were as-
cending. Separated by a narrow channel of water, Britain and France
were especially keen rivals and fought five major wars between 1689 and
1776. The American colonies became entangled in most of them.

The Seven Years' War, or French and Indian War, as Americans have
known it, has been aptly called the "War That Made America."[6] That con-

---

4. Ronald Hoffman and Peter J. Albert, eds., *Peace and the Peacemakers: The Treaty of
1783* (Charlottesville, Va., 1986), ix–xii.
5. Paul Kennedy, *The Rise and Fall of the Great Powers* (New York, 1987), 73.
6. Fred Anderson, *The War That Made America* (New York, 2005).

flict originated in the colonies with fighting between Americans and French in the region between the Allegheny Mountains and the Mississippi River. It spread to Europe, where coalitions gathered around traditional rivals Britain and France, and to colonial possessions in the Caribbean and West Indies, the Mediterranean, the Southwest Pacific, and South Asia. Winston Churchill without too much exaggeration called it the "first world war." After early setbacks in Europe and America, Britain won a decisive victory and emerged the world's greatest power, wresting from France Canada and territory in India and from Spain the territories of East and West Florida, a global empire surpassing that of Rome.[7]

As is often the case in war, victory came at high cost. Americans had played a major part in Britain's success and envisioned themselves as equal partners in the empire. Relieved of the French and Spanish menace, they depended less on Britain's protection and sought to enjoy the fruits of their military success. The war exhausted Britain financially. Efforts to recoup its costs and to pay the expenses of a vastly expanded empire—by closing off the trans-Appalachian region to settlement, enforcing long-standing trade restrictions, and taxing the Americans for their own defense—sparked revolutionary sentiment among the colonists and their first efforts to band together in common cause. The disparate colonies attempted to apply economic pressures in the form of non-importation agreements. Twelve colonies sent delegates to a first Continental Congress in Philadelphia in the fall of 1774 to discuss ways to deal with British "oppression." A second Continental Congress assembled in May 1775 as shots were being fired outside Boston.

American foreign relations began before independence was declared. Once war was a reality, colonial leaders instinctively looked abroad for help. England's rival, France, also took a keen interest in events in America, dispatching an agent to Philadelphia in August 1775 to size up the prospects for rebellion. The Americans were not certain how Europe might respond to a revolution. John Adams of Massachusetts once speculated, with the moral self-righteousness that typified American attitudes toward European diplomacy, that it might take generous bribes, a gift for intrigue, and contact with "some of the Misses and Courtezans in keeping of the statesmen in France" to secure foreign assistance.[8] About the time French envoy Julien-Alexandre Ochard de Bonvouloir arrived in December, the Continental Congress appointed a Committee of Secret

7. Ibid., xxiii, 228.
8. Jack N. Rakove, *The Beginnings of National Politics: An Interpretive History of the Continental Congress* (New York, 1997), 93.

Correspondence to explore the possibility of foreign aid. The committee sounded out Bonvouloir on French willingness to sell war supplies. Encouraged by the response, it sent Connecticut merchant Silas Deane to France to arrange for the purchase of arms and other equipment. Three days before Deane arrived in France, Congress approved a Declaration of Independence designed to bring the American colonies into a union that could establish ties with other nations.[9] Whatever place the Declaration has since assumed in the folklore of American nationhood, its immediate and urgent purpose was to make clear to Europeans, especially the French, the colonies' commitment to independence.[10]

Although their behavior at times suggests otherwise, the Americans were not naive provincials. Their worldview was shaped by experiences as the most important colony of the British Empire, particularly in the most recent war. Colonial leaders were also familiar with European writings on diplomacy and commerce. Americans often expressed moral indignation at the depravity of the European balance-of-power system, but they observed it closely, understood its workings, and sought to exploit it. They turned for assistance to a vengeful France recently humiliated by England and presumably eager to weaken its rival by helping its colony gain independence. Painfully aware of their need for foreign aid, they were also profoundly wary of political commitments to European nations. Conveniently forgetting their own role in provoking the Seven Years' War, they worried that such entanglements would drag them into the wars that seemed constantly to wrack Europe. They feared that, as in 1763, their interests would be ignored in the peacemaking. Americans had followed debates in England on the value of connections with Continental powers. They adapted to their own use the arguments of those Britons who urged avoiding European conflicts and retaining maximum freedom of action. "It is the true interest of America to steer clear of European contentions," Paine advised in *Common Sense*.[11]

Americans also agreed that their ties with Europe should be mainly commercial. Through their experience in the British Empire, they had embraced freedom of trade before the publication of Adam Smith's classic *Wealth of Nations* in 1776. They saw the opportunity to trade with all nations on an equal basis as being in their best interests and indeed

9. Peter S. Onuf, "The Declaration of Independence for Diplomatic Historians," *Diplomatic History* 22 (Winter 1998), 71.

10. William Earl Weeks, *Building the Continental Empire: American Expansion from the Revolution to the Civil War* (Chicago, 1996), 10–11.

11. Gilbert, *Beginnings*, 32–43. The Paine quote is from p. 43.

essential for their economic well-being. Independence would permit them to "shake hands with the world—live at peace with the world—and trade to any market," according to Paine.[12] The enticement of trade would secure European support against Britain. Drawing upon French and Scottish Enlightenment philosophers, some Americans believed that replacement of the corrupt, oppressive, and warlike systems of mercantilism and power politics would produce a more peaceful world. The free interchange of goods would demonstrate that growth in the wealth of one nation would bring an increase for all. The interests of nations were therefore compatible rather than in conflict. The civilizing effect of free trade and the greater understanding among peoples that would come from increased contact would promote harmony among nations.

Keenly aware of their present weakness, the American revolutionaries envisioned future greatness. They embraced views dating back to John Winthrop and the founders of the Massachusetts Bay Colony of a city upon a hill that would serve as a beacon to peoples across the world. They saw themselves conducting a unique experiment in self-government that foreshadowed a new era in world politics. As a young man, John Adams of Massachusetts proclaimed the founding of the American colonies as "the opening of a grand scheme and design in Providence for the elimination of the ignorant, and the emancipation of the slavish part of mankind all over the earth." Americans had gloried in the triumph of the British Empire in 1763. When that empire, in their view, had failed them, they were called into being, in the words of patriot Ezra Stiles, to "rescue & reinthrone the hoary venerable head of the most glorious empire on earth." They believed they were establishing an empire without a metropolis, based on "consent, not coercion," that could serve as an "asylum for mankind," as Paine put it, and inspire others to break the shackles of despotism. Through free trade and enlightened diplomacy they would create a new world order.[13]

Even while Deane was sailing to France in pursuit of money and urgently needed supplies, another committee appointed by Congress was drafting a treaty to be offered to European nations embracing these first precepts of American foreign policy. The so-called Model Treaty, or Plan of 1776, was written largely by John Adams. It would guide treaty-making for years to come. In crafting the terms, Adams and his colleagues agreed as a fundamental principle that the nation must avoid any commitments

12. Fitzsimons, "Paine's New World Order," 576.
13. Peter S. Onuf, *Jefferson's Empire: The Language of American Nationhood* (Charlottesville, Va., 2000), 2, 25, 57; Gilbert, *Beginnings*, 55.

that would entangle it in future European wars. Indeed, Adams specifically recommended that in dealing with France no *political* connections should be formed. America must not submit to French authority or form military ties; it should receive no French troops. France would be asked to renounce claims to territory in North America. In return, the Americans would agree not to oppose French reconquest of the West Indies and would not use an Anglo-French war to come to terms with England. Both signatories would agree in the event of a general war not to make a separate peace without notifying the other six months in advance.

The lure to entice France and other Europeans to support the rebellious colonies would be commerce. Since trade with America was a key element of Britain's power, its rivals would not pass up the opportunity to capture it. The Model Treaty thus proposed that trade should not be encumbered by tariffs or other restrictions. Looking to the time when as a neutral nation they might seek to trade with nations at war, Americans also proposed a set of principles advocated by leading neutral nations and proponents of free trade. Neutrals should be free in wartime to trade with all belligerents in all goods except contraband. Contraband should be defined narrowly. Free ships would make free goods; that is to say, cargo aboard ships not at war should be free from confiscation. The Model Treaty was breathtaking in some of its assumptions and principles. Congress approved it in September 1776 and elected Thomas Jefferson of Virginia (who declined to serve) and elder statesman Benjamin Franklin of Philadelphia to join Deane in assisting with its negotiation and bringing France into the war. The Americans thus entered European diplomacy as heralds of a new age.[14]

Not surprisingly, the French were also nervous about close connections. The architect of French policy toward the American Revolution was the secretary of state for foreign affairs, Charles Gravier, comte de Vergennes. An aristocrat and career diplomat, Vergennes had spent so much time abroad—more than thirty years in posts across Europe—that a colleague dismissed him as a "foreigner become Minister."[15] He was well versed in international politics, cautious by nature, and hardworking. Jefferson said of him that "it is impossible to have a clearer, better argued head." Vergennes's chief concern was to regain French preeminence in

14. Gilbert, *Beginnings*, 56.
15. Orville T. Murphy, "The View from Versailles: Charles Gravier Comte de Vergennes's Perceptions of the American Revolution," in Ronald Hoffman and Peter J. Albert, eds., *Diplomacy and Revolution: The Franco-American Alliance of 1778* (Charlottesville, Va., 1981), 110.

Europe.[16] He saw obvious advantages in helping the Americans. But he also saw dangers. France could not be certain of their commitment to achieve independence or their ability to do so. He worried they might reconcile with Britain and join forces to attack the French West Indies. He recognized that overt aid to the Americans would give Britain cause for a war France was not prepared to fight. French policy therefore was to keep the rebels fighting by "feeding their courage" and offering "hope of efficacious assistance" while avoiding steps that might provoke war with Britain. The French government through what would now be called a covert operation provided limited, clandestine aid to the rebels. It set up a fictitious trading company headed by Pierre-Augustin Caron de Beaumarchais, a colorful aristocrat and playwright whose comedies like *The Barber of Seville* poked fun at his own class, and loaned it funds to purchase military supplies from government warehouses to sell the Americans on credit.

Ninety percent of the gunpowder used by the colonists during the first years of the war came from Europe, and foreign aid was thus indispensable from the outset. By the end of 1776, however, it was increasingly apparent that secret, limited aid might not be enough. Early military operations were disappointing, even calamitous. From the outset, Americans believed that other peoples shared their aspirations. Naively assuming that the residents of Canada, many of them French Catholics, would rally to the cause, they invaded Britain's northernmost province in September 1775. Expecting Canada to fall like "easy prey," in George Washington's words, they also grossly underestimated what was required for the task. Nine months later, on the eve of the Declaration of Independence, the disheartened and defeated invaders limped home in disgrace.[17] In the meantime, Washington had abandoned New York. His army was demoralized, depleted in numbers, short of food, clothing, and arms, and suffering from desertion and disease. Early military reverses hurt American credit in Europe. Designed to attract foreign support, the Declaration of Independence drew little notice in Europe.[18]

From the time he landed in Paris, the energetic but often indiscreet Deane compromised his own mission. He cut deals that benefited the rebel cause—and from which he profited handsomely, provoking later

16. William Howard Adams, *The Paris Years of Thomas Jefferson* (New Haven, Conn., 1997), 185; Murphy, "View from Versailles," 110.
17. Richard W. Van Alstyne, *Empire and Independence: The International History of the American Revolution* (New York, 1965), 104–5.
18. Ibid., 100; Jonathan R. Dull, *A Diplomatic History of the American Revolution* (New Haven, Conn., 1997), 185.

charges of malfeasance and a nasty spat in Congress. He was surrounded by spies, and his employment of the notorious British agent Edward Bancroft produced an intelligence windfall for London.[19] He recruited French officers to serve in the Continental Army and even plotted to replace Washington as commander. He endorsed sabotage operations against British ports, provoking angry protests to France. Even more dangerously, he and his irascible colleague Arthur Lee made the French increasingly uneasy about supporting the Americans. When Franklin landed in France in December 1776, the Revolution was teetering at home; America's first diplomatic mission was doing as much harm as good.

Franklin's mission to Paris is one of the most extraordinary episodes in the history of American diplomacy, important, if not indeed decisive, to the outcome of the Revolution. The eminent scientist, journalist, politician, and homespun philosopher was already an international celebrity when he landed in France. Establishing himself in a comfortable house with a well-stocked wine cellar in a suburb of Paris, he made himself the toast of the city. A steady flow of visitors requested audiences and favors such as commissions in the American army. Through clever packaging, he presented himself to French society as the very embodiment of America's revolution, a model of republican simplicity and virtue. He wore a tattered coat and sometimes a fur hat that he despised. He refused to powder his hair. His countenance appeared on snuffboxes, rings, medals, and bracelets, even (it was said) on an envious King Louis XVI's chamber pot. His face was as familiar to the French, he told his daughter, as "that of the moon."[20] He was compared to Plato and Aristotle. No social gathering was complete without him. To his special delight, women of all ages fawned over *"mon cher papa,"* as one of his favorites called him. A master showman, publicist, and propagandist, Franklin played his role to the hilt. He shrewdly perceived how the French viewed him and used it to further America's cause.[21]

With independence hanging in the balance, Franklin's mission was as daunting as that undertaken by any U.S. diplomat at any time. Seventy years old when he landed, he suffered the agony of gout. In addition to his diplomatic responsibilities, he bore the laborious and time-consuming responsibilities of a consul. The British were enraged with the mere presence in Paris of that "old veteran in mischief," and repeatedly complained

---

19. Rakove, *Beginnings*, 249.
20. Gordon S. Wood, *The Americanization of Benjamin Franklin* (New York, 2004), 177.
21. Ibid., 180.

to the comte de Vergennes about his machinations.[22] His first goal was to get additional money from the French, a task this apostle of self-reliance must have found unsavory at best. He was also to draw France into a war for which it was not yet ready and for which he had little to offer in return. He went months without word from Philadelphia. Most war news came from British sources or American visitors. He was burdened with the presence in Paris of a flock of rival U.S. diplomats including the near paranoid Lee and the imperious and prickly Adams, both of whom constantly fretted about his indolence and Francophilia. The French capital was a veritable den of espionage and intrigue.

With all this, he succeeded brilliantly. The most cosmopolitan of the founders, he had an instinctive feel for what motivated other nations. He patiently endured French caution about entering the war. A master of what a later age would call "spin," he managed to put the worst of American defeats in a positive light. By displaying his affection for things French and not appearing too radical, he made the American Revolution seem less threatening, more palatable, and even fashionable to the court. He won such trust from his French hosts that they insisted he remain when his rivals and would-be replacements sought to have him recalled. He secured loan after loan from Vergennes, sometimes through tactics that verged on extortion. He repeatedly reminded the French that some Americans sought reconciliation with Britain. In January 1778, he conspicuously met with a British emissary to nudge France toward intervention.

That step came on February 6, 1778, when France and the United States agreed to a "perpetual" alliance. By this time, France was better prepared for war and a bellicose spirit was rising in the country. British, French, and Spanish naval mobilization in the Caribbean raised the possibility that war might engulf the West Indies. A major U.S. victory at Saratoga in upstate New York in October 1777 clinched the decision to intervene. British general John Burgoyne's drive down the Hudson Valley was designed to cut off the northeastern colonies, thereby ending the rebellion. The capture of Burgoyne's entire army at Saratoga destroyed such dreams, bolstered sagging American spirits, and spurred peace sentiments in Britain. It was celebrated in France as a victory for French arms. Beaumarchais was so eager to spread the news that his speeding carriage overturned in the streets of Paris. Franklin's friend Madame Brillon composed a march to "cheer up General Burgoyne and his men, as they head

---

22. Stacy Schiff, *A Great Improvisation: Franklin, France, and the Birth of America* (New York, 2005), 68.

off to captivity."[23] Above all, Saratoga provided a convincing and long-sought indication that the Americans could succeed with external assistance, thus easing a French commitment to war.[24]

Negotiations for the treaty proceeded quickly and without major problems. For the Americans, desperation led pragmatism to win out over ideals. They had long since abandoned their scruples about political connections and their naive belief that trade alone would gain French support. The two nations readily agreed not to conclude a separate peace without each other's consent. Each guaranteed the possessions of the other in North America for the present and forever, a unique requirement for a wartime alliance. For the Americans, the indispensable feature of the agreement was a French promise to fight until their independence had been achieved. The United States gave France a free hand in taking British possessions in the West Indies. The two nations also concluded a commercial agreement, which, while not as liberal as the Model Treaty, did put trade on a most-favored-nation basis, a considerable advance beyond the mercantilist principles that governed most such pacts. Americans wildly celebrated their good fortune. Franklin outdid himself in his enthusiasm for his adopted country. Even the normally suspicious Adams declared the alliance a "rock upon which we may safely build."[25]

Like all alliances, the arrangement with France was a marriage of expedience, and the two sides brought to their new relationship long-standing prejudices and sharply different perspectives. French diplomats and military officers were not generally sympathetic to the idea of revolution. They saw the United States, like the small nations of Europe, as an object to be manipulated to their own ends. In the best tradition of European statecraft, French diplomats used bribery and other forms of pressure to ensure that the Continental Congress served their nation's interests. French officers in the United States protested that upon their arrival the Americans stopped fighting.[26] For their part, Americans complained that French aid was inadequate and French troops did not fight aggressively. They worried that France did not support their war aims. Among Americans, moreover, until 1763 at least, France had been the mortal enemy. As an absolute monarchy and Catholic to boot, in the eyes of many it was the epitome of evil. Americans inherited from the British deep-seated prejudices, viewing their

---

23. Ibid., 110–11.
24. Dull, *Diplomatic History*, 89–96, and Van Alstyne, *Empire and Independence*, 131–33, give less significance to Saratoga in the origins of the alliance.
25. Van Alstyne, *Empire and Independence*, 163.
26. Murphy, "View from Versailles," 133.

new allies as small and effeminate, "pale, ugly specimens who lived exclusively on frogs and snails." Some expressed surprise to find French soldiers and sailors "as large & as likely men as can be produced by any other nation." Riots broke out in Boston between French and American sailors. In New York, French troops engaged in looting. To avoid such conflict, French officers often isolated their forces from American civilians, sometimes keeping them on board ships for weeks.[27]

Whatever the problems, the significance of the alliance for the outcome of the Revolution cannot be overstated.[28] The timing was perfect. The news arrived in the United States just after the landing of a British peace commission prepared to concede everything but the word *independence.* The alliance killed a compromise peace by ensuring major external assistance in a war for unqualified independence. Congress celebrated by feting the newly arrived French minister, Conrad Alexandre Gerard, the first diplomat formally accredited to the United States, with food and drink sent by the British commissioners to lubricate the wheels of diplomacy. The French alliance ensured additional money and supplies not only from France but also from other European nations. In all, the United States secured $9 million in foreign military aid without which it would have been difficult to sustain the Revolution. Americans carried French weapons and were paid with money that came from France.[29] The French fleet and French troops played a vital role in the decisive battle of Yorktown.

For a steep price—the promise of assistance in the recapture of Gibraltar—France persuaded Spain to enter the conflict. Spain also provided economic and military aid to the United States and drove the British from the Gulf Coast region of North America. A threatened Franco-Spanish invasion of England in 1779 caused panic, making it difficult for the British government to reinforce its navy and troops in North America. The Dutch would also eventually join the allied coalition. An ill-fated British campaign against Dutch colonial outposts in Africa, Asia, and the Caribbean diverted attention and precious resources from the American theater. In 1780, Russia's Catherine the Great formed an armed neutrality, a group of nations including Sweden, Denmark, Austria, Prussia, Portugal, and the Kingdom of Naples, who joined together to protect by force, if necessary, neutral shipping from British depredations, helping ensure a

27. William C. Stinchcombe, "Americans Celebrate the Birth of the Dauphin," in Hoffman and Albert, *Diplomacy and Revolution,* 44–47.
28. Wood, *Franklin,* 191.
29. Alexander DeConde, "The French Alliance in Historical Speculation," in Hoffman and Albert, *Diplomacy and Revolution,* 18.

flow of supplies to the United States. The Americans were so enthused about the principles of Catherine's program that as a present belligerent but possibly future neutral they tried to join. The French alliance transformed a localized rebellion in North America into a global war that strained even Britain's vast resources and greatly benefited the Americans.[30]

Even with such support, the war went badly. A French ploy to end the conflict quickly by blockading New York and forcing the surrender of the British army failed miserably. Seeking to exploit widespread Loyalist sentiment, Britain in 1779 shifted to a southern strategy, taking Savannah and later Charleston. British success in the South forced Congress to abandon its scruples against foreign troops, evoking urgent pleas that France send military forces along with its navy. It would be the summer of 1780 before they arrived, however, and in the meantime the U.S. war effort hit a low point. Troops in New Jersey and Pennsylvania revolted. The army was in "extreme distress," in Vergennes's words, and he warned French naval commanders not to land forces if the American war effort seemed about to collapse.[31] Chronic money problems required another huge infusion of French funds. By this time, France was also in dire straits militarily. French policymakers briefly contemplated a truce that would have left Britain in control of the southern states.

From Canada to the Floridas, the American Revolution also raged on the western frontier, and here too the war went badly. At the outbreak, the colonists hoped for Native American neutrality. Britain actively sought the Indians' assistance. Perceiving the Americans as the greatest threat to their existence and Britain as the most likely source of arms and protection, most tribes turned to the latter, infuriating the embattled Americans. Adams denounced the Indians as "blood Hounds"; Washington called them "beasts of prey."[32] The Americans seized the opportunities created by Indian affiliation with Britain to wage a war of extirpation, where possible driving the Indians further west and solidifying claims to their lands. Even some tribes who collaborated with the Americans suffered at their hands during and after the revolution. "Civilization or death to all American Savages" was the toast offered at a Fourth of July celebration before an American army marched against the Iroquois in 1779.[33]

30. Ibid., 17–18; Dull, *Diplomatic History*, 163.
31. Murphy, "View from Versailles," 144; Dull, *Diplomatic History*, 107.
32. James M. Merrell, "Declarations of Independence: Indian-White Relations in the New Nation," in Jack P. Greene, ed., *The American Revolution: Its Character and Limits* (New York, 1987), 198–99.
33. Ibid., 198.

This important and often neglected phase of the Revolutionary War began before the Declaration of Independence. In 1774, the governor of Virginia sent an expedition into Shawnee territory in the Ohio Valley, fought a major battle at Point Pleasant on the Ohio River, and forced the Indians to cede extensive land. Three years later, to divert American attention from a British offensive in upstate New York, the British commander at Detroit dispatched Indian raiding parties to attack settlements in Kentucky. Over the next two years, sporadic fighting occurred across the Ohio frontier. The state of Virginia, which had extensive land claims in the region, dispatched George Rogers Clark to attack the British and their Indian allies. In 1778, Clark took forts at Kaskaskia, Cahokia, and Vincennes. The British retook Vincennes the following year. Clark took it back one more time, but he could not establish firm control of the region. Settlements in Kentucky—the "dark and bloody ground"—came under attack the next two years.

The Americans opened a second front in the war against the Indians in western New York. The Iroquois Confederacy split, some tribes siding with the British, others with the Americans. When Indians working with Loyalists conducted raids across upstate New York in 1778, threatening food supplies vital to his army, Washington diverted substantial resources and some of his best troops to the theater with instructions that the Iroquois should be not "merely *overrun* but *destroyed*." In one of the best-planned operations of the war, the Americans inflicted heavy losses on the Iroquois and pushed the frontier westward. But they did not achieve their larger aim of crippling Indian power and stabilizing the region. "The nests are destroyed," one American warned, "but the birds are still on the wing."[34] The Iroquois became more dependent on the British and more angry with the Americans. During the remainder of the war, they exacted vengeance along the northern frontier.

The Americans fared best in the South. Although threatened by the westward advance of the Georgia colony, the Creeks clung to their long-standing tradition of neutrality in wars among whites. They also learned valuable lessons from their neighbors, the Cherokees. Having suffered huge losses in the Seven Years' War, the Cherokees welcomed Britain's post-1763 efforts to stop the migration of colonists into the trans-Appalachian West. Out of gratitude for British support and encouraged by British agents, they rose up against the colonists in May 1776. Their timing could not have been worse. Britain had few troops in the southern states at this time. The Americans seized the chance to eliminate a major

34. Barbara Graymont, *The Iroquois in the American Revolution* (Syracuse, N.Y., 1972), 220.

threat and strengthen their claims to western lands. Georgia and the Carolinas mobilized nearly five thousand men and launched a three-pronged campaign against the Cherokees, destroying some fifty villages, killing and scalping men *and* women, selling some Indians into slavery, and driving others into the mountains. A 1780 punitive expedition did further damage. The Cherokees would in time re-create themselves and develop a flourishing culture, but the war of American independence cost them much of their land and their way of life.[35]

Adoption in March 1781 of a form of government—the Articles of Confederation—marked a major accomplishment of the war years, but it did not come easily and proved at best an imperfect instrument for waging war and negotiating peace. Discussion of formal union began in the summer of 1776. Pressures to act intensified in the fall of 1777 when Congress, faced with rising inflation, requested that the states furnish additional funds, stop issuing paper money, and impose price controls. Foreign policy exigencies proved equally important. Optimistic after Saratoga that an alliance with France would be reality, Congress believed that agreement on a constitution would affirm the stability of the new government and its commitment to independence, strengthening its position with other nations. Much like the Declaration of Independence, the Articles of Confederation were designed to secure foreign support.[36]

It took nearly four years to complete a process initiated to meet immediate demands. Congress moved expeditiously, approving a draft on November 15, 1777. The states were forbidden from negotiating with other nations. They could not make agreements with each other or maintain an army or navy without the consent of Congress. On the other hand, the Confederation government could not levy taxes or regulate commerce. It could not make treaties that infringed on the legislative rights of any state. Affirming the principle of state sovereignty, the articles left with the states any powers not "expressly delegated" to the national government. The Congress rejected numerous amendments proposed by the states, but the process took time, and ratification was delayed until March 1781. By that point, many of the deficiencies of the new instrument had been exposed. Congress addressed a most obvious shortcoming, the lack of executive machinery, by creating in 1781 departments for war, finance, and foreign affairs headed by individuals who were not among its

---

35. Theda Perdue, *The Cherokee* (New York, 1989), 35–36; Allen R. Millett and Peter Maslowski, *For the Common Defense: A Military History of the United States of America* (New York, 1984), 74.
36. Rakove, *Beginnings*, 179.

members. Robert R. Livingston of New York was named secretary of foreign affairs. Even then, many national leaders believed that the Articles of Confederation were obsolete by the time they had been approved.[37]

II

A sudden and dramatic reversal of military fortunes in late 1781 led to negotiations to end the American war. Countering Britain's southern strategy, the United States and France shifted sizeable military forces to Virginia. The French fleet was deployed to the Chesapeake Bay, where the allies in October trapped and forced the surrender of a major British army under the ill-fated Lord Charles Cornwallis on a narrow peninsula along the York River. The victory at Yorktown may have spared the allies from disaster.[38] Although Britain still held Charleston and Savannah, Cornwallis's defeat thwarted the southern strategy. It gave a huge boost to faltering American morale and revived French enthusiasm for the war. Yorktown undermined popular support for the war in Britain and, along with the soaring cost of the conflict, caused the fall of the ministry of Lord North and the emergence of a government intent on negotiating with the United States. The war continued for two more years, but after Yorktown attention shifted to the challenging task of peacemaking.

Victory at Yorktown did not give the United States the upper hand in the peace negotiations, however. Washington's army remained short of food, supplies, arms, and ammunition. Britain retained control of some southern states, where fighting still raged. In fact, after Yorktown, the American theater became a sideshow in the global war. In negotiations involving four major nations and numerous lesser ones and a war that stretched from the Gulf of Mexico to South Asia, events in far-flung areas often had a major impact. British setbacks in the Caribbean combined with Yorktown to encourage peace sentiment in England. French naval defeats in the West Indies in the spring of 1782 made Paris more amenable to separate U.S. negotiations with Great Britain.

For the United States, of course, recognition of its independence was the essential condition for peace.[39] Independence was the reason the war had been fought, and it formed the indispensable principle of the first statement of war aims drafted in 1779. Congress had hesitated even to

---

37. Ibid., 190.
38. Dull, *Diplomatic History*, 120.
39. Gregg L. Lint, "Preparing for Peace: The Objectives of the United States, France, and Spain in the War of the American Revolution," in Ronald Hoffman and Peter J. Albert, eds., *Peacemakers: The Treaty of 1783* (Charlottesville, Va., 1986), 32–33.

raise such issues for fear of exacerbating sectional tensions in wartime. At France's insistence (primarily as a way of bringing U.S. goals into line with its own), the Americans finally did so, and the results made plain the ambitions of the new nation. The territory of the independent republic should extend to the Mississippi River, land that, except for Clark's victories, the United States had not conquered and did not occupy, and to the 31st parallel, the existing border between Georgia and the Floridas. Americans claimed Britain's right acquired from France in 1763 to navigate the Mississippi from its source to the sea.[40] They also sought Nova Scotia. New England's fishing industry was valued at nearly $2 million and employed ten thousand men, and access to North Atlantic fisheries comprised a vital war aim.[41] In his private and unofficial discussions with British diplomats, Franklin went further. Outraged by the atrocities committed by an enemy he denounced as "the worst and wickedest Nation upon Earth," he urged Britons to "recover the Affections" of their former colonies with a generous settlement including the cession of Canada and the Floridas to the United States.[42]

In June 1781, again under French pressure and when the war was going badly, Congress significantly modified the instructions to its diplomats in Europe. Reflecting America's dependence on France, the influence of—and bribes provided by—Gerard and his successor, the comte de la Luzerne, and a widespread fear that French support might be lost, the new instructions affirmed that independence should no longer be a precondition to negotiations. The boundaries proposed in 1779 were also deemed not essential. The commissioners could agree to a treaty with Spain that did not provide for access to the Mississippi. In a truly extraordinary provision, Congress instructed the commissioners to place themselves under French direction, to "undertake nothing...without their knowledge and concurrence; and ultimately to govern yourselves by their advice and opinion."[43] When the military situation changed dramatically after Yorktown, Congress discussed modifying these highly restrictive instructions but did nothing. Fortunately for the United States, its diplomats in Europe ignored them and acted on the basis of the 1779 draft.[44]

French and Spanish war aims complicated the work of the American peace commissioners. France and especially Spain had gone to war to

40. Ibid., 33–35.
41. Richard B. Morris, *The Forging of the Union, 1781–1789* (New York, 1987), 140.
42. Edmund S. Morgan, *Benjamin Franklin* (New Haven, Conn., 2002), 275–76.
43. Bradford Perkins, "The Peace of Paris: Patterns and Legacies," in Hoffman and Albert, *Peacemakers*, 196.
44. Lint, "Preparing for Peace," 49–50.

avenge the humiliation of 1763, weaken their major rival by detaching Britain's most valuable colonies, and restore the global balance of power. France was committed by treaty to American independence, but not to the boundaries Americans sought. Indeed, at various points in the war it was prepared to accept a partition that would have left the southern colonies in Britain's possession. A weaker United States, Vergennes and his advisers reasoned, would be more dependent on France. France did not seek to regain Canada, but it preferred continued British dominance there to keep an independent United States in check. It also sought access to the North Atlantic fisheries.

France's ties with Spain through their 1779 alliance further jeopardized the achievement of U.S. war aims. Although it provided vital assistance to the United States, Spain never consented to a formal alliance or committed itself to American independence. Because France had promised to fight until Spain recovered Gibraltar, America's major war aim could be held hostage by events in the Mediterranean. Spain also sought to recover the Floridas from Britain. Even more than France, it preferred to keep the United States weak and hemmed in as close to the Appalachians and as far north as possible. Spain saw no reason to grant the United States access to the Mississippi.

Ironically, but not surprisingly, given the strange workings of international politics, the United States found its interests more in line with those of its enemy, Great Britain, than its ally, France, and France's ally, Spain. To be sure, Britons acquiesced in American independence only grudgingly. As late as 1782, well after Yorktown, top officials insisted on negotiating on the basis of the *uti possidetis*, the territory actually held at the time, which would have left Britain in control at least of the southernmost American states. King George III contemplated negotiating with the states individually, a classic divide-and-conquer ploy. The British government would have concluded a separate peace with France if expedient. Even after Lord North resigned in March 1782 and a new government took power, there was talk of an "Irish solution," an autonomous America within the British Empire.[45]

Gradually, top British officials and especially William Petty Fitzmaurice, the earl of Shelburne, shifted to a more conciliatory approach. Conservative, aloof, and secretive, known for his duplicity, Shelburne was called "the Jesuit of Berkeley Square." He was persuaded to adopt a more accommodating approach by his friend Richard Oswald, a seventy-six-year-old

45. Esmond Wright, "The British Objectives, 1780–1783: 'If Not Dominion Then Trade,'" in Hoffman and Albert, *Peacemakers*, 8–10.

acquaintance and admirer of Franklin. Oswald owned property in the West Indies, West Florida, and the southern colonies. He had lived six years in Virginia. He and Shelburne, in the latter's words, *"decidedly tho reluctantly"* concluded that Britain's essential aim should be to separate the United States from France. Independence was acceptable if it could accomplish that.[46] They hoped that an America free of France through a shared history, language, and culture would gravitate back toward Britain's influence and become its best customer.[47]

Given the different parties involved and the conflicts and confluences of interests, the peace negotiations were extremely complicated. They resembled, historian Jonathan Dull has written, a "circus of many rings," with all the performers walking a tightrope.[48] Military action on land or sea even in distant parts of the globe could tip the balance one way or the other. Europe and America formed a very small world in the 1780s. The key players knew and indeed in some cases were related to each other. Diplomats moved back and forth between London and Paris with relative ease. At one point, two competing British cabinet ministers had representatives in Paris talking to the Americans. In the latter stages, Franklin's fellow commissioners John Adams and John Jay went off in directions that might have been disastrous.

With North's resignation, an unwieldy government headed by Lord Rockingham took power in England. Two men were nominally responsible for negotiations with the Americans, the Whig Charles James Fox, secretary of state for foreign affairs, who favored immediate independence, and the more cautious Shelburne, secretary of state for home and colonial affairs. Before North's resignation, Franklin, through an especially effusive letter of thanks to Shelburne for a gift of gooseberry bushes sent to a friend in France, had hinted that the Americans might negotiate a separate peace. Shelburne agreed that negotiations could begin in France. Not yet in full control, however, he refused to accept independence except as part of a broader settlement. Franklin again pleaded for British generosity, hinting that in return the United States might help end Britain's wars with France and Spain by threatening a separate peace.

46. Shelburne to Oswald, July 27, 1782, in Mary A. Giunta, ed., *Documents of the Emerging Nation: U.S. Foreign Relations, 1775–1782* (Wilmington, Del., 1998), 91.
47. Perkins, "Peace of Paris," 198; Wright, "British Objectives," 10–15; Charles R. Ritcheson, *Aftermath of Revolution: British Policy Toward the United States* (New York, 1969), 74, 79, 82.
48. Van Alstyne, *Empire and Independence*, 215; Jonathan R. Dull, "Vergennes, Rayneval, and the Diplomacy of Trust," in Hoffman and Albert, *Peacemakers*, 105.

The two sides got past the first major hurdle in July 1782. Shelburne maneuvered Fox out of the negotiations and then out of the cabinet. Rockingham died shortly after, making Shelburne head of the cabinet and giving him control over the negotiations. By this time, Shelburne had resigned himself to full American independence. He named Oswald to negotiate with Franklin. Reflecting the new nation's importance in the balance of power, he instructed his envoy that "if America is to be independent, she must be so of the whole world. No secret, tacit, or ostensible connections with France." Shelburne went along with Franklin's ploy not because of the strength of the American's bargaining position but rather because he was eager for peace with France and Spain and agreed with Franklin that peace with the United States could help end the European war. Oswald accepted in principle Franklin's "necessary" terms: complete and unqualified independence, favorable boundaries, and access to the fisheries.[49]

This left numerous thorny matters unresolved. Britain demanded compensation for property confiscated from those Americans who had remained loyal to the Crown. Americans insisted upon access to the Mississippi. Franklin was furious with Britain's initial reluctance to concede independence and the atrocities he claimed its troops had committed. The fact that his estranged son, William, was a Loyalist gave him a deeply personal reason to oppose for this group the sort of generosity he repeatedly asked of Britain. He exclaimed regarding the Mississippi that "a Neighbour might as well ask me to sell my street Door" as to "sell a Drop of its Waters."[50] Initial discussions produced little progress.

From this point, John Jay, and to a lesser extent Adams, replaced Franklin as the primary negotiators. Both men were profoundly suspicious of Britain—and even more of France. Their approach to the negotiations differed sharply from their elder colleague. From the moment he had arrived in Europe in 1778, Adams had raised a ruckus. "Always an honest Man, often a Wise one, but sometimes in some things out of his Senses," Franklin had said of Adams, and in terms of the younger man's service in Paris, the criticism was understated.[51] Adams repeatedly complained of "the old Conjurer's" indolence, his "continued Discipation," and his subservience to France. He even accused Franklin of conspiring to get him aboard a ship that was captured by the British. Like other Americans, Adams inherited from the British a deep dislike for France, an

49. Dull, *Diplomatic History*, 146.
50. Morgan, *Franklin*, 287–88.
51. Wood, *Franklin*, 195.

"ambitious and faithless nation," he once snarled.[52] His staunch republican ideology bred suspicion of all men of power. Adams railed against the "Count and the Doctor." He insisted that France was determined to "keep us poor. Depress us. Keep us weak."[53] A descendant of French Protestants, Jay came by his suspicions naturally. They were heightened and his disposition soured by the three frustrating and largely fruitless years he spent in Madrid seeking to persuade Spain to ally with the United States. Adams's and Jay's suspiciousness and their often self-righteous, moralistic demeanor, one suspects, were also born of the anxieties afflicting these neophytes in the settled world of European diplomacy. They protested the immorality of that system, but, given their suspicions, they had no qualms about breaking the terms of their treaty with France and negotiating separately with Britain. Jay arrived in Paris in May 1782, but he was bedridden with influenza for several months. When he recovered and Franklin became deathly ill with kidney stones, he turned his worries on the British. Because Oswald's commission did not mention the United States by name and therefore did not explicitly recognize American independence, Jay broke off talks with England.

Within several weeks even more suspicious of France and Spain, Jay abruptly changed course. The trip of one of Vergennes's top advisers to Britain persuaded him that some nefarious Anglo-French plot was afoot. With the consent of Franklin and the enthusiastic support of Adams, he dropped his demand for prior recognition of U.S. independence at about the time Shelburne was prepared to grant it. He sent word to London that the United States would abandon the alliance with France if a separate peace could be arranged. Oswald's commission was revised to include the name of the United States, thus extending formal recognition of independence. It was a curious and costly victory for the Americans. In the hiatus caused by Jay's breaking off of the discussions, the British lifted Spain's siege of Gibraltar, leaving them in a stronger negotiating position and less eager to end the European war. When the talks resumed, Jay compounded his earlier mistake by conceding on the fisheries. He also devised a harebrained scheme to encourage America's enemy, Britain, to attack its backer, Spain, and retake Pensacola. The proposal undoubtedly reflected Jay's passionate hatred for Spain and perhaps his Anglophilia. Had the British gone along, their position on the Gulf Coast would have

52. James H. Hutson, "The American Negotiators: The Diplomacy of Jealousy," in Hoffman and Albert, *Peacemakers*, 54.

53. Ibid., 61–62.

been greatly strengthened, threatening the safety of a new and vulnerable republic.[54]

Despite Jay's dubious maneuvers, a peace settlement was patched together in October and November of 1782. Adams and Jay argued interminably over countless issues—"the greatest quibblers I have ever seen," one British diplomat complained.[55] In the end, they got much of what they wanted and far more than their 1781 instructions called for. Britain agreed to recognize U.S. independence and withdraw its troops from U.S. territory, the essential concessions. Although many complicated details remained to be worked out, the boundary settlement was remarkably generous given the military situation when the war ended: the Mississippi River in the west; the Floridas in the south; and Canada to the north. Britain extended to the United States its rights to navigate the Mississippi, a concession that without Spain's assent was of limited value. The fisheries were one of the most difficult issues, and the United States could secure only the "liberty," not the right, to fish off Newfoundland and the Gulf of St. Lawrence. Other troublesome issues were "resolved" with vague statements that would cause prolonged and bitter disputes. Creditors in each nation were to meet no legal obstacles to the repayment of debts. Congress would recommend to the states the restitution of Loyalist property confiscated during the war.

The American negotiators have often been given the credit for this favorable outcome. They shrewdly played the Europeans against each other, it has been argued, exploiting their rivalries, wisely breaking congressional instructions, and properly deserting an unreliable France to defend their nation's interests and maximize its gains. Such an interpretation is open to question. The Americans, probably from their own insecurities, were anxiety-ridden in dealing with ally and enemy alike.[56] Jay's excessive nervousness about England and then his separate approach to that country not only broke faith with a supportive if not entirely reliable ally but also delayed negotiations for several months. It eased pressure on Shelburne to make concessions and left the United States vulnerable to a possible Shelburne-Vergennes deal at its expense. Jay and Adams had reason to question Vergennes's trustworthiness, but they should have informed him of the terms before springing the signed treaty upon him.

54. Dull, *Diplomatic History*, 149.
55. Hutson, "American Negotiators," 53.
56. Samuel Flagg Bemis, *The Diplomacy of the American Revolution* (Bloomington, Ind., 1957), 255–56, and Richard B. Morris, *The Peacemakers: The Great Powers and American Independence* (New York, 1965), 459, praise Adams and Jay. Perkins, "Peace of Paris," 201, and Dull, *Diplomatic History*, 146–51, are more critical.

Ultimately, the favorable settlement owed much less to America's military prowess and diplomatic skill than to luck and chance: Shelburne's desperate need for peace to salvage his deteriorating political position and his determination to settle quickly with the United States and seek reconciliation through generosity.[57]

News of the preliminary treaty evoked strikingly different reactions among the various parties. Finalization of the terms required a broader European settlement, which would not come until early 1783, but war-weary Americans greeted news of the peace with relief and enthusiasm. At the same time, some members of Congress, encouraged by the ardently pro-French Livingston, sought to rebuke the commissioners for violating their instructions and jeopardizing the French alliance. The move failed, but Franklin was sufficiently offended to muse that the biblical blessings supposedly accorded to peacemakers must be reserved for the next life. Britons naturally recoiled at Shelburne's generosity, and the architect of the peace treaty fell from power in early 1783. His departure and British anger at defeat ensured that the generous trade treaty he had contemplated would not become reality. Vergennes was at least mildly annoyed at the Americans' independence, complaining that if it were a guide to the future "we shall be but poorly payed for all we have done for the United States." He was shocked at British generosity—the "concessions exceed all that I should have thought possible."[58] He was also relieved that the Americans had freed him of obligations to fight until Spain achieved its war aims and thereby helped him secure the quick peace he needed to address European issues. It was Franklin's task to repair the damage done by Jay and Adams (with his consent, of course) and also to secure additional funds without which, Livingston implored him, "we are inevitably ruined."[59] He begged Vergennes's forgiveness for the Americans "neglecting a Point of *bienseance*." Adding a clever twist, he confided that the British "flatter themselves" that they had divided the two allies. The best way to disabuse them of this notion would be for the United States and France to keep "this little misunderstanding" a "perfect Secret."[60] The old doctor even had the audacity to ask for yet another loan. Already heavily invested in his unfaithful allies and hopeful of salvaging something, Vergennes saw little choice but to provide the Americans an additional six million livres.

57. Perkins, "Peace of Paris," 220–21; Dull, *Diplomatic History*, 149–51.
58. Perkins, "Peace of Paris," 215.
59. Morgan, *Franklin*, 289.
60. Franklin to Vergennes, December 17, 1782, in Giunta, *Documents*, 124–25.

The treaties ending the wars of the American Revolution had great significance for the people and nations involved. Most Native Americans had sided with Britain, but the peace treaty ignored them and assigned to the United States lands they regarded as theirs. "Thunder Struck" when they heard the news, they issued their own declarations of independence, proclaiming, in the words of the Six Nations, that they were a "free People subject to no Power upon Earth."[61] For France, an ostensible winner, the war cost an estimated one billion livres, bankrupting the treasury and sparking a revolution that would have momentous consequences in America as well as in Europe. Britain lost a major part of its empire but, ironically, emerged stronger. Its economy quickly recovered, and with the industrial revolution flourished as never before.[62] The treaty sealed U.S. independence. The extensive boundaries provided the springboard for continental empire. Americans would quickly learn, however, that securing the peace could be even more difficult than winning the war.

III

Peace brought scant stability. Debt weighed upon nation and citizens alike. War had ravaged parts of the country. Slaves had been carried off, traditional markets closed, and inflation unleashed. Shortly after the war, the nation plunged into its first full-fledged depression. The economy improved slowly over the next five years, but a Congress lacking real authority could not set economic policies. Wartime unity gave way to snarling rivalry over western lands. Attendance at the Congress was so erratic that there was seldom a quorum. The shift of its meeting place from Philadelphia to Princeton and then to Annapolis, Trenton, and New York City symbolized the instability of the institution and the nation itself.[63]

Challenges from abroad posed greater threats. The rebelling colonies had exploited European rivalries to secure economic and military aid from France and Spain and a generous peace treaty from Britain. Once the war ended, divisions among the major powers receded along with opportunities for the United States. The Europeans did not formally coordinate their postwar approaches, but their policies were generally in tandem. They believed that the United States, like republics before it, would collapse of its own weight. The sheer size of the country worked against it, according to Britain's Lord Sheffield. The "authority of Congress can never be maintained over those distant and boundless regions." Some

61. Merrell, "Declarations," 197.
62. Dull, *Diplomatic History*, 161.
63. Rakove, *Beginnings*, 342.

Britons even comforted themselves that their generosity at the peace table would hasten America's downfall; the time often estimated was five years.[64] A French observer speculated that the whole "edifice would infallibly collapse if the weakness of its various parts did not assure its continuance by making them weigh less strongly the ones over the others."[65]

Europeans were not disposed to help the new nation's survival. To keep it weak and dependent, they imposed harsh trade restrictions and rebuffed appeals for concessions. Britain and Spain blocked the United States from taking control of territory awarded in the 1783 treaty. Lacking the means to retaliate and divided among themselves on foreign policy priorities, Americans were powerless to resist European pressures. More than anything else, their inability to effectively address crucial foreign policy problems persuaded many leaders that a stronger central government was essential to the nation's survival.

One area of progress was in the administration of foreign affairs. Livingston had repeatedly complained of inadequate authority and congressional interference. He resigned before the peace treaty was ratified. Congress responded by strengthening the position of the secretary for foreign affairs. John Jay assumed the office in December 1784 and held it until a new government took power in 1789, providing needed continuity. An able administrator, he insisted that his office have full responsibility for the nation's diplomacy. Remarkably, he also conditioned his acceptance on Congress settling in New York.[66] Assisted by four clerks and several part-time translators, he worked out of two rooms in a tavern near Congress's meeting place. He did not achieve his major foreign policy goals, but he managed his department efficiently. Interestingly, a secret act of Congress authorized him to open and examine any letters going through the post office that might contain information endangering the "safety or interest of the United States." He appears not to have used this authority.[67]

Americans and Europeans confronted each other across a sizeable divide, the product of experience and ideology clearly reflected in diplomatic protocol. Upon arriving as U.S. envoy in England, John Adams quickly wearied of affairs at the Court of St. James's. Good republican— and New Englander—that he was, he complained to Jay after an

64. Peter S. Onuf, "Anarchy and the Crisis of the Union," in Herman Belz, Ronald Hoffman, and Peter J. Albert, eds., *To Form a More Perfect Union* (Charlottesville, Va., 1992), 280.
65. Luis Guillaume Otto to Vergennes, October 1, 1785, in Giunta, *Documents*, 178.
66. Walter Stahr, *John Jay, Founding Father* (New York and London, 2005), 197.
67. Morris, *Forging of the Union*, 194–95; David Patterson, "The Department of State: The Formative Years, 1775–1800," *Prologue* 21 (Winter 1989), 317.

audience with George III that the "essence of things are lost in Ceremony in every Court of Europe." But he responded pragmatically. The United States must "submit to what we cannot alter," he added resignedly. "Patience is the only Remedy."[68] Troubled by the meddling of French diplomats in the United States during the Revolution, Francis Dana, minister to Russia in 1785, urged that the United States abandon diplomacy altogether, warning that "our interests will be more injured by the residence of foreign Ministers among us, than they can be promoted by our Ministers abroad."[69] Americans were much too worldly and practical to go that far, but they did incorporate their republicanism into their protocol and sought to shield themselves from foreign influence. Foreign diplomats were required to make the first visit to newly arriving members of Congress, a sharp departure from European practice. Congressmen made sure never to meet with the envoys by themselves. The "discretion and reserve" with which Americans treated representatives of other countries, a French diplomat complained, "appears to be copied from the Senators of Venice." The "outrageous circumspection" with which Congressmen behaved "renders them sad and silent." Like Adams, the Frenchman saw no choice but to adapt. "Congress insists on the new etiquette," French diplomat Louis Guillaume Otto sighed, "and the foreign Ministers will be obliged to submit to it or to renounce all connection with Members of Congress."[70]

The most pressing issue facing the United States during the Confederation period was commerce. Americans took pride in their independence, but they recognized that economically they remained part of a larger trading community. "The fortune of every citizen is interested in the fate of commerce," a congressional committee reported in 1784, "for it is the constant source of industry and wealth; and the value of our produce and our land must ever rise or fall in proportion to the prosperous or adverse state of our trade."[71] In a world of empires, the republic had to find ways to survive. Americans had often protested the burdens imposed by the Navigation Acts, but they had also benefited from membership in the British Empire. They hoped to retain the advantages without suffering the drawbacks. They assumed that their trade was so important that other nations would accept their terms. In fact, the Europeans and especially Britain set the conditions. And the competition among regions,

68. Adams to Jay, June 2, 1785, in Giunta, *Documents*, 151.
69. Rakove, *Beginnings*, 347.
70. Otto to Vergennes, October 1, 1785, in Giunta, *Documents*, 178–79.
71. Adams, *Jefferson*, 160.

states, and individuals prevented Congress from agreeing on a unified trade policy.[72]

Shelburne's fall from power brought a dramatic shift in British commercial policy. The change toward a hard line reflected persisting anger with the colonies' rebellion, their victory in the war, and what many Britons believed were overly generous peace terms. Despite Adam Smith's fervent advocacy of free trade, the Navigation Acts remained central to British economic thinking. British shipping interests especially feared American postwar competition. The influential Sheffield insisted that since the Americans had left the empire they must be treated as foreigners. This "tribune of shipbuilders and shipowners" argued that America's dependence on British credit and its passion for British manufactures would force trade back into traditional channels. London could fix the terms. On July 2, 1783, ironically the seventh anniversary of Congress's initial resolution for independence, Parliament issued an order in council excluding U.S. ships from the West Indies trade. British policymakers hoped that the rest of the empire could replace the Americans in established trade channels. That did not happen, but the 1783 order devastated New England's fishing and shipping industries. Britain also exploited U.S. removal of wartime trade restrictions and Congress's inability to agree on a tariff to flood the U.S. market with manufactured goods. It restricted the export of any items that would help Americans create their own manufactures. Britain's harsh measures contributed significantly to the depression that caused ruin across the nation.[73]

John Adams assumed the position of minister to England in June 1785 with instructions to press for the elimination of trade restrictions and secure an equitable commercial treaty. Adams sought to hit the British where it hurt, repeatedly warning that the effect of their trade restrictions was to "incapacitate our Merchants to make Remittances to theirs." He carried on a "Sprightly Dialogue" with Prime Minister William Pitt the Younger on trade and other matters and attributed British commercial restrictions to jealousy.[74] After six months, he admitted that he was a "cypher" and that the British were determined to reduce the United States to economic bondage.[75] Minister to France Thomas Jefferson, who joined Adams in London in 1786, flatly labeled the British "our enemies," com-

72. Merrill Jensen, *The New Nation: A History of the United States During the Confederation, 1781–1789* (New York, 1950), 156.
73. Morris, *Forging of the Union*, 130–32.
74. Giunta, *Documents*, 161.
75. Morris, *Forging of the Union*, 205.

plaining that they were "more bitterly hostile to us at present than at any point of the late war." British officials responded to American appeals, he added, by "harping a little on the old String, the insufficiency of the powers of Congress to treat and to compel Compliance with the Treaties."[76] Adams occasionally threatened a Navigation Act discriminating against British imports, but he knew, as did Jay, that such a measure could not be enacted or enforced by a government operating under a constitution that left powers over commerce to the states.

The United States fared little better with other major European powers. Americans hoped that the enticement of their bounteous trade, long circumscribed by British regulations, would lure Spain and France into generous commercial treaties. Spain did open some ports to the United States. Spanish products entered American ports on a de facto most-favored-nation basis. But Spain refused a commercial treaty without U.S. concessions in other areas. More important, once the war ended, Spain closed the ports of Havana and New Orleans to U.S. products and denied Americans access to the Mississippi River.

Of all the European nations, France was the most open to U.S. trade, but this channel failed to meet expectations. Jefferson succeeded the estimable Franklin as minister to France in 1784, "an excellent school of humility," he later mused, and ardently promoted expanded trade with France.[77] The Virginian's cosmopolitan tastes, catholic interests, and aristocratic manners made him a worthy successor and also a hit at court. He believed that if the United States shifted its trade to the French West Indies and opened its ports to French products, British dominance of U.S. commerce could be broken. With his customary attention to detail, Jefferson studied possible items of exchange, urging the French to convert to American whale oil for their lamps and American rice farmers to grow varieties the French preferred. French officials, Vergennes included, went to some lengths to encourage trade, dispatching consuls to most American states and opening four ports to U.S. products. Responding to domestic and colonial interest groups, the French also closed off the French West Indies to major U.S. exports such as sugar and cotton and imposed tariffs on imports of American tobacco. Jefferson pushed for concessions. "If France wishes us to drink her wine," he insisted, "she must let her Islanders eat our bread."[78] But the barriers to trade were greater than the concessions on each side. The French lacked the capital to provide the credits

---

76. Adams, *Jefferson*, 200.
77. Gaye Wilson, "Doctor Franklin," *Monticello* 16 (Winter 2005), 1.
78. Adams, *Jefferson*, 166.

American merchants needed to import their products. France refused to adapt products to American tastes and could not produce others in quantities needed to satisfy American demands. Despite strong efforts from both countries, the trade remained limited to small quantities of luxury goods, wine, and brandy.

The so-called Barbary pirates posed another impediment to commerce. For years, the North African states of Morocco, Algiers, Tunis, and Tripoli had earned a lucrative take by plundering European ships, ransoming or enslaving captive sailors, and extorting from seafaring nations handsome annual fees for safe passage through the Mediterranean. It "was written in their Koran," a Tripolitan diplomat instructed Adams and Jefferson, "that all nations who should not have acknowledged their authority were sinners, that it was their right and duty to make war upon them wherever they could be found, and that every [Muslim] who should be slain in battle was sure to go to paradise."[79]

The Europeans generally found it cheaper to pay than to subdue the pirates by force. As part of the empire, Americans had British protection, and they earned significant profits selling flour, fish, and timber to Mediterranean ports. Jay sought unsuccessfully to get protection for American ships and seamen written into the peace treaty. Once independent, the Americans had to fend for themselves, and the trade was hampered by attacks from the Barbary States. In late 1783, Morocco and Algiers seized three ships and held the crews for ransom. "Our sufferings are beyond our expressing or your conception," an enslaved captive reported to Jefferson.[80] Congress put up $80,000 to free the captives and buy a treaty, a princely sum given the state of the U.S. treasury but not nearly enough to satisfy the captors. Like the Europeans, Adams believed it cheaper to pay than to fight. Jefferson became "obsessed" with the pirates, preferring to cut "to pieces piecemeal" this "pettifogging nest of robbers."[81] In truth, Congress had neither the money nor will to do either. It appealed to the states for funds with no results. Diplomat Thomas Barclay managed to negotiate without tribute a treaty with the emperor of Morocco, mainly because that ruler disliked the British. Otherwise, problems with the Mediterranean trade were left for another day.

The new nation enjoyed some successes during the Confederation period. The small concessions made by some European states were quite

79. Stahr, *Jay*, 218.
80. Richard O'Bryen to Jefferson, August 24, 1785, in Giunta, *Documents*, 229.
81. Adams, *Jefferson*, 202–3.

extraordinary in terms of eighteenth-century commercial policies.[82] The United States negotiated agreements with Sweden and Prussia based on the liberal principles of the 1776 Model Treaty. Enterprising merchants actively sought out new markets. In August 1784, after a voyage of six months, the *Empress of China* became the first American ship to reach the port of Canton, where it exchanged with Chinese merchants pelts and "green gold," the fabled root ginseng believed to restore the virility of old men, for tea, spices, porcelain, and silk. The voyage earned a profit of 25 percent, and the ship's return to New York in May 1785 excited for the first time what would become perennial hopes among U.S. merchants of capturing the presumably rich China market. At first unable to distinguish Americans from the British, Chinese merchants were also enthused by the prospect of trade with these "*New People*" upon seeing from a map the size of this new country.[83] American shippers continued to perfect the fine art of evading European trade restrictions. Especially in the West Indies, they employed various clever schemes to get around the British orders in council, developing a flourishing illicit traffic that even the brilliant young naval officer Horatio Nelson could not stop. Commerce increased steadily during these years, and the United States eased out of the depression, but trade never attained the heights Americans had hoped. To many leaders, the answer was a stronger federal government with authority to regulate commerce and retaliate against those nations who discriminated against the United States.

A second major postwar problem was the windfall the nation acquired from England in the 1783 treaty, the millions of acres of sparsely settled land between the Appalachian Mountains and the Mississippi River. This bounty made the United States an instant great power, but taking control of it and administering it posed enormous challenges. Many of the states held conflicting titles to western lands; Congress's authority was at best uncertain. Already forced westward by the advance of colonial settlements, Native Americans also claimed land in the trans-Appalachian West and were determined to fight for it. They gained support from the British, who hung on to forts granted the United States in the 1783 treaty, and from the Spanish in the Southwest. The problem was complicated when Americans after independence poured westward. The population of Kentucky, according to one estimate, totaled but 150 men in 1775. Fifteen years later, it exceeded 73,000 people. The "seeds of a great people are daily planting beyond the mountains," Jay observed in 1785.[84]

82. Jensen, *New Nation*, 169.
83. Samuel Shaw to Jay, May 19, 1785, in Giunta, *Documents*, 242.
84. Jensen, *New Nation*, 114.

Among the major accomplishments of the Confederation government were the establishment of federal authority over these lands and creation of mechanisms for settling and governing the new territory. The issue of federal versus state control was resolved during the war when the states ceded their land claims to the national government as a condition for adoption of the Articles of Confederation. Virginia had proposed in 1780 that the lands acquired by the national government should be "formed into distinct republican states, which shall become members of the federal union, and have the same rights of sovereignty, freedom, and independence, as the other states."[85] Fearful of the proliferation of thinly populated and weak states with loose bonds to the Confederation, Congress in the Northwest Ordinance of 1787, its most important achievement, put settlement and economic development before statehood. The ordinance did not permit immediate admission to the Union but placed the new settlements under what Virginian James Monroe admitted were "Colonial principles." It did guarantee for those in the territories the fundamental rights and liberties of American citizens and eventual acceptance into the United States on an equal basis with the other states. It became the means by which territory beyond the Mississippi would be incorporated into the Union.[86]

It was one thing to *plan* for governing and incorporating this territory, quite another to control it, and here the Confederation government was far less successful. Continued rapid settlement of the West and effective use of the land required protection from Indians and Europeans and access to markets. The government could provide neither, encouraging among settlers in the western territories rampant disaffection and even secessionist sentiment.

The state and national governments first addressed the Indian "problem" with a massive land grab. Americans rationalized that since most of the Indians had sided with the British they had lost the war and therefore their claim to western lands. The state of New York took 5.5 million acres from the Oneida tribe, Pennsylvania a huge chunk from the Iroquois. Federal negotiators dispensed with the elaborate rituals that had marked earlier negotiations between presumably sovereign entities and instead treated the Indians as a conquered people. The British had not told the Indians of their territorial concessions to the Americans. The Iroquois

85. Morris, *Forging of the Union*, 227.
86. Peter S. Onuf, *Statehood and Union: A History of the Northwest Ordinance* (Bloomington, Ind., 1987), 44–66. The Monroe quote is from p. 49. Also Morris, *Forging of the Union*, 229.

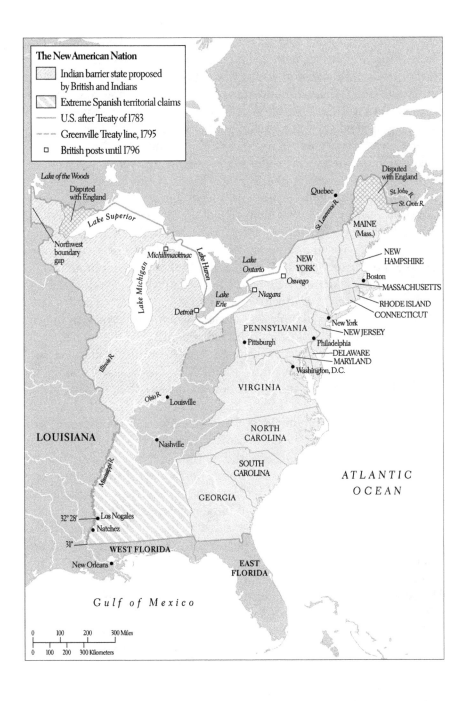

The New American Nation

Indian barrier state proposed by British and Indians

Extreme Spanish territorial claims

U.S. after Treaty of 1783

Greenville Treaty line, 1795

British posts until 1796

Lake of the Woods

Disputed with England

Lake Superior

Quebec

Disputed with England

St. John R.

St. Croix R.

St. Lawrence R.

MAINE (Mass.)

Northwest boundary gap

Michilimackinac

Lake Huron

Lake Michigan

Lake Ontario

NEW YORK

NEW HAMPSHIRE

Oswego

Boston

MASSACHUSETTS

Lake Erie

Niagara

Detroit

RHODE ISLAND

CONNECTICUT

New York

NEW JERSEY

PENNSYLVANIA

Pittsburgh

Philadelphia

DELAWARE

MARYLAND

Washington, D.C.

Illinois R.

VIRGINIA

Ohio R.

Louisville

NORTH CAROLINA

LOUISIANA

Nashville

SOUTH CAROLINA

ATLANTIC OCEAN

GEORGIA

Mississippi R.

32° 28'

Los Nogales

Natchez

31°

WEST FLORIDA

New Orleans

EAST FLORIDA

Gulf of Mexico

0   100   200   300 Miles

0   100   200   300 Kilometers

came to negotiations at Fort Stanwix in October 1784 believing that the lands of the Six Nations belonged to them. Displaying copies of the 1783 treaty awarding the territory to the United States, federal negotiators informed them: "You are a subdued people.... We shall now, therefore declare to you the condition, on which alone you can be received into the peace and protection of the United States." In the Treaty of Fort Stanwix, the Iroquois surrendered claims to the Ohio country.[87] Federal agents negotiated similar treaties with the Cherokees in the South and acquired most Wyandot, Delaware, Ojibwa, and Ottawa claims to the Northwest.

Such heavy-handed tactics provoked Indian resistance. Native American leaders countered that, unlike the British, they had not been defeated in the war. Neither had they consented to the treaty. Britain had "no right Whatever to grant away to the United States of America, their Rights or properties."[88] Leaders such as the Mohawk Joseph Brant and the Creek Alexander McGillivray, both educated in white schools and familiar with white ways, found willing allies in Britain and Spain. Brant secured British backing to build a confederacy of northern Indians to resist American expansion. The Creeks had long considered themselves an independent nation. They were stunned that the British had given away their territory without consulting them. McGillivray tried to pull the Creeks together into a unified nation to defend their independence against the United States. In a 1784 treaty negotiated at Pensacola, he gained Spanish recognition of Creek independence and promises of guns and gunpowder. For the next three years, Creek warriors drove back settlers on western lands in Georgia and Tennessee.[89] By the late 1780s, the United States faced a full-fledged Indian war across the western frontier.

The threat of war pushed Congress into making the pragmatic adjustment from pursuing a policy of confrontation to treating the Indians more equitably. Americans were also sensitive to their historical reputation. Certain that they were a chosen people creating a new form of government and setting higher standards of behavior among nations, they feared that if they did not treat Native Americans equitably, as Secretary of War Henry Knox put it, "the disinterested part of mankind and posterity will be apt to class the efforts of our Conduct and that of the Spanish in Mexico and Peru together."[90] American negotiators reverted to native ritual and custom in the negotiations, admitted that the British had no right to give

87. Merrell, "Declarations," 201; Graymont, *Iroquois*, 278–79.
88. Merrell, "Declarations," 202.
89. Michael D. Green, *The Creeks* (New York, 1990), 41–44.
90. Merrell, "Declarations," 205.

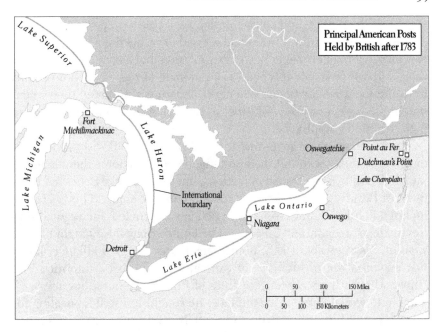

away Indian lands, and even offered to compensate Indians for territory taken in earlier treaties. The Northwest Ordinance provided that Indians should be dealt with in the "utmost good faith" and that "their land and property shall never be taken from them without their consent."[91] Under Knox's direction, Confederation leaders also set out to Americanize the natives, conferring on them the blessings of "civilization" and eventually absorbing them into American society. The goal was the same; the methods changed to salve America's conscience and preserve its reputation. The new approach produced policies that would be followed far into the future. But it did not resolve the immediate problem of quelling Indian resistance.

Equally serious threats came from the British and Spanish, and the Confederation's inability to deal effectively with these problems provided some of the most compelling arguments for a stronger national government. In the Northwest, the British refused to evacuate a string of frontier posts at Detroit, Niagara, and other points along the Great Lakes and used their presence on territory awarded the United States in the treaty to abet Indian resistance to American settlement of the Northwest. British diplomats insisted that they had not upheld their treaty obligations because the United States had not carried out provisions relating to payment of debts

91. Ibid., 204.

owed British creditors and compensation for Loyalist property confiscated during the war. In truth, Britain had refused to vacate the posts as a matter of policy, deliberately using the treaty provision that called for their departure "with all convenient speed" as a rationale to reap maximum profits from the lucrative fur trade. Whenever Americans protested their retention of the posts, however, British officials hurled back at them charges of their own non-compliance.

The Confederation government could not get the British off its territory. Negotiations accomplished nothing; it could not force them to leave. Jay tried hard to meet British objections, but in the case of debts and treatment of Loyalists, the real power resided with the states. They were not inclined to fulfill, and in some cases actively obstructed, the vague promises made to creditors and Loyalists. The United States also sought French support. Nervous about U.S. obligations under the 1778 alliance, Jay at first explored the possibilities of extrication, only to be informed that "those who have once been the allies of France are her allies always."[92] Unable to wriggle free of the alliance, he sought to use it, appealing for French support in getting Britain to abide by its treaty obligations. France refused to meddle in Anglo-American affairs. In any event, French policy after the Revolution was "to have the United States remain in its present state" and not "acquire a force and power" that it "would probably be very easy to abuse."[93] Some French officials, including the comte de Moustier, minister to the United States, were dreaming up an ambitious scheme to restore the French empire to North America.

The United States fared worse with Spain. Of all the European nations, Spain was the most threatened by the new nation and therefore the most hostile. A declining power, Spain was in poor condition to defend its once proud empires in North and South America. It was especially nervous about the Americans, whose restless energy and expansionist thrust endangered its weakly defended colonies in the Southwest. Spain sought to hem in the United States as tightly as possible by treaty or military force. It refused to recognize the Mississippi as the western boundary of the United States and contested the southern boundary set by the United States and Britain in 1783. It rejected American claims to free navigation of the Mississippi from its headwaters to the sea, a crippling blow to the economic viability of the expanding settlements in the Southwest. Spanish officials also negotiated treaties with and provided arms to Southwestern Indians to resist American settlement. They conspired with western

92. DeConde, "French Alliance," 28.
93. Morris, *Forging of the Union*, 209.

settlers and rascals such as the notorious James Wilkinson to promote secession from the United States. After a visit in 1784, George Washington
reported that "the western settlers stand as it were upon a pivot; the touch
of a feather would turn them any way."[94]

Jay and Spain's special envoy Don Diego de Gardoqui set out in 1785 to
resolve these differences. Fearing that the rapid population growth in the
American West might threaten its holdings, Spain sought a treaty as a
shield against an expanding United States. It hoped to exploit northeastern distrust of the West to achieve its goal.[95] The government authorized
Gardoqui to accept the boundary for East Florida specified in the 1783
Anglo-American treaty, but to reject 31° north for West Florida. He was to
insist on Spain's "exclusive right" to navigate the Mississippi and seek a
western boundary for the United States well east of that river and in some
areas as far north as the Ohio River.[96] In return for acceptance of Spain's
essential demands, he could offer a commercial treaty and an alliance
guaranteeing the two nations' possessions in North America. A congressional committee informed Jay, on the other hand, that an acceptable
treaty must include full access to the Mississippi and the borders set forth
in the 1783 peace agreement. The secretary was given some flexibility on
boundaries, but he could conclude no agreement without consulting
Congress.

The Jay-Gardoqui talks took place in the United States, lasted for more
than a year, and eventually produced the outlines of a deal. Gardoqui had
first met Jay in Spain. Viewing him as self-centered, "resolved to make a
fortune," and, most important, dominated by his socialite wife, the
Spanish envoy concluded that "a little management" and a "few timely
gifts" would win over Mrs. Jay and hence her husband. "Notwithstanding
my age, I am acting the gallant," he cheerily advised Madrid, "and accompany Madame to the official entertainments and dances because she likes
it."[97] In the best traditions of European diplomacy, he also presented Jay
the gift of a handsome Spanish horse, which the secretary accepted only
with Congress's approval.

Such extracurricular exertions could not overcome the standoff on the
Mississippi. As Spain had hoped, Jay eventually concluded that Gardoqui
would not give way on that issue and decided on an "expedient" that
waived U.S. access to the river for twenty-five years. In return, Spain

---

94. Jensen, *New Nation*, 171.
95. Francisco Rendon to Don Jose de Galvez, February 12, 1785, in Giunta, *Documents*, 197.
96. Conde de Floridablanca to Don Diego Gardoqui, October 2, 1784, ibid., 190.
97. Jensen, *New Nation*, 172.

would grant the United States a generous commercial treaty, and the two nations would guarantee each other's North American territories. Jay did not discuss the terms with Congress, as he had been instructed—yet another manifestation of his independent cast of mind—although he did consult with individual legislators. A negative response from Virginian Monroe, who had drafted his original instructions, failed to deter him. In May 1786, he offered the agreement to Congress.

Jay's proposal exposed sharp sectional differences and sparked open talk of secession. The onetime Hispanophobe insisted that since Spain was the only European power willing to negotiate, the United States should conclude an agreement. He defended the terms on the basis of the commercial benefits: full reciprocity; the establishment of consulates; Spain's commitment to buy specified American products with much-needed hard currency; full access to the ports of metropolitan Spain. "We gain much, and sacrifice or give up nothing," he claimed. Concession on the Mississippi was "not *at present* important," he added, and "a forbearance to use it while we do not want it, is no great sacrifice."[98] Regarding a concession on the Florida boundary, he argued that it was better to "yield a few acres than to part in ill-humour."[99]

Southerners thought otherwise. They minimized the value of Spain's commercial concessions and maximized the importance of the Mississippi. "The use of the Mississippi is given by nature to our western country," Virginia's James Madison proclaimed, "and no power on earth can take it from them."[100] Failure to gain access to the river would splinter the West from the East. Lurking behind heated southern opposition was the hope that the addition of new states beneath the Ohio River would enlarge their power in the national government. Jay's proposal required them to abandon their expansionist aims for the benefit of northern commerce. Monroe accused him of a "long train of intrigue" to secure congressional approval.[101] Westerners vowed to raise an army of ten thousand men, attack Spanish possessions, and even separate from the United States.[102] To "make us vassals to the merciless Spaniards is a grievance not to be borne," one spokesman thundered.[103] Northern delegates tried to mollify their southern brethren by holding out for the 31st parallel as a Florida boundary. But when seven northern states voted to revise Jay's instructions,

98. Stahr, *Jay*, 215.
99. Morris, *Forging of the Union*, 241.
100. Jensen, *New Nation*, 173.
101. Stahr, *Jay*, 216.
102. Otto to comte de Montmorin, March 5, 1787, in Giunta, *Documents*, 210–11.
103. Jensen, *New Nation*, 173.

southerners questioned the viability of the national government. "If seven states can carry a treaty..., it follows, of course, that a Confederate compact is no more than a rope of sand, and if a more efficient Government is not obtained a dissolution of the Union must take place."[104] It took nine states to ratify, and Jay reluctantly concluded that a "treaty disagreeable to one-half the nation had better not be made for it would be violated." Gardoqui went home empty-handed. The debate over the abortive treaty produced the sharpest sectional divisions yet. Southerners began to suspect that the deadlock threatened the unity of the new nation.[105]

IV

An emerging sense of crisis among leaders of a nationalist bent produced in 1786 urgent calls for changing the Articles of Confederation or scrapping them altogether. The government seemed incapable of relieving the nation's commercial woes. As early as 1784, some delegates had considered asking the states to give Congress power to discriminate against British imports, but the lack of a quorum forestalled action. A congressional committee proposed in early 1785 an amendment to the Articles giving Congress power to regulate commerce. The proposal was debated but never approved, partly from southern fear of northern commercial interests, also because of a more generalized concern about expanded federal power.[106] Although some regions had begun to recover from the postwar depression, commercial problems crippled key sectors of the U.S. economy such as shipbuilding and whaling.[107] Americans deeply resented the indignities heaped upon them by other nations, especially the British.

The situation in the West seemed to nationalists equally menacing. Britain defiantly clung to the Great Lakes forts and continued to exploit the fur trade. From the Canadian border to the Floridas, the United States faced the danger of Indian warfare. Indian attacks killed as many as 1,500 Kentuckians between 1783 and 1790. Two hundred Virginians died in October 1786 alone. In that same year, seven thousand Creeks threatened Savannah on the Georgia coast.[108] The national government was no more effective in dealing with the Indian menace than with commercial problems. It lacked an army and the money to raise one. Its inability to secure access to the Mississippi raised further concerns about its weakness. Jay's

---

104. Morris, *Forging of the Union*, 243.
105. Rakove, *Beginnings*, 350.
106. Ibid., 346–47.
107. Frederick W. Marks III, "Power, Pride, and the Purse: Diplomatic Origins of the Constitution," *Diplomatic History* 11 (Fall 1987), 311–12.
108. Ibid., 310.

apparent willingness to bargain away what southerners considered their birthright threatened dissolution of the Union. The crisis of 1786 posed fundamental questions about whether Congress had the power and backing to defend U.S. interests in a hostile world or even whether it could agree upon those interests that must be protected.[109]

Foreign policy concerns drove nationalist demands to revise the nation's form of government. By 1786, leaders were deeply concerned with the dignity, honor, and respectability of their country. In declaring themselves independent and winning their freedom from Great Britain, Americans were acutely conscious that they were conducting a novel experiment in self-government that could serve as an example to the rest of the world. Their nation's weakness in the face of foreign humiliation threatened that experiment and was therefore especially difficult to accept. Nationalists thus concluded that they must have a government strong enough to command respect abroad. Adams insisted that until the national government could prevent the states from undermining the 1783 treaty it would be impossible to negotiate with England. "Of all the nations on earth," Jefferson protested from Paris, the British "require to be treated with the most hauteur. They require to be kicked into common good manners." The young New York firebrand Alexander Hamilton lamented that the nation was at "almost the last stage of national humiliation."[110] "Is respectability in the eyes of foreign powers a safeguard against foreign encroachments?" he later asked in the *Federalist Papers*. "The imbecility of our government forbids them to treat with us," he answered.[111]

Over the next two years, the nationalists translated their concerns into action. In January 1786, Virginia proposed a convention to be held in Annapolis, Maryland, to deal with commercial issues. Only five states sent representatives—the host state, ironically, was not one of them—but Hamilton used the meeting to enlarge the discussions to other weaknesses of the federal system. The resolution emerging from Annapolis in September described the condition of the union as "delicate and critical" and called upon the states to send delegates to another meeting in Philadelphia to "derive such further provisions as shall appear to be necessary to render the constitution of the Federal Government adequate to

109. Rakove, *Beginnings*, 350.
110. Jonathan R. Dull, "Two Republics in a Hostile World: The United States and the Netherlands in the 1780s," in Greene, *Revolution*, 158.
111. Daniel G. Lang, *Foreign Policy in the Early Republic: The Law of Nations and the Balance of Power* (Baton Rouge, La., 1985), 81.

the exigencies of the Union."[112] Congress gave lukewarm endorsement limited to revising the Articles of Confederation.

A taxpayers' revolt in western Massachusetts led by revolutionary war veteran Daniel Shays just as representatives were preparing to go to Philadelphia provided another boost to the nationalist cause. State military forces raised for the occasion easily suppressed the uprising, but the events confirmed in the minds of nationalists and the propertied classes fears of chaos and even dissolution of the Union. Shays's Rebellion also had foreign policy implications since the rebels had reportedly discussed with the British possible separation from the Union.[113] It strengthened belief in the need for a strong national government that could regulate the militia, maintain order, and hold the Union together. "We are fast verging to anarchy and confusion," Washington warned Madison in November 1786.[114]

The fear of anarchy, although exaggerated, was widely shared and had international implications. Jefferson in Paris worried that signs of chaos would weaken the United States in the eyes of Europeans sympathetic to the Revolution. He and other Americans also viewed events at home in terms of what was happening in Europe. The "partition" of rebellious Poland by outside powers and the plight of the fledgling Dutch republic, divided internally and threatened from within and without, were ever-present reminders of the fragility of the American experiment.[115] Nationalists viewed the American Revolution as a "new chapter in the law of nations" and often comforted themselves that their republic was "immune to the savage enmities of the Old World." By 1786, they feared that the independence of the individual states might lead to the Europeanization of America, its breakup into quarreling entities resembling the European state system. Such a condition could lead to European intervention or the reimposition of despotism. Indeed, Shays's Rebellion and separatist sentiment in Vermont seemed to some nationalists a "stalking horse for counterrevolutionary conspiracy."[116]

The Constitutional Convention met in Philadelphia from May 25 to September 17, 1787. Jefferson hailed it as an "assembly of demigods." A French diplomat agreed that "we will never have seen, even in Europe, an assembly more respectable for the talents, knowledge, disinterestedness,

112. Morris, *Forging of the Union*, 257.
113. Marks, "Diplomatic Origins," 312–13.
114. Morris, *Forging of the Union*, 266.
115. Lawrence S. Kaplan, "Jefferson and the Constitution: The View from Paris, 1786–89," *Diplomatic History* 11 (Fall 1987), 323.
116. Onuf, "Anarchy," 272–74, 281–82.

and patriotism of those who compose it."[117] In 1787, the king of Prussia intervened militarily to crush rebellion in the Netherlands and restore monarchy. The specter of Holland's misfortune clouded the meeting in Philadelphia until it ended.[118] The discussions were dominated by nationalists, but debates were often heated. Crucial differences between large and small states over representation in the legislature were resolved by the "Great Compromise," which provided for equal representation in the upper house, the Senate, and proportional representation in the House of Representatives. The constitution also provided for a president to be elected every four years and a federal judiciary.

Foreign policy issues played a major role in calling the convention and would be important in the deliberations themselves. The fundamental question of the foreign policy powers to be assigned to each branch of government created ambiguities that have vexed the republic ever since. On one issue—commerce—there was little debate. Under the Confederation, the states could not agree on a uniform commercial policy. Other nations had exploited the differences. The need for a unified federal policy "has been so often enforced and descanted upon," a New York newspaper observed, "that the whole subject appears to be worn threadbare."[119] The need for federal authority to regulate commerce was the major reason the convention had been called. All plans proposed in Philadelphia gave the national government that power. A Committee of Detail assigned to Congress "the exclusive power of regulating Trade and levying imposts." Some nervous Deep South states pushed for a two-thirds vote to approve commercial legislation. Madison led the opposition, arguing that "we are laying the foundation of a great empire" and should "take a permanent view of the subject." The great issue, he insisted, was "the necessity of securing the West India trade to this country." The proposal was defeated, but the southerners extracted concessions in the form of provisions preventing any interference with the slave trade before 1808 and prohibiting export duties.[120]

The several branches shared power on other key foreign policy questions such as the making of treaties and diplomatic appointments. Early in the convention, delegates generally agreed that the Senate should be primarily responsible for foreign affairs. They naturally worried that an executive with too much power might replicate the monarchy from which

---

117. Kaplan, "Jefferson," 322; Morris, *Forging of the Union*, 269.
118. Kaplan, "Jefferson," 334.
119. Jacques J. Gorlin, "Foreign Trade and the Constitution," in Robert A. Goldwin and Robert A. Licht, eds., *Foreign Policy and the Constitution* (Washington, 1990), 57.
120. Morris, *Forging of the Union*, 284–85.

they had just escaped. If presidential powers extended to war and peace, South Carolinian Charles Pinckney warned, it "would render the executive a monarchy of the worst kind, to wit an elected one."[121] Since Congress had executive powers under the Articles, it seemed natural to many of the delegates to leave them there. The smaller Senate, composed of more experienced and presumably wiser members, would be better able to deal with foreign policy issues than the popularly elected House. Thus late in the deliberations, when such issues were finally addressed, the power to make treaties and appoint diplomats was given to the Senate.

Ultimately, such powers were shared with the executive. Some delegates believed that the president could act as a check on the Senate and might better serve "as the general Guardian of the national interest."[122] Others felt that a single individual could operate more effectively than a larger legislative body and maintain the secrecy sometimes necessary in handling foreign policy issues. The large states objected to what New York's Rufus King called "the vicious principle of representation," which made them equal with the small. Others disliked the fact that senators were elected by the state legislatures. Madison thus pushed for the president to act on these matters with the "advice and consent" of the Senate. The most controversial proposal was to require a two-thirds vote for approving treaties. The large states objected that a minority of small states could block a treaty. Madison sought to make peace treaties easier to approve by requiring a simple majority, but the two-thirds clause stuck, giving a minority a potent weapon that would be used often in the future.[123]

The constitutional provision that has caused the greatest controversy— the power to make war—was similarly shared yet, ironically, seems to have provoked little discussion in Philadelphia. Some delegates preferred to give the power to the president. Others, not surprisingly, feared granting such power to one person, proposing that it stay with the legislature and even with the Senate. Reflecting the spirit of compromise that marked the proceedings, Madison urged assigning to the president as commander in chief the power to "repel sudden attacks" when Congress could not act but giving Congress the power to declare war. This ambiguous compromise left the president an opening to employ military force without securing a declaration, one of the most persistent and difficult issues to emerge from the Constitution.

121. Jack N. Rakove, "Making Foreign Policy: The View from 1787," in Goldwin and Licht, *Constitution*, 6.
122. Ibid., 13.
123. Ibid., 9–13.

Submission of the document to the states for ratification set off a spirited debate, and foreign policy was central to the discussion. Indeed, the debate over the Constitution was the first in a series of recurring debates over the goals of U.S. foreign policy and the nation's proper role in the world. Those nationalists who shrewdly called themselves Federalists insisted that the weaknesses so blatantly manifest in the Articles of Confederation must be corrected if the United States was to survive and prosper in a hostile world. Those who came to be known as Antifederalists minimized external dangers and warned of the threat to American liberties from a more powerful national government and more active involvement in world affairs.

Federalists saw signs of national decline everywhere.[124] Foreign troops remained on America's soil; ships in its ports flew other flags while U.S. vessels rotted at their moorings. Congress could not enforce treaties. Unpaid debts had destroyed U.S. credit abroad. The lack of respect with which the nation was treated provided the most compelling sign of U.S. weakness. "At the peace . . . America held a most elevated rank among the powers of the earth," a Pennsylvanian lamented, "but how are the mighty fallen! disgraced have we rendered ourselves abroad and ruined at home."[125] The nation's weakness made it "a prey to the nations of the earth," a defender of the Constitution declaimed. "What is there to prevent an Algerine pirate from landing on your coast, and carrying away your citizens into slavery?" a North Carolinian asked with obvious hyperbole. "You have not a single sloop of war."[126] Federalists insisted that the nation's prosperity hinged on a thriving commerce and thus on access to foreign markets. They wanted the United States to take its rightful place among the world's great nations. A constitution that strengthened national power would enable the nation to address its most important foreign policy problems and command respect abroad. It would "raise us from the lowest degree of contempt, into which we are now plunged," a Massachusetts newspaper proclaimed, "to an honorable, and consequently equal station among nations."[127] Some Federalists even championed the Constitution as an "inspirational instrument to the Old World," an essential means to extend to other nations the American model of republican union.[128]

124. Norman A. Graebner, "Isolationism and Antifederalism: The Ratification Debates," *Diplomatic History* 11 (Fall 1987), 337.
125. Ibid.
126. Ibid., 339.
127. Ibid., 340.
128. Onuf, "Anarchy," 300, 303.

Antifederalists took a more sanguine view of the nation's condition, a more limited view of its role in the world. They accused their foes of seeking to terrify the people by concocting "imaginary danger" and of over-promising the benefits of a new constitution. Anticipating arguments that would run throughout future foreign policy debates, they insisted that the United States because of its distance from Europe and the barrier provided by the Atlantic Ocean enjoyed unprecedented security. Should a European nation be so foolish as to attack, it would fight at a distinct disadvantage. Because of the European balance of power, other nations would come to America's aid. The United States could best exploit its geographical advantage by focusing on problems at home and providing the world "an example of a great people, who in their civil institutions hold chiefly in view, the attainment of virtue, and happiness among themselves."[129] It should not seek to influence European politics or intrude in disputes beyond its borders. Southern Antifederalists took issue with the Constitution itself. They feared that assigning to a bare majority the power to regulate commerce would benefit northern merchants at their expense. Opponents from all regions expressed concern over giving Congress unlimited power to tax. A standing army would burden the citizens economically, a Virginian warned; it "must sooner or later, establish a tyranny, not inferiour to the triumvirate...of Rome."[130]

Ratification took place between December 1787 and the summer of 1788. Convention leaders wisely decided not to submit the document to Congress or the state legislatures but rather to state conventions created expressly for that purpose. As a matter of expediency, they sent the draft constitution to Congress in the fall of 1787. That body—soon to be voted out of existence—approved its submission to the states. In many states, the debate provoked frantic political maneuvering and bitter debate. Virginia and New York were vital, and their approval solidified the Union, although New York's endorsement came after the necessary nine states had already ratified, putting the Constitution into effect. More than anything else, the commitment of the Constitution's sponsors to add a Bill of Rights ensured its approval. A new constitution "had been extorted from the grinding necessity of a reluctant nation," the young diplomat John Quincy Adams concluded without exaggeration.[131]

Whatever its ambiguities and defects, the Constitution corrected where foreign affairs were concerned the most glaring deficiencies of the Articles

---

129. Graebner, "Isolationism," 345.
130. Ibid., 340.
131. Morris, Forging of the Union, 317.

of Confederation. It gave the new national government clear authority to handle trade and foreign policy matters and responsibility to protect the nation's security and advance its global interests. These changes came none too soon. In 1789, France was swept by revolution. Three years later, war broke out in Europe, providing for the United States a challenge as great as the Revolution and its aftermath.

2

"None Who Can Make Us Afraid"

The New Republic in a Hostile World, 1789–1801

George Washington's 1796 musings about a United States so powerful that none could "make us afraid" reflected the fear that gripped the nation throughout the turbulent 1790s, a time of dire threats from without and bitter divisions within. They also put into words the first president's vision of an American empire invulnerable to such dangers. If the United States could avoid war for a generation, he reasoned, the growth in population and resources combined with its favorable geographic location would enable it "in a just cause, to bid defiance to any power on earth."[1] Washington and his successor, John Adams, set important precedents in the management of foreign and national security policy. Conciliatory at the brink of war, they managed to avert hostilities with and wring important concessions from both England and France. They consolidated control of the western territories awarded in the 1783 peace treaty with Britain, laying a firm foundation for what Washington called the "future Grandeur of this rising Empire."[2] The Federalists' conduct of U.S. foreign policy significantly shaped the new nation's institutions and political culture. Through skillful diplomacy and great good fortune, the United States emerged from a tumultuous decade much stronger than at the start.

I

During the first years under its new Constitution, the United States faced challenges in foreign relations unsurpassed in gravity until the mid-twentieth century. In 1792, Europe erupted in a war that for more than two decades would convulse much of the world in bitter ideological and military struggle. Americans agreed as a first principle of foreign policy that they must stay out of such wars, but neutrality afforded little shelter. Europe "intruded" on America "in every way," historian Lawrence Kaplan has written, "inspiring fear of reconquest by the mother country, offering opportunity along sparsely settled borderlands, arousing uncertainties

---

1. Quoted in Burton Ira Kaufman, *Washington's Farewell Address: The View from the 20th Century* (Chicago, 1969), 183.
2. Ibid., 184.

over the alliance with a great power."[3] The new nation depended on trade with Europe. The major belligerents attempted to use the United States as an instrument of their grand strategies and respected its neutrality only when expedient. The war also set loose profound divisions within the United States, and the internal strife in turn threatened America's ability to remain impartial toward the belligerents. Nor did the United States, while claiming neutrality, seek to insulate itself from the conflict. Rather, like small nations through history, it sought to exploit great-power rivalries to its own advantage. Sometimes brash and self-righteous in its demeanor toward the outside world, assertive in claiming its rights and aggressive in pursuing its goals, the nation throughout the 1790s was constantly embroiled in conflict. At times its very survival seemed at stake.

The United States in 1789 remained weak and vulnerable. When Washington assumed office, he presided over fewer than four million people, most of them concentrated along the Atlantic seaboard. The United States claimed vast territory in the West, and settlement had expanded rapidly in the Confederation period, but Spain still blocked access to the Mississippi River. The isolated frontier communities had only loose ties to the federal union. British and Spanish agents intrigued to detach them from the United States while encouraging the Indians to resist American expansion. Economically, the United States remained in a quasi-colonial status, a producer of raw materials dependent on European credits, markets, and manufactured goods. Washington and some of his top advisers believed that military power was essential to uphold the authority of the new government, maintain domestic order, and support the nation's diplomacy. But their efforts to create a military establishment were hampered by finances and an anti-militarist tradition deeply rooted in the colonial era. On the eve of war in Europe, the United States had no navy. Its regular army totaled fewer than five hundred men.

The Constitution at least partially corrected the structural weaknesses that had hampered the Confederation's conduct of foreign policy. It conferred on the central government authority to regulate commerce and conduct relations with other nations. Although powers were somewhat ambiguously divided between the executive and legislative branches, Washington sure-handedly established the principle of presidential direction of foreign policy.

3. Lawrence S. Kaplan, "Thomas Jefferson: The Idealist as Realist," in Frank Merli and Theodore A. Wilson, eds., *Makers of American Diplomacy from Benjamin Franklin to Alfred Thayer Mahan* (New York, 1974), 56.

The first president created a Department of State to handle the day-to-day management of foreign relations, as well as domestic matters not under the War and Treasury departments. His fellow Virginian Thomas Jefferson assumed the office of secretary, assisted by a staff of four with an annual budget of $8,000 (including his salary). The other cabinet officers, particularly the secretaries of war and treasury, inevitably ventured into foreign policy. Washington made it a practice to submit important questions to his entire cabinet, resolving the issue himself where major divisions occurred. In keeping with ideals of republican simplicity—and to save money—the administration did not appoint anyone to the rank of ambassador. That "may be the custom of the old world," Jefferson informed the emperor of Morocco, "but it is not ours."[4] The "foreign service" consisted of a minister to France, chargés d'affaires in England, Spain, and Portugal, and an agent at Amsterdam. In 1790, the United States opened its first consulate in Bordeaux, a major source of arms, ammunition, and wine during the Revolution. That same year, it appointed twelve consuls and also named six foreigners as vice-consuls since there were not enough qualified Americans to fill the posts.[5]

A keen awareness of the nation's present weakness in no way clouded visions of its future greatness. The new government formulated ambitious objectives and pursued them doggedly. Conscious of the unusual fertility of the land and productivity of the people and viewing commerce as the natural basis for national wealth and power, American leaders worked vigorously to break down barriers that kept the new nation out of foreign markets. They moved quickly to gain control of the trans-Appalachian West, encouraging emigration and employing diplomatic pressure and military force to eliminate Native Americans and foreigners who stood in the way. Even in its infancy, the United States looked beyond existing boundaries, casting covetous eyes upon Spanish Florida and Louisiana (and even British Canada). Perceiving that in time a restless population that was doubling in size every twenty-two years would give it an advantage over foreign challengers, the Washington administration accepted the need for patience. But it prepared for the future by encouraging settlement of contested territory. Rationalizing their covetousness with the doctrine that superior institutions and ideology entitled them to whatever land they could use, Americans began to think in terms of an empire

4. Quoted in James A. Field Jr., *America and the Mediterranean World, 1776–1882* (Princeton, N.J., 1969), 40.
5. David S. Patterson, "The Department of State: The Formative Years, 1775–1800," *Prologue* 21 (Winter 1989), 323–24.

stretching from Atlantic to Pacific long before the population of existing boundaries was completed.[6]

The most urgent problem facing the new government was the threat of Indian war in the West. The "condition of the Indians to the United States is perhaps unlike that of any other two people in existence," Chief Justice John Marshall would later write, and clashing interests as well as incompatible concepts of sovereignty provoked conflict between them.[7] Most of the tribes scattered through the trans-Appalachian West lived in communal settlements but roamed widely across the land as hunters. American frontier society, on the other hand, was anchored in agriculture, private property, and land ownership, and Americans conveniently rationalized that the Indians had sacrificed claim to the land by not using it properly. The Indians only grudgingly conceded U.S. sovereignty. Increasingly aware that they could not hold back American settlers, they sought to contain them in specified areas by banding together in loose confederations, signing treaties with the United States, seeking assistance from Britain or Spain, or attacking exposed frontier settlements. Following precedents set by the colonial governments, the United States had implicitly granted the Indians a measure of sovereignty and accorded them the status of independent nations through negotiations replete with elaborate ceremony and the signing of treaties. As a way of asserting federal authority for Indian affairs over the states, the Washington administration would do likewise. From its birth, however, the United States had vehemently—and contradictorily—insisted that the Indians were under its sovereignty and that Indian affairs were therefore internal matters. The various land ordinances enacted by the Confederation presumed U.S. sovereignty in the West and sought to provide for orderly and peaceful settlement. But the onrush of settlers and their steady encroachment on Indian lands provoked retaliatory attacks and preemptive strikes.

The Washington administration desperately sought to avoid war. With limited funds in the treasury and no army, the infant government was painfully aware that it could not afford and might not win such a war. At this time, Americans in the more settled, seacoast areas accepted the Enlightenment view that all mankind was of one species and capable of improvement. In addition, Washington and Secretary of War Henry Knox insisted that the United States, a bold experiment in republicanism closely

---

6. Albert K. Weinberg, *Manifest Destiny: A Study of Nationalist Expansionism in American History* (Chicago, 1963), 72–81.

7. Quoted in Francis Paul Prucha, *American Indian Treaties: The History of a Political Anomaly* (Berkeley, Calif., 1991), 1.

watched by the whole world, must be true to its principles in dealing with the Indians. For the short term, the administration sought to avert war by diplomacy, building on the treaties negotiated under the Confederation to keep Indians and settlers apart and achieve cheap and peaceful expansion. For the long term, Knox promoted a policy of expansion with honor that would make available to the Indians the blessings of American civilization in return for their lands, a form of pacification through deculturation and assimilation.[8]

Washington's diplomacy achieved short-term results in the Southwest. The powerful Creeks had traditionally preserved their independence by playing European nations against each other. Eager to bind the autonomous groups that composed the tribe into a tighter union under his leadership and to fend off onrushing American settlers, the redoubtable half-breed Alexander McGillivray journeyed to New York in 1790 and amidst pomp and ceremony, including an audience with the Great Father himself (Washington), agreed to a treaty. In return for three million acres of land, the United States recognized the independence of the Creeks, promised to protect them from the incursions of its citizens, and agreed to boundaries. A seemingly innocent provision afforded a potentially powerful instrument for expansion with honor. "That the Creek nation may be led to a greater degree of civilization, and to become herdsmen and cultivators, instead of remaining in a state of hunters," the treaty solemnly affirmed, "the United States will from time to time furnish gratuitously the said nation with useful domestic animals and implements of husbandry."[9] The United States also provided an annuity of $1,500. The bestowing of such gifts would help civilize the Indians and, in Knox's words, have the "salutary effect of attaching them to the interests of the United States."[10] A secret protocol gave McGillivray control of trade and made him an agent of the United States with the rank of brigadier general and an annuity of $1,200.

In the short run, each party viewed the treaty as a success. It boosted the prestige of the new U.S. government, lured the Creeks from Spain, and averted conflict with the most powerful southwestern tribe. It appeared to the Creeks to recognize their sovereignty and protect them from American

---

8. Robert Berkhofer Jr., *The White Man's Indian: American Images of the Indian from Columbus to the Present* (New York, 1978), 142–44; Reginald Horsman, *Race and Manifest Destiny* (Cambridge, Mass., 1981), 104–6.
9. Michael D. Green, *The Creeks* (New York, 1990), 43–46; Prucha, *Indian Treaties*, 79–84.
10. David Nichols, "The Transformation of Indian Civilization Policy," unpublished paper in possession of author, 8–10.

settlers, buying McGillivray time to develop tribal unity and strength. In fact, the state of Georgia did not respect the treaty and the United States would not or could not force it to do so. Boundaries were not drawn, and settlers continued to encroach on Creek lands. To entice McGillivray away from the United States, Spanish agents doubled the pension provided by Washington. The Creek leader died in 1793, his dream of union unrealized, conditions in the Southwest still unsettled.[11]

The Northwest was far more explosive. The Confederation government had signed treaties with Indians north of the Ohio River, but some tribes had refused to go along, and those who had were dissatisfied. With British encouragement, the Indians sought to create a buffer state in the Northwest. As settlers poured into the area, tensions increased. Frontier people generally viewed the Indians as inferior savages and expendable and preferred to eliminate rather than pacify them. Eventually, their view prevailed.

Eager to avoid war and uphold American honor, the Washington administration capitulated to pressure from land speculators and settlers in Kentucky and elsewhere along the frontier. The administration continued to negotiate with the Indians, but it approached them in a high-handed manner that made success unlikely: "This is the last offer that can be made," Knox warned the northwestern tribes. "If you do not embrace it now, your doom must be sealed forever."[12] By backing its diplomacy with force, moreover, the administration blundered into the war it hoped to avoid. In 1790, to "strike terror into the minds of the Indians," Washington and Knox sent fifteen hundred men under Josiah Harmar deep into present-day Ohio and Indiana. Returning to its base after plundering Indian villages near the Maumee River, Harmar's force was ambushed and suffered heavy losses. To recoup its prestige among its own citizens and the Indians with whom it sought to negotiate, the administration escalated the conflict in 1791, sending fourteen hundred men under Gen. Arthur St. Clair into Indian country north of Cincinnati. St. Clair's small and ill-prepared force was annihilated, losing nine hundred men in what has been called the worst defeat ever suffered by an American army.[13] On the eve of war in Europe, the United States' position in the Northwest was more precarious than before, its prestige shattered.

11. Green, *Creeks*, 46; Lawrence S. Kaplan, *Thomas Jefferson: Westward the Course of Empire* (Wilmington, Del., 1999), 82.
12. Richard H. Kohn, *Eagle and Sword: The Beginnings of the Military Establishment in America* (New York, 1975), 112; Horsman, *Race and Manifest Destiny*, 111–14.
13. Allan R. Millett and Peter Maslowski, *For the Common Defense: A Military History of the United States of America* (New York, 1984), 92.

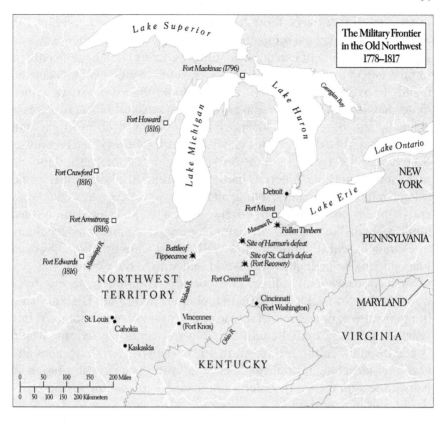

The terrifying reality of slave revolt in the Caribbean and specter of slave rebellion at home further heightened American insecurity in the early 1790s. Inspired by the rhetoric of the French Revolution, slaves in the French colony of Saint-Domingue (the western third of the island of Hispaniola, present-day Haiti) rebelled against their masters in August 1791. At the height of the struggle, as many as one hundred thousand blacks faced forty thousand whites and mulattoes. The fury stirred by racial antagonism and the legacy of slavery produced a peculiarly savage conflict. Marching into battle playing African music and flying banners with the slogan DEATH TO ALL WHITES, the rebels burned plantations and massacred planter families.[14]

Americans' enthusiasm for revolution stopped well short of violent slave revolt, of course, and they viewed events in the West Indies with foreboding. Trade with Saint-Domingue was important, the exports of $3 million

14. Tim Matthewson, "George Washington's Policy Toward the Haitian Revolution," *Diplomatic History* 3 (Summer 1979), 324–28.

in 1790 more than twice those to metropolitan France. Friendship with France also encouraged sympathy for the planters. Some Americans worried that Britain might exploit the conflict on Saint-Domingue to enlarge its presence in the region. But the U.S. response to the revolution derived mainly from racial fears. At this time, attitudes toward slavery remained somewhat flexible, but those who favored emancipation saw it taking place gradually and peacefully. The shock of violent revolt on nearby islands provoked fears of a descent into "chaos and negroism" and the certainty, as Secretary of the Treasury Alexander Hamilton put it, of "calamitous" results. Southerners like Jefferson harbored morbid dread that revolt would extend to the United States, setting off a frenzy of violence that could only end in the "extermination of one or the other race." State legislatures voted funds to help the planters on Saint-Domingue suppress the rebellion. Stretching executive authority, the Washington administration advanced France $726,000 in debt payments and sold arms to the planters.[15]

Such efforts were unavailing. The rebel victory in June 1793 sent shock waves to the North. Defeated French planters fled to the United States, bringing tales of massacre that spread panic throughout the South. While Jefferson privately fretted about the "bloody scenes" Americans would "wade through" in the future, southern states tightened slave codes and began to develop a positive defense of the "peculiar institution."[16] Nervousness on the northwestern frontier was exceeded by the horror of slave revolt in the South.

II

Republican ideology looked upon political parties as disruptive, even evil, but partisan politics intruded into foreign policy early in Washington's first term, a development that the president himself never fully accepted and that, throughout the 1790s, significantly influenced and vastly complicated the new government's dealings with the outside world. The struggle centered around the dynamic personalities of Jefferson and Hamilton, but it reflected much deeper divisions within U.S. society. It assumed a level of special intensity because the participants shared with equal fervor the conviction of revolutionaries that each step they took might determine the destiny of the new nation.[17] In addition, in a new

15. Ibid.
16. Jefferson to James Monroe, July 14, 1793, in Julian P. Boyd, ed., *The Papers of Thomas Jefferson*, vol. 26 (Princeton, N.J., 1995), 503.
17. Stanley Elkins and Eric McKitrick, *The Age of Federalism: The Early American Republic, 1788–1800* (New York, 1993), 4, 77. Classic accounts of the origins of American political parties from very different perspectives are Joseph Charles, *The*

nation any domestic or foreign policy decision could establish a lasting precedent.[18]

Tall, loose-jointed, somewhat awkward in manner and appearance, Jefferson was the embodiment of the southern landed gentry, an aristocrat by birth, an intellectual by temperament, a scholarly and retiring individual who hated open conflict but could be a fierce infighter. Small of stature, born out of wedlock in the West Indies, Hamilton struggled to obtain the social status Jefferson acquired by birth. Handsome and charming, a man of prodigious intellect and boundless energy, he was driven by insatiable ambitions and a compulsion to dominate. Jefferson represented the predominantly agricultural interests of the South and West. Optimistic by nature, a child of the Enlightenment, he had faith in popular government—at least the elitist form practiced in Virginia—viewed agriculture and commerce as the proper bases for national wealth, and was almost morbidly suspicious of the northeastern moneyed groups who prospered through speculation. To Hamilton, order was more important than liberty. A brilliant financier, he believed that political power should reside with those who had the largest stake in society. He attached himself to the financial elite Jefferson so distrusted. The dispute became deeply personal. Hamilton viewed Jefferson as devious and scheming. Jefferson was offended by Hamilton's arrogance and transparent ambition. He especially resented that the secretary of the treasury seemed to have Washington's ear.[19]

The Hamilton-Jefferson foreign policy struggle has often been portrayed in terms of a realist/idealist dichotomy, with Hamilton cast as the realist, more European than American in his thinking, coldly rational and keenly sensitive to the national interest and the limits of power, Jefferson as the archetypical American idealist, intent on spreading the nation's principles even at costs it could not afford. Such a construct, although useful, imposes a modern frame of reference on eighteenth-century ideas and practices and does not do justice to the complexity of the diplomacy of the two men or the conflict between them.[20]

Origins of the American Party System: Three Essays (New York, 1961) and Lance Banning, *The Jeffersonian Persuasion: Evolution of a Party Ideology* (Ithaca, N.Y., 1978).

18. Joseph J. Ellis, *American Sphinx: The Character of Thomas Jefferson* (New York, 1997), 121.

19. Ibid., 25–26, 136–37, 146; Kaplan, *Jefferson*, 73–74, 78.

20. For example, Paul Varg, *Foreign Policies of the Founding Fathers* (New York, 1970) and more recently Robert W. Tucker and David Hendrickson, *Empire of Liberty: The Statecraft of Thomas Jefferson* (New York, 1990) and Walter Russell Mead, *Special Providence: American Foreign Policy and How It Changed the World* (New York, 2001).

Both shared the long-range goal of a strong nation, independent of the great powers of Europe, but they approached it from quite different perspectives, advocating coherent systems of political economy in which foreign and domestic policies were inextricably linked with sharply conflicting visions of what America should be. Hamilton was the more patient. He preferred to build national power and *then* "dictate the terms of the connection between the old world and the new."[21] Modeling his system on that of England, he sought to establish a strong government and stable economy that would attract investment capital and promote manufactures. Through expansion of the home market he hoped in time to get around Britain's commercial restrictions and even challenge its supremacy, but for the moment he would acquiesce. His economic program hinged on revenues from trade with England, and he opposed anything that threatened it. Horrified at the excesses of the French Revolution, he condemned Jefferson's "womanish attachment" to France and increasingly saw England as a bastion of stable governing principles. More accurate than Jefferson and Madison in his assessment of American weakness and therefore more willing to make concessions to Britain, he pursued peace with a zeal that compromised American pride and honor and engaged in machinations that could have undermined American interests. His lust for power could be both reckless and destructive.

Deeply committed to perfecting the republican triumph of the Revolution, Jefferson and his compatriot James Madison, the intellectual force behind republicanism and leader in the House of Representatives, envisioned a youthful, vigorous, predominantly agricultural society composed of virtuous yeoman farmers. Their vision required the opening of foreign markets to absorb the produce of American farms and westward expansion to ensure the availability of sufficient land to sustain a burgeoning population. Britain stood as the major barrier to their dreams—it had "bound us in manacles, and very nearly defeated the object of our independence," Madison declaimed. Still, they were confident that a youthful, dynamic America could prevail over an England they saw as hopelessly corrupt and fundamentally rotten. Confirmed Anglophobes, they were certain from the experience with non-importation in the Revolutionary era that dependence on American necessities would force

A persuasive critique, at least for Jefferson, is Lawrence S. Kaplan, "Jefferson as Idealist-Realist," in *"Entangling Alliances with None": American Foreign Policy in the Age of Jefferson* (Kent, Ohio, 1987), 3–23.

21. Quoted in Michael H. Hunt, *Ideology and U.S. Foreign Policy* (New Haven, Conn., 1987), 24.

Britain to bend to economic pressure. They hoped to divert U.S. commerce to France. Although committed to free trade in theory, they proposed harsh discriminatory duties to force Britain to sign a commercial treaty.[22]

Jefferson and Madison were indeed idealists who dreamed of a world of like-minded republics. They were also internationalists with an abiding faith in progress who accepted, for the moment at least, the existing balance-of-power system and hoped to make it more peaceful and orderly through the negotiation of treaties promoting free trade and international law.[23] Jefferson especially admired France and things French. He welcomed the French Revolution and urged closer ties with the new government. As a French diplomat pointed out, however, his liking for France stemmed in part from his detestation for England, and, in any event, Americans in general were "the sworn enemy of all the European peoples."[24] He was also a tough-minded diplomatist, who advocated playing the European powers against each other to extract concessions. Jefferson and Madison saw Hamilton's policies as abject surrender to England. They viewed the secretary of the treasury and his cronies as tools "of British interests seeking to restore monarchy to America," an "enormous invisible conspiracy against the national welfare."[25] In diplomacy, Jefferson was more independent than Hamilton and could be shrewdly manipulative, but his commitment to principle and his tendency to overestimate American power at times clouded his vision and limited his effectiveness.

The battle was joined when the new government took office. Conflict first broke out over Hamilton's bold initiative to centralize federal power and create a moneyed interest by funding the national debt and assuming state debts, but it quickly extended to foreign affairs. In 1789, an Anglo-Spanish dispute over British fur-trading settlements at Nootka Sound on Vancouver Island in the Pacific Northwest threatened war. Jefferson urged U.S. support for the side that offered the most in return. Hamilton did not openly dissent. Certain that American interests would best be served by siding with Great Britain, however, he confided in British secret agent George Beckwith (the secretary of the treasury was referred to as No. 7 in coded dispatches) that Jefferson's position did not represent U.S. policy.

22. See especially Drew R. McCoy, *The Elusive Republic: Political Economy in Jeffersonian America* (Chapel Hill, N.C., 1980), 146–52.
23. Peter Onuf and Nicholas Onuf, *Federal Union, Modern World: The Law of Nations in an Age of Revolution* (New York, 1994), 92–105.
24. Ellis, *American Sphinx*, 124–25.
25. Kaplan, "Idealist as Realist," 71.

The differences became irrelevant when the threat of war receded, but they widened over commercial policy. Jefferson and Madison pushed for discriminatory duties against British commerce. Hamilton openly used his influence to block their passage in the Senate.[26]

Because of the sharp divisions within its own councils and primarily because of its continued weakness, the new government was little more successful than its predecessor in resolving the nation's major diplomatic problems. Britain in 1792 finally opened formal diplomatic relations, but Jefferson could not secure a commercial agreement or force implementation of the treaty of 1783. The United States was a relatively minor concern to Britain at this point. Content with the status quo, London did not take seriously Jefferson's threats of discrimination, in part because British officials correctly surmised that economic warfare would hurt America more than their own country, in part because of Hamilton's private assurances. In any event, Jefferson's bombastic rhetoric and uncompromising negotiating position left little room for compromise. The secretary of state fared no better with France and Spain. The French government refused even to negotiate a new commercial treaty and imposed discriminatory duties on tobacco and other American imports. Ignoring Jefferson's slightly veiled threats of war, Spain refused commercial concessions and would not discuss the disputed southern boundary and access to the Mississippi. On the eve of war in Europe, the position of the United States seemed anything but promising.

III

The outbreak of war in 1792 offered enticing opportunities to attain long-standing goals but posed new and ominous dangers to the independence and even survival of the republic. The Wars of the French Revolution and Napoleon differed dramatically from the chessboard engagements of the age of limited war. The French Revolution injected ideology and nationalism into traditional European power struggles, making the conflict more intense and all-consuming. Declaring war on Austria in August 1792, France launched a crusade to preserve revolutionary principles at home and extend them across the European continent. Alarmed by developments in Europe, England in February 1793 joined the Continental allies to block the spread of French power *and* the contaminating influence of French radicalism. Monarchical wars gave way to wars of nations; limited war to total war. The belligerents mobilized their entire populations not simply to defeat but to destroy their enemies, creating mass

26. Kaplan, *Jefferson*, 73.

armies that fought with a new patriotic zeal. The conflict spread across the globe. Britain, as always, sought to strangle its adversary by controlling the seas. As with earlier imperial conflicts, colonies formed an integral part of the grand strategies of the belligerents. The war expanded to the Mediterranean, South Asia, and the Western Hemisphere.[27]

These wars of new ferocity and scope left the United States little margin for safety. The great powers of Europe viewed the new nation as little more than a pawn—albeit a potentially useful one—in their struggle for survival. Perceiving the United States as weak and unreliable, neither wanted it as an ally. Each preferred a benevolent neutrality that offered access to naval stores and foodstuffs, shipping as needed, and the use of U.S. ports and territory as bases for commerce raiding and attacks on enemy colonies. They sought to deny their enemy what they wanted for themselves. They were openly contemptuous of America's wish to retain commercial ties with both sides and insulate itself against the war. They blatantly interfered in U.S. politics and employed bribery, intimidation, and the threat of force to achieve their aims.

Americans had long agreed they must abstain from Europe's wars, and the new nation's still fragile position in 1793 underscored the urgency of neutrality. Individuals as different as Hamilton and Jefferson could readily agree, moreover, that to become too closely attached to either power could result in a loss of freedom of action, even independence. Sensitive to the balance-of-power system and their role in it, Americans also quickly perceived that, as in the Revolution, they might exploit European conflict to their own advantage. They also recognized that war would significantly increase demands for their products and might open ports previously closed. As a neutral the United States could trade with all nations, Jefferson observed with more than a touch of self-righteousness, and the "new world will fatten on the follies of the old."[28]

To proclaim neutrality was one thing, to implement it quite another. The United States was tied by treaty to France and by Hamilton's economic system to Britain, posing major threats to neutrality. Establishing a workable policy was also difficult because as a newly independent nation the United States lacked a body of precedent for dealing with the complex issues that arose. International law in the eighteenth century

27. John Lynn, "Revolution in Warfare During the Age of the French Revolution," in Robert A. Doughty et al., *Warfare in the Western World*, vol. 1 (New York, 1996), 173–93.
28. Jefferson to Edward Rutledge, July 4, 1790, in Boyd, *Papers of Jefferson*, vol. 16 (Princeton, N.J., 1961), 600–601.

generally upheld the right of neutrals to trade with belligerents in non-contraband supplies and the sanctity of their territory from belligerent use for military purposes. It was codified only in bilateral treaties, however, which were routinely ignored in times of crisis. Within the general agreement on principles, there was considerable divergence in application. Following the practice of the small, seafaring nations of northern Europe, the United States interpreted neutral rights as broadly as possible. By contrast, Britain relied on sea power as its chief military instrument and interpreted such rights restrictively. Lacking a merchant marine and dependent on neutral carriers, the French accepted America's principles when it was useful, but when the United States veered in the direction of Britain, they reacted strongly. In the absence of courts to enforce international law and especially in the context of total war, power was the final arbiter. From 1793 to 1812, the United States could not maintain a neutrality acceptable to both sides. Whatever it did or refrained from doing, it provoked reprisals from one belligerent or the other.

Growing internal divisions also complicated implementation of a neutrality policy. Still sympathetic to France and seeing in the war an opportunity to free his country from commercial bondage to Britain, Jefferson persuaded himself that the United States could have both neutrality and the alliance with France. Increasingly alarmed by the radicalism of the French Revolution and more than ever persuaded that America's security and his own economic system demanded friendship with Britain, Hamilton leaned in the other direction, grandly indifferent to the consequences for France.[29]

The conflict surfaced when England and France went to war in 1793. In April, Washington requested his cabinet's advice on the issuance of a declaration of neutrality and the more prickly question of U.S. obligations under the 1778 alliance. Hoping to extract concessions from England, Jefferson urged delaying a statement of neutrality. Hamilton favored an immediate and unequivocal declaration, ostensibly to make America's position clear, in fact to avoid any grounds for conflict with London. The French alliance bound the signatories to guarantee each other's possessions in the Western Hemisphere and to admit privateers and prizes to their ports while denying such rights to their enemies. Acceptance of these obligations meant compromising U.S. neutrality; rejection risked antagonizing France. Hamilton advocated what amounted to unilateral abrogation of the alliance, arguing that the change in government in France rendered it void. Jefferson upheld the sanctity of treaties, claiming

29. Kaplan, "Idealist as Realist," 71–72.

that they were negotiated by nations, not governments, and could not be scrapped at whim, but he was motivated as much by a desire to avoid offense to France as by respect for principle. He contended on a practical level that France would not ask the United States to fulfill its obligations, a prediction far off the mark. Washington eventually sided with Hamilton on the issuance of a declaration of neutrality and with Jefferson on the status of the French alliance, a compromise that satisfied neither of the antagonists but established the basis for a reasonably impartial neutrality.[30]

France and its newly appointed minister to the United States, Edmond Charles Genet, challenged the policy at the start. The Girondin government was certain that people across the world—particularly Americans—shared its revolutionary zeal and would assist its crusade to extend republicanism. Genet was instructed to conclude with the United States an "intimate concert" to "promote the Extension of the Empire of Liberty," holding out the prospect of "liberating" Spanish America and opening the Mississippi. Failing this, he was to act on his own to liberate Canada, the Floridas, and Louisiana, and was empowered to issue commissions to Americans to participate. He was also to obtain a $3 million advance payment on America's debt to France. While these matters were under negotiation, he was to secure the opening of U.S. ports to outfit French privateers and bring in enemy prizes. The instructions, if implemented, would have made the United States a de facto ally against England.[31]

The new minister's unsuitability for his position exceeded his chimerical instructions. A gifted linguist and musician, handsome, witty and charming, he was also a flamboyant and volatile individual who had already been thrown out of Catherine the Great's Russia for diplomatic indiscretions. Inflamed with the crusading zeal of the Girondins, he poorly understood the nation to which he was accredited, assuming mistakenly that popular sympathy for France entailed a willingness to risk war with England and that in the United States, as in his country, control of foreign relations resided with the legislature.

From the moment he came ashore, Genet was the proverbial bull in the china shop. Landing in Charleston, South Carolina, where he was widely feted by the governor and local citizenry, he commissioned four privateers that soon brought prizes into U.S. ports. The lavish entertainment he enjoyed along the land route to Philadelphia confirmed his

30. Kaplan, *Jefferson*, 94–98.
31. The standard account is Harry Ammon, *The Genet Mission* (New York, 1973), but see also Elkins and McKitrick, *Age of Federalism*, 330–54.

belief that Americans supported his mission, a conclusion reinforced by early meetings with Jefferson. Hoping to persuade Genet to proceed cautiously lest he give Hamilton reason to adopt blatantly anti-French policies, the secretary of state took the minister into his confidence and spoke candidly, even indiscreetly, about U.S. politics, encouraging the Frenchman's illusions and ardor.

In fact, the two nations were on a collision course. After long and sometimes bitter debates and frequently over Jefferson's objections, the cabinet had hammered out a neutrality policy that construed American obligations under the French alliance as narrowly as possible. The United States denied France the right to outfit privateers or sell enemy prizes in its ports and ordered the release of prizes already brought in. It flatly rejected Genet's offer of a new commercial treaty, as well as his request for an advance payment on the debt, and ordered the arrest of Americans who had enlisted for service on French privateers.

The U.S. policies violated the spirit, if not the letter, of the alliance, giving Genet grounds for protest, but his blatant defiance of American orders undercut his cause. He responded intemperately to Jefferson's official statements, insisting that they did not reflect the will of the American people. Ignoring U.S. instructions, he commissioned a privateer, *La Petite Democrate*, under the government's nose in Philadelphia and began organizing expeditions to attack Louisiana by sea and land, the latter to be manned primarily by Kentuckians headed by revolutionary war hero George Rogers Clark. In defiance of Jefferson's request to delay sailing of the ship and while the cabinet was heatedly debating whether to forcibly stop its departure, he ordered *La Petite Democrate* out of reach of shore batteries and eventually to sea. Responding to repeated official protests, he threatened to take his case to the nation over the head of its president.

Genet's actions sparked a full-fledged, frequently nasty debate in the country at large. Supporters of France and its minister accused the government of pro-British sympathies and monarchical tendencies, calling them "Anglomen" and "monocrats." Those who defended the government denounced the opposition as tools of France and radical revolutionaries. The outlines of political parties began to take form. Jeffersonians took the name Republicans, Hamiltonians became Federalists. Political dialogue was impassioned, street brawls were not uncommon, and old friendships were severed. Newspapers aligned with Hamilton or Jefferson and frequently encouraged by them waged virulent war, debating the basic principles of government while indulging in name-calling and calumny from which even the demigod Washington was not immune.

Discussions in the cabinet reflected the increasingly bitter mood of the nation, provoking a harried and thin-skinned president (the first of many holders of the office, in this regard) to explode that *"by god* he had rather be in his grave than in his present situation."[32]

The Genet affair ended in anticlimax and irony. By July 1793, the administration felt compelled to ask for his recall, even Jefferson agreeing that the appointment had been "calamitous" and confiding in Madison that he saw the "necessity of quitting a wreck which could not but sink all who cling to it."[33] Hamilton and Knox sought to do it in a way that would discredit the French minister and his American supporters. Washington wisely sided with Jefferson, seeking to do so without alienating France. By the time the United States asked for his recall, the Girondins had been replaced by the Jacobins, who, though more radical at home, did not share their predecessors' zeal for a global crusade. Suffering disastrous defeats on land and sea and in desperate need of American food, the new government readily acceded, denouncing Genet's "giddiness." In one of those bizarre twists that marked the politics of the French Revolution, it accused him of complicity in an English plot. Had he returned home, he would likely have been guillotined. Aware of what awaited him, Genet requested, and as a humanitarian gesture was granted, asylum in the United States.[34] He lived out his life as a gentleman farmer and unsuccessful amateur scientist in New York, becoming an American citizen in 1804 and marrying the daughter of New York governor George Clinton.

Genet's shenanigans were generally counterproductive. The escape of *La Petite Democrate* did not provoke British reprisals; the minister's grand scheme for the liberation of Louisiana quickly collapsed from shortage of funds and lack of American support. On the other hand, the cautious and at least mildly pro-British definition of neutral obligations set forth piecemeal by the Washington administration was enacted into law in 1794, forming the basis for U.S. neutrality policies into the twentieth century. Frustration with Genet contributed to Jefferson's decision to leave office in late 1793, removing from the cabinet a voice sympathetic to France and eventually contributing to a tilt in policy toward Britain.

More than anything else, the Genet mission exposed the fragility of American neutrality, the extent to which the European powers would go

32. Quoted in Elkins and McKitrick, *Age of Federalism*, 361.
33. Ellis, *American Sphinx*, 127.
34. Eugene R. Sheridan, "The Recall of Edmond Charles Genet: A Study in Transatlantic Politics and Diplomacy," *Diplomatic History* 18 (Fall 1994), 463–88.

to undermine it, and the depth of internal conflict on foreign policy. It marked the beginning, rather than the end, of a twenty-year effort to steer clear of the European war while profiting from it, and it divided Americans into two deeply antagonistic factions.

IV

Even while the Genet affair occupied center stage, the United States and Britain edged toward war. Still sometimes portrayed by Americans as the ruthless aggression of an arrogant great power against an innocent and vulnerable nation, the crisis of 1794 was considerably more complex in its origins. It provides, in fact, a classic example of the way in which conflicts of interest, exacerbated by intense nationalism on one side, a lack of attention on the other, and the ill-advised actions of poorly informed and sometimes panicky officials miles from the seat of government can create conditions for war even when the governments themselves have reason to avoid it. In this instance, war was averted, but only narrowly and only because both nations and especially the United States found compelling reason for restraint.

By early 1794, the long-simmering conflict along the Great Lakes threatened a clash of arms. Increasingly concerned with the explosive frontier, the British after St. Clair's defeat devised a "compromise" that would have set aside specified lands for the Indians in territory claimed by the United States. By this time, however, neither of the other parties was inclined to negotiate. Buoyed by their victory, the Indians demanded lands from the Canadian border to the Ohio River and murdered under flags of truce several U.S. agents sent to treat with them. Americans never understood the pride and suspicion with which the Indians viewed them. They would concede only limited territory to people Hamilton dismissed as "vagrants." Even after a humiliating defeat, they patronized the victors. They blamed the British for the tribes' exorbitant claims and violently protested their interference in what they viewed a purely internal matter.[35]

In the absence of a settlement, tensions flared. When nervous British officials in Canada learned that the United States was preparing another military expedition to be commanded by General "Mad Anthony" Wayne of Revolutionary War fame, they feared attacks on their frontier posts. Without London's approval, they incited the Indians to resist American advances. As a "defensive" measure, they sent troops to the Maumee River near present-day Detroit. What the British viewed as defensive, Americans

---

35. Kohn, *Eagle and Sword*, 146, 155–57; Elkins and McKitrick, *Age of Federalism*, 436–38.

regarded as further evidence of British perfidy and provocation. As Wayne moved north and British forces south, there was much loose talk of war.

Conflicts over issues of neutrality posed even more difficult problems. From its birth as a nation, the United States had claimed the right to trade with belligerents in non-contraband and defined contraband narrowly to include only specifically military items such as arms and ammunition. It also endorsed the principle that free ships make free goods, meaning that the private property of belligerents aboard neutral ships was immune from seizure. The United States insisted that these "rights" had sanction in international law and incorporated them into treaties with several European countries. But they served the national interest as well. Desperately in need of U.S. foodstuffs, France purchased large quantities of grain and permitted American ships to transport supplies from its West Indian colonies to its home ports, a right generally denied under mercantilist doctrine. Hundreds of American ships swarmed into the Caribbean and across the Atlantic to "fatten on the follies" of the Old World.

Americans' quest for profits ran afoul of Britain's grand strategy. Recognizing France's dependence on external sources of food, the British government set out to starve its enemy into submission, blockading French ports, broadening contraband to include food, and ordering the seizure of American ships carrying grain to France. The British did not want to drive the United States into the arms of France and thus agreed to purchase confiscated grain at fair prices. Preoccupied with the European war, increasingly alarmed at the burgeoning American trade with France, and badly misjudging the Washington administration's handling of Genet, they implemented their strategy in a high-handed and often brutal manner that threatened to provoke war. Without any warning and frequently exceeding their instructions, overzealous British officials in the West Indies seized 250 ships. Egged on by a system that permitted the captors personally to profit from such plunder, ship captains boarded American vessels, stripped them of their sails, and tore down their colors. Hastily assembled kangaroo courts condemned ships and cargoes. Captains and crews were confined, often without provisions. Some Americans were impressed into the Royal Navy; others died in captivity. Britain justified its efforts to curtail trade with France through its so-called Rule of 1756 declaring that trade illegal in time of peace was illegal in time of war. British officials later admitted, however, that the ship seizures of 1794 far exceeded the bounds of this rule.[36]

---

36. Joseph M. Fewster, "The Jay Treaty and British Ship Seizures: The Martinique Cases," *William and Mary Quarterly* 45 (July 1988), 426–52.

London's actions stirred powerful resentment in the United States. What seemed to Britons essential acts of war appeared to Americans a threat to their prosperity and a grievous affront to their dignity as an independent nation. Angry mobs in seaport cities attacked British sailors. In Charleston, a crowd tore down a statue of William Pitt the Elder that had survived the Revolution. Congress assembled in early 1794 in a mood of outrage. Madison's proposals in the House of Representatives for discrimination against British commerce failed in the Senate by the single vote of Vice President John Adams. Even Federalists spoke of war. An angry Congress proceeded to impose a temporary embargo on all foreign shipping and to discuss even more drastic measures such as repudiation of debts owed Britain and creation of a navy to defend American shipping.

The crisis of early 1794 posed a dilemma for the Washington administration. Most top officials regarded a British victory as essential to the preservation of stable government in Europe and hence to the well-being of the United States. On the other hand, they appreciated and indeed shared the rising public anger toward Britain and perceived that their political foes might use it to discredit them. Acquiescence in British high-handedness was unthinkable. Should Madison's quest for economic retaliation succeed, on the other hand, it might provoke a disastrous war. Without precedent to guide him, Washington took the initiative in addressing the crisis, agreeing to Hamilton's proposal to send a special mission to London to negotiate a settlement that might avert war and silence the opposition. Chief Justice John Jay, an experienced diplomat and staunch Federalist, was selected for the mission.[37]

Washington and his advisers perceived that an agreement might be costly. As was customary in a time when communications were slow and uncertain, Jay was given wide latitude. The only explicit requirements were that he agree to nothing that violated the French treaty of 1778 and that he secure access to trade with the British West Indies, both regarded as essential to appease the domestic opposition. He was also instructed to seek compensation for the recent seizures of vessels and cargoes, to settle issues left from the 1783 treaty, particularly British retention of the Northwest posts, and to conclude a commercial treaty that would resolve sticky questions of neutral rights. The administration appears not to have expected major concessions on matters concerning neutrality. It hoped

---

37. The classic accounts are Samuel Flagg Bemis, *Jay's Treaty: A Study in Commerce and Diplomacy* (rev. ed., New Haven, Conn., 1962) and Jerald A. Combs, *The Jay Treaty: Political Battleground of the Founding Fathers* (Berkeley, Calif., 1970).

rather to win enough in other areas to make concessions to the British palatable to its critics.

The British too were in a conciliatory mood, although within distinct limits. Preoccupied with events in Europe and with a political crisis at home, officials were caught off guard by the furious American reaction to ship seizures in the West Indies. Their military position on the Continent precarious, they had no need for war with the United States. Even before Jay arrived in London, they revoked the harsh orders that had led to the West Indian ship seizures. The government received Jay cordially. Its chief negotiator, Lord Grenville, sought to establish an effective working relationship with him. British leaders were prepared to make concessions to avoid conflict with the United States. To have given in on neutral rights would have denied them a vital weapon against France at a critical time, however, and on such issues they stood firm.

The settlement worked out during six months of sporadic and tedious but generally cordial negotiations reflected these influences. The British willingly abandoned an untenable position, agreeing to evacuate the Northwest posts. The treaty was silent on their relations with the Indians. To the annoyance of southern planters, it said nothing about compensation for slaves carried off during the Revolution. A boundary dispute in the Northeast and the question of pre-Revolutionary debts owed by Americans to British creditors were referred to mixed arbitral commissions.[38]

In view of its long-standing opposition to commercial concessions of any sort, Britain was surprisingly liberal in this area. In fact, the home island and especially the colonies depended on trade with the United States. The British Isles were opened to Americans on a most-favored-nation basis. American ships were permitted into British India with virtually no restrictions and also gained access to the much-coveted West Indian trade, although vessels were restricted to less than seventy tons and the Americans were forbidden to reexport certain products including even such items produced in the United States. On balance, for a nation still committed to mercantilist principles, the concessions were generous.

As Hamilton and Jay had feared, Britain stood firm on neutral rights. Grenville readily agreed to compensate the United States for ships and cargoes seized in the West Indies but would go no further. Jay conceded the substance, if not the principle, of British definitions of contraband and the Rule of 1756. For all practical purposes, he scrapped the principle

38. The negotiations are discussed in Bemis, *Jay's Treaty*, 318–73, and from the British perspective in Charles R. Ritcheson, *Aftermath of Revolution: British Policy Toward the United States, 1783–1795* (New York, 1971), 318–59.

of free ships and free goods and agreed to admit British privateers and prizes to American ports, a direct violation of the 1778 treaty.

Critics then and later have argued that Jay gave up more than was necessary and secured less than he should have in return. He was too eager for a settlement, they claim, and refused to hold out, bargain, or exploit his strengths and British weaknesses. Some scholars have also contended that Hamilton undercut Jay's position by confiding in the British minister to Washington, George Hammond, that the United States would not join a group of nations then forming an armed neutrality to defend their shipping against Britain.[39] As in earlier cases, Hamilton's machinations cannot be condoned, but, in this instance, their practical effects appear limited. The armed neutrality lacked support from major European neutrals such as Russia. In any event, the United States had little to contribute or gain from it. Hamilton's assurances reached London only after the negotiations were all but concluded and told the British little they did not know. Jay was indeed anxious for a settlement. He might have gained a bit more by dragging out the negotiations. But on neutral rights Britain could not be moved. Their backs to the wall on the Continent and in the Caribbean, London officials could not relinquish their most effective weapon. Without an army or navy and standing to lose huge revenues from war with England, the United States could not make them do so.

Although desperate for peace, Hamilton and Washington were themselves keenly disappointed with the terms. For a time, the president hesitated to submit the document to the Senate, but he eventually rationalized that a bad treaty was better than none at all. He sent Jay's handiwork to the upper house without any recommendation, but he was so concerned with possible public reaction that he insisted it be considered in secret. The Senate approved the treaty by the barest majority, 20–10, and then only after the article on West Indian trade was excised because the limits on tonnage effectively eliminated American ships from the trans-Atlantic trade.

No other treaty in U.S. history has aroused such hostile public reaction or provoked such passionate debate, even though, ironically, the Jay Treaty brought the United States important concessions and served its interests well. The explanation must be sought not only in rampant political partisanship but also in ideology and the insecurities of a new and fragile nation.[40] The treaty provoked such anger because it touched Americans in areas

39. Bemis argues this in *Jay's Treaty*, 337–40. For persuasive rebuttals, see Elkins and McKitrick, *Age of Federalism*, 410, and Bradford Perkins, *The First Rapprochement: England and the United States, 1795–1805* (Berkeley, Calif., 1967), 42–43.

40. Elkins and McKitrick, *Age of Federalism*, 416.

where they were most sensitive. The mere fact of negotiations with Britain was difficult for many to accept. To some Americans, Jay's concessions smacked of subservience. Moreover, to an extent that was not true in Europe, foreign policy in the United States was subject to debate by a public whose understanding of the issues and mechanisms was neither sophisticated nor nuanced, that sought clear-cut and definitive solutions, and defined outcomes in terms of victory and defeat. By the very nature of diplomacy, such high expectations were bound to be disappointed and the results to be received with something less than enthusiasm. American insecurity thus manifested itself in a frenzy of anger and an outpouring of patriotic fervor.

When the text of the treaty was published by a Republican newspaper less than a week after approval by the Senate, popular indignation swept the land. The aura of secrecy that had shrouded the treaty and its disclosure on the eve of emotional July 4 celebrations heightened the intensity of the reaction. Even in Federalist strongholds, the document and its author were publicly condemned. In towns and villages across the country, incensed citizens lowered flags to half mast and hangmen ceremoniously destroyed copies of the treaty. Burning effigies of that "damned arch traitor Jay" lit the night. The British minister was publicly insulted by a hostile crowd. When Hamilton took the stump in New York to defend the treaty, he was struck by a stone. Once again, the venerable Washington came under attack, irate critics labeling him a dupe and a fool and even accusing him of misusing public funds.

Outraged by the terms of the treaty and smelling political blood, Republican leaders fanned the popular indignation. Southerners and westerners, suspicious of Jay since his negotiations with Spain a decade earlier, saw their worst fears confirmed in the obnoxious document. Failure to deal with the issue of confiscated slaves and submission of the debt controversy to an arbitral commission touched southern interests directly. From the Republican point of view, the commercial treaty and the cave-in on neutral rights totally undermined the principles essential for a truly independent status for the United States. By prohibiting interference in Anglo-American trade for ten years, it surrendered the instrument— commercial discrimination—needed to attain that end. It represented a humiliating capitulation to the archenemy Britain and a slap in the face to France. Madison and Jefferson saw treaties as a means to reform the balance-of-power system and international law. To them, the Jay Treaty represented an abject retreat to the old ways. It was "unworthy [of] the voluntary acceptance of an Independent people," Madison fumed.[41]

41. Onuf and Onuf, *Federal Union*, 161.

Jefferson was more outspoken, denouncing the treaty as a "monument of folly and venality," an "infamous act," nothing more than a "treaty of alliance between England and the anglomen of this country against the legislature and people of the United States." Those who had been "Samsons in the field and Solomons in the council," he privately exclaimed, "have had their heads shorn by the harlot England."[42]

The treaty survived the storm. Hamilton, now a private citizen, joined Jay in mounting a vigorous and generally effective defense of their handiwork. Despite their compunctions about mobilizing a presumably ignorant public, the Federalists effectively rallied popular support, highlighting the concessions made by Britain and emphasizing that, whatever its deficiencies, the treaty preserved peace with the nation whose friendship was essential to U.S. prosperity and well-being.[43] Perhaps persuaded by Hamilton and Jay, Washington overcame persistent reservations about ratifying the treaty. The bitter personal attacks on him by foes of the treaty probably contributed to his decision. A harried president finally signed the Jay Treaty in August 1795.

Defeated in the Senate and by the executive, the Republicans mounted a bitter rearguard effort that would delay implementation of the treaty for almost a year and raise important constitutional questions. Insisting that the House also had the power to approve treaties, a position Jefferson himself had explicitly rejected some years earlier, the Republican-controlled lower chamber demanded that the president submit to it all documents relating to negotiation of the treaty. Washington refused, setting an important precedent on executive privilege. The House quickly approved a resolution reaffirming its right to pass on any treaty requiring implementing legislation. Some Republicans shied away from direct confrontation with the president, however, and in April 1796 the House appropriated funds to implement the treaty by a narrow margin of three votes, setting a precedent that has never been challenged.

Remarkable and fortuitous economic and diplomatic gains facilitated public acceptance of the treaty. There is no better balm for wounded pride than prosperity. As a neutral carrier for both sides, the United States enjoyed a major economic boom in the aftermath of the treaty. Exports more then tripled between 1792 and 1796. "The affairs of Europe rain

42. Tucker and Hendrickson, *Empire of Liberty*, 67; Jefferson to Philip Mazzei, April 14, 1796, in Paul Leicester Ford, ed., *The Writings of Thomas Jefferson* (10 vols., New York, 1892–99), 7:72–78.

43. Todd Estes, "Shaping the Politics of Public Opinion: Federalists and the Jay Treaty Debate," *Journal of the Early Republic* 20 (Fall 2000), 393–422.

riches on us," one American exulted, "and it is as much as we can do to find dishes to catch the golden shower."[44]

While Jay was negotiating in London and the treaty was being debated at home, Wayne settled the future of the Northwest on U.S. terms. Following the St. Clair debacle, he gathered an imposing army eventually numbering 3,500 men and prepared his campaign with the utmost care. In August 1794, he routed a small force of Indians at Fallen Timbers near British-held Fort Miami. Despite earlier inciting them to battle, the British refused to back the Indians or even allow them into the fort when Wayne had them on the run. After a tense standoff outside the fort where, perhaps miraculously, neither Britons nor Americans fired a shot, Wayne systematically plundered Indian storehouses and burned villages in the Ohio country. In August 1795, he imposed on the defeated and dispirited tribes the Treaty of Greenville that confined them to a narrow strip of land along Lake Erie. It was certainly not expansion with honor, but in the eyes of most Americans the ends justified the means. Wayne's campaign crippled the hold of Indians and British in the Old Northwest, restoring the prestige of the American government and strengthening its hold on the Ohio country. Removal of the British was the last step in completing the process Wayne had begun, a point defenders of the Jay Treaty hammered home in speech after speech.[45]

An unanticipated and quite astounding diplomatic windfall from the Jay Treaty also eased its acceptance. A declining power, Spain found itself in a precarious position between the major European belligerents. Allied for a time with Britain, it changed sides when the advance of a French army into the Iberian peninsula threatened its very survival. Fearing British reprisals and suspecting—incorrectly, as it turned out—that the Jay Treaty portended an Anglo-American alliance that might bring combined expeditions against Spanish America, a panicky Madrid government moved quickly to appease the United States. The U.S. minister, Thomas Pinckney, was astute enough to seize the opportunity. In the Treaty of San Lorenzo, signed in October 1795 and sometimes called Pinckney's Treaty, Spain recognized the boundary claimed by the United States since 1783. It also granted the long-coveted access to the Mississippi and for three years the right to deposit goods at New Orleans for storage and transshipment without duties. Resolving at virtually no cost to the United States issues that had plagued Spanish-American relations and

44. Quoted in Elkins and McKitrick, *Age of Federalism*, 441.
45. Kohn, *Eagle and Sword*, 156–57, 182.

threatened the allegiance of the West, Pinckney's Treaty pacified the restless westerners and made the Jay Treaty more palatable.[46]

From the vantage point of more than two hundred years, the verdict on Jay's Treaty is unambiguous. Jay was dealt a weak hand and might have played it better. In seeking and pushing the treaty, Hamilton and Jay acted for blatantly partisan and self-serving reasons, promoting their grand design for foreign relations and domestic development. Their dire warnings of war may have been exaggerated. The most likely alternative to the treaty was a continued state of crisis and conflict that could have led to war. On the other hand, Republican ranting was also driven by partisanship and was certainly overstated. Diplomacy by its very nature requires concessions, a point Americans even then were inclined to forget. The circumstances of 1794 left little choice but to sacrifice on neutral rights. Jay secured concessions Jefferson could not get that turned out to be very important over the long run. Most important, Britain recognized U.S. independence in a way it had not in 1783. Rarely has a treaty so bad on the face of it produced such positive results. It initiated a period of sustained prosperity that in turn promoted stability and strength. It bound the Northwest and Southwest to a still very fragile federal union. It bought for a new and still weak nation that most priceless commodity—time.

V

Whatever its long-term benefits, the treaty afforded the United States no immediate respite. Conflict with France dominated the remainder of the decade, provoking a sustained diplomatic crisis, blatant French interference in American internal affairs, and an undeclared naval war. The war scare of 1798 heightened already bitter divisions at home. Federalist exploitation of the rage against France for partisan advantage provoked fierce Republican reaction that could not be silenced through repression. Suspicions on each side ran wild, Federalists claiming that Republicans were joining with France to bring the excesses of the French Revolution to America, Republicans insisting that the Federalists, allied with Britain, were seeking to destroy republicanism at home. The war scare also set the Federalists squabbling among themselves, producing cabinet intrigues and rumors of plots akin to coups.

Absorbed with the European war and its own internal politics, France viewed the United States as a nuisance and possible source of exploitation rather than a major concern. The Directory then in power represented

46. The standard account is Samuel Flagg Bemis, *Pinckney's Treaty: America's Advantage from Europe's Distress, 1783–1800* (rev. ed., New Haven, Conn., 1960).

the low point of the revolution, unpopular, divided against itself, and rife with corruption. French policy toward the United States, if indeed it could be called that, reflected the whim of the moment, a need for food, a lust for money. The French naturally protested the Jay Treaty, claiming they had been "betrayed and despoiled with impunity." But the treaty was as much pretext as cause for attacks on the United States that were reckless to the point of stupidity. Flushed with victories on the Continent, France arrogantly toyed with the United States and plundered its shipping, outraging a profoundly insecure people whose nerves were already frayed from years of mistreatment at the hands of the great powers.[47]

Following the Jay Treaty, France retaliated against the United States. Genet's successors, Joseph Fauchet and Pierre Adet, lobbied vigorously to defeat the treaty in the Senate and House, offering bribes to some congressmen. Failing, they tried intimidation to mitigate its effects. Proclaiming that the treaty of 1778 was no longer in effect and hinting ominously at a severance of diplomatic relations, they insisted that U.S. concessions to Britain compelled them to scrap the principle of free ships, free goods. They seized more than three hundred American ships in 1795 alone. Hoping to exploit popular anger with Jay's Treaty, they used the threat of war to secure the election of a more friendly government. Adet interfered in the election of 1796 in a way not since duplicated by a foreign representative by warning that war could be avoided only by the election of Jefferson. A furious Washington denounced French treatment of the United States as "outrageous beyond conception."[48]

French meddling provoked a sharp presidential response in the form of Washington's Farewell Address. Drafted partly by Hamilton, the president's statement was at one level a highly partisan political document timed to promote the Federalist cause in the approaching election. Washington's fervid warnings against the "insidious wiles of foreign influence" and "passionate attachments" to "permanent alliances" with other nations unmistakably alluded to the French connection and Adet's intrigues. They were designed, at least in part, to discredit the Republicans.[49]

At another level, the Farewell Address was a political testament, based on recent experience, in which the retiring president set forth principles to guide the nation in its formative years. Washington's admonitions

47. Elkins and McKitrick, *Age of Federalism*, 506, 511, 538.
48. Alexander DeConde, *Entangling Alliance: Politics and Diplomacy Under George Washington* (Durham, N.C., 1958), 488.
49. The text of the Farewell Address and various interpretations of it can be conveniently found in Kaufman, *Washington's Farewell Address*.

against partisanship reflected his sincere and deep-seated fears of the perils of factionalism at a delicate stage in the national development. His references to alliances set forth a view common among Americans that their nation, founded on exceptional principles and favored by geography, could best achieve its destiny by preserving its freedom of action. Although it would later be used as a justification for isolationism, the Farewell Address was *not* an isolationist document. The word *isolationism* did not become fixed in the American political lexicon until the twentieth century. No one in the 1790s could have seriously entertained the notion of freedom from foreign involvement.[50] Washington vigorously advocated commercial expansion. He also conceded that "temporary alliances" might be required in "extraordinary emergencies." Influenced by experience dating to the colonial period, he stressed the importance of an independent course free of emotional attachments and wherever possible binding political commitments to other nations. When the country had grown strong and the interior was tied closely to the Union, it would be able to fend off any threat, a blueprint for future empire.[51]

For whatever reason, Americans heeded Washington's warnings, and France's efforts to swing the election of 1796 backfired. The Federalists took the high ground of principle and nationalism, charging their opponents with serving a foreign power. Although it is impossible to weigh with any precision the impact of Adet's interference, it likely contributed to the Federalist victory. Despite a split between those Federalists supporting Vice President John Adams and those, including Hamilton, who preferred Thomas Pinckney, Adams won seventy-one electoral votes to sixty-eight for Jefferson. At a time when the runner-up automatically became vice president, the nation experienced the anomaly of its two top officials representing bitterly contending parties.

Failing to "revolutionize" the U.S. government, France sought to punish the upstart nation for its independence. Proclaiming that it would treat neutrals as neutrals allowed England to treat them, Paris officially sanctioned what had been going on for months, authorizing naval commanders and privateers to seize ships carrying British property. They quickly equaled the haul of 1795. Atrocities sometimes accompanied the seizures—one American ship captain was tortured with thumbscrews until he declared his cargo British property and liable for seizure. By 1797, French raiders boldly attacked U.S. ships off the coast of Long Island and

50. Kaplan, *Entangling Alliances*, 94.
51. Fred Anderson, *The War That Made America: A Short History of the French and Indian War* (New York, 2005), 163.

Philadelphia. France also refused to receive the newly appointed U.S. minister, Charles C. Pinckney, insisting that an envoy would not be accredited until the United States redressed its grievances.[52]

In seeking to intimidate the United States, France badly misjudged the mood of the nation and the character of its new president. Sixty-one years old, vain, thin-skinned, and impulsive, John Adams was also a man of keen intelligence and considerable learning. In many ways, he was the most stubbornly independent of the Founders. Pessimistic in his view of human nature and conservative in his politics, he had been skeptical of the French Revolution from the outset.[53] A staunch nationalist, he reacted indignantly to French high-handedness. And some of his advisers would have welcomed war. In awe of his predecessor, he retained not only the cabinet system but also Washington's cabinet: the querulous and narrow-minded Timothy Pickering as secretary of state and Oliver Wolcott, the mediocre Hamilton confidant, as secretary of the treasury. Adams never shared the pro-British sympathies of his colleagues. Short and plump, by his own admission "but an Ordinary Man," he lacked his illustrious predecessor's commanding presence. Unsure of himself in the presidency and deeply angered by France, he tolerated his advisers' virulently anti-French policies to the brink of war.

Adams's initial approach to France combined a willingness to employ force with an openness to negotiations. Shortly after taking office, he revived long-dormant plans to build a navy to protect U.S. shipping. Still hoping to avert war, he emulated Washington's 1794 approach to England by dispatching to France a special peace mission composed of John Marshall, Elbridge Gerry, and Charles C. Pinckney. He instructed his commissioners to ask compensation for the seizures of ships and cargoes, secure release from the articles of the 1778 treaty binding the United States to defend the French West Indies, and win French acceptance of the Jay Treaty. They were authorized to offer little in return.

Given American terms, a settlement would have been difficult under any circumstances, but the timing was especially inopportune. Revolutionary France was at the peak of its power. Napoleon Bonaparte had won great victories on the Continent. Britain was isolated and vulnerable. France was willing to settle with the United States, but it saw no need for haste. In need of money and accustomed to manipulating the small states of

---

52. Alexander DeConde, *The Quasi-War: The Politics and Diplomacy of the Undeclared War with France, 1797–1801* (New York, 1966), 124–25.
53. Joseph J. Ellis, *Passionate Sage: The Character and Legacy of John Adams* (New York, 2001).

Europe through a "vast network of international plunder," the Directory set out to extort what it could from the United States. Its minister of foreign relations, the notorious Charles Maurice de Talleyrand-Périgord, an aristocrat, former Roman Catholic bishop, and notorious womanizer, had lived in exile in the United States and had little respect for Americans. Certain that the new nation "merited no more consideration than Genoa or Geneva," he preferred at least for the moment a condition he described as "half friendly, half hostile," which permitted France to enrich itself by looting U.S. ships.[54] A master of survival in the hurly-burly of French politics, conniving, above all venal, Talleyrand also hoped to enrich himself at American expense. He treated Adams's commissioners as representatives of a European vassal state. When the delegation arrived in France, it was told by mysterious agents identified only as X, Y, and Z that negotiations would proceed more smoothly if the United States paid a bribe of $250,000 and loaned France $12 million.[55]

The so-called XYZ mission failed not because France insulted American honor but because the U.S. diplomats concluded that no settlement was attainable. Pinckney's much publicized response — "No, no, not a sixpence" — did not reflect the initial view of the commissioners. They were prepared to pay a small douceur if persuaded that negotiations could succeed. Although doubtful the U.S. treasury could sustain a loan of the magnitude requested, they considered asking for new instructions if they could convince France to stop attacking American ships. Eventually, however, it became clear that Talleyrand had no intention of easing the pressure or compensating their country for earlier losses. Certain that their mission was hopeless, Pinckney and Marshall returned home, playing for all it was worth the role of aggrieved republicans whose honor had been insulted by a decadent old world.

The XYZ Affair set off a near hysterical reaction in the United States, providing an outlet for tensions built up over years of conflict with the Europeans. Adams was so incensed with the treatment of his diplomats that he began drafting a war message. Publication of correspondence relating to the mission unleashed a storm of patriotic indignation. Angry crowds burned Talleyrand in effigy and attacked supposed French sympathizers. Memorials of support for the president poured in from across the country. The once popular tricolor cockade gave way to the more traditional black cockade, French songs to American. Frenzied public gatherings sang new patriotic songs such as "Hail Columbia" and "Adams and

54. William Stinchcombe, *The XYZ Affair* (Westport, Conn., 1981), 35.
55. Stinchcombe's *XYZ Affair* is the standard account.

Liberty" and drank toasts to the popular slogan "Millions for defense but not one cent for tribute." Militia rolls swelled. Old men joined patriotic patrols, while little boys played war against imaginary French soldiers. Exulting in the "most magical effects" of the XYZ furor on public attitudes, Federalists fanned the flames by disseminating rumors of French plans to invade the United States, incite slave uprisings in the South, and burn Philadelphia and massacre its women and children. Basking in the glow of unaccustomed popularity, Adams stoked the martial spirit. "The finger of destiny writes on the wall the word: 'War,'" he told one cheering audience.[56]

The president eventually settled for a policy of "qualified hostility." Some Republicans challenged the war fever—Jefferson sarcastically talked of the "XYZ dish cooked up by Marshall" to help the Federalists expand their power.[57] With only a narrow majority in the House, Adams feared that a premature declaration might fail. Moreover, he learned from reliable sources that France did not want war, giving him pause. Although he remained willing to consider war, he determined to respond forcibly to French provocations without seeking a declaration. A firm American posture might persuade France to negotiate on more favorable terms or provoke the United States to declare war. Continued conflict might eventually goad Congress into acting.

Adams thus pushed through Congress a series of measures that led to the so-called Quasi-War with France. The 1778 treaty was unilaterally abrogated, an embargo placed on trade with France. Secretary of State Pickering reversed Washington's policy toward Saint-Domingue, cutting a deal with the independent black republic to restore trade and employing warships to help solidify its power.[58] Congress approved the creation of a separate Department of the Navy, authorized the government to construct, purchase, or borrow a fleet of warships, approved the arming of merchant vessels and the commissioning of privateers, and permitted U.S. ships to attack armed French vessels anywhere on the high seas. Over the next two years, the United States and France waged an undeclared naval war, much of it in the Caribbean and West Indies, the center of U.S. trade with Europe and the focal point of British and French attacks on American shipping. Supported by a fleet of armed merchantmen, the infant U.S. Navy drove

56. Adams quoted in DeConde, *Quasi-War*, 81; Thomas M. Ray, " 'Not One Cent for Tribute': The Public Addresses and American Popular Reaction to the XYZ Affair, 1798–1799," *Journal of the Early Republic* 3 (Winter 1983), 389–411.
57. Kaplan, *Jefferson*, 118.
58. Tim Matthewson, "Jefferson and Haiti," *Journal of Southern History* 61 (May 1995), 215.

French warships from American coastal waters, convoyed merchant ships into the West Indies, and successfully fought numerous battles with French warships. Americans cheered with especial nationalist fervor the victory of Capt. Thomas Truxtun's *Constellation* over *Insurgente*, reputedly the fastest warship in the French navy.[59]

Adams's more belligerent advisers saw in the conflict with France a splendid opportunity to achieve larger objectives. The war scare provided a pretext for the standing army Federalists had long sought. In the summer of 1798, Congress authorized an army of fifty thousand men to be commanded by Washington in the event of hostilities. Federalists in the cabinet and Senate also sought to rid the nation of recent immigrants from France and other countries who were viewed as potential subversives — and even worse as Republican political fodder — enacting laws making it more difficult to acquire American citizenship and permitting the deportation of aliens deemed dangerous to public safety. Striking directly at the opposition, the Federalists passed several vaguely worded and blatantly repressive Sedition Acts that made it a federal crime to interfere with the operation of the government or publish any "false, scandalous and malicious writings" against its officials. Egged on by Hamilton, some extremists fantasized about an alliance with England and joint military operations against the Floridas, Louisiana, and French colonies in the West Indies.[60]

The war scare of 1798 waned as quickly as it had waxed. When the hostile U.S. reaction made clear the extent of his miscalculations, Talleyrand shifted direction. French officials feared driving the United States into the arms of England, solidifying the power of the Federalists, and denying France access to vital products. Already negotiating with Spain an agreement to regain Louisiana as part of a larger design to restore French power in North America, nervous officials perceived that war with the United States would invite an assault on Louisiana and destroy France's dreams of empire before implementation had begun. The demonstrated ability of the United States to defend its commerce reduced the profits from plunder, rendering the "half friendly, half hostile" policy counterproductive. As early as the summer of 1798, Talleyrand began sending out signals of reconciliation. His message grew stronger by the end of the year.

As belligerent as anyone at the outset, Adams in time broke with his more extreme colleagues. Gerry, who had remained in Paris, the Quaker

---

59. The standard account is DeConde, *Quasi-War*.
60. Kohn, *Eagle and Sword*, 219–55; Paul Douglas Newman, "The Federalists' Cold War: The Fries Rebellion, National Security, and the State, 1787–1800," *Pennsylvania History* 67 (Winter 2000), 63–104.

George Logan, then on an unofficial and unauthorized peace mission in France, Adams's son John Quincy, and other U.S. diplomats in Europe all reported unmistakable signs of French interest in negotiations. Adams had never taken seriously the threat of a French invasion of the United States. Lord Nelson's destruction of the French fleet at Aboukir Bay in Egypt in October 1798 rendered it a practical impossibility. There was "no more prospect of seeing a French army here, than there is in Heaven," the president snarled.[61]

Within the United States, peace sentiment grew. In the absence of formal hostilities, the war fever dissipated, turning to apathy and then protest against the high taxes and repressive measures adopted by the government. Adams gradually recognized, moreover, that Hamilton was behind the more aggressive measures proposed by his cabinet. He suspected, not without reason, that the ambitious New Yorker might be conspiring to gain control of the government. The president was enraged when his cabinet, Federalist senators, and Washington pressured him to appoint Hamilton inspector general of the army, a post everyone recognized, in view of Washington's age and increasing infirmity, was tantamount to actual command. Adams thus decided in early 1799 to send another peace mission to France.

The decision set off a struggle that sundered Adams's administration and in time destroyed his party. Still eager for war—or at least the threat of war—and stunned by Adams's decision, extreme Federalists resisted. A group of senators vowed to block the nomination of an envoy to France, provoking an enraged president to threaten resignation—which would have left the government in the hands of the despised Jefferson. Adams eventually agreed to enlarge the delegation to three persons. While the president was in Massachusetts tending his ill wife, Pickering, Wolcott, and Secretary of War James McHenry continued to obstruct his policy, delaying issuing instructions to the commissioners and trying to persuade them to resign. There was even talk of something akin to a palace coup, in which Hamilton would have been a major participant, with the cabinet taking control from the president. Returning to the temporary capital at Trenton at the urging of loyal cabinet members, Adams was stunned to find the inspector general conferring with some of his advisers. Without consulting the cabinet, he ordered the delegation to leave for France at once. Upon learning that Pickering and McHenry were plotting with Hamilton to unseat him in the election, Adams forced McHenry to resign. Pickering refused resignation on grounds that he needed the salary

---

61. Quoted in Elkins and McKitrick, *Age of Federalism*, 606.

to support his large family. Adams was compelled to fire him, making him the only secretary of state to leave office in this manner. The president denounced Hamilton as "the greatest intriguant in the world—a man devoid of every moral principle—and a bastard."[62]

A settlement would not come easily. The instructions Pickering drafted for the delegation asked a great deal: formal release from the treaty of 1778; compensation for seizures of American ships and property (estimated at $20 million); and French acceptance of the Jay Treaty. From France's standpoint, the Americans asked everything and offered nothing. French officials desperately wanted to regain exclusive right to bring privateers and prizes into American ports and insisted that they would compensate the United States for damages only if the treaties remained in effect. The negotiations quickly deadlocked, causing an agitated and impatient Adams to reconsider a declaration of war.

Both sides found reason to compromise. Napoleon by late 1800 had assumed near dictatorial powers and was busy promoting schemes to end the European war on favorable terms and restore the French empire to North America. The reacquisition of Louisiana was nearing fruition. The United States had to be pacified at least until France could take control of its new territory. Napoleon was also encouraging European neutrals to arm against Britain. He saw an opportunity to loosen Anglo-American ties and win over the neutrals by demonstrating his commitment to liberal maritime principles. Sensing that France was daily growing stronger in Europe and further delay might be costly, the U.S. delegation departed from its instructions and agreed to compromise. The Convention of 1800 restored diplomatic relations, tacitly terminated the alliance of 1778, postponed (forever as it turned out) further consideration of treaties and financial claims, and included a statement of neutral rights that did not conflict with Jay's Treaty. To impress Europe with his achievement, Napoleon staged an elaborate signing ceremony at Mortefontaine on October 3, 1800, complete with sumptuous banquets, rounds of toasts, fireworks and booming cannon, and plays and concerts.[63]

Although unpopular in the United States, the convention was eventually approved. Americans' expectations continued to exceed their nation's power. As with the Jay Treaty, critics protested that the commissioners had paid too much for peace. Jefferson complained of "bungling negotiations."[64]

62. Quoted in Page Smith, *John Adams* (2 vols., New York, 1962), 2:1027–28.
63. The Mortefontaine negotiations and celebrations are covered in DeConde, *Quasi-War*, 223–58.
64. Kaplan, *Jefferson*, 123.

Extreme Federalists complained of further humiliation at the hands of France. Upon first submission to the Senate, the convention failed to receive a two-thirds majority. The prospect of continued hostilities with France provoked sober second thoughts, however. Many senators concluded that the United States could not do better and might do worse. Adams quickly resubmitted the agreement. It was narrowly approved with an amendment striking out the provisions calling for further discussion of treaties and indemnities. The document was ratified by his successor, Thomas Jefferson, in December 1801.

The Convention of 1800 represented a giant step toward an independent U.S. foreign policy. To be sure, the commissioners abandoned substantial, if inflated, financial claims against France. As with the Jay Treaty, however, when viewed from the longer perspective, the advantages far outweighed the shortcomings. The convention ended five years of conflict with France and eliminated, at least temporarily, the threat of a war the United States could ill afford. It stopped French plunder of American commerce and secured the release of ships. France recognized the independence of the United States as it had not before and tacitly accepted the Anglo-American connection set forth in Jay's Treaty. Most important, although it could not be fully appreciated at the time, the United States freed itself from the alliance of 1778, a source of tension with France and domestic discord since the outbreak of the European war. Continuation of that conflict until 1815 perpetuated the threat to the United States, but severance of ties with France rendered its situation much less complicated. The nation would not be a party to another "entangling alliance" until the mid-twentieth century.

If the price for peace and freedom of action was relatively low for the nation, it was high for its principal author and his party. Adams's belated commitment to negotiations with France irreparably divided his party, sealing his defeat in the election of 1800 and contributing to the demise of Federalism. At least in retrospect, he insisted that the price was worth paying. "I desire no other inscription over my gravestone," he later wrote, "than: 'Here lies John Adams, who took upon himself the responsibility for peace with France in the year 1800.'"[65]

Despite their partisanship and occasional excess, the Federalists skillfully guided the United States through a perilous era. Displaying opportunism and pragmatism in time of crisis, they exploited the European war to America's advantage while scrupulously avoiding the full-scale involvement that would have been disastrous at this stage of the nation's growth.

---

65. Quoted in DeConde, *Quasi-War*, 339.

Insisting on its rights to trade with both major belligerents, the United States suffered heavy losses in shipping but achieved major gains in foreign trade. Exports increased from $20 million in 1792 to more than $94 million in 1801, imports from $23 million in 1790 to $110 million in 1801, and the reexport trade jumped from $1 million in 1792 to nearly $50 million in 1800. This prosperity was based on unusual conditions, to be sure, but it provided a foundation for future economic growth. The removal of British troops from U.S. soil, along with Spanish recognition of the southern boundary and granting of access to the Mississippi, eased the foreign threat to frontier communities, curbed secessionist impulses among westerners, and facilitated incorporation of the West into the Union. By the end of the decade, moreover, restless Americans had begun to filter into Spanish Florida and Louisiana, preparing the way for future acquisition. Federalists gained a measure of international respect for the United States not forthcoming in the 1780s. They secured release from the French alliance, making possible a truly independent foreign policy. Few decades in U.S. history have been as dangerous and yet as rich in accomplishment.

The Federalists also bequeathed an enduring legacy of practice and doctrine. Inheriting a distrust of executive or legislative control of foreign policy, the Founders created a mixed constitutional arrangement with little basis in historical experience. Without precedent to guide him, Washington molded the vagaries of the Constitution into a workable system. The result was not a democratic foreign policy in any real sense of the word. Constitutional ambiguities would lead to executive abuses of power and intense executive-legislative conflict. But the system subjected foreign policy to the popular will to a greater degree than in other governments to that time. The Washington administration also put into practice a body of doctrine that neatly assimilated the American experience and accurately reflected popular aspirations. Based on the premise of American exceptionalism, it called for independence from Europe and looked to the day when the American empire would rival the Old World in size and strength. Significantly, although Jefferson hailed what he called the "revolution of 1800," he did not repudiate the Federalist heritage. Rather, he and his successors refined it into a foreign policy of independence and expansion that would guide the nation for years to come.

3

"Purified, as by Fire"

Republicanism Imperiled and Reaffirmed, 1801–1815

No one personifies better than Thomas Jefferson the essential elements of a distinctively American approach to foreign policy. "He thought of America the way we like to think of ourselves," Robert Tucker and David Hendrickson have written, "and saw its significance as we still do, in terms larger than itself." Like his countrymen at the time and since, Jefferson drew a sharp distinction between the "high moral purpose" that animated America and the "low motives of power and expediency that drove others." He disclaimed ambition for the United States, and when engaged in disputes with other nations often took the high ground of moral principle. In theory, at least, he rejected the mechanisms of traditional European diplomacy. Viewing war as the foremost enemy of liberty, he claimed to spurn force as an instrument of diplomacy, preferring, as he put it, the "Quaker system." After the buffeting of the 1790s, he yearned for disengagement from Europe, speaking of "divorce" from Britain and France and even a China-like isolation from the outside world. "The promise of Jefferson's statecraft," Tucker and Hendrickson conclude, "was thus of a new diplomacy, based on the confidence of a free and virtuous people, that would secure ends founded on the natural and universal rights of man, by means that escaped war and its corruptions."[1]

Jefferson was also a "practical idealist" (often more practical than idealistic), and in this too he set an enduring tone for his nation's foreign policy. His invocation of principle masked grandiose ambitions. Republican ideology rested on the twin pillars of commercial and landed expansion, each of which required contact and on occasion provoked conflict with the outside world, rendering Jefferson's dream of economic engagement and political separation a chimera. Whether he came to recognize this is unclear. What is clear is his willingness to put aside his scruples to achieve his goals. He sought to exploit the European system to America's advantage, all the while proclaiming his nation's moral superiority. He was

---

1. Robert W. Tucker and David C. Hendrickson, *Empire of Liberty: The Statecraft of Thomas Jefferson* (New York, 1992), 6, 19.

willing, at times, to employ devious and even duplicitous means to achieve ends he considered noble or simply necessary.

Jefferson's successes and failures were of epic proportions, also typifying those of his nation. His ideological fervor and self-confidence gave a steely strength to his diplomacy. Through skillful maneuvering and extraordinary good fortune, he secured for the United States in his first term the great windfall of the vast Louisiana territory. As so often happens, success gave rise to a near-fatal hubris. His subsequent efforts to "conquer without war" in the bitter struggle with England over neutral rights failed miserably. He refused to compromise his principles or to fight for them, pushing his confidant and successor James Madison toward a war they both dreaded and that could have been disastrous. The United States survived, however, and that alone seemed to vindicate its policies and confirm in the eyes of its leaders and people the strength of its principles and institutions.[2]

I

Jefferson took office under unusually favorable circumstances. By the end of 1800, the European combatants had bludgeoned each other to a draw. Napoleon's defeat of Austria solidified French control of the Continent and left England without allies, but British dominance of the seas stood in the way of a complete French victory. Each side felt compelled to regroup. After a year of negotiations, the Peace of Amiens (March 1802) formally ended the war. The treaty left most of the central issues unresolved and would last less than a year. But it gave Jefferson precious breathing space to effect the transfer of power, what he called "the revolution of 1800," consolidate his position, and calm the divisions that had sundered the nation during Adams's last years in office.

Although much stronger and more secure in 1801 than when Washington had assumed the presidency, the United States remained weak by European standards. The population had doubled since 1776, exceeding by the turn of the century five million people (approximately one-fifth slaves) and reinforcing visions of future power and greatness, but it was still scattered in largely isolated communities over a great expanse of land. Admission of Vermont, Tennessee, and Kentucky as states and the

2. Lawrence S. Kaplan, "Thomas Jefferson: The Idealist as Realist," in Frank J. Merli and Theodore A. Wilson, eds., *Makers of American Diplomacy: From Benjamin Franklin to Alfred Thayer Mahan* (New York, 1974), 53–79; Peter Onuf and Nicholas Onuf, *Federal Union, Modern World: The Law of Nations in an Age of Revolution* (New York, 1994), 174–75.

organization of territories in Indiana and Mississippi consolidated the domain of the original union. The ties between western settlements and the seaboard remained tenuous, however, and disunionist schemes and foreign intrigue persisted through the War of 1812. The United States had fattened on the European wars. Agriculture and commerce flourished. But prosperity hinged on war-induced foreign trade, making it highly vulnerable to external forces. The new capital in Washington, graced by a few pretentious buildings but otherwise a "place with a few bad houses, extensive swamps, hanging on the skirts of a too thinly peopled, weak and barren country," symbolized the grand aspirations and continuing backwardness of the new republic.[3]

In spite of his radical preelection image, Jefferson retained the instruments and followed the basic thrust of his predecessors' foreign policy. A champion of state power and congressional prerogatives in the Federalist era, in office he greatly enlarged the power of the central government and through personal persuasion and party discipline exercised firm control of Congress. He retained the cabinet system inherited from Washington. Having observed firsthand Adams's problems, he kept his own cabinet on a close rein, a system his secretary of state, Madison, found entirely acceptable. Anti-militarist in his philosophy and determined to slash government expenditures, Jefferson eagerly seized the occasion of peace in Europe to drastically scale back the army and navy. Adhering to republican doctrine, he shifted the focus of military policy from the regular army to the militia and from an oceangoing navy to small gunboats designed for harbor defense. But he maintained the basic military structure created by the Federalists. He even added to it by establishing the U.S. Military Academy at West Point to train an officer corps.[4]

The allure France once held for Jefferson waned with Napoleon's rise to power, and the third president was even more determined than his predecessors to pursue an independent foreign policy. His inaugural commitment to "peace, commerce, and honest friendship with all nations — entangling alliances with none" echoed in less qualified terms the sentiments of Washington's Farewell Address and reaffirmed to skeptics his independence of spirit. Viewing separation from the "cankers" and "sores" of European society and the "madmen" and "tyrants" of European politics as essential to the purity of American institutions, he scrupulously avoided any foreign ties, which, like the French alliance, might compromise

3. Quoted in Merrill D. Peterson, *Thomas Jefferson and the New Nation* (New York, 1970), 653.
4. Forrest McDonald, *The Presidency of Thomas Jefferson* (Lawrence, Kans., 1976), 43–44.

America's freedom of action, inflame its domestic politics, or contaminate its councils. He refused to associate the United States with a league of armed European neutrals committed to defending freedom of the seas, even though it supported principles Americans agreed with. Jefferson was in no sense an isolationist, however, and his diplomacy was flexible and pragmatic. A shrewd observer of world affairs, he understood the workings of the European system of politics and was quick to exploit it. He was prepared to depart from principle to advance American interests, even to the point of contemplating an alliance with England during the Louisiana crisis.[5]

While following the paths staked out by his predecessors, Jefferson also introduced important changes in style and substance. Confirmed in his Americanism and republicanism, he integrated them into his diplomacy and even flaunted them. He had long viewed professional diplomats and diplomacy as the "pest of the peace of the world," and he reduced U.S. representation abroad to the essential minimum. Eschewing the pomp and display of the courts of Washington and Adams, he dressed plainly — slovenly, critics said — and opened the doors of the presidential mansion on equal terms to visitors of high station and low. His personal warmth and glittering conversation, along with the simplicity and studied casualness of his style, charmed some European visitors. His disdain for protocol scandalized other members of the small and generally unhappy diplomatic community in Washington. Outraged when received by the president in a tattered bathrobe and slippers and forced at a presidential dinner to conform to "pell-mell" seating arrangements respecting no rank, the British minister to Washington, Anthony Merry, bitterly protested the affront suffered at the president's table. Jefferson no doubt privately chuckled at the arrogant Englishman's discomfiture, but his subsequent codification of republican practices into established procedures betrayed a larger purpose. By adapting the new nation's forms to its principles, he hoped to establish a uniquely American style in diplomacy.[6]

Republican ideology influenced Jefferson's foreign policy in more important ways. In his view, the preservation of the principles of the American Revolution at home was inextricably linked to the nation's foreign policy. Genuine political and economic freedom required a population of independent landowners engaged in productive enterprises, as distinct from the stockjobbers and manipulators who held power in England and the

5. Ibid., 54. For Jefferson's flexibility, see especially Kaplan, "Idealist as Realist," 58–59.
6. McDonald, *Jefferson*, 39, 54–55; Dumas Malone, *Jefferson the President: First Term, 1801–1815* (Boston, 1970), 379–92.

wage-labor class they dominated. A republican population demanded, in turn, access to foreign markets to ensure continued outlets for America's agricultural surpluses and the availability of sufficient land to provide an economic basis for freedom for a rapidly expanding people. Commercial and territorial expansion were therefore indispensable to the preservation of republican institutions, and thus essential ingredients of Republican foreign policy.[7]

Despite its relative weakness, moreover, Jefferson believed that the United States could achieve its goals. Persuaded that the virtue of its people and the nature of its institutions were more important measures of a nation's strength than military or even economic power, he viewed the United States as the "strongest government on earth." He clung doggedly to the belief that Europe depended on the "necessities" produced by the United States, while Americans could do without the "superfluities" manufactured by Europe, giving them a potentially powerful weapon in the form of trade restrictions. Certain of America's strength, Jefferson was less inclined than the Federalists to accommodate other nations in times of crisis. Philosophically, he tended toward pacifism—"peace is my passion," he proclaimed—but he was not above using force to uphold principles he believed in. In dealings with the Barbary States of North Africa, Spain, and France during the Louisiana crisis, and Britain and France in conflicts over neutral rights, he was more belligerent and assertive than his predecessors. Certain that the United States was a "chosen country," the "world's best hope," he was less inclined to respect foreign holdings in North America. He was aggressively expansionist.[8] If Washington and the Federalists charted the basic course of U.S. foreign policy, Jefferson and the Republicans infused into it a peculiarly American spirit and style.

II

Jefferson's assertiveness is manifest in his handling of the Tripolitan War, America's first foreign war and the first of numerous intrusions into a region that, more than two centuries later, remained terra incognita for most Americans. Raiders from the Barbary States continued to prey on American shipping in the 1790s; Algiers captured eleven ships and more than a hundred sailors in 1793 alone. An irate Congress voted the next year to create a navy to defend U.S. commerce, but crises with Britain and France forced a bow to expediency. Concluding that it would cost less to

7. Drew McCoy, *The Elusive Republic: Political Economy in Jeffersonian America* (Chapel Hill, N.C., 1980), 188–201.
8. Peterson, *Jefferson*, 657, 665.

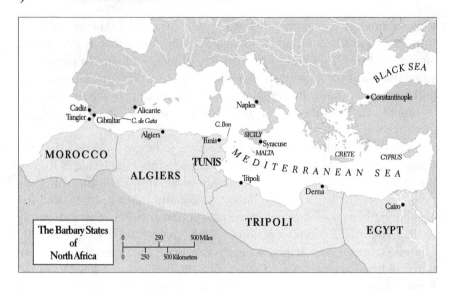

The Barbary States of North Africa

pay than to fight, Washington and Adams ransomed the release of prisoners. They concluded treaties with Morocco, Algiers, and Tripoli at a cost of more than $1 million that protected U.S. trade in return for annual payments of money or the provision of ships, gunpowder, and naval supplies. As a gesture to local sensibilities, the treaty with Tripoli even explicitly avowed that the United States was "not, in any sense, founded on the Christian religion."[9]

Never comfortable with what he considered extortion, Jefferson reversed Federalist policy. Like most Westerners, he viewed the Islamic states as hopelessly despotic and oppressive. The actions of these "lawless pirates" violated his standards of civilized behavior and his commitment to free trade. He was certain that appeasement encouraged more outrageous demands. As minister to France and secretary of state he had advocated the use of force to uphold U.S. honor and keep vital shipping lanes open. "I think it is to our interest to punish the first insult," he insisted, "because an insult unpunished is the parent of many others."[10]

Upon assuming office, Jefferson found ample reason for reprisal. Annoyed that the United States had not sent its tribute on time and in the amount promised, the dey of Algiers commandeered an American ship, the *George Washington*, and compelled its humiliated captain to undertake

9. James A. Field Jr., *America and the Mediterranean World, 1776–1882* (Princeton, N.J., 1969), 32–43; Robert J. Allison, *The Crescent Obscured: The United States and the Muslim World, 1776–1815* (New York, 1995), 17–24.
10. Dumas Malone, *Jefferson and the Rights of Man* (Boston, 1951), 27.

a personal tribute mission for him to Turkey. Upset that he was receiving less booty than Algiers and therefore presumably was viewed as inferior, the pasha of Tripoli raised his demands and ceremoniously declared war on the United States by hacking down the flag at the U.S. consulate. The United States was "too high-minded to endure the degradation of others," Jefferson declaimed. Tripoli's demands were "unfounded either in right or compact," and the "style of the demand admitted but one answer."[11] Eager to prove to North Africans—and Europeans—that the United States would meet force with force, he dispatched four ships to the Mediterranean to "protect our commerce and chastise their insolence" by "sinking, burning, or destroying their ships and Vessels." Setting a major precedent in terms of executive authority, he did not seek congressional authorization to commit forces abroad, reasoning that war already existed by act of Tripoli.[12]

The Tripolitan War lasted from 1801 to 1805. Torn between his desire to punish his foes on the one hand and hold down federal expenditures on the other, Jefferson kept the conflict strictly limited and did not provide sufficient forces to patrol a fifteen-hundred-mile coast and "chastise the insolent." His naval commanders faced horrendous logistical problems and consequently displayed understandable caution, provoking an angry president to complain of a "two year sleep." Indecisiveness turned to near disaster in 1803 when the frigate *Philadelphia* ran aground off Tripoli and its captain and crew were held for $3 million ransom.[13]

His hands freed by the easing of the Louisiana crisis, Jefferson in late 1803 sharply escalated the war. He attempted unsuccessfully to organize an international naval force to curb piracy in the Mediterranean. He dispatched every available ship to the region. In what British naval hero Horatio Lord Nelson called "the most bold and daring act of the age," U.S. sailors slipped through the pasha's heavy defenses without the loss of a single life and burned the *Philadelphia*. The navy blockaded the coast off Tripoli and bombarded the city itself. In an early example of what would come to be called "mission creep," Jefferson and Madison approved the first U.S. attempt to replace a hostile foreign government. Madison conceded that to "intermeddle in the domestic contests of other countries" violated American principles, but, he reasoned, "it cannot be unfair, in the prosecution of a just war" to exploit "the enmity and

---

11. Allison, *Crescent Obscured*, 24.
12. David A. Carson, "Jefferson, Congress and the Question of Leadership in the Tripolitan War," *Virginia Magazine of History and Biography* 94 (1986), 411–12.
13. Field, *Mediterranean World*, 50–51.

pretenses of others against a common foe."[14] With authorization from Washington, the U.S. consul at Tunis, William Eaton, plotted with the pasha's exiled brother to overthrow the government of Tripoli. Assembling a motley force of eight U.S. Marines and some four hundred Greek and Arab adventurers, he marched five hundred miles across the desert and "liberated" Derna, the second most important city of Tripoli.[15]

The war ended in 1805 on terms less than satisfactory to some Americans. Facing serious embarrassment, even possible military defeat and deposition, the pasha agreed to a commercial treaty without tribute, although he did manage to extort $60,000 to ransom the hostages and secured U.S. agreement to the continued exile of his brother. Some Americans vigorously protested the ransom, insisting that the United States could have dictated terms. Eaton bitterly complained of the abandonment of the unfortunate pretender. By this time, however, the war was costing more than $1 million per year, provoking growing concern from a frugal president and Congress. The pasha's frequent warnings that, having killed his father and brother, he would have no scruples about a "few infidels" evoked concern for the hostages. Despite persistent grumbling, the treaty was approved.[16]

The Tripolitan War has been dismissed as unimportant, and in strictly practical terms it was.[17] It cost far more than the price of tribute. It did not end American difficulties with the Barbary States. When the threat of war with Britain forced U.S. withdrawal from the region in 1807, Algiers, Tunis, and Tripoli resumed harassment of U.S. shipping. Only after the War of 1812 was the United States, by another show of force, able to secure free passage of the Mediterranean.

To consider the war in such narrow terms badly misses the point. It had enormous psychological and ideological significance for the United States. The effective use of force stimulated the self-pride of the new nation; the exploits of the U.S. Navy and Marines on the "shores of Tripoli" formed an important part of its patriotic folklore. Coming at the same time as the acquisition of Louisiana, it gave Americans a renewed sense of mission and destiny. For some, it became a morality play. They perceived Islamic despotism as the most backward form of governance, depriving people of liberty and the fruits of their labor, restraining progress, and

14. James R. Sofka, "The Jeffersonian Idea of National Security: Commerce, the Atlantic Balance of Power, and the Barbary War, 1786–1805," *Diplomatic History* 21 (Fall 1997), 540.

15. Field, *Mediterranean World*, 52–54; McDonald, *Jefferson*, 78.

16. Field, *Mediterranean World*, 52–53; Dumas Malone, *Jefferson the President: Second Term, 1805–1809* (Boston, 1974), 40.

17. McDonald, *Jefferson*, 76.

breeding lethargy, misery, poverty and ignorance. They exulted that republican ideals had given them the courage and strength to defeat the "plundering vassals of the tyrannical bashaw," striking a blow for liberty *and* Christianity. Americans had proven themselves, in the words of a contemporary nationalist poet, "a race of beings! of equal spirit to the first of nations." Proud that they rather than the Europeans had taken the lead in chastising the Barbary pirates, Americans were confirmed in their view of themselves as the agents of a new order of justice and freedom. Jefferson even speculated that his nation's success might encourage the European powers to emancipate themselves from that "degrading yoke."[18]

III

Jefferson's expansionism represents the fullest expression of his nationalism and republicanism. He shared with others of his generation a keen sense of America's exceptionalism and destiny. "A chosen country," he hailed it in his eloquent first inaugural address, "kindly separated by nature and a wide ocean from the exterminating havoc of one quarter of the globe" with "room enough for our descendants to the thousandth and thousandth generation." He was among the first to envision the extension of the nation's institutions to the Pacific Ocean. "However our present interests may restrain us...," he wrote in 1801, "it is impossible not to look forward to distant times when our rapid multiplication will...cover the whole northern if not the southern continent with people speaking the same language, governed in similar forms, and by similar laws."[19] His vision of that "union" was vague, in some ways paradoxical, almost ethereal. He did not foresee the incorporation of this territory into a single political entity. Certain that geography and distance would inhibit unity and that small, self-governing republics were best suited to preserve individual liberties, he saw rather a series of "distinct but bordering establishments" bound by "relations of blood [and] affection." Formal ties would not be required because such like-minded states, in contrast to Europe, would not be hostile to each other. As president, Jefferson perceived the immediate limits to U.S. expansion, but he was also alert to opportunities to reduce foreign influence on the continent. He used every available instrument, including the threat of war, to enlarge his "empire for liberty."[20]

18. Allison, *Crescent Obscured*, 46–54, 189, 193, 204; Jefferson to John Taylor, March 29, 1805, in Paul Leicester Ford, ed., *The Writings of Thomas Jefferson* (10 vols., New York, 1892–99), 4:574.
19. Jefferson to Monroe, November 24, 1801, in Ford, *Writings* 8:105.
20. Peter S. Onuf, *Jefferson's Empire: The Language of American Nationhood* (Charlottesville, Va., 2000), 118–19.

A chance to do so to an extent he could not possibly have imagined came with the Louisiana crisis of 1802–3 and the acquisition of a vast new territory. This greatest achievement of Jefferson's presidency is often and rightly regarded as a diplomatic windfall—the result of accident, luck, and the whim of Napoleon Bonaparte—but it also owed much to design. Americans had coveted Louisiana and especially the crucial port of New Orleans since the colonial era. Through commercial and agricultural penetration, the United States had acquired significant influence there by the end of the century. The American presence in Louisiana, combined with Jefferson's shrewd and sometimes belligerent diplomacy, played a part in Napoleon's decision to sell to the United States territory he never occupied.

Throughout the last half of the eighteenth century, Louisiana was a pawn on the chessboard of European politics. Originally claimed by Spain but explored and settled by France, this enormous, uncharted region stretched from the source of the Mississippi to its mouth on the Gulf of Mexico and westward along its tributaries to the Rockies. Scattered Indian tribes, with whom Europeans and Americans carried on a lively and lucrative trade in furs, roamed its vast distances. Under French administration, it was sparsely settled and weakly defended. Having lost Canada to Britain in the Seven Years' War, France in 1763 ceded New Orleans and Louisiana west of the Mississippi to Spain, which acquired it mainly to keep it from British hands. Dreams of an American empire died hard in France, however, and for the rest of the century some officials pressed for reacquisition of Louisiana.

Americans also had designs on the Spanish colony. The United States early mastered the arts of infiltration and subversion and first employed with Spanish Louisiana the tactics later successfully used in the Floridas, Texas, California, and Hawaii. As early as the Revolution, restless frontiersmen began to filter into Louisiana. The reliance of trans-Appalachian settlers on the Mississippi River and New Orleans quickened interest in the region. Spain's refusal to grant access to the river provoked talk of secession or a war of conquest. Pinckney's Treaty temporarily eased the problem and sharply expanded American influence in Spanish territory. Flatboats loaded with foodstuffs, tobacco, and whiskey and skillfully maneuvered by the wild river men—the "half-horse, half-alligators" of popular legend—floated down the Mississippi in droves. By the end of the century, the United States dominated commerce at the port of New Orleans. Encouraged at times by their own government, at times by the Spanish, who saw them as a buffer against a possible British invasion from Canada, and often acting on their own, American settlers continued to drift into Louisiana. Although living on foreign soil, they retained allegiance to the United States and displayed open contempt for their nominal rulers. In some areas, they composed a majority of the population, in others an unassimilable minority compared by increasingly nervous Spanish officials to the "Goths at the gates of Rome."[21] Some even ventured illegally into upper Louisiana west of the Mississippi River. By the time Jefferson took office, Americans were actually taking control of territory under nominal European jurisdiction.[22]

As long as Louisiana remained in the hands of "feeble" Spain, Americans were content to be patient, and Jefferson was certain that in time the United States would acquire it "piece by piece." Should it be taken by a stronger power, however, a "profound reconsideration" of U.S. policy would be necessary.[23] Jefferson's fears were soon realized. Upon becoming First Consul in 1799, Napoleon took up long dormant schemes to restore French grandeur in North America. Persuaded that an empire composed of the Floridas, Louisiana, and the Caribbean sugar islands would enrich his treasury, enhance his prestige, undermine British trade, and give him leverage against the United States, he set out to relieve Spain of its colonies. In the secret Treaty of San Ildefonso (October 1800), Spain relinquished costly and increasingly vulnerable Louisiana for a piece of European territory, but it refused to give up the Floridas and extracted from Napoleon a pledge not to transfer his new possession to a third party. Once peace was established in Europe in 1801, Napoleon dispatched a military expedition to regain control of rebellious Saint-Domingue. His next move was to occupy New Orleans.

Bonaparte's maneuvers sent shock waves across the Atlantic. Rumors of French acquisition of Louisiana began to reach America as early as the spring of 1801. Subsequent confirmation of the retrocession provoked an immediate and nervous response. "This little event of France possessing herself of Louisiana ...," Jefferson wrote a friend in April 1802, "is the embryo of a tornado which will burst on the countries on both sides of the Atlantic and involve in its effects their highest destinies."[24] Through unofficial emissaries, he dispatched stern warnings to France. "There is on the globe one single spot, the possessor of which is our natural and habitual enemy," he admonished. Should France take possession of New Orleans,

21. Alexander DeConde, *This Affair of Louisiana* (New York, 1976), 64.
22. Stephen E. Ambrose, *Undaunted Courage: Meriwether Lewis, Thomas Jefferson, and the Opening of the American West* (New York, 1996), 56.
23. Malone, *First Term*, 250.
24. Jefferson to Pierre Samuel DuPont, April 25, 1802, quoted in DeConde, *Louisiana*, 114–15.

the United States would have no choice but to "marry" itself to the "British fleet and nation" and use the outbreak of war in Europe as an excuse to take Louisiana by force.[25] To threaten war over territory to which the United States had no claim and that had been exchanged in a perfectly legal manner was, to say the least, extraordinary. Given Jefferson's history of Anglophobia, the prospect of an alliance with Britain was perhaps even more so. Justifying his position on the dubious grounds that "natural law" entitled Americans to security and the free navigation of rivers adjoining their territory, he softened the threat by suggesting that France could avert war by ceding New Orleans to the United States.

Sudden revocation in October 1802 of Americans' rights to deposit goods at New Orleans for transshipment to other ports without duty inflamed an already tense situation. Spain had delayed executing the treaty. Spanish officials in New Orleans sought to curb the rampant and costly American smuggling, but most Americans saw the sinister hand of Bonaparte behind what they viewed as a pretext for French seizure of the port. Westerners demanded war. To embarrass the administration and fulfill their old expansionist designs, Federalists joined forces. "It belongs of right to the United States to regulate the future destiny of North America," one Federalist newspaper declared. Anxious to undercut the opposition and resolve the crisis without war, Jefferson combined continued threats with diplomacy. He reiterated earlier warnings that French occupation of Louisiana could bring war and backed them by mobilizing forces along the frontier. Under the guise of a "scientific expedition," he ordered Meriwether Lewis and William Clark to reconnoiter upper Louisiana and the Missouri River valley, in part to gain intelligence about Spanish military power. In January 1803, he dispatched to Paris as his special envoy James Monroe, a man respected in the West, authorizing him to purchase New Orleans and the Floridas (which he mistakenly assumed had also been transferred to France). If that failed, Monroe was to proceed to London to discuss an alliance. "On the event of this mission, depends the future destinies of this republic," Monroe himself exclaimed. Toasts drunk to the departing envoy revealed the bellicose mood of the nation: "Peace, if peace is honorable; war, if war is necessary."[26]

Jefferson's fears for Louisiana even prompted him to abandon—temporarily—efforts to subvert the rebellion on Saint-Domingue. Shortly after taking office, he had reversed Adams's policy toward the rebellious French

25. Jefferson to Robert R. Livingston, April 18, 1802, in Ford, *Writings* 8:143–47.
26. Quoted in Joseph J. Ellis, *American Sphinx: The Character of Thomas Jefferson* (New York, 1997), 206.

colony. Labeling the rebels "cannibals" and fearing that the "combustion" they had sparked might spread to North America, he quietly suspended relations with the government of charismatic rebel leader Toussaint L'Ouverture and agreed to support French efforts to regain the colony. The threat of a French empire in North America gave Jefferson pause, however. Southern slaveholders fretted that a prolonged racial war on the sugar island posed a greater threat to slavery in the United States and that, once in control of Louisiana, the French might seek to abolish slavery there. The ever agile Jefferson shifted gears once again, withholding aid promised France and initiating a lively trade with Toussaint's forces including arms and ammunition. "St. Domingo delays their taking possession of Louisiana," Jefferson exulted, "and they are in the last distress for money for current purposes."[27]

By the time Monroe arrived in Paris in late winter 1803, a sequence of calamitous events in Europe and the Caribbean—fortuitous for the United States—pulled the props from beneath Napoleon's scheme for empire. Spanish officials procrastinated until late 1802 executing the treaty, delaying French plans to take possession of Louisiana and allowing time for U.S. hostility to build. They also refused to relinquish the Floridas, without which, Napoleon realized, Louisiana was indefensible. The First Consul had dispatched to Saint-Domingue in 1802 one of the largest expeditionary forces ever sent to the New World. His brother-in-law, Gen. Victor LeClerc, enjoyed early military successes. He tricked Toussaint into surrendering under the false pretense that blacks would be given their freedom. The rebel leader was instead sent to France and thrown into prison, where he subsequently died. Even without Toussaint, blacks fiercely resisted French rule—the women "die with incredible fanaticism; they laugh at death," LeClerc lamented.[28] Yellow fever decimated French forces. In all, some twenty-four thousand French troops died in the futile effort to reconquer Saint-Domingue, denying Napoleon the centerpiece of his projected empire. The expedition to take control of Louisiana was icebound in Holland. "Damn sugar, damn coffee, damn colonies," a frustrated Napoleon blurted out in a moment of rage. By this time, the resumption of war with England was imminent. Desperate for money and angry at Spain, he ignored the Treaty of San Ildefonso and sold the United States all of Louisiana instead of simply New Orleans for

27. Tim Matthewson, "Jefferson and Haiti," *Journal of Southern History* 61 (May 1995), 217–29; Donald R. Hickey, "America's Response to the Slave Revolt in Haiti," *Journal of the Early Republic* 2 (Winter 1982), 368–69.
28. Quoted in Matthewson, "Jefferson and Haiti," 230.

funds to underwrite war against England. His precise motives will never be known. Events in Europe and the Caribbean were certainly most important. But Jefferson's threats appear to have made an impression. Napoleon probably reasoned that it would be better to secure much-needed cash and U.S. goodwill than risk losing by force a territory he did not control and could not defend. After some haggling, the two nations agreed on a price of $15 million.[29]

Having acquired far more than he had sought, Jefferson quickly cleared away obstacles to possession of his empire for liberty. Troubled that the Constitution did not explicitly authorize acquisition of new lands, he considered an amendment remedying the omission. But when told that Napoleon might be having second thoughts about the transaction, he waved aside his scruples and presented the treaty to Congress without reference to the constitutional issue. A few die-hard Federalists complained of paying an exorbitant price for a vast wasteland, poorly masking their fears that the purchase would solidify Republican control of the government. But the treaty was generally popular, and Congress quickly approved it. When Spain protested the illegality of the transfer and threatened to block it, Jefferson mobilized troops along the frontier and vowed to seize Louisiana *and* the Floridas, leaving hapless Spain little choice but to acquiesce.

Governing the new territory caused more serious problems. Deeming the Creoles and Indians unfit for self-government, Jefferson readily abandoned his principles of representative government, delaying full admission to the Union until the natives had served an apprenticeship and the American population had increased. Only after vigorous protest from the inhabitants did he speed up the timetable, in 1805 creating a representative assembly.[30]

In a move fraught with great portent for the future of the republic, Congress allowed national security concerns to thwart efforts to limit slavery in the Louisiana territory. Taking a modest step toward gradual abolition, Congress in 1804 prohibited the international and domestic slave trade in Louisiana. White Louisianans, some of them refugees from Caribbean sugar islands eager to replicate what they had left behind, warned they would not accept U.S. rule unless slavery was protected. They even threatened to approach Napoleon. Many Americans feared that the republic was dangerously overextended. The inhabitants of Louisiana, in their view, were not ready for self-government; "a more ignorant and

29. DeConde, *Louisiana*, 147–75.
30. Ibid., 210–11.

depraved race of civilized men did not exist," Treasury Secretary Albert Gallatin observed. Without assurances about slavery, they would be susceptible to foreign, especially French, influence and prime candidates for disunionist schemes. To ensure U.S. control of the new territory, it was also deemed essential to encourage emigration of Americans there, and bans on slavery could hinder that process. Southerners increasingly feared that the rapid growth of the slave population in their states posed the threat of rebellions like the one on Saint-Domingue. Diffusion of the existing slave population through emigration into the new territories provided a safety valve. Responding to these multiple pressures, Congress in 1805 refused to renew its ban on the domestic slave trade in Louisiana or take measures to check the expansion of slavery, laying the foundation for the crisis of the Union a half century later.[31]

By any standard, the Louisiana Purchase was a monumental achievement. The nation acquired 828,000 square miles, doubling its territory at a cost of roughly three cents per acre, one of history's greatest real estate steals. Control of the Mississippi would tie the West firmly to the Union, enhance U.S. security, and provide enormous commercial advantages. Napoleon's sale of Louisiana all but eliminated a French return to North America, leaving the Floridas hopelessly vulnerable and Texas exposed. The United States' acquisition of Louisiana established a precedent for expansion and empire and gave substance to the idea that would later be called Manifest Destiny. This stunning achievement increased the self-confidence of the nation and reinforced an already deeply entrenched sense of destiny. For Republicans, it assumed special significance. By making available the land necessary for continued expansion of agriculture, ensuring commercial growth, and easing the European threat, thus seemingly eliminating the need for a large military establishment, the purchase appeared to ensure the preservation of the essentially republican character of American society. All of this was accomplished without the use of force—"truth and reason have been more powerful than the sword," a pro-administration newspaper exulted—thus vindicating republican statecraft.[32]

His appetite whetted and self-confidence inflated beyond reason, Jefferson set out to relieve Spain of the Floridas. Americans had long viewed that land as essential to their security and prosperity. Rapidly

31. John Craig Hammond, " 'They Are Very Much Interested in Obtaining an Unlimited Slavery': Rethinking the Expansion of Slavery in the Louisiana Purchase Territories," *Journal of the Early Republic* 23 (Fall 2003), 353–80.
32. Quoted in Tucker and Hendrickson, *Empire of Liberty*, 89.

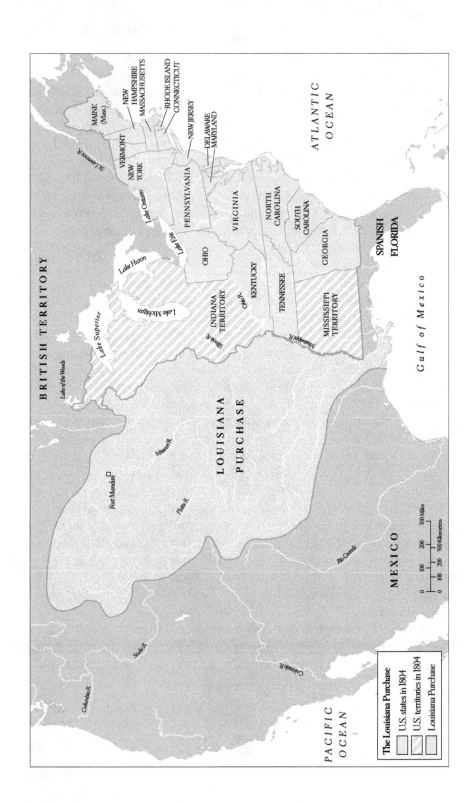

expanding settlements in the Mississippi territory required access to the port of Mobile. The commerce of the Gulf Coast promised great riches. Resting astride the Gulf of Mexico, the Floridas, as Napoleon had perceived, were vital to the defense of Louisiana. In Spanish hands, they represented a nuisance rather than a threat, but Jefferson was tempted by Spain's weakness and harbored near paranoid fears these lands might be seized by Britain. Americans now insisted that the Floridas were manifestly useless to Spain and interpreted the ever adaptable and useful laws of nature as entitling them to a water boundary on the South.

Displaying an obsessiveness not easy to comprehend, Jefferson used every conceivable means to attain his object. Permitting his wishes to drive his claims, he argued with more force than logic that since Louisiana under French control had extended to the Perdido River, including a sizeable chunk of West Florida, the United States was entitled to the same boundary, a position Spain quickly and rightly dismissed. Confident that if he "pushed Spain strongly with one hand, holding out a price in the other, we shall certainly obtain the Floridas and in all good time," he employed the same bullying tactics used with France. He combined offers to purchase the Floridas with only slightly veiled threats to seize them by force. He concentrated troops along the Spanish frontier and secured congressional passage of the Mobile Act, a vague document that appeared unilaterally to assert U.S. jurisdiction over much of West Florida. Again rebuffed, he swallowed his republican scruples and responded positively to hints from Paris that for a price Napoleon would intercede with the stubborn Spain.[33]

Jefferson's lust for Florida, along with pressures from southern slaveholders, also prompted abandonment of his brief and altogether expedient flirtation with the rebellion on Saint-Domingue. On January 1, 1804, victorious rebels proclaimed the independent republic of Haiti and began systematically killing French citizens who remained on the island. These events sent a chill through already nervous American slaveholders. At the very time the cotton gin was infusing new life into the institution of slavery in the United States, Haiti appeared a major threat. It was demonized and used as an argument against emancipation. A Georgia senator even insisted that "the government of that unfortunate island must be destroyed." Still not ready to concede defeat, France demanded that the United States cease its "shameful" and "scandalous" trade with the rebels. The administration went well beyond that modest request, in effect

33. DeConde, *Louisiana*, 214–15; Jefferson to John Breckinridge, August 12, 1803, in Ford, *Writings* 10:5n.

denying the very existence of the new country. It refused to recognize the new republic or even to use the word *Haiti*. Fearing, as Jefferson's son-in-law put it, that trade with the island could result in "the immediate and horrible destruction of the fairest part of America," and hoping to curry French support on Florida, the United States imposed a trade embargo. For reasons of race and diplomatic expediency, it conceded to the British the wealth of the sugar island trade and moral leadership in its own hemisphere. As a result of persisting slaveholder opposition, the first republic in the Western Hemisphere outside the United States went unrecognized by Washington until 1862.[34]

Jefferson's Florida diplomacy reveals him at his worst. His lust for land trumped his concern for principle and obscured his usually clear vision. Having lost Louisiana as a result of French duplicity, Spain was not in a generous mood. It was determined to hold on to its last bit of leverage against an expansive America. Timing is crucial in international negotiation. In this instance, the twists and turns of European politics worked against the United States. At the outset, Napoleon eagerly played Washington against Madrid to see what he could get, but when Spain and France joined forces in 1805 he supported his ally. In the meantime, the revelation of a possible bribe to France provoked intense opposition from old-school Republicans such as Virginian John Randolph, who denounced this "base prostration of the national character," weakening Jefferson's hand. A frustrated president would voice righteous indignation at Spanish "perfidy and injustice," but he was unable to secure the object of his ambitions.[35]

Jefferson's successor, James Madison, shared his fixation with the Floridas and evinced a willingness to use the presence of Americans there and the exigencies of the European war to take them. Drawn to West Florida by cheap and fertile land and easy access to the Gulf, American settlers made up a majority of the population by 1810. They resented Spanish rule—such as it was—and especially the duties they paid to use Spanish ports. Encouraged by Washington to form a "convention" should Spanish authority collapse, a collection of gentleman planters, hooligans, and fugitives from Spanish *and* American justice seized the fort at Baton Rouge. With no money in hand but a flag already designed, they proclaimed the independent republic of West Florida and requested

34. Matthewson, "Jefferson and Haiti," 234–39; Hickey, "Slave Revolt," 374–76; Tim Matthewson, "Jefferson and the Nonrecognition of Haiti," *Proceedings of the American Philosophical Society* 140 (March 1996), 22–47.
35. Malone, *Second Term*, 73; Ford, *Writings* 9:381–82.

annexation by the United States. By not waiting for the end of Spanish rule to declare independence, the rebels moved much further and faster than Madison intended. Fearful, on the other hand, that France or Britain might seize the territory, he acted preemptively to back up America's contested claim. Refusing to negotiate with the rebels, whose legitimacy he questioned, he ordered the occupation of West Florida to the Perdido River.[36] In 1811, he asserted U.S. jurisdiction over the province; the following year, he incorporated it into the state of Louisiana. Using the possibility of a British invasion as a pretext, Madison completed the conquest of Spanish West Florida in 1813 by annexing Mobile.

The administration's actions in East Florida in 1812 represent an embarrassing episode in early national history, a failed attempt to take by force territory to which the United States had little claim. Fearing the collapse of Spanish rule, Madison in 1810 dispatched Georgia adventurer George Mathews to inform the residents of East Florida that if they were to separate from Spain they would be welcomed into the United States. The following year, he secured from Congress authorization to use force to prevent a foreign takeover of East Florida, instructing Mathews in such an eventuality to occupy the province or negotiate with the locals. Mathews subsequently sought authority to foment revolution there. The administration's non-response was interpreted by him—and has been seen by some historians—as tantamount to silent complicity in the scheme. Others persuasively argue that this was standard operating procedure and did not imply consent. Whatever the case, the overzealous Mathews organized a group of local "Patriots" who seized Amelia Island off the Georgia coast and laid siege to St. Augustine. Complaining that Mathews's "extravagance" had put the administration in "the most distressing dilemma," Madison disavowed his reckless agent. On the verge of war with Britain, however, and more than ever concerned about the threat to East Florida, he authorized the Patriots to hold on to territory they had taken.[37] Furious with his abandonment, Mathews started home to expose the administration's complicity. In a rare bit of good luck during his embattled presidency, Madison was spared further embarrassment when Mathews died en route.[38]

36. Thomas P. Abernethy, *The South in the New Nation, 1789–1819* (Baton Rouge, La., 1961), 340–66; J.C.A. Stagg, "James Madison and George Mathews: The East Florida Revolution of 1812 Reconsidered," *Diplomatic History* 30 (January 2006), 29–31.

37. Stagg, "Madison and Mathews," 32–55.

38. Robert Allen Rutland, *The Presidency of James Madison* (Lawrence, Kans., 1990), 92.

While consolidating his Louisiana prize and pressing Spain on the Floridas, Jefferson had taken the first steps toward an American empire on the Pacific. During the height of the Louisiana crisis, he instructed his aide Meriwether Lewis to explore what was then Spanish territory. To the Spanish, he justified the mission in scientific and "literary" terms; to Congress, he spoke of exploiting the lucrative fur trade, "civilizing" the Indians, and finding the fabled water route to the Pacific. By the time Lewis and William Clark got under way, Louisiana belonged to the United States and Jefferson's vision had expanded to acquiring all of the West. He instructed the explorers to bring the Indians into the U.S. orbit, wrest the fur trade from Britain, and lay claim to the Pacific Northwest.[39]

One of the great adventures of all times, Lewis and Clark's dramatic and arduous journey to the Columbia River and back covered more than seven thousand miles and took more than two years. Confident that Indians, in contrast to blacks, were "noble savages" who could be civilized, Jefferson contemplated keeping the West as a vast reservation where those already settled and tribes transplanted from the East could be civilized and in time assimilated. Using the combination of threats and bribes that had long stamped American Indian policy, Lewis and Clark parleyed with tribes along the way, urging them to accept U.S. sovereignty, make peace among themselves, and welcome American traders. This initial approach to the Plains Indians had mixed results for the United States and largely negative results for the Indians. Representatives of some tribes actually visited Washington; some trade ties were established. Lewis and Clark did not seek to befriend the hostile Sioux and Blackfeet, however, and they were unable to make peace among the other tribes. Most important for the long run, reports from the expedition excited trappers and eventually settlers to head West, in time re-creating there and with the same results the wars of extermination already under way to the east.[40]

The explorers discovered no water route to the Pacific—dashing long-standing geographical assumptions—and their reports underlined the formidable barriers to settling the trans-Mississippi West. The expedition did produce priceless geographical and scientific discoveries, however, and it greatly facilitated U.S. expansion to the Pacific. Encouraged by Jefferson's offer of "every reasonable [government] patronage," the New York merchant John Jacob Astor immediately set out to capture the fur trade by constructing a series of posts from the Missouri River to the Columbia. In 1811, he established a fort at the mouth of the Columbia,

39. Peterson, *Jefferson*, 762–64.
40. Ambrose, *Undaunted Courage*, 140–395.

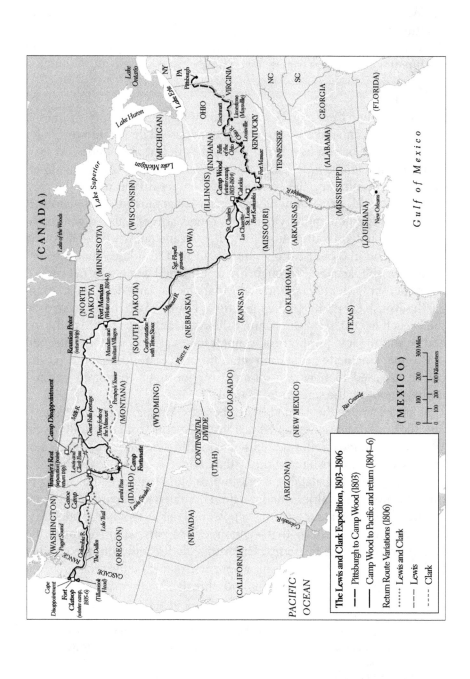

The Lewis and Clark Expedition, 1803–1806

— Pittsburgh to Camp Wood (1803)

— Camp Wood to Pacific and return (1804–6)

Return Route Variations (1806)

······ Lewis and Clark

— — — Lewis

---- Clark

laying the first substantial American claim to the Oregon territory. During the War of 1812, Astor loaned a near bankrupt United States $2.5 million in return for promises to defend Astoria it could not keep. The advance to the Pacific was delayed by geography and war, but Jefferson's vision of continental empire was eagerly taken up by his successors.[41]

IV

At best an armed truce, the Peace of Amiens broke down in 1803, and the European war entered an even more bitter phase, a desperate struggle for survival not to be resolved until Napoleon's defeat at Waterloo in 1815. During much of this time, the major combatants were locked in a stand-off, France dominating the continent of Europe, Britain ruling the seas. Combining with devastating effectiveness his genius for battlefield ma-neuver and the new military concept of mass armies imbued with patri-otic zeal, Napoleon routed Austria and Prussia and quickly brought Russia to terms. The master of Europe, he sought next to subdue that despised "nation of shopkeepers" through his Continental System, a network of blockades set forth in his Berlin and Milan decrees and designed to stran-gle the British economy. In the meantime, Lord Nelson in 1805 destroyed the French fleet at Trafalgar, giving Britain uncontested control of the sea and permitting it to position and support forces anywhere along the coast of Europe. Unable to get at each other through conventional means, the powers resorted to new and all-inclusive forms of economic warfare, blithely ignoring the screams of neutrals.[42]

As in the 1790s, the United States became entangled in the struggle, but this time it did not escape direct involvement. Unlike Hamilton and Washington in 1794, Jefferson refused to sacrifice American commerce or acquiesce in the British maritime system. His visceral dislike for England made such steps unpalatable if not impossible. He persisted in trying to exploit European rivalries, and for a time hesitated to jeopardize his quest for the Floridas by antagonizing Napoleon. True to republican ideology, he continued to believe that economic weapons would compel the Europeans to accept his terms. Unfortunately for Jefferson, the conflict had reached a level of intensity where the major belligerents were no longer subject to manipulation and threats. Neither would appease

---

41. Peterson, *Jefferson*, 904; John M. Belohlavek, "Economic Interest Groups and the Formation of Foreign Policy in the Early Republic," *Journal of the Early Republic* 14 (Winter 1994), 480–81.

42. Robert Doughty, Ira Gruber, et al., *Warfare in the Modern World*, vol. 1, *Military Operations from 1600 to 1871* (Lexington, Mass., 1996), 212–34.

America. As the European war had brought Jefferson the twin windfalls of prosperity and Louisiana in his first term, so also it was the source of his unremitting misfortune in the second. Caught between what he angrily called the "tyrant of the ocean" and the "scourge of the land," he and his successor, Madison, reeled from crisis to crisis between 1805 and 1812.[43] Relations with France remained tense, but Britain's control of the seas impinged more directly on U.S. interests, provoking a sustained and particularly bitter dispute that eventually brought war.

The resumption of war in Europe brought to the forefront the volatile issue of the carrying trade. When France and Spain opened their colonies to American shipping in the 1790s, Britain had invoked the Rule of 1756, declaring that trade illegal in time of peace was also illegal in war. As part of the larger rapprochement following the Jay Treaty, the two nations had reached an unwritten compromise. American shippers had skirted British regulations by what was called the "broken voyage," picking up wares in French or Spanish colonies, returning to U.S. ports and observing normal customs procedures, then reexporting the cargoes to Europe. Eager to preserve U.S. friendship and certain that the awkwardness and expense of the procedure would limit the size of the trade, London had accepted the broken voyage. In the case of the ship *Polly* (1800), an admiralty court had even sanctioned its legality.[44]

When war resumed, Americans jumped back into the carrying trade with a vengeance, and as profits soared they became less and less scrupulous about observing the niceties of the broken voyage. Acts of Congress permitted merchants to recover much of the import duties on reexported items. Some shippers paid no duties at all. In many cases, they did not even bother to unload the cargoes. In a life-and-death situation, the carrying trade threatened to deprive Britain of the presumed advantages of control of the seas. In the 1805 *Essex* case, admiralty courts held that the final destination of the cargo determined the nature of the voyage, thus rendering the broken voyage illegal. Even before this, Britain had begun to seize American ships and confiscate cargoes. British measures jeopardized a trade that by 1805 exceeded $60 million, comprised nearly two-thirds of U.S. exports, and had become the basis of American prosperity. Some Americans conceded that this commerce was unnatural and temporary and therefore not worth the risk of war. But Jefferson viewed it as a

43. Peterson, *Jefferson*, 916.
44. These issues are discussed in depth in Bradford Perkins, *Prologue to War: England and the United States* (Berkeley, Calif., 1961), 75–95, and Paul A. Varg, *Foreign Policies of the Founding Fathers* (Baltimore, Md., 1970), 172–79.

way to make up an unfavorable balance of trade with Britain. He insisted that its loss would leave the United States vulnerable to British pressure and might force undesirable changes in the domestic economy. Many Americans denounced what seemed an obvious attempt to impoverish their country.

An even more difficult issue, the British practice of impressing sailors, allegedly deserters, from U.S. ships stemmed at least indirectly from proliferation of the carrying trade. Where impressment was concerned, the two nations took conflicting legal positions on the most basic of issues. Britain adhered to the doctrine of "indefeasible allegiance," the principle that a person born under its flag could not legally change citizenship. The United States permitted and even encouraged such changes by making naturalization easy and conferring full citizenship on those naturalized. Under the laws of each nation, therefore, an individual could be a citizen of both at the same time. The United States did not dispute Britain's right to search its merchant vessels for deserters in British ports. Britain did not claim the right to search men-of-war anywhere or U.S. merchant vessels in neutral ports. But the United States advanced the position—not then accepted by any other nation—that Britain could not search its merchant vessels on the high seas, a claim the British flatly rejected.

The issue touched vital interests and deep-seated emotions on both sides. Britain's survival depended on the Royal Navy, which, in turn, required an ample supply of seamen. Manpower was chronically short, a problem made worse by wholesale desertion to U.S. ships. As the carrying trade grew after 1803, the American merchant marine expanded enormously in size. Thousands of British sailors eagerly fled to ships where working conditions were far better and pay as much as five times higher. Some U.S. ship captains openly enticed sailors from the Royal Navy. The ease with which legal or forged citizenship papers could be acquired facilitated the practice. Albert Gallatin admitted that half of the sailors employed in the U.S. merchant marine were English—even according to American definitions of citizenship. To the great annoyance of London, U.S. courts frequently refused to turn over deserters. Britain found this intolerable at a time of crisis and adamantly upheld its right to recover deserters.

Each side handled the issue in ways that exacerbated their differences. Had Britain exercised some discretion in implementing impressment, conflict might have been mitigated, but responsibility rested with officers of the Royal Navy, for whom restraint was not a desirable or even acceptable personality trait. Operating far from home and desperate for seamen, they cared little about American sensitivities. British ships hovered off the

U.S. coastline, imposing a virtual blockade of many ports, a practice that galled an independent and insecure people. Ship captains often did not bother to investigate whether men taken were in fact deserters or even British citizens. Between three thousand and six thousand innocent Americans were pressed into British service from 1803 to 1812. On occasion, overzealous captains exceeded bounds recognized by both nations, stopping and searching U.S. naval vessels or merchant vessels in American waters. Americans thus viewed impressment as an affront to the dignity of a free nation and a gross assault on human rights. They also perceived that to surrender on the issue could wreck the merchant marine upon which their prosperity depended. The rigid position assumed by the United States left Britain no means to recover the thousands of sailors who deserted.

Attitudes and emotions on both sides of the Atlantic made already difficult conflicts of interest impossible to resolve. Engaged in a desperate struggle against Napoleonic tyranny, the British saw themselves defending the liberties of the "free world." They deeply resented U.S. interference with what they regarded as essential measures of war. They dismissed America's insistence on neutral rights as Francophilia in disguise or the product of a grasping desire to profit at the expense of a nation fighting for its life. Outraged Britons expressed open contempt for the Americans, "less popular and esteemed among us than the base and bigotted Portugeze, or the ferocious and ignorant Russians," a leading journal of opinion exclaimed. They minimized the threat of retaliation from "a nation three thousand miles off—scarcely held together by the weakest government in the world."[45]

Americans from Jefferson down failed to comprehend the extent to which the European war dominated British policy, attributing the harsh maritime measures to sheer vengeance or greed. The residue of Anglophobia left from the Revolution deepened as the crisis intensified. Outraged by British insults to their honor, Americans insisted on demands London could not possibly meet, placing the two nations on a collision course.

An incident off the coast of Virginia in June 1807 brought the two nations to the brink of war. The frigate USS *Chesapeake* had taken on board a number of British deserters, some of whom had flaunted their new status before their former officers on the streets of Norfolk. Infuriated, the British naval commander in America, Adm. Sir George Berkeley, ordered tough measures. When the *Chesapeake* passed into international waters

45. Perkins, *Prologue*, 7; Onuf and Onuf, *Federal Union*, 213–15.

en route to its station in the Mediterranean, HMS *Leopard* opened fire. The outmanned, unprepared, and totally unsuspecting American ship struck colors virtually without a fight. The British took four men, one a deserter, the others impressed Americans who had fled British service.[46] American anger exceeded that provoked by the XYZ Affair. Mass meetings in seaboard cities denounced the outrage and demanded satisfaction. Mobs attacked British sailors. In Philadelphia, angry citizens nearly destroyed a British ship. "This country has never been in such a state of excitement since the battle of Lexington," Jefferson declared.[47]

Unlike Adams a decade earlier, the president did not fan the martial spirit. He closed American ports to Royal Navy ships and demanded not merely reparation but British abandonment of impressment. But he would go no further. Recognizing that the nation was unprepared to fight, fearing for the large number of U.S. ships at sea, and still hoping for a diplomatic solution, he contented himself with quiet preparations for a war that seemed likely if not inevitable. Jefferson's hesitant and even contradictory response prolonged the crisis without providing any means to resolve it. In the absence of presidential direction, the war fever quickly dissipated, making it difficult to ready the nation's defenses. The tough line with Britain precluded a diplomatic solution. Jefferson's quiet public response and the apparent acquiescence of the nation reinforced British certainty of American weakness.

Alone in Europe at this point, and faring poorly in the war, London was in no mood to compromise. The navy demonstrated its disdain for neutrality by bombarding Copenhagen and seizing the entire Danish fleet. The government recalled Berkeley but refused even to consider the larger issue of impressment. Foreign Minister George Canning provocatively blamed the *Chesapeake-Leopard* incident on the United States. A new order in council of November 1807 required ships bound for Europe to pass first through Britain and secure a license. The French responded by announcing that ships abiding by British regulations would be seized. Any ships now attempting to trade across the Atlantic were liable to seizure by one power or the other.[48]

Unwilling to compromise and unable to fight, Jefferson fell back on an embargo of American commerce. Publicly, he justified the step in terms

---

46. Spencer C. Tucker and Frank T. Reuter, "The *Chesapeake-Leopard* Affair," *Naval History* (March/April 1996), 40–44.
47. Peterson, *Jefferson*, 876.
48. Burton I. Spivak, *Jefferson's English Crisis: Commerce, Embargo, and the Republican Revolution* (Charlottesville, Va., 1979), 99–102.

of immediate, practical needs. It would keep ships and sailors "out of harm's way" and insulate the United States from belligerents who had reverted to the "vandalism of the fifth century." His private motives were more complex. Unless he could disabuse Europeans of the notion that the United States was wedded to "Quaker principles," he reasoned, it would be subject to the "plunder of all nations."[49] He and Madison had long agreed that European dependence on American necessities gave the United States the means to force them to respect its "rights." For Americans to do without the "superfluities and poisons" provided by Europe, on the other hand, would encourage domestic manufactures, thus promoting the independent and virtuous republic of which he and Madison dreamed. Jefferson hoped that his experiment in "peaceable coercion" might even offer an alternative to war to peace-loving peoples across the world and force the European powers to alter their methods of warfare. He seems to have perceived the pitfalls of a long-term embargo, but he depended on Europe's vulnerability and his own people's tolerance for sacrifice to ensure the success of his policy.[50]

Jefferson miscalculated on both counts. The embargo had no effect in France and indeed played into Napoleon's hands by depriving Britain of trade with the United States and increasing Anglo-American antagonism. Openly mocking America, Napoleon appointed himself an enforcer, ordering seizure of U.S. ships entering European ports. During its first year, the embargo caused a slight rise in prices and some unemployment in England, but little more. The timing was unfortunate. The unusually large trade of 1806 left British warehouses bulging with American goods. Revolution in Spain's Latin American colonies opened new markets to offset the loss of American buyers. The short-term pain was not sufficient to compel a shaky British ministry, engaged in a war for survival, to capitulate to the United States. By the time England had begun to feel the pinch, support for "peaceable coercion" had dissipated in the United States.

Jefferson's greatest miscalculation was of his own people's willingness to endure economic hardship for the sake of principle. Accustomed to fat profits and intolerant of government interference, fiercely individualistic Americans evaded the law at will and resisted the stern measures used to enforce it. At the outset, loopholes made evasion easy. The coastal trade was essential for the seaboard cities. Ships licensed to trade among American ports transferred cargoes to British vessels waiting at sea or, claiming to be blown off course, slipped away to the West Indies or

49. Ibid., 103.
50. McCoy, *Elusive Republic*, 218–19.

Canada's maritime provinces. Posting bond made no difference since profits obtained from illicit trade far exceeded the amount required. When the administration tightened the loopholes, merchants resorted to outright smuggling, a practice Americans had long since perfected. Hundreds of ships escaped the detection of overworked port officials. Large quantities of American foodstuffs, potash, and lumber went into Canada overland, by boat, or even by sled in winter. On occasion, wares were placed on hillsides and rolled north across the border! The British encouraged evasion by offering top prices and protecting smugglers from law enforcers. From the Great Lakes to the Atlantic, distinct borderland societies had emerged where people on each side were linked through business, friendship, and family ties. These communities were closer to each other than to their governments. Defiance verged on insurrection. Smuggled goods seized as evidence mysteriously disappeared. Federal agents were bribed or intimidated, or themselves joined in the plunder. Juries refused to convict smugglers.[51]

Jefferson sought to "legalize all *means* which may be necessary to attain its *end*," using the military to enforce the law, declaring the borderlands in a state of rebellion, and ordering out the militia.[52] The passage in January 1809 of additional enforcement measures sharply circumscribing individual liberties did not stop smuggling and provoked near-rebellion in New England. Angry crowds revived songs of protest from the revolution. Speakers compared Jefferson—unfavorably—to George III. The Massachusetts and Connecticut legislatures declared the embargo not legally binding. There was open talk of secession. Outside New England, the opposition was scattered and muted, but the obvious failure of the embargo abroad and the hardships it imposed at home brought growing demands for repeal.[53]

Jefferson's failures of leadership contributed to the inglorious end of his experiment. He never adequately explained the purposes of the embargo, leaving the field to critics who accused him of oppressing and impoverishing his own people for the benefit of Napoleon. He could not fathom the nature or the depth of the opposition, dismissing his critics as die-hard Federalists, Anglophiles, or plain "rascals." Throughout 1808, friends begged him to reassess his policy. Stung by the bitter personal attacks, at times seemingly paralyzed by indecision, he clung stubbornly to the

---

51. Reginald C. Stuart, *United States Expansion and British North America, 1775–1871* (Chapel Hill, N.C., 1988), 42–52.
52. Tucker and Hendrickson, *Empire of Liberty*, 224.
53. Peterson, *Jefferson*, 913–14.

embargo and resorted to even more rigorous enforcement. After Madison was elected to succeed him, he virtually abdicated to a confused, divided, and sometimes panicky Congress. Jefferson and Madison had hoped to sustain the embargo until summer and then, if it had still not succeeded, couple repeal with steps toward war. Frightened by the specter of rebellion in New England, Congress moved repeal to March and rejected any moves toward war. To save face, the legislators approved a lame substitute, the Non-Intercourse Act, which resumed trade with all nations but Britain and France and offered to restore it with either of the belligerents who lifted its obnoxious decrees. Fittingly, the embargo expired the day Jefferson left office, having produced tragically ironic results. Designed as a substitute for the war that would undermine republican ideals, it produced a form of warfare at home. A president profoundly committed to individual freedom became trapped into imposing repressive measures that starkly violated his most basic convictions about civil liberties.[54]

V

Between 1809 and 1812, two nations with every reason to avoid conflict drifted inexorably into a war that could have been disastrous for either, providing a textbook example of how not to conduct diplomacy.

The United States clung stubbornly to the futile course set by Jefferson. Madison inherited a policy in shambles, a divided party, and an increasingly unruly Congress—Senate "malcontents" even blocked his appointment of the able Gallatin as secretary of state.[55] A small and retiring individual, lacking Jefferson's commanding presence and enormous prestige, Madison tended to defer in situations that demanded firm leadership. Faithful to principle to the point of folly, he refused concessions on neutral "rights." Equally fearful of the threat war posed to republican institutions, he hesitated to accept it even as a last resort. He retained faith in "peaceable coercion" long after its limits had become palpable. Thus Non-Intercourse was followed in May 1810 by Macon's Bill No. 2, which opened trade with Britain and France but indicated that if either dropped its restrictions the United States would impose an embargo on the other. Eager for peace to the point of gullibility, Madison leaped at French and British proposals when he ought to have been cautious. He accepted at face value the wily Napoleon's announcement, hedged with conditions, that he had repealed the Berlin and Milan decrees and reimposed nonintercourse on England. This ill-considered move soured relations with

54. McDonald, *Jefferson*, 139.
55. Rutland, *Madison*, 16–17.

Britain while Napoleon used escape clauses to harass American shipping. Even when Madison finally concluded that war was inevitable, he moved in such a slow and circuitous fashion that friends and foes on both sides of the Atlantic were uncertain where he was heading.[56]

British diplomacy was also flawed. The European war reached its climactic stages during these years. Absorbed with the Peninsular War in Spain and Portugal and Napoleon's invasion of Russia, British officials gave little attention to America. Certain that the United States would not go to war, they also refused concessions. Although clearly in the wrong on the *Chesapeake* affair, they showed "contemptuous indifference" by taking four years to apologize.[57] Ironically, just when Madison and Congress were moving toward war, British manufacturing interests were lobbying to revoke the restrictive orders in council. But the London government accepted compromise as hesitantly as Madison accepted war. The direction of its policy was no more clear.[58]

In crises, diplomats can make a difference, but here the diplomats made things worse. Viewing the United States as a secondary theater, Britain made a series of unfortunate appointments to the Washington post. The youthful, inexperienced, and overeager David Erskine submitted to the Americans an agreement his government rejected, infuriating both capitals. Erskine was replaced by the arrogant, obnoxious, and blustering Francis James Jackson, already notorious—and given the sobriquet "Copenhagen"—for his prominent role in the destruction inflicted on neutral Denmark. Jackson confidently informed London that the United States would not fight: "Dogs that bark don't bite."[59] He made no effort to disguise his contempt for America and Americans, describing Madison as a "plain and rather mean-looking man" and his wife, the gracious and charming Dolley, as "fat and forty, but not fair." His demeanor provoked so much hostility in such a short time that Madison demanded his recall. London complied but delayed replacing him for months, leaving a vacuum at a critical time. Even after his recall, Jackson hung around longer, provoking more ire from outraged Americans. "Base and Insolent in the Extreme," furious citizens called him, "a miscreant so vile." Even the mild-mannered Madison described him as "mean" and "insolent." His replacement, the playboy Augustus John Foster, was less openly obnoxious if no less arrogant. But he listened to Federalist friends rather than

56. Ibid., 64; J.C.A. Stagg, *Mr. Madison's War* (Princeton, N.J., 1983), 116.
57. George F. G. Stanley, *The War of 1812: Land Operations* (Ottawa, 1983), 21.
58. Rutland, *Madison*, 96.
59. Ibid., 44–45.

trying to sense the changing mood in Washington, underscoring London's belief that America would not fight and reinforcing its complacency.[60]

During the last critical months, the United States had no ministers in key European capitals. John Armstrong left Paris and William Pinkney left London in 1811, Armstrong apparently to avoid being tainted with Madison's weak policies and to promote his own presidential ambitions, Pinkney out of sheer frustration with the impossibility of his assignment. "The Prime of my Life is passing away in barren Toil and Anxiety," the financially strapped diplomat lamented.[61] The U.S. chargé in London, the hapless Jonathan Russell, did not sense and thus could not inform Washington of subtle shifts in British policy.

The threat of Indian warfare on the frontier, which Americans also conveniently blamed on Britain, added to an already long list of grievances. In fact, the problem was self-inflicted. Disease, alcohol, commerce, and the relentless pressure of U.S. expansion placed the traditional culture of northwestern Indians under full assault. Some acquiesced, accepting American annuities and supplies and missionary efforts to turn them into farmers. Some found escape in whiskey. Others resisted. They found a leader in a Shawnee and former drunkard who, after claiming in 1805 to have a vision, took the name Tenskwatawa and initiated a revivalist movement to save Native American culture. Fusing traditional ways with Western ideas, including some borrowed from Christianity, the man also called "the Prophet" urged Indians to put aside the evil habits of the "Long Knives" and return to their ancient traditions. As Jefferson and Madison negotiated more treaties taking more Indian lands, Tenskwatawa's message fell on increasingly receptive ears, especially among the young. He attracted as many as three thousand followers and in 1808 established a village called Prophetstown in Indiana. Building on Tenskwatawa's revivalist movement, his half-brother, the redoubtable Tecumseh, set out to unite southern and northwestern tribes to resist further land cessions. Following in the footsteps of Mohawk visionary Joseph Brant, he traveled from the Great Lakes to the Mississippi territory in the daunting and ultimately futile task of bringing together disparate tribes into a pan-Indian confederation. "They have driven us from the sea to the lakes," Tecumseh warned in 1809. "We can go no farther."[62]

60. For sample attacks on Jackson, see J.C.A. Stagg, ed., *The Papers of James Madison*, Presidential Series, vol. 2 (Charlottesville, Va., 1992), 27, 123, 263.
61. Pinkney to Madison, August 13, 1810, in Stagg, *Madison Papers* 2:478–82.
62. R. David Edmunds, *The Shawnee Prophet* (Lincoln, Neb., 1983), 34–79; the Tecumseh quote is from R. David Edmunds, *Tecumseh and the Quest for Indian Leadership* (New York, 1984), 131. See also John Sugden, *Tecumseh: A Life* (New York, 1998).

Americans viewed these developments with growing alarm. Neither understanding nor respecting Indian culture, they failed to perceive that Tenskwatawa's movement was the natural response of a people overwhelmed by change. They were inclined then—as historians have been since—to dismiss him as a charlatan and fanatic.[63] The British in fact responded with notable caution to Indian unrest, but Americans could not concede the legitimacy of Indian grievances without admitting their own guilt. They blamed the agitation on the British. From the relative security of Washington, Jefferson and Madison counted on American benevolence to solve the problem. As was often the case, however, the commander on the scene took a quite different approach. Certain that Indians understood only force, Governor William Henry Harrison sought to drive the Prophet from the Indiana territory. If he did not conspire to provoke an Indian attack, the result was the same. When Harrison established position outside Prophetstown, claiming to wish to parley, the Prophet ordered an attack. In the battle of Tippecanoe, November 7, 1811, each side suffered heavy losses. The Americans claimed victory, and indeed Harrison did destroy Prophetstown and discredit the Prophet as a leader. Formerly settled in one place, the Indians now scattered. Violence erupted across the frontier.[64] Americans increasingly feared a general Indian war, for which they blamed the British.

By the summer of 1812, anger and frustration reached the breaking point. Neither diplomacy nor economic retaliation had wrenched concessions from England. Americans from Madison down increasingly accepted the necessity for war. Madison appears to have reached such a conclusion as soon as late 1811, but his halting and ineffectual efforts to mobilize Congress failed.[65] A sizeable bloc of congressmen, the so-called War Hawks, were already committed to fight, but the rest were badly divided. The Federalist minority blamed the impasse on the Republicans. One group of Republicans opposed both war and acquiescence; another wavered uncertainly. Persuaded by May that no settlement was likely, and with the approaching election putting a premium on action of some kind, Madison submitted a war message to Congress. It was approved on June 17 without enthusiasm and by the closest vote of any declaration of war in U.S. history (79–49 in the House; 19–13 in the Senate).

Ironically, at the very time Americans were drifting toward war, Britain was lurching toward concessions. Years of trade restrictions had

63. Edmunds, *Prophet*, 187–92.
64. Edmunds, *Tecumseh*, 159–60; Stagg, *Madison's War*, 189–92.
65. Rutland, *Madison*, 86; Stagg, *Madison's War*, 189–90.

finally worked significant hardships, especially among the rising manufacturing class, producing growing pressures for changes in policy. In
1812, the Admiralty ordered the navy to avoid clashes with U.S. ships and
stay clear of the coast. In late June, the ministry revoked the orders in
council for one year. But each step was taken on an ad hoc basis without
publicity or explanation of the larger forces that drove it. At a time when
it could take as long as twelve weeks to exchange dispatches across the
Atlantic, word of changes in policy on one side did not arrive in time to
influence the other. The British found out about the American decision
for war long after they had revoked the orders. The Americans did not
learn about revocation of the orders until August, two months after declaring war.[66]

It has often been speculated that faster communication in 1812 might
have averted an unnecessary war, but this may assume too much. The
new British ministry, while more conciliatory, was not prepared to go as
far as Madison wished. On several occasions after war began, the belligerents or outside powers such as Russia attempted to promote an armistice.
Each effort failed because of persisting deadlock on impressment. Revocation
of the orders in council was only temporary, not enough to satisfy the
United States. In any event, had he known of them, Madison might have
interpreted British concessions as a sign of weakness and pushed ahead
with war.[67]

At least on the American side, the question of war or peace by 1812 tran-
scended disagreements on specific issues. For many Americans, war provided an opportunity to fulfill long-standing expansionist designs on
Florida and Canada. Southern War Hawks such as Kentucky's Henry
Clay and Tennessee's Felix Grundy had their eyes firmly fixed on East
Florida. Vast in size, weakly defended, its population small and presumed
of dubious loyalty to the Crown, Canada also seemed irresistibly ripe for
the plucking. "I verily believe," Clay boasted to Madison, "that the militia
of Kentucky are alone competent to place Upper Canada at your feet."[68]
More important, Canada was the one place where mighty Britain seemed
vulnerable. Its conquest would plug a major leak in the embargo and
eliminate an alternative means of supply for the British West Indies, thus
making U.S. trade restrictions more effective and giving the United States
a way to wring concessions from Britain. Eliminating their primary means
of support would help quell the Indian menace and open the Northwest

66. Donald R. Hickey, *The War of 1812: A Forgotten Conflict* (Urbana, Ill., 1989), 42.
67. Stagg, *Madison's War*, 118–19.
68. Quoted in Rutland, *Madison*, 95.

to American expansion. In a broader sense, the elimination of British power from North America would enhance U.S. security.[69] Whether or not American expansion was essentially defensive, the conquest of Canada served urgent national needs. Manifest Destiny would be the "rallying cry of the next generation," Robert Rutland has written, "but as a political force it was first unleashed by the War Hawks of 1812."[70]

The vote of 1812 was along strict party lines, and for Republicans, by this time, war also seemed the only means to defend honor, principle, and party. Republicans in all sections felt a deep sense of humiliation at having endured for so long affronts to American sovereignty. The United States was being treated as though the war of independence had never occurred. Some form of redemption was essential to restore its self-respect. "By war, we should be purified, as by fire," Massachusetts Republican Elbridge Gerry told Madison.[71] For many Republicans, it was not only a matter of honor but also one of defending their principles and indeed their embattled party. Republican political economy depended on the right to export. By 1812, in the face of crippling threats from abroad, war seemed the only way to preserve the ideals of republican political economy.[72] Viewing the American Revolution as a unique experiment in constructing a society based on principles of individual liberty and their party as the guarantor of those principles, Republicans saw that experiment as imperiled by the great powers abroad and Federalists at home. If the government could not withstand that dual challenge, it would surely collapse, demonstrating the invalidity of republican principles. Republicans accepted war as the only way to preserve the party and the heritage of the Revolution. Younger Americans who had not participated in the Revolution felt this with particular keenness. They must show "the World," War Hawk John C. Calhoun of South Carolina proclaimed, "that we have not only inherited the liberty which our Fathers gave us, but also the will and power to maintain it."[73]

69. Reginald Horsman, "On to Canada: Manifest Destiny and United States Strategy in the War of 1812," *Michigan Historical Review* 13 (Fall 1987), 1–24, and "The War of 1812 Revisited," *Diplomatic History* 15 (Winter 1991), 122–23.
70. Rutland, *Madison*, 96.
71. Quoted in Hickey, *War of 1812*, 28; Roger Brown, *The Republic in Peril: 1812* (New York, 1971) develops the theme of embattled Republicanism.
72. McCoy, *Elusive Republic*, 235; Brown, *Republic in Peril*, 182–86.
73. Quoted in Merrill D. Peterson, *The Great Triumvirate* (New York, 1987), 4. The generational concept is developed in Steven Watts, *The Republic Reborn: Politics, Diplomacy, and Warfare in the Early Republic, 1783–1830* (Baltimore, Md., 1987).

VI

Madison accepted war in 1812 in the confidence that it would be relatively short, inexpensive, and bloodless—more talk than fight—and that the United States could achieve its objectives without great difficulty. In fact, the War of 1812 lasted two and a half years and cost more than two thousand American lives and $1.6 billion.[74] For Britain, the war was a military and diplomatic sideshow to the main performance in Europe; for the United States, it became a struggle for survival.

The Americans hoped to conquer Canada quickly and use it to extract concessions from Britain on neutral rights and Indian issues. Fearing that delay would permit Britain to reinforce its colony, Madison rejected London's proposals for a truce and urged vigorous prosecution of the war. "The sword once drawn, full justice must be done," Jefferson thundered from Monticello. "'Indemnification for the past and security for the Future,' should be painted on our banners."[75]

As in previous crises, the aims of Republican strategy exceeded the means available to attain them. Canada *was* poorly defended and Britain *was* preoccupied with Europe, but the United States could not exploit these advantages. As a result of Republican frugality, the army had languished. Preparedness measures belatedly enacted by Congress after the declaration did little to rectify the deficiencies. The Madison administration attempted the unique experiment of sending an army to war without any staff organization. At the outset, the army consisted of but seven thousand men (more officers than soldiers), poorly trained and equipped and led by superannuated and incompetent commanders. The desertion rate was so high (often justified by lack of food and pay) that Madison pardoned deserters to fill rolls. Liberal dispensation of liquor and handsome bounties failed to secure enough enlistments. The vaunted militia turned out to be disorganized and even cowardly. Some units simply refused to cross the border into Canada.[76]

Inadequately manned and poorly conceived, the much talked-about "holiday campaign" into Canada met disaster. British regulars supported by Tecumseh's Indians repulsed an invasion of Detroit in July 1812, removing any threat to Canada and leaving the American Northwest vulnerable. A later assault by the Niagara River met a similar fate. Its dreams of

---

74. Rutland, *Madison*, 105. American battle deaths are numbered at 2,260. British and Canadian casualties have been estimated at 8,744, American at 7,738. Hickey, *War of 1812*, 302–3; Stanley, *War of 1812*, 433–34.

75. Dumas Malone, *The Sage of Monticello* (Boston, 1981), 105.

76. Stagg, *Madison's War*, 160–76.

easy success quickly dashed, the United States found itself on the defensive.

During the first year and a half of the war, neither belligerent could gain the upper hand. Dismissed by some Royal Navy officers as a few ships "manned by a handful of bastards and out laws," the U.S. Navy acquitted itself honorably in individual encounters with British men-of-war. American privateers inflicted costly losses on enemy merchant shipping.[77] But the Royal Navy enforced a tight blockade of the U.S. coast, exacerbating economic problems. Raiding parties wreaked havoc among the seaboard population. On the Canadian frontier, U.S. Navy forces under Oliver Hazard Perry won a major victory on Lake Erie in September 1813. In October, Harrison inflicted a crushing defeat on the British and Indians at the battle of the Thames on the north shore of Lake Erie. The two victories, combined with Tecumseh's death in battle, eased the threat to the Old Northwest and even permitted a modest American incursion into Canada. In the meantime, a two-pronged U.S. invasion of Montreal was repulsed.

The fighting was not at all like the quaint eighteenth-century war Madison had foreseen. Action at the Thames was as savage as that in the especially brutal Peninsular War in Spain and Portugal. According to a British sailor who had seen both, the fire at Lake Erie made Trafalgar seem a "mere fleabite by comparison."[78] The Kentucky militia dressed in war paint and carried—and used—scalping knives. A British soldier described them as "wretches...capable of the greatest villainies." When Americans complained that British use of Indians led to atrocities, the British retorted that, after all, the Americans used Kentuckians.[79]

In 1814, America's position worsened measurably. Instead of relieving the nation's problems, the stalemated war compounded them. At least until Vietnam, the War of 1812 was easily the most unpopular conflict in U.S. history, and Madison encountered enormous difficulties mobilizing his people. The British blockade denied the United States access to war materials from abroad. Creating domestic industries virtually from scratch posed nearly insuperable problems. Unable to find buyers for its bonds and reluctant for political reasons to raise taxes, the government faced near bankruptcy by 1814. The smuggling initiated during the embargo persisted in wartime in the form of trading with the enemy. "Self, the great ruling principle [is] more powerful with Yankees than any people I ever

77. Hickey, War of 1812, 135.
78. Quoted in ibid., 216.
79. Stanley, War of 1812, 208.

saw," sneered one British officer.[80] Many parts of the nation were decidedly apathetic toward the war. Open disaffection in Federalist New England was far more serious. Governors refused to order the militia beyond state borders. Congressmen attempted to block administration war measures. Extremists talked openly of seceding and creating an independent nation tied closely to England.

Developments abroad were even more ominous. Napoleon abdicated in April, and the imminent end of war in Europe permitted Britain to shift resources to North America. To exact revenge upon the United States, protect Canada, and improve its strategic position and bargaining power, Britain devised a three-pronged offensive: a diversionary strike in the Chesapeake Bay area, an invasion by Lake Champlain to isolate the disaffected northeastern states, and an attack on New Orleans to gain control of the Mississippi Valley. "Chastise the savages," thundered the London *Times*.[81]

To add to Madison's difficulties, formal Anglo-American peace negotiations were scheduled to begin just as the British launched their offensive. By the time the peace commissioners actually assembled in August 1814 in the British-controlled Flemish town of Ghent, Britain had gained the edge militarily. Its harsh demands reflected its change in fortunes. To repay their allies and protect Canada from the United States, the British demanded creation of an Indian buffer state comprising 250,000 square miles (about 15 percent of U.S. territory) between the Ohio River and the Great Lakes. They also insisted upon unrestricted access to the Mississippi, a northeastern boundary giving Canada a sizeable chunk of Maine, banishment of U.S. vessels from the Great Lakes, and exclusion of Americans from fishing grounds off Nova Scotia. London aimed to reverse major results of the 1783 Treaty of Paris.

In this supreme crisis, diplomacy salvaged for the United States what could not be won on the battlefield. Madison had already abandoned demands that Britain accept his position on neutral rights and impressment. The end of the European war seemed to make such issues irrelevant. Britain would relent only to the extent of a settlement on the basis of the *uti possidetis*, meaning that territory held at the time the war ended would go to the occupant. The U.S. delegation, headed by Clay, Gallatin, and John Quincy Adams, was perhaps the ablest ever put together by the nation. A master of card games—at Ghent he was often stumbling to bed about the time Adams was rising to pray—Clay sensed that the British

80. Quoted in Hickey, *War of 1812*, 216.
81. Ibid., 182.

were bluffing and persuaded his colleagues to stall. The delegation thus ignored Washington's instructions to break off the negotiations.[82]

Clay's high-stakes gamble paid off handsomely. In the last months of 1814, the U.S. position changed dramatically. In one of the most significant battles of the war, U.S. Navy forces under Capt. Thomas Macdonough destroyed an enemy fleet on Lake Champlain (September 11, 1814), giving the United States control of the lake and thwarting Britain's northeastern campaign. The British expedition into the Chesapeake Bay enjoyed initial success. Militia defending the makeshift capital at Bladensburg ran so fast they could not be captured. British forces entered and burned Washington, one of the most humiliating events in the nation's history.[83] The looting was left to American hooligans. But while poet Francis Scott Key watched and pondered and wrote what would later become the national anthem, a British attack on the vital commercial city of Baltimore was repulsed. The invaders retreated to their ships.

Luck once more smiled on the United States. The imminent breakdown of peace negotiations at Vienna and political turmoil in France threatened resumption of the European War. Faced with abandoning its inflated war aims in America or fighting an extended and costly war in which, according to the prime minister, Britain was "not likely to attain any glory or renown at all commensurate to the inconvenience it will occasion," London chose the better part of valor.[84] The negotiators signed a treaty on Christmas Eve. The next day they celebrated with beef, plum pudding, and toasts to the unlikely duo of George III and James Madison.

Dismissed as the "Treaty of Omissions" by a cynical French diplomat, the peace of Ghent accurately reflected the stalemate on the battlefield. It said nothing about impressment and other issues over which the United States had gone to war. Britain scrapped its vindictive and expansive war aims for the *status quo ante bellum*. The treaty fixed the northern boundary of the United States from the Lake of the Woods to the Rocky Mountains at the 49th parallel and referred the disputed northeastern boundary to arbitration. The U.S. delegation was itself bitterly divided on British demands regarding the Mississippi River and fisheries. The New Englander Adams was willing to trade British access to the Mississippi for the fisheries; Clay vehemently opposed sacrificing western interests. Not for the first time mediating among his contentious colleagues, the

82. Rutland, *Madison*, 170.
83. Ibid., 159–65.
84. Ibid., 177.

Swiss-born Gallatin proposed deferring these issues for future discussion, a wise decision as it turned out. The British went along.

Despite its inconclusive outcome, the War of 1812 had a huge impact on the future of North America. The United States had gone to war in 1812—as in 1775—confident of the dubious loyalty of British North Americans and even hopeful they might rally to appeals to throw off British "tyranny and oppression." Ironically, U.S. efforts to relieve Britain of its provinces and the bitter fighting along the border helped stimulate in Canada's disparate population a sense of cohesion and even nascent nationalism. The former Loyalists of Upper Canada, in particular, took enormous pride in repulsing the Yankee invaders, fueling an anti-Americanism that persisted into the future. The war gave Canadians a sense of their own distinct history and helped create a "national idea."[85]

The War of 1812 also sealed the tragic fate of Native Americans—the ultimate losers of a stalemated conflict. The Battle of the Thames opened the Northwest for U.S. expansion. The death of Tecumseh dashed fragile dreams of an Indian confederacy. In the South, conflict between those Creeks who sought accommodation with the United States and those who chose resistance exploded in July 1813 into war. The Americans invaded the Creek nation from three directions, destroying villages and inflicting heavy losses. At Horseshoe Bend in March 1814, Andrew Jackson's militia crushed the Creeks and their Cherokee allies, killing close to a thousand braves, causing even that hardened Indian fighter to admit that "the carnage was dreadfull." In all, some three thousand Creeks were killed, 15 percent of the population. "My people are no more!" the half-breed Creek leader William Weatherford lamented.[86] In the subsequent Treaty of Fort Jackson, imposed on accommodationist Creeks over bitter objections, the Indians surrendered without any compensation twentyfive million acres, roughly half their land, and forswore any future contact with the British and Spanish. The Treaty of Ghent was to restore the *status quo ante bellum* in Indian affairs and might have been interpreted as nullifying the earlier Treaty of Fort Jackson, but in fact both were ratified the same day. As a result of the War of 1812, foreign nations would never intercede with the Indians again, depriving them of what little leverage they had. The Indians would never again threaten U.S. expansion. From this point, the United States imposed its will on them. Councils were no longer matters of sovereign nations negotiating on the basis of rough equality. By the force of events, if not of law and equity, Indian affairs

85. Stanley, *War of 1812*, 411–12.
86. Quoted in Hickey, *War of 1812*, 151.

became a matter of domestic policy rather than foreign relations for the United States. The War of 1812 opened the way for removal of the Indians and their destruction as a people.[87]

Although the United States had achieved none of its aims and barely averted disaster, the war marked a major step in its development. With peace in Europe, the issues that had led to war lost their significance. It would be another fifty years—and with the roles reversed—before questions of neutral rights would resurface. The United States had survived a major challenge without external assistance, demonstrating to a skeptical Europe that hopes of its imminent collapse were unfounded. Henceforth, Europeans would treat the new nation with greater respect.

Probably most important was the impact on the national psyche. From 1783 to 1814, Europeans had subjected the United States to repeated indignities and challenged its existence as an independent nation. At home, Federalists questioned the validity of the government's principles and defied its authority. Many Republicans themselves began to doubt whether a government such as theirs could survive in a hostile world. The nation's demonstrated ability to withstand the test of war eased growing self doubts. Twenty-six Federalist delegates from the New England states had assembled at Hartford, Connecticut, in December 1814 to consider demands to be made to the national government. The news from Ghent and New Orleans rendered the Hartford Convention irrelevant and made it the butt of national ridicule. The Federalist party was discredited, never to recover. The Republican party emerged from the war more firmly entrenched, its prestige greatly increased. National unity was enhanced. "They are more Americans," Gallatin observed of his adopted countrymen, "they feel and act more as a nation."[88] Through that remarkable process by which memory becomes history, the repeated embarrassments and near disaster that had marked the war were forgotten. Victories over the world's greatest power avenged old wrongs and restored national self-confidence. In particular, the decisive victory of Jackson's strange assortment of frontiersmen, pirates, free blacks, Creoles, and Indians over eight thousand seasoned British veterans in the monthlong Battle of New Orleans was seen as confirming the superiority of virtuous republican militiamen over European conscripts. Americans learned of New Orleans and the Treaty of Ghent at about the same time, and this sudden turn of events had a huge psychological impact. "Never did a country occupy

87. Michael D. Green, *The Creeks* (New York, 1990), 50–53; Francis Paul Prucha, *American Indian Treaties: The History of a Political Anomaly* (Berkeley, 1994), 129–32.
88. Quoted in Rutland, *Madison*, 188.

more lofty ground," Massachusetts Republican and Supreme Court Justice Joseph Story exclaimed with unrestrained hyperbole. "We have stood the contest single-handed against the conqueror of Europe."[89] "What is our present situation?" Clay asked in jubilation. "Respectability and character abroad—security and confidence at home. . . . Our character and Constitution are placed on a solid basis, never to be shaken."[90] The War of 1812 thus "passed into history not as a futile and costly struggle in which the United States barely escaped dismemberment and disunion, but as a glorious triumph in which the nation had single-handedly defeated the conqueror of Napoleon and the Mistress of the Seas."[91] Now resting on a firm foundation, the United States was poised for conquest of the continent.

89. Quoted in ibid., 189.
90. Perkins, *Prologue to War*, 435.
91. Hickey, *War of 1812*, 299–309.

4

"Leave the Rest to Us"

The Assertive Republic, 1815–1837

During a tense exchange on January 27, 1821, Secretary of State John Quincy Adams and the British minister to the United States, Stratford Canning, debated the future of North America. Emphasizing the extravagance of Britain's worldwide pretensions, Adams pointedly remarked: "I do not know what you claim nor what you do not claim. You claim India; you claim Africa; you claim—" "Perhaps," Canning sarcastically interjected, "a piece of the moon." Adams conceded he knew of no British interest in acquiring the moon, but, he went on to say, "there is not a spot on *this* habitable globe that I could affirm you do not claim." When he dismissed Britain's title to the Oregon country, implying doubts about all its holdings in North America, an alarmed Canning inquired whether the United States questioned his nation's position in Canada. No, Adams retorted. "Keep what is yours and leave the rest of the continent to us."[1]

That a U.S. diplomat should address a representative of the world's most powerful nation in such tones suggests how far the United States had come since 1789 when Britain refused even to send a minister to its former colony. Adams's statement also expressed the spirit of the age and affirmed its central foreign policy objective. Through individual initiative and government action, Americans after the War of 1812 became even more assertive in foreign policy. They challenged the European commercial system and sought to break down trade barriers. Above all, they poised themselves to take control of North America and seized every opportunity to remove any obstacle. Indeed, only to the powerful British would they concede the right to "keep what is yours." They gave Spaniards, Indians, and Mexicans no such consideration.

I

The quest for continental empire took place in an international setting highly favorable to the United States. Through the balance-of-power system, the Europeans maintained a precarious stability for nearly a century

---

1. Quoted in Samuel Flagg Bemis, *John Quincy Adams and the Foundations of American Foreign Policy* (New York, 1973), 491–92.

after Waterloo. The absence of a major war eased the threat of foreign intervention that had imperiled the very existence of the United States during its early years. Europe's imperial urge did not slacken, and from 1800 to 1878 the amount of territory under its control almost doubled.[2] But the focus shifted from the Americas to Asia and Africa. The Europeans accorded the United States a newfound, if still grudging, respect. Britain and, to a lesser extent, France clung to vague hopes of containing U.S. expansion but exerted little effort to do so. Periodic European crises distracted them from North America. The vulnerability of Canada and growing importance of U.S. raw materials and markets to Britain's industrial revolution constrained its interference. While Americans continued to fret nervously about the English menace, the Royal Navy protected the hemisphere from outside intervention, freeing the United States from alliances and a large military establishment. The nation enjoyed a rare period of "free" security in which to develop without major external threats.[3]

Revolutions in South America during and after the Napoleonic wars provided opportunities and posed dangers for the United States. Sentiment for independence had long simmered on the continent. When Napoleon took control of Spain and Portugal in 1808, rebellion erupted. A new republic emerged in Buenos Aires. Revolutionary leaders Simón Bolívar and Francisco de Miranda led revolts in Colombia and Venezuela, forming a short-lived republic of New Granada. After 1815, revolutions broke out in Chile, Mexico, Brazil, Gran Colombia, and Central America. Many North Americans sympathized with the revolutions. Speaker of the House Henry Clay hailed the "glorious spectacle of eighteen millions of peoples, struggling to burst their chains and to be free."[4] Some saw opportunities for a lucrative trade. Preoccupied with its own crises and eager to gain Spanish territory, the United States remained neutral, but in a way that favored the rebellious colonies. Madison and Monroe cautiously withheld recognition. United States officials feared Spain might attempt to recover its colonies or Britain might seek to acquire them, threatening another round of European intervention.

2. Paul Kennedy, *The Rise and Fall of the Great Powers* (New York, 1987), 150, 160; Stephen Pelz, "Changing International Systems, the World Balance of Power, and the United States, 1776–1976," *Diplomatic History* 15 (Winter 1991), 51–63.
3. Charles Sellers, *The Market Revolution: Jacksonian America* (New York, 1991), 93; for U.S. nervousness about British territorial and commercial expansion, see Kinley J. Brauer, "The United States and British Imperial Expansion, 1815–1860," *Diplomatic History* 12 (Winter 1988), 19–37.
4. Quoted in Kyle Longley, *In the Eagle's Shadow: The United States and Latin America* (Wheeling, Ill., 2002), 38.

After 1815, the United States surged to the level of a second-rank power. By 1840, much of the territory extending to the Mississippi River had been settled; the original thirteen states had doubled to twenty-six. As the result of immigration and a high birth rate—what nationalists exuberantly labeled "the American multiplication table"—a population that had doubled between 1789 and 1815 doubled again between 1820 and 1840. Despite major depressions in 1819 and 1837, the nation experienced phenomenal economic growth. An enterprising merchant marine monopolized the coastal trade and challenged Britain's preeminence in international commerce. Wheat and corn production proliferated in the Northwest. Cotton supplanted tobacco as the South's staple crop and the nation's top export. The cotton boom resuscitated a moribund institution of slavery and added pressures for territorial expansion. Indeed, slavery and expansion merged in the prolonged political crisis over admission of Missouri to the Union in 1819—Thomas Jefferson's "fire bell in the night" that raised in a more ominous form the old threat of disunion. The crisis was resolved and disunion perhaps thwarted by the Missouri Compromise of 1820 that admitted Maine as a free state and Missouri as a slave state and prohibited slavery in the Louisiana Purchase territory north of 36° 30′.

Between 1820 and 1840, the U.S. economy began to mature. Construction of roads and canals brought scattered communities together and, along with the steamboat, shrank distances. These innovations dramatically transformed the predominantly agricultural, subsistence economy of Jefferson's time. Americans increasingly prided themselves on political separation from Europe, but the United States was an integral part of an Atlantic-centered international economy. European capital and technology fueled U.S. economic growth. Particularly in agriculture, the nation produced far more than could be consumed at home. Commerce with Europe remained essential to its prosperity.[5]

Purposeful leaders actively employing the organized power of the national government pushed this process along. Republican ideology was tempered by the exigencies of war. Shortages of critical items forced even Jefferson to concede the necessity of manufactures. Clay went further, promoting an "American System" that aimed at national self-sufficiency by developing domestic manufactures and expanding the home market through such Federalist devices as protective tariffs, a national bank, and federally financed internal improvements. Some Republicans clung to

5. See especially Daniel Walker Howe, *What Hath God Wrought: The Transformation of America, 1815–1848* (New York, 2007), 46–48.

MEXICO

ATLANTIC

OCEAN

Gulf of Mexico

BELIZE
(disputed)

CUBA
(still Spanish)

HAITI

PUERTO RICO
(still Spanish)

GUATEMALA
EL SALVADOR

HONDURAS
NICARAGUA

CARIBBEAN SEA

CENTRAL
AMERICA

COSTA RICA

VENEZUELA

GUYANA (British)
SURINAM (Netherlands)
GUIANA (France)

COLOMBIA

ECUADOR

EMPIRE
OF
BRAZIL

PERU

PACIFIC

OCEAN

BOLIVIA

PARAGUAY

UNITED
PROVINCES

CHILE

URUGUAY

(ARGENTINA)

PATAGONIA
(disputed)

0   500   1000 Miles

0   500   1000 Kilometers

Post-Colonial
América

the Jeffersonian vision of a virtuous republic of small farmers. But with
the market revolution, new National Republicans dreamed of national
wealth and power based on commercial and territorial expansion. Like
Clay, they adopted a neo-mercantilist approach that sought to expand exports of agricultural and raw materials and protect domestic manufactures
through tariffs.[6]

6. Ibid., 270–76, 283.

The War of 1812 gave a tremendous boost to nationalism. Americans entered the postwar era more optimistic than ever. Their faith in themselves and their nation's destiny knew few bounds. Their boastful pride in their own institutions often annoyed visitors. "A foreigner will gladly agree to praise much in their country," the perceptive Frenchman Alexis de Tocqueville complained, "but he would like to be allowed to criticize something and that he is absolutely refused." "I love national glory," one congressman exulted.[7] American horizons broadened. Even the optimistic Jefferson could envision nothing more than a series of independent republics in North America. His successor as the architect of U.S. expansion, John Quincy Adams, foresaw a single nation stretching from Atlantic to Pacific. As secretary of state and president he worked tirelessly to realize this destiny.

The quality of American statecraft remained high in the postwar era. Most policymakers had acquired practical experience in the school of diplomatic hard knocks. Cosmopolitan representatives of a still provincial republic, they generally acquitted themselves with distinction. The last—usually viewed as the least—of the Virginia Dynasty, James Monroe was an experienced and capable diplomatist. Described by contemporaries as a "plain man" with "good heart and amiable disposition," he was industrious, a shrewd judge of people and problems, and excelled at getting strong-willed men to work together.[8]

Monroe's secretary of state, John Quincy Adams, towered above his contemporaries and is generally regarded among the most effective of all those who have held the office. The son of a diplomat and president, Adams brought to his post a wealth of experience and extraordinary skills. He knew six European languages. His seventeen years abroad gave him unparalleled knowledge of the workings of European diplomacy. A man of prodigious industry, he oversaw, with the assistance of eight clerks, the workings of the State Department, writing most dispatches himself and creating a filing system that would be used until 1915. He regularly rose before dawn to pray. His early morning swims in the Potomac, clad only in green goggles and a skullcap, were the stuff of Washington legend. Short, stout, and balding, with a wandering eye—his frequent adversary Stratford Canning called him "Squinty"—Adams could be cold and austere. Throughout his life, he struggled to live up to the high expectations set by his illustrious parents, John and Abigail. Haunted by self-doubt and fears of failure, he drove himself relentlessly. He was proud that his foes

7. Sellers, *Market Revolution*, 76.
8. Noble E. Cunningham Jr., *The Presidency of James Monroe* (Lawrence, Kans., 1996), 187.

found him an "unsocial savage." Through force of intellect and mastery of detail he was a diplomat of enormous skill.[9]

Adams was also an ardent expansionist whose vision of American destiny was well ahead of his time. A profoundly religious man, he saw the United States as the instrument of God's will and himself as the agent of both. Sensitive to the needs of the shipping and mercantile interests of his native New England, he viewed free trade as the basis for a new global economic order. He fought doggedly to break down mercantilist barriers. His vision extended literally to the ends of the earth. He relished in 1820 the possibility of a confrontation with Britain over newly discovered Graham Land on the northwest coast of Antarctica, a region he conceded was "something between Rock and Iceberg."[10]

The focus of Adams's attention was North America. As early as 1811, he had foreseen a time when all of the continent would be "one nation, speaking one language, professing one general system of religious and political principles, and accustomed to one general tenor of social usage and customs." That the United States in time should acquire Canada and Texas, he believed, was "as much the law of nature as that the Mississippi should flow to the sea." He told the cabinet in 1822 that "the world should become familiarized with the idea of considering our proper dominion to be the entire continent of North America." As secretary of state, he took giant steps toward achieving that goal. As president from 1825 to 1829, he—with his own secretary of state, Clay—continued to pursue it.[11]

Monroe introduced important modifications to U.S. diplomatic practice. In keeping with republican principles, he instructed his envoys to "respectfully but decisively" decline the gifts that were the lubricant of European diplomacy. Adams recommended that individuals who had served abroad for more than six years should return home to be "new tempered."[12] At the same time, Monroe had suffered numerous slights at the hands of the great powers during his own diplomatic career, and he was eager to command their respect. Persuaded that Jefferson's pell-mell "protocol" had lowered American prestige among Europeans, he reverted to the more formal practice of Washington, receiving foreign envoys by appointment and in full diplomatic dress. U.S. diplomats wore a "uniform," a blue cloth coat with silk lining and gold or silver embroidery, and

9. Bemis, *Adams*, 255–57, 262–77; William Earl Weeks, *John Quincy Adams and American Global Empire* (Lexington, Ky., 1992), 9–17, 52–61.
10. Cunningham, *Monroe*, 119.
11. Walter LaFeber, ed., *John Quincy Adams and American Continental Empire* (Chicago, 1965), 36; Dexter Perkins, *A History of the Monroe Doctrine* (rev. ed., Boston, 1963), 28.
12. Bemis, *Adams*, 264.

a plumed hat. When Monroe took office, the capital still showed scars of the British invasion. When he left, the city's appearance and social life had begun to rival European capitals, achieving a "splendour which is really astonishing," according to one American participant. As much as Jefferson's style had symbolized the republican simplicity of an earlier era, Monroe's marked the rise of the United States to new wealth and power.[13]

The formulation of policy changed little under Monroe and Adams. Monroe employed Washington's cabinet system, submitting major foreign policy issues for the full consideration of department heads. The demise of Federalism after 1815 left only one party for the next decade, but foreign policy remained an area of heated political battle. The so-called Era of Good Feelings was anything but. Throughout the administrations of Monroe and Adams, ambitious cabinet members exploited foreign policy issues to gain an edge on potential rivals. As the economy expanded and diversified, interest groups pushed their demands on the government. In the 1820s, foreign policy, like everything else, became locked in the bitter sectional struggle over slavery. By 1824, partisan politics was back with a vengeance as the followers of war hero Andrew Jackson challenged the Republican ascendancy.

II

Monroe's and Adams's administrations set commercial expansion as a paramount goal and employed numerous distinctly unrepublican measures to achieve it. Abandoning Jefferson's disdain for diplomats, they expanded the number of U.S. missions abroad. Between 1820 and 1830, they almost doubled the number of consuls, many of them assigned to the newly independent governments of Latin America. These men performed numerous and sometimes difficult tasks, looking after the interests of U.S. citizens and especially merchants, negotiating trade treaties, and seeking out commercial opportunities. When fire devastated Havana, Cuba, in 1826, for example, consul Thomas Rodney alerted Americans to the newly created market for building materials.[14] The National Republicans also put aside traditional fears of the navy, maintaining a sizeable fleet after the War of 1812 and employing it to protect and promote U.S. commerce.

13. Cunningham, *Monroe*, 133–37; Robert Ralph Davis Jr., "Diplomatic Plumage: American Court Dress in the Early National Period," *American Quarterly* 20, no. 1 (1968), 170–71.
14. Peter T. Dalleo, "Thomas Kean Rodney: U.S. Consul in Cuba: The Havana Years, 1825–1829," *Delaware History* 22 (Spring/Summer 1987): 204–18; David W. McFadden, "John Quincy Adams, American Commercial Diplomacy, and Russia, 1809–1825," *New England Quarterly* 66 (December 1993), 620–22.

Squadrons of small, fast warships were posted to the Mediterranean, the West Indies, Africa, and the Pacific, where they defended U.S. shipping from pirates and privateers, policed the illegal slave trade, and looked for new commercial opportunities. While sailing the Pacific station during the 1820s, Thomas ap Catesby Jones, commander of the USS *Peacock*, negotiated trade treaties with Tahiti and the Hawaiian Islands.[15]

Monroe and Adams also pushed to secure payment of claims from the spoliation of American commerce, not simply for the money but also as a matter of principle. Payment of such claims would at least imply endorsement of the U.S. position on free trade and neutral rights. The United States pressed France for payment of more than $6 million for seizure of ships and cargoes under Napoleonic decrees and sought additional claims against smaller European states acting under French authority. It tried to collect money from Russia and, during Adams's presidency in particular, from the Latin American governments, most of the claims arising from privateering and other alleged violations of neutral rights by governments or rebels or in disputes between governments during the wars of independence. United States diplomats vigorously defended the nation's interests. Before demanding his passports (a diplomatic practice indicating extreme displeasure that often preceded the breaking of relations), the colorful consul to Rio de Janeiro, Condy Raguet, exclaimed that if U.S. ships wanted to break Brazil's blockade of the Rio de la Plata they would not ask permission and would be stopped only "by force of balls."[16]

Monroe and Adams used reciprocity as a major weapon of commercial expansion. In its last days, the Madison administration launched an all-out attack on the restrictive trading policies of the European powers. Responding to the president's call to secure for the United States a "just proportion of the navigation of the world," Congress in 1815 enacted reciprocity legislation that legalized the program of discrimination Jefferson and Madison had advocated since 1789. Passed in a mood of exuberant nationalism, the measure made the abolition of discriminatory duties and shipping charges contingent on similar concessions from other countries. Reciprocity was designed to strengthen the hands of U.S. diplomats in negotiations with European powers. As opposed to the most-favored-nation principle, the basis for earlier treaties, it provided, in Clay's words, a "plain and familiar rule" for the two signatories, uncomplicated by deals with

---

15. John H. Schroeder, *Shaping a Maritime Empire: The Commercial and Diplomatic Role of the American Navy, 1829–1861* (Westport, Conn., 1985), 15–18.

16. Mary W. M. Hargreaves, *The Presidency of John Quincy Adams* (Lawrence, Kans., 1985), 73.

other nations, thus reducing the chances for misunderstanding and conflict.[17] Reciprocity also made clear U.S. willingness to retaliate. Americans and Europeans increasingly recognized, moreover—the latter sometimes to their chagrin—that reciprocity did not always operate equally on all parties. Such was the superiority of the U.S. merchant marine and mercantile skill that often, as a diplomat pointed out, American shippers could secure a monopoly of trade "whenever anything like fair and equal terms [are] extended to us."[18] Through the 1820s, the United States used reciprocity to break down European commercial restrictions and gain access on favorable terms to newly opened markets in Latin America and elsewhere across the world.

For the effort expended, the Monroe-Adams trade offensive produced limited results. The United States settled a small claims dispute with Russia, but not much else. Negotiations with France provoked a nasty diplomatic spat. The United States pushed these claims with great vigor, at one point even discussing naval retaliation. Their treasury exhausted from years of war, the French perceived that if they paid the United States other claimants would get in line. Thus they stalled, reminding U.S. officials that loans made by French citizens during the American Revolution remained unpaid. The issue persisted into the Jackson administration, poisoning relations between onetime allies.[19]

In all, Monroe and Adams concluded twelve commercial agreements. They managed to secure reciprocity with Britain in direct commerce, giving the United States a huge advantage in the North Atlantic carrying trade. They concluded a most-favored-nation treaty with Russia in 1824 and reciprocity agreements with several smaller European nations. On the other hand, U.S. support for the Greek revolution thwarted negotiations with Turkey. Once again, discussions with France were especially frustrating. The United States attempted to batter down France's commercial restrictions by imposing discriminatory duties, provoking a brief but bitter trade war. A limited commercial treaty negotiated in 1822 left most major issues unresolved.[20]

Adams and Clay entertained high hopes for trade with Latin America and invested great energy in negotiations with that region, but they achieved little. For reasons of race and politics, more than economics,

17. Quoted in ibid., 76.
18. Quoted in Paul A. Varg, *United States Foreign Relations, 1820–1860* (East Lansing, Mich., 1979), 75.
19. Hargreaves, *Adams*, 70–72.
20. Ibid., 68, 72, 85–86.

southerners continued to block trade with Haiti. Raguet's provocative behavior killed a treaty with Brazil, and no treaties were negotiated with Buenos Aires, Chile, or Peru. Minister Joel Poinsett's blatant meddling in Mexican politics, as well as major differences on issues of reciprocity, limited the treaty negotiated in 1826 to most-favored-nation status. It was not ratified until much later. Clay did conclude a treaty with the Central American Federation, a political grouping of the region's five states, something he viewed as his greatest accomplishment as secretary of state and a model for a new world trading system. The federation collapsed within a short time, however, and Clay's dreams died with it.[21]

Most frustrating was U.S. inability to open the British West Indies. Since the Revolution, Americans had sought access to the lucrative triangular trade with Britain's island colonies. London clung stubbornly to restrictive policies. In the commercial convention of 1815, Britain limited American imports to a small number of specified goods and required that they come in British ships. With large numbers of its own vessels rotting at the docks, the United States retaliated. A Navigation Act of 1817 limited imports from the West Indies to U.S. ships. The following year, Congress closed America's ports to ships from any colony where its ships were excluded. Seeking to get at the West Indies through Canada, the United States in 1820 imposed virtual non-intercourse on Britain's North American colonies. The issue took on growing emotional significance. Americans protested British efforts to gain "ascendancy over every nation in every market of the world."[22] Britons feared for their merchant marine and fretted about U.S. penetration of the empire. Even the normally conciliatory prime minister Lord Castlereagh insisted he would let the West Indies starve rather than abandon the colonial system.

Mainly because of U.S. intransigence, the conflict stalemated. Under pressure from West Indian planters and the emerging industrial class, Britain in 1822 opened a number of West Indian ports with only modest duties. Three years later, it offered to crack the door still wider if the United States would drop duties on British ships entering its ports. As secretary of state and president, Adams stubbornly persisted in trying to end the British imperial preference system, perhaps with the notion, as one of his New England constituents put it, that with full reciprocity the United States could "successfully compete with any nation on earth."[23] Even the British free trader William Huskinson denounced the U.S.

21. Ibid., 77–84.
22. Quoted in Varg, *United States Foreign Relations*, 63.
23. Quoted in Hargreaves, *Adams*, 97.

position as a "pretension unheard of in the commercial relations of independent states."[24] When the United States refused to remove its duties, the British closed their West Indian ports. At this point, the issue became entangled in presidential politics. Jackson's supporters in Congress frustrated the administration's efforts to reopen negotiations, leaving Adams no choice but to reimpose restrictions on Britain. The Jacksonians ridiculed "Our diplomatic President," who, they claimed, had destroyed "colonial intercourse with Great Britain."[25] By this time the West Indian trade had declined in practical importance, but it remained a major symbol of the clash of empires. Neither would give in.

III

Although much stronger after the War of 1812, the United States still faced threats around its periphery. The European political situation was potentially explosive. The Latin American revolutions brought dangers as well as possible advantages. The world's greatest power remained in Canada with a long border contested at various points. Americans continued to fear British intrusion in the Pacific Northwest and Central America. The boundaries of the vast Louisiana territory were hotly disputed. For years, Spain had refused to recognize the legality of the purchase. Even after conceding on that issue, it sought to confine the United States east of the Mississippi. The United States claimed at times from the Louisiana acquisition the Floridas, Texas, and even the Oregon territory. Madison had returned East Florida to Spain in 1813. Spain's continued presence there, along with hostile Indian tribes, menaced the southern United States. In 1815, Americans still viewed the outside world with trepidation. While postponing some disputes in hopes that delay would work to their benefit, U.S. leaders continued to pursue security through expansion. In the case of Spain, Monroe and Adams enjoyed predictable success, negotiating at gunpoint a treaty securing not only the Floridas but also Spanish claims to the Pacific Northwest.

The War of 1812 underscored the importance of the Floridas, reinforced U.S. covetousness, and strengthened the nation's already advantageous position. Britain's wartime invasion of West Florida, its alliances with southwestern Indians, and its rumored plans to incite slave revolts in the southern United States all highlighted how essential it was to gain a land often likened to a pistol pointed at the nation's heart. Spain was further

24. Quoted in George Dangerfield, *The Awakening of American Nationalism, 1815–1828* (New York, 1965), 157.
25. Robert Remini, *Henry Clay: Statesman for the Union* (New York, 1991), 309.

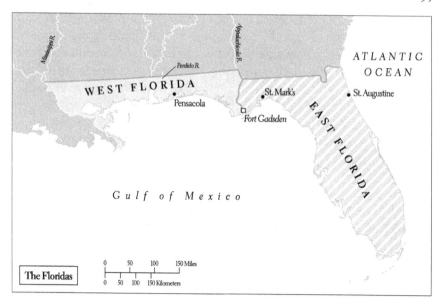

ATLANTIC
OCEAN

WEST FLORIDA

Perdido R

Pensacola

St. Mark's

St. Augustine

Fort Gadsden

EAST FLORIDA

Gulf of Mexico

Mississippi R

Appalachicola R

0   50   100   150 Miles

0   50   100   150 Kilometers

The Floridas

weakened by the Napoleonic wars. Americans believed that the long-sought territory might be detached with relative ease.[26]

Even when the outcome is obvious, negotiations can be difficult. The terms on which the Floridas would come to the United States were important to both nations. Spain was prepared to abandon a colony it could not defend, but it hoped to protect its territories in Texas and California against the on-rushing Americans and naively counted on British support. When negotiations began in early 1818, the able Spanish minister Don Luis de Onis proposed setting the western boundary of the United States at the Mississippi River. He also sought a U.S. pledge not to recognize the new Latin American republics. Monroe and Adams insisted on a line following the Colorado River into what is now northern Texas and from there north along the 104th parallel to the Rocky Mountains. The United States was willing to delay Latin American recognition, perceiving that doing so might complicate acquisition of the Floridas or even encourage European intervention to restore monarchical governments. On the other hand, a public pledge of non-recognition would antagonize new nations with whom the United States hoped to establish a thriving commerce and anger people like Clay who sympathized with the Latin Americans. The negotiations quickly deadlocked.[27]

26. William Earl Weeks, *Building the Continental Empire: American Expansion from the Revolution to the Civil War* (Chicago, 1996), 32–34.
27. Weeks, *Adams*, 71–80.

At this point, the United States began to apply not so subtle pressure against the hapless Madrid government. Under Spain's lax administration, the Floridas had become a volatile no-man's-land, a center for international intrigue and illicit commercial activities, a refuge for those fleeing oppression—and justice. The area had more than its share of pirates, renegades, and outlaws, as U.S. officials charged, but it also attracted other people, many with legitimate grievances against the United States. Latin American rebels used Atlantic and Gulf Coast ports to stage military operations against Spanish forces. Fugitive slaves sought escape from bondage. After the 1814 Treaty of Fort Jackson, Creeks expelled from their lands fled into the Floridas, some hoping to exact retribution against the United States. Outraged when the United States purchased from the Creeks lands they claimed and then forcibly removed them, the Seminoles launched a bloody war. Conflict thus raged along the Florida border. Americans drew a picture of outlaws attacking innocent settlers. In reality, all parties contributed to the melee.[28]

Under intense pressure from nervous settlers in the Southwest and land speculators who feared for their investments, the Monroe administration mounted military expeditions to quell the violence that could also be used as leverage in negotiations with Spain. In December 1817, the president authorized seizure of Amelia Island from Latin American rebels whose presence threatened eventual U.S. control. Shortly after, he authorized Gen. Andrew Jackson to invade Florida and "pacify" the Seminoles.

The nature of Jackson's instructions aroused bitter controversy. In a letter to Monroe, the general indicated that if given the go-ahead he could seize Florida within sixty days. When his behavior later provoked outrage at home and abroad, he insisted that he had received this authority. Monroe adamantly denied giving Jackson such orders, leaving critics to charge that the general had acted impetuously and illegally. Although Monroe seems not to have sent the requested signal, he did give the general "full powers to conduct the war in the manner he may judge best." The president had long favored forcibly dislodging Spain from Florida. He knew Jackson well enough to predict what he might do when unleashed. Thus, although he never sent explicit instructions, he gave the general virtual carte blanche and left himself free to disavow Jackson if he went too far.[29]

28. Ibid., 142.
29. Ibid., 109; Sellers, *Market Revolution*, 98.

Whatever his instructions, this *"Napoleon de bois,"* as the Spanish called him, moved with a decisiveness that likely shocked Monroe. A lifelong Indian fighter whose code of pacification was "An eye for an eye, a toothe for a toothe, a scalp for a scalp," Jackson hated Spaniards even more than native peoples. He had long believed that U.S. security demanded that the "Wolf be struck in his den." Indeed, he preferred simply to take the Floridas.[30] With a force of some three thousand regulars and state militia along with several thousand Creek allies, he plunged across the border. Unable to bring the Seminoles to battle, he destroyed their villages and seized livestock and stores of food, crippling their resistance. Claiming to act on the "immutable principle of self-defense," he occupied Spanish forts at St. Marks and Pensacola. At St. Marks, he captured a kindly Scots trader named Alexander Arbuthnot, whose principal offense was to have be-friended the Seminoles, and a British soldier of fortune, Richard Armbrister, who was assisting Seminole resistance to the United States. Jackson had long believed that such troublemakers "must feel the keenness of the scalp-ing knife which they excite." He vowed to deal with them "with the greatest rigor known to civilized Warfare."[31] Accusing the two men of "wickedness, corruption, and barbarity at which the heart sickens," he tried and executed them on the spot. Arbuthnot was hanged from the yardarm of his own ship, appropriately named *The Chance*. The hastily assembled military court at first shied away from a death sentence for Armbrister. Jackson restored it. This trial of two British subjects before an American military court on Spanish territory was an unparalleled example of frontier justice in action. "I have destroyed the babylon of the South," Jackson excitedly wrote his wife. With reinforcements, he informed Washington, he could take St. Augustine and "I will insure you cuba in a few days."[32]

Jackson's escapade provoked loud outcries. Spain demanded his punish-ment, indemnity, and the restoration of seized property. Angry British citi-zens urged reprisals for the execution of Arbuthnot and Armbrister. Clay proposed that Jackson be punished for violating domestic and international law. Panicky cabinet members pressed Monroe to disavow his general.

In fact, Monroe and especially Adams skillfully exploited what Adams called the "Jackson magic" to pry a favorable treaty from Spain. Adams

30. Jackson to George Graham, December 17, 1817, in Harold D. Moser, ed., *The Papers of Andrew Jackson*, vol. 2 (Knoxville, Tenn., 1994), 161.

31. Jackson to Graham, April 22, 1817, ibid., 111–12. See also David Heidler and Jeanne Heidler, *Old Hickory's War: Andrew Jackson's Quest for Empire* (Mechanicsburg, Pa., 1996).

32. Jackson to Rachel Jackson, June 2, 1818, ibid., 212–13; to James Monroe, June 2, 1818, ibid., 215.

correctly surmised that Spanish protests were mostly bluff. To permit them to retreat with honor, Monroe agreed to return the captured forts. But the United States also demanded that Spain strike a deal quickly or risk losing everything for nothing in return. The United States also threatened to recognize the Latin American nations. In a series of powerful state papers, Adams vigorously defended Jackson's conduct on grounds that Spain's inability to maintain order compelled the United States to do so. He warned the British that if they expected their citizens to escape the fate of Arbuthnot and Armbrister they must prevent them from engaging in acts hostile to the United States. Adams's spirited defense of Jackson played fast and loose with the facts and provided a classic example, repeated often in the nation's history, of justifying an act of aggression in terms of morality, national mission, and destiny. It marked an expedient act on the part of a man known for commitment to principle. It facilitated the expansion of slavery and Indian removal, two evils Adams would spend his later life fighting.[33] It also had the desired effect, breaking the back of domestic opposition, forestalling British intervention, and persuading Spain to come to terms.

The two nations reached a settlement in February 1819. Monroe abandoned his demand for Texas, perceiving that its acquisition would exacerbate an already dangerous domestic crisis over slavery in the Missouri territory. Instead, on Adams's suggestion, the United States asked for Spanish claims to the Pacific Northwest, territory also claimed by Britain and Russia. Onis at first hesitated. But in the face of U.S. adamancy and without British support, he backed down. The so-called Transcontinental Treaty left Texas in the hands of Spain but acquired for the United States unchallenged title to all of the Floridas and Spanish claims to the Pacific Northwest. The United States agreed to pay some $5 million U.S. citizens insisted they were owed by the Spanish government. The heartland of the United States was at last secure against foreign threat. A weak U.S. claim to the Pacific Northwest was greatly strengthened against a stronger British claim by acquiring Spanish interests, the most valid of the three. Even before Americans became accustomed to thinking of a republic west of the Mississippi, Adams had secured Spanish recognition of a nation extending to the Pacific and made a first move toward gaining a share of East Asian commerce.[34] Taking justifiable pride in his handiwork, he hailed in his diary a "great epocha in our history" and offered "fervent gratitude to the Giver of all Good."[35] He might also have thanked Andrew Jackson.

33. Weeks, *Adams*, 139.
34. Ibid., 178.
35. Quoted in Bemis, *Adams*, 338–39.

The United States also aggressively challenged British and Russian pretensions in the Pacific Northwest. Anglo-American relations improved markedly after the War of 1812. Recognizing a growing commonality of economic and political interests, the former enemies negotiated a limited trade agreement, began the difficult process of fixing a Canadian boundary, and, through the Rush-Bagot agreement of 1817 providing for reduction of armaments on the Great Lakes, averted a potentially dangerous naval arms race. The ever alert Adams also pried from Britain acceptance of the *alternat*, a diplomatic practice providing that the names of the two nations would be alternated when used together in the text of treaties, a symbolic achievement of no small importance.[36]

While moving toward rapprochement, the established imperial power and its upstart competitor also vied for preeminence in the Pacific Northwest. Many observers dismissed the mountainous Oregon country with its rocky, windblown coastline as bleak and inhospitable. Others, Adams included, saw the ports of Puget Sound and the prevalence of sea otters as keys to capturing the fabled East Asian trade. At the insistence of merchant prince John Jacob Astor, the United States after the War of 1812 reasserted claims to the mouth of the Columbia River abandoned during the war. The aggressive Adams also sought to further U.S. interests by extending the boundary with Canada along the 49th parallel to the Pacific, a move that would have left Puget Sound, the Columbia River basin, and the Oregon country in U.S. hands. Britain would not go this far. Nor did it wish to confront the United States. In the Anglo-American Convention of 1818, the two nations agreed to leave the Oregon country open to both countries for ten years, tacitly accepting the legitimacy of U.S. claims. Persuaded that America was poised to extend its "civilization and laws to the western confines of the continent," Secretary of War and then ardent nationalist John C. Calhoun in 1817 drew up plans to locate a string of forts extending to the mouth of the Yellowstone River. Again under the guise of a scientific and literary expedition, the administration in 1819 dispatched Stephen Long to survey the Great Plains and Rocky Mountain regions. He was also to seize control of the fur trade and chip away at British influence.[37]

Anglo-American rivalry quickened after 1818. The Hudson's Bay Company bought out the old Northwest Company and under the

36. The standard account of the postwar Anglo-American rapprochement is Bradford Perkins, *Castlereagh and Adams: England and the United States, 1812–1823* (Berkeley, Calif., 1964). For the importance of the *alternat*, see Bemis, *Adams*, 225–27.
37. Weeks, *Adams*, 122–23; Sellers, *Market Revolution*, 92; Cunningham, *Monroe*, 86–88.

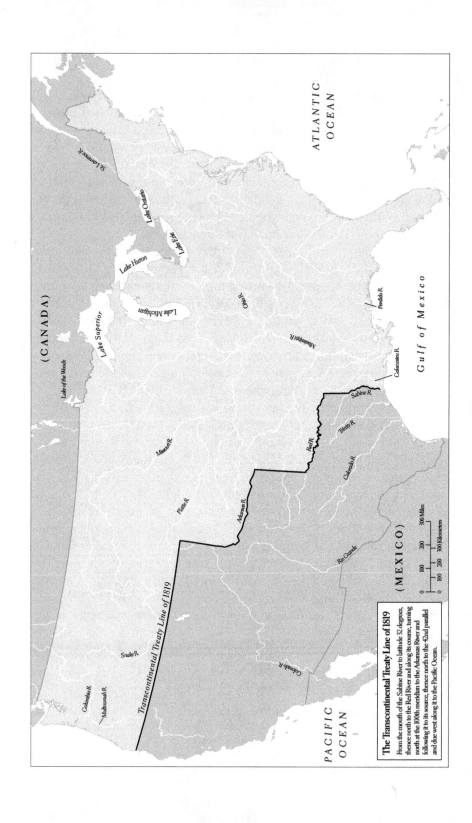

(CANADA)

ATLANTIC
OCEAN

St. Lawrence R.

Lake of the Woods

Lake Superior

Lake Huron

Lake Michigan

Lake Ontario

Lake Erie

Ohio R.

Mississippi R.

Gulf of Mexico

Perdido R.

Calcasieu R.

Sabine R.

Trinity R.

Red R.

Colorado R.

Missouri R.

Platte R.

Arkansas R.

Rio Grande

(MEXICO)

Columbus R.

Multnomah R.

Snake R.

Transcontinental Treaty Line of 1819

Colorado R.

PACIFIC
OCEAN

0   100   200   300 Miles

0 100 200 300 Kilometers

The Transcontinental Treaty Line of 1819

From the mouth of the Sabine River to latitude 32 degrees, thence north to the Red River and along its course, turning north at the 100th meridian to the Arkansas River and following it to its source, thence north to the 42nd parallel and due west along it to the Pacific Ocean.

watchful eye of the Royal Navy began systematically exploiting the area south of the Columbia River, hoping to discourage Americans from settling there. Astor's plans never reached fruition. Although Adams hesitated to challenge Britain directly, members of Congress such as Dr. John Floyd of Virginia and Thomas Hart Benton of Missouri increasingly warned of a British menace and urged settlement of the Oregon country. Congressional pressures were driving the United States toward a confrontation with Britain when Russia added a third side to the triangle.[38]

IV

Russia's challenge in the Northwest, along with a revolution in Greece and the threat of European intervention to restore monarchical governments in Latin America, brought forth in December 1823 what came to be known as the Monroe Doctrine, one of the most significant and iconic statements of the principles of U.S. foreign policy and a ringing affirmation of U.S. preeminence in the Western Hemisphere and especially North America.[39]

Tsar Alexander's ukase (imperial edict) of 1821 is often viewed as a typical expression of Russia's age-old propensity for aggrandizement, but it was considerably less. On the basis of explorations, Russia claimed the Pacific coast of North America. The tsar had given the Russian-American Company a trade monopoly as far south as 55° north. The company established scattered trading posts along the Alaskan coast, but it lacked government support and faced growing U.S. competition. New England traders and poachers took most of the region's sea otters and began supplying the indigenous population with guns and whiskey. Further alarmed by talk of American settlements in the northwest, the Russian-American Company secured Alexander's assistance. Apparently without much thought, he issued on September 4, 1821, another ukase granting Russians exclusive rights for trading, whaling, and fishing in the area of Alaska and the Bering Sea and south along the coast to 51° (far south of Russia's main settlement near the present site of Sitka, Alaska). Under threat of confiscation

---

38. Norman A. Graebner, *Empire on the Pacific: A Study in Continental Expansion* (rev. ed., Claremont, Calif., 1983), 37; Howard Jones and Donald Rakestraw, *Prologue to Manifest Destiny: Anglo-American Relations in the 1840s* (Wilmington, Del., 1997), 159.

39. The classic study is Dexter Perkins, *The Monroe Doctrine, 1823–1826* (Cambridge, Mass., 1927).

and capture, the ukase also forbade foreign ships from approaching within 100 Italian miles (115 English miles) of Russian claims.[40]

The ukase aroused grave concern in the United States. Russia's territorial aspirations posed no direct threat, since the United States had never claimed above 49°. The hostile reaction reflected more U.S. pretensions than those of Russia. But the coastal restrictions challenged the principle of freedom of the seas and threatened one of the most profitable enterprises of Adams's New England constituents. Congressmen agitated for settlement of the Columbia basin and urged Monroe to defend U.S. interests. The tsar at precisely this time was arbitrating an Anglo-American dispute over slaves carried away during the War of 1812, so Monroe and Adams proceeded cautiously. At the first opportunity, however, Adams informed the Russian minister "that we should contest the right of Russia to *any* territorial establishment on this continent, and that we should assume distinctly the principle that the American continents are no longer subjects for any new colonial establishments."[41]

The outbreak of revolution in Greece posed the equally significant and not entirely unrelated issue of America's commitment to republican principles and the role it should play in supporting liberation movements abroad. In the spring of 1821, the Greeks revolted against Turkish rule. Early the following year, various resistance groups coalesced, issued an American-style declaration of independence, and appealed to the world— and especially the "fellow-citizens of Penn, of Washington, and of Franklin"—for assistance.

Widely acknowledged as the birthplace of modern democracy, Greece became the cause célèbre of the era. "Greek fever" took hold in the United States. Americans viewed the revolution as an offspring of their own and the Turks as the worst form of barbarians and infidels. Pro-Greek rallies were staged in numerous towns and cities; speakers called for contributions and volunteers. In one of the most famous exhortations, Harvard professor Edward Everett enjoined Americans to fulfill "the great and glorious part which this country is to act, in the political regeneration of the world."[42]

The issue divided the U.S. government. Always the skeptic, Adams dismissed the Greek infatuation as "all sentiment" and feared that support

40. Normal E. Saul, *Distant Friends: The United States and Russia, 1763–1867* (Lawrence, Kans., 1991), 96–98.
41. Bemis, *Adams*, 368.
42. James A. Field Jr., *America and the Mediterranean World, 1776–1882* (Princeton, N.J., 1969), 122.

for the rebels would jeopardize trade negotiations with Turkey. On the other hand, minister to France Gallatin urged employment of the U.S. Navy's Mediterranean squadron against the Turks. Former president Madison advocated a public declaration in favor of Greek independence. Congressmen Clay and Daniel Webster of Massachusetts used their famed eloquence to press for the dispatch of an official agent to Greece. Clay indignantly protested that U.S. support for liberty was being compromised by a "miserable invoice of figs and opium." Monroe was leaning toward recognition when a more pressing challenge led the administration to take a public stand on the several issues it confronted.[43]

The possibility of European intervention to suppress the Latin American revolutions was the most serious threat to face the United States since the War of 1812. Following the Napoleonic wars, Tsar Alexander had taken the lead in mobilizing the Continental powers to check the forces of revolution. A religious fanatic whose propensity for prayer was said to have caused calluses on his knees, Alexander later became obsessed with a fear of revolution and increasingly associated opposition with godlessness. For reasons of state, he refused to help the Turks suppress the Greeks. At the Congress of Verona in November 1822, however, he secured an allied commitment to restore the fallen monarchy in Spain. French troops subsequently accomplished this mission. With the Spanish monarchy restored, talk swept Europe of an allied move to restore Spain's Latin American colonies or establish in Latin America independent monarchies.[44]

The United States had responded cautiously to the Latin American revolutions. Adams was delighted with the further dissolution of European colonialism and hoped eventually to secure trade advantages from an independent Latin America. At the same time, he believed that the Spanish and Catholic influence was too strong to permit the growth of republicanism among the new nations. He did not share the enthusiasm of Clay and others who foresaw a group of Latin American nations that were closely tied to the United States and that might build institutions resembling those of the North Americans. Nor did he wish to antagonize Spain as long as the Florida question was unresolved and the *threat* of recognition gave him leverage with Onís. Over the protests of Clay and others, the administration withheld recognition until 1822 and sought to implement an "impartial neutrality." Clay's position was popular, however, and clandestine organizations in East Coast ports provided arms, supplies, and

43. Remini, *Clay*, 222–25; Hargreaves, *Adams*, 118.
44. Perkins, *Monroe Doctrine*, 22–24, 34.

mercenaries for the rebels. Loopholes in the neutrality laws permitted the fitting-out in U.S. ports of privateers that preyed on Spanish shipping.[45]

Whatever its attitudes toward Latin America, the United States could only view with alarm the possibility of European intervention. The threat revived memories of those early years when the omnipresent reality of foreign intrusion endangered the very survival of the new republic. It could foreclose commercial opportunities that now seemed open in the hemisphere.

Curiously, in light of past antagonisms, it was the old Yankeephobe British foreign secretary George Canning who brought the issue of European intervention to the forefront. During conversations with a shocked U.S. minister Richard Rush in the summer of 1823, Canning proposed a joint statement opposing European intervention to restore the Spanish colonies and disavowing American and British designs on the new nations. The motives for this quite extraordinary proposal remain a matter of speculation. Canning may already have committed himself to recognition of the Latin American nations and was seeking U.S. support against critics at home and abroad. Many Americans, Adams included, suspected a clever British trick to keep Cuba out of U.S. hands.[46]

Whatever the case, Canning's "great flirtation" set off a prolonged debate in Washington. As was his custom, Monroe consulted with his illustrious Virginia predecessors before going to his cabinet. Jefferson and Madison swallowed their Anglophobia and counseled going along with Canning. Persuaded that European intervention was likely if not certain, Calhoun agreed.[47] Adams disagreed, and on most issues he prevailed. He astutely and correctly minimized the likelihood of European intervention. As secretary of state and a presidential aspirant, he may have feared that joining with Britain would leave him vulnerable to charges of being too cozy with an old enemy.[48] He was also alert to the advantages of acting

---

45. Arthur P. Whitaker, *The United States and the Independence of Latin America, 1800–1830* (New York, 1964), 217.

46. See, for example, William W. Kaufmann, *British Policy and Latin America* (New Haven, Conn., 1951), 142–53.

47. Jefferson to Monroe, October 24, 1823, in Paul Leicester Ford, ed., *The Works of Thomas Jefferson* (New York, 1904), 12:318–21; Madison to Monroe, October 30, November 1, 1823, in Stanislaus Murray Hamilton, ed., *The Writings of James Monroe* (7 vols., New York, 1898–1903), 6:394–95.

48. Ernest R. May advances this argument in *The Making of the Monroe Doctrine* (Cambridge, Mass., 1976). For a persuasive rebuttal, see Harry Ammon, "Monroe Doctrine: Domestic Politics or National Decision," *Diplomatic History* 5 (Winter 1981), 53–70.

alone. Acceptance of Canning's proposal might for the short run jeopardize chances of getting Cuba or Texas. An independent stance might advance prospects of trade with Latin American nations. "It would be more candid, as well as more dignified," he advised the cabinet, "to avow our principles explicitly to Russia and France than to come in as a cock-boat in the wake of the British man-of-war."[49] Reaffirming his long-held view that U.S. political interests lay primarily on the North American continent and warning against an unnecessary affront to the European powers, Adams talked Monroe out of recognizing Greece. The president overruled his secretary of state only on the form the statement should take, including it in his annual message to Congress rather than the diplomatic dispatches Adams would have preferred (as that would have given him more credit).

What much later came to be called the Monroe Doctrine, in whose formulation Adams played the crucial role, was contained in separate parts of the president's December 2, 1823, message to Congress. Asserting the doctrine of the two spheres, which had some precedent in European treaties, he sharply distinguished between the political systems of the Old World and the New and affirmed that the two should not impinge on each other. He went on to enunciate a "non-colonization principle," a bold and pretentious public reiteration of the position Adams had taken privately with the Russian and British ministers: The American continents "by the free and independent conditions which they have assumed and maintain, are henceforth not to be considered as subjects of colonizations by any European power." Monroe went on to affirm that generally, and in the specific case of Greece, the United States would not interfere in the "internal affairs" of Europe. On the most pressing issue, he set forth a non-intervention principle, warning the Holy Allies and France that the United States would regard as "dangerous" to its "peace and safety" any European effort to "extend their system to any portion of the hemisphere."[50]

Monroe's statement raised as many questions as it answered. It left unclear whether the non-colonization principle applied with equal weight to all of North and South America and what—if anything—the United States might do to defend the independence of Latin America. The Greek issue was settled when Congress subsequently tabled a resolution calling for recognition, but Monroe's statement did not close the door entirely to

49. Quoted in Bemis, *Adams*, 385.
50. Seventh Annual Message, December 2, 1823, in James D. Richardson, ed., *A Compilation of the Messages and Papers of the Presidents of the United States* (20 vols., Washington, 1897–1916), 2:776–789.

U.S. involvement in Europe. It did not even represent a definitive exposition of U.S. policy. The administration, Adams included, was prepared to consider an Anglo-American alliance should the threat of European intervention materialize.[51]

The immediate response gave little indication that Monroe's pronunciations would assume the status of holy writ. Americans lustily cheered and then largely forgot the ringing reaffirmation of America's independence from Europe. European reaction ranged from outright hostility to incredulity at the pretentiousness of such strong words from such a weak nation. That high priest of the old order, Austria's Prince Metternich, privately denounced the statement as a "new act of revolt" and warned that it would "set altar against altar" and give "new strength to the apostles of sedition and reanimate the courage of every conspirator."[52] When Canning realized that he had been outmaneuvered, he released a statement given him by the French government making clear that Britain had been responsible for deterring European intervention. Many Latin Americans had minimized the threat of European intervention from the outset. Those who took it seriously perceived that Britain, not the United States, had headed it off. Latin American leaders were eager to ascertain whether Monroe's apparent offer of support had substance, but they also feared a North American threat to their independence. The practical effects of the "doctrine" were also limited. Indeed, for many years, the United States stood by while Britain violated—and enforced—its key provisions.

The Monroe "doctrine" was by no means a hollow statement. It neatly encapsulated and gave public expression to goals Monroe and Adams had pursued aggressively since 1817. That it was issued at all reflected America's ambitions in the Pacific Northwest and its renewed concerns for its security. That it was done separately from Britain reflected the nation's keen interest in acquiring Texas and Cuba and its commercial aspirations in Latin America. It expressed the spirit of the age and provided a ringing, if still premature, statement of U.S. preeminence in the hemisphere. It publicly reaffirmed the continental vision Adams had already privately shared with the British and Russians: "Keep what is yours but leave the rest of the continent to us."

Monroe, Adams, and Clay continued to pursue this vision, pushing relentlessly against foreign positions in the Northwest and Southwest. Adams's vigorous protests against the ukase and Monroe's message were

51. Gale W. McGee, "The Monroe Doctrine—A Stopgap Measure," *Mississippi Valley Historical Review* 38 (September 1951), 233–50.
52. Perkins, *Monroe Doctrine*, 73–75. Metternich is quoted on pp. 55–57.

heard in St. Petersburg. This time listening to his foreign policy advisers rather than the Russian-American Company, the tsar made major concessions in treaties of 1824 and 1825, dividing Russian and United States "possessions" at 54° 40′, opening the ports and coasts of the Russian Pacific to U.S. ships, and leaving the unsettled stretches of the Pacific Northwest open to American traders as long as they did not sell firearms and whiskey to the indigenous peoples.[53]

Chosen president by the House of Representatives after a hotly disputed 1824 election, Adams immediately ratcheted up the pressure on Britain. He sent the veteran diplomat Gallatin to London with instructions to extend the boundary along the 49th parallel to the Pacific. Still determined to protect British interests in the Oregon country, Canning insisted on the Columbia River as a boundary. When it was evident that neither nation would back down, they agreed in 1827 to leave the territory open indefinitely to the citizens of each. Adams found it expedient to delay rather than risk conflict at a time when the U.S. position was still weak.

The United States also tried to roll back Mexico's boundaries in the Southwest. Clay had bitterly attacked Monroe and Adams for abandoning Texas in 1819. As Adams's secretary of state, he lamented that the Texas border "approached our great western Mart [New Orleans], nearer than could be wished."[54] With the president's blessings, he pushed the newly independent and still fragile government of Mexico to part with territory into which large numbers of U.S. citizens were already flocking. He authorized his minister to Mexico, South Carolinian Joel Poinsett, to negotiate a boundary at the Brazos River or even the Rio Grande, arguing, with transparently self-serving logic, that the detachment of Texas would leave the capital, Mexico City, closer to the nation's center, making it easier to administer. Not surprisingly, Mexico rejected Poinsett's overtures and Clay's logic. An outspoken champion of U.S.-style republicanism, the ebullient diplomat (better known for giving his name to a brightly colored Christmas flower native to Central America) was instructed by Clay to represent to Mexicans the "very great advantages" of the (North) American system. Poinsett took his instructions much too seriously, openly expressing his disdain for Mexican institutions and aligning himself with the political opposition. The triumph of the group he backed changed nothing. The new government resisted the meddlesome minister's offers of

53. Saul, *Distant Friends*, 101–3.
54. James E. Lewis Jr., *John Quincy Adams: Policymaker for the Union* (Wilmington, Del., 2001), 103.

$1 million for the Rio Grande boundary and in 1829 requested his recall. As with Britain in the Northwest, Adams and Clay refused to press the matter, certain that in time Texas would fall into U.S. hands.[55]

V

Implicit in the Monroe Doctrine was a commitment to the extension of the ideology and institutions of the United States, a key issue throughout much of the mid-1820s. The Greek and Latin American revolutions made it a practical and tangible matter. The marquis de Lafayette had dedicated his life to liberal causes. His triumphal pilgrimage across the United States in 1825 evoked an orgy of speeches and celebrations, reminding Americans of the glories of their revolution and stimulating sympathy for the cause of liberty elsewhere. The fiftieth anniversary of the Declaration of Independence on July 4, 1826, also brought forth talk of a rededication to freedom. The remarkable, coincidental deaths of Thomas Jefferson and John Adams on that very day seemed to President John Quincy Adams a "visible and palpable" sign of "Divine favor," a reminder of America's special role in the world.[56]

Much of the initiative for the extension of American ideals came from individuals, and the impetus was mainly religious. Inspired by the American Revolution and by a revival that swept the nation in the 1820s (the Second Great Awakening), troubled by the rampant materialism that accompanied frenzied economic growth, a small group of New England missionaries set out to evangelize the world. Originating primarily in the seaport communities and often backed by leading merchants, they saw religion, patriotism, and commerce working hand in hand. They were committed to the view of Congregationalist minister Samuel Hopkins that the spread of Christianity would bring about "the most happy state of public society that can be enjoyed on earth."[57] In the beginning, American evangelicals worked with the British. The first missionary traveled to India in 1812. In the 1820s, they struck out on their own. They did not seek or expect government support. Certain that the millennium was at hand — the estimated date was 1866 — they brought to their work a special urgency and believed the task could be done in a generation. A mission went to Latin America in 1823 to survey the prospects of liberating that continent from Catholicism and monarchy. "If one part of this new national family

---

55. Hargreaves, Adams, 116–17; Karl M. Schmitt, Mexico and the United States, 1821–1973: Conflict and Coexistence (New York, 1974), 35–41.

56. Hargreaves, Adams, 114–15.

57. Quoted in Field, Mediterranean World, 92.

should fall back under a monarchical system, the event must threaten, if not bring down evils, on the part remaining."[58] Two African American Baptist ministers were among the first Americans to go to Africa. The major thrust was the Middle East. An intrepid group of missionaries left for Jerusalem in 1819 to liberate the birthplace of Christianity from "nominal" Christians, "Islamic fanaticism," and "Catholic superstition." Plunged into the deadly maelstrom of Middle Eastern religion and politics, the mission moved on to Beirut and barely survived. But it established the foundation for a worldwide movement that would play an important role in U.S. foreign relations before the end of the century.[59]

The concept of mission assumed a major place in the foreign policy of Adams and Clay. The zealous, romantic Kentuckian had always championed the cause of freedom, often to the discomfiture of Monroe and Adams. As secretary of state, Adams had rebuffed Clay's proposals to support the Greek and Latin American revolutions—the United States should be the "well-wisher to the freedom and independence of all…, the champion and vindicator only of her own," he proclaimed in an oft-quoted July 4, 1821, oration responding to Clay.[60] But as president he moved in that direction. Shortly after Lafayette's visit, he dispatched a secret agent to offer U.S. sympathy to the Greeks and assess their ability to "sustain an independent Government." Whether Adams saw this as preliminary to recognition is unclear. It became irrelevant. The agent died en route. In April 1826, the Greeks suffered a crushing defeat, seemingly answering the question he was sent to ask. Adams nonetheless expressed sympathy for them in subsequent speeches. He hailed the outbreak of war between Russia and Turkey in 1828 as offering them renewed hope.[61]

Closer to home, Adams and Clay sought to encourage republicanism in Latin America. For years, Clay had ardently championed Latin American independence. As secretary of state, he aspired to commit hemispheric nations to a loose association based on U.S. political and commercial principles. Although skeptical, Adams too came to envision the United States providing leadership to the hemisphere in those "very fundamental maxims which we from our cradle at first proclaimed and partially succeeded to introduce into the code of national law." The two men feared that the

58. Quoted in Hargreaves, *Adams*, 114.
59. Field, *Mediterranean World*, 68–101; Ussama Makdisi, "Reclaiming the Land of the Bible: Missionaries, Secularism, and Evangelical Modernity," *American Historical Review* 102 (June 1997), 680–90.
60. Adams's July 4, 1821, speech to the House of Representatives may be conveniently found at www.millercenter.virginia.edu/academic/americanpresidents/jqadams.
61. Hargreaves, *Adams*, 119–21.

Latin American republics might fall back under European sway or as independent nations compete with each other and the United States in ways that threatened U.S. interests. The best solution seemed to be to reshape them according to North American republican principles and institutions.[62]

There is a fine line between encouraging change in countries and interfering in their internal affairs, and Adams, Clay, and their diplomats often crossed it. Raguet publicly expressed contempt for Brazil's monarchy and the corruption and immorality that, he claimed, inevitably accompanied it. Poinsett used the Freemasons' organization to foment opposition to the government of Mexico. The U.S. chargé actively intruded in a debate among Chileans over the principles of government.[63] During the revolutions against Spain, North Americans hailed Simón Bolívar as the George Washington of Latin America. But his advocacy of a presidency for life for Bolivia and Colombia aroused suspicions of British influence and fears of a turn toward monarchy. Clay privately enjoined the Liberator to choose the "true glory of our immortal Washington, to the ignoble fame of the destroyers of liberty." The U.S. chargé in Peru denounced Bolívar as a usurper and "madman" and backed his opponents. Minister to Colombia William Henry Harrison openly consorted with Bolívar's enemies and was asked to leave. An admirer of the United States, the Liberator observed that this rich and powerful northern neighbor "seemed destined by Providence to plague America with torments in the name of freedom."[64]

Adams and Clay never permitted the cause of freedom to interfere with more important interests. They were willing to recognize the Brazilian monarchy as long as Brazil's ports were open to U.S. trade. When the threat of European intervention caused Latin American leaders to ask how the United States might respond, they got only vague responses. Monroe's statement had not conveyed "any pledge or obligation the performance of which foreign nations have a right to demand," Clay asserted. The United States flatly rejected proposals by Colombia and Brazil for alliances. When wars or rumors of war among the Latin nations themselves threatened Hemispheric stability, Clay and Adams stuck to a policy of "strict and impartial neutrality."[65]

62. Ibid., 127; Lewis, *Adams*, 87–88.
63. Hargreaves, *Adams*, 128.
64. Ibid., 127; David Bushnell, "Simon Bolivar and the United States: A Study in Ambivalence," *Air University Review* 37 (July–August 1986), 106–12.
65. Hargreaves, *Adams*, 129–31.

With Haiti and Cuba, race, commerce, and expediency dictated support for the status quo. Clay was inclined to recognize Haiti, but southerners like Calhoun fretted about "social relations" with a black diplomat and the participation of his children "in the society of our daughters and sons." Adams opposed recognition as long as the black republic granted exclusive trade privileges to France and showed "little respect" for "races other than African."[66] The United States preferred the certainties of continued Spanish control of Cuba to the risks of independence. Its rule threatened throughout the 1820s by rebellion from within and a possible British takeover or Mexican or Colombian invasion from without, Spain maintained at best a precarious hold on its island colony. United States officials, on the other hand, saw Cuba as a natural appendage of their country, certain, as Adams put it, that, like an "apple severed by the tempest from its native tree," Cuba, once separated from Spain, could "gravitate only towards the North American union." For the moment, they were content with the status quo. A premature move to acquire Cuba might provoke British intervention. The "moral condition, and discordant character" of Cuba's predominantly black population raised the specter of the "most shocking excess" of the Haitian revolution. Clay and Adams thus rebuffed schemes proposed by Cuban planters for U.S. annexation and rejected British proposals for a multilateral pledge of self-denial. They warned off Mexico and Colombia, proclaiming that if Cuba was to become a dependency of any nation "it is impossible not to allow that the law of its position proclaims that it should be attached to the United States." They did nothing to encourage Cuban independence, preferring the status quo as long as the island was open to U.S. trade.[67]

Adams and Clay's efforts to promote closer relations with hemispheric neighbors through participation in an inter-American conference in Panama became hopelessly entangled in the bitter partisan politics that afflicted their last years in office. Bolívar conceived the idea of an inter-American congress to build closer ties among the new nations to help fend off European intervention and perhaps also support his own ambitions for Hemispheric leadership. Some Latin American leaders saw inviting the United States as a means to secure the pledges of support Washington had been unwilling to give on a bilateral basis. Adams and Clay were not prepared to go this far, but they were willing to participate,

66. Sellers, *Market Revolution*, 273; Remini, *Clay*, 299; Lars Schoultz, *Beneath the United States: A History of U.S. Policy Toward Latin America* (Cambridge, Mass., 1998), 80–81.
67. Hargreaves, *Adams*, 140–46; Remini, *Clay*, 301–3.

Clay to further his dreams of an American System, Adams, who critics sneered had caught the "Spanish American fever" from his secretary of state, to promote U.S. commerce and demonstrate goodwill. Their missionary impulse was manifest in Clay's instructions to the delegates. They were not to proselytize actively, but they should be ready to respond to questions about the U.S. system of government and the "manifold blessings" enjoyed by the people under it.[68]

The Panama Congress became a political lightning rod, drawing increasingly bitter attacks from the followers of presidential aspirants former secretary of the treasury William Crawford, Vice President Calhoun, and especially Andrew Jackson. Critics ominously warned that participation would violate Washington's strictures against alliances and sell out U.S. freedom of action to a "stupendous Confederacy, in which the United States have but a single vote." Southerners protested association with nations whose economies were competitive, expressed concern that the congress might seek to abolish slavery, and objected to association with Haitian diplomats. A Georgia senator issued dire warnings against meeting with "the emancipated slave, his hands yet reeking in the blood of his masters." The acerbic Virginia congressman John Randolph of Roanoke declaimed against a "Kentucky cuckoo's egg, laid in a Spanish-American nest." Condemning the political "bargain" that had allegedly given Adams the presidency and made Clay secretary of state, he sneered at the union of the "Puritan with the black-leg," a "coalition of Blifil and Black George" (the reference to especially unsavory characters from Henry Fielding's novel *Tom Jones*). Randolph's charges provoked a duel with Clay more comical than life-threatening, the only casualty of which was the Virginian's greatcoat.[69]

United States participation never materialized. A hostile Senate delayed for months voting on Adams' nominees. By the time they were finally approved, one refused to go to Panama during the "sickly season," and the other died before receiving his instructions. When the congress finally assembled in June 1826 after repeated delays, no U.S. representative was present. After a series of sessions, it adjourned with no plans to reconvene. Adams gamely persisted, appointing a new representative, but the congress never met formally again. The Senate refused even to publish the administration's instructions to its delegates, writing a fitting epitaph to a comedy of errors. For the first time but by no means the last, a major foreign policy initiative fell victim to partisan politics.[70]

68. Quoted in Hargreaves, *Adams*, 157.
69. Ibid., 147–148; Remini, *Clay*, 292–95.
70. Remini, *Clay*, 300–301.

The Panama Congress fiasco typified the travails of Adams's presidency. Perhaps the nation's most successful secretary of state, he met frustration and failure in its highest office.[71] Although he brought to the White House the most limited mandate, he set ambitious goals. He and Clay achieved some important accomplishments, especially in the construction of roads and canals and the passage of a highly controversial protective tariff in 1828. In most areas, they failed. Outraged at losing an election in which they had won a plurality of the popular vote, Jackson and his supporters built a vibrant political organization and obstructed administration initiatives. Caught off guard by the opposition, Adams often seemed incapable of asserting effective leadership. Perhaps like Jefferson and also from hubris, he too overreached, refusing to bend from principle in trade negotiations with England and badly misjudging the willingness of weak nations such as Mexico to succumb to U.S. pressure.

This said, the era of Monroe and Adams was rich in foreign policy accomplishment. Through the Transcontinental Treaty, the United States secured its southern border, gained uncontested control of the Mississippi, and established a foothold in the Pacific Northwest. The threat of European intervention diminished appreciably. Britain was still the major power in the Western Hemisphere, but the United States in a relatively short time emerged as a formidable rival, already larger than all the European states except for Russia. Still threatened by manifold dangers in 1817, the U.S. continental empire was firmly established by 1824. Well might Adams observe in his last months as secretary of state that never had there been "a period of more tranquility at home and abroad since our existence as a nation than that which prevails now."[72]

VI

The election of Andrew Jackson in 1828 provoked alarm among some Americans and many Europeans, especially in the realm of foreign policy. The first westerner to capture the White House, Jackson, unlike his predecessors, had not served abroad or as secretary of state. His record as a soldier, especially in the invasion of Florida, raised legitimate concerns that he would be impulsive, even reckless, in the exercise of power.

Jackson introduced important institutional changes. His cabinet met sparingly and rarely discussed foreign policy. He went through four secretaries of state in eight years, much of the time assuming for himself the primary role in policymaking. He instituted the first major reform of the

71. Lewis, Adams, 99.
72. Ibid., 95; Weeks, Continental Empire, 58–59.

State Department, creating eight bureaus and elevating the chief clerk to a status roughly equivalent to a modern undersecretary. He expanded the consular service and sought to reform it by paying salaries, thus reducing the likelihood of corruption, only to have a penurious Congress reject his proposal and try to reduce U.S. representation abroad. With much fanfare, he institutionalized the principle of rotation in office—a spoils system, critics called it. He used the diplomatic service for political ends. Ministers William Cabell Rives, Louis McLane, Martin Van Buren, and James Buchanan distinguished themselves in European capitals, but they were among the major exceptions to a generally weak group of diplomatic appointments. The eccentric John Randolph—sent to St. Petersburg to get him out of Washington—left after twenty-nine days, finding the Russian weather unbearably cold even in August. Jackson crony and world-class scoundrel Anthony Butler was the worst of a sorry lot of appointments to Latin America.[73]

In keeping with the democratic spirit of the day, Jackson altered the dress of the diplomatic corps. His Democratic Party followers accused Monroe and Adams of trying to "ape the splendors...of the monarchical governments"; Jackson himself thought the fancy diplomatic uniform "extremely ostentatious" and too expensive. He introduced an outfit more in keeping with "pure republican principles," a plain black coat with gold stars on the collar and a three-cornered hat.[74]

Jackson's changes were more of style and method than substance. Cadaverous in appearance with strikingly gray hair that stood on end, chronically ill, still bearing the scars from numerous military campaigns and carrying in his body two bullets from duels, the rough-hewn but surprisingly sophisticated hero of New Orleans embodied the spirit of the new republic. His rhetoric harked back to the republican virtues of a simpler time, but he was both the product and an ardent promoter of an emerging capitalist society. Domestic struggles such as the nullification controversy and the bank war occupied center stage during Jackson's presidency. There were no major foreign policy crises. At the same time, Jackson saw foreign policy as essential to domestic well-being and gave it high priority. He was less concerned with promoting republicanism abroad than with commanding respect for the United States. He readily embraced the global destiny of a rising nation. More than his predecessors,

---

73. Donald B. Cole, *The Presidency of Andrew Jackson* (Lawrence, Kans., 1993), 41–42, 93, 241–42; John M. Belohlavek, *"Let the Eagle Soar!" The Foreign Policy of Andrew Jackson* (Lincoln, Neb., 1985), 34–36.

74. Davis, "Diplomatic Plumage," 171–72.

he sought to project U.S. power into distant areas. He energetically pursued the major goals set by Monroe, Adams, and the despised Clay: to expand and protect the commerce upon which America's prosperity depended; to eliminate or at least roll back alien settlements that threatened its security or blocked its expansion.[75]

Jackson's methods represented a combination of frontier bluster and frontier practicality. In his first inaugural, he vowed to "ask nothing but what is right, permit nothing that is wrong." He did not live up to this high standard, but he did establish a style distinctly his own. Like Monroe and Adams, he had been profoundly influenced by the menacing and sometimes humiliating experiences of the republic's infancy. He was extremely sensitive to insults to the national honor and threats to national security. He claimed to stand on principle. He insisted that other nations be made to "sorely feel" the consequences of their actions; he was quick to threaten or use force if he thought his nation wronged. In actual negotiations, however, he was conciliatory and flexible. If, on occasion, he raised relatively minor issues to the level of crises, he also solved by compromise problems that had frustrated Adams, a man renowned for diplomatic skill. His gracious manner and folksy charm won over foreigners who expected to find him offensive.[76]

Like Monroe and Adams before him, Jackson gave high priority to expanding U.S. trade. A product of the southwestern frontier, he recognized the essentiality of markets for American exports. Despite the efforts of his predecessors, commerce had stagnated in the 1820s, and surpluses of cotton, tobacco, grain, and fish threatened the continued expansion of agriculture, commerce, and manufacturing. He thus moved vigorously to resolve unsettled claims disputes, break down old trade barriers, and open new markets.[77]

Jackson perceived that securing payments of outstanding claims would bind grateful merchants to him, stimulate the economy, and facilitate new trade agreements. Through patient negotiation and the timely deployment of naval power, he extracted $2 million from the Kingdom of Naples. The threat of a trade war helped secure $650,000 from Denmark. Settlement of the long-standing French claims dispute represented a major success of his first administration and reveals much about his methods

75. Belohlavek, *Eagle*, 92–106.
76. Walter Russell Mead, *Special Providence: American Foreign Policy and How It Changed the World* (New York, 2001) uses Jackson to represent a belligerent strain in U.S. foreign policy. Arthur Schlesinger Jr. depicts a gentler, more diplomatic Jackson in *New York Review of Books* (May 15, 2003), 19.
77. Cole, *Jackson*, 121–23.

of operation. He attached great importance to the negotiations, believing that other nations would view failure as a sign of weakness. Informed by minister Rives that France would not pay unless "made to believe that their interests…require it," Jackson took a firm position. But after months of laborious negotiations, when the fragile new government of Louis Philippe offered to settle for $5 million, he readily assented, conceding that, although less than U.S. demands, the sum was fair. The United States promised to pay 1,500,000 francs to satisfy French claims from the American Revolution.[78]

Jackson almost undid his success by pressing too hard for payment. Without bothering to determine when the first installment was due or notify the French government, he ordered a draft on the French treasury. It was returned unpaid, and the Chamber of Deputies subsequently rejected appropriations for the settlement. At this point, an angry Jackson impulsively threatened to seize French property. "I know them French," he reportedly exclaimed. "They won't pay unless they are made to."[79] The Chamber appropriated the funds but refused to pay until Jackson apologized. The dispute quickly escalated. The French recalled their minister from Washington, asked Rives to leave Paris, and sent naval forces to the West Indies. Jackson drafted a bellicose message and ordered the navy to prepare for war. A totally unnecessary conflict over a relatively trivial sum was averted when a suddenly conciliatory Jackson in his December 1835 message to Congress refused to apologize but insisted he meant no offense. Paris viewed the apology that was not an apology as sufficient and paid the claims.[80]

Jackson also broke the long-standing and often bitter deadlock over access to the British West Indies. The departure of Adams and the death of Canning in 1827 greatly facilitated settlement of an apparently intractable issue. More interested in markets than shipping, Jackson's southern and western constituents exploited Adams's blunders in the 1828 campaign. To prove his mettle as a diplomat, Jackson sought to succeed where his predecessor had failed. British planters and industrialists had long pressed the government to resolve the issue. At least for the moment, instability on the Continent made good relations with the United States especially important.[81]

78. Belohlavek, *Eagle*, 92–106.
79. Quoted in Marvin R. Zahniser, *Uncertain Friendship: American-French Relations Through the Cold War* (New York, 1975), 102.
80. Cole, *Jackson*, 126–27.
81. Ibid., 124–25.

The two nations thus inched toward resolving an issue that had vexed relations since the American Revolution. Persuaded that Adams's rigidity had frustrated earlier negotiations, Jackson abandoned his predecessor's insistence that Britain give up imperial preference. He continued to talk tough, at one point threatening to cut off trade with "Canady." But when advised by McLane in 1830 that the issue might be settled more easily by action than negotiation, he removed the retaliatory measures prohibiting entry into U.S. ports of ships from the British West Indies. London responded by opening the West Indies to direct trade. An issue that had grown in symbolic importance while declining in practical significance was at last settled, removing a major impediment to amicable relations. Britons especially had feared accession of the allegedly Anglophobic Jackson, executioner of Arbuthnot and Armbrister. His demeanor in these negotiations won him an esteem in London given none of his predecessors and evoked a determination, in the words of King William IV, to "keep well with the United States."[82]

Jackson also energetically pursued new trade agreements. James Buchanan's dismal later performance as president has obscured his considerable skill as minister to Russia. He endured the St. Petersburg weather and the constant surveillance placed on foreigners. He ingratiated himself at court through his storytelling and dancing, even his flattery of the tsar. He negotiated a treaty providing for reciprocity in direct trade and access to the Black Sea.[83]

The United States also managed to achieve the treaty with Turkey that had eluded it for thirty years. Destruction of the Turkish navy by a combined European fleet at Navarino in 1827 convinced the sultan that closer relations with the United States would be useful. In return for a "separate and secret" U.S. promise to assist in rebuilding its navy, Turkey agreed to establish diplomatic and consular relations, trade on a most-favored-nation basis and admit American ships to the Black Sea. Although the Senate rejected the secret article, Americans without official sanction helped design ships and train sailors for the Turkish navy. The commercial treaty did not live up to expectations, only the exchange of rum and cotton goods in Smyrna for opium, fruit, and nuts turning out to be significant, but it established, along with the missionaries in Beirut, a basis for U.S. involvement in the Middle East.[84]

82. Quoted in Charles R. Ritcheson, "Van Buren's Mission to London, 1831–1832," *International History Review* 8 (May 1986), 198–211.
83. Belohlavek, *Eagle*, 84–88; Saul, *Distant Friends*, 121–22.
84. Field, *Mediterranean World*, 141–53; Belohlavek, *Eagle*, 128–38.

Jackson eagerly sought out trade with Asia. In January 1832, he appointed New England merchant and veteran sailor Edmund Roberts as a special agent to negotiate treaties with Muscat, Siam (Thailand), and Cochin China (southern Vietnam). To keep his mission secret, Roberts was given "ostensible employment" as clerk to the commander of the sloop *Peacock*. This first encounter between the United States and Vietnam was not a happy one. The ship landed near present-day Qui Nhon in January 1833. The discussions that followed constituted a classic cross-cultural exercise in futility. Low-level Vietnamese officials raised what Roberts called "impertinent queries," namely, whether the visitors had brought the obligatory presents for the king. Himself an imperious figure and like most Americans of the time strongly nationalistic, Roberts staunchly refused to use the "servile forms of address" the Vietnamese demanded in dealing with the emperor. They would accept nothing less, insisting that since the U.S. president was elected he was obviously inferior to a king. Roberts took a strong dislike to his hosts, describing them as untrustworthy and "without exception the most filthy people in the world." Most important, he refused to submit to "any species of degradation"—notably the elaborate ritual known as the ko-tow—to "gain commercial advantage." After a month of unproductive discussions, the *Peacock* sailed away.

Roberts's frustrations with Vietnam persisted. The *Peacock* went on to insular Southeast Asia, where he negotiated treaties with the rulers of Siam and Muscat, the former a model of commercial liberality. Jackson was so pleased that he asked his envoy to go back to Cochin China and then proceed to Japan, pragmatically imploring him, this time, to conform to local custom "however absurd." Wined and dined by rulers across the world, the venturesome Roberts had survived shipwrecks, pirates, and disease. This time his luck ran out. He contracted cholera en route. His ship landed at Da Nang in May 1836, but after a week of futile discussions, this time hampered by his illness, he sailed to Macao, where he died before completing his mission. The emperor Ming-Mang summed up the experience with a poem:

> We did not oppose their coming,
> We did not pursue them on their departure,
> We behaved according to the manners of a civilized nation
> What good would it do for us to complain of foreign barbarians.[85]

85. Robert Hopkins Miller, *The United States and Vietnam, 1787–1941* (Washington, 1990), 32–40. Also Ronald Spector, "The American Image of Southeast Asia, 1790–1865: A Preliminary Assessment," *Journal of Southeast Asian Studies* 111 (September 1972), 299–305, and Belohlavek, *Eagle*, 162–77.

Building on Adams and Clay's foundation, Jackson negotiated ten commercial treaties in all. Exports nearly doubled during his two terms. Much of the increase was with Europe, still the major U.S. market, but the new treaties established a foundation for future commercial interests in the Middle East and East Asia.

Far more than his predecessors, Jackson thought in global terms, and he was committed to extending American influence into remote areas. He endorsed a plan for exploring the South Pole, agreeing, with its promoter, that it was important to show the flag "to every portion of the globe, to give to civilized and savage man a just impression of the power we possess."[86]

He upgraded the navy and used it to defend the nation's commercial interests and uphold its honor. For years, Americans had fished and sealed in the gray and icy South Atlantic and dried sealskins on the shores of the barren Falkland/Malvinas Islands. In the early 1820s, the new republic of Buenos Aires laid claim to the islands, established a tiny settlement of gauchos and ex-convicts, and restricted foreigners from fishing and sealing. When U.S. sailors in 1831 violated the orders, local authorities seized three American ships. Recently arrived in the area, the powerful USS *Lexington* proceeded to the Falkland/Malvinas under general instructions to protect U.S. commercial interests. Exceeding more specific orders issued by a diplomat in Buenos Aires without standing or instructions, and flying the French flag for purposes of deception, Capt. Silas Duncan neutralized Argentine defenses, declared the islands without government, placed the settlers under arrest, and took several hostages. Far from disavowing Duncan's actions, Jackson endorsed them. The new U.S. minister in Buenos Aires defended the captain to the point of demanding his passport to return home.[87]

A more serious incident occurred in 1831 along the "pepper coast" of present-day Indonesia. Malayan pirates attacked an American merchantman (ironically named *The Friendship*) in the West Sumatran port of Quallah Battoo, killing several sailors, taking $12,000 in specie and $8,000 in opium, and adding insult to injury by taunting the captain and his crew: "Who is greater now, Malay or American?" Outraged by this affront and persuaded that the "piratical perpetrators" were in "such a state of

86. Schroeder, *Maritime Empire*, 34.

87. Christian J. Maisch, "Falkland/Malvinas Islands Clash of 1831–1832," *Diplomatic History* 24 (Spring 2000), 185–210. Jackson's gunboat diplomacy is vigorously defended in Craig Evan Klafter, "United States Involvement in the Falklands Islands Crisis of 1831–1833," *Journal of the Early Republic* 4 (Winter 1984), 395–420.

society that the usual course of proceedings between civilized nations could not be perused," Jackson dispatched the fifty-gun USS *Potomac* to the East Indies, instructed Capt. John Downes to demand indemnity and restitution of the stolen property, and authorized him to use force if no satisfaction was obtained. Arriving at the scene in early 1832, the impulsive captain decided to shoot first and talk later. He landed marines on Quallah Battoo, plundered the port, and burned the town, killing as many as two hundred Malays, women and children included. Annoyed that Downes had exceeded his orders, Jackson assigned him to finish his career as an inspector of lighthouses. But he publicly defended the captain, condemning the Malays as a "band of lawless pirates" and admitting that his purpose was to "inflict a chastisement as would deter them from like aggressions."[88]

Jackson's gunboat diplomacy reveals much about U.S. foreign policy in the 1830s. It makes clear the nation's contempt for "lesser" peoples, its determination to command respect as a great power, and its conviction that military force could be used to alter the behavior of others. Jackson's political foes denounced him for being trigger-happy and bloodthirsty, and for usurping a war-making power rightly belonging to Congress. His defenders, in turn, dismissed as "unmanly" the notion that the president could not chastise "pirates" without an act of Congress. Americans in general applauded his actions as a "necessary lesson to be taught ignorant savages who would violate the rights of a young republic with a world destiny to fulfill."[89] The United States was justified in defending its interests, but in each case naval officers exceeded their orders and, in Sumatra in particular, inflicted destruction far out of proportion to the losses suffered. Moreover, the lessons administered seem to have been lost on their intended students. Numerous incidents along the pepper coast made clear that Downes's reprisals had not deterred "like aggression." In an ironic twist, Duncan's escapade left the Falkland/Malvinas vacant. When Britain filled the vacuum by seizing the islands in early 1833, Argentina asked for U.S. support under the Monroe Doctrine. It was one thing, of course, to take on Argentina, quite another Great Britain, and the United States did nothing. Jackson's action—and subsequent inaction—confirmed Latin American and especially Argentine suspicions of the United States. His gunboat diplomacy put the United States very much in the mainstream of Western imperialism rather than outside of it, as Americans have boasted, belying the nation's claims of its exceptionalism.

88. Belohlavek, *Eagle*, 152–62.
89. Schroeder, *Maritime Empire*, 28; Belohlavek, *Eagle*, 162.

Like Monroe and Adams, Jackson moved vigorously to eliminate obstacles to U.S. expansion on the North American continent. This involved, on the one hand, removal of the Indians to unoccupied land west of the Mississippi, and on the other, efforts to acquire Texas from Mexico through purchase or negotiation. Jackson's inaugural pledge to ask nothing "not clearly right" and "permit nothing that is wrong," did not apply in these cases.

Defeat in the War of 1812 had crippled Indian resistance to white expansion, and in its aftermath the United States moved to solve the Indian "problem." It was a solution devised by whites for Native Americans. Indians "neither are, in fact, nor ought to be considered as independent nations," Calhoun observed in 1818. "Our views of their interest, and not their own, ought to govern them."[90] That view came to center on removal. Monroe endorsed the policy as early as 1817. The cotton boom in the South and discovery of gold in Georgia prompted land-hungry settlers in Georgia, Alabama, and Mississippi to agitate for removing the southeastern Indians west of the Mississippi. Ironically, the main targets of removal, the so-called Five Civilized Tribes, had taken the greatest strides toward assimilation, but by this time that concept had fallen into disrepute. Some Americans viewed the degeneracy that "civilization" had brought to Indians as evidence that assimilation had failed. Most fell back on the blatantly racist and entirely expedient position that Indians were an inferior people beyond redemption. Even Clay, whose views were relatively humane, affirmed that the Indians "were not an improvable breed, and their disappearance from the human family will be no great loss to the world."[91]

In this atmosphere, drastic change in Indian policy was inevitable. Jackson was elected by states eager for removal. He had concluded that the Indians could not remain—it was impossible for separate peoples to coexist within a nation. Thus, even though the United States had signed numerous treaties with the various tribes, he rejected outright their claim to sovereignty. He rationalized removal as a way of saving Indian civilization—the only alternative to annihilation—although he must have foreseen that in time the same pressures might drive them from the lands to which they were being removed.[92]

90. Robert L. Meriwether et al., *The Papers of John C. Calhoun* (28 vols., Columbia, S.C., 1959–2003), 3:350.
91. Reginald Horsman, *Race and Manifest Destiny* (Cambridge, Mass., 1981), 198.
92. Cole, *Jackson*, 67–74.

One of the great tragedies of U.S. history thus unfolded during the Jackson years. Violating earlier treaty obligations, Congress passed in 1830 by a very thin margin a bill for removal. In theory, it was voluntary. Jackson insisted that he would not forcibly remove those Indians who submitted to state law, but state officials ignored his qualification and applied the law to Indians in a discriminatory and oppressive manner. Removal was accomplished by force, bribery, fraud, and the grossest exploitation. Jackson himself warned recalcitrant chiefs, if they rejected removal, not to call upon their "great father hereafter to relieve you of your troubles." When his old adversaries, the Creeks and Cherokees, resisted and sued the United States, he made clear he must leave those "poor deluded" tribes "to their fate and annihilation."[93]

Jackson's claims that his policy toward his "red children" was "just and humane" ring hollow. Removal may indeed have been inevitable, but he might have done more to protect the rights of those who chose to remain and make the process of removal more humane. The government acquired 100 million acres of Indian land for $70 million plus 30 million acres in the West. Amidst horrific suffering, more than forty-six thousand Indians were forced from their ancestral lands into the wilderness across the Mississippi. The human losses were incalculable. Members of the tribes were divided against themselves. Efforts to remove the Seminoles sparked a war that lasted seven years and cost millions of dollars and thousands of lives. The cold winter of 1831–32, a cholera epidemic, and Congress's refusal to appropriate adequate funds added to the misery of those removed. The Cherokees resisted longest. They were herded into prison camps and eventually removed by force, resulting under Jackson's successor, Martin Van Buren, in the infamous "Trail of Tears." Jackson's removal policy spelled the doom of the American Indian. "What is history but the obituary of nations," one pro-removal congressman sighed.[94]

With no more scruples but much less success, the administration also attempted to push back the frontiers of Mexico. Like other southerners, Jackson viewed the exclusion of Texas from the treaty with Spain as a huge mistake. He feared leaving a foreign power in control of the lower branches of the Mississippi. He rationalized that national security and good relations with Mexico required a natural boundary. The "god of the universe had intended this great valley to belong to one nation," he exclaimed. "I shall keep my eye on this object, and the first propitious

93. Robert V. Remini, *Andrew Jackson and the Course of American Freedom, 1822–1832* (New York, 1981), 270, 272.
94. Horsman, *Race*, 202.

moment make the attempt to *regain* the Territory as far south and west as the great Desert."[95]

Jackson was not terribly troubled about the means employed. In August 1829, he empowered Poinsett to offer as much as $5 million for a boundary at the Rio Grande. The minister had already been discredited by his interference in Mexican politics. When Mexico demanded his recall, Jackson made a bad situation worse by replacing him with an old pal, Colonel Anthony Butler of Mississippi. A wheeler-dealer and notorious rascal, Butler also speculated in Texas lands. Jackson probably encouraged his aggressiveness and unscrupulousness by advising him that "I scarcely ever knew a Spaniard who was not the slave of avarice, and...this weakness may be worth a great deal to us in this case."[96]

Upon arriving at his post, Butler made obvious his contempt for the Mexicans and his determination to get Texas by fair means or foul. Alternately pushy and indolent, happily ignorant of and insensitive to his hosts, Butler completely misread his opposite number in negotiations, the clever and sophisticated secretary of foreign affairs, Lucas Alaman, who had no intention of selling Texas. Certain of success, Butler promised his chief that he would get what he wanted or "forfeit my head." He tried first to purchase the coveted territory. That failing, he urged Jackson to occupy strategic parts of Texas and then open negotiations. When Jackson rejected that proposal, he suggested in an uncoded communication the bribery of that "vile hypocrite and most unprincipled man," the Mexican leader Antonio Lopez de Santa Anna. This was too much even for Jackson. "A. Butler. What a scamp!" the president snarled as he ordered his minister recalled. Without Texas, still in possession of his head, and not content with the damage already done, Butler tarried for two years, among other things, challenging the Mexican secretary of war to a duel and threatening to cane and whip him in public. He is also alleged to have molested Mexican women. When ordered to leave the country, he had the effrontery—as well as the good sense—to request an armed guard to escort him to the border.[97]

The Butler mission represents the low point of Jacksonian diplomacy. The president sent perhaps the worst possible person on a mission of great delicacy, encouraged his bad behavior by sharing his own negative

95. Remini, *Jackson*, 202, 218.
96. Belohlavek, *Eagle*, 225.
97. Quinton C. Lamar, "A Diplomatic Disaster: The Mexican Mission of Anthony Butler, 1829–1834," *Americas* 45 (July 1988), 1–18; Joe Gibson, "'A. Butler: What a Scamp!'" *Journal of the West* 2 (1972), 235–47.

assessment of Mexicans, and refused to recall his agent when his conduct demanded it. Butler could not accomplish his mission. His arrogance and crudeness further poisoned Mexican-American relations, already strained by Poinsett's meddling, creating an atmosphere of anger and distrust conducive to war.

In the meantime, a revolution among Americans in Texas created a new set of problems—and opportunities. The United States did not incite the revolution; nor did the Jackson administration do anything to stop it. The president proclaimed U.S. neutrality but did not rigorously enforce it. When the Texans won independence after the April 1836 Battle of San Jacinto and asked for recognition and annexation, Jackson demurred, fearing that the explosive issue of the expansion of slavery would tear apart his Democratic Party and cost his chosen successor, Van Buren, the election. Even after Van Buren had won, the ailing, outgoing president declined to act decisively, passing the buck to Congress. After an equally hesitant legislature finally enacted a resolution favoring recognition in March 1837, Jackson in one of his last acts recognized the Republic of Texas, leaving annexation for another day.

Despite his dedication to empire and his considerable foreign policy achievements, Jackson failed to complete a central task of continental expansion left undone by Monroe and Adams. In this case, the exigencies of politics won out over his commitment to expansionist goals. The annexation of Texas would form perhaps the defining event in the era of Manifest Destiny, helping to provoke a war with Mexico that in turn would round off U.S. continental expansion and inflame internal divisions that would lead to Civil War.

5

A Dose of Arsenic

Slavery, Expansion, and the Road to Disunion, 1837–1861

"The United States will conquer Mexico," philosopher Ralph Waldo Emerson predicted at the outbreak of war in May 1846, "but it will be as the man swallows the arsenic, which brings him down in turn. Mexico will poison us."[1] Emerson correctly predicted that America's first major foreign war would have disastrous consequences, but he was wrong about what they would be. The assumptions of Anglo-Saxon superiority he shared with his countrymen caused him to fear that absorption of Mexico's alien people would sully the purity of America's population and the strength of its institutions. In fact, it was the cancer of slavery within U.S. society that, when linked with disposition of the territory taken from Mexico, poisoned the body politic, provoking the irrepressible crisis that eventually sundered the Union.

Indeed, throughout the 1840s and 1850s, slavery and expansion marched hand in hand. Certain of the superiority of their institutions and greatness of their nation, a bumptious people continued to push out against the weak restraints that bound them. Through negotiation and conquest, they more than doubled the nation's territory by 1848. By the time of the Mexican-American War, however, the future of the South's "peculiar institution" had provoked passionate controversy. Even before the war, slavery had become for southerners the driving force behind expansionism and for abolitionists the reason to oppose acquisition of new territory. The conquest of vast new lands in the war with Mexico brought to the fore the pressing question of whether new slave states would be created, the issue that would tear the Union apart. Fears of the further extension of slavery and absorption of alien races, in turn, stymied southern efforts in the 1850s to acquire additional territory in the Caribbean and Central America. In foreign policy, as in domestic affairs, slavery dominated the politics of the antebellum era.

---

1. William H. Gilman et al., *Journals of Ralph Waldo Emerson* (14 vols., Cambridge, Mass., 1960–78), 9:430–31.

I

The mid-nineteenth century marked a transitional stage between the post-Napoleonic international system and the disequilibrium leading to World War I. The European great powers sustained a general peace interrupted only by limited, regional wars. England solidified its position as hegemonic power. The Royal Navy controlled the seas; by 1860, Britain produced 20 percent of the world's manufactures and dominated global finance. The industrial revolution generated drastic economic changes that would produce profound political and social dislocations. Revolutions in France and Central Europe in 1848 shook the established order momentarily and threatened general war. The two nations that prevented war at this point, Britain and Russia, fought with each other in 1854. The Crimean War, in turn, stirred "revisionist" ambitions across Europe and heightened British isolationism, helping to initiate in the 1850s a period of mounting instability. While avoiding a major war, the European powers used the "firepower gap" created by new technology to further encroach on the non-Western world. The opening of China and Japan to Western influence, in particular, had enormous long-range implications for world politics.[2]

America's global position changed significantly. The United States took steps toward becoming a Pacific power, asserting its interests in Hawaii, participating in the quasi-colonial system the European powers imposed on China, and taking the lead in opening Japan. Its relations with Europe were more important and more complex. Economically, the United States was an integral part of the Atlantic trading community. Politically, it remained a distant and apparently disinterested observer of European internal politics and external maneuvering. Americans took European interest in the Western Hemisphere most seriously. Still nominally committed to containing U.S. expansion, Britain and France dabbled in Texas and California. The British quietly expanded in Central America. In fact, the powers were preoccupied with internal problems and continental rivalries, and European ambitions in the Western Hemisphere were receding. Nevertheless, U.S. politicians used the European threat to generate support for expansion. Increasingly paranoid slaveholders saw the sinister force of abolitionism behind the appearance of every British gunboat and the machinations of every British diplomat.

The 1840s and 1850s brought headlong growth for the United States. As a result of a continued high birth rate and the massive immigration of

---

2. Paul Kennedy, *The Rise and Fall of the Great Powers* (New York, 1987), 150; Stephen Pelz, "Changing International Systems, the World Balance of Power, and the United States, 1776–1976," *Diplomatic History* 12 (Winter 1988), 57–58.

Germans and Irish Catholics, the population nearly doubled again, reaching 31.5 million by 1860. Eight new states were admitted, bringing the total to thirty-three. Described with wonderment by foreign visitors as a "people in motion," Americans began spilling out into Texas and Oregon even before the region between the Mississippi River and Rocky Mountains was settled. Technology helped bind this vast territory together. By 1840, the United States had twice as much railroad track as all of Europe. Soon, there was talk of a transcontinental railroad. The invention of the telegraph and the rise of the penny press provided means to disseminate more information faster to a larger reading public, making it possible, in the words of publisher James Gordon Bennett, "to blend into one homogeneous mass...the whole population of the Republic." The antebellum era was the age of U.S. maritime greatness. Sleek clipper ships still ruled the seas, but in 1840 steamboat service was initiated to England, cutting the trip to ten days and quickening the pace of diplomacy.[3]

The economy grew exponentially after the Panic of 1837. Freed from dependence on Britain through development of a home market, America was no longer a colonial economy. In agriculture, cotton was still king, but western farmers with the aid of new technology launched a second agricultural revolution, challenging Russia as the world's leading producer of food. Mining and manufacturing became vital segments of an increasingly diversified economy. The United States was self-sufficient in most areas, but exports could make the difference between prosperity and recession; U.S. exports, mostly cotton, swelled from an average of $70 million during 1815–20 to $249 million in the decade before the Civil War.[4]

American approaches to the world appeared contradictory. On the one hand, technology was shrinking the globe. The United States was becoming part of the broader world community. Major metropolitan newspapers assigned correspondents to London and Paris. The government dispatched expeditions to explore Antarctica and the Pacific, the interior of Africa and South America, and the exotic Middle East. Curious readers devoured their reports. On their own initiative, merchants and missionaries in growing numbers went forth to spread the gospel of Americanism. Each group looked beyond its immediate objectives to the larger goal of uplifting other peoples. "One should not forget," *New York Tribune*

3. William Earl Weeks, *Building the Continental Empire: American Expansion from the Revolution to the Civil War* (Chicago, 1996), 85.
4. Kinley J. Brauer, "The United States and British Imperial Expansion, 1815–1860," *Diplomatic History* 12 (Winter 1988), 36–37.

London correspondent Karl Marx wrote, "that America is the youngest and most vigorous exponent of Western Civilization."[5]

Americans observed the outside world with great fascination. They longed "to see distant lands," observed writer James Fenimore Cooper, to view the "peculiarities of nations" and the differences "between strangers and ourselves."[6] Some promoted development in other countries. The father of artist James McNeill Whistler oversaw the building of a railroad between Moscow and St. Petersburg. Growing numbers traveled abroad, many to Europe. These tourists carried their patriotism with them and found in the perceived inferiority of other nations confirmation of their own greatness. Those dissatisfied with America should tour the Old World, a Tennessean wrote, and they would "return home with national ideas, national love and national fidelity."[7]

On the other hand, U.S. policymakers and diplomats, once an experienced and cosmopolitan lot, were increasingly parochial, sometimes amateurish—and often proud of it. The presidential domination of foreign policy institutionalized by Jackson persisted under Polk. Of the chief executives who served in these years, only James Buchanan had diplomatic experience. Reflecting an emerging world role, the secretary of state had a staff of forty-three people by the 1850s; twenty-seven diplomats and eighty-eight consuls were posted abroad. Reforms limited consular appointments to U.S. citizens and restricted their ability to engage in private business.[8] The diplomatic corps was composed more and more of politicians and merchants. Some served with distinction; others made Anthony Butler look good.

Americans wore their republicanism on their sleeves and even enshrined it in protocol. Polk displayed "American arrogance" toward diplomats who addressed him in a language other than English and dismissed as "ridiculous" the repeated ceremonial visits of the Russian minister to announce such trivia as the marriage of the tsar's son.[9] Secretary of State William Marcy's "dress circular" of 1853 went well beyond Jackson's republicanism by requiring diplomats to appear in court in plain black evening clothes, the "simple dress of an American citizen." Parisians scornfully

5. Quoted in Larry Gara, *The Presidency of Franklin Pierce* (Lawrence, Kans., 1991), 129.
6. Quoted in Robert W. Johannsen, *To the Halls of the Montezumas: The Mexican War in the American Imagination* (New York, 1987), 144–45.
7. Quoted in Edwin T. Greninger, "Tennesseans Abroad in 1851–1852," *Tennessee Historical Quarterly* 49 (Summer 1990), 81–82. See also Reginald C. Stuart, *United States Expansionism and British North America* (Chapel Hill, N.C., 1988), 148–66.
8. Gara, *Pierce*, 57–59.
9. Paul H. Bergeron, *The Presidency of James K. Polk* (Lawrence, Kans., 1987), 218–19.

dubbed the U.S. minister "the Black Crow." Americans applauded. The person who represented his nation abroad should "look like an American, talk like an American, and be an American example," the *New York Post* proclaimed.[10] New World ways some times rubbed off on Old World diplomats. Russian Eduard Stoeckl married an American and during his time in Washington served in a fire company where, in his words, he "run wid de lantern."[11]

II

The catchphrase "Manifest Destiny" summed up the expansionist thrust of the pre–Civil War era. Coined in 1845 by the Democratic Party journalist John L. O'Sullivan to justify annexation of Texas, Oregon, and California, the phrase meant, simply defined, that God had willed the expansion of the United States to the Pacific Ocean—or beyond. The concept expressed the exuberant nationalism and brash arrogance of the era. Divine sanction, in the eyes of many Americans, gave them a superior claim to any rival and lent an air of inevitability to their expansion. Manifest Destiny pulled together into a potent ideology notions dating to the origins of the republic with implications extending beyond the continent: that the American people and their institutions were uniquely virtuous, thus imposing on them a God-given mission to remake the world in their own image.[12]

Many Americans have accepted the rhetoric of Manifest Destiny at face value, seeing their nation's continental expansion as inevitable and altruistic, a result of the irresistible force generated by a virtuous people. Once viewed as a great national movement, an expression of American optimism and idealism, and the driving force behind expansion in the 1840s, Manifest Destiny's meaning and significance have been considerably qualified in recent years.[13]

10. Quoted in Ralph Davis Jr., "Diplomatic Plumage: American Court Dress in the Early National Period," *American Quarterly* 20, no. 2 (1968), 175–79; Gara, *Pierce*, 58–59.

11. Norman E. Saul, *Distant Friends: The United States and Russia, 1763–1867* (Lawrence, Kans., 1991), 253.

12. Weeks, *Continental Empire*, 59–62.

13. The classic study, an intellectual history, remains Albert K. Weinberg, *Manifest Destiny: A Study of Nationalist Expansionism in American History* (Baltimore, Md., 1935). Other major works include Frederick Merk, *Manifest Destiny and Mission in American History: A Reinterpretation* (New York, 1966), Thomas R.Hietala,*Manifest Design: Anxious Aggrandizement in Jacksonian America* (Ithaca, N.Y., 1985), and Anders Stephanson, *Manifest Destiny—American Expansion and the Empire of Right* (New York, 1995).

For some Americans, no doubt, the rhetoric expressed idealistic senti-ments. The acquisition of new lands and the admission of new peoples to the Union extended the blessings of liberty. Territorial expansion pro-vided a haven for those fleeing oppression in other lands. Some Americans even believed that their nation had an obligation to uplift and regenerate "backward" peoples like Mexicans.

More often than not, Manifest Destiny covered and attempted to legit-imate selfish motives. Southerners sought new land to perpetuate an eco-nomic and social system based on cotton and slavery and new slave states to preserve their power in Congress. People from all sections interested in the export trade coveted the magnificent ports of the Oregon country and California as jumping-off points to capture the rich commerce of East Asia. Restless, land-hungry westerners sought territory for its own sake. Some Americans argued that if the United States did not take Texas and California, the British and French would. At least, they might try to sus-tain independent republics that could threaten the security of the United States.

Manifest Destiny was also heavily tinged with racism. At the time of the Revolution and for years after, some Americans had sincerely be-lieved that they could teach other peoples to share in the blessings of republicanism. The nation's remarkable success increasingly turned optimism into arrogance, however, and repeated clashes with Indians and Mexicans created a need to justify the exploitation of weaker peo-ple. "Scientific" theories of superior and inferior races thus emerged in the nineteenth century to rationalize U.S. expansion. Inferior races did not use the land properly and impeded progress, it was argued. They must give way before superior races, some, like African Americans, doomed to perpetual subservience, others, like Indians, to assimilation or extinction.[14]

Manifest Destiny was a sectional rather than national phenomenon, its support strongest in the Northeast and Northwest and weakest in the South, which supported only the annexation of Texas. It was also highly partisan. A second American party system emerged in the 1840s with the rise of two distinct political entities, roughly equal in strength, that set the agenda for national politics and took well-defined positions on major issues. The lineal descendants of Jefferson's Republicans, the Democrats rallied around the policies of the charismatic hero Andrew Jackson. The Whigs, a direct offshoot of the National Republicans along with some disaf-fected Democrats, formed in opposition to what its followers saw as the

14. Reginald Horsman, *Race and Manifest Destiny* (Cambridge, Mass., 1981), 301.

dangerous consolidation of executive power by "King Andrew I." Henry Clay was the leading national figure.[15]

The two parties differed sharply on the crucial issue of expansion. Looking backward to an idyllic agricultural society, the Democrats, like Jefferson, fervently believed that preservation of traditional republican values depended on commercial and territorial expansion. The Panic of 1837 and a growing surplus in agricultural production aroused their anxieties. Deeply alarmed by the rise of industrialization, urbanization, and class conflict in the Northeast, the very evils Jefferson had warned about, they saw expansion as a solution to the problems of modernization. The availability of new land in the West and acquisition of new markets for farm products would preserve the essentially agricultural economy upon which republicanism depended. An expanding frontier would protect Americans against poverty, concentration of population, exhaustion of the land, and the wage slavery of industrial capitalism. A sprawling national domain would preserve liberty rather than threaten it. Fortuitously, new technology like the railroad and telegraph that annihilated distance would permit administration of a vast empire. Expansion was fundamental to the American character, the Democrats insisted. The very process of the westward movement produced those special qualities that made Americans exceptional.[16]

More cautious and conservative, Whigs harbored deep fears of uncontrolled expansion. Change must be orderly, they insisted; the existing Union must be consolidated before the nation acquired more territory. The more rapidly and extensively the Union grew, the more difficult it would be to govern and the more it would be imperiled. The East might be left desolate and depopulated and sectional tensions increased. Whigs welcomed industrialism. In contrast to the Democrats, who promoted an activist role for government in external matters, they believed government's major task was to promote economic growth and disperse prosperity and capital in a way that would avert internal conflict, improve the lot of the individual, and enrich society. Government should promote the interests of the entire nation to ensure harmony and balance, ease sectional and class tensions, and promote peace. Like the Democrats, the

15. Richard P. McCormick, *The Second American Party System* (Chapel Hill, N.C., 1966); Ronald P. Formisano, *The Birth of Mass Political Parties, Michigan, 1827–1861* (Princeton, N.J., 1971); Michael F. Holt, *Rise and Fall of the American Whig Party: Jacksonian Politics and the Onset of the American Civil War* (New York, 1999).
16. Michael A. Morrison, "Westward the Curse of Empire: Texas Annexation and the American Whig Party," *Journal of the Early Republic* 10 (Summer 1990), 226–29; Hietala, *Manifest Design*, 95–131, 196.

Whigs talked of extending freedom, but their approach was passive rather than active. "The eyes of the world are upon us," Edward Everett asserted, "and our example will probably be decisive of the cause of human liberty."[17]

The increasingly inflammatory debate over slavery heightened conflict over expansion. As early as the 1830s, abolitionists began to attack slaveholder domination of the political system, creating one of the first pressure groups to influence U.S. foreign policy. The still volatile issue of Haiti became their cause célèbre. Abolitionists such as Lydia Maria Child and their frequent supporter John Quincy Adams condemned those who opposed recognition of the black republic because a "colored ambassador would be so disagreeable to our prejudice." They pleaded for recognition as a matter of principle and for trade. They pushed for opening of the British market for corn and wheat to spur prosperity in the Northwest, breaking the stranglehold of the "slavocracy" on the national government. Urging the United States to join Britain in an international effort to police the slave trade and abolish slavery, they passionately opposed the acquisition of new slave states.[18]

Increasingly paranoid slaveholders, on the other side, warned that a vast abolitionist conspiracy threatened their peculiar institution and indeed the nation. Haiti also had huge symbolic importance for them, the bloodshed, political chaos, and economic distress there portending the inevitable results of emancipation elsewhere. They saw abolitionism as an international movement centered in London whose philanthropic pretensions covered sinister imperialist designs. By abolishing slavery, the British could undercut southern production of staples, destroy the U.S. economy, and dominate world commerce and manufacturing. They denounced British high-handedness in policing the slave trade. They mongered among themselves morbid rumors of nefarious British plots to foment revolution among slaves in Cuba, incite Mexicans and Indians against the United States, and invade the South with armies of free blacks. They conjured graphic images of entire white populations being murdered except for the young and beautiful women reserved for "African lust." They condemned the federal government for not defending their

17. Morrison, "Westward," 230–33; Norma Lois Peterson, *The Presidencies of William Henry Harrison and John Tyler* (Lawrence, Kans., 1989), 138. See also Major Wilson, *Space, Time, and Freedom: The Quest for Nationality and the Irrepressible Conflict* (Westport, Conn., 1974).

18. Edward P. Crapol, "The Foreign Policy of Anti-slavery, 1833–1846," in Lloyd C. Gardner, ed., *Redefining the Past: Essays in Diplomatic History in Honor of William Appleman Williams* (Corvallis, Ore., 1986), 88–102.

rights from "foreign wrongs." They spoke openly of taking up the burden of defending slavery and even of secession. They ardently promoted the addition of new slave states. Pandering to the racial fears of northern Democrats, they suggested that extension of slavery into areas like Texas would draw the black population southward, even into Central America, ending the institution by natural processes and sparing the northern states and Upper South concentrations of free blacks.[19]

American expansionism in the 1840s was neither providential nor innocent. It resulted from design, rather than destiny, a carefully calculated effort by purposeful Democratic leaders to attain specific objectives that served mainly U.S. interests. The rhetoric of Manifest Destiny was nationalistic, idealistic, and self-confident, but it covered deep and sometimes morbid fears for America's security against internal decay and external danger. Expansionism showed scant regard for the "inferior" peoples who stood in the way. When combined with the volatile issue of slavery, it fueled increasingly bitter sectional and partisan conflict.[20]

III

Manifest Destiny had limits, most notably along the northern border with British Canada. Anglophobia and respect for Britain coexisted uneasily during the antebellum years. Americans still viewed the former mother country as the major threat to their security and prosperity and resented its refusal to pay them proper respect. At election time, U.S. politicians habitually twisted the lion's tail to whip up popular support. Upper-class Americans, on the other hand, admired British accomplishments and institutions. Responsible citizens understood the importance of economic ties between the two nations. A healthy respect for British power and a growing sense of Anglo-Saxon unity and common purpose—their "peculiar and sacred relations to the cause of civilization and freedom," O'Sullivan called it—produced very different attitudes and approaches toward Britain and Mexico. Americans continued to regard Canada as a base from which Britain could strike the United States, but they increasingly doubted it would be used. They also came to accept the presence of their northern neighbor and evinced a willingness to live in peace with it.

19. Hietala, *Manifest Design*, 30–32. For a sampling of slaveholder fear mongering, see Edmund P. Gaines to Calhoun, May 5, 1844, in Clyde Wilson, ed., *The Papers of John C. Calhoun*, vol. 18 (Columbia, S.C., 1989), 440–44, Calhoun to Ana Maria Calhoun Clemson, May 16, 1844, ibid., 469, Calhoun to William King, August 12, 1844, ibid., vol. 19 (Columbia, S.C., 1990), 574–75, Robert M. Harrison to Calhoun, August 12, 1844, ibid., 634–36, and Wilson introduction to ibid., xiii–xviii.
20. Hietala, *Manifest Design*, passim.

Even the zealot O'Sullivan conceded that Manifest Destiny stopped at the Canadian border. He viewed Canadians as possible junior partners in the process of Manifest Destiny but did not press for annexation when the opportunity presented itself, envisioning a peaceful evolution toward a possible merger at some unspecified future time.[21]

Rebellions in Canada in 1837–38 raised the threat of a third Anglo-American war, but they evoked from most Americans a generally restrained response. At the outset, to be sure, some saw the Canadian uprisings, along with events in Texas, as part of the onward march of republicanism. Along the border, some Americans offered the rebels sanctuary and support. Incidents such as the burning of the American ship *Caroline* by Canadian soldiers on U.S. territory in December 1837 inflamed tensions. As it became clear that the rebellions were something less than republican in origin and intent, tempers cooled. Borderland communities where legal and illegal trade flourished feared the potential costs of war. President Martin Van Buren declared U.S. neutrality and after the *Caroline* incident dispatched War of 1812 hero Gen. Winfield Scott to enforce it. Traveling the border country by sled in frigid temperatures, often alone, Scott zealously executed his orders, expressing outrage at the destruction of the *Caroline* and promising to defend U.S. territory from British attack but warning his countrymen against provocative actions. On one occasion, he admonished hotheads that "except it be over my body, you shall *not* pass this line." Another time, as a preemptive measure, he bought out from under rebel supporters a ship he suspected was to be used for hostile activities. Scott's intervention helped ease tensions along the border. In terms of Manifest Destiny, Americans continued to believe that Canadians would opt for republicanism, but they respected the principle of self-determination rather than seeking to impose their views by force.[22]

Conflict over the long-disputed boundary between Maine and New Brunswick also produced Anglo-American hostility — and restraint. Local interests on both sides posed insuperable obstacles to settlement. For years, Maine had frustrated federal efforts to negotiate. Washington did nothing when the state government or its citizens defied federal law or international agreements. When Canadian lumberjacks cut timber in the

21. Stuart, *United States Expansionism*, 85–99.
22. Ibid., 126–47; Howard Jones and Donald A. Rakestraw, *Prologue to Manifest Destiny: Anglo-American Relations in the 1840s* (Wilmington, Del., 1997), 21–41; Scott Kaufman and John A. Soares Jr., "'Sagacious Beyond Praise'? Winfield Scott and Anglo-American-Canadian Border Diplomacy, 1837–1860," *Diplomatic History* 30 (January 2006), 58–66.

disputed Aroostook River valley in late 1838, tempers flared, sparking threats of war. The tireless and peripatetic Scott hastened to Maine to re-assure its citizens and encourage local officials to compromise. As with the Canadian rebellions, cooler heads prevailed. The so-called Aroostook War amounted to little more than a barroom brawl, the major casualties bloody noses and broken arms. But territorial dispute continued to threaten the peace.[23]

Conflict over the slave trade added a more volatile dimension to Anglo-American tension. In the 1830s, Britain launched an all-out crusade against that brutal and nefarious traffic in human beings. The United States outlawed the international slave trade in 1808 but, because of south-ern resistance, did little to stop it. Alone among nations, it refused to par-ticipate in multilateral efforts. Slave traders thus used the U.S. flag to cover their activities. The War of 1812 still fresh in their minds and highly sensitive to affronts to their honor, Americans South *and* North loudly protested when British ships began stopping and searching vessels flying the Stars and Stripes. An incident in November 1841 raised a simmering dispute to the level of crisis. Led by a cook named Madison Washington, slaves aboard the *Creole* en route from Virginia to New Orleans mutinied, took over the ship, killed a slave trader, and sailed to the Bahamas. Under pressure from the local population, British authorities released all 135 of the slaves because they landed on free territory. Furious with British inter-ference with the domestic slave trade and more than ever convinced of a sinister plot to destroy slavery in the United States, southerners demanded restoration of their property and reparations. But the United States had no extradition treaty with Britain and could do nothing to back its citizens' claims.[24]

The Webster-Ashburton Treaty of 1842 solved several burning issues and confirmed the limits of Manifest Destiny. By this time, both sides sought to ease tensions. An avowed Anglophile, Secretary of State Daniel Webster viewed commerce with England as essential to U.S. prosperity. The new British government of Sir Robert Peel was friendly toward the United States and sought respite from tension to pursue domestic reform and address more urgent European problems. By sending a special mis-sion to the United States, Peel struck a responsive chord among insecure Americans — "an unusual piece of condescension" for "haughty" England, New Yorker Philip Hone conceded.[25] The appointment of Alexander

23. Jones and Rakestraw, *Prologue*, 8–11, Kaufman and Soares, "Scott," 66–71.
24. Jones and Rakestraw, *Prologue*, 81–89.
25. Quoted in ibid., 105.

Baring, Lord Ashburton, to carry out the mission confirmed London's good intentions. Head of one of the world's leading banking houses, Ashburton was married to an American, owned land in Maine, and had extensive investments in the United States. He believed that good relations were essential to the "moral improvement and the progressive civilization of the world." Ashburton steeled himself for the rigors of life in the "colonies" by bringing with him three secretaries, five servants, and three horses and a carriage. He and Webster entertained lavishly. Old friends, they agreed to dispense with the usual conventions of diplomacy and work informally. Webster even invited representatives of Maine and Massachusetts to join the discussions, causing Ashburton to marvel how "this Mass of ungovernable and unmanageable anarchy" functioned as well as it did.[26]

The novice diplomats used unconventional methods to resolve major differences. On the most difficult issue, the Maine–New Brunswick boundary, they worked out a compromise that satisfied hotheads on neither side and then used devious means to sell it. Each conveniently employed different maps to prove to skeptical constituents their side had got the better of the deal—or at least avoided losing more. Webster had more difficulty negotiating with Maine than with his British counterpart. He used $12,000 from a secret presidential slush fund to propagandize his fellow New Englanders to accept the treaty. This knot untied, the two men with relative ease set a boundary between Lake Superior and the Lake of the Woods. They defused the still-sensitive *Caroline* issue and agreed on an extradition treaty to help deal with matters like the *Creole*. Resolution of differences on the slave trade was most difficult. Eventually, the treaty provided for a joint squadron, but the United States, predictably, did not uphold the arrangement. The Webster-Ashburton Treaty testified to Anglo-American good sense when that quality seemed in short supply. It confirmed U.S. acceptance of the sharing of North America with British Canadians. It resolved numerous problems that might have provoked war and set the two nations on a course toward eventual rapprochement. The threat of war eased in the Northeast, the United States could turn its attention to the Pacific Northwest and the Southwest.[27]

26. Ibid., 114.
27. Charles S. Campbell, *From Revolution to Rapprochement: The United States and Great Britain, 1783–1900* (New York, 1974), 62; Stuart, *United States Expansionism*, 101–2; Jones and Rakestraw, *Prologue*, 149. The standard account is Howard Jones, *To the Webster-Ashburton Treaty: A Study in Anglo-American Relations, 1783–1843* (Chapel Hill, N.C., 1977). See also Francis M. Carroll, *A Good and Wise Measure; The Search for the Canadian-American Boundary, 1783–1842* (Toronto, 2001).

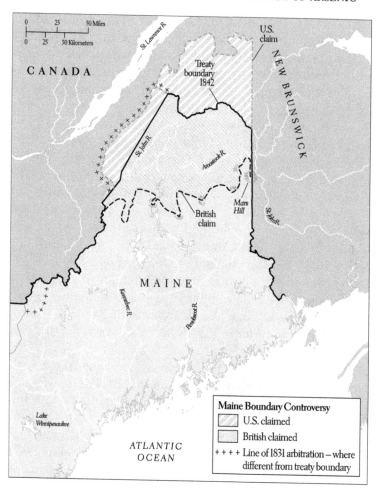

Oregon was a major exception to the budding Anglo-American accord. The joint occupation had outlived its usefulness by the mid-1840s. The Pacific Northwest became the focal point of a dangerous conflict sparked largely by bungling diplomacy and exacerbated by domestic politics in both countries and especially by the intrusion of national honor. The Oregon crisis brought out old suspicions and hatreds, nearly provoking an unnecessary and costly war.

In the 1840s, a long-dormant conflict in the Pacific Northwest sprang to life. British interests remained essentially commercial and quickened with the opening of China through the 1842 Treaty of Nanking. The ports of Oregon and Mexican California were perfectly situated for exploiting the commerce of East Asia, and merchants and sea captains pressed the government to take possession. Americans too saw links with the fabled commerce of the Orient, but their major interest in Oregon had shifted to settlement. Missionaries first went there to proselytize the Indians but established the permanent settlements that provided the basis for U.S. occupation. Driven from their homes by the depression of 1837 and enticed west by tales of lush farm lands, thousands of restless Americans followed in making the rugged, costly, and hazardous two-thousand-mile, six-month trek from St. Louis across the Oregon Trail. The return of the Great United States Exploring Expedition in June 1842 after an eighty-seven-thousand-mile voyage around the world stirred the American imagination and drew special attention to Oregon, "a storehouse of wealth in its forests, furs and fisheries," a veritable Eden on the Pacific.[28] Oregon "fever" became an epidemic. By 1845, some five thousand Americans lived in the region and established a government to which even the once mighty Hudson's Bay Company paid taxes. They talked of admission to the Union, a direct challenge to the 1827 agreement with Britain. The "same causes which impelled our population . . . to the valley of the Mississippi, will impel them onward with accumulating force . . . into the valley of the Columbia," Secretary of State John C. Calhoun informed the British minister in 1844. The "whole region . . . is destined to be peopled by us."[29]

Along with Texas, Oregon became a volatile issue in the hotly contested presidential campaign of 1844. Western expansionists advanced outrageous claims all the way to 54° 40′, the line negotiated with Russia in 1824 but far beyond the point ever contested with Britain. The bombastic Senator Thomas Hart Benton of Missouri even threatened war, proclaiming that "30–40,000 rifles are our best negotiators." Expansionist Democrats tried to link Texas with Oregon, trading southern votes for Oregon with western votes for Texas. The Democratic platform thus affirmed a "clear and unquestionable" claim to all of Oregon. The dark horse candidate, ardent expansionist James K. Polk of Tennessee, campaigned on the dubious slogan of the "re-annexation of Texas" and "reoccupation of Oregon."[30]

A crisis erupted within months after Polk took office. The forty-nine-year-old Tennessean was short, thin, and somewhat drab in appearance with a sad look, deep piercing eyes, and a sour disposition. Vain and driven, he set lofty expansionist goals for his administration, and by pledging not to seek reelection he placed self-imposed limits on his ability to

28. Peterson, *Harrison and Tyler*, 136–37.
29. Calhoun to Pakenham, September 3, 1844, in Wilson, *Calhoun Papers* 19:705.
30. The "reannexation" of Texas suggested, wrongly, that Texas had once belonged to the United States but had been carelessly squandered in the 1819 treaty with Spain.

achieve them. He was introverted, humorless, and a workaholic. His shrewdness and ability to size up friends and rivals had served him well in the rough-and-tumble of backcountry politics, and he had an especially keen eye for detail. But he could be cold and aloof. Parochial and highly nationalistic, he was impatient with the niceties of diplomacy and lacked understanding of and sensitivity to other nations and peoples.[31]

Polk's initial efforts to strike a deal provoked a crisis. Despite his menacing rhetoric, he realized that the United States had never claimed beyond the 49th parallel. Thus while continuing publicly to claim all of Oregon, he professed himself bound by the acts of his predecessors. He privately offered a "generous" settlement at the 49th parallel with free ports on the southern tip of Vancouver Island. An experienced and skillful diplomat, British minister Richard Pakenham might have overlooked Polk's posturing, but he too let nationalist pride interfere with diplomacy. Infuriated by Polk's pretensions of generosity, he refused to refer the proposal to London. The Foreign Office subsequently disapproved Pakenham's action, but the damage was done. Stung by the rejection of proposals he believed generous, Polk was probably relieved that Pakenham had taken him off the hook. He defiantly withdrew the "compromise," rejected British proposals for arbitration, reasserted claims to all of Oregon, and asked Congress to abrogate the joint occupation provision of the 1827 treaty. The "only way to treat John Bull is to look him straight in the eye," the tough-talking Tennessean later informed a delegation of congressmen.[32]

Polk's ill-conceived effort to stare down the world's greatest power nearly backfired. In the United States, at least momentarily, the breakdown of diplomacy left the field to the hotheads. "54-40 or fight," they shouted, and O'Sullivan coined the phrase that marked an era, proclaiming that the U.S. title to Oregon was "by the right of our manifest destiny to overspread and to possess the whole of the continent which Providence has given us for the development of the great experiment of Liberty." Conveniently forgetting his earlier willingness to compromise, Massachusetts congressman John Quincy Adams now found sanction in the Book of Genesis for possession of all of Oregon.[33]

31. Bergeron, *Polk*, 45; Hietala, *Manifest Design*, 249.
32. Jones and Rakestraw, *Prologue*, 235. Daniel Walker Howe, *What Hath God Wrought: The Transformation of America, 1815–1845* (New York, 2007), 715–22, argues that Polk took a hard line on Oregon to gain northern Democrats' support for a tough stance with Mexico.
33. Ibid., 240.

Its future imperiled by domestic disputes over trade policy, the Peel government wanted to settle the Oregon issue, but not at the price of national honor. American pretensions aroused fury in London. Foreign Minister Lord Aberdeen retorted in Polk's own phrase that British rights to Oregon were "clear and unquestionable." Peel proclaimed that "we are resolved—and we are prepared—to maintain them."[34] Responding directly to Adams, the *Times* of London sneered that a "democracy intoxicated with what it mistakes for religion is the most formidable apparition which can startle the world."[35] Hotheads pressed for war. The army and navy prepared for action. Some zealots welcomed war with the United States as a heaven-sent opportunity to eliminate slavery. Whigs stood poised to exploit any sign of Tory weakness. In early 1846, the government emphasized that its patience was wearing thin. Revelation of plans to send as many as thirty warships to Canada underscored the warning.

The two nations steadied themselves in mid-1846 just as they teetered on the brink of war. Polk perceived that his bluster had angered rather than intimidated the British and that more of the same might lead to war. Congressional debates in early 1846 made clear that despite the political bombast a war for *all* of Oregon would not have broad support. Also on the verge of war with Mexico, the United States was not prepared to fight one enemy, much less two. Polk thus set out to ease the crisis he had helped to provoke by putting forth terms he might have offered earlier. Shortly after Congress passed the resolution giving notice of abrogation of the 1827 treaty, he quietly informed London of his willingness to compromise. Reports from Oregon that American settlers were firmly entrenched and that Britain should cut its losses reinforced Peel's eagerness for a settlement. London thus responded with terms nearly identical to those earlier outlined by the United States. Ever cautious, Polk took the extraordinary step of securing Senate approval before proceeding. Already at war with Mexico, the United States approved the treaty as drafted in London, a mere nine days passing between its delivery to the State Department and ratification. "Now we can thrash Mexico into decency at our leisure," the *New York Herald* exclaimed.[36]

The Oregon settlement accorded reasonably well with the specific interests of each signatory. It extended the boundary along the 49th parallel from the Rockies to the coast, leaving Vancouver Island in British

34. Ibid, 206.
35. Quoted in David M. Pletcher, *The Diplomacy of Annexation: Texas, Oregon, and the Mexican War* (Columbia, Mo., 1973), 339.
36. Ibid., 414.

hands and Juan de Fuca Strait open to both countries. Against Polk's wishes, it also permitted the Hudson's Bay Company to navigate the Columbia River. The United States had no settlements north of the 49th parallel and had never claimed that area before the 1840s. Despite the sometimes heated rhetoric, few Americans thought all of Oregon worth a war. Britain had long sought a boundary at the Columbia River, but the fur trade in the disputed area was virtually exhausted. Possession of Vancouver Island and access to Juan de Fuca Strait adequately met its maritime needs.

In each nation, other crises put a premium on settlement. The war with Mexico and Britain's refusal to interfere there made peace both urgent and expedient for the United States. Strained relations with France, problems in Ireland, and an impending political crisis at home made a settlement with the United States desirable, if not absolutely essential, for the British. Both sides recognized the importance of commercial ties and a common culture and heritage. In the United States, respect for British power and a reluctance on racial grounds to fight with Anglo-Saxon brethren made war unthinkable. Most important, both sides realized the foolishness of war. Often praised for his diplomacy, Polk deserves credit mainly for the good sense to extricate the nation from a crisis he had helped provoke.[37]

The Oregon treaty freed the United States to turn its attention southward. It also provided the much-coveted outlet on the Pacific as well as clear title to a rich expanse of territory including all of the future states of Washington, Oregon, Idaho, and parts of Montana and Wyoming. Along with the Webster-Ashburton Treaty, it eased a conflict that had been a fact of life since the Revolution. Americans generally agreed that their "Manifest Destiny" did not include Canada. Having contained U.S. expansion in the North, Britain increasingly learned to live with the upstart republic. Conflict would continue, but only during the American Civil War would it assume dangerous proportions. Increasingly, the two nations would find that more united than divided them. Despite the rhetoric of Manifest Destiny, the United States and Britain had reached an agreement on the sharing of North America.[38]

IV

"No instance of aggrandizement or lust for territory has stained our annals," O'Sullivan boasted in 1844, expressing one of the nation's most

37. Ibid., 402–17; Howe, *What Hath God Wrought*, 718–22.
38. Stuart, *United States Expansionism*, 104–5.

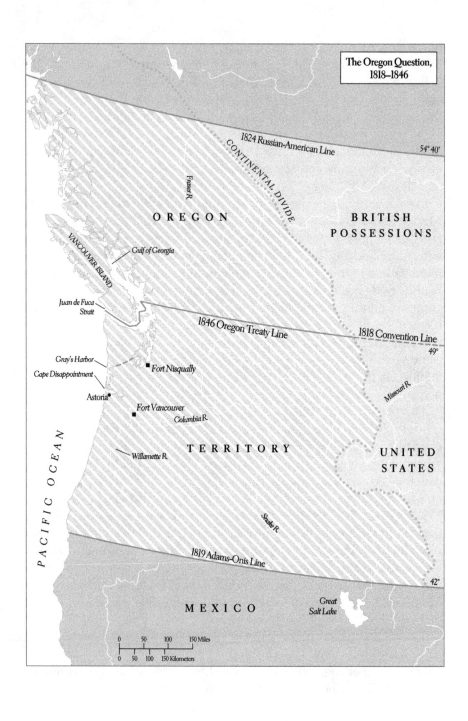

The Oregon Question,
1818–1846

1824 Russian-American Line

CONTINENTAL DIVIDE

54° 40'

Fraser R.

OREGON

BRITISH
POSSESSIONS

Gulf of Georgia

VANCOUVER ISLAND

Juan de Fuca
Strait

1846 Oregon Treaty Line

1818 Convention Line

49°

Gray's Harbor

Cape Disappointment

Fort Nisqually

Astoria

Missouri R.

Fort Vancouver

Columbia R.

Willamette R.

TERRITORY

UNITED
STATES

PACIFIC OCEAN

Snake R.

1819 Adams-Onis Line

42°

MEXICO

Great
Salt Lake

0   50   100   150 Miles

0   50   100   150 Kilometers

cherished and durable myths.[39] Dubious when it was written, O'Sullivan's affirmation soon proved completely wrong. The Mexican-American conflict of 1846–48 was in large part a war of lust and aggrandizement. The United States had long coveted Texas. In the 1840s, California and New Mexico also became objects of its desire. With characteristic single-mindedness, Polk set his sights on all of them. He employed the same bullying approach used with the British, this time without backing off, provoking a war that would have momentous consequences for both nations.

The United States government did not orchestrate a clever conspiracy to steal Texas, as Mexicans charged, but the result was the same. Lured to the "New El Dorado" by the promise of cheap cotton land, thirty-five thousand Americans with five thousand slaves had spilled into Texas by 1835. Alarmed by an immigration it once welcomed, the newly independent government of Mexico sought to impose its authority over the newcomers and abolish slavery. To defend their rights—and slaves—the Texans took up arms. After a crushing defeat at the Alamo, the subject of much patriotic folklore, they won a decisive victory at San Jacinto in April 1836.

An independent Texas presented enticing opportunities and vexing problems. Americans had taken a keen interest in the revolution. Despite nominal neutrality—and in marked contrast to the strict enforcement of neutrality laws along the Canadian border—they assisted the rebels with money, arms, and volunteers. Many Americans and Texans assumed that the "sister republic" would join the United States. From the outset, however, Texas got entangled with the explosive issue of slavery. Politicians handled it gingerly. Jackson refused to recognize the new nation until his successor, Van Buren, was safely elected. Eager for reelection, Van Buren warily turned aside Texas proposals for annexation.

By 1844, Texas had become the focal point of rumors, plots and counterplots, diplomatic intrigue, and bitter political conflict. Many Texans favored annexation, others preferred independence, some straddled the fence. Although unwilling to risk war with the United States, Britain and France sought an independent Texas and urged Mexico to recognize the new nation to keep it out of U.S. hands. Alarmist southerners fed each other's fears with lurid tales of sinister British schemes to abolish slavery in Texas, incite a slave revolt in Cuba, and strike a "fatal blow" against slavery in the United States, provoking a race war "of the most deadly and desolating character." In the eyes of some southerners, Britain's real aim was to throw an "Iron Chain" around

39. Hietala, *Manifest Design*, 193.

the United States to gain "command of the commerce, navigation and manufactures of the world" and to reduce its former colonies to economic "vassalage."[40]

For Americans of all political persuasions, the Union's future depended on the absorption of Texas. Whigs protested that annexation would violate principles Americans had long believed in and might provoke war with Mexico.[41] Abolitionists warned of a slaveholders' conspiracy to retain control of the government and perpetuate the evils of human bondage.[42] On the annexation of Texas "hinges the very existence of our Southern Institutions," South Carolinian James Gadsden warned Calhoun, "and if we of the South now prove recreant, we will or must [be] content to be Heawers of wood and Drawers of Water for our Northern Brethren."[43]

In 1844, with an independent Texas a distinct possibility, the Virginian and slaveholder John Tyler, who had become president in 1841 on the death of William Henry Harrison, took up the challenge Jackson and Van Buren had skirted. A staunch Jeffersonian, Tyler is often dismissed as an advocate of states' rights who sought to acquire Texas mainly to protect the institution of slavery. In fact, he was a strong nationalist who pushed a broad agenda of commercial and territorial expansion in hopes of uniting the nation, fulfilling its God-given destiny, and gaining reelection.[44] Seeking to win over the Democrats or rally a party of his own, he pressed vigorously for annexation of Texas. A treaty might have passed the Senate in 1844 had not Calhoun stiffened the opposition by publicly defending slavery. Once the 1844 election was over, lame duck Tyler again proposed admission. Instead of a treaty of annexation, which would have required a two-thirds vote in the Senate, he sought a joint resolution for admission as a state, requiring only a simple majority, on the questionable constitutional grounds that new states could be admitted by act of Congress. The resolution passed after heated debate and drawn-out maneuvering, winning in the Senate by a mere two votes. Texas agreed to the proposals, initiating the process of annexation.[45]

40. Robert Paquette, "The Everett–Del Monte Connection: A Study in the International Politics of Slavery," Diplomatic History 11 (Winter 1987), 1–22; Edmund P. Gaines to Calhoun, May 5, 1844, in Wilson, Calhoun Papers 18:440–441, and Calhoun to William King, August 12, 1844, ibid. 19:568, 578.
41. Morrison, "Westward the Curse," 235.
42. Crapol, "Anti-slavery," 84–87, 89–91.
43. Gadsden to Calhoun, May 3, 1844, in Wilson, Calhoun Papers 18:84–85.
44. Edward P. Crapol, "John Tyler and the Pursuit of National Destiny," Journal of the Early Republic 17 (Fall 1997), 476–79.
45. Peterson, Harrison and Tyler, 176–80, 256–58.

Mexico considered annexation an act of war. Born in 1821, the nation had great expectations because of its size and wealth in natural resources but had suffered economic devastation during its war of independence. The flight of capital abroad in its early years reduced it to bankruptcy. It was also afflicted by profound class, religious, and political divisions. The central government exercised at best nominal authority over the vast outer provinces. Political instability was a way of life. Rival Masonic lodges contended for power, ironic in a predominantly Catholic country. Coup followed coup, sixteen presidents serving between 1837 and 1851. The "volcanic genius" Antonio Lopez de Santa Anna embodied the chaos of Mexican political life. Brilliant but erratic, skilled at mobilizing the population but bored with the details of governance, he served eleven times as president. A master conspirator, he switched sides with alacrity and was said even to intrigue against himself. Noted for his flamboyance, he buried with full military honors the leg he had lost in battle. When he was later repudiated, his enemies dug up the leg and ceremoniously dragged it through the streets.[46]

Too proud to surrender Texas but too weak and divided to regain it by force, Mexicans justifiably (and correctly) feared that acquiescence in annexation could initiate a domino effect that would cost them additional territory. In their view, the United States had encouraged its citizens to infiltrate Texas, incited and supported their revolution, and then moved to absorb the renegade state. They denounced U.S. actions as "the most scandalous violation of the law of nations," the "most direct spoliation, which has been seen for ages."[47] When the annexation resolution passed Congress, Mexico severed diplomatic relations.

A dispute over the Texas boundary exacerbated Mexican-American conflict. Under Spanish and Mexican rule, the province had never extended south of the Nueces River; Texas had never established its authority or even a settlement beyond that point. On the basis of nothing more than an act of its own congress and the fact that Mexican forces withdrew south of the Rio Grande after San Jacinto, Texas had claimed territory to the Rio Grande. Despite the dubious claim and the uncertain value of the barren land, Polk firmly supported the Texans. He ordered Gen. Zachary Taylor to the area to deter a possible Mexican attack and subsequently instructed him to take a position as close to the Rio Grande as "prudence will dictate."[48]

46. Enrique Krauze, *Mexico, Biography of Power: A History of Modern Mexico* (New York, 1997), 99–135, 142.

47. J. M. de Bocaneara to Ben Green, June 6, 15, 1844, in Wilson, *Calhoun Papers* 19:67, 79.

48. Bergeron, *Polk*, 58–63.

Polk also set out to acquire California. Only six thousand Mexicans lived there. Mexico had stationed in its northernmost province an army of fewer than six hundred men to control a huge territory. In October 1842, acting on rumors of war with Mexico, Cmdre. Thomas ap Catesby Jones sailed into Monterey, captured the local authorities, and raised the U.S. flag. When he learned there was no war, he lowered the flag, held a banquet of apology for his captives, and sailed away.[49] Americans were increasingly drawn to California. Sea captains and explorers spoke with wonderment of the lush farmland and salubrious climate of this land of unlimited bounty and "perpetual spring," "one of the finest countries in the world," in the words of consul Thomas Larkin. The "safe and capacious harbors which dot her western shore," an Alabama congressman added, "invite to their bosoms the rich commerce of the East."[50] American emigration to California grew steadily, raising the possibility of a replay of the Texas game. Signs of British interest increased the allure of California and the sense of urgency in Washington. Polk early committed himself to its acquisition, alerted Americans in the area to the possibility of war, and ordered his agents to discourage foreign acquisition.

Polk also wielded a "diplomatic club" against Mexico in the millions of dollars in claims held by U.S. citizens against its people and government. Many of the claims were inflated, some were patently unjust, and most derived from profiteering at Mexico's expense. They were based on the new international "law" imposed by the leading capitalist powers that secured for their citizens the same property rights in other countries they had at home.[51] A commission had scaled the claims back to $2.5 million. Mexico made a few payments before a bankrupt treasury forced suspension in 1843. Americans charged Mexico with bad faith. Mexico denounced the claims as a "tribute" it was "obliged to pay in recognition of U.S. strength."[52]

Polk's approach to Mexico was dictated by the overtly racist attitudes he shared with most of his countrymen. Certain of Anglo-Saxon superiority, Americans scorned Mexicans as a mixed breed, even below free blacks and Indians, "an imbecile, pusillanimous race of men...unfit to control the destinies of that beautiful country," a "rascally perfidious race," a "band

49. Peterson, *Harrison and Tyler*, 139.
50. Larkin to Calhoun, August 18, 1844, in Wilson, *Calhoun Papers* 19:606–7; Hietala, *Manifest Design*, 87.
51. Charles G. Sellers, *The Market Revolution: Jacksonian America, 1815–1846* (New York, 1991), 420.
52. Gene M. Brack, *Mexico Views Manifest Destiny, 1821–1846: An Essay on the Origins of the Mexican War* (Albuquerque, N.M., 1975), 95.

of pirates and robbers."[53] Indeed, they found no difficulty justifying as part of God's will the taking of fertile land from an "idle, thriftless people." They assumed that Mexico could be bullied into submission or, if foolish enough to fight, easily defeated. "Let its bark be treated with contempt, and its little bite, if it should attempt it, [be] quickly brushed aside with a single stroke of the paw," O'Sullivan exclaimed.[54] Some Americans even assumed that Mexicans would welcome them as liberators from their own depraved government.

Given the intractability of the issues and the attitudes on both sides, a settlement would have been difficult under any circumstances, but Polk's heavy-handed diplomacy ensured war. There is no evidence to confirm charges that he plotted to provoke Mexico into firing the first shot.[55] He seems rather to have hoped that by bribery and intimidation he could get what he wanted without war and to have expected that if war did come, it would be short, easy, and inexpensive. His sense of urgency heightened in the fall of 1845 by new and exaggerated reports of British designs on California, he tightened the noose. In December 1845, he revived the Monroe Doctrine, warning Britain and France against trying to block U.S. expansion. He deployed naval units off the Mexican port of Veracruz and ordered Taylor to the Rio Grande. He sent agents to Santa Fe to bribe provincial authorities of the New Mexico territory and persuade its residents of the benefits of U.S. rule. He dispatched secret orders to the navy's Pacific squadron and Larkin that should war break out or Britain move overtly to take California they should occupy the major ports and encourage the local population to revolt. He may also have secretly ordered the adventurer—and notorious troublemaker—John Charles Frémont to go to California. In any event, Frémont in the spring of 1846 turned abruptly south from an expedition in Oregon and began fomenting revolution in California.[56]

Having encircled Mexico with U.S. military power and begun to chip away at its outlying provinces, Polk set out to force a deal. Mistakenly concluding that Mexico had agreed to receive an envoy, he sent Louisianan John Slidell to Mexico City. The president's instructions make clear the sort of "negotiations" he sought. Slidell was to restore good relations with Mexico while demanding that it surrender on the Rio Grande boundary

53. Horsman, *Race and Manifest Destiny*, 210; Hietala, *Manifest Design*, 156.
54. Quoted in Hietala, *Manifest Design*, 154.
55. The major "revisionist" study is Glenn W. Price, *Origins of the War with Mexico: The Polk-Stockton Intrigue* (Austin, Tex., 1967).
56. Bergeron, *Polk*, 73–74.

and relinquish California, no mean task. The United States would pay Mexico $30 million and absorb the claims of its citizens.

The predictable failure of Slidell's mission led directly to war. Mexico had agreed only to receive a commissioner to discuss resumption of diplomatic relations. Slidell's mere presence destabilized an already shaky government. When he moved on to the capital, violating the explicit instructions of Mexican officials, his mission was doomed.[57] After Mexico refused to receive him, he advised Polk that the United States should not deal further with them until it had "given them a good drubbing."[58] Polk concurred. After learning of Slidell's return, he began drafting a war message. In the meantime, Taylor took a provocative position just north of the Rio Grande, his artillery trained on the town of Matamoros. Before the war message could be completed, Washington learned that Mexican troops had attacked one of Taylor's patrols. American blood had been shed on American soil, Polk exclaimed with exaggeration. The administration quickly secured its declaration of war.

The Mexican-American War resulted from U.S. impatience and aggressiveness and Mexican weakness. Polk and many of his countrymen were determined to have Texas to the Rio Grande and all of California on their own terms. They might have waited for the apples to fall from the tree, to borrow John Quincy Adams's Cuban metaphor, but patience was not among their virtues. Polk appears not to have set out to provoke Mexico into what could be used as a war of conquest. Rather, contemptuous of his presumably inferior adversaries, he assumed he could bully them into giving him what he wanted. Mexico's weakness and internal divisions encouraged his aggressiveness. A stronger or more united Mexico might have deterred the United States or acquiesced in the annexation of Texas to avoid war, as the British minister and former Mexican foreign minister Lucas Alaman urged. By this time, however, Yankeephobia was rampant. Mexicans deeply resented the theft of Texas and obvious U.S. designs on California. They viewed the United States as the "Russian threat" of the New World. Incensed by the racist views of their northern neighbors, they feared cultural extinction. Newspapers warned that if the North Americans were not stopped in Texas, Protestantism would be imposed on the Mexican people and they would be "sold as beasts."[59] Fear,

---

57. Sellers, *Market Revolution*, 421.
58. Quoted in Norman A. Graebner, "The Mexican War: A Study in Causation," *Pacific Historical Review* 49 (August 1980), 418.
59. Brack, *Mexico Views*, 82, 99. A recent excellent analysis is Timothy Henderson, *A Glorious Defeat: Mexico and Its War with the United States* (New York, 2007).

anger, and pride made it impossible to acquiesce in U.S. aggression. Mexico chose war over surrender.

Polk's strategy for fighting Mexico reflected the racist assumptions that got him into war. Certain that an inferior people would be no match for Americans, he envisioned a war of three to four months. The United States would secure control of Mexico's northern provinces and use them to force acceptance of the Rio Grande boundary and cession of California and New Mexico.

In a strictly military sense, Polk's estimate proved on the mark. Using artillery with devastating effect, Taylor drove Mexican attackers back across the Rio Grande. Over the next ten months, he defeated larger armies at Monterrey and Buena Vista, fueling popular excitement, making himself a national hero, and gaining control of much of northern Mexico. In the meantime, Cmdre. Robert Stockton and Frémont backed the so-called Bear Flag Revolt of Americans around Sacramento and proclaimed California part of the United States. Colonel Stephen Kearney's forces took New Mexico without resistance. To facilitate negotiations, Polk permitted the exiled Santa Anna to go back to Mexico where, in return, he was to arrange a settlement.

War is never as simple as its planners envision, however, and despite smashing military successes, Polk could not impose peace. Mexico turned out to be an "ugly enemy," in Daniel Webster's words. "She will not fight—& will not treat."[60] Despite crushing defeats, the Mexicans refused to negotiate on U.S. terms. They mounted a costly and frustrating guerrilla war against the invaders, "hardly...a legitimate system of warfare," Americans snarled, additional evidence (if any was needed) of Mexican debasement.[61] Santa Anna did Polk's deviousness one better, using the United States to get home and then mobilizing fierce opposition to the invaders. "The United States may triumph," a Mexican newspaper proclaimed defiantly, "but its prize, like that of the vulture, will lie in a lake of blood."[62]

The United States by mid-1847 faced the grim prospect of a long and costly war. Annoyed that Taylor had not moved more decisively and alarmed that the general's martial exploits could make him a formidable political rival, the fiercely partisan Polk shifted his strategy southward, designing a combined army-navy assault against Veracruz, the strongest fortress in the Western Hemisphere, to be led by Gen. Winfield Scott and

60. Pletcher, *Diplomacy of Annexation*, 461.
61. Hietala, *Manifest Design*, 158.
62. Pletcher, *Diplomacy of Annexation*, 493.

followed by an overland advance on Mexico City. Demonstrating the emerging professionalism of U.S. forces, Scott in March 1847 launched the first large-scale amphibious operation in the nation's history. After a siege of several weeks, he took Veracruz. In April, he defeated the ubiquitous Santa Anna at Cerro Gordo and began a slow, bloody advance to Mexico City. In August, five miles from the city, he agreed to an armistice.

Even this smashing success did not end the conflict. Fearing Scott as a potential political rival, Polk denied him the role of peacemaker, dispatching a minor figure, State Department clerk Nicholas Trist, to negotiate with Mexico. Shortly after his arrival, Trist fell into a childish and nasty spat with Scott that left the two refusing to speak to each other. The untimely feud may have botched an opportunity to end the war. More important, despite the imminent threat to their capital, the Mexicans stubbornly held out, insisting that the United States give up all occupied territory, accept the Nueces boundary, and pay the costs of the war. Santa Anna used the armistice to strengthen the defenses of the capital. With the breakdown of negotiations, Polk angrily recalled Trist, terminated the armistice, and ordered Scott to march on Mexico City.

The Mexican-American War was the nation's first major military intervention abroad and its first experience with occupying another country. Americans brought to this venture the ethos of the age, clearly defined notions of their own superiority, and the conviction that they were "pioneers of civilization," as contemporary historian William H. Prescott put it, bringing to a benighted people the blessings of republicanism. Given the crushing impediment of racism they also brought with them, and the difficulties of living in a different climate and sometimes hostile environment, U.S. forces comported themselves reasonably well. There were atrocities, to be sure, and the Polk administration imposed a heavy burden on a defeated people by forcing them to pay taxes to finance the occupation. As a matter of military expediency, however, and to behave as they felt citizens of a republic should, the Americans tried to conciliate the population in most areas they moved through. Little was done to impose republicanism, and the impact of U.S. intervention on Mexico appears to have been slight. The areas occupied were briefly Americanized and some elements of American culture survived in Mexico, but the mixing of peoples was at best superficial and the gap between them remained wide. Ironically, the impact of intervention may have been greater on the occupiers, manifesting itself in such things as men's fashions and hair-styles and the incorporation of Spanish words and phrases into the language and as U.S. place names. The experience of fighting in a foreign land

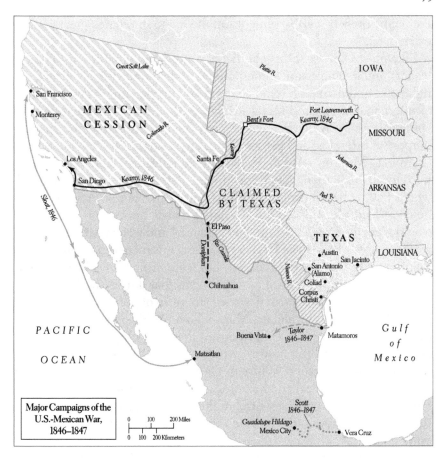

Major Campaigns of the
U.S.-Mexican War,
1846–1847

exposed Americans to a foreign culture, challenging their parochialism
and contributing to the growth of national self-awareness.[63]

The war bitterly divided the United States. Citizens responded to its
outbreak with an enthusiasm that bordered on hysteria. The prospect of
fighting in an exotic foreign land appealed to their romantic spirit and
sense of adventure. War provided a diversion from the mounting sectional
conflict and served as an antidote for the materialism of the age. In the
eyes of some, it was a test for the republican experiment, a way to bring
the nation back to its first principles. "Ho, for the Halls of the Montezumas"
was the battle cry, and the call for volunteers produced such a response
that thousands had to be turned away. This was the first U.S. war to rest on
a popular base. Stirring reports of battles provided to avid readers through

63. Johannsen, *Halls of the Montezumas*, 32–33, 50, 171–73, 205; Howe, *What Hath God Wrought*, 789–90, 797–98.

the penny press by correspondents on the scene stimulated great popular excitement.[64]

Like most U.S. wars, this conflict also provoked opposition. Religious leaders, intellectuals, and some politicians denounced it as "illegal, unrighteous, and damnable" and accused Polk of violating "every principle of international law and moral justice."[65] Abolitionists claimed that this "piratical war" was being waged "solely for the detestable and horrible purpose of extending and perpetuating American slavery."[66] Whigs sought to exploit "Mr. Polk's War." The young congressman Abraham Lincoln introduced his famous "spot resolution," demanding to know precisely where Polk believed American blood had been shed on American soil. Senator Tom Corwin of Ohio declared that if he were a Mexican he would greet the invaders "with bloody hands" and welcome them to "hospitable graves." Polk's own Democratic Party was increasingly divided, the followers of both Calhoun and Van Buren opposing him. The opposition to the Mexican War was not as crippling as that during the War of 1812. Anti-war forces were weakened by the extremism of people such as Corwin and by their own ambivalence. Many who fervently opposed the war saw no choice but to support U.S. troops in the field. Opponents of the war also recognized that the nation as a whole supported the war. Remembering the fate of the Federalists, Whigs in Congress tempered their opposition. In any event, they lacked the votes to block administration measures. Until after the Whigs won control of the House of Representatives in the 1846 elections, they could do little more than protest and make life difficult for Polk.[67]

Pinched economically from the growing cost of the war and frustrated that an unbroken string of military successes had not produced peace, Americans by 1848 grew impatient. Divisions in both parties sharpened. When the Wilmot Proviso, banning slavery in any territory acquired from Mexico, was introduced in Congress in August 1846, it brought that explosive issue to the surface. Outraged by Mexico's continued defiance and excited by tales of vast mineral wealth, "All Mexico" Democrats pushed for annexation of the entire country. At the other extreme, critics urged Polk's impeachment "as an indemnity to the American people for the loss of 15,000 lives...in Mexico."[68]

64. Johannsen, *Halls of the Montezumas*, 10, 12–13, 16, 25.
65. Graebner, "Mexican War," 405.
66. John H. Schroeder, *Mr. Polk's War: American Opposition and Dissent, 1846–1848* (Madison, Wisc., 1973), 99.
67. Ibid., 72–73, 160–63; Johannsen, *Halls of the Montezumas*, 275–79.
68. Schroeder, *Mr. Polk's War*, 143.

A peace settlement emerged almost by accident. After two weeks of heavy fighting, Scott's army forced the surrender of the heavily defended capital. "I believe if we were to plant our batteries in Hell the damned Yankees would take them from us," a stunned Santa Anna remarked after the fall of the supposedly impregnable fortress of Chapultepec.[69] Fearing a drawn-out war, Trist ignored Polk's orders to come home. Acting without authority, he negotiated a treaty that met the president's original demands. Mexico recognized the Rio Grande boundary and ceded upper California and New Mexico. The United States was to pay $15 million plus U.S. claims against Mexico.

Outraged by Trist's disobedience, Polk would have liked to take more territory to punish Mexico for its insolence. Ironically, the very racism that drove the United States into Mexico limited its conquests. "We can no more amalgamate with her people than with negroes," the former president's nephew and namesake Andrew Jackson Donelson observed. "The Spanish blood will not mix well with the Yankee," Prescott added.[70] Concern about the absorption of an alien population and the prospect of peace took the steam out of the All Mexico movement. Facing sharpening divisions at home, Polk felt compelled to accept the treaty negotiated by that "impudent and unqualified scoundrel." Some Whigs opposed it because it gave the United States too much territory, others because the price was too high. In the final analysis, peace seemed preferable to more bloodshed. The treaty passed the Senate on March 10, 1848, by a bipartisan vote of 36 to 14. The Treaty of Guadalupe Hidalgo, in Philip Hone's apt phrase, was "negotiated by an unauthorized agent, with an unacknowledged government, submitted by an accidental president to a dissatisfied Senate."[71]

For Trist, the diplomat who had taken peace into his own hands, the reward was abuse from a vindictive boss. He was fired from his State Department post and not paid for his service until some twenty-five years later, shortly before his death.

For Mexico, the war was a devastating blow to the optimism that had marked its birth, perhaps the supreme tragedy in its history. When Santa Anna was shown maps of his country making clear for the first time the enormity of its losses, he wept openly. Mexico plunged deeper into debt. With half its territory gone, war raging in Yucatán, agrarian revolts

69. Robert A. Doughty et al., *Warfare in the Western World* (2 vols., Lexington, Mass., 1996), 1:321.
70. Hietala, *Manifest Design*, 163; Johannsen, *Halls of the Montezumas*, 299.
71. Quoted in K. Jack Bauer, *The Mexican War, 1846–1848* (New York, 1974), 399.

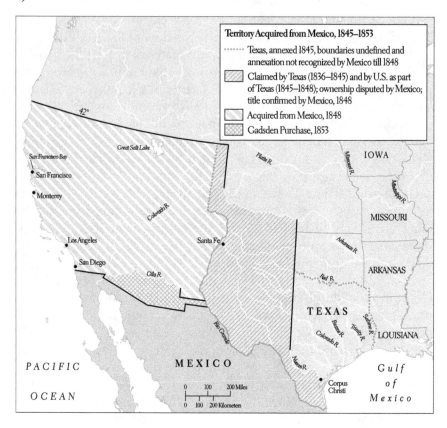

Territory Acquired from Mexico, 1845–1853

······· Texas, annexed 1845, boundaries undefined and annexation not recognized by Mexico till 1848

Claimed by Texas (1836–1845) and by U.S. as part of Texas (1845–1848); ownership disputed by Mexico; title confirmed by Mexico, 1848

Acquired from Mexico, 1848

Gadsden Purchase, 1853

sweeping the heartland, and Indian unrest in the north, the nation seemed near falling apart. Military defeat brought despair to leadership groups. Liberals questioned Mexico's capacity for nationhood. Conservatives concluded that republicanism was tantamount to anarchy and that they should look to Europe for models, even to monarchy. It was the "most unjust war in history," Alaman lamented, "provoked by the ambition not of an absolute monarchy but of a republic that claims to be at the forefront of nineteenth century civilization."[72]

For the United States, the war brought a vast bounty, adding 529,000 square miles to the national domain, coveted outlets on the Pacific, and the unanticipated boon of California gold. If Texas is added, the booty totals about 1.2 million square miles, one-third of the nation's present territory. All of this for thirteen thousand dead, an estimated $97 million

72. Krauze, *Mexico*, 143, 147–49; Johannsen, *Halls of the Montezumas*, 301.

in war costs, and the $15 million paid Mexico. North Americans saw the war as a great event in their own and indeed in world history. Success against Mexico demonstrated, Polk insisted, the "capacity of republican governments to prosecute successfully a just and necessary foreign war with all the vigor usually attributed to more arbitrary forms of government."[73] For a people still unsure of their bold experiment, the war confirmed their faith in republicanism and seemed to earn them new respect abroad. Some Americans even saw the European revolutions of 1848 as extensions of the great test between monarchy and republicanism that began on the battlefields of Mexico. "The whole civilized world resounds with American opinions and American principles," declared Speaker of the House of Representatives Robert Winthrop in a victory oration on July 4, 1848.[74]

The celebration of victory obscured only momentarily the war's darker consequences. It aroused among Latin Americans growing fear of what was already commonly labeled the "colossus of the North." Most important, acquisition of the vast new territory opened a veritable Pandora's box of troubles at home. From the Wilmot Proviso to Fort Sumter, the explosive issue of extending slavery into the territories dominated the political landscape, setting off a bitter and ultimately irreconcilable conflict. Polk's victory thus came at a huge price, setting the nation on the road to civil war.[75]

V

Rising with each word to new heights of exuberance, Secretary of State Daniel Webster proclaimed in 1851 that it was America's destiny to "command the oceans, both oceans, all the oceans."[76] Some of the same forces that drove the United States across the continent in the 1840s propelled it into the Pacific and East Asia. Trade, of course, was a major factor. The Panic of 1837 and growing concern with surplus agricultural productivity heightened the importance of finding new markets. Whigs like Webster saw commercial expansion as essential to domestic well-being and international stability. Democrats viewed it as essential to sustain the agricultural production that would safeguard the nation from the threats of manufacturing, economic distress, and monopoly. The lure of East Asian trade played a

73. Bergeron, *Polk*, 110.
74. Johannsen, *Halls of the Montezumas*, 5.
75. Sellers, *Market Revolution*, 425.
76. Quoted in Kenneth E. Shewmaker, "Forging the 'Great Chain': Daniel Webster and the Origins of American Foreign Policy Toward East Asia and the Pacific, 1841–1852," *Proceedings of the American Philosophical Society* 129 (September 1985), 250–51.

crucial role in the quest for Oregon and California; their acquisition, in turn, quickened interest in the Pacific and East Asia. "By our recent acquisitions in the Pacific," Secretary of the Treasury Robert Walker proclaimed in 1848, "Asia has suddenly become our neighbor, with a placid intervening ocean inviting our steamships upon the trade of a commerce greater than all of Europe combined."[77] It was no accident that in the 1840s the United States began to formulate a clear-cut policy for the Pacific region.

The Pacific Ocean was a focal point of international rivalry in the mid-nineteenth century, the United States an active participant. American merchants entered the China trade before 1800. From the first years of the century, sea captains and traders sailed up and down the west coast of the American continents and far out into the Pacific. Americans dominated the whaling industry, pursuing their lucrative prey from the Arctic Ocean to Antarctica and California to the Tasman Sea. Americans were the first to set foot on Antarctica. During its dramatic four-year voyage around the world, the Great United States Exploring Expedition, commanded by Capt. Charles Wilkes, charted the islands, harbors, and coast lines of the Pacific. The U.S. Navy assumed a constabulary role, supporting enterprising Americans in far-flung areas. United States citizens on their own initiative carved out interests and pushed the government to defend them.[78]

This was especially true in Hawaii, where Americans predominated by midcentury. Missionaries and merchants began flocking there as early as 1820 and by the 1840s played a major role in the life of the islands. United States trade far surpassed that of the nearest rival, Great Britain. New England Congregationalist missionaries established schools and printing presses and enjoyed unusually large conversion rates. As in other areas, Western disease ravaged the indigenous population and Western culture assaulted local customs. But the missionaries also helped Hawaii manage the jolt of Westernization without entirely giving in. Americans assisted Hawaiian rulers in adapting Western forms of governance and in protecting their sovereignty. On the advice of missionary William Richards, King Kamehameha II mounted a diplomatic offensive in the 1840s to spare his people from falling under European domination, pushing Hawaii toward the U.S. orbit.[79]

77. Walter LaFeber, *The Clash: U.S.-Japanese Relations Throughout History* (New York, 1997), 11.
78. Arthur Power Dudden, *The American Pacific: From the Old China Trade to the Present* (New York, 1992), 11–17; William Stanton, *The Great United States Exploring Expedition of 1838–1842* (Berkeley, Calif., 1975); Nathaniel Philbrick, *Sea of Glory: America's Voyage of Discovery, the U.S. Exploring Expedition, 1838–1842* (New York, 2003).
79. Dudden, *American Pacific*, 56–57.

A result was the so-called Tyler Doctrine of 1842, the end of official indifference toward Hawaii. Protestant missionaries had also persuaded the Hawaiians to discriminate against French Catholics. When the French government threatened to retaliate, a nervous and opportunistic Kamehameha sought from the United States, Britain, and France a tripartite guarantee of Hawaiian independence. To get action from Washington, Richards even hinted at Hawaii's willingness to accept a British protectorate. Webster and the "Pacific-minded" Tyler perceived Hawaii's importance as the "Malta of the Pacific," a vital link in the "great chain" connecting the United States with East Asia. Unwilling to take on risky commitments, they rejected a tripartite guarantee and refused even to recognize Hawaii's sovereignty. The Tyler Doctrine did, however, claim special U.S. interests in Hawaii based on proximity and trade. It made clear that if other powers threatened Hawaii's independence the United States would be justified in "making a decided remonstrance." Seeking to protect U.S. interests at minimum cost, the doctrine claimed Hawaii as a U.S. sphere of influence and firmly supported its independence, establishing a policy that would last until annexation.[80]

As secretary of state under Millard Fillmore, Webster in 1851 went a step further. Under the Tyler Doctrine, U.S. interests expanded significantly. Hawaii resembled a "Pacific New England" in culture and institutions.[81] The development of oceangoing steam navigation increased its importance as a possible coaling station. Again threatened by French gunboat diplomacy, Kamehameha II in 1851 signed a secret document transferring sovereignty to the United States in the event of war. Webster and Fillmore steered clear of annexation and warned missionaries against provoking conflict with France. At the same time, in a strongly worded message of July 14, 1851, the secretary of state asserted that the United States would accept no infringement on Hawaiian sovereignty and would use force if necessary. Webster's willingness to go this far reflected the increased importance of Hawaii due to the acquisition of Oregon and California and rising U.S. interest in East Asia. His threats infuriated the French, but extracted from them a clear statement respecting Hawaiian sovereignty.[82]

The United States' concern for Hawaii was tied to the opening of China. Until the 1840s, East Asia remained largely closed to the West because of policies rigorously enforced by both China and Japan.

80. Shewmaker, "Great Chain," 231–33.
81. Ibid., 239.
82. Ibid., 239–43.

China's isolationist policy reflected a set of highly ethnocentric ideas that viewed the Celestial Kingdom as the center of the universe and other peoples as "barbarians." The notion of equal relations among sovereign states had no place in this scheme of things. Ties with other nations were permitted only on a "tributary" basis. Foreign representatives had to pay tribute to the emperor through various rituals including the elaborate series of prostrations known as the ko-tow. In the 1790s, China began to permit limited trade—to make available to the barbarians necessities such as tea and rhubarb, its officials said—but it was restricted in volume and tightly regulated by Chinese merchants. Japanese exclusion was less ideological but more rigid. Viewing outsiders and especially missionaries as threats to internal stability, they kept out all but a handful of Dutch traders, who operated only on an island in Nagasaki harbor. Indeed, the Japanese so feared contamination that they prohibited their own people from going abroad and forbade those who did so from returning.[83]

By the 1840s, the European powers had far outstripped the isolated Asians in economic and military power. Eager for expanded trade and outlets for missionary activity, they challenged Chinese and Japanese restrictions. In the United States, producers of cotton and tobacco fancied huge profits from access to China's millions. Some Americans even envisioned their country as an entrepôt for a global trade in which European goods would be imported, transshipped across the continent, and then sent from San Francisco to East Asian ports by steamship.

The missionary impulse reinforced commercial drives. The 1840s was a period of intense religious ferment in the United States, and numerous Protestant sects stepped up evangelizing activities around the world. China and Japan, which seemed particularly decadent and barbaric, offered perhaps the greatest challenge. The Chinese empire was "so vast, so populous, and so idolatrous," one missionary exclaimed, "that it cannot be mentioned by Christians without exciting statements of the deepest concern." The handful of American missionaries already in China questioned its rulers' right to make "a large part of the earth's surface...impassable." They also emphasized China's weakness and pressed for its opening—by force if necessary.[84]

83. Ssu-Yu Teng and John K. Fairbank, *China's Response to the West: A Documentary Survey, 1839–1923* (New York, 1954), 17–19; Edwin O. Reischauer, *The United States and Japan* (rev. ed., New York, 1957), 5–11.

84. Murray A. Rubinstein, "The Wars They Wanted: American Missionaries' Use of the *Chinese Repository* Before the Opium War," *American Neptune* 48 (Fall 1988), 277–82.

Britain took the lead. To redress a balance of trade chronically favoring China, Western merchants, Americans included, had taken to the illegal and profitable sale of opium. Chinese officials objected on economic grounds and also because of the baneful effects on their people. When they attempted to stop the trade, the British responded with force and used their trouncing of China in the so-called Opium War as leverage to pry it open. The Treaty of Nanking (1842), imposed on China by the British, marked the end of Chinese exclusion, putting into effect a system of blatantly discriminatory unequal treaties that reversed China's traditional way of dealing with other nations. The Chinese opened five ports to trade with Britain, eliminated some of the more obnoxious regulations imposed on British merchants, and opened their tariff to negotiation. They also ceded Hong Kong and agreed to a practice called extraterritoriality by which British citizens in China were tried under their own law rather than Chinese.

Through what came to be known as hitchhiking imperialism, the United States took advantage of British gains. Shortly after the Treaty of Nanking, Tyler sent Massachusetts merchant Caleb Cushing to negotiate with China. The two nations approached each other across a yawning geographical and cultural chasm. Contemptuous of Chinese pretensions of superiority, the administration instructed its delegation to take with them a globe (if one could be found) so that "the celestials may see that they are not the Central Kingdom." Cushing was to use religion as an excuse not to perform the ko-tow.[85] Chinese viewed the United States as "the most remote and least civilized" of Western nations—an "isolated place outside the pale." Their chief negotiator instructed the emperor to use a "simple and direct style" so his meaning would be clear. Hoping to play the barbarians against each other, the Chinese were willing to deal. In the Treaty of Wang-hsia (1844), they granted the United States the same commercial concessions as Britain. Most important, they agreed to a most-favored-nation clause that would automatically concede to the United States terms given any other nation.[86]

During the 1850s, the West made further inroads, implementing an increasingly exploitative form of quasi-colonialism. Capitalizing on China's prolonged and bloody civil war—the so-called Taiping Rebellion lasted

85. Kenneth E. Shewmaker, ed., *The Papers of Daniel Webster: Diplomatic Papers* (Hanover, N.H., 1983), 1:907–10; Webster to Caleb Cushing, May 8, 1843, ibid., 922–26.

86. Warren I. Cohen, *America's Response to China: An Interpretive History of Sino-American Relations* (New York, 1974), 14.

fifteen years and took as many as forty million lives—and rewarding its intransigence and insults with high-handedness, the Europeans negotiated at gunpoint treaties that opened additional ports, permitted navigation into the interior, forced toleration of missionaries, legalized the opium trade, and, by fixing a maximum tariff of 5 percent, deprived China of control over its own economy.

Americans then and later fancied themselves different from the Europeans in dealing with China, and to some extent they were. Until the end of the century, at least, the United States remained a minor player. Trade with China increased significantly but remained only a small portion of China's commerce with the West. American missionaries were few in number and small in impact. "Our preaching is listened to by a few, laughed at by many, and disregarded by most," one missionary lamented.[87] Americans generally refrained from the use of force. Some, like minister John Ward, sent to ratify the 1858 treaties of Tientsin, observed Chinese conventions; Ward even rode in a mule cart traditionally deserved for tributaries, earning the contempt of his European counterparts and praise from his countrymen for Yankee practicality.[88]

The differences were more of form than substance. The United States sometimes participated in gunboat diplomacy and regularly used the most-favored-nation clause to secure concessions extorted by the Europeans at cannon's mouth. Like the Europeans, Americans generally looked down on the Chinese—one diplomat described a "china-man" as "surely the most grotesque animal."[89] Some Chinese perceived a subtle difference and tried to exploit it, but in general they made little distinction. "The English barbarians' craftiness is manifold, their proud tyranny is uncontrollable," one Chinese official observed. "Americans do nothing but follow in their direction."[90]

The United States took the lead in opening Japan. Encouraged by Britain's success in China and viewing Japan as a vital coaling station en route to the Celestial Kingdom, the last link in Webster's "great chain," Fillmore in 1852 named Cmdre. Matthew Perry to head a mission to Japan. Regarding the Japanese as a "weak and semi-barbarous people," Perry decided to deal forcibly with them. In July 1853, he steamed defiantly into

87. Michael H. Hunt, *The Making of a Special Relationship: The United States and China to 1914* (New York, 1983), 26.
88. William M. Gabard, "John Eliot Ward: A Georgia Elitist in the Celestial Empire, 1858–1860," *Studies in the Social Sciences* 22 (June 1983), 56–60.
89. Hunt, *Special Relationship*, 35.
90. Earl Swisher, China's *Management of the American Barbarians* (New Haven, Conn., 1951), 46.

Edo (later Tokyo) Bay with a fleet of four very large, black-hulled ships, sixty-one guns, and a crew of nearly one thousand men. He maneuvered his ships closer to the city than any foreigner had previously gone. Japanese initially responded to the "burning ships" with panic, then by official stalling. Fearing they might simply wait until his provisions were exhausted, Perry, after preliminary discussions with low-level officials, sailed to China, informing them he would return the following year to negotiate.

Perry came back in March 1854 with a larger fleet, threatening this time that if Japan did not treat with him it might suffer the fate of Mexico. Instructed by the State Department to "do everything to impress" the Japanese "with a just sense of the power and greatness" of the United States, he brought with him large quantities of champagne and vintage Kentucky bourbon to grease the wheels of diplomacy, a pair of Sam Colt's six-shooters and a scale model train to display U.S. technological advancement, and a history of the Mexican War to validate its military superiority. He employed Chinese coolies and African Americans in his entourage in ways that highlighted the power of whites over peoples of color. He used uniforms, pageants, and music—even a blackface minstrel show—as manifestations of Western cultural supremacy. Perry's reluctant hosts most likely negotiated in spite of rather than because of his forceful demeanor and cultural symbols. Aware of the West's technological advances, they disagreed whether to resist or accommodate with and learn about this new threat. Alarmed by developments in China, they decided to deal with the United States rather than Britain and make limited concessions rather than have more exploitative agreements forced on them. Thus in the Treaty of Kanagawa, they opened two relatively isolated and inaccessible ports and agreed to provide refuge to crews of wrecked U.S. ships. The treaty got the Americans a foot in the door.[91]

It remained for Townsend Harris, a diplomat of undistinguished credentials with no force at his disposal, to establish the foundation for Japan's relations with the West for the remainder of the century. Arriving in 1856 as the first U.S. consul, he was shunted to the small and inaccessible village of Shimoda by a government that would have preferred he stay home. He was forced to share a run-down temple with rats, bats, and enormous spiders. Sometimes going months without word from Washington, Harris rightly considered himself the "most isolated American official in the world." Frustrated by Japanese obstructionism, he also came to admire

---

91. Jeffrey A. Keith, " 'An Entirely Peaceful Spirit of Conquest': Commodore Matthew Galbraith Perry's Cultural Diplomacy, 1852–1854" (M.A. thesis, University of Kentucky, 2006).

the Japanese people and appreciate their culture, perhaps through the influence of a mistress, assigned him by the government, who may have been the inspiration for Giacomo Puccini's opera *Madama Butterfly*. Confident that with patience the West could elevate Japan to "our standards of civilization," Harris stubbornly persisted, repeatedly warning his hosts that it would be better to deal peaceably with the United States than risk China's fate at the hands of the Europeans. Eventually, he prevailed. In 1858, the Japanese agreed to permit trade, opened five new ports, established diplomatic relations, and accepted extraterritoriality. Within a decade, Harris's treaty would cause a revolution in Japan, but the immediate result was more resistance. As the first U.S. minister to the country, he faced continued obstruction and what his British counterpart called the "perpetual menace of massacre"—seven foreign diplomats were killed in eighteen months (including Harris's translator), some of them hacked to pieces by gangs of sword-wielding assassins. Ironically, as other nations arrived in Japan, U.S. influence waned. By 1861, when Harris left, it was, as in China, a junior partner to the British.[92] Although a secondary power in East Asia, the United States established significant interests and framed a coherent policy based on the principle of equality of commercial opportunity, laying the foundation for a more active and influential role in the future.

VI

"The American destiny did not seem so manifest in the 1850s," historian Reginald Stuart has written.[93] During these years, Americans remained an aggressive, acquisitive, competitive breed certain of their own righteousness and the evil of their foes.[94] Victorious in war, having more than doubled the size of their nation, they began to see themselves as an emerging world power, even a rival to Britain. Expansionist sentiment remained alive. Some Democrats viewed an aggressive foreign policy as a way to divert the nation from growing internal divisions and hold an embattled Union together. Combining ardent nationalism with blatant racism, the Young America movement in the name of promoting republicanism hoped to project the nation's power abroad. Southerners sought salvation through expansion. They deemed the acquisition of new slave states essential to maintain a balance of power in the Senate. The expansion of

---

92. LaFeber, *Clash*, 18–23; Jack M. Hammersmith, *Spoilsmen in a "Flowery Fairland": The Development of the U.S. Legation in Japan, 1859–1906* (Kent, Ohio, 1998), 1–25.
93. Stuart, *United States Expansionism*, 96.
94. Elbert B. Smith, *The Presidencies of Zachary Taylor and Millard Fillmore* (Lawrence, Kans., 1988), 18.

slavery would also disperse the black population and thereby help solve the nation's race problem. "The safety of the South is to be found only in the extension of its peculiar institutions," *DeBow's Review* exclaimed, "and the security of the Union in the safety of the South."[95]

In the heyday of the so-called filibusters, U.S. expansion turned southward and assumed even more aggressive forms. The name "filibuster" originated through the French and Spanish languages from a Dutch word meaning pirate or freebooter. By no means unique to the United States, these patently illegal, privately organized and funded military expeditions against foreign territory became a staple of American life in the 1850s. The leadership included such well-known adventurers as the charismatic Venezuelan and former Spanish army officer Narciso López, Mexican War hero and Mississippi governor John Quitman, and, most prominently, the onetime physician and would-be ruler of Nicaragua, William Walker. The ranks drew from discharged Mexican War soldiers, restless young men who sought companionship, adventure, and military glory, the urban unemployed, including recent immigrants and refugees from failed European revolutions, southerners who hoped to expand slavery, and Freemasons who aspired to expand liberty—and constrict Catholicism. Celebrated in the popular press, stage productions, and song, the filibusters captured the romantic spirit of the age. Mexico was the target of countless attacks, most designed to detach its northern provinces. Cuba and Canada also drew attention. There were expeditions against Honduras, Nicaragua, and even Ecuador. A planned "invasion" of Hawaii was aborted. British officials, not without reason, fretted about a possible attack on Ireland. Americans joked about expeditions to the North Pole.[96]

In contrast to the previous decade, expansionism produced few results in the 1850s. The Franklin Pierce administration through the 1853 Gadsden Purchase extorted from Santa Anna, once again in power and out of pocket, thirty-nine million additional acres of Mexican territory to secure a southern route for the transcontinental railroad. It also seized— for its rich deposits of guano, widely used as fertilizer—Parker Island in the South Pacific, the first non-contiguous territory acquired.[97] But there were no other annexations. Brash self-confidence was tempered by escalating sectional divisions. The Compromise of 1850, which admitted California as a free state, exacerbated rather than resolved internal con-

95. Gara, *Pierce*, 150.
96. Robert E. May, *Manifest Destiny's Underworld: Filibustering in Antebellum America* (Chapel Hill, N.C., 2002), 1–116.
97. Gara, *Pierce*, 129–32, 147–48.

flict. From the agony of "Bleeding Kansas" to the firing on Fort Sumter, the nation tore itself apart over the extension of slavery. Southern determination to expand the peculiar institution into new areas aroused passionate opposition in the North. Northern frustration of southern designs in turn provoked secessionist sentiment in the South. Expansionism thus tore the nation apart instead of pulling it together, making a mockery of the grand pretensions of Manifest Destiny.

For all the excitement they generated, the filibusters achieved nothing. Private citizens found it difficult to raise the necessary funds and organize and execute complex, often seaborne military operations. Though the Pierce and Buchanan administrations privately sympathized with filibusters' goals, they dutifully enforced the neutrality laws, deterring, hampering, and sometimes stopping expansionist schemes. In no case did local populations rise up to welcome the American invaders as liberators, as the filibusters so naively expected. Once in country, the outsiders suffered from cholera and other deadly diseases. Many who sought adventure were wounded or killed in battle. Some were captured and executed. Aside from Walker in Nicaragua, none of the expansionist plots brought even short-term success.[98]

In terms of promoting republican principles abroad, the United States remained properly cautious. The nation by this time was firmly established as the center of world democratic revolution. European reformers conceded the Old World's preeminence in things aesthetic but praised America's political freedoms, religious tolerance, lack of poverty, and technological prowess. They looked to the New World for inspiration and support. Americans in turn hailed the European revolutions of 1848 as extensions of their own. As always preeminently concerned about slavery, southerners feared precedents that might be turned against them. "If we sanction interference, we will be the first who will be interfered with," a New Orleans newspaper warned.[99] But others enthusiastically endorsed the European revolutions and even urged active support of them.

Americans responded with special fervor to Hungary's rebellion against Austria's rule. The flamboyant Hungarian leader Louis Kossuth consciously modeled his declaration of independence after that of the United States and became a folk hero. Some Americans even urged active

---

98. May, *Filibustering*, 117–248.

99. Quoted in Joseph A. Fry, *Dixie Looks Abroad: The South and U.S. Foreign Relations, 1789–1973* (Baton Rouge, La., 2002), 67. Also Jozsef Gellen, "The American Experiment and Reform-Age Hungary, 1828–1848," in Jacques Portes, ed., *Europe and America: Criss-Crossing Perspectives, 1788–1848* (Paris, 1987), 131–48.

support for the "Noble Magyar." The U.S. government handled Kossuth with great care. Adhering to a long-standing convention of European diplomacy, President Zachary Taylor refused recognition until certain that the Hungarians could sustain an independent government on their own. When Austria, with Russian assistance, crushed the revolution, Webster dismissed the oppressor as "but a patch on the earth's surface" and made clear America's sympathy for people seeking self-determination.[100] The United States helped Kossuth get out of a Turkish prison and welcomed him to its shores. Fillmore openly sympathized with the Hungarian struggle. Webster exclaimed that he would "rejoice to see our American model upon the lower Danube and on the mountains of Hungary." But the United States offered no more than verbal support. Turning aside Kossuth's request for aid, Fillmore cautiously proclaimed America's true mission was "to teach by example and show by our success, moderation, and justice the blessings of self-government and the advantages of our free institutions."[101]

The United States spurned opportunities for new annexations, even when offered on a silver platter. In the case of Yucatán, race proved the sticking point. This strategic peninsula, gateway to the Gulf of Mexico, erupted into the unusually brutal Caste War in 1847, Indians rising in revolt against their Spanish rulers. Some Americans wanted to save the embattled whites from extermination. Others warned that the British might seek control of a strategic area. The United States did mount a show of force in support of Yucatán's rulers in early 1848, but it turned back their proposals for annexation. Americans grew increasingly disenchanted with the Yucatán whites, who seemed "cowardly" and unworthy of their race. More important, they were not inclined to risk contamination by absorbing the "uncivilized, perfidious" Indians, who, Calhoun said, "were too ignorant to appreciate liberty, or exercise the rights if conferred."[102] Similarly, Pierce rebuffed Hawaiian proposals for annexation conditioned on the islands' admission as a state and the granting of full citizenship to their people.[103]

Persistent efforts to acquire Cuba ran afoul of the explosive slavery issue. Slaveholders saw the creation of new slave states there as a means to redress a congressional balance that had tipped against them. They feared

100. Smith, *Taylor/Fillmore*, 231.
101. Ibid., 230–33.
102. Mark J. White, "The Case of the Yucatecan Request: American Foreign Policy at the Close of the Mexican War," *Mid-America* 72 (October 1990), 177, 184, 189.
103. Gara, *Pierce*, 147.

that Britain might acquire Cuba and abolish slavery or push the Spanish toward abolition. They especially worried about what they ominously labeled "Africanization," a Cuban slave revolt as in Haiti that might spread the horrors of race war to the United States. Cuba took on added strategic significance with talk of a canal across the Central American isthmus.

Throughout the 1850s, Cuba was the object of various schemes for acquisition. Administrations from Polk to Buchanan tried to purchase it from Spain. Between 1849 and 1851, Narciso López launched four filibustering expeditions, appealing to southerners to "advance the cause of civilization and humanity"—and to seize the island "while the present condition of her slaves is untouched."[104] The pro-southern Pierce and Buchanan administrations assigned high priority to acquisition. Pierre Soulé, minister to Spain and a diplomat notoriously lacking in diplomatic skills, made Cuba a personal obsession and tried to get it by fair means and mostly foul. He connived with Spanish rebels to overthrow the monarchy in hopes of getting a more compliant government, all the while shamelessly flattering the queen to do his bidding. In 1854, he and other pro-southern U.S. diplomats in Europe issued the so-called Ostend Manifesto (actually released at Aix-la-Chapelle without approval of Washington and hence without official standing), claiming that Cuba was essential to the United States and the institution of slavery. Should Spain refuse to sell it, the United States "by every law human and divine" would be "justified in wresting it from Spain."[105] When Britain and France seemed likely to go to war in 1859, southerners urged exploiting the opportunity to take Cuba. England could be kept quiet by maintaining a "defiant attitude toward France."[106]

All efforts failed. Spanish officials stubbornly insisted that they would rather see Cuba beneath the ocean than as part of the United States. Taylor and Fillmore scrupulously applied the neutrality laws, limiting U.S. support for López's ill-fated expeditions. The popular uprisings the adventurer counted on never materialized. On his last mission, he and some of his motley band of "freedom fighters," Americans included, were captured and executed. The Ostend Manifesto was too much even for the sympathetic Pierce, who saw no choice but to repudiate his reckless appointees. Cuba became as emotional an issue for opponents of slavery as

104. Cristobal Madam to William Preston, November 2, 1849, William Preston Papers, Special Collections, University of Kentucky Library, Box 46. My thanks to Dr. Randolph Hollingsworth for bringing these documents to my attention.
105. Gara, *Pierce*, 150–55; "The Ostend Manifesto," October 18, 1854, in Ruhl Bartlett, ed., *The Record of American Diplomacy* (New York, 1950), 240–42.
106. Preston to James Buchanan, May 8, 1859, Preston Papers, Box 46.

for southerners. Free Soilers who staunchly opposed the extension of slavery blocked Buchanan's efforts to appropriate funds for its purchase. Some southerners expressed skepticism about acquiring a territory filled with alien races. The failure to acquire Cuba turned others toward secession.

Central America drew more U.S. attention than Cuba. Some North Americans had long viewed the region as an outlet for slavery and a possible solution to the nation's race problem. The establishment of trading interests in Asia, the acquisition of California and Oregon, and the gold rush of 1849 heightened interest in a passage across the isthmus. Henry Clay had dreamed of a canal to shorten the distance between Atlantic and Pacific. By the 1850s, Clay's dream had become a national priority. "Central America is destined to occupy an influential position in the family of nations," the *New York Times* proclaimed in 1854, "if her advantages of location, climate and soil are availed of by a race of 'Northmen' who shall supplant the tainted, mongrel and decaying race which now occupies the region."[107]

Central America in the 1850s was a uniquely volatile region. Bolívar's federation had long since collapsed, giving way to five separate, insecure, and combative nations. Disputes between the countries over boundaries and resources were exceeded by the conflict within them. The chronic instability and sudden importance of the region drew foreign entrepreneurs, adventurers, and filibusters. Britain had long-standing strategic and economic interests in the area. As the United States began to assert itself, Anglo-American tensions escalated sharply. The 1850 Clayton-Bulwer Treaty, providing for joint construction and control of a canal, was negotiated to ease tensions, but its vague language actually sparked new conflicts.

From the late 1840s, the United States steadily expanded its role in Central America. In separate treaties with Colombia and Nicaragua, it acquired rights to build an isthmian canal. The treaty with Colombia gave it a virtual protectorate over the northernmost province of Panama. North Americans bought up Central America's lands and exploited its mines. Entrepreneurs such as the swashbuckling Cornelius Vanderbilt constructed land and water routes across the isthmus. In 1855, Americans completed a forty-eight-mile railroad across Panama, a triumph of Yankee skill and the "marvel" of an age full of remarkable technological advances.[108]

107. Quoted in Thomas M. Leonard, *Central America and the United States: The Search for Stability* (Athens, Ga., 1991), 22.
108. Gara, *Pierce*, 145.

Whatever benefits they brought to Central America, the "Northmen" hailed by the *New York Times* were also meddlesome and aggressive. Even in the golden age of gunboat diplomacy, minister to Nicaragua Solon Borland gave diplomats a bad name. A physician turned politician, former senator from Arkansas, and avowed expansionist, Borland's self-proclaimed "greatest ambition" was to "see the State of Nicaragua forming a bright star in the flag of the United States." He managed to convert a relatively trivial incident into a near war with Britain. Seeking to protect a U.S. citizen wanted for murder, he claimed diplomatic immunity when local officials tried to arrest the accused and himself for interfering. When struck in the face with a randomly thrown bottle, he demanded a formal apology. A U.S. Navy vessel was sent to collect reparations for damage to American property and the treatment of Borland. When officials predictably rejected U.S. demands, the captain, exceeding his instructions, bombarded the British-controlled port of Greytown and sent marines ashore to burn what was left, doing an estimated $3 million damage. Some Americans protested this grossly excessive use of force. Experienced in such matters, the British denounced it as an unparalleled outrage and might have retaliated had they not been tied down by the Crimean War. Embarrassed but unwilling to apologize, the Pierce administration clumsily tried to shift blame elsewhere.[109]

The notorious William Walker put Borland to shame. Also a former physician—and lawyer, journalist and gold rusher—the hundred-pound "grey-eyed man of destiny" plunged headlong into the maelstrom of Nicaraguan politics. Attaching himself to the faction out of power, he and a band of adventurers he called "the Immortals" landed in Nicaragua in June 1855, imposed peace on the group holding power, and established a puppet government giving Walker control. Walker subsequently "won" the presidency through sham elections, reinstituted slavery, and established English as a second language. An overt racist who dismissed the local elite as "drivelers," he dreamed of creating a Central American union, based on slavery and run by white men, with himself as head and closely tied to the southern states. In time, he overextended himself. Otherwise unable to cooperate, the Central American nations banded together in what is still proudly called the "National War" to throw out the Yankee intruder. They received crucial support from Vanderbilt, whose interests Walker had challenged, and from the British, who saw him as an instrument of U.S. designs. Walker managed to escape and returned to New Orleans a hero. The U.S. Navy foiled a second expedition in 1859.

109. James M. Woods, "Expansionism as Diplomacy: The Career of Solon Borland in Central America, 1853–1854," *Americas* 40 (January 1984), 410–15.

The following year, on yet a third try to regain power, he was captured in Honduras, tried, and executed.[110]

United States intervention in Central America had significant results. No new territory was annexed, but U.S. interests and involvement expanded significantly. The nation acquired rights to the major canal routes, increased its political influence, and established a naval presence. North American companies controlled the existing routes across the isthmus. Most important, as the United States established its preeminence, Britain began to withdraw. Preoccupied with events in Europe, officials refused, as Lord John Russell put it, to permit the "miserable States in Central America" to provoke a needless war. They may even have developed a certain admiration for their offspring as an imperialist "chip off the old block."[111] They rationalized that U.S. control might be expedient politically and profitable economically. Britain thus initiated a gradual withdrawal from a region it had once dominated.[112]

For Central Americans, U.S. intrusion was at best a mixed blessing. The United States contributed to their economic development. Central Americans on occasion exploited the U.S. presence to their advantage. But North American racism and expansionism left a bitter legacy. Following the Walker affair, Costa Rica and Nicaragua declared themselves under the protection of Britain, France, and Sardinia against the "barbarians of the United States."[113] While Walker has remained an object of amusement for later generations of Americans, and has even been hailed as a "valiant idealist," his intervention in Nicaragua remains a major event in Central American history, a stark symbol of the ambitions and aggressiveness of the colossus to the north.[114]

The Buchanan presidency typifies the contradictions of U.S. expansionism in the 1850s. An experienced and successful diplomat, Buchanan, like his mentor Polk, was his own secretary of state. Indecisive and even timid in dealing with the nation's increasingly urgent domestic problems, he was belligerent with other nations and pursued numerous expansionist schemes. Like Polk, he looked John Bull straight in the eye. He defended Walker beyond the point of propriety. He dispatched a naval force of

110. Leonard, *Central America*, 22–30; John H. Coatsworth, *Central America and the United States: The Clients and the Colossus* (New York, 1994), 27–29.

111. Quoted in Paul A. Varg, *United States Foreign Relations, 1820–1860* (East Lansing, Mich., 1979), 230.

112. Elbert B. Smith, *The Presidency of James Buchanan* (Lawrence, Kans., 1975), 71.

113. Quoted in ibid., 73.

114. Coatsworth, *Central America*, 27; Albert Z. Carr, *The World and William Walker* (New York, 1963).

nineteen ships to avenge tiny Paraguay's killing of a single U.S. seaman. To secure payment for dubious financial claims against Mexico, he asked Congress for authority to detach its northern provinces and then to invade. He vigorously pursued the acquisition of Cuba. Anticipating twentieth-century chief executives, he sought and nearly secured from Congress a resolution giving him a blank check to use military force in Latin America. Caught up in the secession crisis, a preoccupied Congress wisely rejected Buchanan's wilder schemes, sealing the fate of expansion.[115]

DURING THE AGE OF MANIFEST DESTINY, the United States greatly expanded its territory and acquired vast riches in natural resources, swelling national pride and laying the foundation for its future status as the world's greatest power. Popular myth to the contrary, foreign policy was central to the national experience in the antebellum era. Even in the 1850s, when little territory was added, Americans continued to operate across the globe. The United States expanded its involvement and interests in places like East Asia and Central America.

In terms of solving the nation's immediate problems, expansion did not live up to its billing. The Asian market did not meet expectations and did not absorb the nation's agricultural surplus. Commercial and territorial expansion did not head off industrialization and urbanization, as the Jeffersonians had hoped. The expansionism of the 1850s had generally negative results. To be sure, U.S. government aggressiveness, along with the filibusters, helped spur British withdrawal from Central America, a region deemed increasingly important to the United States. The "Yankees" were such "ingenious Rogues," Prime Minister Lord Palmerston complained, that they would get their way in Central America through the "indirect agency" of people like Walker—"Texas all over again." British withdrawal in turn ensured eventual U.S. dominance of the region. On the other hand, the filibuster expeditions provoked staunch opposition in Mexico and Cuba to the sale of territory to the United States. Along with relentless U.S. efforts to purchase territory to the south, the filibusters aroused fear and hatred of the United States in Central and indeed South America. Even Chileans feared that the "Yankee nation" was awaiting a chance to "devour them." Some Latins turned to Europe for protection against their rapacious northern neighbor. At least for the short term, filibustering slowed U.S. commercial expansion in Central America.[116]

---

115. Smith, *Buchanan*, 69–80.
116. Robert M. May, "Agents of Manifest Destiny," unpublished paper in possession of author, and *Manifest Destiny*, 240, 246–47.

Most important, expansion exacerbated rather than solved the nation's most urgent problem. Southern efforts to preserve their way of life through expansion aroused growing opposition in the North. Northern frustration of their designs sapped southern confidence in their ability to survive within the federal union, sparking secessionist sentiment. The emergence by 1856 of the Republican Party, a political alignment committed to stopping the expansion of slavery, suggested the extent to which Manifest Destiny had become a sectional issue. Rejection by leaders on both sides of the 1860 Crittenden Compromise, which would have extended the Missouri Compromise line to the Pacific—and possibly beyond—made clear the issue could not be resolved. Foreign policy was important to the calculations on each side. Southerners feared their loss of control of U.S. foreign policy doomed them to inferior status in the Union. For Republicans, on the other hand, slavery prevented the United States from achieving its higher global mission. It "deprives our republican example of its just influence in the world," Abraham Lincoln asserted in 1854; it "enables the enemies of free institutions to taunt us as hypocrites."[117] The irrepressible conflict over expansion and slavery led straight to Fort Sumter. The nation had swallowed Emerson's dose of arsenic.

117. Weeks, *Continental Empire*, 163; Fry, *Dixie*, 72–74.

FRANKLIN'S RECEPTION AT THE COURT OF FRANCE. 1778.
RESPECTFULLY DEDICATED TO THE PEOPLE OF THE UNITED STATES

"Franklin and the Ladies of Paris": While in Paris, Benjamin Franklin took special delight in the company of French women. His dour—and perhaps envious—fellow diplomat John Adams complained that "one was not enough for him but he must have one on each side, and all the ladies both young and old were ready to eat him up." *Library of Congress Prints and Photographs Division. LC-DIG-pga-01591, Library of Congress, Washington, D.C.*

This painting by Benjamin West portrays the peacemakers of the American Revolution, from left to right John Jay, John Adams, Benjamin Franklin, Henry Laurens, and William Temple Franklin. British diplomats refused to sit for the painting, leaving it unfinished. *Library of Congress.*

Thomas Jefferson's idealism and hard-nosed practicality epitomized what would become a distinctively American approach to foreign policy. His expansionist vision and skillful diplomacy, along with a huge dose of good luck, secured the windfall of the Louisiana Purchase. *Library of Congress.*

A brilliant financier, Secretary of the Treasury Alexander Hamilton put the new nation on a sound economic footing. His bitter struggle with Secretary of State Thomas Jefferson in the early 1790s helped shape the foreign policy of the United States during its infancy. *Library of Congress.*

The multi-talented, ebullient, and zealous French diplomat, Edmond-Charles Genet, sought American help in spreading the revolution. His blatant violations of U.S. neutrality prompted George Washington's administration to seek his recall, and, when a more radical government took power in France, to grant him asylum. *Courtesy of Wikimedia Creative Commons.*

A hero of the Haitian revolution, known as the "Black Napoleon," the charismatic Toussaint Louverture led struggles for the abolition of slavery and freedom from Spanish and French rule on the island of Saint-Domingue. He was captured by French forces in 1802 and died in a French prison. *Courtesy of Wikimedia Creative Commons; PD-old-70.*

The so-called Barbary Wars were the nation's first foreign war. They evoked among Americans powerful nationalist sentiments tinged with anti-Muslim prejudices as demonstrated in this engraving of Stephen Decatur and Daniel Fraser in mortal conflict with the enemy. *U.S. Naval Historical Center.*

The British warship *Leopard*'s mauling of the U.S. vessel *Chesapeake* off the coast of Virginia in June 1807 provoked war fever among Americans. Instead of fueling the outrage, President Thomas Jefferson tried what he called "peaceable coercion" with an embargo of British goods. *Fred S. Cozzens, "The incident between HMS 'Leopard; and USS 'Chesapeake' that sparked the Chesapeake-Leopard Affair," 1897. Courtesy of Wikimedia Creative Commons. PD-old-70.*

This 1807 political cartoon shows an American smuggler being bitten by a large snapping turtle called "Ograbme" (embargo spelled backwards). Jefferson's embargo sought to punish Britain for its trade restrictions but inflicted great harm on U.S. merchants and made smuggling a national pastime.

A Native American spiritual and political leader and brother of the better known Tecumseh, Tenskwatawa sought to mobilize Shawnees to resist American encroachment on their lands. Routed at the Battle of Tippecanoe (1811), he fled to Canada to continue the fight. Following the War of 1812, he joined his people in their removal west of the Mississippi River. *Courtesy of Wikimedia Creative Commons.*

John Quincy Adams is generally regarded as the nation's greatest secretary of state. His shrewd diplomacy brought to the United States East and West Florida and Spanish claims to the Pacific Northwest. He was instrumental in formulating the Monroe Doctrine. *Library of Congress.*

This hand-colored lithograph made near the end of Andrew Jackson's presidency by N. Currier of Currier and Ives fame portrayed him in the heroic pose in which Americans pictured him. *Library of Congress.*

The removal of Native Americans to lands across the Mississippi in the 1830s brought forth great tragedy, as portrayed in this rendition of the infamous Trail of Tears that went with Cherokee removal to the West. *Woolaroc Museum, Bartlesville, Oklahoma.*

Col. Harney and U.S. dragoons pursue Mexicans at the Battle of Churubusco, August 20, 1847. The Mexican-American War reinforced in the minds of Americans the singular virtues of their republic. *Library of Congress.*

N.Trist.

After dispatching Nicholas Trist to Mexico in 1847 to negotiate a peace treaty, President James K. Polk upped his demands and recalled his emissary. Certain that the war was "iniquitous" and determined to end it, Trist defied Polk and concluded a treaty based on the original demands. The president declared Trist "devoid of honour or principle" and fired him–but accepted his treaty. *The Miriam and Ira D. Wallach Division of Art, Prints and Photographs: Print Collection, The New York Public Library.*

This Japanese print portrays a U.S. naval officer (not Perry) in the most fearsome manner. *Library of Congress*.

This portrait of Commodore Matthew C. Perry was produced around the time of his landmark voyage that led to the opening of Japan. *Library of Congress*.

A physician and lawyer, William Walker, the "grey-eyed man of destiny," was one of the 1850s' leading filibusterers. He got himself elected president of Nicaragua. Thrown out of office, he was executed in Honduras in 1860 on a third attempt to regain power. *Library of Congress*.

Abraham Lincoln, portrayed in this 1863 Alexander Gardner photograph, presided over a bloody war to preserve a Union free of slavery that could stand as the "last best hope" for freedom in the world. *Library of Congress.*

Lincoln's secretary of state, William Henry Seward, skillfully employed a combination of bluster and conciliation to defend Union interests during the Civil War. *Library of Congress.*

U.S. Navy Capt. Charles Wilkes's November 1861 seizure of two Confederate diplomats from the British mail packet Trent provoked the first diplomatic crisis of the Civil War. Seward's timely concessions smoothed Anglo-American relations at a crucial time. *Library of Congress.*

An educator and abolitionist, Ebenezer Don Carlos Bassett was America's first African American diplomat. From 1869 to 1877, he served as Minister Resident in Haiti. After returning home, he became Haiti's Consul General in New York. *Photo by: Universal History Archive/UIG via Getty Images.*

This portrait of the colorful James G. Blaine, the "Plumed Knight of Maine," hangs in the Department of State where he twice served as the nation's chief diplomat. An ardent expansionist, Blaine prepared the way for the U.S. overseas thrust in the 1890s. *Library of Congress.*

Chinese immigrants played an important part in the building of the United States, especially in the completion of the transcontinental railroad. They were also the object of bitter resentment among many Americans, resulting in restrictive Congressional legislation and anti-Chinese riots such as this one in Denver on October 31, 1880. *Library of Congress.*

A SIMPLE DEFINITION.

Master Johnny Bull. "MONROE DOCTRINE! WHAT *IS* THE 'MONROE DOCTRINE'?"
Master Jonathan. "WA-AL—GUESS IT'S THAT EVERYTHING EVERYWHERE BE-LONGS TO *US!*'"

This biting cartoon from the British magazine *Punch* mocked the extravagant claims for the Monroe Doctrine asserted by U.S. Secretary of State Richard Olney during an 1895 dispute. The British government also denounced Olney's notion that the United States "was practically sovereign" in Latin America, but in the interest of building friendship with a rising power acquiesced in the U.S. position.

This sensationalist drawing by the renowned artist Frederic Remington appeared in the New York *Journal* February 12, 1897 under the headline "DOES OUR FLAG PROTECT WOMEN?" and was intended to inflame American readers. An incident like this in fact occurred, but the searching took place below decks and was done by women. *The Granger Collection, New York.*

Portrayed here in dress uniform, Emilio Aguinaldo led the Philippine rebellion against U.S. occupation forces. *Library of Congress.*

Filipino insurgents at prayer before surrendering to U.S. forces. National Archives (photo no. 395-pi-1-50_wc0322).

THE DRAGON'S CHOICE

In this August 1900 cartoon during the Boxer Rebellion, a burly and obviously vigilant Uncle Sam awaits the Chinese dragon's choice of war or peace. *The Granger Collection, New York.*

President Theodore Roosevelt once boasted that he took Panama while others debated the issue. A person who loved to be at the center of everything, TR is shown here in November 1906 operating a steam shovel at the Panama Canal construction site. Theodore Roosevelt Collection, Harvard College Library.

Roosevelt's chief diplomatic trouble shooter, William Howard Taft, is pictured here seated on an unfortunate water buffalo. Taft served as governor-general of America's new Philippines colony. U.S. Army Military History Institute.

The United States was determined to be a good colonialist in the lands it took from Spain. An American is shown here conducting classes in schools established for Filipino children. National Archives (photo no. 350-P-CA-5-1).

One of America's most distinguished public servants, corporate lawyer Elihu Root as secretary of war modernized the U.S. Army and as secretary of state balmed Latin American anger at Theodore Roosevelt's aggressiveness. A person of towering intellect and searing wit, Root is generally regarded as the founder of the eastern "Establishment" that shaped U.S. foreign policy during much of the twentieth century. *Library of Congress Prints and Photographs Division. LC-USZ62-100792, Library of Congress, Washington, D.C.*

Mexican revolutionary and folk hero Francisco "Pancho" Villa is shown in this 1914 photo with U.S. Army general John J. Pershing. American support for Villa's rival Venustiano Carranza provoked him to raid Columbus, New Mexico, on March 9, 1916, which in turn prompted the dispatch of U.S. forces headed by Pershing into Mexico, bringing the two nations to the brink of war. *Bettmann/Getty Images.*

Wilson received a hero's welcome in Paris and other European cities in early 1919, encouraging his belief that peoples everywhere sought the kind of peace he had so eloquently advocated. Princeton University Library.

The Council of Four (left to right, British prime minister David Lloyd George, Italian leader Vittorio Orlando, French premier Georges Clemenceau, and U.S. president Woodrow Wilson) did much of the work of drafting the controversial Treaty of Versailles that ended the First World War. National Archives (photo no. 111-sc-055456_wc0722).

Massachusetts Republican senator Henry Cabot Lodge and President Woodrow Wilson thoroughly despised each other, and Lodge's opposition to Wilson's League of Nations was thus personal as well as political. Lodge and other foes also raised legitimate questions about America's future role in the world that Wilson's refusal even to consider helped doom his brainchild. *Courtesy of Wikimedia Creative Commons.*

6

"Last Best Hope"

The Union, the Confederacy, and Civil War Diplomacy, 1861–1877

The American Civil War was an event of great international importance.[1] Union and Confederate leaders recognized that their success or failure might swing on actions taken or not taken by the European great powers. European leaders, in turn, saw enticing opportunities and grave threats in the conflagration across the Atlantic. For Europeans, the Civil War also had momentous ideological implications. Conservatives welcomed the breakup of the Union, which some had long predicted, hoping that it would eliminate the menace of U.S.-style democracy throughout the world. Along with President Abraham Lincoln, on the other hand, liberals viewed the Union as the "last best hope of earth," agreeing that upon its survival hinged the future of republicanism for "the whole family of man."[2] The triumph of the Union, as Lincoln seems to have understood, ensured that within a short time the United States would emerge as a major world power.

I

The Civil War was part of a worldwide mid-nineteenth-century flowering of nation-building, a broader effort on the part of peoples across the globe to affirm, often through force of arms, their national identity. In Europe, Hungarians and Poles rose up in unsuccessful revolts against Austria and Russia. Modern nations took shape in Italy and Germany through military conquest. After a short war, the Swiss formed a federal union binding together cantons previously divided by religion. The Taiping "rebellion" raged for years in China at gruesome cost; the 1868 Meiji Restoration converted Japan from a feudal entity into a modern nation-state. The quest for national identity extended to North America. With indirect U.S. support, Mexicans frustrated France's attempt to reestablish an American

1. Robert E. May, ed., *The Union, the Confederacy and the Atlantic Rim* (Lafayette, Ind., 1995), 1–2.
2. James M. McPherson, " 'The Whole Family of Man': Lincoln and the Last Best Hope Abroad," in ibid., 136–38.

empire. The threat of U.S. annexation during the Civil War forced Britain to shore up Canada's vulnerability, leading in 1867 to creation of a united nation under a federal constitution with a centralized government.

The war also had enormous global implications. In the United States before 1861, union was an incomplete concept, especially in the South. The Civil War can thus be seen as an effort to establish a nation still not completely formed. Like similar struggles elsewhere, this was accomplished by force of arms. The Union victory also marked a turning of the tide internationally in favor of nationalism, solidifying a worldwide trend toward nation-states. More important, the Civil War fused nationalism with liberalism, giving significant moral purpose to nationalism, assuring that popular government could survive, and renewing hope among liberals across the world.[3] The steamship, telegraph, and trade brought nations closer at the same time nationalism was highlighting differences and provoking conflict. Other nations closely watched the U.S. internal struggle. Americans were more aware of events elsewhere because of increased immigration, faster and cheaper communication, growing literacy, and mass-circulation newspapers.[4]

Still clinging to dreams of imperial glory in the Western Hemisphere, Europeans attempted to exploit America's absorption in its domestic struggles. Spain invaded Santo Domingo in March 1861. In the spring of 1863, France's Napoleon III sent troops into Mexico. Europe itself was wracked with conflict during these years, however, putting a premium on caution in its handling of the American war. Crises erupted in 1862 from the Italian *Risorgimento* and Austria's conflict with Prussia. In 1863, the Polish rebellion against Russia threatened a general European war. By dividing the great powers against each other, these events rendered less likely any form of intervention in U.S. affairs. By increasing problems for France in Europe, German and Italian unification influenced Napoleon's eventual withdrawal from Mexico.[5]

For both Union and Confederacy, diplomacy was vital. Should the Europeans recognize the belligerency and eventually the independence

3. Carl N. Degler, "One Among Many: The United States and National Unification," in Carl J. Guarneri, *America Compared* (New York, 1997), 335–52; David M. Potter, "Civil War," in C. Vann Woodward, ed., *The Comparative Approach to American History* (New York, 1968), 138–45.

4. Norman E. Saul, *Distant Friends: The United States and Russia, 1763–1867* (Lawrence, Kans., 1991), 329.

5. Paul Kennedy, *The Rise and Fall of the Great Powers* (New York, 1987), 187–93; D. P. Crook, *Diplomacy During the American Civil War* (New York, 1975), 21, 99, 107, 121, 155, 180–83.

of the South, offer economic and military aid, perhaps even send military forces, they could ensure its survival and ultimate independence. Their neutrality and refusal to intervene, on the other hand, would help the Union, perhaps even seal Confederate doom. Americans on both sides remembered, in this regard, that French intervention in 1778 had ensured the success of their revolution.[6]

Confederate diplomacy was founded on naïveté and illusion. Facing a huge disadvantage in such essential sinews of war as population, natural resources, and industrial capacity, the South might have looked abroad to make up the deficiency. In fact, southerners were strangely ambivalent toward the outside world. They believed themselves sophisticated and in touch with European elites. But they were quite out of tune with the prevailing currents of liberal nationalism in Europe.[7] Certain of their rectitude and invincibility, they badly misread European attitudes toward their cause and their own need for outside assistance. Especially in the Confederacy's first years, they undervalued the importance of diplomacy. President Jefferson Davis appointed incompetents to the vital position of secretary of state. He and his advisers did not actively seek foreign recognition and aid. If recognition was not forthcoming, some leaders arrogantly reasoned, so what? The "sovereign State of Mississippi can do a great deal better without England than England can do without her," its governor boldly—and recklessly—proclaimed.[8]

For years, southerners had fancied that they held a trump card. King Cotton, it was called, and it was based on the fundamental—and ultimately flawed—assumption that Europe in general and Britain in particular so depended on southern cotton that they had to ensure its continued import. In theory, at least, it made sense. When the Civil War broke out, about one-fifth of the population of Great Britain made a living from the manufacture of cotton, 80 percent of which came from the American South. France imported 90 percent of its cotton from the South; its textile factories employed 250,000 people. Should the cotton supply be cut off, the theory went, the European powers would be reduced to economic ruin and threatened with revolution. Southerners thus concluded that if the Union attempted a blockade, which they fully anticipated, Britain and France would have to intervene to ensure their own survival. To

6. Gary W. Gallagher, *The Confederate War* (Cambridge, Mass., 1997), 145.
7. Emory M. Thomas, *The Confederate Nation, 1861–1865* (New York, 1979), 167–68.
8. Henry Blumenthal, "Confederate Diplomacy: Popular Notions and International Rivalries," *Journal of Southern History* 32 (May 1966), 153; Joseph A. Fry, *Dixie Looks Abroad: The South and U.S. Foreign Relations, 1789–1973* (Baton Rouge, LA., 2002), 75–78.

underscore the point, they burned some 2.5 million bales at the start of the war.[9]

The architect of Union diplomatic strategy and the individual mainly responsible for its implementation was Secretary of State William Henry Seward. Seward was in many ways a strange person: "I am an enigma even to myself," he once remarked. A man of enormous energy, sloppy in appearance, he was also a genial host, a lover of fine cigars and brandy, a great raconteur, a person of such magnetism, Henry Adams once said, that he could "charm a cow to statesmanship." A man of considerable vision and sophistication, he was also earthy and a total political animal. He was brash, impulsive, and hot-tempered, given to bluster and threats. But he was most dangerous, associates said, "when he pretends to agree a good deal with you."[10]

More than a bit vainglorious, he fancied himself at the outset a prime minister to the younger and less experienced Lincoln, and he concocted schemes that bordered on the bizarre. For example, on April Fools' Day, 1861 (appropriately), he proposed that the crisis of secession might be averted if the United States declared war on France and Spain simultaneously. This "wrap the world in fire" proposal had the presumed advantage of holding the Union together by instigating a foreign war. Lincoln had the good sense to reject it.

After this inauspicious beginning, Seward matured and went on to conduct Union diplomacy with distinction, maneuvering astutely through a series of crises. Employing a policy of controlled anger, he repeatedly emphasized to European powers the dangers of sticking their noses in America's troubles. More than once, he demonstrated that rarest and most essential of diplomatic skills, talking tough enough to satisfy his domestic constituency and give an adversary pause while compromising when the situation demanded it. He carefully cultivated a madman image, encouraging other nations to believe him reckless. He often reminded Britain and France of the dangers of intervention in U.S. affairs, warning that a Union victory would mean a high price to pay later on. He became a fervent spokesman for the Union and the republican principles upon which it was founded. Once remembered for little more than the

9. Fry, *Dixie*, 76–77.

10. Howard Jones, *Union in Peril: The Crisis over British Intervention in the Civil War* (Chapel Hill, N.C., 1992), 7, 11, 88. On Seward, see also Gordon H. Warren, "William Henry Seward," in Frank J. Merli and Theodore A. Wilson, *Makers of American Diplomacy: From Benjamin Franklin to Alfred Thayer Mahan* (New York, 1974), 195–219.

purchase of Alaska, which, of course, was labeled his "folly," Seward now ranks among the nation's best secretaries of state.

Lincoln proved a perfect complement to his brilliant and sometimes volatile adviser. The president brought no diplomatic experience to the White House. He had traveled only to Canada, knew no foreign languages, and even by nineteenth-century-American standards would be considered provincial. But he appointed able people to key positions. He was a master at managing the strong men who worked with him. A natural-born politician, he had an instinctive feel for the diplomatic art. Rivals for the presidency, he and Seward formed what Lincoln's personal secretary John Hay called an "official connection hallowed by a friendship so absolute and sincere," a true rarity in government. Lincoln found relief from the pressures of war in Seward's convivial Lafayette Square parlor. For the most part, he left the secretary of state free to do his job, only occasionally reining in his excesses. Above all, Lincoln was the quintessentially American practical idealist. As the war wore on, he eloquently voiced the importance of a Union victory for the worldwide cause of freedom and shrewdly maneuvered between sometimes conflicting domestic and foreign pressures to realize the ideals he preached.[11]

At the start of the Civil War, only tsarist Russia, among the European powers, stood squarely with the Union. This curious entente between autocratic Russia and the world's leading democracy was deeply rooted in recent history. In the 1840s, the two nations had followed non-conflicting expansionist courses. Each saw the other as a potential check against Britain. Americans played an important role in Russia's economic development, especially in transportation and communications. The two nations developed a remarkable cultural affinity. During the Crimean War, the United States became "considerably Russified," in Secretary of State William Marcy's words, maintaining a benevolent neutrality that verged on the alliance Americans professed to abhor. The United States sold Russia large quantities of coal, cotton, and war supplies. American volunteers fought with Russia; U.S. doctors served with its army. Contacts between the two nations increased after the war, and the rise of abolitionism in both countries in the 1850s provided another important link.[12]

11. Hay is quoted in Doris Kearns Goodwin, *Team of Rivals: The Political Genius of Abraham Lincoln* (New York, 2005), 745. On Lincoln, see Howard Jones, *Abraham Lincoln and a New Birth of Freedom: The Union and Slavery in the Diplomacy of the Civil War* (Lincoln, Neb., 1999) and Jan Morris, *Lincoln: A Foreigner's Quest* (New York, 2000).

12. Saul, *Distant Friends*, 166–237, 398–99; the quotation is from p. 201.

Russians feared with the outbreak of the Civil War that the United States would not be able to balance Britain during a period of instability in Europe. They were determined to repay U.S. support during the Crimean War. Tsar Alexander welcomed to St. Petersburg in June 1861 the Union minister, Cassius Clay of Kentucky, hailing two nations "bound together by a common sympathy in the common cause of emancipation." Throughout four years of bloody warfare in America and turbulence in Europe, his country never wavered from that position.[13]

The other major powers, France and England, were sharply divided on the American Civil War. In England, the rising forces of liberalism despised slavery and saw the United States as a beacon of democracy in a conservative world. Despite reservations about slavery, more conservative Britons and indeed the European ruling classes generally considered the breakup of the "American colossus" as "good riddance of a night mare."[14] They felt some kinship with the stability, order, and gentility of the southern social system, in contrast to the money-grubbing plutocracy and dangerous mobocracy that, in their eyes, characterized the Union.

Those Europeans responsible for the conduct of diplomacy, balance-of-power politicians in the great age of European realpolitik, saw advantages in a divided America as opposed to a *United* States. Some Britons, in particular, concluded that Canada and other vital interests in the Western Hemisphere might be more secure with a balance of power in North America instead of U.S. hegemony. Seeking to emulate his famous uncle and fire French national pride through foreign adventurism, Napoleon III thoroughly despised the United States and saw the Monroe Doctrine as a major obstacle to his grand scheme for restoring national glory and containing republicanism by rebuilding in America a French empire centered upon Mexico.

Finally, to some Europeans, the principle of self-determination, as manifested in southern secessionism, had an appealing ring. The staunchly pro-Confederate *Times* of London, undoubtedly with a twinkle in its journalistic eye, found an "exact analogy between the government in Washington and the Government of George III, and the South and the Thirteen Revolted Provinces."[15] Misjudging U.S. determination to restore the Union and taking Lincoln's early caution on slavery at face value, some

13. Ibid., 312–25; the quotation is from p. 305.
14. *Times* of London, quoted in McPherson, "Whole Family," 136. The authoritative study of British opinion is R.J.M. Blackett, *Divided Hearts: Britain and the American Civil War* (Baton Rouge, La., 2001).
15. November 7, 1861.

British leaders viewed the war as a "meaningless bloodbath." They hoped for peace, and saw separation as an acceptable means to that end.

Although sympathetic to the South and the idea of secession, European leaders were not disposed to intrude. The adventurism that had raised southern hopes of support in fact had left France overextended. A newly cautious Napoleon increasingly deferred to British leadership. British leaders saw advantages in separation and felt some urge to end the war on humanitarian grounds, but they refused to take risks. They listened to Seward's warnings and carefully avoided steps that might provoke war with the United States. They recognized the importance of U.S. trade to their economy and refused to jeopardize it. Much like the United States in the Napoleonic era, they wanted to avoid entanglement *and* trade with both sides. Neutrality was thus the obvious choice. They sought to steer a delicate course between the two belligerents while protecting their interests and keeping their own people from involving their nation in war. Above all, they sought to stay out of the war and ensure that France did the same.

II

The combatants themselves provoked the first international crisis of the Civil War. The Lincoln administration adamantly insisted that it faced nothing more than an insurrection, but it employed means appropriate for full-scale war. Seeking to strangle the Confederacy at birth, it proclaimed a blockade, even though, technically, a blockade was an act of war, and, practically, it did not have enough ships to seal off a three-thousand-mile coastline. The Confederacy sent three commissioners to Europe seeking recognition. Using precedents set by the United States, it authorized the employment of privateers—the "militia of the sea"—as an "efficient and admirable instrument of defensive warfare." The Union threatened to treat privateers as pirates.[16]

Britain responded on May 13, 1861, by proclaiming its neutrality. To some extent the declaration reflected rising hostility toward the United States. The British resented the protective tariff passed by the Republican Congress in 1861 and the Union blockade. They may have moved too fast. They announced their neutrality without consulting Washington. Union leaders considered the move at best premature, at worst outright hostile. Still, the actions taken by the combatants, especially the blockade, left

16. Davis message to Second Provisional Congress, April 29, 1861, in James D. Richardson, ed., *The Messages and Papers of Jefferson Davis and the Confederacy* (2 vols., New York, 1966), 1:75.

little choice. British leaders saw the rebellion for what it was—a war. They cleverly harked back to precedents set by George Washington in 1793.

The British correctly insisted that they were not taking sides, but their actions appeared to favor the South. The declaration of neutrality automatically conceded belligerent status to the Confederacy. It was seen in both North and South (incorrectly as it turned out) as a precursor to recognition of independence and perhaps even aid. Foreign Secretary Lord John Russell further angered the Union by receiving the Confederate commissioners informally and announcing that Britain and France would act in concert in issues dealing with the war.

"God damn them!" Seward roared in response. His famous Dispatch No. 10 of May 21, 1861, although toned down by Lincoln, still threatened a break in relations if Britain continued to meet with southern representatives and otherwise moved closer to recognizing Confederate independence.[17] He demanded respect for the Union blockade. When the British and French ministers visited him together, he insisted on seeing them separately. The U.S. minister to England, Charles Francis Adams, underscored the secretary's warnings. Arriving at his post just as the neutrality crisis erupted, Adams went out of his way to avoid antagonizing his hosts by appearing at court in the traditional stockings and lace rather than the black republican garb required by Marcy's 1853 dress circular. Echoing Seward's warnings, he threatened to depart before beginning his mission if Britain gave further comfort to the enemy.

Taking heed of Union protests and warnings, the British maintained a proper neutrality, offending both sides but increasingly leaning toward the Union. Recognizing the future value of precedents set by Washington, they did not challenge the blockade, despite its questionable legality. To the consternation of southerners, Russell did not receive the Confederate commissioners again. Britain refused to admit privateers to its ports, depriving the Confederacy of the presumed advantages of its "militia of the sea." British leaders did not want to appear to be supporting slavery. They were well aware of the long-run threat of diminishing cotton imports, but because of large crops in 1860 their warehouses were full and they could accept the short-term loss rather than provoke the Union. For the moment, they adopted a wait-and-see demeanor, letting the American dust settle before they acted. Sometimes in diplomacy the "wisest strategy was to do nothing," Russell explained. "They who in quarrels interpose, will often get a bloody nose," Prime Minister Lord Palmerston, the consummate

---

17. Phillip S. Paludan, *The Presidency of Abraham Lincoln* (Lawrence, Kans., 1994), 89–90.

realist, pointedly reminded his colleagues.[18] Even the Confederate victory at First Bull Run in July 1861, which momentarily encouraged the South and demoralized the North, failed to budge Britain from its strategy. Now the Confederacy protested British "truckling" to Seward's "arrogant demands" and acceptance of the "so-called blockade."

This changed suddenly in November 1861 when an incident at sea brought the United States and Britain to the verge of war. The *Trent* affair was the handiwork of the brilliant and eccentric Capt. Charles Wilkes. An accomplished scientist as well as naval officer, Wilkes had headed the Great United States Exploring Expedition on its worldwide journey in the 1840s.[19] Arrogant, overbearing, as paranoid as the legendary Capt. William Bligh, he was also impulsive and ambitious—he once promoted himself to captain while at sea and ostentatiously donned the uniform he had packed for the occasion. His actions in 1861 made clear the way an impetuous individual could provoke a major crisis.[20] Learning that recently appointed southern diplomats James Mason and John Slidell were aboard the British ship *Trent* en route from Havana to Europe via St. Thomas, Wilkes, on his own authority, stopped and boarded the neutral ship. Taking upon himself the role of international lawyer and prize court judge, he captured Mason and Slidell. Without searching the ship or taking it to prize court, he sent it on its way. In fact, the neutral vessel was carrying southern dispatches, generally recognized as contraband, but by not following the proper rules of search and seizure Wilkes rendered his actions illegal.

The capture of Mason and Slidell reversed the traditional roles of America and Britain in maritime disputes and provoked anger across the Atlantic. Britons were furious; there was much loose talk of war.[21] The cabinet was understandably outraged and demanded that the United States disavow Wilkes's actions, release Mason and Slidell, and apologize. The dying Prince Albert, Queen Victoria's closest adviser, softened the tone of the cabinet's ultimatum, giving diplomacy a chance to work, but British leaders were still prepared to break relations, the last step before war. The nation began to mobilize and took steps to fortify Canadian defenses. France backed Britain and even proposed joint intervention in the Civil War, a step London quickly and wisely rejected.

18. Jones, *Union in Peril*, 50.
19. William Stanton, *The Great United States Exploring Expedition of 1838–1842* (Berkeley, Calif., 1975).
20. Geoffrey S. Smith, "Charles Wilkes and the Growth of American Naval Diplomacy," in Merli and Wilson, *Makers of American Diplomacy*, 152.
21. Jones, *Union in Peril*, 87.

All "the world is disgusted by the insolence of the American Republic," Russell exclaimed.[22]

The U.S. reaction was mixed. To a nation starved for victories, the capture of the two Confederate diplomats was welcome news, especially since Mason and Slidell had been among the most rabid of southern disunionists. Northerners hailed Wilkes's audacity. Some hotheads responded to British war fever with bellicose talk of their own. Others recognized that Wilkes had violated the nation's traditional stand for freedom of the seas. In time, moreover, even the hottest of heads perceived the difficulty of defeating Britain and the Confederacy at once and recognized that a war with Britain might ensure southern independence. At first complacent, Lincoln and Seward gradually recognized the hornet's nest Wilkes had stirred. Near-panic in financial circles encouraged their desire for compromise. In this instance, Lincoln continued to talk tough to his domestic audience while letting Seward arrange a face-saving compromise. The secretary readily assented to British demands to give up the two diplomats. Since they were contraband, he insisted, their seizure had been legal, but Wilkes's failure to follow the rules forced their release. He also justified his action in terms of America's long-standing support for freedom of the seas and its opposition to impressment.

The *Trent* affair was both ominous and useful, forcing the United States and Britain at an early stage to confront the risks and possible costs of war. By eliminating a very real threat of conflict with Britain, it left the Union free to concentrate on defeating the Confederacy. But it did not end the possibility of recognition of southern independence or British intervention. And British leaders appear to have concluded from the experience that the best way to deal with the United States was to take a hard line.[23]

III

Following the *Trent* crisis, while Union and Confederate armies settled into their bloody struggle, diplomats from both sides competed for advantages that might determine the outcome of the war. Southern diplomacy could never quite rise above its considerable limits. Communications posed especially difficult problems. The blockade and lack of access to a cable made it extremely difficult to issue instructions and receive dispatches. Confederate officials often had to get news from the northern press. Dispatches were lost or captured and sometimes appeared in Union

22. Ibid., 87.
23. Paludan, *Lincoln*, 93; Crook, *Diplomacy*, 57–60; Jones, *Union in Peril*, 98–99.

newspapers.[24] In dealing with Caribbean countries, southerners had to explain away their aggressive past, something they tried to do—with only limited success—by noting that they had sought additional territory only to preserve a "balance of power in a Government from whose dominant majority they feared oppression and injury."[25] The Confederacy faced a huge challenge in persuading Britain and France to do things that threatened war with the Union. Most important, it could never overcome the stigma of slavery.

Ironically, although the Confederacy inherited through the national Democratic Party a corps of experienced diplomats, it made notably poor appointments. The first commissioners sent to England were an undistinguished group not well suited to a difficult assignment. William Lowndes Yancey, their spokesman, defended slavery with such passion that he quickly made himself unpopular in England.[26] Slidell and Mason were both seasoned diplomats, but they were not especially effective. Mason was an intelligent individual, but his boorish behavior, his errant aim with tobacco juice, and his reputation as an apologist for slavery limited his efforts in England. Slidell was astute and experienced and presumably had an affinity with the French through his background in Louisiana and fluency in the language, but he never grasped what motivated French officials or how the government operated. Historian Charles Roland has wryly observed that the two did more good for their cause while incarcerated in a northern prison than when they actually took their posts. Mexican recognition could have been a huge boon to the Confederacy, but John Pickett of Kentucky was as bad a choice for that country as Joel Poinsett and Anthony Butler. Like those two notorious predecessors, he blustered and threatened and displayed open contempt for the Mexican nation and people. His personal behavior was reprehensible—he was jailed for assaulting another American in Mexico City and eventually bribed his way out. In all, southern diplomats were a provincial lot who, even by the standards of the time, evinced enormous insensitivity to foreign cultures. They were much less astute than their Union counterparts when dealing with world affairs.[27]

Southern foreign policy was poorly conceived. Confederate leaders did not give diplomacy high priority or adequate attention at the outset. By the

24. Crook, *Diplomacy*, 80; Richardson, *Davis Messages* 2:326, documents a case where it took five months to receive a dispatch from Paris.

25. R.M.T. Hunter to William L. Yancey, Pierre A. Rost, and A. Dudley Mann, August 24, 1861, in Richardson, *Davis Messages* 2:74.

26. Charles P. Roland, *The Confederacy* (Chicago, 1960), 102.

27. May, *Union, Confederacy*, 12; Roland, *Confederacy*, 103–6.

time they recognized its importance, it was too late. Confident of victory, they did not seek alliances or even foreign assistance. Inexplicably, the Confederacy did not try to establish ties with Russia despite its size and the importance of cotton exports. It did not appoint a mission until late 1862; the commissioner never made it to St. Petersburg.[28] The South perceived the importance of an alliance with Mexico to secure access to the outside world through its ports, but it pursued this important goal in a bumbling way. Much in the mode of Butler, Pickett tried to bribe Mexico into recognition. That failing, like Poinsett, he backed the political opposition. When Mason met unofficially with Russell, he did not press the case for recognition and aid, perhaps the South's only hope for survival, letting Britain off the hook.

Even where it achieved some success, southern diplomacy was hemmed in by sharp limitations. Displaying a rare shrewdness born perhaps of necessity, the Confederacy negotiated in 1861 treaties with the Five Civilized Tribes living in Indian Territory in Oklahoma, even pledging that the Indians would not be "troubled or molested" by individuals or the states. The key provision for the Indians was the protection offered against the Union; in return, they vowed fealty to the South and even promised to fight. When the Confederacy could no longer provide such protection, however, and this came as early as the spring of 1862, the alliance disintegrated. The Indians were not inclined to assist a Confederacy that could do nothing for them.[29]

Confederate propaganda also revealed limitations. The key figure was Henry Hotze, a Swiss-born Mobile journalist who in May 1862 launched on his own the *Index*, a weekly newspaper propounding the southern point of view. In time, the Richmond government began to subsidize Hotze's work. It also sponsored a propaganda effort in France. Late in 1863, the Confederacy promoted the founding of a Society to Promote the Cessation of Hostilities, a pro-southern organization that used fact sheets, handbills, and lectures to sway British opinion toward recognition. Confederate propaganda evinced some sophistication, revealing a growing maturity in southern foreign relations. Propagandists shrewdly concentrated on the hardest-hit areas of Britain, where they presumed their message would be best received. They admitted, however, that they could not get their point of view across even in these areas because of fierce working-class opposition to slavery.[30]

28. Saul, *Distant Friends*, 335–36.
29. Thomas, *Confederate Nation*, 188–89.
30. Ibid., 177–79; R.J.M. Blackett, "Pressure from Without: African Americans, British Public Opinion, and Civil War Diplomacy," in May, *Union, Confederacy*, 80–90.

The South continued to rely on King Cotton. The voluntary embargo requested by the Confederate government was remarkably effective, far more so than Jefferson's leak-plagued efforts before 1812, making clear the power of southern nationalism. By the spring of 1862, the shortage of cotton began to have significant effects in Europe. Baron Rothschild spoke of a "whole continent in convulsion." Many British mills closed in 1862, prices skyrocketed, and unemployment steadily increased.

Whatever its effects, the cotton embargo did not live up to the faith placed in it. Economic sanctions take time to work, and time was not on the Confederacy's side. It was also a matter of strategy. The South tried to use the embargo as a "lever" to force European recognition. It might have done better to bargain shipments of cotton in return for recognition and assistance. The British blamed the South rather than the Union for the shortages. The virtual embargo of cotton undermined its value as a diplomatic weapon.[31]

Timing also worked against King Cotton. When war broke out in 1861, England had a huge surplus in its warehouses, in large part because of a bumper crop in 1860 and record imports. There was also a surplus of manufactured cotton goods, so much so, in fact, that many factory owners had shut down or drastically cut back production to keep prices from plummeting. Despite the effectiveness of the voluntary embargo, greed could not be eliminated, and some cotton made it through the embargoes and the Union blockade. Later in the war, the loss of southern cotton was offset by new sources in Egypt and British India. As the Union began to occupy parts of the South, it made sure to get as much cotton as possible to England.

Other factors limited the presumed clout of King Cotton. However important southern cotton may have been to its economy, Britain also had vital economic ties to the North. Bad crops at home during the war forced it to turn to the United States for grain. King Wheat thus proved as important as King Cotton. British citizens had also invested heavily in U.S. canals, railroads, and banks, and these sizeable investments might be threatened if Britain moved too close to the Confederacy. Finally, and perhaps ironically, the Civil War stimulated an economic boom in England in various industries, more than compensating for the loss of cotton. King Cotton may have worked as well as economic sanctions ever have, but it was still not enough. Not for the first time or the last did a nation, or in this case an aspirant nation, fall victim to the chimera of what Jefferson called "peaceable coercion."

31. Blumenthal, "Confederate Diplomacy," 170.

The central task of northern diplomacy was easier, of course: to keep the British and French on the cautious path toward which they were already predisposed rather than persuade them to take drastic steps. A new political party, the Republicans had no reservoir of diplomatic experience to draw on, but their diplomats in key positions performed effectively, in some cases remarkably so. Seward matured quickly. He worked diligently to maintain the harmony in Anglo-American relations that followed the *Trent* affair. He attempted to use Union military success to deter any European move toward intervention and to turn cotton against the South by opening captured southern ports to European ships as a gesture of goodwill.[32] Although ignorant of the language and unschooled in diplomacy, William Dayton of New Jersey proved a competent minister in Paris, establishing good relations with Napoleon III and working hard to head off French intervention.[33] Nominally minister to Belgium, the wealthy Henry Sanford of Connecticut did much more. Imaginative, indefatigable, often meddlesome in the eyes of colleagues, Sanford was a one-man diplomatic wrecking crew, organizing a number of Union propaganda initiatives, establishing an "octopus-like" secret service network of private investigators and paid informants to track Confederate activities on the Continent, and overseeing and sometimes funding with his own money preemptive purchases to keep crucial war supplies out of Confederate hands. A colleague referred to Sanford without exaggeration as a "Legation on Wheels."[34]

Cassius Clay of Kentucky earned both notoriety and a measure of distinction in Russia. Clay was one of those anti-slavery radicals Charles Francis Adams labeled "the noisy jackasses," and his militance worried Lincoln. He was sent to St. Petersburg because, it was said, he could do no harm there and — more important — it would get him out of Washington. Clay wore a dazzling array of Bowie knives and brought to his post his notoriously thin skin and propensity for the duel. His "pigeon wing" dancing provided amusement at court. Despite his characteristically eccentric behavior — maybe in part because of it — he proved a good choice. He came to admire the Russian people and to see Russia as "our sincere friend" and "most powerful ally." A surprisingly sophisticated diplomatist with a keen understanding of balance of power politics, he did nothing to harm the existing friendship. In many ways, he actively promoted it.[35]

---

32. Crook, *Diplomacy*, 72–73.
33. *Dictionary of American Biography* (26 vols., New York, 1934–61), 3:167.
34. Joseph A. Fry, *Henry S. Sanford: Diplomacy and Business in Nineteenth-Century America* (Reno, Nev., 1982), 35–65.
35. Saul, *Distant Friends*, 317–19.

Charles Francis Adams in London was even more effective—and much more significant. Like his illustrious father—and indeed grandfather—he also was a "bulldog among spaniels," relentless, tireless in bringing to British attention alleged violations of neutrality and warning of the pitfalls of intervention. Less combative than his distinguished forebears, characterized even by Russell as "calm and judicious," he also employed friendly persuasion to mitigate and reinforce Seward's threats. Adams is generally viewed as one of the most skillful diplomats to have served his nation, a person who made a difference during a critical period.

From expediency, the Union shelved its expansionist ambitions for the duration. Lincoln was in the Whig mold, believing that America's mission could best be carried out by demonstrating "before an admiring world...the capacity of a people to govern themselves."[36] Seward, in contrast, was an avowed expansionist, whose vision of empire exceeded that of John Quincy Adams. But he understood that such ambitions must be put aside to deal with the emergency. Early in the war, Lincoln and Seward toyed with colonization schemes as a means to address domestic problems and expand U.S. influence abroad. The dispatch of freed slaves into Central America and Mexico, they reasoned, would not only ease racial tensions at home but also help ensure U.S. control over raw materials, harbors, and transit facilities in a vital area. The national security argument gained force as Europeans intervened in Mexico and Central America, In 1862, Congress appropriated funds for a colonization program. African Americans and abolitionists bitterly opposed the idea, however. When Central Americans expressed fears of "Africanization" and especially of the intrusion of a nation that had already revealed its true colors "in the aggression of Walker," Seward and Lincoln backed off.[37]

In large part to promote U.S. diplomatic objectives, Lincoln slowly and with the utmost caution seized the moral high ground. The United States recognized Haiti and Liberia in 1862. Still wary of measures long urged by abolitionists and opposed by southerners, the president took the unusual step of asking Congress to endorse the move. The first U.S. representative to Haiti held the relatively lowly rank of commissioner. Also in 1862, the United States and Britain agreed to a treaty providing for mutual searches to end the slave trade. "If I have done nothing else worthy of self-congratulation,"

36. Paludan, Lincoln, 88–89.
37. Thomas Schoonover, "Miscontrued Mission: Expansionism and Black Colonization in Mexico and Central America During the American Civil War," Pacific Historical Review 44 (November 1980), 607–20.

Seward boasted, "I deem this treaty worthy to have lived for."[38] In February 1863, the first American was executed for participation in that illegal activity. At least compared to the days when southerners controlled Congress, U.S. diplomacy was becoming increasingly color-blind.[39]

The issue of slavery had huge domestic and international implications, and Lincoln handled it with special care. As a young man, he had come to view the institution as morally wrong, but he accepted its protection by the Constitution. He had staunchly opposed the expansion of slavery but, like his idol Henry Clay, looked upon colonization as a possible solution to America's racial problems. The 1854 Kansas-Nebraska Act pushed him toward a harder line. Claiming to be "thunderstruck and stunned" by a measure that infused new life into a moribund institution, he opposed the further expansion of slavery with great moral force. He insisted that the demise of this "monstrous injustice" was essential to preserve the United States as a beacon of freedom throughout the world. When the war began, he was sufficiently concerned about the loyalty of border states such as Kentucky, Missouri, and Maryland and the support of moderates North and South to downplay slavery, focusing instead on preserving the Union. By July 1862, in the face of battlefield defeat and possible European intervention, he concluded that emancipation was a military necessity. Freeing the slaves in territory held by the Confederacy could undermine the southern war effort. It might fend off British and French intervention. It would preserve and indeed perfect the Union by securing the promises of freedom enunciated in the Declaration of Independence. "I shall not surrender the game leaving any available card unplayed," Lincoln affirmed.[40] On Seward's advice, to avoid the appearance of desperation, he delayed any move until the Union achieved some battlefield success.

Like the Confederacy, the Union waged an active propaganda war across the Atlantic. Seward sent former *New York Evening Post* editor John Bigelow to influence the French press favorably toward the Union. Bigelow and Republican politico Thurlow Weed carefully cultivated European journalists and sent letters to the editors of major newspapers. Sanford provided material to friendly newspapers across Europe and used his slush fund to hire European journalists to write favorable articles. African Americans played an important part. Fugitive slaves and freed slaves including Jefferson Davis's former coachman, Andrew Jackson, gave speeches discussing the horrors of slavery as they had experienced it

38. Crook, *Diplomacy*, 68–69.
39. Paludan, *Lincoln*, 133–34.
40. Quoted in Jones, *Lincoln*, 87.

to generate support for the Union and opposition to the Confederacy. Speeches in the mill areas in particular helped to focus the debate on the issue of freedom when it could have turned narrowly on cotton. Southern sympathizers, it was said, "breathed a sigh of relief" when Jackson returned to the United States at the end of 1863.[41]

IV

The summer and fall of 1862 were the closest the American Civil War came to becoming a world war, "the very crisis of our fate," in the anxious words of Charles Francis Adams.[42] While Union and Confederate armies slugged it out in the Mississippi Valley and especially across the bloody corridor between Richmond and Washington, the European great powers and especially Great Britain teetered on the brink of intervention. Cotton provides a partial explanation. By the summer of 1862, one-half of Britain's textile workers were unemployed, one-third of its mills had closed, and stocks were dwindling. The trans-Atlantic trade, vital to Britain's economy, suffered severe dislocation. Government revenues declined. Nervous manufacturers pressed the cabinet to do something. The economic crisis was even more severe in France. "We are nearly out of cotton, and cotton *we must have*," the French foreign minister told Sanford in April.[43]

For many Europeans, ending the war for geopolitical *and* humanitarian reasons became increasingly urgent. The longer the conflict dragged on, the greater its impact on the Old World, the more Europeans sought to end it before the conflagration spread. For Victorians, the carnage produced in America by the harnessing of modern technology to warfare came as a profound shock, provoking growing cries to stop what Britons labeled this "bloody and purposeless war," this "suicidal frenzy."[44] General George McClellan's failure to take Richmond in the Peninsular Campaign of 1862 and his adversary Robert E. Lee's dazzling maneuvers persuaded many Europeans that the Union could not win. The war might go on indefinitely. As Lee's armies moved north in August 1862 for what might be a knockout blow, Europeans anticipated that another Union defeat might provide the occasion for intervention.

Although increasingly disposed to do something, British leaders remained cautious. Seward's warnings that the Civil War could become a "war of the world" could not be ignored. There was little inclination to

41. Blackett, *Divided Hearts*, 189.
42. Crook, *Diplomacy*, 93.
43. Jones, *Union in Peril*, 156.
44. Ibid., 145, 150.

risk war with the Union by challenging the blockade until Confederate independence, as Palmerston put it, was "a Truth and a Fact."[45] By the late summer of 1862, however, British leaders were increasingly disposed to mediate the American struggle as a way to end the bloodletting, ease Europe's economic problems, and perhaps even destroy slavery by stopping its expansion. Still failing to perceive Lincoln's steadfast determination to preserve the Union, British leaders assumed that European mediation would lead to an armistice, the end of the blockade, and the acceptance of two separate governments.

A Union military victory in the fall of 1862 gave Lincoln the opportunity to take the initiative on emancipation. Lee's advancing armies met Union forces at Antietam Creek near Sharpsburg, Maryland, on September 17. In the most gruesome day of the war, the two sides together lost five thousand killed and suffered twenty-four thousand casualties. The battle was at best a draw, but Lee's retreat back into Virginia permitted the Union to claim victory. Antietam stopped the Confederate offensive into the North and provided a much-needed boost to Union morale. Five days later, Lincoln issued a preliminary Emancipation Proclamation. The order did not go into effect until January 1, 1863. Reflecting the president's persisting concern for the border states, it applied only to areas held by the Confederacy. Prosaic in tone, it disappointed abolitionists. On the other hand, it further bolstered northern spirits and spurred black enlistments in the Union army. In his annual message to Congress, December 1, 1862, Lincoln remained cautious on slavery, again speaking of colonization and compensated emancipation. He also eloquently took the moral high ground. Warning that the "dogmas of the quiet past are inadequate to the stormy present" and calling upon Americans to "think anew and act anew," he insisted that only by eradicating slavery could the United States be true to its principles. "In *giving* freedom to the slaves," he proclaimed, "we *assure* freedom to the *free*." He cast emancipation in global terms. At a time when republicanism appeared to be losing out across the world and the threat of European intervention still loomed over America, he insisted that the nation must eliminate the blot of slavery to ensure that it remained "the last best hope of earth."[46] The Emancipation Proclamation represented a crucial point in the war. It set in motion the process of ending slavery. It shifted U.S. war aims from mere preservation

45. Ibid., 128.
46. James D. Richardson, ed., *A Compilation of the Messages and Papers of the Presidents of the United States* (20 vols., Washington, 1897–1916), 8:3343–44.

of the Union to its betterment by making the nation faithful to the ideals enunciated in its Declaration of Independence.[47]

Often cited as eliminating the threat of foreign intervention, Antietam and the Emancipation Proclamation for the short term actually increased pressures on Britain and France to do something. The bloodbath in Maryland and the absence of a decisive victory merely confirmed for European statesmen that the two combatants, without external intervention, might fight on indefinitely at horrendous cost. Lincoln had issued his Emancipation Proclamation in part to gain foreign support for the Union cause, but many Britons initially saw it as an act of desperation. Viewing emancipation through the prism of mid-nineteenth-century Anglo-Saxon racism, they also feared it might unleash slave insurrections throughout the South and even set off a race war that could spread beyond the United States. British leaders thus grew more inclined to intervene. Russell discussed with France the possibility of a joint intervention aimed at an armistice. Should the Union reject such proposals, they agreed, southern independence might be recognized. Liberal leader William Evart Gladstone's dramatic October 7, 1862, speech proclaiming that southern leaders had "made an army; they are making, it appears a navy; and they have made what is more than either, they have made a nation," seemed to portend recognition of Confederate independence.

Caution once again prevailed. Gladstone's speech was not authorized. It did not reflect the views of the government or even a pro-southern view on his part. Its main concern was to end the carnage. It evoked a negative reaction throughout England and forced the cabinet to examine the consequences of intervention. Russell was most inclined to act, but the more prudent eventually won the day. Seward's strong words helped persuade British leaders that neither side would accept compromise. Intervention posed varied and considerable dangers, especially the threat of war with the United States. It thus seemed better, as Secretary of War Cornewall Lewis quoted Hamlet, to "endure the ills we have, Than to fly to others we know not of." To this point, France had been more inclined toward intervention than Britain, but a crisis in Italy and turmoil within the French government drew attention away from America at a critical point, rendered Napoleon more cautious, and divided France and Britain. The Yankeephobic but ever careful Palmerston agreed that with Lee retreating into Virginia "the Pugilists must fight a few more Rounds before the Bystanders can decide that the State Should be divided between them."[48]

47. Jones, *Lincoln*, 146.
48. Jones, *Union in Peril*, 193.

As is so often the case at times of momentous decision, doing nothing seemed the best course.[49]

Another crisis followed in October, largely the work of France's Napoleon III. The French emperor's interventionism was motivated partly by the demand for cotton, but its roots went much deeper. Gaining power through elections after the 1848 revolution, the ambitious and mercurial Napoleon in time assumed the title of emperor and set out to emulate his more illustrious uncle and namesake by restoring France's imperial glory. He challenged British dominance in the Mediterranean and South Asia. He schemed to attain the American empire pursued fleetingly by his uncle. Taking advantage of Mexico's civil strife and chronic indebtedness, he hoped to establish there a base to promote French economic and political power in the Americas. He contemplated a canal across the Central American isthmus. He saw French hegemony in Mexico as a bulwark against U.S. expansion and a springboard to restore monarchy to other Latin American states, thereby heading off the "degradation of the Latin race on the other side of the ocean," in the words of one of his advisers, and containing the advance of republicanism.

Napoleon sent French troops into Mexico in late 1861, ostensibly to collect debts, in fact to establish an imperial foothold. An independent Confederacy would provide an invaluable buffer against the United States, he reasoned. He was increasingly inclined to recognize the Richmond government to further his grand design. Frustrated by British indecisiveness, Napoleon in October 1862 proposed joint French, British, and Russian mediation calling for a six-month armistice and the lifting of the Union blockade. Should the Lincoln administration say no, he told Slidell, the powers might recognize southern independence, perhaps even provide military assistance to force an end to hostilities. Early November 1862 thus became the most perilous time for the Union.[50]

Again after advancing to the brink of intervention, the Europeans drew back. Russia was eager to end the war but unwilling to antagonize Washington. Its opposition helped kill Napoleon's proposal. Russell was inclined to act, but his colleagues remained cautious. Lewis remained the major voice of restraint, warning that Britain should wait until southern independence was firmly established or the North concluded from events on the battlefield that it could not win. Napoleon would not act without British support. His proposal died. Although it was not clear at the time, any possibility of European intervention expired with it.

49. Crook, *Diplomacy*, 100.
50. Jones, *Lincoln*, 16, 56, 59, 70–71, 131–32, 163–66.

Refusing to give up entirely, Napoleon through the instrumentation of a meddlesome and inept British member of Parliament made one last attempt in the summer of 1863. Determined to get cotton and to protect his Mexican venture by ensuring a balance of power in North America, he offered assurances to the pro-Confederate J. A. Roebuck that he would work with Britain toward recognition of the South. The bumbling Roebuck proved a poor choice. His indiscreet statement that the French feared being double-crossed by England infuriated the British, deepening their already considerable—and well-founded—suspicions of Napoleon. He further discredited himself by overstating French eagerness to act. His bitter attacks on the United States as a "mongrelised" democracy and the "great bully of the world" antagonized Union sympathizers and aroused concerns even among southern enthusiasts of the pitfalls of intervention. Once disposed to do something to stop the bloodletting, most British leaders had concluded that no outside power could stop the war except at great risk and cost to itself. British support was simply not forthcoming. Slidell could not persuade Napoleon to organize the Continental powers to act without Britain. A failed intervention could do more damage to his Mexican ambitions than none at all. Napoleon thus concluded that it would be better to do nothing and hope that the Confederacy could somehow secure its independence.[51]

A crisis over Poland in the summer of 1863 ended already dim prospects of European intervention. When the Poles rose up against Russia early in the year, France, Britain, and Austria demanded a settlement on the basis of amnesty and Polish independence. The apparent European support for the concept of self-determination seemed to offer hope to the Confederacy, but appearances were deceptive. The threat of war in Europe diverted attention from North America during an especially critical time. Napoleon could not resist meddling in the Polish crisis. His actions aroused British and Russian suspicions, closing the option of concerted action in America. Most important, European support for self-determination proved weak. When Russia rejected the powers' proposal and forcibly suppressed the revolt, they did nothing. National interest took precedence over concern for the Poles and commitment to an ideal.[52]

The Polish crisis also cemented the emerging entente between the Union and Russia, providing yet another reason for European caution. The United States had traditionally given verbal support to self-determination. Thousands of Poles had fled to America after failed rebellions in the 1830s

---

51. Crook, *Diplomacy*, 139–42.
52. Ibid., 121–24, 144–46.

and 1840s; twenty-five hundred Poles fought for the Union in the Civil War. The Lincoln administration might also have traded support for the Poles for a French pledge of non-intervention. But when caught between its ideals and self-interest, the Union behaved like the Europeans. U.S. officials were pleased, Adams noted, that the Polish crisis had "done something to take continental pressure from us." For reasons of expediency, Seward rebuffed a French proposal to join in protest, expressing contentment to leave the Poles to the tender mercies of the tsar. The Russian-American convergence on Poland reinforced European fears of an "unholy alliance" between the two rising powers that might, French writer Alexis de Tocqueville and others speculated, produce a major shift in the balance of power. This specter increased great-power reluctance to act either in Central Europe or in America.[53]

While Europe fretted about a Russian-American alliance, the appearance of a Russian "fleet" of six warships in New York harbor in September 1863 created a sensation in America—and abroad. At the time, grateful Americans hailed the visit as an overt display of Russian support for their cause, sharply contrasting it with British and French perfidy. More cynical contemporaries and subsequent historians argued that the Russians acted out of self-interest: to keep their fleet from being bottled up in Baltic ports if war broke out over Poland. In fact, Russian motives appear to have been even more complex. The fleet was conducting a normal training exercise and would have left port that summer without the threat of war. Russian officers wanted to observe the new ironclad warfare taking place in America and to demonstrate their country's rising naval capability. They also carried double crews in hopes of purchasing additional ships from the United States. Once the threat of war in Europe eased, they could achieve these practical aims while solidifying already strong ties with the United States.

Whatever the reasons, the Russian "invasion" of New York was a significant time in the Civil War. For two months, three thousand Russian visitors attended parades, balls, and dinners, while U.S. bands played "God Save the Tsar" and toastmasters hailed Lincoln and Alexander II. The visit boosted northern morale and had a negative impact in the South. It aroused further European concern of an alliance, eliminating any possibility of intervention in North America.[54]

To a large degree, as Horace Greeley suggested at the time, the Union was spared foreign intervention by the "unprincipled egotism that is the

53. Saul, *Distant Friends*, 338, 351–52.
54. Ibid., 399–52.

soul of European diplomacy."[55] Although they quickly recognized southern belligerency, the powers cautiously withheld recognition until the
Confederacy proved it could stand on its own. In the wake of southern
battlefield success in 1862, they edged warily toward intervention. But the
Union victory at Antietam and the more decisive victories at Vicksburg
and Gettysburg in the summer of 1863 eliminated any real prospect that
the Confederacy could survive. Every time they began seriously to consider acting, the British concluded that the possible gains of war with the
Union would not be worth the risks. For all his bluster and meddlesome-
ness, Napoleon followed London's lead. The Union was also lucky that
the Civil War took place when Europe was as unstable as at any time
since Waterloo. The distractions caused by its internal conflict and the
resulting great power divisions rendered intervention less likely.

Ideology as well as realpolitik accounted for European non-involvement. The American Civil War aroused passionate feelings in Europe.
The British and French governments, although far from democratic,
could not ignore domestic opinion. Slavery, of course, was the crucial
issue. British philosopher John Stuart Mill warned that Confederate success would be a "victory for the powers of evil which would give courage
to the enemies of progress and damp the spirits of its friends all over the civilized world." As long as the North fought merely for union, foreigners saw
little difference between the two combatants. But Lincoln's Emancipation
Proclamation in time evoked a powerful pro-Union reaction in Britain,
especially among liberals and the working class, that drowned out voices
favorable to the Confederacy and influenced, if it did not determine, the
government's policy. His firm stand against slavery also made it easier for
onetime British proponents of intervention to rationalize inaction. A
French citizen bluntly informed Slidell that "as long as you maintain and
are maintained by slavery, we cannot offer you an alliance. On the contrary, we believe and expect you will fail."[56]

V

The Civil War was also fought on the high seas, and here too the great
powers, especially Britain, became involved, with traditional roles reversed. Union attacks on neutral shipping caused outrage in Britain,
threatening war by the side door. British shipbuilders constructed for the
Confederacy commerce raiders that devastated the U.S. merchant marine, provoking threats of war from Seward and Adams. As with the *Trent*,

---

55. Crook, *Diplomacy*, 186.
56. McPherson, "Whole Family," 141–43; Jones, *Lincoln*, 154–57.

caution and good sense prevailed. Seward spoke loudly but acted quietly to mitigate conflict with England. The British permitted the Union to stretch belligerent rights in ways possibly useful in a future war.

Union interference with British shipping became a major problem by 1863. A thriving trade had developed in which cotton was exchanged for contraband. Neutral ships deposited goods bound for the Confederacy at ports in the Bahamas, Bermuda, and Cuba. There they were loaded aboard blockade runners, often shipped to Matamoros, Mexico, and then overland to the Confederacy. To cut down or eliminate this trade, Union warships harassed neutral shipping between Havana and Matamoros. Assigned to the region with his Flying Squadron, the indomitable Wilkes hovered off West Indian ports, establishing a virtual blockade of Nassau and Bermuda, plundering neutral shipping, and, as with the *Trent*, interpreting international law to suit himself. To justify its actions, Washington hurled back at the British the once despised doctrine of continuous voyage, even exceeding British precedent by declaring that overland trade to an enemy port made goods liable to seizure. Britain screamed about freedom of the seas and illegal search and seizure and denounced that "ill-informed and violent naval officer" Wilkes.[57]

Both sides exercised restraint. Without abandoning measures it considered essential, the Union took steps to mitigate conflict with England. It transferred the abrasive Wilkes where he could do less damage and commanded U.S. naval officers to observe proper rules of search and seizure. While going through the motions of backing its shipowners, the British government acquiesced in American actions and court rulings and ordered warships in the West Indies not to interfere with Union seizure of ships outside territorial waters.

In time, Britain also acceded to Union demands to stop private shipbuilders from constructing ships for the Confederacy. The shipbuilding program was one of the few major successes of Confederate diplomacy. Early in the war, Confederate agent James Bulloch arranged to have built in Britain a small fleet of fast, propeller-driven cruisers to prey on enemy shipping. Commerce raiding, it was reasoned, could hamper Union logistics, drive up shipping and insurance costs, and force trade to neutral carriers. The first products of this program, the *Florida* and *Alabama*, went to sea in 1862. Since the two ships left port without armament, they did not violate British neutrality laws. The *Florida* steamed to Nassau in the spring of 1862, where it was armed and began to attack Union ships. Over loud Union protests, the *Alabama* also slipped out of port, sailed to

57. Smith, "Wilkes," 156.

the Azores, and acquired armaments. During its nearly two years at sea, it destroyed or captured sixty northern ships. Meanwhile, Bulloch contracted with British shipbuilders for more commerce raiders and also frigates and ironclad rams to break the blockade.[58]

In a very real sense, the Confederacy was the victim of its success. As the *Alabama*'s tally mounted, Union protests grew louder. The Confederate raiders caused alarm up and down the eastern seaboard. Insurance rates skyrocketed, and trade moved to neutral carriers. Union officials especially feared that the ironclad rams could shatter the flimsy wooden ships manning the blockade. The United States, of course, had been among the foremost neutral profiteers during the Napoleonic wars, but as a belligerent it saw things quite differently. Union officials demanded that the British government stop building ships for the Confederacy, threatening to unleash privateers against British shipping and seek reparations for damages. *New York Herald* editor James Gordon Bennett thundered that the United States would seize Canada in return for Britain's "villainous treachery" and hold it until "full and satisfactory retribution be made."[59]

The British gradually acceded to Union demands. From the outset, Foreign Office lawyers had urged that the ships be detained, but the ministry had adhered to the more narrow requirements of domestic law. In time, it came around. Union agents snooped around British shipyards and hired private investigators to confirm that the ships were intended for the Confederacy. Adams issued stern warnings, at times even threatening war. As the tide of battle turned against the South and the likelihood of European intervention diminished, the British government grew more cautious. Adams's warnings had an impact. Perhaps more important, Britons grew increasingly concerned about setting precedents that the United States or some other neutral might use in some future war to build ships for their enemies, depriving them of their historic advantage of control of the seas.

Thus in the spring and summer of 1863, the government acted to prevent additional vessels from getting to sea. In April, officials seized the *Alexandra* on suspicion of intent, indicating a major shift in position. More important, in the summer of 1863, Britain first detained, then seized, and eventually purchased to spare the shipbuilder financial loss the first of the Laird rams, a ship ostensibly built for the pasha of Egypt. With understandable familial pride and exaggeration, Minister Adams's

58. Thomas, *Confederate Nation*, 182–83.
59. Crook, *Diplomacy*, 116.

son Henry called it a "second Vicksburg...the crowning stroke of our diplomacy."[60]

For the Confederacy, it was the last straw. An embattled Jefferson Davis bitterly protested the bias of British neutrality, complaining that while taking measures hostile to the Confederacy, Britain, in defiance of the law of nations, permitted thousands of its Irish subjects to come to America in its ships and fight for the Union. Without these "armies from foreign countries," he claimed, the "invaders would ere this have been driven from our soil." In August 1863, Mason left the increasingly hostile environs of London for Paris. The Richmond government expelled British consular officials.[61]

Davis's tone suggested his government's desperation, and in early 1865, almost as an afterthought, the Confederacy tried one last diplomatic gambit to secure foreign recognition. Suffering military defeat on all fronts, with Atlanta having fallen and Gen. Ulysses S. Grant advancing on Richmond, Davis authorized Louisiana congressman Duncan Kenner to travel secretly to Europe and propose emancipation of the slaves in return for recognition. It was too little, too late. Kenner slipped through the blockade, but the Europeans were not buying. Napoleon affirmed what was already manifest—France would follow England's lead. Britain indicated that under no circumstances would it recognize the South. The mission made clear the extent to which a Confederacy on the verge of defeat would go to somehow salvage its independence. It confirmed once again Europe's unwillingness to intrude.

The Confederate surrender at Appomattox on April 9, 1865, saved the Union and destroyed slavery, resolving by force of arms the two great issues that had divided Americans throughout the nineteenth century. By establishing that the United States would indeed be united with a free-labor economic system, it answered the great question of American nationhood. It ensured that the nation would become a great power.[62] The Union's survival of the bloody test of war gave a tremendous boost to national pride and brought a resurgence of self-confidence and optimism. Americans marveled at their power, the largest army in the world, a navy of 671 ships, and a huge industrial base. "We shall be the greatest power on earth," Gen. Joseph Hooker exulted.[63] European monarchs had exploited

60. Ibid., 152.
61. Davis messages, December 7, 1863, and November 7, 1864, in Richardson, *Davis Messages* 1:356, 487.
62. Crook, *Diplomacy*, 9.
63. Morris, *Lincoln*, 198.

America's internal conflict to reintrude in the Western Hemisphere, but they were soon in full flight. Spain withdrew from the Dominican Republic as the war ended; France and Russia were not far behind. "One by one they have retreated...," Massachusetts senator Charles Sumner proclaimed, "all giving way to the absorbing Unity declared in the national motto, *E pluribus unum*." Expressing ideas many Americans fervently shared, Sumner foresaw a not too distant time when through stages "republican principles under the primacy of the United States must embrace the whole continent."[64]

The Civil War also restored faith in the viability of those principles and certainty in the future destiny of the republic. The Union victory affirmed as Lincoln had so eloquently proclaimed in his Gettysburg Address that "government of the people, by the people, for the people" would not "perish from this earth." The abolition of slavery purified American republicanism, producing a "new birth of freedom." Lincoln's assassination just five days after Appomattox added the force of martyrdom to the cause he had so nobly espoused and so diligently pursued. Americans thus emerged from the war with their traditional faith in the superiority of their ideals and institutions revivified. On April 21, 1865, Grant privately hailed a United States "that is now beginning to loom far above all other countries, modern or ancient. What a spectacle it will be to see a country able...to put half a Million soldiers in the field....That Nation, united," he added, "will have a strength which will enable it to dictate to all others, [to] *conform to justice and right*."[65]

VI

The outburst of nationalism and rebirth of Manifest Destiny that accompanied the Union victory did not set loose a new wave of expansionism. Some Republican leaders clung to Whiggish views that America had enough land. Further expansion would hinder effective governance. The nation could best promote its ideals through example. War-weariness certainly played a part, as did a huge war debt and the enormous problems of Reconstruction: reunification of a defeated but still defiant South and consolidation of the vast western territory acquired before the war. The especially bitter struggle between Lincoln's successor, Vice President

64. Charles S. Campbell, *The Transformation of American Foreign Relations, 1865–1900* (New York, 1976), 20.
65. To Julia Grant Dent, April 21, 1865, in John Simon, ed., *The Papers of U.S. Grant*, vol. 14 (Carbondale, Ill., 1985), 428–29. My thanks to Charles Bracelen Flood for bringing this document to my attention.

Andrew Johnson of Tennessee, and the Radical Republicans over reconstruction policy spilled over into foreign policy issues. In the case of Mexico, Central America, and the Caribbean, Americans remained reluctant to acquire territory populated by alien races. Thus, although opportunities presented themselves, Seward's purchase of Alaska was the only major acquisition during Reconstruction.[66]

This does not mean that expansionist sentiment did not exist or that foreign policy was not important in these years. On the contrary, the Civil War in many ways confirmed the importance of foreign policy to the survival of the republic. An expansionist vision persisted, especially in the persons of Seward and his successor, Hamilton Fish. If there were few new acquisitions, Seward and Fish nonetheless resumed the push to the Caribbean and Pacific initiated in the 1840s and 1850s, charting the course of a new empire and taking the first steps toward its realization. Those historians who view the postwar years as a great hiatus between two eras of expansion miss the essential continuity of America's outward thrust.

Toward its southern and northern neighbors, Mexico and Canada, the United States demonstrated remarkable restraint during and immediately after the war, accepting as permanent the boundaries carved out in the antebellum period. In furtherance of Napoleon's grand design, French troops occupied Mexico City in June 1863. Later that year, Napoleon installed as ruler of Mexico the well-meaning but dull-witted Archduke Maximilian, brother of Emperor Franz Josef of Austria. Maximilian and his equally naive wife, Carlotta, undertook with enthusiasm the "holy work" of saving Mexicans from their own fecklessness, stabilizing the country, and fending off the march of republicanism in the Western Hemisphere.[67]

Civil War combatants perceived the dangers and opportunities of these developments to their respective causes and dealt with them accordingly. Despite its professed commitment to the principle of self-determination, the Confederacy sought to accommodate the new Mexican government to curry favor with Napoleon and perhaps gain recognition. Fearful of antagonizing the Union, Napoleon politely rebuffed southern overtures. Seward responded with a policy of "cautious moderation." He had refused to recognize the puppet government and warned that at some future point the United States might remove it by force. On the other hand, he also declined to assist the Mexican resistance forces of Benito Juarez.

---

66. Crook, *Diplomacy*, 178; Reginald C. Stuart, *United States Expansionism and British North America, 1775–1871* (Chapel Hill, N.C., 1988), 220.
67. Jones, *Lincoln*, 181–82.

The United States would practice in regard to Mexico "the non-interven-tion which they require all foreign powers to observe in regard to the United States," he informed the Europeans.[68] To keep Napoleon off bal-ance, he left uncertain what the United States might do in the future.

As the Civil War ended, pressures mounted to do something. Congress and the press denounced foreign intervention. "Defenders of the Monroe Doctrine" organizations sprang up across the country. Defying the neu-trality laws, Americans began to provide sizeable clandestine assistance to Juarez.[69] Before replacing Lincoln, Vice President Johnson had talked of war with Mexico as "recreation" for Union soldiers.[70] "Now for Mexico!" General Grant shouted on the day after Appomattox. Like Johnson, Grant and other generals saw a Mexican operation as a means to keep a large and increasingly restive army occupied. Warning that the establishment of a monarchical government in Mexico was an "act of hostility" against the United States and might provide a haven for Confederates leading to a "long, expensive and bloody war," Grant proposed to Johnson possible military action or at least disposing of America's huge arms surplus by sell-ing weapons to Mexican resistance forces.[71]

Bogged down in a struggle with Congress over intractable Reconstruction problems, Johnson left diplomacy in the capable hands of Seward. The secretary of state dealt with Mexico in a way that belied his carefully cul-tivated reputation for recklessness. He saw a needless war as a threat to an already embattled administration and to his lingering presidential ambi-tions. Grant positioned fifty thousand troops along the Rio Grande. Their commander, the dashing cavalryman Gen. Philip Sheridan, declared substantial stocks of weapons surplus and placed them along the border after informing Mexicans of their location. But Seward blocked Grant's more aggressive proposals, contenting himself with ratcheting up diplo-matic pressure on Napoleon and Austria. In November 1865, he warned that failure to remove European troops could mean war. He sent Gen. John Schofield to Paris with instructions to "get his legs under Napoleon's mahogany and tell him he must get out of Mexico."[72] When Austria ap-peared on the verge of sending troops to back Maximilian, Seward warned

68. Stephen J. Vallone, "'Weakness Offers Temptation': William H. Seward and the Reassertion of the Monroe Doctrine," *Diplomatic History* 19 (Fall 1995), 585.
69. Karl M. Schmitt, *Mexico and the United States, 1821–1973: Conflict and Coexistence* (New York, 1974), 86.
70. Albert Castel, *The Presidency of Andrew Johnson* (Lawrence, Kans., 1979), 39–42.
71. Ibid.; Grant to Johnson, June 19, 1965, July 15, 1865, in LeRoy P. Graf and Ralph W. Haskins, *The Papers of Andrew Johnson*, vol. 8 (Knoxville, Tenn., 1989), 257–58, 410.
72. Vallone, "Monroe Doctrine," 588.

he would consider it an act of war and the United States could not remain a "silent or neutral spectator." Aware that Austria was already deeply entangled in a crisis with Prussia, Seward exploited its vulnerability. His warning signaled France to speed its exit. Seward may also have hoped through diplomatic firmness to salvage a faltering administration.[73]

Pressure from the United States was not the only or perhaps even the most important reason for Napoleon's retreat. Juarez's forces waged deadly guerrilla warfare against the invaders. The inept Maximilian could never rally Mexican support, and his power did not extend beyond the presence of French troops. Increasingly absorbed with European problems, the unpredictable Napoleon quickly lost interest in Mexico and began to search for a way out without appearing to capitulate to the United States. Lacking French support and facing a crisis in Europe, Austria declined to test the sincerity of Seward's threats. Both governments left the hapless Maximilian to his own devices. He was thrown out of office and executed by a Mexican firing squad in June 1867. Without giving in to the more belligerent voices inside and outside of the government, Seward served notice on the Europeans that the temporary suspension of the Monroe Doctrine as a result of the Civil War had ended.[74]

A hotbed of intrigue and conflict during and immediately after the Civil War, Canada was also a potentially explosive issue. Easy access across the border made the northern neighbor a refuge for draft dodgers, bounty jumpers, and anti-war Copperheads, and therefore a source of great resentment to staunch Unionists. Canada also served as a base for Confederate guerrillas, including the legendary John Hunt Morgan. After 1864, the Confederate government mounted a desperate last-ditch effort to open a second front in Canada by embroiling the Union in conflict with Great Britain. A series of cross-border raids was designed to harass Union territory and provoke conflict with Canada. The attacks amounted to little more than pinpricks and at times verged on comic opera, except for a raid into the Vermont town of St. Albans by Kentuckians in October 1864. The raiders robbed a bank, shot up, looted, and burned the town, and then fled back across the border. Local authorities and federal troops pursued them, threatening a clash. Canada's refusal to extradite the raiders or make prompt restitution infuriated the Union. Americans naturally resented the use of Canadian soil for hostile purposes and threatened to gain restitution by seizing it after the war or taking it in compensation for claims for damage done by the *Alabama*. Sensitive to Canada's vulnerability,

73. Ibid., 599.
74. Ibid.

the British took Union threats seriously, fearing that a victorious—or de-feated—Union might seek revenge by attacking Canada.

Tensions persisted after Appomattox. Hotheads demanded cession of Canada as payment for the *Alabama* claims and other alleged British breaches of neutrality. Rebellions in Canada's western provinces and an-nexationist sentiment on the British Columbia frontier after the U.S. pur-chase of Alaska created opportunities for American troublemakers and aroused nervousness in Canada. The most divisive postwar issue was a series of raids into Canada by the so-called Fenians, Irish expatriates, some of them Union veterans, operating from bases in the United States. Neither Johnson nor Seward at first took the Fenians seriously. They may have taken secret pleasure at Canada's discomfiture now that the incur-sionist shoe was on the other foot. Their failure to enforce the neutrality laws swiftly and effectively caused anger and resentment in Canada.

Despite persisting provocations, officials on both sides kept tensions in check. The British were determined to prevent border conflicts from get-ting out of control. Canadian officials made serious if not always effective efforts to enforce neutrality laws, and after initial hesitation offered resti-tution for the St. Albans raid. A New Yorker, Seward knew and under-stood the cross border neighbors and gave no encouragement to those who urged supporting rebellions in Canada or even annexation as com-pensation. Grant and Fish acted more effectively than Johnson and Seward to enforce the neutrality laws and curb the Fenians.

Partly in response to the perceived American threat, Britain created a federal union in Canada through the British North American Act of 1867. Most U.S. citizens quietly acquiesced, even though the word *dominion* in the new dependency's title gave some republican souls pause. Just as the British in 1776 had been certain that the new United States was not a via-ble entity, so also Americans believed that the new dominion of Canada would collapse. They accepted as an article of faith what has been called the convergence theory, the belief that because U.S. ideology, trade, and culture were so important to a people so similar to themselves the two nations would converge and Canada would join the United States. Dominion status was a transitional stage. There was no need to push for annexation.[75]

The 1871 Treaty of Washington helped ease escalating post–Civil War tensions and laid the basis for a growing Anglo-American accord. The treaty is most often noted for its agreement to arbitrate the especially con-tentious *Alabama* claims dispute and for its resolution of long-standing

75. Stuart, *United States Expansionism*, xi, 216–17.

spats over U.S.-Canadian boundaries and access to fisheries. It evoked from both sides quite extraordinary concessions, a British apology for damages done by the Confederate raiders and eventual U.S. abandonment of its exorbitant "indirect" claims against Britain for Civil War damages, the latter occasioned in large measure by a desperate U.S. need for British capital to finance its enormous war debt.[76] A complex three-sided negotiation between the United States, Britain, and the Dominion of Canada, the Treaty of Washington also had major implications for North America. Much of the time was spent on Canadian issues. The result was tacit U.S. recognition of Canada's new status.[77]

Seward's moderation toward Mexico and Canada reflected his acceptance of the convergence theory, an integral part of his larger concept of America's destiny. Historians have vigorously debated whether his expansionism was opportunistic and ad hoc or reflected a larger design.[78] The distinct pattern of his goals and the purposefulness of his actions strongly suggest the latter. But there is no debating that he was the key figure in mid-nineteenth-century expansion, the link between the Manifest Destiny movement of the 1840s and the overseas expansionism of the 1890s. In terms of his vision of the nation's destiny, he was the logical successor to Jefferson and John Quincy Adams, the latter of whom he referred to as a "patron, a guide, a counsellor, and a friend."[79] His horizons extended well beyond the continentalism of his illustrious predecessors to the Caribbean and the Pacific.

Like the expansionists of the 1840s, Seward fused commercial with territorial objectives and moved a step beyond them in promoting the acquisition of overseas territory. He added to Henry Clay's views on economic development specific new concerns arising out of the nation's industrial growth and technological advancement. He strongly endorsed the Republican program of economic development: a national banking system; federal support for internal improvements such as a transcontinental railroad and cable to bind western territories to the Union; and a tariff to protect nascent industries. He added a vigorous commitment to promote investments and markets abroad. Moving beyond his Whig roots, he

76. Jay Sexton, "The Funded Loan and the *Alabama* Claims," *Diplomatic History* 27 (September 2003), 449–78.

77. Stuart, *United States Expansionism*, 252.

78. See Castel, *Johnson* for the former, Ernest N. Paolino, *The Foundations of American Expansionism: William Henry Seward and U.S. Foreign Policy* (Ithaca, N.Y., 1973) for the latter.

79. Walter LaFeber, *The New Empire: An Interpretation of American Expansionism* (Ithaca, N.Y., 1973), 25.

conceived various expansionist schemes to establish bases and coaling stations for a steam-powered navy in the Caribbean and Pacific. This naval
power would in turn protect existing markets and help add new ones.
Seward thus also provides a crucial link between U.S. foreign policy in
the nineteenth century and in the twentieth.

Never satisfied with a "small policy," in Henry Adams's words, the secretary of state pursued multifarious projects to fulfill his expansive vision
of nation's destiny. The seat of empire was moving steadily westward, he
believed, and the struggle for world power would occur in Asia. He saw no
need for colonies or wars of conquest. Territory would accrue to the
United States by natural processes and should be acquired, as Andrew
Johnson put it, "peacefully and lawfully, while neither doing nor menacing injury to other states."[80] Seward's vision extended from the Caribbean
and the Gulf of Mexico to the North Pole to East Asia (what he referred
to, ethnocentrically, as the "Far West"). He had long envisioned the
Caribbean as an American domain. The difficulty of chasing Confederate
raiders "from our own distant shores" during the Civil War underscored
the urgency of U.S. control. In January 1866, ostensibly for reasons of
health, he toured the area in search of locations for naval bases and coaling stations in the Caribbean and Gulf of Mexico. He negotiated treaties
for acquisition of the Virgin Islands and Danish West Indies and for a
naval base at Samana Bay in the Dominican Republic. He contemplated
acquisition of Cuba, Puerto Rico, Haiti, and Tiger Island off the coast of
Honduras. Laying the groundwork for fulfillment of a dream dating back
to Clay, he negotiated with Colombia a treaty for the right-of-way to build
a canal across the isthmus of Panama. His vision extended to the North
Atlantic, where he eyed the purchase of Iceland and Greenland, and to
the Pacific, where he looked into acquisition of the Hawaiian and Fiji islands, proposed a naval base on the island of Formosa, and initiated preparations for an expedition to open the "hermit kingdom" of Korea to trade
and Western influence. His cabinet colleague and sometime foe Secretary
of the Navy Gideon Welles called him a "monomaniac" on expansion. If
he could live another thirty years, Seward once boasted, he would gain for
the United States "possession of the American continent and the control
of the world."[81]

Seward's reach exceeded the nation's grasp, or at least the vision of his
contemporaries. Some of his schemes fell victim to events abroad or
forces of nature. The Colombian Senate refused to ratify the canal treaty;

---

80. Annual message, December 3, 1867, in Graf and Haskins, *Johnson Papers* 13:304.
81. Castel, *Johnson*, 144–45; Warren, "Seward," 215.

a revolution in Santo Domingo doomed the Samana Bay deal. A hurricane that devastated the Danish West Indies and the opposition of General Grant helped thwart acquisition of those islands. Some of his projects died from lack of interest or support. Most ran afoul of the tempestuous politics of the time. While Seward was busily trying to expand the nation's horizons, Johnson was paralyzed by the conflict within his own party that led to his impeachment. A hostile Senate tabled a treaty for reciprocity with Hawaii and scuttled other Seward projects. "How sadly domestic disturbances of ours demoralize the national ambition," the secretary lamented in October 1868.[82]

Seward's tangible accomplishments were limited but significant. The navy took Midway Island in the Pacific in 1867 under an 1850s "Guano Law" that permitted acquisition of uninhabited Pacific islands. Strategists were disappointed when it proved unsuitable for a deepwater port. Only many years later would its strategic importance be realized as an airstrip.

Far more important was the windfall purchase of Alaska in the same year. Seward had long viewed this Russian possession as a potentially vital way station toward domination of the East Asian trade. Devastating Confederate attacks on Union shipping in the Aleutian Islands in 1865 had reinforced his certainty of its strategic significance in the north Pacific. Alaska was also seen as a way to pressure Canada to join the United States. For Russia, in the meantime, this vast frozen territory had become a financial and strategic liability. Some Russians feared with good reason that an expansive United States would simply take Alaska and reasoned that they had best get something while they could. The Russian-American Company's hold was weakening. Letting go was made easier since Russia was gaining new, more defensible, territory in Central and East Asia. Some Russians also believed that the sale of Alaska would be a good way to solidify friendship with the United States, a proper ending for a period of good relations.[83]

Scorned by many at the time, the purchase became Seward's greatest triumph. Eager for something to offset the administration's domestic failures, he jumped at the chance to purchase Alaska. The price of $7.2 million was $2 million more than he wanted to pay and $2 million more than the Russians originally sought, but the secretary was in a hurry to consummate the deal; he and Russian minister Eduard Stoeckl worked until 4:00 A.M. to draw up a treaty. Critics dismissed Alaska as a "sucked orange," "Seward's folly," or Johnson's "polar bear garden." Editor Horace Greeley

82. Castel, *Johnson*, 205.
83. Saul, *Distant Friends*, 396.

called it "Walrussia." Foes of the purchase accused Johnson and Seward of trying to deflect attention from failures at home. Seward lobbied furiously and effectively, however, emphasizing the land's commercial and strategic potential and the importance of obliging good friends like the Russians. Congress was in full revolt against Johnson by this time, and the House of Representatives out of pique threatened not to appropriate funds. While complaining about the "wholly exceptional" difficulties of conducting diplomacy in the American democratic system, Stoeckl, who stood to profit handsomely from the deal, bribed key congressmen. At the time of its purchase, the main product of "Seward's ice-box" was indeed ice, sold in large quantities to the bustling communities along the West Coast. More quickly than anyone might have imagined, the secretary's vision was vindicated, his prize acquisition, like California earlier, bringing the added bonus of gold.[84]

Like Seward, Grant's secretary of state, Hamilton Fish, was a New Yorker. In contrast to his flamboyant predecessor, the wealthy and socially prominent Fish was dignified and stodgy. Where Seward had coveted his cabinet post as a stepping-stone to the presidency, Fish dismissed it as one "for which I have little taste and less fitness." Taste and fitness notwithstanding, he ranks among the nation's better secretaries of state, in large part because of his settlement of the *Alabama* claims dispute with Britain. Unimaginative and somewhat rigid in his thinking, he was a person of good judgment and distinguished himself in an administration not noted for the integrity or accomplishments of its top officials. He served longer than any other individual who held the post in the nineteenth century.

Along with Johnson's successor, war hero General Grant, who instinctively sought to project American power abroad, Fish was a spiritual heir to Seward's expansionism.[85] In Latin America, Fish and Grant sought to replace European influence with that of the United States. The secretary of state envisioned a time, as he put it, when "America shall be wholly American," when the "prominent position" of the United States on the continent would entitle it to a "leading voice" and impose on it "duties of right and of honor regarding American questions, whether these questions affected emancipated colonies, or colonies still subject to European domination."[86] To expand U.S. influence, they tied to the Monroe Doctrine

84. Ronald J. Jensen, *The Alaska Purchase and Russian-American Relations* (Seattle, 1975), 81–85, 94.
85. James B. Chapin, "Hamilton Fish and American Expansion," in Merli and Wilson, *Makers of American Diplomacy*, 225; Campbell, *Transformation*, 25, 50.
86. Chapin, "Fish," 245.

the no-transfer principle first enunciated by Jefferson in 1808, proclaiming unequivocally that "hereafter no territory on this continent shall be regarded as subject to transfer to a European power."[87] They anticipated that the erosion of European power would lead to increased U.S. trade and political influence. They pushed ahead with plans for an isthmian canal. When Colombia blocked yet another treaty, Grant ordered surveys of alternate canal routes, producing a recommendation to build across Nicaragua that would be accepted policy until the turn of the century.

The islands of Hispaniola and Cuba had long been of special concern to Americans. Seward had cast a covetous eye on Samana Bay, a magnificent natural harbor in the Dominican Republic that could guard the eastern approaches to a canal and protect U.S. commercial and strategic interests in the Caribbean. In the Dominican Republic, as elsewhere, internal rivalries created opportunities for U.S. expansion, and the object of American desires took the initiative. With Spain gone, contending factions could no longer play the Europeans against the United States and thus could only seek from Americans the money and guns to remain in power and deter the threat of a hostile Haiti. Between 1869 and 1873, various Dominican factions developed proposals for the lease of Samana Bay, a U.S. protectorate over the Dominican Republic, and even formal annexation. A fraudulent plebiscite was conducted to demonstrate popular support for joining the United States.[88]

Despite support for annexation on both sides, the scheme faltered. Prodded by cronies with investments in the Dominican Republic, Grant was especially eager to oblige Dominican annexationists or at least acquire Samana Bay. He gave the issue top priority in his scandal-ridden administration. In 1869, the two countries actually agreed to a treaty incorporating the Dominican Republic as a territory. Grant lobbied vigorously for Senate approval, but he met massive and unrelenting opposition. Haiti bitterly opposed a U.S. presence next door, and its minister to the United States spent $20,000 to defeat the treaty. In the United States, expansion into the Caribbean had acquired a bad name among Republicans from Democratic exploits in the 1850s. Many Americans opposed the incorporation of territory with a large non-white population. "Beware of the tropics," warned soldier, diplomat, journalist, and Missouri senator Carl

87. LaFeber, New Empire, 36–37.
88. Louis Martinez-Fernandez, "Caudillos, Annexationism, and the Rivalry Between Empires in the Dominican Republic, 1844–1874," Diplomatic History 17 (Fall 1993), 595–96.

Schurz. "Do not trifle with that which may poison the future of this great nation."[89] On the other hand, some idealists opposed absorbing tropical territory they claimed nature had set aside for darker-skinned people. Much of the opposition, including that from the formidable Senator Sumner, was personal and political. Undeterred by the defeat of annexation, Grant pushed for the lease of Samana Bay to private U.S. interests. He might have succeeded had not a revolution in the Dominican Republic in 1873 led to revocation of the offer.[90]

As always, Cuba posed especially complex challenges. The Spanish colony had been a major object of prewar expansionists, many of them seeking to protect the institution of slavery. Yet another rebellion against Spanish rule in 1868 brought it back to the forefront. Americans were deeply divided. Still infused with idealistic zeal, some Republicans urged continuation of the "noble work" of the Civil War by abolishing slavery in Cuba. African American leaders like Frederick Douglass went further, advocating aid for the Cuban rebels, the abolition of slavery in Cuba, and even its annexation. Harking back to America's traditional sense of mission, other Republicans urged extending Lincoln's "new birth of freedom" by eliminating one of the last bastions of European imperialism in the Western Hemisphere. Spain's brutal treatment of the rebels gave moral urgency to the pleas of interventionists. On the other hand, conservative Republicans opposed the taking of territory inhabited by mixed races and especially worried that acquisition of tropical lands would "degrade" the American people and their institutions. Some former Whigs insisted that the United States should continue to adhere to non-interventionism. Its ideals could best be spread by example.[91]

Grant and Fish approached the Cuban rebellion with great caution. Although Americans were eager to remove Spain from the Western Hemisphere, the Civil War remained fresh in their minds, and they were unwilling to risk war to abolish slavery or free Cuba. Fish refused to recognize Cuban belligerency, arguing that it could hurt their cause by expanding Spain's right of search. Premature recognition, he also perceived, would undercut the U.S. position in the ongoing dispute with Britain over the *Alabama* claims. Even when Spanish officials in 1873 seized the *Virginius*, an arms-running ship flying the American flag, and shot the

89. Lars Schoultz, *Beneath the United States: A History of U.S. Policy Toward Latin America* (Cambridge, Mass., 1998), 83.

90. Campbell, *Transformation*, 50–52; Martinez-Fernandez, "Caudillos," 592–97.

91. Jay Sexton, "The United States, the Cuban Rebellion, and the Multilateral Initiative of 1875," *Diplomatic History* 30 (June 2006), 339–48.

captain, thirty-six of the crew, and sixteen passengers, the administration responded calmly. The ship was falsely registered in the United States and carrying arms to rebels and therefore liable to seizure.

United States officials were also leery of the consequences of Cuban independence. They doubted Cubans' capacity for self-government and feared that chaos might engulf the island, threatening U.S. economic and strategic interests. There was little support for annexation. The staunchly conservative Fish viewed Cubans as inferior even to African Americans and unfit to be U.S. citizens. He would have preferred an autonomous Cuba under informal U.S. economic and political control. A lawyer himself and a devotee of the emerging specialty of international law, Fish followed British Liberal Party leader Gladstone in advocating multilateral solutions to world problems. To resolve an issue that caused much turmoil in Congress, he proposed in late 1875 a six-nation approach to Spain to end the fighting. The European powers were then embroiled in a crisis in the Balkans and declined the overture, but Fish's ploy was quite extraordinary in its deviation from traditional American unilateralism. After ten years of brutal fighting in which as many as a hundred thousand people were killed, the Cuban rebellion fizzled out. Moving in the direction Fish preferred, U.S. investors took advantage of bankrupt and desperate Cuban and Spanish planters to buy up their property, considerably expanding America's economic stake and preparing the way for a very different outcome in 1898.[92]

Grant and Fish enjoyed greater success in the Pacific. As in the Caribbean, the Civil War highlighted the value of naval bases in the Pacific. Completion of the transcontinental railroad in 1869 raised hopes for vastly expanded commerce with Asia. Trans-Pacific steamship lines looked for stopping-off places en route to the Orient. Hawaii seemed an ideal midpoint and Pearl Harbor a potentially vital naval base to guard western approaches to a canal and protect the western coast of the United States. With the British and other European nations lopping off Pacific islands one by one, pressures developed for the United States to do the same.[93]

As in the Dominican Republic, much of the impetus for closer U.S.-Hawaiian ties came from forces outside Washington, in this case Americans with business interests and political clout in the islands.[94] The

92. Ibid., 353–65; Louis A. Pérez, Cuba Between Empires, 1878–1902 (Pittsburgh, 1983), 62–64; LaFeber, New Empire, 37–38.
93. Campbell, Transformation, 72.
94. Barry Rigby, "The Origins of American Expansion in Hawaii and Samoa," International History Review 10 (May 1988), 222.

Civil War also had a huge impact in Hawaii. Confederate raiders destroyed the whaling business. The Union blockade increased demands for raw sugar, encouraging enterprising Americans to expand sugar cultivation. After the war, American entrepreneurs in Hawaii sought an expanded U.S. naval presence to defend a thriving commerce and a protected U.S. market for their sugar. They insinuated themselves with the Hawaiian government to achieve their goals. At one time or another, American sugar planters served as Hawaii's foreign minister and minister to Washington. They made up the delegation that negotiated the treaty. Talk of possible annexation found little support in Washington. "The indisposition to consider important questions of the future in the Cabinet is wonderful," Fish complained. "A matter must be imminent to engage attention—indifference and reticence—alas!"[95] Proposals for a naval base at Pearl Harbor also aroused opposition among native Hawaiians. Eventually, to win U.S. support for the free entry of sugar into the U.S. market, American sugar planters sent to Washington to negotiate a reciprocity treaty agreed that Hawaii would not grant such trade terms or naval bases to any other nation, thus limiting Hawaii's sovereignty in return for a secure market for their commodity. The idea, as the American who served as Hawaii's minister to the United States put it, was to "make Hawaii an American colony with the same laws and institutions as our own."[96] To seal the deal, Hawaii's King Kalakaua visited the United States in 1874, the first reigning monarch to do so.

As Fish observed, the 1873 reciprocity treaty bound Hawaii to the United States with "hoops of steel." It set off a period of frantic development for Hawaii's sugar plantations, increasing the islands' dependence on U.S. capital and the U.S. market. The demand for cheap labor to work the plantations led to a huge influx of Asians. Hawaiians now controlled only 15 percent of the land and 2 percent of the capital and were relegated to a "dispossessed minority." These demographic changes in turn aroused U.S. fears of Asian control. It was only a short step to annexation.[97]

The United States' interest in Samoa also originated from local forces. Again, the Civil War played a role, the worldwide demand for raw cotton fueling a land rush on that remote South Pacific island that drew attention to its other advantages. About halfway between Hawaii and Australia, Samoa and particularly the harbor of Pago Pago—"the most perfectly landlocked harbor that exists in the Pacific Ocean"—attracted the attention of

95. Campbell, *Transformation*, 67–68.
96. Rigby, "Hawaii and Samoa," 226.
97. Ibid., 225–27.

New York shipping interests. These shippers encouraged Commander Richard Meade of the Pacific squadron to claim the harbor for the United States. Meade dutifully obliged, but a contentious Senate in 1873 scrapped his treaty. Undeterred, Grant dispatched an agent to inquire about a naval base. A treaty was subsequently negotiated giving the United States the right to a base at Pago Pago and obliging it to use its good offices should Samoa encounter problems with third-party countries. Remarkably, the Senate approved this treaty in 1878, Samoa's first treaty with a foreign nation, perhaps reflecting Grant's departure from office or that body's appreciation of the growing importance of the Pacific. That treaty provided the basis for expanded U.S. involvement in the 1880s and subsequent annexation.[98] The treaties with Hawaii and Samoa mark major steps in the establishment of the United States as a Pacific power. They make clear the persistence of expansionist forces during the Civil War and Reconstruction.

THE YEAR 1877 MARKED AN END to the Civil War era. The political compromise worked out in March resolved the deadlocked Hayes-Tilden presidential election of 1876 by keeping the Republicans in the White House in return for restoration of home rule in the South. That year also marked the end of an epoch in U.S. foreign policy. The sections would continue to disagree on foreign policy issues, sometimes heatedly, but the Union victory definitively settled the fundamental question of American nationhood. Postwar non-intervention in Mexico and acquiescence in the Dominion of Canada fixed the boundaries of the continental United States. The Civil War and the Thirteenth Amendment abolished slavery. The major issues on which U.S. foreign policy had focused throughout much of the nineteenth century were resolved. Over the next three decades, the nation would be dramatically transformed through immigration, urbanization, and industrialization. It would take its place among the world's great powers. Continental expansion would give way to overseas expansion.

98. Campbell, *Transformation*, 76.

7

"A Good Enough England"

Foreign Relations in the Gilded Age, 1877–1893

By 1882, many Americans insisted that their country must control an isthmian canal, and when Great Britain showed no willingness to scrap the 1850 Clayton-Bulwer Treaty, providing for joint ownership and operation, the ever brash *New York Herald* offered its trans-Atlantic cousin some gratuitous advice. If Britain felt compelled to impose its designs on other peoples, the *Herald* opined, it should "take another turn" at the Boers, the Zulus, or the Afghans. "She need not bother with this side of the sea. We are a good enough England for this hemisphere."[1]

The newspaper's boast was more than a bit inflated when rendered, but by the 1890s it would approximate reality. During the so-called Gilded Age, a reunited and increasingly industrialized America lurched in fits and starts toward great power status. Absorbed in domestic problems and less concerned with external threats than at any time in their nation's history, Gilded Age Americans elevated traditional doctrines of non-entanglement to holy writ. At the same time, they were more than ever drawn to far-flung areas in search of adventure, opportunity, commerce, and "heathen" souls to be saved. Conscious of their rising power, they were more disposed to intervene in their own hemisphere and indeed beyond. During these years, such intrusions were often clumsy and counterproductive. Expansionist initiatives were frequently thwarted by a hostile Congress or junked by incoming administrations. By the turbulent 1890s, however, an increasingly powerful and anxiety-ridden United States began to assert its claims more vociferously and back them with action. Especially under the aggressive and sometimes bellicose leadership of President Benjamin Harrison and Secretary of State James G. Blaine, the United States between 1889 and 1893 moved decisively to strengthen its position at the expense of potential rivals in the Pacific Basin region and the Caribbean. At least for the Western Hemisphere, it was a "good enough England" indeed.

1. Quoted in Milton Plesur, *America's Outward Thrust: Approaches to Foreign Affairs, 1865–1890* (DeKalb, Ill., 1971), 176.

I

The world of the late nineteenth century was a turbulent place of rapid—and, to contemporaries, often bewildering—change. The railroad, steam-ship, and telegraph shrank distances dramatically, providing the means, contemporaries believed, to "erase ignorance and isolation, erode away the misunderstandings between peoples, and facilitate the getting and dis-tribution of the new plenty."[2] People, goods, and capital moved freely across international boundaries in this first rush of what is now called "globalization," connecting disparate areas through an intricate network of commerce and investments. "The world is a city!" French banking magnate Carl Meyer von Rothschild approvingly exclaimed in 1875.[3]

Technological advances also made the world more dangerous. The transportation revolution permitted more rapid movement of larger mili-tary forces over larger areas, enabling the Western imperial powers to ad-minister colonial holdings from greater distances. After almost a decade of false starts and frustrations such as fires, breaks in the line, and storms at sea, the United States and Britain in 1866 were linked by cable. Such ties soon extended to continental Europe and East Asia. The cost of sending telegraph messages initially limited the cable's utility in diplomacy, but its wider use over time speeded up communications, accelerating the pace of diplomatic activity, giving diplomatic crises a new urgency, and shifting control from diplomats on the scene to Washington.[4] The era also brought innovations in printing that, when combined with rising literacy rates in the Western industrialized countries, produced a rapt audience for excit-ing events in other places, creating both opportunities for mobilization of disparate peoples and popular pressures on those who wielded power. Above all, as the American Civil War so grimly demonstrated, the har-nessing of modern technology to the once genteel "art" of war created enormous and still not fully appreciated powers of destruction.

The ethos of the age stressed competition and struggle, adding to the turbulence that marked the international system. Published in 1859, Charles Darwin's *Origin of Species* theorized that plant and animal life had evolved through an ongoing competition in which only the "fittest"

2. David Healy, *U.S. Expansionism: The Imperialist Surge in the 1890s* (Madison, Wisc., 1970), 13.
3. Nicholas Kristoff, "At This Rate We'll Be Global in Another Hundred Years," *New York Times*, May 23, 1999.
4. James A. Field Jr., "American Imperialism: The Worst Chapter in Almost Any Book," *American Historical Review* 83 (June 1978), 661; David Paull Nickles, "Telegraph Diplomats: The United States' Relations with France, 1848 and 1870," *Technology and Culture* 40 (January 1999), 1–25.

flourished; the weak fell by the wayside. As popularized and applied to international politics, Darwin's ideas emphasized a struggle among nations and survival of the strongest, encouraging peoples already inclined toward the pursuit of power and wealth to compete more aggressively for the world's resources and use force to achieve their goals. "Nations, like men, will shrink and decline when they fail to grasp firmly the opportunities for success and use them to the utmost," Alabama senator John Tyler Morgan grimly proclaimed.[5]

Britain remained the number-one power in a still Europe-centered world. The empire on which the sun never set encompassed by century's end some twelve million square miles of territory and nearly one-fourth of the world's population, the largest the world had ever seen. London also maintained a precarious industrial and commercial supremacy, but its strengths had increasingly become its weakness. Its vast holdings and commitments compelled it to struggle merely to hang on to its existing position.[6]

Newcomers to the great game of international politics increasingly challenged Britain and the other traditional powers, rattling the post-1815 equilibrium. Although still weak by European standards, a newly unified Italy posed a regional danger to declining powers such as France and Austria-Hungary. The main threat to the existing order came from Germany, which emerged with stunning speed. By late century, it had surpassed France and was beginning to challenge Britain in industry and commerce. Germany was the first power to realize the military potential of the modern nation-state. Its crushing of Austria in 1866 and even more shocking defeat of France in 1871 marked its coming of age. Through artful diplomacy, the "Iron Chancellor," Otto von Bismarck, managed to expand his nation's interests without arraying the other powers against him. The Germany of Wilhelm II (1888–1918) was more aggressive and less clever, arousing growing fears in Europe, Britain, and even the United States.

In the 1880s and 1890s, the Europeans again took their competition on the road. Colonies had fallen out of fashion at midcentury, but in the eighties they once again became sought after as sources of power and wealth, setting off a new and furious scramble for political and economic advantages in unclaimed areas across the globe. Now joined by the Germans

5. Joseph A. Fry, *John Tyler Morgan and the Search for Southern Autonomy* (Knoxville, Tenn., 1992), 74.
6. Paul Kennedy, *The Rise and Fall of the Great Powers: Economic Change and Military Conflict from 1500 to 2000* (New York, 1987), 176–77.

and Italians, the British and French competed for colonies in the Middle East, North and sub-Saharan Africa, and East and Southeast Asia and even, to the alarm of Americans, made gestures in the direction of Latin America. Between 1870 and 1900, Britain added more than four million square miles to its imperial holdings, France more than three and a half million, and Germany one million. The new rush for empire further destabilized an already unsettled world.[7]

Even as Europe expanded into new areas, its centuries-old preeminence was under challenge from emerging powers. Russia's vast size and wealth of resources were more than offset by its administrative and political weakness, but its enormous potential made its Continental rivals uneasy. Emulating the Europeans, Japan after the Meiji Restoration of 1868 set out to modernize, industrialize, and build a Western-style military apparatus. The Japanese remained well behind the Europeans to the turn of the century, but their remarkable advance in a short time gained notice. Their defeat of hapless China in the so-called Pigtail War of 1894–95 marked their advent as a rising power in East Asia.

No nation surpassed the United States in economic growth, and nothing was more decisive for the future of the international system than America's emergence as a world power. Powerful and prosperous, with relatively greater individual liberties, at least for white men, than any other nation, the United States after the Civil War continued to attract millions of people searching for opportunity. Before the war, most immigrants had come from northern and western Europe; after, they came mainly from southern and eastern Europe. These millions of so-called new immigrants dramatically altered the makeup of the nation, provoked rising domestic tensions, and had profound implications for the future of U.S. foreign relations. Hordes of immigrants combined with continued high birth rates to push the population of the United States to more than seventy-five million people by 1900, second only to Russia among the world's leading nations.

Consolidation proceeded apace. The South was slowly and at times painfully reintegrated—often at the expense of African Americans on whose behalf the Civil War had presumably been fought. Railroads and the telegraph bound the vast territory acquired before the Civil War. Six new states entered the Union between 1889 and 1893, the most in any four-year period, bringing the total to forty-four.

During the last third of the nineteenth century, at the expense of Native Americans, the United States solidified its hold on the trans-Mississippi

7. Healy, U.S. Expansionism, 11–13.

West. The discovery of gold and silver, the 1862 Homestead Act offering cheap land to settlers, and the completion of a network of western railroads sparked yet another mass migration after the Civil War. Americans settled more land between 1870 and 1900 than in all their previous history. The population of the last frontier beyond the Mississippi more than quadrupled. As before, the mass influx of white settlers sparked conflict with Indians native to the region and some tribes removed from the East. As in the East, the government sought to deal with the problem by confining the Indians to reservations on generally undesirable lands. It was left to the U.S. Army to implement a policy the fiercely independent western Indians despised and resisted by force. For nearly a quarter century, the western tribes waged relentless guerrilla warfare against the frontier army, fighting nearly one thousand mostly small engagements. As on earlier frontiers, the outcome was a foregone conclusion. The army used its mobility, firepower, superior numbers, and ruthless attacks on winter encampments to cripple resistance. Even more important was the massive influx of settlers whose crops and cattle destroyed the grass and wildlife, especially the buffalo, that provided the basis of Indian society, forcing them to the reservation—or death.[8]

The United States' Indian policy changed markedly during this last stage of forced displacement to western reservations. At one time treated as independent nations, by the 1830s they were viewed as what Chief Justice John Marshall called "a domestic dependent nation," what amounted to protectorate status. Treaties continued to provide a measure of self-rule, but in 1871 the government stopped making agreements with the Indians, and the Supreme Court empowered Congress legally to nullify earlier commitments. After this point, Indians were treated as dependent peoples, indeed colonial subjects. George Washington and Henry Knox's well-intentioned ideal of civilization with honor gave way to an attitude of civilization or else. Rather than enticing the Indian to white man's ways with trinkets, tools, and Bibles, the government imposed civilization on them by requiring them to use the English language, accept Christianity, hold private property, and adopt subsistence agriculture. Agents were sent to the reservations to implement the new policies. The Bill of Rights did not apply. Indians could not even leave the reservation without permission. There was a direct line between the handling of Native Americans in the Gilded Age and the acquisition of overseas empire in the 1890s. "The ties between the Indian and foreign policy...were

8. Allan R. Millett and Peter Maslowski, *For the Common Defense: A Military History of the United States of America* (New York, 1984), 236–41.

not so much broken as transformed," historian Michael Hunt has concluded. "The rationale used to justify the defeat and dispossession of one people would in the future serve to sanction claims to American superiority and dominion over other people."[9]

The Union's triumph in the Civil War positioned the nation to exploit its enormous economic assets: rich land; a wealth of natural resources; a growing and energetic population; the absence of foreign threat or other obstacles to growth. Possessing numerous advantages and few disadvantages, the United States transformed itself at near miraculous pace. Agricultural and industrial production soared. By 1900, the United States surpassed even Britain in manufacturing output. The nation began to pour its agricultural and industrial products across the world while maintaining a high tariff to protect its own industries from foreign competition. American "hyperproductivity," along with recurrent and increasingly serious economic crises, fed rising fears among elites that the home market could not absorb a mounting surplus, the so-called glut thesis, provoking agitation for the acquisition of new markets abroad and a more active foreign policy. Only in military power did the United States lag behind the Europeans, but even here the gap was closing by the turn of the century. In any event, America's smaller military expenditures provided an advantage obscured in an age where the trappings of power often masked its essentials. The costs of maintaining an empire in fact could be a source of weakness rather than strength. The rapid expansion of two new powers caused Europeans increasingly to fret about a world order dominated by a crude and backward Russia and a rich and vulgar America. The explosive growth of the United States—an "entire rival continent"—provoked the first of repeated European warnings about the Americanization of the world.[10]

II

Once dismissed by internationalist historians as an isolationist backwater and the nadir of statesmanship, Gilded Age diplomacy has been rehabilitated in recent years. Revisionist writers have found in the post–Civil War era the roots of the modern American empire. Drab and colorless the diplomatists may have been, it is argued, but they were hardworking

---

9. Michael H. Hunt, *Ideology and U.S. Foreign Policy* (New Haven, Conn., 1987), 55. The connection between the Plains Indians and 1890s imperialism is explicated at length in Walter L. Williams, "United States Indian Policy and the Debate over Philippine Annexation: Implications for the Origins of American Imperialism," *Journal of American History* 66 (March 1980), 810–31.

10. Kennedy, *Great Powers*, 242–45.

and dedicated public servants who pursued the national interest with dogged determination. Concerned with the economic crisis produced by mounting agricultural and industrial surpluses, they were especially energetic in searching out foreign markets. They developed the rationale and began to create the instruments for the acquisition of overseas territory in the 1890s.[11]

Foreign relations have thus been brought back into the mainstream of Gilded Age history and the Gilded Age into the mainstream of U.S. foreign relations. To be sure, as critics have pointed out, "the era was marked by uncoordinated diplomacy, amateurish emissaries, shallow rhetoric, and much public and congressional indifference."[12] There was strong opposition to international involvement and especially commitment. Anti-imperialists defeated numerous expansionist initiatives. There was no master plan for empire. Still, diplomacy was much more important, active, systematic, and deliberate than previously allowed. During this period, the ideology and instruments that provided the basis for America's global involvement in the twentieth century took form. The Gilded Age was a transition period between the continental empire of Jefferson and Adams and the insular empire of the early twentieth century.[13]

Attitudes toward the outside world were paradoxical. For the first time in its short history, the new nation did not face a major external threat. Its position in North America was firmly established. Europe was retreating from the Western Hemisphere. The relative stability on the Continent spared the danger of a general European war. America's headlong economic growth and consolidation of the Union absorbed the energies and attention of its people after the Civil War. Under these circumstances, world events naturally receded in the scale of national priorities. Americans did not think of themselves as isolationists—indeed, the term *isolationism* was just beginning to creep into the national political vocabulary by the end of the century. But the nation's leaders did speak in reverential tones of the foreign policy principles bequeathed by Washington, Jefferson, and Monroe. Our "traditional rule of noninterference in the affairs of foreign nations has proved of great value in past times and ought to be strictly observed," President Rutherford B. Hayes proclaimed in 1877, a mantra

11. Walter LaFeber, *The New Empire: An Interpretation of American Expansion, 1860–1898* (Ithaca, N.Y., 1963), 39–149; Joseph A. Fry, "Phases of Empire: Late Nineteenth Century U.S. Foreign Relations," in Charles W. Calhoun, ed., *The Gilded Age: Essays on the Origins of Modern America* (Wilmington, Del., 1996), 261–72.

12. Justus D. Doenecke, *The Presidencies of James A. Garfield and Chester A. Arthur* (Lawrence, Kans., 1981), 55.

13. Fry, "Phases of Empire," 283.

ritualistically repeated by his Gilded Age successors.[14] Some ultra-nationalists even echoed in less qualified terms Jefferson's dream of scrapping an unrepublican and allegedly unnecessary diplomatic corps.

In the Gilded Age, as before and after, of course, Americans were anything but isolated from the outside world. From the beginning of the republic, U.S. foreign relations had been driven as much by private citizens as by government, and in these years, a society bursting with energy sent Americans abroad in varied roles.[15] The growing ease of travel, increased wealth, and the emergence of a tourism industry produced an explosion of overseas travel after the Civil War. By the end of the century, the State Department issued thirty thousand passports each year. Children of the elite took a Grand Tour modeled on that long practiced by the British aristocracy. Students flooded prestigious European universities. Immigrants returned home for visits. Some critics worried that foreign travel might taint the purity of the American character; the rude behavior of some of these travelers eternally stereotyped Americans to their European hosts. Visitors from the United States still found through exposure to foreign cultures confirmation of the virtues of their own society. After an extended stay in Europe, a young Harvard graduate and future ambassador to Germany and Britain in 1888 "bade adieu...to the 'effete despotisms of the old world.' " A year later, humorist Mark Twain boasted that "there is today only one real civilization in the world."[16] Nevertheless, the burst of tourism helped broaden America's perspectives and break down its parochialism. The experience of foreign travel significantly shaped the views of those who made up the nation's foreign policy elite in the twentieth century.[17]

Often on their own, sometimes with public sponsorship, Americans took part in multifarious activities in distant lands. The charting of North America completed, adventurers set off to explore the new frontier in Alaska. The government sponsored expeditions into the Arctic region. Private groups explored the Holy Land and the rain forests of South America.

14. Inaugural Address, March 5, 1877, in James D. Richardson, ed., A Compilation of the Messages and Papers of the Presidents of the United States (20 vols., Washington, 1897–1916), 10:4397.
15. Field, "Worst Chapter," 659.
16. Quoted in Jeffrey J. Matthews, Alanson B. Houghton: Ambassador of the New Era (Wilmington, Del., 2004), 24; Manfred Putz, "Mark Twain and the Idea of American Superiority at the End of the Nineteenth Century," in Serge Ricard, ed., An American Empire: Expansionist Cultures and Politics (Aix-en-Provence, 1990), 215–35.
17. Plesur, Outward Thrust, 103–8.

The Gilded Age also saw the first organized and officially sponsored efforts to export Yankee know-how, especially in Japan. As part of its effort to beat the West by joining it, the Japanese government recruited some three thousand foreign experts (*oyatoi*) to facilitate its rush toward modernization. Japanese leaders were not drawn to American democracy, preferring the German system of government. They relied mainly on Europeans to build a Western-style military establishment, although Japanese students did enroll at the U.S. Naval Academy and a U.S. citizen directed Japan's first naval school. Americans also assisted the Japanese in mastering Western diplomatic protocol and international law as a means to free them from the burdens of the Western-imposed unequal treaties. Americans played their most important role in education and agriculture. They helped establish a system of public education modeled loosely on that recently instituted in the United States. Experts from U.S. colleges, sponsored by the commissioner of agriculture, disseminated the latest methods of dairy farming and growing corn and wheat. Specialists from the Massachusetts agriculture college sought to extend the land grant model to Japan by helping establish at Sapporo an experimental farm and agricultural school that would become the University of Hokkaido. Americans brought to Japan such things as the McIntosh apple and Concord grapes. As expatriates seeking recreation, they introduced the Japanese to baseball, helping to start teams that in time would compete with Americans residing in that country. To the dismay of British observers, baseball by the end of the century had become more popular in Japan than cricket.[18]

Born earlier in the century, the Protestant missionary movement exploded after the Civil War. The number of foreign missions jumped from eighteen in 1870 to ninety in 1890. In China alone, the number of missionaries increased from 81 in 1858 to 1,296 in 1889. The missionaries fanned out across the world, from Catholic South America to the Muslim Middle East. They were especially active in "pagan" China and Japan and even began to establish an American presence in Africa.

The role and impact of American missionaries have been subjects of much controversy. Persuaded that God had blessed them with modern technology to facilitate their evangelizing of the world and fervently committed to "bring light to heathen lands," they brought to their task a self-righteous arrogance that would make them an easy target for critics in later centuries. In some areas, they were the advance guard for American commercial penetration. While spreading their gospel, they were often guilty of the worst kind of cultural imperialism. They invariably ran afoul of local customs and provoked nationalist opposition that, in places like Japan, sharply limited their influence. On the other hand, they stimulated American philanthropy. They opposed the introduction of opium into treaty ports in China and took the unpopular position of opposing exclusion of Chinese immigrants in debates that raged across the United States in these years. For better or worse, they introduced the modernization process into lands where they served. They were among the leading agents of the internationalization of America. They brought distant areas to the attention of a sometimes parochial nation and shaped popular attitudes toward other peoples. Their appeals for support and protection sometimes forced the government to act in areas where its role had been nonexistent.[19]

Missionary work provided opportunities abroad for Americans whose roles were constricted at home. African American missionaries sought converts in Africa while promoting colonization schemes with distinctly imperialist overtones. Increasingly frustrated with their place in U.S. society, ministers such as Alexander Crummell and Henry McLeod Turner advocated missionary work in Africa *and* "back to Africa" colonization schemes like those Henry Clay and Abraham Lincoln had once endorsed. They sought through return to the continent from which their race had come escape from their growing oppression in the United States and a means to establish their American national identity. While hailing Africa's higher morality, they shared with European colonialists a belief that the "dark continent" was in need of a civilizing mission and brought to their task a sense of their own superiority. Some even rationalized that slavery had been part of a divinely inspired master plan to prepare African Americans to regenerate a backward Africa. In the 1890s, Turner promoted missions in Liberia and Sierra Leone as bases for his larger colonization project. Crummell went to Liberia as a missionary and proposed a U.S. protectorate over the nation founded by freed American slaves. These early pan-African schemes got little support from the African American middle class—the churches were dubious precisely because they smacked too much of earlier colonization plans. "We have no

---

19. Plesur, *Outward Thrust*, 75–86; Michael H. Hunt, *The Making of a Special Relationship: The United States and China to 1914* (New York, 1983), 24–32, 154–65.

business in Africa," a bishop protested.[20] An indifferent U.S. government provided no backing. The only results were to provide intellectual justification for and indirect encouragement to European colonialism of Africa.[21]

Missionary work and other international charitable activities offered outlets and opportunities for women still denied full equality at home. By 1890, wives of male missionaries or groups of unwed women operating on their own made up roughly 60 percent of the total number. Their contributions were unique. Their approach to missionary work was more personal than that of men, resembling the sort of nurturing work they did in the domestic sphere at home. In China, women more often than men identified with and expressed concern for the powerlessness of the local population in dealing with the West. Dominated by their husbands, they protested the way outsiders dominated Chinese. By standing up for China, they stood up for themselves. In doing so, they took an important step toward their own liberation. Paradoxically, although empathizing with the Chinese, by promoting Westernization they exercised authority over them.[22]

Women also took a leading role in late-century international relief programs. When famine struck Russia in 1891, women at the local and national level under the leadership of legendary Civil War nurse and American Red Cross president Clara Barton organized a massive campaign to get corn and flour to the victims. Congress refused to appropriate funds, so the entire effort had to be privately financed. The women managed to secure some free transportation from the railroads and steamship companies. Some women traveled to Russia with the food to ensure that good meals were prepared for recipients. Critics groused that the autocratic tsarist government had inflicted the disaster on its own people, but the organizers appealed to the nation's humanitarian instincts, traditional Russian-American friendship, and Russia's timely support during the Civil War. Americans helped feed as many as 125,000 people in one of their first major overseas relief efforts. Women's involvement in the famine relief campaigns expanded their area of influence by

20. Quoted in James T. Campbell, *Surge of Zion: The African Methodist Episcopal Church in the United States and South Africa* (Chapel Hill, N.C., 1998), 88–99.

21. Tunde Andeleke, *UnAfrican Americans: Nineteenth-Century Black Nationalists and the Civilizing Mission* (Lexington, Ky., 1998), especially 111–39.

22. Jane Hunter, "Women Missionaries and Cultural Conquest," in Dennis Merrill and Thomas G. Paterson, *Major Problems in American Foreign Relations*, vol. 1, *To 1920* (Boston, 2005), 383–92.

pushing them into the traditionally male-dominated realm of international relations.[23]

In an era and nation where business reigned supreme, no segment of American society was more active abroad. It would be wrong, of course, to exaggerate the commitment of U.S. business to overseas expansion. Preoccupied with production for the home market, many businessmen were among the last to appreciate the importance of foreign markets. Congress was sometimes indifferent. The Republican devotion to a protective tariff hampered foreign trade. Americans were rank amateurs at overseas marketing, and the dumping of inferior and even dangerous products sometimes deservedly gave them a bad name.

Still, after the Civil War, U.S. business became more involved internationally. Government and business sponsored participation in expositions and world fairs to attract immigrant laborers and foreign capital and peddle their wares. For the first time, the nation had surplus capital to export. American entrepreneurs exploited mines and built railroads in other countries, especially in such friendly environs for foreign investors as Porfirio Diaz's Mexico. With the backing of J. P. Morgan & Co., James Scrymers linked the United States to much of South America by cable. United States companies dominated Russian markets in such diverse areas as farm machinery and life insurance. No firm exceeded John D. Rockefeller's Standard Oil in the breadth of its overseas operations. From the outset, Rockefeller set out aggressively to capture "the utmost market in all lands." Assisted by U.S. consuls who even bought lamps with their own funds and distributed them to create demand, his oil and kerosene found a huge market in a rapidly industrializing Europe. According to a Standard Oil representative, the corporation "forced its way into more nooks and corners of civilized and uncivilized countries than any other product in business history emanating from a single source." Throughout East Asia, Standard Oil's blue tin cans were a mainstay of the local economies, used to make tile roofs, opium cups, and hibachis. As late as the 1940s, "Rockefeller lamps" were status symbols in Vietnam.[24]

America's Gilded Age foreign policies reflected these crosscurrents. Statesmen devoted relatively little time to foreign policy because there was no need to do so and because domestic issues were generally more

23. Shannon Smith, "From Relief to Revolution: American Women and the Russian-American Relationship, 1890–1917," *Diplomatic History* 19 (Fall 1995), 601–6.
24. Plesur, *Outward Thrust*, 14–22; Normal Saul, *Concord and Conflict: The United States and Russia, 1867–1914* (Lawrence, Kans., 1996), 276–81; Daniel Yergin, *The Prize: The Epic Quest for Oil, Money, and Power* (New York, 1991), 50–57.

pressing. "The President has rarely leisure to give close or continuous attention to foreign policy," Englishman James Bryce observed.[25] Most leaders understandably hesitated to take on major commitments abroad. As far as Europe was concerned, they absolutely refused to do so. What has been called "old paradigm" foreign policy generally consisted of improvised and ad hoc responses to developments abroad.[26]

But that was only one side of the picture. Many younger Americans, especially offspring of the elite, shared a growing sense of the nation's rising power and status in the world. Some warned of dangers in a changing international situation and urged reconsideration of traditional foreign policy principles. Some saw domestic imperatives as demanding more active policies. There was no master plan or grand design, to be sure, but many Americans agreed upon the need to expand foreign markets and increase U.S. influence in the Western Hemisphere and the Pacific. Some even expressed interest in acquiring territory.

In an era when political parties were fragmented and nearly equal in strength and when domestic issues held center stage, party positions on foreign policy were not sharply drawn. Republicans and Democrats agreed that the United States should abstain from involvement in Europe's politics, alliances, and wars. Most Americans supported expanding their nation's influence in the Western Hemisphere.

Composed of diverse regional and socioeconomic interests, the Democratic Party remained true to its Jeffersonian roots in supporting laissezfaire, limited government, and public frugality. Most Democrats advocated free trade and opposed protectionism. Some like Alabama's Morgan kept alive the expansionism of southern Democrats in the 1850s, advocating aggressive pursuit of foreign markets, a large modern navy, and construction of an isthmian canal to help free the South from "foreign" oppression at the hands of British creditors and northern reconstructionists. Morgan even endorsed the acquisition of overseas territory to boost the South's political power and provide a haven for colonized blacks. The great majority of southerners, on the other hand, opposed policies that might result in the absorption of non-white peoples, strengthening of the federal government, and competition with their agricultural products. Most Democrats viewed commercial and territorial expansion as contrary to American traditions and principles. Some like Georgia's

25. Quoted in John A. Garraty, *The New Commonwealth, 1877–1890* (New York, 1968), 283n.
26. Robert L. Beisner, *From the Old Diplomacy to the New, 1865–1900* (2nd ed., 1986), 37.

James Blount saw colonial acquisitions as all too reminiscent of the North's imposition of outside rule on the defeated South.[27]

The Republican Party had in many ways outlived the anti-slavery platform that brought it into being. Most Republicans still believed in a strong central government and subsidizing economic growth through a protective tariff. Some clung to cautious Whiggish notions opposing expansion. Others followed Seward in pushing for a more assertive foreign policy, a large navy, and a canal. The party was changing from its Whig roots to outright support of expansion and even imperialism.

Because the times did not demand it (and probably would not have permitted it), no Jefferson, John Quincy Adams, or Seward arose among Gilded Age diplomatists, and efforts on the part of historians to make one of James G. Blaine remain unconvincing. Secretaries of State William Evarts (1877–81), Frederick Frelinghuysen (1881–85), and Thomas Bayard (1885–89) were in most matters cautious. They managed American diplomacy without bravado but with quiet competence.[28] President Grover Cleveland, a Democrat, was stubborn, unimaginative, and insular in his thinking, but he was not afraid to make tough foreign policy decisions. He displayed on occasion an admirable tendency to do the right thing for the right reason, injecting an element of morality into an area of endeavor and political climate where it was normally absent.

Blaine served at the beginning of the 1880s and 1890s and was far and away the most colorful, controversial, and important of the lot. Charming, energetic, and hugely ambitious—"When I want a thing, I want it dreadfully," he once said—the "Plumed Knight" was a total political animal and a rabidly partisan Republican.[29] Intense, suspicious, and given to intrigue, he was often linked with the corruption that marked the age. If he *was* involved, he was too clever to get caught. As secretary of state, he was much more inclined to project American power abroad than the lawyers who preceded and followed him. He pursued with characteristic energy the expansion of U.S. trade and influence in the Western Hemisphere and the Pacific. He shared with earlier generations of Americans a sense of the nation's greatness and destiny. He developed a vision of empire that included U.S. preeminence in the hemisphere, commercial domination of the Pacific, an American-owned canal, and even the acquisition of

27. Fry, *Morgan*, 48, 74–75; Tennant S. McWilliams, "James H. Blount, the South, and Hawaiian Annexation," *Pacific Historical Review* 57 (February 1988), 39.
28. Doenecke, *Garfield and Arthur*, 142; Richard E. Welch Jr., *The Presidencies of Grover Cleveland* (Lawrence, Kans., 1988), 161.
29. Doenecke, *Garfield and Arthur*, 14.

Hawaii, Cuba, and Puerto Rico. Especially in his first term as secretary of state, "Jingo Jim," as he was called, could be impulsive, heavy-handed, and insensitive to other peoples. His diplomacy was also sometimes marked by demagoguery.[30] He was denied greatness in part because of such deficiencies in his leadership but even more because his tangible accomplishments were few and because the times did not provide the sort of foreign policy challenges faced by his more illustrious predecessors. At the same time, his "blueprint" for U.S. expansion and his mentoring of such future leaders as William McKinley and John Hay establish him as a major link between antebellum expansionism and late nineteenth-century U.S. imperialism.[31]

The instruments of Gilded Age foreign policy reflected more the nation's insular past than its global future. The State Department escaped the worst abuses of the era of spoilsmen, but its staff of eighty-one people remained small for an incipient world power. Work hours were a leisurely 9:00 A.M. to 4:00 P.M.; the pace was very slow.[32] State's methods of operation dated to John Quincy Adams. Much of the work was done by a single person, the legendary Alvey Adee, a bureaucrat par excellence who served nearly forty years as second assistant secretary of state. The State Department's institutional memory and a master of diplomatic practice, Adee drafted most of its instructions and dispatches. "Why there isn't a kitten born in a palace anywhere on earth that I don't have to write a letter of congratulation to the peripatetic tomcat that might have been its sire," Theodore Roosevelt would later joke, "and old Adee does that for me!"[33]

The rank of ambassador was still considered too pretentious for a republic, and U.S. diplomats were often outranked by representatives of much smaller nations. All were political appointees. Some such as James Russell Lowell in England and Andrew Dickson White in Germany distinguished themselves. Most of the "foreign service" consisted of "second-rate personnel frequently forced to live in third-rate surroundings," provoking John Hay to compare the diplomatic vocation to the "'Catholic Church, calculated only for celibates.'"[34] In places like Japan, because of recurrent attacks on foreigners and devastating fires, diplomatic service could be life-threatening. A remarkable informality and ease of movement

30. Ibid., 74.
31. Edward P. Crapol, *James G. Blaine: Architect of Empire* (Wilmington, Del., 2000), xiv, 137–46.
32. Doenecke, *Garfield and Arthur*, 56–57.
33. Peter Bridges, "An Appreciation of Alvey Adee," *American Diplomacy* Web site, www .unc.edu/depts/diplomat/archives_roll/2001_10-12/bridges_adee/bridges_adee.html.
34. Doenecke, *Garfield and Arthur*, 56–57.

characterized the diplomatic community. Ebenezar Don Carlos Bassett became the first U.S. minister to Haiti and the first African American to hold a diplomatic position. When his term expired, he entered the Haitian foreign service and subsequently became consul-general in the United States.[35] The number of consulates had grown to two hundred by this time, supplemented by four hundred agencies in less important areas. Some consulates provided respectable pay; most compensated scant money with an exotic place to live.[36]

The state of the military reflected the mood of a nation without major external threat and still suffering from the fallout of a long and bloody war. The mighty army that had defeated the Confederacy was demobilized. A tiny remnant scattered in posts across the West occupied itself with eliminating Indian resistance. The once proud U.S. Navy was also scuttled, by the 1870s ranking below the "fleets" of Paraguay and Turkey. "The mention of our Navy only excites a smile," a shipbuilder snarled. "We have not six ships that would be kept at sea in war by any maritime power," the future high priest of sea power Capt. Alfred Thayer Mahan protested.[37]

Even in the Gilded Age, however, there were signs of the institutional changes that would mark America's rise to world power. Substantive reform of the State Department awaited the twentieth century, but the consular service was upgraded and focused toward finding markets. The army sought to improve the quality of its enlisted personnel and better educate its officers, created an intelligence arm, and in 1885 conducted its first large-scale maneuvers. The real focus of Gilded Age reform was the navy. Spurred by aggressive and sometimes alarmist naval officers and by a war scare with Chile, the Chester A. Arthur administration in the early 1880s initiated major efforts to build a modern fleet, establishing a Naval War College and the Office of Naval Intelligence and commissioning three new armor-plated cruisers to protect merchant ships in remote areas. Cleveland continued the naval building program. Modernization was well under way by the 1890s.

Symbolic of an emerging nation—if still way ahead of the upgrading of the agencies it housed—was the completion in 1888 of the State, War, Navy Building just west of the White House. Built at a cost of more than

35. Wanda Faye Jackson, "The Diplomatic Relationship Between the United States and Haiti, 1862–1900" (Ph.D. dissertation, University of Kentucky, 1999), 49–50.
36. Ari Hoogenboom, *The Presidency of Rutherford B. Hayes* (Lawrence, Kans., 1988), 105, 108.
37. Doenecke, *Garfield and Arthur*, 146.

$10 million, this masterpiece of Victorian excess had a total floor area of ten acres and almost two miles of corridors. Some Americans boasted that it was the largest and finest office building in the world. At the very least, a Washington newspaper proclaimed, it was the "finest in the United States, and in every way worthy... [of] the uses to which it is to be devoted."[38]

III

Immigration strikingly reshaped U.S. society in the late nineteenth century, and some of the most complex problems for Gilded Age diplomacy stemmed from the increasing number, size, and diversity of ethnic groups in the United States. The pattern of immigration during the Gilded Age shifted from northern to eastern and southern Europe and Asia, bringing to U.S. shores millions of so-called new immigrants much less familiar in terms of their ethnicity, language, religion, and culture. The presence of immigrants from exotic races provoked growing internal tensions and in different ways sparked conflict with other countries. The harsh treatment of the new ethnic groups by bigoted Americans provoked diplomatic crises with the nations of their origin. The involvement of immigrants or naturalized Americans with revolutions in their homelands brought the United States into conflict with the threatened governments. Anticipating one of the major problems of twentieth-century foreign relations, some ethnic groups sought to get the U.S. government to defend their compatriots from oppression. The emergence of such problems in the Gilded Age highlighted the uniqueness of the American political system, the changing nature of U.S. foreign relations, and the nation's increasingly close connections with the outside world.

An old standby, the Irish problem, flared up anew in the late nineteenth century. Naturalized Americans played an increasingly prominent role in the ongoing Irish rebellion against British rule. The United States became a leading source of arms and explosives for Irish terrorists. The British Parliament sought to contain the flare-up in 1881 with a Coercion Act that permitted detention without trial of suspected revolutionaries. Some U.S. citizens were imprisoned under the act and appealed to Washington for help. The British also pressed Washington to shut down the Irish-American newspapers that encouraged arms shipments. A notorious Anglophobe, Blaine at first demanded release of the Americans. His successor, the usually calm Frelinghuysen, stood firmly for freedom of the press. Long-standing tensions in Anglo-American relations and Britain's

---

38. Lee Burke, *Homes of the Department of State* (Washington, 1977), 43–47.

traditional role as a whipping boy of U.S. politics created the potential for a crisis.

Sanity eventually prevailed. Some of the arrested Americans turned out to be shady characters, not the sort of persons causes célèbres are made of. It became increasingly obvious that they were using U.S. citizenship to protect themselves from British law. Blaine dismissed one who had falsified passport information as "a pestiferous fellow" who "deserved what he got."[39] Generally, he came to regard the agitators as "the scum of Europe." Some Americans continued to protest the treatment of their fellow citizens and the government's apparent indifference. "Oh, that we only had as much protection given to a live American citizen as . . . a dead Cincinnati hog!" a Brooklyn congressmen protested, an obvious reference to the simultaneous dispute with Britain and other European countries over U.S. exports of pork.[40] Most Americans sympathized with Irish nationalism, but not to the point of sparking a crisis with Britain. The increasingly overt and brazen activities of Irish nationalists in the United States and the explosion of bombs in the House of Commons and several English railroad stations provoked a backlash in America. Protest subsided. The Arthur administration took forceful measures to reduce illegal arms shipments. The British adamantly refused to modify the Coercion Law, but in time for reasons of their own released some Americans. The crisis eased, but similar disputes would recur in various forms as the Irish question festered over the next century.[41]

The problem of Chinese immigrants in the United States was more complex. Lured to America to perform backbreaking work in western mines and on the transcontinental railroad, the Chinese played an instrumental role in developing the nation. But their growing numbers, pronounced cultural differences, resistance to assimilation, and willingness to work for cheap wages provoked a vicious nativist backlash. Chinese were beaten, lynched, and brutally murdered, giving rise to the saying that a doomed person did not have a "Chinaman's chance." There was also rising agitation, especially in the West, for the exclusion of Chinese immigrants. China had once been indifferent to the treatment of its nationals abroad, but American actions were so egregious that it could not but express outrage. It must have wondered too at the pretenses of people who claimed to have established a superior civilization. Because of the unequal treaties, China was not even sovereign in its own territory. It

39. Doenecke, *Garfield and Arthur*, 70.
40. Ibid, 138.
41. Ibid, 70–71, 138–39.

could do little but protest. While Westerners enjoyed the protection of extraterritoriality in China, the Chinese government could not safeguard the lives of its citizens who were victimized in America.

The United States settled the issue on its own terms. Congress in 1879 passed a bill limiting the number of Chinese who could come into the country on any ship. As anti-Chinese as he was anti-British, then-Senator Blaine defended the legislation as a blow for the "civilization of Christ" against the "civilization of Confucius."[42] Arguing that the bill violated U.S. treaty obligations, Hayes courageously vetoed it. Recognizing the political strength of the agitators, however, the government negotiated a new treaty with China permitting the United States to limit or suspend but not to "absolutely prohibit" Chinese immigration. Congress immediately suspended immigration for twenty years, provoking an Arthur veto. The legislators responded with a new bill suspending Chinese immigration for ten years, the first such exclusion in U.S. history. More exclusionist laws followed. With no choice but to acquiesce, the Chinese in 1894 agreed to a new treaty that "absolutely prohibited" the immigration of Chinese laborers for ten years. Diplomatic relations worsened during the 1890s.[43]

The brutal mob killing of eleven Italians in New Orleans provoked an 1891 mini-crisis with Italy. A sharp rise in the number of Italian immigrants and an increase in gang warfare caused rising tensions in that tradition-bound southern city. The murder of a popular young police superintendent, allegedly by Italians with connections to a sinister "mafia," set off popular outrage. When the first group of those charged was found not guilty—a "thunderbolt of surprise," screamed the *Times-Picayune*—an angry mob including some of the city's leading citizens descended upon the jail, gunned down eight of the accused inside the walls, and removed and lynched three more from nearby tree limbs and lampposts. A dishonored and furious Italian government denounced this "atrocious deed," demanded protection for Italians in the United States, and insisted upon reparations. Belying his nickname "Jingo Jim," an ill and preoccupied Blaine at first responded complacently. Rising to the occasion as the dispute heated up, he retorted in notably undiplomatic language that some of the victims were U.S. citizens, explained that the federal government could not impose its will on the state of Louisiana, and expressed to Italy's minister his indifference what Italians might think about U.S. institutions.

42. Crapol, *Blaine*, 57.
43. Warren I. Cohen, *America's Response to China: An Interpretive History of Sino-American Relations* (New York, 1971), 35–38; Hoogenboom, *Hayes*, 177–84.

"You may do as you choose," he snarled in conclusion. Italy recalled its minister from Washington. Both nations strutted and blustered, and there was talk of war. After months of irresolution, Italy finally backed away from its threats, Harrison expressed regret for the killings, and the Italian minister returned to Washington. The perpetrators went unpunished, but an indemnity of $25,000 was eventually paid to the families of three of the victims. In the United States, the affair stoked a sharp rise in anti-immigrant sentiment leading to pressure for additional exclusionist legislation. Sea power advocates used the threat of war and the alleged vulnerability of U.S. ports even to the Italian fleet to drum up support for a larger navy.[44]

Quite different and much more significant was an increasingly assertive American response to the treatment of Jews in Russia. Russian anti-Semitism was deeply rooted. It grew much worse in the 1880s when famine ravaged the country and Jews were scapegoated for mounting revolutionary activities and assassination of the tsar. The issue involved the United States in several ways. American Jews traveling to Russia on business suffered various kinds of discrimination and appealed to their government for help. In addition, as their treatment in Russia became unbearable, thousands of Jews fled to a seemingly welcoming United States and through public protests called attention to the plight of those left behind. Americans were reading more about events abroad and beginning to sense that, as an emerging power, their country might exert some influence over other societies. Some began to view Russia's treatment of Jews as an outrage against humanity. Immigration officials and relief societies were overwhelmed by floods of immigrants and pleaded for surcease. Some Americans, including Secretary of State Walter Gresham, privately accused Russia of conspiring to undermine American society by "forcing upon our shores a numerous class of immigrants destitute of resources and unfitted in many important respects for absorption into our body politic."[45]

The "Jewish Question" assumed growing importance in U.S. foreign relations. The State Department managed to protect the interests of most American Jews through quiet and persistent diplomacy. While affirming U.S. reluctance "officiously and offensively to intermeddle," diplomats

44. Homer E. Socolofsky and Allan B. Spetter, *The Presidency of Benjamin Harrison* (Lawrence, Kans., 1987), 152–54; Campbell, *Transformation*, 166–68; David A. Smith, "From the Mississippi to the Mediterranean: The 1891 New Orleans Lynching and its Effects on United States Diplomacy and the American Navy," *Southern Historian* 19 (Spring 1988), 60–85.

45. Saul, *Concord and Conflict*, 397.

also appealed to the Russian government in the most carefully phrased language and on the grounds of its own self-interest to cause the mistreatment of "these unfortunate fellow beings to cease."[46] Russian officials retorted that the United States had effectively dealt with problems posed by Chinese immigrants. If the influx of Jews grew too burdensome, they too could be excluded. Heightened Russian repression stimulated further Jewish emigration to the United States. The St. Petersburg government opened a new area of conflict by refusing to issue visas to American Jews. Along with Russian-speaking journalist and lecturer George Kennan's inflammatory mid-1880s expose of the horrific conditions in Siberian prisons, the ongoing dispute over treatment of Jews soured traditional Russian-American friendship and provoked some Americans to call for revolution in Russia. The issue was as important as any other in getting the American public involved in the "new foreign policy" of the 1890s. It was the first of numerous cases where pressure from ethnic groups and humanitarian concerns pushed the United States to challenge other governments, even friendly ones, on issues of human rights.[47]

IV

The U.S. economy was the marvel of the world in the late nineteenth century. The gross national product quadrupled from $9 billion during 1869–73 to $37 billion between 1897 and 1901. Production soared. Steel output increased from 77,000 tons in 1870 to 11,270,000 in 1900. Wheat and corn production doubled. The quality of American products, their low prices, and improved transportation produced a surge in trade. Exports jumped from $234 million in 1865 to $1.5 billion in 1900. In 1876, the centennial year, exports for the first time began regularly to surpass imports. As a result of rampant industrialization, exports of manufactured goods started to catch up with traditionally dominant agricultural products and would pass them in 1913. Britain was the major consumer of U.S. exports, followed by Germany and France—in all, Europe absorbed close to 80 percent of the total by the late 1880s. Closer to home, Canada and Cuba were the major purchasers. For the first time, Americans had capital to invest elsewhere. By the end of the century, the nation was second only to Britain as an economic power. Americans hailed their rising prowess in the most exuberant terms. It is "our manifest destiny to rise to the

46. Ibid., 249; John Lewis Gaddis, *Russia, the Soviet Union, and the United States: An Interpretive History* (2nd ed., New York, 1990), 29.

47. Saul, *Concord and Conflict*, 235–40; Gaddis, *Russia, The Soviet Union, and the United States*, 26–31.

first rank among the manufacturing nations," one enthusiast proclaimed. We have sent "coals to Newcastle, cotton to Manchester, cutlery to Sheffield, potatoes to Ireland, champagne to France, watches to Switzerland," boasted another.[48]

Some Americans increasingly feared that their blessing could become their curse. A severe depression in 1873 wreaked devastation across the land, raising concerns among some businessmen and government leaders that producing more than could be absorbed at home threatened economic stability. Exports still represented only about 7 percent of the gross national product, but they came to be seen as the key to economic wellbeing. "The house we live in has got too small," economist David Wells warned. Without an expansion of foreign markets, "we are certain to be smothered in our own grease."[49] Gilded Age politicians and businessmen thus set out to protect existing foreign markets and find new ones. The government began to play a more important role in this process. Such efforts were not always determined or systematic. Most businesses continued to focus on the domestic market. Devotion to protectionism inhibited the negotiation of new trade agreements and overturned existing ones. The results thus did not match up to the rhetoric.[50] At the same time, a growing concern for foreign markets spurred the United States to project its influence into new areas and even participate in an international conference, use old weapons with new vigor, and take a tough line with the European powers on vital trade issues.

The search for markets took Americans to distant shores. As early as 1867, Cdr. Robert W. Shufeldt had sought to emulate Perry by opening Korea, the "Hermit Kingdom," but he was twice rebuffed. Finally, in 1882, with the help of Chinese intermediaries, he negotiated the Treaty of Chemulpo, providing for trade on a most-favored-nation basis, the establishment of diplomatic relations, and, as in earlier treaties with China and Japan, extraterritoriality. The Chinese hoped to use the United States to strengthen their own control over a neighboring country, but the Americans insisted, in Frelinghuysen's words, that "Corea is an independent, sovereign power." Seeking to exploit the United States to secure its independence, Korea agreed to an exchange of missions. A group of Koreans visited the Brooklyn Navy Yard and the U.S. Military Academy at West Point.

48. David M. Pletcher, "Rhetoric and Results: A Pragmatic View of American Economic Expansionism, 1865–1898," *Diplomatic History* 5 (Spring 1981), 94–95; Campbell, *Transformation*, 85–86.
49. Pletcher, "Economic Expansionism," 95.
50. Ibid., 103–5.

A U.S. naval officer served as adviser to the Korean court. The Yankees quickly learned that Seoul was an especially precarious place to work. Minister Lucius Foote helped arrange a settlement between pro-Chinese and Japanese factions, but the result was to reduce U.S. influence. In any event, the United States quickly contented itself with being a minor player in a country torn by rivalries between larger and nearby nations. Trade was negligible.[51]

Some Americans also looked to the Congo River basin of West Africa for markets. A series of reports in the *New York Herald* first drew notice to the region. The newspaper in 1869 sent Scottish-born adventurer Henry M. Stanley to the Congo to find the long-missing medical missionary David Livingstone, who had gained international notoriety by "discovering" the Zambezi River and Victoria Falls. Stanley's 1871 encounter with his fellow Scotsman near Lake Tanganyika in present-day Tanzania, immortalized in the oft-quoted greeting "Dr. Livingstone, I presume," caused a worldwide sensation, attracting more attention to Africa. After a triumphant return to the United States, the intrepid explorer ranged deep into the Congo region, extolling its commercial possibilities. Some timely lobbying by Civil War diplomat and entrepreneur Henry Sanford, at this time serving as an agent for Belgium's King Leopold II, further promoted the Congo as a market for U.S. products. President Arthur himself spoke of "covering those unclad millions with our domestic cottons," calculating that "but three yards per capita would make an enormous aggregate for our cotton mills."[52]

The lure of African markets caused the United States in 1884 to break long-standing precedent by participating in an international conference held in Berlin to deal with the Congo region. The U.S. delegates were instructed to promote freedom of trade and steer clear of European entanglements—no mean task. The result was far less than America's Congo publicists had hoped. The conference solemnly declared itself in favor of free trade, but it also recognized Leopold's African International Association as the governing body. The association turned out to be a thinly veiled cover for exclusive trading arrangements and the most brutal exploitation of Africans. In any event, Republicans and Democrats denounced the agreement as an "entangling alliance." Cleveland took office in March 1885 just as the act was negotiated and, as with several other expansionist measures, refused to submit it to the Senate. The "noble dream" produced negligible results.[53]

51. Doenecke, *Garfield and Arthur*, 153–56.
52. Quoted in Campbell, *Transformation*, 100–102.
53. Doenecke, *Garfield and Arthur*, 162.

Republican efforts to use reciprocity treaties to expand foreign trade met a similar fate. Monroe and Adams had employed the device earlier in the century to challenge mercantilist trade barriers. More recently, Hamilton Fish through reciprocity had bound Hawaii economically to the United States. At a time when Europeans threatened to shut America out of foreign markets, reciprocity had a special attraction. It seemed an ideal means to secure new outlets for U.S. products when free trade was impossible and retaliation dangerous while still permitting some protection. In dealing with less developed nations, it had special advantages. It could gain free entry for foreign raw materials and markets for U.S. manufactured goods. As the Hawaiian example had shown, it established a means of control without resort to colonial rule.

Reciprocity was the "linchpin" of Arthur and Frelinghuysen's foreign trade policy. They especially targeted Latin America, a "natural mart of supply and demand," in Arthur's words, hoping to tie Latin economies to the United States, weaken European influence, and promote larger U.S. political aims. They attached special importance to a treaty with Mexico, naming former president U.S. Grant as a negotiator and working out an agreement that exchanged American manufactured goods for Mexican foods and raw materials. Diplomat John W. Foster bludgeoned Spain into agreements for Cuba and Puerto Rico that eliminated virtually all barriers to trade. The Cuban deal, Foster boasted, was "the most perfect reciprocity treaty our Government has ever made," giving the United States "an almost complete commercial monopoly" and thus "annexing Cuba in the most desirable way."[54] Foster negotiated an even more favorable agreement with Santo Domingo making the U.S. dollar the unit of currency in bilateral trade.

The Arthur trade offensive met insuperable obstacles at home. The tariff was the most contentious political issue of the age. Democrats who preferred broad and general tariff reductions and Republicans who supported protection both opposed reciprocity. The tariff brought to the fore the competing interests of farmers, manufacturers, and consumers, and any specific proposal could draw fire from a range of groups. Critics of the Mexican treaty complained it would subsidize foreign investors and favor railroad interests. American cigar makers and sugar interests fought the Cuban treaty. In any event, the Arthur treaties were completed as Cleveland took office. A throwback to Jefferson and Jackson, he doubted the validity of the "glut thesis" and sought to reduce tariffs to lower consumer prices and eliminate special privileges for business. Viewing reciprocity as a

54. Ibid., 176.

"conspiratorial device to prevent passage of a general tariff reduction act," he scrapped the treaties negotiated by his predecessor.[55]

The so-called Pork War with Europe exemplified America's concern with markets and its growing assertiveness and produced better results. A horrible famine on the Continent in 1879 proved a bonanza for the United States, leading to massive exports of agricultural products and full recovery from the Panic of 1873. Alarmed at the flood of American imports, European nations began to limit and then ban them. American meats were probably no less safe than European, but rumors of disease were used to justify what was economically and politically expedient. The British consul bemoaned the fate of one poor victim who found worms "in his flesh by the millions, being scraped and squeezed from the pores of his skin." Britain limited imports of U.S. pork and beef. France and Germany banned all imports even though America's meats had been certified safe by the French Academy of Medicine and its pork was reputedly safer than German.

The European measures provoked fury in the United States. Outraged farmers and producers urged retaliation by banning imports of French and German wines. The *Chicago Tribune* denounced the "rule or ruin" policies of the European aristocracy. The *New York Herald* urged "avenging the American hog."[56] Responding to domestic pressures, Blaine protested vigorously, but he also proposed that all meat products be inspected before exportation and offered to lower tariffs if the Europeans would rescind their bans. Arthur and Frelinghuysen also handled the matter cautiously. Arthur created an independent commission to study American meat-producing methods. He endorsed "equitable retaliation" but refused to act, fearing that a trade war might hurt the United States more than Europe. Their stopgap measures avoided a dangerous conflict while keeping some European markets open.[57]

A more assertive United States in 1890 launched all-out war on European restrictions. The issue was of more than passing political importance. "It does not comport with the self-respect and dignity of this government to longer tolerate such a policy," Secretary of Agriculture Jeremiah Rusk advised President Benjamin Harrison. The United States established mechanisms to inspect meat to be exported, thus presumably removing the rationale for European bans. The Harrison administration also threatened to ban imports of German sugar and French wines (known,

55. Welch, *Cleveland*, 85.
56. Campbell, *Transformation*, 103.
57. Doenecke, *Garfield and Arthur*, 67–69, 136–38.

in some cases, to be adulterated), and Congress in 1890 provided the means to retaliate. When the German government proposed lifting the ban if the United States agreed not to shut off imports of German sugar, Blaine urged acceptance, but a determined Harrison demurred, making clear his readiness to retaliate. In the face of this determination, Germany lifted its ban in return for American promises to keep sugar on the free list. Other European nations followed suit. Exports of U.S. meat products doubled between May 1891 and May 1892.[58]

V

In areas of traditional concern such as the Western Hemisphere and the Pacific basin, the United States during the Gilded Age mounted a concerted effort to expand its influence. Americans harbored vague and generally unfounded fears that Europeans might use their strong existing position to extend their colonizing tendencies to the Western Hemisphere. Certain of the superiority of their institutions and conscious of their rising power, they increasingly claimed that their rightful place was at the head of the American nations. They believed they could assist their southern neighbors to be more stable and orderly. For reasons of both economics and security, they sought to roll back European influence and increase their own.

Part of the work was done by individuals without direction or even encouragement from government. Following the devastation of the Ten Years' War, U.S. entrepreneurs bought up sugar estates, mines, and ranches in Cuba. By the 1890s, they dominated the island's economy. Exploiting the generous subsidies and tax breaks offered foreign investors by dictator Porfirio Diaz, Americans came to view Mexico as a "second India, Cuba, Brazil, Italy, and Troy all rolled into one." U.S. capital poured across the border into railroads, mines, and oil, totaling $500 million by 1900, transforming Mexico into a virtual satellite of the United States, and causing growing alarm among Mexican nationalists.[59] Some Central American rulers also welcomed U.S. capital as a means to modernize their economies, boost their nations' wealth, and uplift their people. They too granted generous concessions, permitting North Americans to buy up mines and plantations, control great wealth, and wield enormous power.[60]

58. Socolofsky and Spetter, *Harrison*, 132–36.
59. Enrique Krauze, *Mexico, Biography of Power: A History of Modern Mexico* (New York, 1997), 6; Karl M. Schmitt, *Mexico and the United States, 1821–1973* (New York, 1974), 101–5.
60. Thomas M. Leonard, *Central America and the United States: The Search for Stability* (Athens, Ga., 1991), 42–44.

For the first time, the United States came out openly and insistently for an American-owned and -controlled isthmian canal. From the outset, some Americans had demanded that they must build and operate such a canal. The 1850 Clayton-Bulwer Treaty had provoked bitter opposition on precisely such grounds. By the 1880s, a canal had assumed greater importance to the United States. Central American nations sought to exploit its anxieties. Nicaraguan overtures to British bankers and Colombia's deal with Ferdinand de Lesseps, builder of the Suez Canal, to construct a canal across Panama, stunned a complacent Washington into action. Former Union general Ambrose Burnside pronounced a French-built canal "dangerous to our peace and safety"; Congress responded with a flurry of resolutions. In terms of commerce and security, the normally laconic Rutherford B. Hayes declared, a canal would be "virtually a part of the coast line of the United States." The "true policy" of the United States must be "either a canal under American control, or no canal." Hayes did not stop the de Lesseps venture, but he did secure from the French government an affirmation that it was a private venture without official support.[61]

Hayes's successors went further. Blaine and Frelinghuysen stood firmly for an American-owned and -controlled canal and made sporadic efforts to modify or abrogate the Clayton-Bulwer Treaty. Blaine called an isthmian canal as much a "channel of communication" between the East and West coasts of the United States as "our own transcontinental railroad." It was "strictly and solely . . . an American question, to be dealt with and decided by the American governments." Rejecting such claims, the British firmly retorted that any Central American canal concerned "the whole civilized world."[62] To counter de Lesseps, Frelinghuysen negotiated a treaty with Nicaragua permitting the United States to build and operate a canal in return for a promise to defend that nation's sovereignty. The treaty was one-sided, the New York Times explained, because the "will of a mighty nation of 55,000,000 of homogenous, progressive and patriotic people is of course irresistible when it runs counter to the wishes of feeble and unstable governments like Central and South America."[63] As with so many other Arthur-Frelinghuysen initiatives, the incoming Cleveland administration junked the treaty because it viewed the commitment to Nicaragua as an entangling alliance.

To reduce foreign influence in the hemisphere and increase its own, the United States claimed for itself a new leadership role and initiated a

61. Hoogenboom, *Hayes*, 189–90.
62. Doenecke, *Garfield and Arthur*, 66–67.
63. Leonard, *United States and Central America*, 39–40.

habit of "paternalistic meddling" that would persist far into the future. Blaine was the ringleader in both areas. His efforts reflected his assertive personality but also his conviction that exposure to the United States would have a positive "moral influence" and raise "the standard of...civ- ilization" of peoples he regarded as congenitally quarrelsome and conten- tious, thus eliminating any excuses for European intrusion.[64] He first in- tervened in a boundary dispute between Mexico and Guatemala in 1881, foolishly encouraging Guatemala, which had the weaker claim, and thereby delaying a settlement. His intervention in the War of the Pacific the same year was even more clumsy in execution and harmful in results. Spying Britain's sinister hand behind Chile's efforts to gain territory dis- puted with Peru, he dispatched two singularly inept diplomats to the scene. One got involved in a shady scheme from which he stood to profit handsomely. Together, the two undercut each other's efforts and alien- ated both sides, Peru counting on U.S. support that was not forthcoming, Chile correctly viewing the United States as thwarting its ambitions. The British minister dismissed the U.S. intervention as "pretentious incapac- ity." Frelinghuysen liquidated it as quickly as possible. But it left a deep legacy of suspicion and anger on the west coast of South America.[65]

The pace of U.S. overseas activity quickened from 1889 to 1893 under the aggressive leadership of President Benjamin Harrison and Secretary of State Blaine. Defeated by Cleveland for the presidency in 1884, Blaine de- clined to run four years later. The Republicans nominated instead the Indiana lawyer, U.S. senator, and grandson of President William Henry Harrison. As a Senate mentor, Blaine had helped convert the Indianan to expansionism. The cold, aloof president and his dynamic, charismatic ad- viser never formed a close working relationship; their collaboration was often beset with rivalry and tension. But the two pursued an activist, some- times belligerent foreign policy that jump-started a decade of expansion- ism, energetically reasserting U.S. leadership of the hemisphere, pushing reciprocity with renewed vigor, escalating a minor crisis with Chile to the point of war, aggressively pursuing naval bases in the Caribbean and Pacific, and even giving the green light to a coup d'état in Hawaii. Small of stature with a high-pitched voice, "Little Ben" was especially bellicose and on sev- eral occasions had to be restrained by the man known as "Jingo Jim."[66]

Under Blaine's direction, the United States in 1889 hosted the first inter-American conference since the ill-fated Panama Congress of 1826.

64. Schoultz, *Beneath the United States*, 94.
65. Ibid., 94–97; Doenecke, *Garfield and Arthur*, 57–62.
66. Crapol, *Blaine*, 107–8, 112.

Concerned that interhemispheric conflict might invite European intervention, the secretary of state had first proposed such a meeting in 1881 so
that the hemisphere nations could find ways to prevent war among themselves. The invitations were canceled after Garfield's assassination, partly
to spite Blaine. Appropriately, the Plumed Knight was back in office when
the conference finally convened in 1889. By this time, the focus had
shifted to trade issues. The delegates were immediately whisked off on a
six-week, six-thousand-mile tour of U.S. industrial centers, a crude brand
of huckstering that annoyed some Latin visitors. Blaine's ambitious
agenda for the six-month conference included such things as arbitration
of disputes, a customs union, and copyright agreements. It produced little
except the resolve to meet again and establishment of a bureaucracy
based in Washington that would evolve into the Pan American Union.
Blaine's efforts brought few immediate, tangible gains, but they made
clear U.S. determination to assume hemispheric leadership and initiated
"the modern era of an institutionalized hemispheric community."[67]

Given broad authority by a measure Blaine had included in the tariff
bill of 1890 to negotiate agreements without congressional oversight, the
Harrison administration also mounted a new drive for reciprocal trade
treaties in Latin America. Food and raw materials would be permitted to
enter duty free, but if other nations did not respond with similar generosity the United States would reimpose duties. The administration used the
first treaty with Brazil to pressure Spain into new agreements with Cuba
and Puerto Rico. Of the former, steel magnate Andrew Carnegie observed, Cuba "hereafter will be of as little good to Spain as Canada is to
Britain."[68] As with many other Republican initiatives, however, the
Democrats' return to power in 1893 and passage of the Wilson-Gorman
tariff in 1894 undercut Harrison's efforts, leaving little to show for two decades of effort.

The Harrison administration's assertiveness was most blatantly manifested in its handling of a minor dispute with Chile. During a drunken
brawl in a seedy part of Valparaiso in late 1891, two sailors from the USS
Baltimore were killed, seventeen wounded, and thirty-six jailed. The incident quickly escalated. As nationalistic as Americans, Chileans saw themselves as a rival to the United States for hemispheric leadership. Relations
between the two nations had been strained since Blaine's ill-conceived
intrusion into the War of the Pacific and worsened in 1889 when the United
States openly interfered in Chile's internal politics. The *Baltimore's*

67. Schoultz, *Beneath the United States*, 283, 318; Socolofsky and Spetter, *Harrison*, 117–18.
68. Socolofsky and Spetter, *Harrison*, 119–23.

captain insisted that his sailors had been "properly drunk," the victims of an unprovoked attack. Blaine was ill, and therefore not involved in the negotiations. A notably bellicose Harrison far exceeded traditional U.S. practice by demanding not only an apology but also "prompt and full" reparation. Still furious at the United States for its earlier meddling, Chile at first denied the charges and accused Washington of lying, but it subsequently expressed "very sincere regret for the unfortunate events." Unappeased and very much in keeping with the mood of the time, Harrison exclaimed that "we must protect those who in foreign ports display the flag or wear its colors." He continued to demand a "suitable apology" and reparation and threatened to break relations. As the two nations edged toward an especially foolish war, Chile blinked first, offering an apology and $75,000 in reparations. Belying his reputation for bellicosity, Blaine persuaded Harrison to accept. To Adm. Bancroft Gherardi, the incident made clear that the United States was "no longer to be trifled with."[69]

Harrison and Blaine employed economic and diplomatic pressure and gunboat diplomacy in a futile effort to secure naval bases in the Caribbean. The more U.S. leaders talked of a canal, the greater the perceived need for bases to protect it. Haiti's Môle St. Nicolas was especially attractive, and Blaine exerted strong pressure against a government threatened by revolution to acquire it. When that government balked, the United States permitted arms shipments to the rebels, hoping that its generosity would be repaid. After the rebels took power, the administration dispatched the distinguished African American leader Frederick Douglass, himself an ardent expansionist, to negotiate with Haiti. When those negotiations stalled, Blaine sent Admiral Gherardi to take over; when he also failed to budge Haitian leaders, the United States conducted a naval demonstration off its shores. Haiti refused to be cowed. Santo Domingo was no more obliging. The United States' efforts to use the leverage provided by a reciprocity treaty to acquire Samana Bay produced nothing. Blaine resigned in June 1892 and died the following year without realizing his dream of a Caribbean naval base. To the end, he remained confident that the United States would acquire Cuba and Puerto Rico within a generation.[70]

The Harrison administration also sought to strengthen the U.S. position in the Pacific basin. Through a bizarre set of circumstances, not at all atypical for this turbulent era, the United States assumed a quite remarkable role on Samoa. Shortly after the 1878 treaty, the U.S. consul had signed an agreement neutralizing the town of Apia and establishing a

69. Schoultz, *Beneath the United States*, 102–6; Socolofsky and Spetter, *Harrison*, 146–51.
70. Crapol, *Blaine*, 129–30.

multilateral governing body composed of himself and the British and German consuls. The agreement was never submitted to the Senate, but it operated anyway, "an unprecedented collaboration with European countries on a distant South Sea archipelago."[71] Such cooperation soon embroiled the United States in a mini-crisis with Germany. When German naval officers seized Apia in 1885 and then asserted their intention to take control of Samoa, the Cleveland administration balked. On his own, the U.S. consul launched a preemptive strike by declaring an American protectorate over all Samoa. An embarrassed secretary of state Bayard beat a hasty retreat, disavowing the overzealous consul and temporarily easing tensions. In 1887, however, Germany sent warships to Samoa and deported the pro-American king. Claiming sanctimoniously that the United States' "first allegiance" was to the "rights of the natives in Samoa," Cleveland and Bayard also sent warships. Already annoyed with Germany over the Pork War, the American press expressed outrage. Congress appropriated funds to defend U.S. interests on that distant isle.[72]

The Samoan crisis eased as quickly as it had flared up. The master diplomatist Bismarck did not want war with the United States over a faraway Pacific island and invited America and Britain to discuss the issue at a conference in Berlin. A timely hurricane, along with tidal waves, struck Apia in March 1889, sinking or disabling all German and U.S. warships and killing 150 men. This act of God diverted attention from the great power conflict, removed the instruments of war, and cooled tempers. The Berlin conference later that year, in which the United States was a full participant, quickly reached an agreement declaring Samoa independent but establishing a complex mechanism for what was in effect a tripartite agreement dividing power among the great powers while leaving Samoa nominally autonomous. At Blaine's insistence, the United States retained control over the superb harbor of Pago Pago. Some Americans cheered that their secretary of state had stood up to Germany's Iron Chancellor. For the first time in its history, the United States was formally committed to govern an overseas people. It was also a participant in an entangling agreement with two European nations in an area where it had scant interests.[73]

In Hawaii, Blaine and Harrison almost pulled off a replay of the methods used to secure Florida, Texas, and California. The reciprocity treaty of 1875 had done its job. By the 1880s, Hawaii was a virtual satellite of the United States, and any foreign challenge met a firm rebuff. When the

71. Campbell, *Transformation*, 77.
72. Ibid., 80–81.
73. Ibid., 83.

British and French sought to defend their dwindling interests by insisting on most-favored-nation status, the Senate Foreign Relations Committee proclaimed Hawaii a part of "the physical and political geography of the United States." Blaine called it part of an "American Zollverein," the name given to a contemporaneous German customs union. In 1884, the two nations renewed the treaty for an additional seven years. Even Cleveland went along, although he opposed reciprocity in principle, insisting that Hawaii was essential to U.S. commerce in the Pacific.[74] Because of opposition from domestic sugar producers, Senate approval came only after three years and after an amendment giving the United States exclusive right to a naval base at Pearl Harbor. The British consul correctly predicted that the base agreement would "lead to the loss of Hawaiian independence."[75] Indeed, upon taking power in 1889, Blaine and Harrison negotiated with the American serving as Hawaiian minister to the United States an agreement making Hawaii a U.S. protectorate. The king resisted the provision permitting the United States to use military force to protect Hawaii's independence. The idea died — momentarily.

An abortive move to annex Hawaii made clear the lengths the Harrison administration would go to achieve its expansionist aims. The McKinley tariff of 1890 deprived Hawaiian sugar of its privileged position and spread economic distress on the islands. Along with the determined efforts of the new Queen Liliuokalani to regain the royal powers squandered to the Americans by her late brother and to restore "Hawaii for the Hawaiians," it threatened the economic well-being and political power of U.S. planters. In early 1892, the Americans formed a secret "Annexation Club," sounded out U.S. minister to Hawaii John L. Stevens, an old friend and business partner of Blaine, and instigated a plot to overthrow the queen. Harrison carefully maintained what would later be called plausible deniability. Neither he nor Blaine encouraged Stevens's actions, but they presumably agreed with the plan and did nothing to stop it. Indeed, in June 1892, the administration assured a Stevens crony that if the Hawaiian people applied for annexation the United States could not say no. When the queen proclaimed a new constitution, the conspirators made their move. In January 1893, on orders from Stevens, the USS *Boston* landed sailors to preserve order, a step crucial to the outcome. The plotters seized power in a bloodless takeover. Stevens declared the new government under U.S. protection. "The Hawaiian pear is now fully ripe and this is the golden

---

74. Doenecke, *Garfield and Arthur*, 177; Welch, *Cleveland*, 169.
75. Campbell, *Transformation*, 71.

hour for the United States to pluck it," he advised the State Department.[76] Hawaiian representatives hustled to Washington, where, with embarrassing speed, a treaty of annexation was negotiated, signed, and submitted to the Senate. Disclaiming responsibility for the coup, Harrison nevertheless denounced the queen as "effete," warned that the United States must act decisively lest the ripe pear fall into the waiting lap of some rival nation, and urged annexation. Like other expansionist moves, this effort to acquire Hawaii would die—at least temporarily—at the hands of a second Cleveland administration, but it made quite clear the new commitment to expansionist goals and the willingness to use extraordinary means to achieve them. One hundred years later, without acknowledging United States responsibility, Congress would pass a bill formally apologizing to the people of Hawaii for the overthrow of its government.[77]

FOREIGN POLICY WAS NOT A HIGH NATIONAL PRIORITY in the Gilded Age. There was no threat to the nation's security. The Pork War was the closest thing to a real crisis; the overblown war scares with Italy and Chile, so typical of an age of flag-waving nationalism, patriotic posturing, and inflated concern with honor, were not far behind. Gilded Age diplomatists have been dismissed for not being "internationalists," but there was no need for them to be nor any reason to expect that of them. Dull and plodding they may have seemed, sometimes clumsy in the execution of policies, but they took their jobs seriously. They began to develop the accoutrements of national power. Although the results would not be seen until later, they vigorously pursued new outlets for trade. They defended the nation's interests. They had no master plan or fixed agenda, but the goals they pursued and the decisions they made reflected their commitment to the extension of American power.[78] They achieved few tangible results, but in the Caribbean and the Pacific, areas of greatest U.S. interest, they shored up the nation's already strong position. They provided a springboard for another burst of expansionism in the 1890s.

76. Quoted in Crapol, *Blaine*, 128.
77. Ibid., 125–26.
78. Crapol in Joseph A. Fry, "From Open Door to World Systems: Economic Interpretations of Late Nineteenth-Century American Foreign Relations," *Pacific Historical Review* 65 (May 1996), 302.

8

The War of 1898, the New Empire, and the Dawn of the American Century, 1893–1901

The great transformation in U.S. foreign relations that culminated in the globalism of the American Century began in the 1890s. During that tumultuous decade, the pace of diplomatic activity quickened. Americans took greater notice of events abroad and more vigorously asserted themselves in defense of perceived interests. The War with Spain in 1898 and the acquisition of overseas colonies have often been viewed as accidents of history, departures from tradition, a "great aberration," in the words of historian Samuel Flagg Bemis, "empire by default," according to a more recent writer.[1] In fact, the United States in going to war with Spain acted much more purposefully than such interpretations allow. To be sure, the nation broke precedent by acquiring overseas colonies with no intention of admitting them as states. At the same time, in its aims, its methods, and the rhetoric used to justify it, the expansionism of the 1890s followed logically from earlier patterns, built on established precedents, and gave structure to the blueprints drawn up by expansionists such as Thomas Jefferson, John Quincy Adams, James K. Polk, William H. Seward, and James G. Blaine.

I

During the 1890s, Americans became acutely conscious of their emerging power. "We are sixty-five million of people, the most advanced and powerful on earth," a senator observed in 1893 with pride and more than a touch of exaggeration.[2] "We are a Nation—with the biggest kind of N," Kentucky journalist Henry Watterson added, "a great imperial Republic destined to exercise a controlling influence upon the actions of mankind and to affect the future of the world."[3]

1. Samuel Flagg Bemis, A Diplomatic History of the United States (5th ed., New York, 1965), 463; Ivan Musicant, Empire by Default: The Spanish-American War and the Dawn of the American Century (New York, 1998).
2. Robert L. Beisner, From the Old Diplomacy to the New, 1865–1900 (2nd ed., Arlington Heights, Ill., 1986), 78.
3. David Healy, U.S. Expansionism: The Imperialist Urge in the 1890s (Madison, Wisc., 1970), 46.

Acknowledgment of this new position came in various forms. In 1892, the Europeans upgraded their ministers in Washington to the rank of ambassador, tacitly recognizing America's status as a major power.[4] One year later, Congress without debate scrapped its republican inhibitions and the practices of a century by creating that rank within the U.S. foreign service, a move of more than symbolic importance. United States diplomats had long bristled at the lack of precedence accorded them in foreign courts because of their lowly rank of minister. They viewed the snubs and shabby treatment as an affront to the prestige of a rising power. An ambassador also had better access to sovereigns and prime ministers, it was argued, and could therefore negotiate more easily and effectively.[5]

The Columbian Exposition in Chicago in 1893 both symbolized and celebrated the nation's coming of age. Organized to commemorate the four-hundredth anniversary of Columbus's "discovery" of America, it was used by U.S. officials to promote trade with Latin America.[6] Its futuristic exhibits took a peek at life in the twentieth century. It displayed high culture and low, the latter including Buffalo Bill's Wild West Show, the first Ferris wheel, and the exotic performances of belly-dancer Little Egypt. It highlighted American technology and the mass culture that would be the nation's major export in the next century. Above all, it was a patriotic celebration of U.S. achievements, past, present, and to come. Frenchman Paul de Bourget was "struck dumb...with wonderment" by what he saw, "this wonderfully new country" in "advance of the age."[7]

Wonder and pride were increasingly tempered by fear and foreboding. During the 1890s, Americans experienced internal shocks and perceived external threats that caused profound anxieties and spurred them to intensified diplomatic activity, greater assertiveness, and overseas expansion. Ironically, just a month after the opening of the Columbian Exposition, the most severe economic crisis in its history stunned the nation. Triggered by the failure of a British banking house, the Panic of 1893 wreaked devastation across the land, causing some fifteen thousand business failures in that year alone and 17 percent unemployment. The depression shook

4. Paul Kennedy, *The Rise and Fall of the Great Powers: Economic Change and Military Conflict from 1500 to 2000* (New York, 1987), 194.
5. Warren Frederick Ilchman, *Professional Diplomacy in the United States: An Administrative History* (Chicago, 1961), 71–72.
6. Frank A. Cassell, "The Columbian Exposition of 1893 and United States Diplomacy in Latin America," *Mid-America: A Historical Review* 67 (October 1985), 109–24.
7. Robert Muccigrosso, *Celebrating the New World: Chicago's Columbian Exposition of 1893* (Chicago, 1998), 179, 193; Emily S. Rosenberg, *Spreading the American Dream: American Economic and Cultural Expansion, 1890–1945* (New York, 1982), 3.

the nation to its core, eroding optimism and raising serious doubts about the new industrial system.[8]

Social and political concerns combined with a malfunctioning economy to produce confusion about the present and anxiety for the future.[9] Close to a half million immigrants arrived in the United States each year in the 1880s. The ethnic makeup of these newcomers—Italians, Poles, Greeks, Jews, Hungarians—was even more unsettling to old-stock Americans than their numbers, threatening a homogenous social order. The sprawling, ugly cities they populated produced fears for the survival of a simpler, agrarian America.

Democracy itself seemed in jeopardy. At first enthusiastically hailed for their productive capacity, giant corporations such as Standard Oil, Carnegie Steel, and the Pennsylvania Railroad, and the huge banking houses such as J. P. Morgan and Co. that financed them, became increasingly suspect because of the allegedly corrupt and exploitative practices used by the so-called robber barons to build them, the enormous power they wielded, and their threat to individual enterprise. At the Chicago exposition, historian Frederick Jackson Turner presented a paper attributing American democracy to the availability of a western frontier. Coming at a time when demographers were claiming (incorrectly, as it turned out) that the continental frontier had closed, Turner's writings aroused concerns that the nation's fundamental values were in jeopardy. Such fears produced a "social malaise" that gripped the United States through much of the decade.[10]

The crisis was evidenced in various ways. The growing militancy of labor—there were 1,400 strikes in the year 1894 alone—and the use of force to suppress it produced a threat to social order that frightened solid middle-class citizens. The violence that accompanied the 1892 Homestead "massacre" in Pennsylvania, where private security forces battled workers, and the Pullman strike in Illinois two yeas later in which thirteen strikers were killed was particularly unsettling. The march on Washington of Jacob Coxey's "army" of unemployed in the spring of 1894 to demand federal relief and the Populist "revolt" of embattled southern and western farmers proposing major political and economic reforms portended a radical upheaval that might alter basic institutions.

The nation also appeared threatened from abroad. The uneasy equilibrium that had prevailed in Europe since Waterloo seemed increasingly

8. Charles S. Campbell, *The Transformation of American Foreign Relations, 1865–1900* (New York, 1976), 142.
9. Beisner, *Old Diplomacy to the New*, 74.
10. Ibid., 74–76.

endangered. The worldwide imperialist surge quickened in the 1890s. The partition of Africa neared completion. Following Japan's defeat of China in their 1894–95 war, the European powers turned to East Asia, joining their Asian newcomer in marking out spheres of influence, threatening to eliminate what remained of the helpless Middle Kingdom's sovereignty, perhaps shutting it off to American trade. Some Europeans spoke of closing ranks against a rising U.S. commercial menace. Some nations raised tariffs. Britain's threat to impose imperial preference in its vast colonial holdings portended a further shrinkage of markets deemed more essential than ever in years of depression.[11]

The gloom and anxiety of the 1890s produced a mood conducive to war and expansion. They triggered a noisy nationalism and spread-eagle patriotism, manifested in the stirring marches of John Philip Sousa and outwardly emotional displays of reverence for the flag. The word *jingoism* was coined in Britain in the 1870s. Xenophobia flourished in the United States in the 1890s in nativist attacks upon immigrants at home and verbal blasts against nations that affronted U.S. honor. For some Americans, a belligerent foreign policy offered a release for pent-up aggressions and diversion from domestic difficulties. It could "knock on the head...the matters which have embarrassed us at home," Massachusetts senator Henry Cabot Lodge averred.[12]

The social malaise also aroused concern about issues of manhood. The depression robbed many American men of the means to support their families. A rising generation that had not fought in the Civil War and remembered only its glories increasingly feared that industrialism, urbanization, and immigration, along with widening divisions of class and race, were sapping American males of the manly virtues deemed essential for good governance. The emergence of a militant women's movement demanding political participation further threatened men's traditional role in U.S. politics. For some jingoes, a more assertive foreign policy, war, and even the acquisition of colonies would reaffirm their manhood, restore lost pride and virility, and legitimize their traditional place in the political system. "War is healthy to a nation," an Illinois congressman proclaimed. "War is a bad thing, no doubt," Lodge added, "but there are far worse things both for nations and for men," among which he would have included dishonor and a failure vigorously to defend the nation's interests.[13]

11. Ibid., 77; Campbell, *Transformation*, 146.

12. Healy, *U.S. Expansionism*, 108.

13. Kristin L. Hoganson, *Fighting for American Manhood: How Gender Politics Provoked the Spanish-American and Philippine-American Wars* (New Haven, Conn., 1998), 35–40.

Changes at home and abroad convinced some Americans of the need to reexamine long-standing foreign policy assumptions. The further shrinkage of distances, the advent of menacing weapons, the emergence of new powers such as Germany and Japan, and the surge of imperialist activity persuaded some military leaders that the United States no longer enjoyed freedom from foreign threat. Isolated from civilian society, increasingly professionalized, their own interests appearing to be happily aligned with those of the nation, they pushed for a reexamination of national defense policy and the building of a modern military machine. They promoted the novel idea (for Americans, at least) that even in time of peace a nation must prepare for war. Army officers added Germany and Japan to the nation's list of potential enemies and warned of emerging threats from European imperialism, commercial rivalries, and foreign challenges to an American-controlled canal. They began to push for an expanded, more professional regular army based on European models.[14]

Advocates for the new navy offered more compelling arguments and achieved greater results. The most fervent and influential late nineteenth-century advocate of sea power was Capt. Alfred Thayer Mahan, son of an early superintendent of West Point. A mediocre sailor who detested sea duty, the younger Mahan salvaged a flagging career by accepting the post of senior lecturer at the new Naval War College. While putting together a course in naval history, he wrote his classic *The Influence of Seapower upon History* (1890). Mahan argued that the United States must abandon its defensive, "continentalist" strategy based on harbor defense and commerce raiding for a more outward-looking approach. Britain had achieved greatpower status by controlling the seas and dominating global commerce. So too, he contended, the United States must compete aggressively for world trade, build a large merchant marine, acquire colonies for raw materials, markets, and naval bases, and construct a modern battleship fleet, "the arm of offensive power, which alone enables a country to extend its influence outward." Such moves would ensure U.S. prosperity by keeping sea lanes open in time of war and peace. A skilled publicist as well as an influential strategic thinker, Mahan won worldwide acclaim in the 1890s; his book became an international best seller. At home, a naval renaissance was already under way. Mahan's ideas provided a persuasive

---

14. Beisner, *Old Diplomacy to the New*, 79; Allen R. Millett and Peter Maslowski, *For the Common Defense: A Military History of the United States of America* (New York, 1984), 255–58.

rationale for the new battleship navy and a more aggressive U.S. foreign policy.[15]

Some civilians also called for an activist foreign policy, even for abandoning long-standing strictures against alliances and inhibitions against overseas expansion. Such policies had done well enough "when we were an embryo nation," a senator observed, but the mere fact that the United States had become a major power now demanded their abandonment.[16] As a rising great power, the United States had interests that must be defended. It must assume the responsibility for its own welfare and for world order that went with its new status. "The mission of this country is not merely to pose but to act...," former attorney general and secretary of state Richard Olney proclaimed in 1898, "to forego no fitting opportunity to further the progress of civilization."[17]

Since Jefferson's time, Americans had sought to deal with pressing internal difficulties through expansion, and in the 1890s they increasingly looked outward for solutions to domestic problems. With the disappearance of the frontier, it was argued, new outlets must be found abroad for America's energy and enterprise. In a world driven by Darwinian struggle where only the strongest survived, the United States must compete aggressively. The Panic of 1893 marked the coming of age of the "glut thesis." America's traditional interest in foreign trade now became almost an obsession. Businessmen increasingly looked to Washington for assistance.[18] Many Americans agreed that to compete effectively in world markets the United States needed an isthmian canal and island bases to protect it. In the tense atmosphere of the 1890s, some advocates of the socalled large policy even urged acquisition of colonies.

The idea of overseas empire ran up against the nation's tradition of anticolonialism, and in the 1890s, as so often before, Americans heatedly debated the means by which they could best fulfill their providential destiny. A rising elite keenly interested in foreign policy followed closely similar debates on empire in Britain and adapted their arguments to the United States.[19] Some continued to insist that the nation should focus on perfecting its domestic institutions to provide an example to others. But as Americans became more conscious of their rising power, others insisted

15. Russell F. Weigley, *The American Way of War: A History of United States Military Strategy and Policy* (New York, 1977), 78.
16. Beisner, *Old Diplomacy to the New*, 78.
17. Ibid., 84.
18. Ibid., 77; also Walter LaFeber, *The New Empire: An Interpretation of American Expansion, 1866–1898* (Ithaca, N.Y., 1967), especially 190–97.
19. Ernest R. May, *American Imperialism: A Speculative Essay* (rev. ed., Chicago, 1991).

they had a God-given obligation to spread the blessings of their superior institutions to less fortunate peoples across the world. God was "preparing in our civilization the die with which to stamp nations," Congregationalist minister Josiah Strong proclaimed, and was "preparing mankind to receive our impress."[20]

Racism and popular notions of Anglo-Saxonism and the white man's burden helped justify the imposition of U.S. rule on "backward" populations. Even while the United States and Britain continued to tangle over various issues, Americans hailed the blood ties and common heritage of the English-speaking peoples. According to Anglo-Saxonist ideas, Americans and Britons stood together at the top of a hierarchy of races, superior in intellect, industry, and morality. Some Americans took pride in the glory of the British Empire while predicting that in time they would supplant it. The United States was bound to become "a greater England with a nobler destiny," proclaimed Indiana senator and staunch expansionist Albert Jeremiah Beveridge.[21] Convictions of Anglo-Saxonism helped rationalize harsh measures toward lesser races. While disfranchising and segregating African Americans at home, some Americans promoted the idea of extending civilization to lesser peoples abroad. Recent experiences with Native Americans provided handy precedents. Expansionists thus easily reconciled imperialism with traditional principles. The economic penetration or even colonization of less developed areas would allegedly benefit those peoples by bringing them the advantages of U.S. institutions. Arguing for the Americanization and eventual annexation of Cuba, expansionist James Harrison Wilson put it all together: "Let us take this course because it is noble and just and right, and besides because it will pay."[22]

The new mood was early manifest in the assertive diplomacy of President Benjamin Harrison and Secretary of State James G. Blaine. In response to attacks on American missionaries, Harrison joined other great powers in seeking to coerce the Chinese government to respect the rights of foreigners. He also ordered the construction of specially designed gunboats to show the flag in Chinese waters. The bullying of Haiti and Santo Domingo in a futile quest for a Caribbean naval base, the bellicose handling of minor incidents with Italy and Chile, and the abortive 1893 move to annex Hawaii all indicated a distinct shift in the tone of U.S. policy and the adoption of new and more aggressive methods.

20. Quoted in Healy, U.S. Expansionism, 38.
21. Michael H. Hunt, Ideology and U.S. Foreign Policy (New Haven, Conn., 1987), 77–81.
22. Healy, U.S. Expansionism, 95.

A second Grover Cleveland administration (1893–97) killed the Republican effort to acquire Hawaii. Anti-expansionist and anti-annexation, Cleveland had a strong sense of right and wrong in such matters. He recalled the treaty of annexation from the Senate and dispatched James Blount of Georgia on a secret fact-finding mission to Hawaii. Blount also opposed overseas expansion both in principle and on racial grounds. "We have nothing in common with those people," he once exclaimed of Venezuelans. He ignored the new Hawaiian government's frenzied warnings that Japan was waiting to seize the islands if the United States demurred. He concluded, correctly, that most Hawaiians opposed annexation and that the change of government had been engineered by Americans to protect their own profits. His report firmly opposed annexation.[23] Facing a divided Congress and a nation absorbed in economic crisis, Cleveland was inclined to restore Queen Liliuokalani to power, but he also worried about the fate of the rebels. The queen had threatened to have their heads—and their property. Unable to get from either side the assurances he sought and unwilling to decide himself, he tossed the issue back to Congress. After months of debate, the legislators could agree only on the desirability of recognizing the existing Hawaiian government. Cleveland reluctantly went along.[24]

Even the normally cautious and anti-expansionist Cleveland was not immune to the spirit of the age. In January 1894, his administration injected U.S. power into an internal struggle in Brazil. Suspecting (probably incorrectly) that Britain sought to use the conflict to enhance its position in that important Latin American nation, Cleveland dispatched five ships of the new navy, the most imposing fleet the nation had ever sent to sea, to break a rebel blockade and protect U.S. ships and exports. When the navy moved on to show the flag elsewhere, private interests took on the task of gunboat diplomacy. With Cleveland's acquiescence or tacit support, the colorful industrialist, shipbuilder, and arms merchant Charles Flint equipped merchant and passenger ships with the most up-to-date weapons, including a "dynamite gun" that could fire a 980-pound projectile. He dispatched his "fleet" to the coast of Brazil. The mere threat of the notorious dynamite gun helped cow the rebels and keep the government in power, solidifying U.S. influence in Brazil. In November

23. Tennant S. McWilliams, "James H. Blount, the South, and Hawaiian Annexation," *Pacific Historical Review* 57 (February 1988), 25–46.
24. Richard E. Welch Jr., *The Presidencies of Grover Cleveland* (Lawrence, Kans., 1988), 171–75.

1894, Brazilians laid the cornerstone to a monument in Rio de Janeiro to James Monroe and his doctrine.[25]

The following year, the Cleveland administration intruded in a boundary dispute between Britain and Venezuela over British Guiana, rendering a new and more expansive interpretation of that doctrine. The dispute had dragged on for years. Venezuela numerous times sought to draw the United States into it by speaking of violations of Monroe's statement. Each time, Washington had politely declined, and it is not entirely clear why Cleveland now took up a challenge his predecessors had sensibly resisted. He had a soft spot for the underdog. He may have been moved by his fervent anti-imperialism. He was undoubtedly responding to domestic pressures, stirred up in part by the lobbying of a shady former U.S. diplomat now working for Venezuela. Britain appeared particularly aggressive in the hemisphere, and the United States was increasingly sensitive to its position. Some Americans feared the British might use the dispute to secure control of the Orinoco River and close it to trade. More generally, Cleveland responded to the broad threat of a surging European imperialism and the fear that the Europeans might turn their attention to Latin America, thus directly threatening U.S. interests. He determined to use the dispute to assert U.S. preeminence in the Western Hemisphere.[26]

Significantly, Richard Olney replaced Walter Gresham as secretary of state at this point. Not known for tact or finesse—as attorney general, Olney had just forcibly suppressed the Pullman strike—he quickly set the tone for U.S. intrusion. In what Cleveland called his "twenty-inch gun" (new Dreadnought battleships were equipped with twelve-inch guns), Olney's July 20, 1895, note insisted in prosecutor's language that the Monroe Doctrine justified U.S. intervention and pressed Britain to arbitrate. More important, it claimed hegemonic power. Today "the United States is practically sovereign on this continent," he proclaimed, "and its fiat is law upon the subjects to which it confines its interposition." The New York World spoke excitedly of the "blaze" that swept the nation after Olney's message.[27]

Even more surprising than the fact of U.S. intrusion and the force of Olney's blast was Britain's eventual acquiescence. At first shocked that the United States should take such an extravagant stand on a "subject so

25. Steven C. Topik, *Trade and Gunboats: The United States and Brazil in the Age of Empire* (Stanford, Calif., 1996), 120–76.

26. Welch, *Cleveland*, 187–90; Beisner, *Old Diplomacy to the New*, 112–15. See also LaFeber, *New Empire*, 243–50.

27. Robert C. Hilderbrand, *Power and the People: Executive Management of Public Opinion in Foreign Affairs*, 1877–1921 (Chapel Hill, N.C., 1981), 8.

comparatively small," Prime Minister Lord Salisbury delayed four months before replying. He then lectured an upstart nation on how to behave in a grown-up world, rejecting its claims and telling it to mind its own business. Now "mad clean through," as he put it, Cleveland responded in kind. On both sides, as so often in the nineteenth century, talk of war abounded. Once again, U.S. timing was excellent. Britain was distracted by crises in the Middle East, East Asia, and especially South Africa, where war loomed with the Boers. As before, the threat of war evoked from both nations ties of kinship that grew stronger throughout the century. London proposed, then quickly dropped over U.S. objections, a conference to define the meaning of the Monroe Doctrine, a significant concession. It also tacitly conceded the U.S. definition of the Monroe Doctrine and its hegemony in the hemisphere.[28]

The larger principle more or less settled, the two nations, not surprisingly, resolved their differences at the expense of Venezuela. Neither Anglo-Saxon country had much respect for the third party, "a mongrel state," Thomas Bayard, then serving in London as the first U.S. ambassador, exclaimed dismissively. They were not about to leave questions of war and peace in its hands. Britain agreed to arbitrate once the United States accepted its conditions for arbitration. The two nations then imposed on an outraged Venezuela a treaty providing for arbitration and giving it no representation on the commission. Britain got much of what it wanted except for a strip of land controlling the Orinoco River, precisely what Washington sought to keep from it. Venezuela got very little. Despite Olney's bombast, the United States secured British recognition of its expanded interpretation of the Monroe Doctrine and a larger share of the trade of northern South America. Olney's blast further announced to the world and especially to Britain that the United States was prepared to establish its place among the great powers, whatever Europeans might think. It elevated the Monroe Doctrine to near holy writ at home and marked the end of British efforts to contest U.S. preeminence in the Caribbean.[29]

From 1895 to 1898, the expansionist program was clearly articulated and well publicized and gained numerous adherents. In the 1896 election campaign between Republican William McKinley of Ohio and Democrat William Jennings Bryan of Nebraska, domestic issues, especially Bryan's

---

28. Lars Schoultz, *Beneath the United States: A History of U.S. Policy Toward Latin America* (Cambridge, Mass., 1998), 119.

29. Ibid., 124; Welch, *Cleveland*, 192; Campbell, *Transformation*, 221; LaFeber, *New Empire*, 278–83.

pet program, the coinage of silver, held center stage. But the Republican platform set forth a full-fledged expansionist agenda: European withdrawal from the hemisphere; a voluntary union of English-speaking peoples in North America, meaning Canada; construction of a U.S.-controlled isthmian canal; acquisition of the Virgin Islands; annexation of Hawaii; and independence for Cuba. The War of 1898 provided an opportunity to implement much of this agenda—and more.[30]

II

What was once called the Spanish-American War was the pivotal event of a pivotal decade, bringing the "large policy" to fruition and marking the United States as a world power. Few events in U.S. history have been as encrusted in myth and indeed trivialized. The very title is a misnomer, of course, since it omits Cuba and the Philippines, both key players in the conflict. Despite four decades of "revisionist" scholarship, popular writing continues to attribute the war to a sensationalist "yellow press," which allegedly whipped into martial frenzy an ignorant public that in turn drove weak leaders into an unnecessary war.[31] The war itself has been reduced to comic opera, its consequences dismissed as an aberration. Such treatment undermines the notion of war by design, allowing Americans to cling to the idea of their own noble purposes and sparing them responsibility for a war they came to see as unnecessary and imperialist results they came to regard as unsavory.[32] Such interpretations also ignore the extent to which the war and its consequences represented a logical culmination of major trends in nineteenth-century U.S. foreign policy. It was less a case of the United States coming upon greatness almost inadvertently than of it pursuing its destiny deliberately and purposefully.[33]

The war grew out of a revolution in Cuba that was itself in many ways a product of the island's geographical proximity to and economic dependence on the United States. As with the Hawaiian revolution, U.S. tariff policies played a key role. The 1890 reciprocity treaty with Spain sparked

---

30. Joseph A. Fry, "Phases of Empire: Late Nineteenth-Century U.S. Foreign Relations," in Charles W. Calhoun, ed., *The Gilded Age: Essays on the Origins of Modern America* (Wilmington, Del., 1996), 277.

31. *New York Times*, February 15, 1998.

32. Louis A. Pérez, "The Meaning of the *Maine*: Causation and the Historiography of the Spanish-American War," *Pacific Historical Review* 58 (August 1989), 319–21.

33. Ernest R. May, *Imperial Democracy: The Emergence of America as a Great Power* (New York, 1973), 270, and the commentary in Thomas G. Paterson, "United States Intervention in Cuba, 1898: Interpretations of the Spanish-American-Cuban-Filipino War," *History Teacher* 29 (May 1996), 345.

an economic boom on the island. But the 1894 Wilson-Gorman tariff, by depriving Cuban sugar of its privileged position in the U.S. market, inflicted economic devastation and stirred widespread political unrest. Revolutionary sentiment had long smoldered. In 1895, exiles such as the poet, novelist, and patriot leader José Martí returned from the United States to foment rebellion. Concerned about possible U.S. designs on Cuba, Martí, Máximo Gómez, and Antonio Maceo sought a quick victory through scorched earth policies—"abominable devastation," they called it—seeking to turn Cuba into a desert and by doing so drive Spain from the island. Spanish general Valeriano "Butcher" Weyler retaliated with his brutal *"reconcentrado"* policies, herding peasants into fortified areas where they could be controlled. The results were catastrophic: Ninety-five thousand people died from disease and malnutrition. On the other side, weather, disease, and Cuban arms took a fearsome toll on young and poorly prepared Spanish forces, an estimated thirty-five thousand of them killed each year. The rebels used the machete with especially terrifying effect, littering the sugar and pineapple fields with the heads of Spanish soldiers.[34]

From the outset, this brutal insurgent war had an enormous impact in the United States. Since Jefferson's day, Cuba's economic and strategic importance had made it an object of U.S. attention. Like Florida, Texas, and Hawaii, the island was Americanized in the late nineteenth century. The Cuban elite was increasingly educated in the United States. By the end of the century, the United States dominated Cuba economically. Exports to the United States increased from 42 percent of the total in 1859 to 87 percent in 1897. United States investments have been estimated at $50 million, trade at $100 million. The war threatened American-owned sugar estates, mines, and ranches and the safety of U.S. citizens. A junta located mainly in Florida and New York and led by Cuban expatriates, some of them U.S. citizens, lobbied tirelessly for *Cuba Libre*, sold war bonds in the United States, and smuggled weapons onto the island. Cubans naturalized as U.S. citizens returned to fight. Not surprisingly, Cubans had mixed feelings about U.S. assistance. Some conservative leaders lacked confidence in their peoples' ability to govern themselves and feared chaos if the African, former slave population took power. They were amenable to U.S. tutelage—even annexation—to maintain their positions and property. Others like Martí, Gómez, and Maceo, while eager

---

34. Alistair Hennessey, "The Origins of the Cuban Revolt," in Angel Smith and Emma Dávila-Cox, eds., *The Crisis of 1898: Colonial Redistribution and Nationalist Mobilization* (New York, 1998), 81–88.

for American backing, feared that military intervention might lead to U.S. domination. "To change masters is not to be free," Martí warned.[35]

The "yellow press" (so named for the "Yellow Kid," a popular cartoon character that appeared in its newly colored pages) helped make Cuba a cause célèbre in the United States. The mass-circulation newspaper came into its own in the 1890s. The New York dailies of William Randolph Hearst and Joseph Pulitzer engaged in a fierce, head-to-head competition with few restraints and fewer scruples about the truth. They eagerly disseminated stories furnished by the junta. Talented artists such as Frederic Remington and writers such as Richard Harding Davis portrayed the revolution as a simple morality play featuring the oppression of freedom-loving Cubans by evil Spaniards.[36] The yellow press undoubtedly contributed to a war spirit, but Americans in areas where it did not circulate also strongly sympathized with Cuba. The Dubuque, Iowa, *Times*, for example, appealed to "men in whose breast the fire of patriotism burns" for the "annihilation of the Spanish dogs."[37] The press did not create the differences between Cuba, Spain, and the United States that proved insoluble. War likely would have occurred without its agitation.

Sympathy for Cuba and outrage with Spain produced demands for intervention and war. Anxieties in the country at large fed a martial fever. Businessmen worried that the Cuban problem might delay recovery from the depression. Some Americans, like the Cuban Creoles, feared that an insurgent victory would threaten U.S. investments and trade. The rising furor quickly took on political ramifications. Divided Democrats sought to reunite their party over the Cuban issue and embarrass the Republicans; Republicans tried to head off the opposition. Elites increasingly agreed that the United States must act. National pride, a resurgent sense of destiny, and a conviction that the United States as a rising world power must take responsibility for world events in its area of influence gave an increasing urgency to the Cuban crisis.[38]

From the time he took office in 1897, President William McKinley was absorbed in the Cuban problem. Once caricatured as a weakling, the puppet of big business, McKinley has received his due in recent years. His retiring demeanor and refusal to promote himself concealed strength of character and resoluteness of purpose. A plain, down-home man of simple tastes, McKinley had extraordinary political skills. His greatest asset was his

35. Louis A. Pérez Jr., *Cuba Between Empires, 1878–1902* (Pittsburgh, 1983), 94.
36. Schoultz, *Beneath the United States*, 131.
37. Hilderbrand, *Power and the People*, 23.
38. Lewis L. Gould, *The Presidency of William McKinley* (Lawrence, Kans., 1980), 63.

understanding of people and his ability to deal with them. Accessible, kindly, and a good listener, he was a master of the art of leading by indirection, letting others seem to persuade him of positions he had already taken, appearing to follow while actually leading. "He had a way of handling men," his secretary of war Elihu Root observed, "so that they thought his ideas were their own."[39] He entered the presidency with a clearly defined agenda, including the expansionist planks of the Republican platform. In many ways the first modern president, he used the instruments of his office as no one had since Lincoln, dominating his cabinet, controlling Congress, and skillfully employing the press to build political support for his policies.[40]

For two years, McKinley patiently negotiated with Spain while holding off domestic pressures for war. Reversing America's long-standing acceptance of Spanish sovereignty, he sought by steadily increasing diplomatic pressure to end Weyler's brutal measures and drive Spain from Cuba without war. For a time, he appeared to succeed. The Madrid government recalled Weyler and promised Cuban autonomy. But his success was illusory. By this time, Spain was willing to concede some measure of self-government. But the insurgents, having spent much blood and treasure, would accept nothing less than complete independence. Spanish officials feared that to abandon the "ever faithful isle," the last remnant of their once glorious American empire, would bring down the government and perhaps the monarchy. They tried to hold off the United States by a policy of "procrastination and dissimulation," deluding themselves that somehow things would work out.[41]

Two incidents in early 1898 brought the two nations to the brink of war. On February 9, Hearst's New York World published a letter written by Enrique Dupuy de Lôme, Spanish minister in Washington, to friends in Cuba describing McKinley as weak and a bidder for the crowd and speaking cynically of Spain's promises of reforms in Cuba. It was a private letter, of course, and Americans themselves had publicly said much worse things about McKinley. But in the supercharged atmosphere of 1898, this "Worst Insult to the United States in Its History," as one newspaper hyperbolically headlined it, provoked popular outrage. More important, de Lôme's cynical comments about reforms caused McKinley to doubt Spain's good faith.[42]

39. Hilderbrand, *Power and the People*, 18, 40.
40. Ibid., 10–11; Gould, *McKinley*, 56; Joseph A. Fry, "William McKinley and the Coming of the Spanish-American War: A Study of the Besmirching and Redemption of an Historical Image," *Diplomatic History* 3 (Winter 1979) 77–97.
41. Gould, *McKinley*, 61–62.
42. H. Wayne Morgan, *America's Road to Empire: The War with Spain and Overseas Expansion* (New York, 1965), 41–43.

Less than a week later, the battleship USS *Maine* mysteriously exploded in Havana harbor, killing 266 American sailors. The catastrophe almost certainly resulted from an internal explosion, but Americans pinned responsibility elsewhere. "Remember the *Maine*, to hell with Spain" became a popular rallying cry. Without bothering to examine the facts, the press blamed the explosion on Spain. Theater audiences wept, stamped their feet, and cheered when patriotic songs were played. Jingoes wrapped themselves in flags and demanded war. When McKinley pleaded for restraint, he was burned in effigy. Congress threatened to take matters into its own hands and recognize the Cuban rebels or even declare war.[43]

McKinley's last-ditch efforts to achieve his aims without war failed. Phrasing his demands in the language of diplomacy to leave room for maneuver, he insisted that Spain must get out of Cuba or face war. In Spain also, opposition to concessions grew. The Spanish resented being blamed for the *Maine*. The threat of U.S. intervention in Cuba provoked among students, middle-class urbanites, and even some working-class people a surge of patriotism not unlike that in the United States. A jingoist spirit marked bullfights and fiestas. Street demonstrations rocked major Iberian cities. In Málaga, angry mobs threw rocks at the U.S. consulate amidst shouts of "*Viva España! Muerte a los Yanques! Abajo el armisticio!*" As in the United States, the press incited popular outrage.[44] Fearing for its survival and even for the monarchy, the government recognized that it could not win a war with the United States and feared disastrous consequences. In keeping with the spirit of the era, however, it preferred the honor of war to the ignominy of surrender. It offered last-minute concessions to buy time but refused to surrender on the fundamental issue.

Since he left scant written record, it is difficult to determine why McKinley finally decided upon war. He was understandably sensitive to the mounting political pressures and stung by charges of spinelessness. But he appears to have found other, more compelling reasons to act. Historians disagree sharply on the state of the insurgency, some arguing that the rebels were close to victory, others that the war had ground into a

---

43. Hyman G. Rickover, *How the Battleship* Maine *Was Destroyed* (Washington, 1976). For the reaction, see May, *Imperial Democracy*, 139–47.
44. John L. Offner, *An Unwanted War: The Diplomacy of the United States and Spain over Cuba, 1895–1898* (Chapel Hill, N.C., 1992), 191; Angel Smith, "The People and the Nation: Nationalist Mobilization and the Crisis of 1895–98 in Spain," in Smith and Dávila-Cox, *Crisis of 1898*, 164.

bloody stalemate.[45] McKinley found either prospect unacceptable. An insurgent triumph threatened American property and investments as well as ultimate U.S. control of Cuba. Memories of another Caribbean revolution a century earlier had not died, and in the eyes of some Americans Cuba raised the grim specter of a second Haiti. Continued stalemate risked more destruction on the island and an unsettled situation at home. It was therefore not so much the case of an aroused public forcing a weak president into an unnecessary war as of McKinley choosing war to defend vital U.S. interests and remove "a constant menace to our peace" in an area "right at our door."[46]

The ambiguous manner in which the administration went to war belied its steadfastness of purpose. True to form, the president did not ask Congress for a declaration. Rather, he let the legislators take the initiative, the only instance in U.S. history in which that has happened. He sought "a neutral intervention" that would leave him maximum freedom of action in Cuba. His supporters in Congress warned that it would be a "grave mistake" to recognize a "people of whom we know practically nothing." They affirmed that the president must be in a position to "insist upon such a government as will be of practical advantage to the United States." McKinley successfully headed off those zealots who sought to couple intervention with recognition of Cuban independence. But he could not thwart the so-called Teller Amendment providing that the United States would not annex Cuba once the war ended. The amendment derived from various forces, those who opposed annexing territory containing large numbers of blacks and Catholics, those who sincerely supported Cuban independence, and representatives of the domestic sugar business, including sponsor Senator Henry Teller of Colorado, who feared Cuban competition. McKinley did not like the amendment, but he acquiesced. Cubans remained suspicious, warning that the Americans were a "people who do not work for nothing."[47]

III

By modern military standards, the War of 1898 did not amount to much. On the U.S. side, the last vestiges of nineteenth-century voluntarism and amateurism collided with an incipient twentieth-century military

---

45. Offner, *Unwanted War*, 227–28; Pérez, *Cuba Between Empires*, 177–78; Louis A. Pérez Jr., *The War of 1898: The United States and Cuba in History and Historiography* (Chapel Hill, N.C., 1998), 89.

46. Gould, *McKinley*, 85.

47. Pérez, *Cuba Between Empires*, 188–89.

professionalism, creating confusion, mismanagement, and indeed, at times, comic opera. Volunteers responded in such numbers that they could not be absorbed by a sclerotic military bureaucracy. Large numbers of troops languished in squalid camps where they fought each other and eventually drifted home. Americans arrived in Cuba's tropical summer sun in woolen uniforms left over from the Civil War. They were fed a form of canned beef variously described as "embalmed" and "nauseating." The U.S. commander, Gen. William Shafter, weighed more than three hundred pounds and resembled a "floating tent." Mounting his horse required a complicated system of ropes and pulleys, a feat of real engineering ingenuity.

Despite ineptitude and mismanagement, victory came easily, causing journalist Richard Harding Davis to observe that God looked after drunkards, babies, and Americans. With McKinley's approval, Assistant Secretary of the Navy Theodore Roosevelt had ordered Adm. George Dewey's fleet to steam to the Philippines. In a smashing victory that set the tone for and came to symbolize the war, Dewey's six new warships crushed the decrepit Spanish squadron in Manila Bay, setting off wild celebrations at home, sealing the doom of Spain's empire in the Philippines, and creating an opportunity for and enthusiasm about expansionism. Victory in Cuba did not come so easily. United States forces landed near Santiago without resistance, the result of luck as much as design. But they met stubborn Spanish resistance while advancing inland and in taking the city suffered heavy losses from Spanish fire and especially disease. Exhausted from three years of fighting Cubans, Spanish forces had no desire to take on fresh U.S. troops. Food shortages, mounting debt, political disarray, and a conspicuous lack of support from the European great powers sapped Spain's enthusiasm for war.[48] It took less than four months for U.S. forces to conquer Cuba (just as disease began to decimate the invading force). Victory cost a mere 345 killed in action, 5,000 lost to illness, and an estimated $250 million.

The ease and decisiveness of the victory intoxicated Americans, stoking an already overheated chauvinism. "It was a splendid little war," Ambassador John Hay chortled from London (giving the conflict an enduring label), "begun with the highest motives, carried on with magnificent intelligence and spirit, favored by that fortune which loves the brave." "No war in history has accomplished so much in so short a time with so little loss," concurred the U.S. ambassador to France. The ease

48. A good military history is David F. Trask, *The War with Spain in 1898* (New York, 1981).

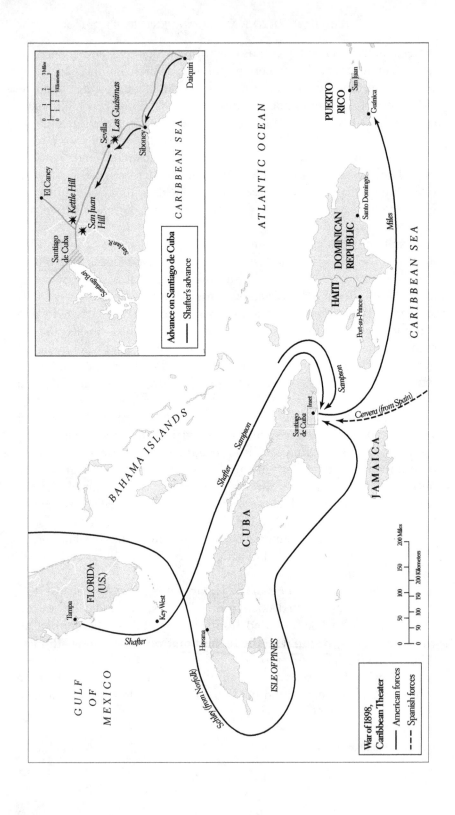

Advance on Santiago de Cuba
—— Shafter's advance

War of 1898,
Caribbean Theater
—— American forces
- - - Spanish forces

of victory confirmed the rising view that the nation stood on the brink of greatness.[49]

In the national mythology, the acquisition of empire from a war often dismissed with caricature has been viewed as accidental or aberrational, an ad hoc response to situations that had not been anticipated. In fact, the administration conducted the war with a clarity and resoluteness of purpose that belied its comic opera qualities. The first modern commander in chief, McKinley created a War Room on the second floor of the White House and used fifteen telephone lines and the telegraph to coordinate the Washington bureaucracy and maintain direct contact with U.S. forces in Cuba.[50] More important, he used the war to advance America's status as a world power and achieve its expansionist objectives. He set out to remove Spain from the Western Hemisphere, completing a process begun one hundred years earlier. Moving with characteristic stealth, he kept rebel forces in Cuba and the Philippines at arm's length to ensure maximum U.S. control and freedom of choice. Until the war ended, he asserted, "we must keep all we get; when the war is over we must keep what we want."[51]

McKinley used the exigencies of war to fulfill the old aim of annexing Hawaii. Upon taking office, he had declared annexation but a matter of time—not a new departure, he correctly affirmed, but a "consummation."[52] "We need Hawaii as much as in its day we needed California. It was Manifest Destiny," he stated on another occasion.[53] A perceived threat from Japan underscored the urgency. Hawaii had encouraged the immigration of Japanese workers to meet a labor shortage, but by the mid-1890s an influx once welcomed had aroused concern. When the government sought to restrict further immigration, a Japan puffed up by victory over China vigorously protested and dispatched a warship to back up its words. McKinley sent a new treaty of annexation to the Senate in June 1897, provoking yet another Japanese protest and a mini war scare (one U.S. naval officer actually predicted a Japanese surprise attack on the Hawaiian Islands). Advocates of annexation insisted that the United States must "act NOW to preserve the results of its past policy, and to prevent the dominancy of Hawaii by a foreign people."[54] The anti-imperialist opposi-

49. Walter Millis, *The Martial Spirit* (New York, 1931), 340; Morgan, *Road to Empire*, 83.
50. Gould, *McKinley*, 93.
51. Ibid., 101.
52. Ibid., 49.
53. María Dolores Elizalde, "1898: The Coordinates of the Spanish Crisis in the Pacific," in Smith and Dávila-Cox, *Crisis of 1898*, 191.
54. Campbell, *Transformation*, 237.

tion had the votes to forestall a two-thirds majority. The administration thus followed John Tyler's 1844 precedent by seeking a joint resolution. In any event, by early 1898 the emerging crisis with Spain put a premium on caution.

What had once been a deterrent soon spurred action. Relentlessly pursuing annexation, Hawaii's pro-American government opened its ports and resources to the United States instead of proclaiming neutrality. The war made obvious Hawaii's strategic importance. Worries about German and Japanese expansion in the Pacific reinforced the point. Hawaii assumed a major role in supplying U.S. troops in the Philippines. McKinley even talked of annexing it under presidential war powers. Shortly after the outbreak of war, he submitted to Congress a resolution for annexation. Legislators declared Hawaii a "naval and military necessity," the "key to the Pacific"; not to annex would be "national folly," one exclaimed. The resolution passed in July by sizeable majorities. The *haole* (non-Hawaiian) ruling classes cheered. Some native Hawaiians lamented that "Annexation is Rotten Bananas." One group issued a futile protest against "annexation...without reference to the consent of the people of the Hawaiian Islands." The Women's Patriotic League sewed hatbands declaring "*Ku'u Hae Aloha*"(I Love My Flag).[55]

While fighting in Cuba, the United States also moved swiftly to take Puerto Rico before the war ended. Named "wealthy port" by its first Spanish governor, the island occupied a commanding position between the two ocean passages. It was called the "Malta of the Caribbean" because it could guard an isthmian canal and the Pacific coast as that Mediterranean island protected Egypt. In contrast to Cuba, the United States had little trade with and few investments in Puerto Rico. But Blaine had put it on his list of necessary acquisitions, mainly as a base to guard a canal. By preventing the United States from taking Cuba, the Teller Amendment probably increased the importance of Puerto Rico. Once the United States was at war with Spain, Puerto Rico provided another chance to remove European influence from the hemisphere. From his debarkation point in Texas, Rough Rider and ardent expansionist Theodore Roosevelt urged his imperialist cohort Senator Lodge to "prevent any talk of peace until we get Porto Rico and the Philippines as well as secure the independence of Cuba."[56] Once war began, some businessmen recommended taking Puerto Rico for its commercial and strategic value. Protestant

---

55. Ibid., 295; Mehmed Ali, "Ho'ohui'aina Palaka Mai'a: Remembering Hawaiian Annexation One Hundred Years Ago," *Journal of Hawaiian History* 32 (1998), 141–54.

56. Healy, *U.S. Expansionism*, 112.

missionaries expressed interest in opening the island—already heavily Roman Catholic—to the "Gospel of the Lord Jesus Christ."[57] By late June, if not earlier, the administration was committed to its acquisition, ostensibly as payment for a costly intervention.

The main U.S. concern was to seize Puerto Rico before Spain sued for peace. On July 7, the White House ordered Gen. Nelson A. Miles to proceed to Puerto Rico as soon as victory in Cuba was secured. Miles landed at Guánica on July 25 without significant opposition—indeed, the invaders were greeted with shouts of *"viva"* and given provisions. Puerto Rico was relatively peaceful and prosperous. Its people enjoyed a large measure of autonomy under Spain. They looked favorably upon the United States; many were prepared to accept its tutelage. Thus even after the invaders made clear they intended to take possession of the island, they encountered only sporadic and scattered opposition and suffered few casualties. United States forces characterized the invasion as a "picnic." The only shortage was of American flags for the Puerto Ricans to wave.[58] The occupation was completed just in time. On August 7, Spain asked for peace terms. It had hoped to hang on to Puerto Rico, but the United States insisted upon taking the island in lieu of "pecuniary indemnity."[59]

The island land grab extended to the Pacific. Increased great-power interest in East Asia heightened the importance of the numerous islands scattered along Pacific sea routes. Prior to 1898, Germany, Great Britain, and the United States were already engaged in a lively competition. To secure a coaling station for ships en route to the southwest Pacific, McKinley on June 3 ordered the navy to seize one of the Mariana Islands strategically positioned between Hawaii and the Philippines. Three U.S. ships subsequently stopped at Guam. In a scene worthy of a Gilbert and Sullivan operetta, they announced their arrival by firing their guns. Not knowing the two nations were at war, the Spanish garrison apologized for not being able to answer what they thought was an American salute because they had no ammunition. Spanish defenders were taken prisoner and the island seized. With Guam and the Philippines, the United States saw the need for a cable station to better communicate with its distant possessions. Wake Atoll, a tiny piece of uninhabited land in the central Pacific, seemed suitable. Although Germany had strong claims, U.S. naval

57. Julius W. Pratt, *Expansionists of 1898* (Chicago, 1964), 274, 277, 287.
58. Millis, *Martial Spirit*, 335–38; Emma Dávila-Cox, "Puerto Rico in the Hispanic-Cuban-American War: Re-assessing 'the Picnic,'" in Smith and Dávila-Cox, *Crisis of 1898*, 115–18.
59. Pratt, *Expansionists of 1898*, 330.

officers seized Wake for the United States in January 1899. Mainly eager to solidify its claims to Samoa, Germany did not contest the U.S. claim. As it turned out, Wake Island did not prove feasible for a cable relay station. The United States did nothing more to establish its sovereignty.[60]

McKinley moved with more circumspection on the Philippines. It remains unclear exactly when he decided to annex the islands. He first hinted they might be left in Spanish hands; the United States would settle for a port. He later suggested that the issue might be negotiated. Even before he received official confirmation of Dewey's victory, however, he dispatched twenty thousand soldiers to establish U.S. authority in the Philippines. Permitting missionary and business expansionists to persuade him of what he may already have believed, he apparently decided as early as the summer of 1898 to take all the islands. Moving with customary indirection, he helped shape the outcome he sought. He used extended speaking tours through the Middle West and South to mobilize public opinion. He stacked the peace commission with expansionists. He made a conscious decision appear the result of fate and destiny, proclaiming by the time negotiations began that he could see "but one plain path of duty—the acceptance of the archipelago." In December 1898, his negotiators thus imposed on a reluctant but hapless Spain the Treaty of Paris, calling for the cession of Cuba, Puerto Rico, and the Philippines. The United States awarded Spain a booby prize of $20 million.[61]

Dealing with insurgent forces in Cuba and the Philippines proved more complex and costly. Americans took to Cuba genuine enthusiasm for a noble cause, "the first war of its kind," a fictional soldier averred. "We are coming with Old Glory," a popular song proclaimed.[62] Their idealism barely outlasted their initial encounters with Cuban rebels. Viewing *Cuba Libre* through the idealized prism of their own revolution, Americans were not prepared for what they encountered. They had no sense of what a guerrilla army three years in the field might look like. They brought with their weapons and knapsacks the heavy burden of deeply entrenched racism. The Cubans thus appeared to them "ragged and half-starved," a "wretched mongrel lot," "utter tatterdemalions." From a military standpoint, they seemed useless, not worthy allies. Their participation was quickly limited to support roles, the sort of menial tasks African Americans

60. Thomas Schoonover, *Uncle Sam's War of 1898 and the Origins of Globalization* (Lexington, Ky., 2003), 89; Dirk Spennerman, "The United States Annexation of Wake Atoll, Central Pacific Ocean," *Journal of Pacific History* 33 (September 1998), 239–47.

61. Trask, *War with Spain*, 441–42.

62. Pérez, *War of 1898*, 24.

were expected to perform at home. The proud rebels' rejection of such assignments reinforced negative stereotypes. Indeed, Americans came to look more favorably upon the once despised Spanish soldiers, viewing them as a source of order, a safeguard for property, and a protection against a possible race war.[63]

Popular perceptions nicely complemented the nation's political goals. Cuba in fact had made significant progress toward self-government in the last days of Spanish rule, but this was lost on the invaders. The ragtag Cubans were no more fit for self-government than "gunpowder is for hell," General Shafter thundered, and from the moment they landed Americans set out to establish complete control regardless of the Teller Amendment.[64] The United States ignored the provisional government already in place and refused to recognize the insurgents or army. It did not consult Cubans regarding peace aims or negotiations and did not permit them even a ceremonial role in the surrender at Santiago or the overall surrender of the island. They were required to recognize the military authority of the United States, which, to their consternation, refused any commitment for future independence.

The United States handled the Philippines in much the same way. There as in Cuba, Americans encountered revolution, the first anticolonial revolt in the Pacific region, a middle-class uprising launched in 1896 by well-educated, relatively prosperous Filipinos such as the twenty-nine-year-old Emilio Aguinaldo. Seeing the exiled Aguinaldo as possibly useful in undermining Spanish authority, U.S. officials had helped him get home, perhaps deluding him into believing they would not stay. Once there, he declared the islands independent, established a "provisional dictatorship" with himself as head, and even designed a red, white, and blue flag. Americans on the scene conceded that Aguinaldo's group included "men of education and ability" but also conveniently concluded that it did not have broad popular support and could not sustain itself against European predators. McKinley gave no more than fleeting thought to independence and rejected a U.S. protectorate. He instructed the U.S. military to compel the rebels to accept its authority. The United States refused to recognize Aguinaldo's government, as with the Cubans, keeping it at arm's length. In December 1898, McKinley proclaimed a military government. He vowed to respect the rights of Filipinos but made no promises of self-government. On the scene, tensions mounted between

63. Pérez, *Cuba Between Empires*, 197–201; Pérez, *War of 1898*, 94–95.
64. Pérez, *Cuba Between Empires*, 218.

U.S. occupation forces and the thirty thousand Filipinos besieging Manila.[65]

From the late summer of 1898 until after the election of 1900, one of those periodic great debates over the nation's role in the world raged in the United States. The central issue was the Philippines. Defenders of annexation pointed to obvious strategic and commercial advantages, fine harbors for naval bases, a "key to the wealth of the Orient." The islands would themselves provide important markets and in addition furnish a vital outpost from which to capture a share of the fabled China market. The imperialists easily rationalized the subjugation of alien peoples. Indeed, they argued, the United States by virtue of its superior institutions had an obligation to rescue lesser peoples from barbarism and ignorance and bring them the blessings of Anglo-Saxon civilization. As McKinley allegedly put it to a delegation of visiting churchmen, there seemed nothing to do but to "educate the Filipinos, and uplift them and civilize them and Christianize them, and by God's grace do the very best we could by them."[66] If America were to abandon the islands after rescuing them from Spain, they might be snapped up by another nation—Germany had displayed more than passing interest. They could fall victim to their own incapacity for self-government. The United States could not in good conscience escape the responsibilities thrust upon it. "My countrymen," McKinley proclaimed in October 1898, "the currents of destiny flow through the hearts of the people.... Who will divert them? Who will stop them?"[67]

An anti-imperialist movement including some of the nation's political and intellectual leaders challenged the expansionist argument on every count. Political independents, the anti-imperialists eloquently warned that expansion would compromise America's ideals and its special mission in the world.[68] The acquisition of overseas territory with no prospect for statehood violated the Constitution. More important, it undermined the republican principles upon which the nation was founded. The United States could not join the Old World in exploiting other peoples without betraying its anti-colonial tradition. The acquisition of overseas empire would require a large standing army and higher taxes. It would compel U.S. involvement in the dangerous power politics of East Asia and the Pacific.

65. Brian Linn, *The Philippine War, 1899–1902* (Lawrence, Kans., 2000), 42–46.

66. May, *Imperial Democracy*, 252–53.

67. Gould, *McKinley*, 136–37.

68. Robert L. Beisner, *Twelve Against Empire: The Anti-Imperialists, 1898–1900* (New York, 1968), 17.

At the outbreak of war in 1898, the philosopher William James marveled at how the nation could "puke up its ancient soul...in five minutes without a wink of squeamishness." He denounced as "snivelling," "loathsome" cant talk of uplifting the Filipinos. The U.S. Army was at that time suppressing an insurrection with military force, and that, he argued, was the only education the people could expect. "God damn the U.S. for its vile conduct in the Philippines," he exploded.[69] Industrialist Andrew Carnegie, contending that the islands would drain the United States economically, offered to buy their independence with a personal check for $20 million. Other anti-imperialists warned that any gains from new markets would be offset by harmful competition with American farmers. Some argued that the United States already had sufficient territory. "We do not want any more States until we can civilize Kansas," sneered journalist E. L. Godkin.[70] Many anti-imperialists objected on grounds of race. "Pitchfork Ben" Tilman of South Carolina vehemently opposed injecting into the "body politic of the United States...that vitiated blood, that debased and ignorant people."[71] The nation already had a "black elephant" in the South, the *New York World* proclaimed. Did it "really need a white elephant in the Philippines, a leper elephant in Hawaii, a brown elephant in Porto Rico and perhaps a yellow elephant in Cuba?"[72]

The anti-imperialists may have made the stronger case over the long run, but the immediate outcome was not determined by logic or force of argument. The administration had the advantage of the initiative, of offering something positive to a people still heady from military triumphs. Many Americans found seductive the February 1899 appeal of British poet Rudyard Kipling to take up the "white man's burden," first published just days before the Senate took up the issue of annexation. The Republicans also had a solid majority in the Senate. A remarkably heterogeneous group, the anti-imperialists were divided among themselves and lacked effective leadership. They had to "blow cold upon the hot excitement," as James put it.[73] In an early example of foreign policy bipartisanship, William Jennings Bryan, the titular leader of the Democratic opposition, vitiated the anti-imperialist cause and infuriated its leaders by instructing his followers to vote for the peace treaty with Spain, which provided for annexation of the Philippines, in order to end the war. The Philippines

69. Ibid., 44, 48.
70. H. W. Brands, *The Reckless Decade: America in the 1890s* (New York, 1998), 330.
71. Stanley Karnow, *In Our Image: America's Empire in the Philippines* (New York, 1989), 137.
72. Beisner, *Twelve Against Empire*, 219.
73. Ibid., 228.

could be dealt with later. The outbreak of war in the Philippines on the eve of the Senate vote solidified support for the treaty. In what Lodge called "the hardest, closest fight I have ever known," the Senate approved the treaty 57–21 in February 1899, a bare one vote more than necessary, and a result facilitated by the defection of eleven Democrats.[74] McKinley was easily reelected in 1900 in a campaign in which imperialism was no more than a peripheral issue.

IV

As the great debate droned on in the United States, the McKinley administration set about consolidating control over the new empire. The president vowed that the Teller pledge would be "sacredly kept," but he also insisted that the "new Cuba" must be bound to the United States by "ties of singular intimacy and strength." Many Americans believed that annexation was a matter of time and that, as with Texas, California, and Hawaii, it would evolve through natural processes—"annexation by acclamation," one official labeled it. Some indeed thought that the way the United States implemented the occupation would contribute to this outcome. "It is better to have the favors of a lady by her consent, after judicious courtship," Secretary of War Elihu Root observed, "than to ravish her."[75] The United States established close ties with Cuban men of property and standing—"our friends," Root called them—many of them expatriates, some U.S. citizens. It created an army closely tied to the United States. It carried out good works. The occupation government imposed ordinances making it easy for outsiders to acquire land, built railroads, and at least indirectly encouraged the emigration of Americans. "Little by little the whole island is passing into the hands of American citizens," a Louisiana journal exclaimed in 1903, "the shortest and surest way to obtain its annexation to the United States."[76]

The expected outcome did not materialize, and other means had to be found to establish the ties McKinley sought. Except for a small minority of pro-Americans, sentiment for annexation did not develop in Cuba. Nationalism remained strong and indeed intensified under the occupation. The first elections did not go as Americans wanted; some officials continued to fear that Cubans of African descent might plunge the nation

74. Healy, U.S. Expansionism, 227.
75. Pérez, Cuba Between Empires, 279.
76. Carmen Diana Deere, "Here Come the Yankees: The Rise and Decline of United States Colonies in Cuba," Hispanic American Historical Review 78 (November 1998), 734.

into a "Hayti No. 2." The outbreak of war in the Philippines in early 1899 aroused similar fears for Cuba.

Eager to get out but determined to maintain control of a nominally independent Cuba, the United States settled on the so-called Platt Amendment to create and sustain a protectorate. Drafted by Root and attached to a military appropriation bill approved by Congress in March 1901, it forbade Cuba from entering into any treaty that would impair its independence, granting concessions to any foreign power, or contracting a public debt in excess of its ability to pay. It explicitly empowered the United States to intervene in Cuba's internal affairs and provided two sites for U.S. naval bases. "There is, of course, little or no independence left Cuba under the Platt Amendment," military governor Gen. Leonard Wood candidly conceded.[77] When Cubans resisted this obvious infringement on their sovereignty with street demonstrations, marches, rallies, and petitions, the United States demanded that they incorporate the amendment into their constitution or face an indefinite occupation. It passed by a single vote. "It is either Annexation or a Republic with an Amendment," one Cuban lamented; "I prefer the latter." "Cuba is dead; we are enslaved forever," a patriot protested.[78]

A 1903 reciprocity treaty provided an economic counterpart to the Platt Amendment. The war left Cuba a wasteland. In its aftermath, the United States set out to construct a neo-colonial economic structure built around sugar and tobacco as major cash crops and tied closely to the U.S. market. Without prodding from their government, Americans stepped in to buy up the sugar estates from fleeing Spaniards and destitute Cubans. Using Hawaii as a model, U.S. officials saw in free trade a means to promote annexation by "natural voluntary and progressive steps honorable alike to both parties." Reciprocity would allegedly revive the sugar industry, solidify the position of Cuba's propertied classes, and promote close ties to the United States. It would deepen Cuba's dependence on one crop and one market. The arrangement naturally provoked complaints from U.S. cane and beet growers. Cuban nationalists protested that it would substitute the United States for "our old mother country." Approved in 1903, the agreement provided the basis for Cuban-American economic relations for more than a half century. The War of 1898 thus ended with Cuba as a protectorate of the United States. Not surprisingly, it remained for Cubans a "brooding preoccupation." While Americans remembered the war as something

---

77. Ibid.
78. Pérez, *Cuba Between Empires*, 327; Ramon Ruiz, *Cuba: The Making of a Revolution* (Amherst, Mass., 1968), 33.

they had done *for* Cubans and expected Cuba to show gratitude, Cubans saw it as something done *to* them. The betrayal of 1898 provided the basis for another Cuban revolution at midcentury.[79]

The acquisition of a Pacific empire elevated the expansionist dream of an isthmian canal to an urgent priority. Defense of Hawaii and the Philippines required easier access to the Pacific, a point highlighted during the war when the battleship *Oregon* required sixty-eight days to steam from Puget Sound to Cuba. A canal would also give the United States a competitive edge in Pacific and East Asian markets. The availability of long-sought naval bases in the Caribbean now provided the means to defend it. Thus after the war with Spain, the McKinley administration pressed Britain to abrogate the Clayton-Bulwer Treaty. The threat of congressional legislation directing the United States to build a canal without reference to the 1850 treaty pushed the British into negotiations. When the Senate vehemently objected to a treaty giving the United States authority to build and operate but not to fortify a canal, the State Department insisted on reopening negotiations. Preoccupied with European issues and its own imperial war in South Africa and eager for good relations with Washington, London conceded the United States in a treaty finally concluded in November 1901 exclusive right to build, operate, and fortify a canal, an unmistakable sign of acceptance of U.S. preeminence in the Caribbean. The way was clear for initiation of a project that would be carried forward with great gusto by McKinley's successor, Theodore Roosevelt.[80]

Pacification of the Philippines proved much more difficult and costly. McKinley spoke eloquently of "benevolent assimilation" and insisted that "our priceless principles undergo no change under a tropical sun. They go with the flag."[81] But he also ordered the imposition of unchallenged U.S. authority. The United States soon found itself at war with Aguinaldo's insurgents. The Filipinos naively expected to gain recognition of their independence and then counted on the U.S. Senate to defeat the peace treaty. Many Americans viewed the Filipinos with contempt. Tensions increased along their adjoining lines around Manila until an incident in February 1899 provoked war. Americans called it the "Philippine Insurrection," thus branding the enemy as rebels against duly constituted

79. Pérez, *War of 1898*, 125; Louis A. Pérez Jr., "Incurring a Debt of Gratitude: 1898 and the Moral Sources of U.S. Hegemony in Cuba," *American Historical Review* 104 (April 1999), 358, 381.

80. Schoultz, *Beneath the United States*, 161; Walter LaFeber, *The Panama Canal: The Crisis in Historical Perspective* (New York, 1979), 18.

81. Linn, *Philippine War*, 30.

authority. The Filipinos viewed it as a war for independence fought by a legitimate government against an outside oppressor. It became an especially brutal war, hatreds on both sides fueled by nationalism, race, and a tropical sun. It provoked enormous controversy in the United States for a time and then was largely forgotten until obvious if often overdrawn parallels with the war in Vietnam revived interest in the 1960s.

The army of occupation and U.S. civilian officials took seriously McKinley's charge of "benevolent assimilation," seeking to defuse resistance through enlightened colonial policies. The military developed a "pacification" program to win Filipino support, building roads and bridges, establishing schools, tackling the twin scourges of smallpox and leprosy with public health facilities, and distributing food where it was most needed. They began to restructure the Spanish legal system, reform the tax structure, and establish local governments. McKinley sent fellow Ohioan William Howard Taft to the Philippines in 1900 to implement his policies. Taft shared the general American skepticism of Filipino capacity for self-government, but he also accepted McKinley's earnest sense of obligation to America's "little brown brothers." He launched a "policy of attraction," drawing to the United States upper-class *ilustrados* to govern the islands under colonial tutelage. They helped establish a Filipino political party with its own newspaper and American-style patronage. The United States' colonial policies drained support from Aguinaldo while sparing the nation some of the cost and stigma of direct imperialism. At the same time, U.S. officials on the scene reinforced ties with the old elite from the Spanish era, ensuring that it would remain in power long after they left. They began the process of Americanization of the islands.[82]

In time, U.S. forces also suppressed the insurgency, no mean feat in an archipelago of seven thousand islands, covering an area of half a million square miles, with a population of seven million people. American volunteers and regulars fought well and maintained generally high morale against an often elusive enemy under difficult conditions, suffocating heat and humidity, drenching monsoon rains, impenetrable jungles, and rugged mountains. After a period of trial and error, the army developed an effective counterinsurgency strategy. Its civic action programs helped win some Filipino support and weaken the insurgency. Later in the war, it added a "policy of chastisement," waging fierce and often brutal campaigns against pockets of resistance. The United States did not commit genocide in the Philippines; atrocities were neither authorized nor condoned. Under the pressures of guerrilla warfare in the tropics, however,

82. Karnow, *In Our Image*, 171–77.

brutal measures were employed. Americans came to view the war in racial terms, a conflict of "civilization," in Roosevelt's words, against the "black chaos of savagery and barbarism." The U.S. troops often applied to their Filipino enemy racial epithets such as "nigger," "dusky fellow," "black devil," or "goo-goo" (the last a word of uncertain origin and the basis for "gook" as used by GIs in the Korean and Vietnam wars). The war also gave rise to the word *boondock*, derived from the Tagalog *bonduk*, meaning remote, which to soldiers had dark and sinister connotations.[83] To secure information about the guerrillas, U.S. troops used the notorious "water cure," allegedly learned from Filipinos who worked with them, in which a bamboo tube was thrust into the mouth of a captive and dirty water — "the filthier the better" — was poured down his "unwilling throat." In Batangas, late in the war, Americans resorted to tactics not unlike those employed by the despised Weyler in Cuba, forcing the resettlement of the population into protected areas to isolate the guerrillas from those who served as their sources of supply. Following the "Batangiga massacre" in which forty-eight Americans were killed, Gen. Jacob Smith ordered that the island of Samar be turned into a "howling wilderness." Although not typical of the war, these events were used to discredit it and came to stamp it. They aroused outrage at home, provoked congressional hearings that lasted from January to June 1902, and revived a moribund anti-imperialist movement.[84]

Americans too often ascribe the outcome of world events to what they themselves do or fail to do, but in the Philippine War the insurgents contributed mightily to their own defeat. Aguinaldo and his top field commander, a pharmacist, military buff, and admirer of Napoleon, foolishly adopted a conventional war strategy, suffering irreplaceable losses in early frontal assaults against U.S. troops before belatedly resorting to guerrilla tactics. By the time they changed, the war may have been lost.[85] Although the Filipinos fought bravely — the bolo-men sometimes with the machetes for which they were named — they lacked modern weapons and skilled leadership. Given the difficulties of geography, they could never establish centralized organization and command. Split into factions, they were vulnerable to U.S. divide-and-conquer tactics. Aguinaldo and other insurgent

83. Linn, *Philippine War*, 223; for a more critical view, see Paul A. Kramer, "Race-Making and Colonial Violence in the U.S. Empire," *Diplomatic History* 30 (April 2006), 169–210.

84. Kramer, "Race-Making," 189, 197, 201–3.

85. Glenn Anthony May, "Why the Filipinos Fired High: Popular Participation in the Philippine Revolution and the Philippine-American War," *Biblion* 7 (Spring 1999), 87–104.

leaders came from the rural gentry and never identified with the peasantry or developed programs to appeal to them. In some areas, the guerrillas alienated the population by seizing food and destroying property—some Filipinos, ironically, found their needs better met by Americans.[86] The insurgents placed far too much hope in the election of Bryan in 1900 and found his defeat hugely demoralizing. The capture of Aguinaldo in March 1901 in a daring raid by Filipino Scouts allied with the United States and posing as rebel reinforcements came at a time when the insurgents were already reeling from military defeats. If not the turning point in the war, it helped break the back of the rebellion, although fighting persisted in remote areas for years.

On July 4, 1902, new president Theodore Roosevelt chose to declare the war ended and U.S. rule confirmed. Victory came at a cost of more than 4,000 U.S. dead and 2,800 wounded, a casualty rate of 5.5 percent, among the highest of any of the American wars. The cost through 1902 was around $600 million. The United States estimated 20,000 Filipinos killed in action and as many as 200,000 civilians killed from war-related causes. At home, the war brought disillusionment with the nation's imperial mission.

V

The United States had taken an interest in the Philippines in part from concern about its stake in China, and it is no coincidence that acquisition of the islands almost immediately led to a more active role on the Asian mainland. By the late 1890s, China had become a focal point of intense imperial rivalries. For a half century, the European powers—joined by the United States—had steadily encroached on its sovereignty. Following the Sino-Japanese war of 1894–95, the great powers exploited China's palpable weakness to stake out spheres of influence giving them exclusive concessions over trade, mining, and railroads. Germany initiated the process called "slicing the Chinese melon" in 1897. Using the killing of two German missionaries as a pretext, it secured from the hapless imperial government a naval base at Qing Dao along with mining and railroad concessions on the Shandong peninsula. Russia followed by acquiring bases and railroad concessions on the Liaodong peninsula. Britain secured leases to Hong Kong and Kowloon, France concessions in southern China. The powers threatened to reduce the once proud Middle Kingdom to a conglomeration of virtual colonies.[87]

86. Linn, *Philippine War*, 197.
87. Schoonover, *War of 1898*, 68–77.

The U.S. government had shown little interest in China during the Gilded Age, but in the 1890s pressures mounted for greater involvement. Trade and investments enjoyed a boomlet, once again stirring hopes of a bounteous China market. The threat of partition after the Sino-Japanese War produced pressures from the business community to protect the market for U.S. exports. By this time, missionaries had increased dramatically in numbers and penetrated the interior of China. As certain of the rectitude of their cause as the Chinese were of the superiority of their civilization, the missionaries promoted an ideology very much at odds with Confucianism and undermined the power of local elites. Scapegoats in Chinese eyes for growing Western influence, the missionaries were increasingly subjected to violent attacks and appealed to their government to defend them against the barbaric forces that threatened their civilizing mission. Missionaries, along with the "China hands," a small group of diplomats who became self-appointed agents for bringing China into the mainstream of Western civilization, constituted a so-called Open Door constituency that sought to make the United States responsible for preventing further assaults on China's sovereignty and reforming it for its own betterment. Some influential Americans indeed came to view China as the next frontier for U.S. influence, the pivot on which a twentieth-century clash of civilizations might hinge.[88]

These pressure groups were pushing for an active role in China at precisely the point when the United States was becoming more sensitive to its rising power and prestige in the world. For years, the U.S. government had resisted appeals from missionaries for protection, reasoning that it could hardly ask the Chinese government to take care of Americans when it did not protect Chinese and when its exclusionist policies incurred their wrath. Secretary of State Olney initiated the change. Acting as assertively with China as with the British in Latin America, he proclaimed in 1895 that the United States must "leave no doubt in the mind of the Chinese government or the people in the interior" that it is an "effective factor for securing due right for Americans resident in China."[89] To support his strong words, he beefed up the U.S. naval presence in Chinese waters. The United States in the 1890s "dramatically broadened" the definition of missionary "rights" and made clear its intent to defend them.[90]

88. Michael H. Hunt, *The Making of a Special Relationship: The United States and China to 1914* (New York, 1983), 143–68.
89. Warren I. Cohen, *America's Response to China: An Interpretative History of Sino-American Relations* (New York, 1971), 54.
90. Hunt, *Special Relationship*, 162.

Once the Spanish crisis had ended, the McKinley administration also took a stand in defense of U.S. trade in China. The task fell to newly appointed Secretary of State John Hay. At one time Lincoln's private secretary, the dapper, witty, and multitalented Hay had worked in business and journalism and was also an accomplished poet, novelist, and biographer. He had served in diplomatic posts in Vienna, Paris, Madrid, and London before returning to Washington. Independently wealthy, urbane, and extraordinarily well connected, the Indianan was a shrewd politician. Like many Republicans, he had once opposed expansion, but he gave way in the 1890s to what he called a "cosmic tendency."[91] Pressured by China hands like W. W. Rockhill, Hay concluded that a statement of the U.S. position on freedom of trade in China would appease American businessmen and possibly earn some goodwill among the Chinese that might benefit the United States commercially. It would convince expansionists the United States was prepared to live up to its responsibilities as an Asian power. In addition, according to one State Department operative, it could be a "trump card for the Administration and crush all the life out of the anti-imperialist agitation."[92] Thus in September 1899, Hay issued the first Open Door Note, a circular letter urging the great powers involved in China not to discriminate against the commerce of other nations within their spheres of influence.

The following year, the United States joined Japan and the Europeans in a military intervention in China. Simmering anti-foreign agitation fed by bad harvests, floods, plague, and unemployment boiled over in the summer of 1900 into the Boxer Rebellion, so named because its leaders practiced a form of martial arts called spirit boxing. Blaming foreigners for the ills that afflicted their country, the "Righteous and Harmonious Fists" sought to eliminate the evil. They bore placards urging the killing of foreigners. Certain that their animistic rituals made them invincible—even against bullets—they fought with swords and lances. Armed bands of Boxers numbering as high as 140,000 burned and pillaged across North China, eventually killing two hundred missionaries and an estimated two thousand Chinese converts to Christianity. With the complicity of the empress dowager, the Boxers moved on Beijing. In June 1900, joined by troops of the imperial army, they killed two diplomats—a German and a Japanese—and besieged the foreign legations, leaving some 533 foreigners

91. Foster Rhea Dulles, "John Hay," in Norman A. Graebner, ed., *An Uncertain Tradition: American Secretaries of State in the Twentieth Century* (New York, 1961), 22–27.
92. A. Whitney Griswold, *The Far Eastern Policy of the United States* (rev. ed., New Haven, Conn., 1962), 71.

cut off from the outside world. Often dismissed as fanatical and reaction-ary, the uprising, as one sensitive and empathetic China hand presciently warned, was also "today's hint to the future," the first shot of a sustained nationalist challenge to the humiliation inflicted on a proud people by the West.[93]

The great powers responded forcibly. After a first military assault failed to relieve the siege of the legations, they assembled at Tianjin an eight-nation force of some fifty thousand troops and on July 7 took the city. In August 1900, while the world watched, the multilateral force fought its way over eighty miles in suffocating heat and against sometimes stubborn opposition to Beijing. After some hesitation, McKinley dispatched A China Relief Expedition of 6,300 troops from the Philippines to assist in relieving the siege, setting an important precedent by intervening militar-ily far from home without seeking congressional approval.[94] Although col-laboration among the various powers was poor—each nation's military force sought to grab the glory—the troops relieved the siege, in the proc-ess exacting fierce retribution against the Chinese through killing, raping, and looting. Although late in arriving, the Germans were especially vi-cious. Kaiser Wilhelm II enjoined his troops to act in the mode of Attila's Huns and "make the name of Germany become known in such a manner in China, that no Chinese will ever again dare look askance at a German."[95] The kaiser's statement and the Germans' brutal behavior gave them a name that would follow them into World War I. In a protocol of September 1901, the powers demanded punishment of government officials who had supported the Boxers, imposed on China an indemnity of more than $300 million, and secured the right to station additional troops on Chinese soil.

While acting with the great powers, the United States was also quite sensitive to its own interests and sought some degree of independence. An unspoken reason for sending U.S. troops was to help protect China from further foreign encroachments. McKinley ordered the Americans to act separately from the powers when they could and cooperate when they must. He insisted that they treat the Chinese firmly but fairly. In general, U.S. troops comported themselves well. The United States sought to use its influence to prevent the conflict from spreading beyond northern China and the peace settlement from resulting in partition. Even while the foreign troops were gathering for the expedition to relieve the siege,

93. Hunt, *Special Relationship*, 187.
94. Walter LaFeber, "The 'Lion in the Path': The U.S. Emergence as a World Power," *Political Science Quarterly* 101, no. 5 (1986), 714.
95. Peter Fleming, *The Siege of Peking* (London, 1959), 135–36.

Hay in July 1900 issued another statement, this one nothing more than an affirmation of U.S. policy. This second Open Door Note made clear the United States' intention to protect the lives and property of its citizens in China, its commitment to lifting the siege of Beijing, and its determination to protect "all legitimate interests." It expressed concern about the "virtual anarchy" in Beijing and hope that it would not spread elsewhere. The words that drew the most attention then and since affirmed that the policy of the United States was to promote "permanent safety and peace to China, preserve Chinese territorial and administrative entity...and safeguard for the world the principle of equal and impartial trade with all parts of the Chinese empire."[96]

The Open Door Notes have produced as much mythology as anything in the history of U.S. foreign relations. Although he knew better, Hay encouraged and happily accepted popular praise for America's bold and altruistic defense of China from the rapacious powers. These contemporary accolades evolved into the enduring myth that the United States in a singular act of beneficence at a critical point in China's history saved it from further plunder by the European powers and Japan. More recently, historians have found in the Open Door Notes a driving force behind much of twentieth-century U.S. foreign policy. Scholar-diplomat George F. Kennan dismissed them as typical of the idealism and legalism that he insisted had characterized the American approach to diplomacy, a meaningless statement in defense of a dubious cause—the independence of China—which had the baneful effect of inflating in the eyes of Americans the importance of their interests in China and their ability to dictate events there.[97] Historian William Appleman Williams and the so-called Wisconsin School have portrayed the notes as an aggressive first move to capture the China market that laid the foundation for U.S. policy in much of the world in the twentieth century.[98]

As historian Michael Hunt has observed, the original Open Door Notes, while important, amounted to much less than has been attributed to them. The United States by issuing the notes was looking out for its own interests; any benefit to China was incidental. McKinley and Hay had little concern for China. Hay was contemptuous even of those Chinese who sought to befriend the United States and did not bother to consult them before

96. The text is in Ruhl Bartlett, ed., *The Record of American Diplomacy* (New York, 1950), 413.
97. George F. Kennan, *American Diplomacy, 1900–1950* (New York, 1952), 23–37.
98. William A. Williams, *The Tragedy of American Diplomacy* (rev. ed., New York, 1988), 49–57; Thomas J. McCormick, *China Market: America's Quest for Informal Empire, 1893–1901* (Chicago, 1967).

acting on their behalf. To the great anger of the Chinese, he did not challenge the despised unequal treaties. The United States took for itself $25 million of the huge indemnity imposed upon China. It participated in forcing the Chinese to accept permanent stationing of Western military forces between Beijing and the sea, additional evidence of China's impotence, and increased its own military forces there.[99] It did not even rule out the acquisition of its own sphere of influence. "May we not want a slice, if it is to be divided?" the ever alert McKinley inquired.[100]

The notes had little immediate impact for China or the United States. The United States, in Hunt's words, had taken a "token nod at the future possibility of the China market," but it did little subsequently to promote trade with China. The first note did not even address the important issue of investments in spheres of influence.[101] The powers' response to the first note was qualified and evasive, something Hay for political expediency managed to twist into "final and definitive." The second time, a wiser secretary of state did not ask for a response. The notes did less to save China from partition than the fact that the Europeans and Japan for their own reasons chose not to push for it. The Open Door Notes satisfied the need for action at home and threatened no one abroad. Their issuance did signal the beginning of an independent U.S. role in East Asian politics, a course fraught with difficulties and destined to occupy a central place in twentieth-century American foreign policy.

ALTHOUGH SHORT IN DURATION and relatively low in cost—at least for the victor—the War of 1898 had significant consequences. For Cuba, Puerto Rico, and the Philippines, it exchanged one colonial master for another and brought changes in the form of external control. Spaniards viewed it as "the Disaster," a defeat that raised basic questions not simply about the political system but also about the nation and its people. The "question for us...the only and exclusive question," a popular magazine observed, "is one of life and death,...of whether we can continue to exist as a nation or not." "Everything is broken in this unhappy country," a Madrid newspaper added, "all is fiction, all decadence, all ruins."[102] Although the Disaster did not spark a revolution or even major political

99. Cohen, *America's Response to China*, 59.
100. Hunt, *Special Relationship*, 182.
101. Ibid., 152–54.
102. Sebastian Balfour, "The Impact of War within Spain: Continuity or Crisis?" in Smith and Dávila-Cox, *Crisis of 1898*, 102.

changes, it accentuated the class and regional divisions that would lead to the Spanish Civil War.

"No war ever transformed us quite as the war with Spain transformed us," Woodrow Wilson, then president of Princeton University, wrote in 1902.[103] "The nation has stepped forth into the open arena of the world." Wilson's statement was filled with the hyperbole that marked many contemporary assessments, but it contained more than a grain of truth. As a result of the war with Spain, the United States became a full-fledged member of the imperial club, assuming a protectorate over Cuba and taking Hawaii, Puerto Rico, and the Philippines as outright colonies. Its acquisitions in the Pacific made it a major player, if not the dominant power, in that region. With the Open Door Notes and the China Relief Expedition, it became an active participant in the volatile politics of East Asia. The War of 1898 reinforced Americans' sense of their rising greatness and reaffirmed their traditional convictions of national destiny. It sealed the post–Civil War reconciliation of the Union. By 1898, the South had come to terms with its defeat in the Civil War and eagerly accepted the conflict with Spain to prove its loyalty. The North came to recognize the nobility of Confederate sacrifice. Certain that the Civil War had reaffirmed America's mission in the world, former Union and Confederate soldiers eagerly took up the cause of *Cuba Libre*.[104]

The War of 1898 did not produce a realignment in the global balance of power, but it did mark the onset of a new era in world politics. The revolutions in Cuba and the Philippines and the conflicts that followed set the tone for a sustained struggle between colonizers and colonized, one of the major phenomena of the twentieth century. The war brought the end of the Spanish empire and sealed the demise of Spain as a major power. It represented both symbolically and tangibly America's emergence as a world power. The War of 1898 drew European attention as few other events of the decade. Europeans erred in believing that the United States would immediately become a major player in world politics. It possessed the capability, but not yet the will, to act on a global basis. They correctly recognized, however, that it had emerged from war as the seventh great power.[105] Indeed, although it was by no means clear at the

103. "The Ideals of America," *The Atlantic Monthly*, December, 1902. www.theatlantic .com/issues/o2dec/wilson.htm.
104. Gaines Foster, "Coming to Terms with Defeat: Post–Vietnam War America and the Post–Civil War South," *Virginia Quarterly Review* 66 (Winter 1990), 27.
105. Kennedy, *Great Powers*, 248; May, *Imperial Democracy*, 221, 239, 264–65.

time, the War of 1898 also marked the beginning of what would come to be called the American Century.

William McKinley presided over and in many ways guided these changes in U.S. foreign policy. More a practical politician than a thinker, he did not articulate a new vision of America's role in the world. Rather, he took full advantage of the opportunities provided by the War of 1898, responding to and helping to popularize the expansionist doctrines of duty, dollars, and destiny. He fashioned an overseas empire, rooted U.S. influence more deeply in the Caribbean and Pacific Basin, and began to stake out an independent role in East Asia. In his last months in office, he pushed for economic reciprocity and greater world involvement. Speaking at an exposition in Buffalo on September 5, 1901, he warned his countrymen that with the speed of modern communications American "isolation was no longer possible or desirable."[106] A week later, he was dead, the victim of an assassin's bullet. His successor, Theodore Roosevelt, his polar opposite in personality and leadership style, would take up the challenge.

106. James D. Richardson, ed., *A Compilation of the Messages and Papers of the Presidents of the United States* (20 vols., Washington, 1897–1916), 15:662.

9

"Bursting with Good Intentions"

The United States in World Affairs, 1901–1913

Contrary to European predictions, the United States did not become a major player in world politics immediately after the War of 1898. An avowed Anglophile, President Theodore Roosevelt flirted with the idea of an alliance with Great Britain, but he knew that such an arrangement was not feasible because of the relative security the nation continued to enjoy and its long-standing aversion to foreign entanglements. The brief flurry of enthusiasm for empire barely outlasted the war with Spain. The need to consolidate territory already acquired consumed great energy and resources. The Philippine War soured many Americans on colonies. Once an enthusiast for empire, Roosevelt himself would admit by 1907 that the Philippines was America's Achilles' heel. While busy solidifying its position in such traditional areas of influence as the Caribbean and the Pacific Basin, the United States did not acquire new colonies or involve itself in the frantic jockeying for alliances that stamped European politics before World War I. It was a great power but not yet a participant in the great-power system.[1]

The United States between 1901 and 1913 did take a much more active role in the world. Brimming over with optimism and exuberance, their traditional certainty of their virtue now combined with a newfound power and status, Americans firmly believed that their ideals and institutions were the way of the future. Private individuals and organizations, often working with government, took a major role in meeting natural disasters across the world. Americans assumed leadership in promoting world peace. They began to press their own government and others to protect human rights in countries where they were threatened. The perfect exemplar of the nation's mood in the new century, Roosevelt promoted what he called "civilization" through such diverse ventures as building the Panama Canal, managing the nation's imperial holdings in the Philippines and the Caribbean, and even mediating great-power disputes and wars. "We are bursting today with good intentions," journalist E. L. Godkin proclaimed in 1899.[2]

1. Paul Kennedy, *The Rise and Fall of the Great Powers* (New York, 1987), 248.
2. Pedro A. Cabán, *Constructing a Colonial People: Puerto Rico and the United States, 1898–1932* (Boulder, Colo., 1999), 109.

I

"What a playball has this planet of ours become," novelist Jack London exclaimed at the turn of the century. "Steam has made its parts accessible The telegraph annihilates space and time."[3] Indeed, the world had shrunk appreciably by the year 1900. Steamships crossed the Atlantic in less than a week—"giant ferryboats" traversing the "straits of New York," Americans called them.[4] Cable joined much of the globe. Passports were unnecessary in many areas; people moved easily from one country to another to visit or work. The revolutions in technology and transportation permitted large-scale trade and international investments. Commerce and capital moved with relative freedom across national borders. This early globalization of capitalism led some enthusiasts to proclaim a new era of world peace. Applying modern ideas to Enlightenment theories, British businessman Norman Angell in his 1910 best seller *The Great Illusion* proclaimed capitalism an inherently peaceful system that rendered unnecessary formal empires based on possession of territory and thus might eliminate great-power rivalries and make war unthinkable because of the potential cost to winners as well as losers.

Angell also recognized the destructive capacity of modern nation-states, which, in fact, along with the expansion of capitalism and technological and geopolitical changes, was opening the way to history's bloodiest century. The early 1900s represented the high-water mark of imperialism. In 1901, the great powers maintained 140 colonies, protectorates, and dependencies covering two-thirds of the earth's surface and one-third of the world's population. "No land is occupied that is not stolen," humorist Mark Twain quipped after a global tour in the 1890s.[5] The rise of Germany, Japan, and the United States and the demise of the Spanish empire upset the existing order and aroused uncertainty and fear among the established powers, manifested in heated colonial rivalries, a spiraling arms race, and shifting alliances. In a diplomatic revolution of mammoth proportions, traditional enemies Britain and France joined to face the emerging threat of Germany. Britain's accommodation with its ancient rival Russia in turn aroused German fear of encirclement. The increasing rigidity of alliances and the escalating arms race raised the possibility that a crisis in the most remote part of the world could plunge Europe into conflagration.

3. Judy Crichton, *America 1900: The Turning Point* (New York, 1998), 5.
4. Ibid., 70.
5. Mark Twain, *Following the Equator* (New York, 1897), quotation taken from *Mark Twain: A Film Directed by Ken Burns* (PBS, 2002), part 2.

The Russo-Japanese War of 1904–5 further jostled an already wobbly international system. Revelations of Russia's stunning weakness gave Germany a fleeting edge in great-power rivalries, adding anxiety in Britain and France. The surprisingly easy victory of an Asian nation over Europeans assaulted the theories of racial supremacy that undergirded a Eurocentric world order and excited hope among Asians groaning under imperialism. It was "like a strange new world opening up," Vietnamese patriot Phan Boi Chau recorded. "We have become increasingly enthusiastic and intense in our commitment to our ideals."[6]

The years 1900 to 1912 also witnessed the first stirring of the revolutions that would rock the twentieth century. The war with Japan helped spark an abortive revolution in Russia in 1905, a forerunner of the more radical upheaval to come. Republicans overthrew the decaying Manchu regime in China in 1911, setting off nearly four decades of internal strife and agitation against foreign domination. Revolutions also erupted in Mexico and Iran. In all these early twentieth-century upheavals, peasants, industrial workers, the petty bourgeoisie, and provincial elites challenged established governments while meeting the threats posed by foreign powers and each other. Their success was limited, but they hinted at the shakiness of the established order and the turmoil ahead.[7]

In terms of size and population, the United States was clearly a great power. Between 1900 and 1912, the last of the original forty-eight states were admitted to the union, completing the organization of the continental United States. The territory of the mainland exceeded three million square miles; the new overseas empire covered 125,000 square miles extending halfway across the world. A still rapidly expanding population surpassed seventy-seven million in 1901 and was becoming daily more diverse. Almost eight million immigrants entered the United States during the Roosevelt presidency alone. By 1910, America's twelve largest cities had populations one-third foreign born. New York, it was said, "had more Italians than Naples, more Germans than Hamburg, twice as many Irish as Dublin, and more Jews than the whole of western Europe."[8] The influx of these new immigrants inflamed nativist passions and significantly influenced U.S. foreign relations.

6. Robert J. McMahon, ed., *Major Problems in the History of the Vietnam War* (New York, 1990), 31–32.
7. Richard H. Collin, "Symbiosis Versus Hegemony: New Directions in the Foreign Relations Historiography of Theodore Roosevelt and William Howard Taft," *Diplomatic History* 19 (Summer 1995), 493.
8. Lewis L. Gould, *The Presidency of Theodore Roosevelt* (Lawrence, Kans., 1991), 36.

Economically, the United States was first among equals. Per capita income was the highest in the world, although the average concealed gross and growing disparities between rich and poor. Agricultural and industrial productivity soared; the national wealth doubled between 1900 and 1912. A favorable balance of trade permitted a dramatic rise in foreign investments—from $700 million in 1897 to $3.5 billion by 1914. A once yawning gap between what Americans owed abroad and were owed closed by that same year, eliciting predictions that New York would soon be the center of world finance. "London and Berlin are standing in perfectly abject terror," novelist Henry James observed in 1901, "watching Pierpont Morgan's nose flaming over the waves, and approaching horribly nearer their bank vaults."[9] The consolidation of industry that began in the late nineteenth century continued apace in the early twentieth. More and more corporations fell under the control of the great New York banking houses.

The nation's political life centered around adaptations to these changes. The Progressive movement comprised an almost bewildering mélange of sometimes conflicting groups. What they shared was a faith in progress and a conviction that problems could be solved by professional expertise. The progressives set out to deal with the disorders of the 1890s by applying modern problem-solving techniques. They put great stock in bureaucracy and saw government as the essential instrument of order and progress.[10]

The American mood at the turn of the century was one of unbounded optimism and unalloyed exuberance. The return of prosperity salved the wounds opened in the 1890s. Americans again marveled at their productivity and gloried in their material well-being. The defeat of Spain filled the nation with pride. "There is not a man here who does not feel four hundred percent bigger in 1900...," New York senator Chauncey Depew observed, "[now] that he is a citizen of a country that has become a world power."[11] Americans, and indeed some Europeans, more than ever believed that their way of doing things would prevail across the world. Woodrow Wilson told a 1906 audience that the great vitality of the United States would thrust it into new frontiers beyond Alaska and the Philippines: "Soon...the shores of Asia and then Autocratic Europe shall hear us knocking at their back door, demanding admittance for American ideas,

9. Jean Strouse, *Morgan: American Financier* (New York, 1999), 412.
10. Emily S. Rosenberg, *Spreading the American Dream: American Economic and Cultural Expansion, 1896–1945* (New York, 1982), 42.
11. Crichton, *America 1900*, 10.

customs and arts."[12] The first generation of historians of U.S. foreign policy shared this excitement for the nation's new role in the world. Archibald Cary Coolidge hailed the emergence of his country as one of those nations "directly interested in all parts of the world and whose voices must be heard."[13]

The internationalization of America and the Americanization of the world was under way by 1900. Another spurt in tourism manifested the nation's emerging internationalism. The growing ease and luxury and declining cost of travel increased the number of Americans going to Europe from 100,000 in 1885 to nearly 250,000 by 1914. Americans proudly referred to themselves as the "world's wanderers" and boasted that in the "century of travel, Americans are the nation of travelers." Some tourists approached Europe much like their ancestors, their experiences abroad confirming their Americanness. Others viewed travel as a way to broaden their horizons and spread American values and influence. Some hoped to liberalize and Americanize the Old World—even to improve French hygiene by flaunting the newest brand of American-made soap. Some saw travel as a way to promote peace, reasoning that the better people got to know each other the more difficult it would be to go to war. Most saw increased travel as a manifestation of their nation's power and influence. "To be a world power was to travel," it was said, "and to travel was to be a world power." Whatever the rationalization, travel influenced Americans' views of other nations and of their own place in the world. It shaped the culture from which twentieth-century policymakers and an elite keenly interested in foreign policy would emerge. In the spirit of the age, it led to calls for a more professional foreign service, even for improved foreign language skills.[14]

Once scorned by Europeans for its cultural backwardness, the United States by the turn of the century had assumed an important role in the international cultural establishment. American artists and writers took advantage of French encouragement of the arts; wealthy Americans sponsored such artists as Picasso, Matisse, and Cézanne. Henry James and James McNeill Whistler were among England's cultural elite. Americans

---

12. Speech, March 22, 1906, in Arthur S. Link, ed., *The Papers of Woodrow Wilson* (69 vols., Princeton, N.J., 1966–94), 16:341.

13. Archibald Cary Coolidge, *The United States as a World Power* (New York, 1912), 7. See also John H. Latané, *America as a World Power* (New York, 1907), Carl Russell Fish, *American Diplomacy* (New York, 1919), and Albert Bushnell Hart, *The Foundations of American Foreign Policy* (New York, 1901).

14. Christopher Endy, "Travel and World Power: Americans in Europe, 1890–1917," *Diplomatic History* 22 (Fall 1998), 565–94.

bought and collected foreign art. J. P. Morgan acquired so many treasures that Europeans began to impose limits on art exports. Charles Freer's gift of Asian art spurred the creation of the first national gallery.[15]

In terms of its technological and manufacturing feats, the United States was widely recognized as *the* world power by 1900. At the Paris Universal Exposition that year, a huge dome topped by an oversized eagle towering above everything else marked the U.S. pavilion. It contained six thousand exhibits, second only to France, displaying everything from steam engines to meats. "It seems almost incredible," reveled a *Munsey's Magazine* writer, "that we should be sending cutlery to Sheffield, pig iron to Birmingham, silks to France, watch cases to Switzerland...or building sixty locomotives for British railways."[16] Europeans expressed fascination with U.S. methods of mass production and especially Frederick Taylor's principles of scientific business management. Some urged their emulation. Others warned that to copy U.S. techniques would lead to shoddy products. Europeans also feared the mass consumption and democracy that were presumably the inevitable by-products of mass production and would, they fretted, undermine their high culture and threaten their elites. British journalist William Stead's 1901 best seller *The Americanization of the World* sounded an alarm bell that would echo repeatedly throughout the century.[17]

United States citizens, sometimes working with the government, eagerly took up the cause of humanitarian relief for peoples stricken by natural disaster. The wealth generated by the industrial revolution created a strong sense of noblesse oblige. Many citizens also agreed that their nation's status as a world power entailed global responsibilities. Modern communications brought to their attention disasters in far-flung areas; modern transportation made it possible to provide timely assistance. San Franciscans in the wake of their own horrendous earthquake in 1906 contributed $10,000 to victims of a similar disaster in Chile. Dr. Louis Klopsch of the *Christian Herald*, called the "twentieth-century captain of philanthropy," used his paper to collect contributions for famine relief in China and Scandinavia. In 1902, Roosevelt set aside $500,000 for victims of an earthquake on the islands of Martinique and St. Vincent. In 1907 and 1909, sailors from U.S. Navy ships helped with earthquake relief in Jamaica

15. Collin, "Symbiosis," 483–84.
16. Crichton, *America 1900*, 30.
17. Volker Berghahn, "Philanthropy and Diplomacy in the 'American Century,'" *Diplomatic History* 23 (Summer 1999), 393–96; Richard Pells, *Not Like Us: How Europeans Have Loved, Hated, and Transformed American Culture Since World War II* (New York, 1997), 7.

and Messina, Italy. Reorganized in 1905 under a congressional charter giving it status as a semiofficial government agency, the American Red Cross took the lead in many emergency operations. America's "habit of giving" saved countless lives and provided hope across the world. United States aid provoked some criticism, even from recipients, but also earned praise. According to the empress dowager of China, America was "known as the one foreign nation that is really a friend and whose people though barbarians, are really kind."[18]

The United States' rise to world power led to increased citizen activism on foreign policy issues. Americans agitated for reform of and even revolution against the oppressive tsarist government of Russia, in 1911 pressuring Congress into abrogating the commercial treaty of 1832. They took up the cause of world peace. In 1910, steel magnate Andrew Carnegie established the first foundation with an "explicit international orientation." Funded with $10 million of U.S. Steel stock, the Carnegie Endowment for International Peace sought to promote peace through law, international exchanges, and research.[19]

Increased citizen activism led to growing interest in and involvement with foreign policy issues on the part of American women. The realm of diplomacy, like that of politics, remained an exclusive male preserve, but women moved easily from agitation for suffrage and temperance at home into causes abroad. Philanthropy was more open to female participation than the political system. Reformer Alice Stone Blackwell took a leading role in efforts to promote revolution in Russia, even advocating a form of terrorism.[20] Women had early taken up the cause of world peace, urging arbitration of the controversy with Britain in 1895 lest men "deluge the world in blood for a strip of land in Venezuela." After the turn of the century, they campaigned for disarmament and international arbitration of disputes and to publicize their cause designated May 15 as "Peace Day." In promoting peace, they took a position at odds with their male counterparts, singling out what they saw as misguided and dangerous notions of manliness. Deploring modern industrialism, which they viewed as the triumph of male values, they fought against military appropriations, the sale of real and toy guns, and even the sport of boxing.[21]

18. Merle Curti, *American Philanthropy Abroad* (New Brunswick, N.J., 1963), 216–17, 222–23; Berghahn, "Philanthropy," 397–98.
19. Berghahn, "Philanthropy," 397–98.
20. Shannon Smith, "From Relief to Revolution: American Women and the Russian-American Relationship, 1890–1917," *Diplomatic History* 19 (Fall 1995), 607–15.
21. Judith Papachristou, "American Women and Foreign Policy, 1898–1905," *Diplomatic History* 14 (Fall 1990), 493–509.

In an age of internationalization, even African Americans, the most oppressed of American minorities, looked abroad. Leading educational institutions like Hampton Institute in Virginia and Tuskegee Institute in Alabama, each committed to uplifting African Americans by teaching self-help, industrial arts, and Christian morality, sought to project their values abroad. Samuel Armstrong, the founder of Hampton, envisioned a "Girdle Around the World" and encouraged Hawaiians, Africans, Cubans, even Japanese minority groups to come to Hampton, learn its ways, and return home to uplift their peoples by introducing a "little Hampton" there. Booker T. Washington sought to spread his Tuskegee model to Africa by bringing students to the Alabama school and dispatching Tuskegee students to Togo, Sudan, Liberia, and South Africa. Like elites at home, the colonial authorities in Africa found Washington's ideas and programs congenial as ways to help manage the "natives" and make them more productive workers.[22] As on domestic issues, the more radical W.E.B. DuBois, a founder of the National Association for the Advancement of Colored People, took issue with the Tuskegee-Hampton approach. Linking discrimination against African Americans at home with the exploitation of black people, especially Africans, abroad, he vigorously advocated an end to racial oppression at home and imperialism abroad.[23]

II

Although thrust into office by an assassin's bullet, Theodore Roosevelt perfectly fitted early twentieth-century America. He had traveled through Europe and the Middle East as a young man, broadening his horizons and expanding his views of other peoples and nations. An avid reader and prolific writer, he was abreast of the major intellectual currents of his day and had close ties to the international literary and political elite. From his early years, he had taken a keen interest in world affairs. He was a driving force behind, as well as an active participant in, the "large policy" of the 1890s. In his first address to Congress, in December 1901, he preached the gospel of international noblesse oblige: "Whether we desire it or not, we

22. Jeanne Zeidler, "Samuel Chapman Armstrong's Vision: Hampton's Girdle Around the World," paper presented at the Pacific Coast Branch, American Historical Association, August 1995; Michael O. West, "The Tuskegee Model of Development in Africa: Another Dimension of the African/African American Connection, *Diplomatic History* 16 (Summer 1992), 371–87.

23. Tunde Adeleke, *Nineteenth-Century Black Nationalists and the Civilizing Mission* (Lexington, Ky., 1998), 137–139.

must henceforth recognize that we have international duties no less than international rights."[24]

The youngest president to this time, Roosevelt brought to the office a flamboyant style that neatly reflected the America of his time. A "steam engine in trousers," he was called, "an avalanche that the sound of your voice might loosen," and his youthful exuberance and frenetic energy mirrored the pent-up vitality of his emerging nation. Henry James labeled him "Theodore Rex" and described him as "the mere monstrous embodiment of unprecedented and monstrous noise."[25] A supreme egoist—his memoir of the war with Spain should have been titled "Alone in Cuba," one wit observed—he loved to be the center of attention. At the beginning of the age of mass media, he and his attractive family made excellent copy, fascinating and captivating the public and making TR, as he was called, the first politician to attain celebrity status. Building on precedents set by McKinley, he mastered the art of press relations and especially the press release to monopolize the news.[26]

Unlike his predecessors at least back to John Quincy Adams, he demonstrated a particular zest and flair for diplomacy, placing himself at the center of policymaking and setting precedents for executive dominance that became a hallmark of twentieth-century U.S. foreign policy. He reveled in intimate exchanges at the top level and in the stealth and secrecy that were part of the process. He disdained the "pink tea" protocol of formal diplomacy. He delighted in vigorous walks and horseback rides that left the stuffed shirts panting in the rear. He often short-circuited regular channels, using personal friends such as British ambassador Cecil Spring-Rice and his French and German counterparts, Jules Jusserand and Speck von Sternburg, the famous "tennis cabinet," as sources of information and diplomatic intermediaries.

Roosevelt was not a free agent in making foreign policy. In the days before scientific polling, it was impossible to determine what the public thought and how public opinion affected policy. The press could provoke excitement on specific issues as with Cuba in the mid-1890s, especially in the metropolitan areas on the two coasts. When the nation was not threatened from abroad, however, the mass public, especially in the rural Midwest and South, showed little interest in foreign policy. Americans

24. Gould, *Roosevelt*, 13.
25. Jacob Heilbrun, "Larger than Life," *New York Times Book Review* (December 30, 2001), 7.
26. Robert C. Hilderbrand, *Power and the People: Executive Management of Public Opinion in Foreign Affairs, 1877–1921* (Chapel Hill, N.C., 1981), 53–55.

firmly believed that their country should not join alliances or assume commitments that could lead to war. Congress to some extent reflected popular attitudes and set additional barriers to presidential freedom of action. Partisan politics could play a crucial role. Especially at a time when presidents were steadily expanding their power, Congress jealously guarded its prerogatives.

Roosevelt believed that America's new role required a strong executive. He often lamented that "this people of ours simply does not understand how things are outside our boundaries." He understood that Americans would not support some of the things he wished to do in foreign policy. Borrowing from the "social control" theories of sociologist Edward Ross, he saw his role as managing and manipulating a presumably ignorant or indifferent public and Congress to do what he deemed right and necessary.[27] On occasion, he used the "bully pulpit" to educate the nation about things he believed in its best interest. More often, he stretched presidential powers as far as he could without provoking outright rebellion. He frequently operated in secrecy to keep the public and Congress from knowing what he was up to. During most of his presidency, he enjoyed comfortable majorities in Congress. But in his second term he encountered stubborn opposition from fiercely partisan southern Democrats who feared he might use expanded presidential powers to challenge their racial policies and Republicans who worried about the direction of his domestic programs and his accumulation of power. Numerous times, when thwarted by congressional opposition, he used executive agreements to implement his policies. Building on precedents set by McKinley, he established a firm basis for what would later be called the imperial presidency.[28]

TR was not above using foreign policy for partisan political advantage. In 1904, on the eve of the Republican nominating convention, he instructed Secretary of State John Hay to make public the ringing ultimatum "Perdicaris Alive or Raisuli Dead," purportedly to force the release of an American held hostage by a local chieftain in Morocco. The ostensibly bold threat set off wild cheers at the convention and has been hailed since as an example of the virtues of tough talk in diplomacy. In fact, Perdicaris was not a U.S. citizen. Roosevelt had no intention of using force to retrieve him. Most important, his release had already been secured

---

27. Ibid.; Walter LaFeber, "The 'Lion in the Path': The U.S. Emergence as a World Power," *Political Science Quarterly* 101, no. 5 (1986), 716–18.

28. Joseph A. Fry, *Dixie Looks Abroad: The South and U.S. Foreign Relations, 1789–1973* (Baton Rouge, La., 2002), 134–37.

by diplomacy before the telegram was sent. "It is curious how a concise impropriety hits the public," Hay chortled.[29] Although Americans were sometimes uneasy with TR's activism, they delighted in his growing international notoriety and the importance it signified for their young nation. They guffawed when he uttered such outrageous statements as "If I ever see another king, I will bite him."

A quintessentially American figure and a legitimate American hero, Roosevelt has been a subject of controversy. Especially during periods when interventionism has been out of fashion, he has been denounced as a heavy-handed imperialist, insensitive to the nationalism of people he considered backward. During the Cold War years, on the other hand, he was widely praised as a realist, more European than American in his thinking, a shrewd and skillful diplomatist who understood power politics, appreciated the central role America must play in the world, and vigorously defended its interests.

Roosevelt understood power and its limits, to be sure, but he was no Bismarck. On the contrary, he was quintessentially American in his conviction that power must be used for altruistic purposes. He was very much a person of his times. Cosmopolitan in his views, he hailed the advance of Western and especially Anglo-Saxon civilization as a world movement, the key to peace and progress. He believed his most important task was to guide his nation into the mainstream of world history. He viewed "barbaric" peoples as the major threat to civilization and thus had no difficulty rationalizing the use of force to keep them in line. "Warlike intervention by the civilized powers would contribute directly to the peace of the world," he reasoned, and could also spread American virtues and thereby promote the advance of civilization.[30] He was less clear how to keep peace among the so-called civilized nations. Pure power politics ran counter to the morality that was such an essential part of his makeup. In any event, he recognized that Americans' traditional aversion to intervention in European matters limited his freedom of action. The more appropriate role for the United States was as a civilizing power carrying out its moral obligations to maintain peace.[31]

Almost as important, if much less visible, was Elihu Root, who served Roosevelt ably as secretary of war and of state. A classic workaholic, Root

29. Gould, *Roosevelt*, 136.
30. Frank Ninkovich, "Theodore Roosevelt: Civilization as Ideology," *Diplomatic History* 10 (Summer 1986), 233.
31. Ibid.; Serge Ricard, "Theodore Roosevelt and the Diplomacy of Righteousness," *Theodore Roosevelt Association Journal* 12 (Winter 1986), 3–4.

rose to the top echelons of New York corporate law and the Republican Party by virtue of a prodigious memory, mastery of detail, and the clarity and force of his argument. A staunch conservative, he profoundly distrusted democracy. He sought to promote order through the extension of law, the application of knowledge, and the use of government. He shared Roosevelt's internationalism and was especially committed to promoting an open and prosperous world economy. He was more cautious in the exercise of power than his sometimes impulsive boss. For entirely practical reasons, he was also more sensitive to the feelings of other nations, especially potential trading partners. A man of great charm and wit—when the 325-pound Taft sent him a long report of a grueling horseback ride in the Philippines' heat, he responded tersely: "How's the horse?"—he sometimes smoothed over his boss's rough edges. He was a consummate state-builder who used his understanding of power and his formidable persuasiveness to build a strong national government.[32] He was the organization man in the organizational society, "the spring in the machine," as Henry Adams put it.[33] He founded the eastern foreign policy establishment, that informal network connecting Wall Street, Washington, the large foundations, and the prestigious social clubs, which directed U.S. foreign policy through much of the twentieth century.[34]

Roosevelt and Root devoted much attention to modernizing the instruments of national power. Their reforms were part of a worldwide trend toward professionalization of military and diplomatic services based on the notion that modern war and diplomacy required specialized training and highly skilled personnel. They believed that, as an emerging great power in a world filled with tension, the United States must have well-trained public servants to defend its interests, promote its commerce, and carry out its civilizing mission. The call to public service was also a way to combat the selfishness and decadence that threatened the nation from within.

Learning from the chaos that accompanied mobilization for war in 1898, Root had begun to reform the army when Roosevelt took office. Generally acknowledged as the father of the modern U.S. Army, he initiated its conversion from a frontier constabulary to a modern military force

32. Richard Hume Werking, *The Master Architects: Building the United States Foreign Service, 1890–1913* (Lexington, Ky., 1977), 93.

33. Walter LaFeber, "Technology and U.S. Foreign Relations," *Diplomatic History* 24 (Winter 2000), 7.

34. George Mowry, *The Era of Theodore Roosevelt, 1900–1912* (New York, 1958), 43, 121; Walter Isaacson and Evan Thomas, *The Wise Men: Six Friends and the World They Made* (New York, 1986), 28–29, 186–87, 244, 336.

and introduced the radical idea of military professionalism to a nation proud of its citizen-soldier tradition. He created the Army War College in 1903 to prepare senior officers for war. Attacking the army's antiquated and conflict-ridden bureaucracy and following European and especially German models, he secured congressional approval in 1903 for a general staff to better plan for and conduct war. By trading federal funds for increased federal control, he also initiated the difficult and politically sensitive process of building a national reserve force from state-run militias. The so-called Root Reforms aroused bitter opposition inside and outside the army. Although they did not go as far as Root and others would have liked, they represented a major step toward modernization.[35]

Much closer to the president's heart and more acceptable to the nation was the further expansion and upgrading of the navy. A disciple of Alfred Thayer Mahan and sea power, Roosevelt retained throughout his life a boyish enthusiasm for ships and the sea. An "adequate" navy, he declared, was the "cheapest and most effective peace insurance" a nation could buy. He brought to the task his special zeal and skill at public relations.[36] Under his guidance, the U.S. Navy completed the shift from harbor defense to a modern battleship fleet, expanding from eleven battleships in 1898 to thirty-six by 1913 and rising to third place behind Britain and Germany. Direct naval appropriations during Roosevelt's tenure exceeded $900 million; the fleet grew from 19,000 sailors to 44,500. As was his wont, Roosevelt intervened personally to improve the accuracy of naval gunners. His dispatch of the Great White Fleet on its world tour in 1907 was, to him, a crowning achievement. "Did you ever see such a fleet and such a day?" an unusually exuberant (even for him!) president crowed. "By George, isn't it magnificent?" The cruise exposed major technical problems with the fleet and a serious shortage of bases in crucial areas, but it represented a coming-out party of sorts for the modern U.S. Navy.[37]

Roosevelt and Root also initiated reform of the consular and diplomatic services. At a time when competition for markets was a national priority, changes in the consular service aroused little controversy. Some Americans continued to see little need for diplomats — consuls were quite enough — but they were increasingly shouted down by the voices of modernization. Diplomats as well as consuls could serve the demands of an expanding commerce. Greater foreign travel and commerce required more and better

35. Gould, *Roosevelt*, 123; Allan R. Millett and Peter Maslowski, *For the Common Defense: A Military History of the United States of America* (New York, 1984), 299–319.
36. Gould, *Roosevelt*, 43.
37. Ibid., 263; Millett and Maslowski, *Common Defense*, 299–309.

representation. Most important, as TR put it, was the "growth of our present weight in the councils of the world." The United States needed skilled professional diplomats to compete with other nations. To level the playing field, it must eliminate politics, patronage, and amateurism. "The nation is now too mature to continue in its foreign relations these temporary expedients natural to a people to whom domestic affairs are the sole concern," Roosevelt's successor, William Howard Taft, exclaimed.[38] TR took up the cause, and Root applied his considerable skills to institution-building. The unlikely combination of Massachusetts Republican senator Henry Cabot Lodge and Alabama Democratic senator John Tyler Morgan spearheaded reform in Congress.

To remove patronage and politics, consuls and diplomats were selected by examination, carefully evaluated, and promoted on the basis of performance. As a practical business matter, the consular service was restricted to U.S. citizens. Consuls were paid better salaries and forbidden to do business on the side. Emphasis was placed on language skills. As secretary of state, Root shook the hidebound State Department from top to bottom. There was talk of specialized training for diplomats. Universities from New York to California began to create courses and programs—the Harvard Business School actually began as a venue for public service training. Following European models, geographical divisions were established in the State Department to provide the sort of expertise needed to deal with specialized problems.[39] Diplomats rotated between Washington and the field. Some of the changes were undone when Democrat Woodrow Wilson became president in 1913, but the process of reform was under way. To this point, U.S. diplomats had leased space for missions in other countries. Responding to the slogan "Better Embassies Mean Better Business," bankers, businessmen, and lawyers joined forces in 1909 to create improved working facilities for diplomats and consuls. In 1911, Congress authorized the State Department to buy land upon which to build new embassies.[40]

III

As the United States became more and more a nation of nations, ethnic groups played an increasingly important part in U.S. foreign relations.

---

38. Warren Frederick Ilchman, *Professional Diplomacy in the United States, 1779–1939* (Chicago, 1961), 111.
39. Werking, *Master Architects*, 129.
40. Jane C. Loeffler, "The Architecture of Diplomacy," *Journal of the Society of Architecture Historians* 49 (September 1990), 251–55.

Some immigrant groups sought to use their rising power to influence policy on issues affecting the lands from which they had come, on occasion provoking conflict with these nations. More often, the persecution of immigrants by Americans sparked protest from the countries of their origin, threatening good relations, and with Japan raising the possibility of war.

Russia's persecution of Jews became an especially volatile issue in the early twentieth century. Large numbers of Jews had emigrated to the United States from Russia and eastern Europe. Like other immigrant groups, many sought to return to visit or stay. The Russian government viewed Jews as a major source of revolutionary activity and hence a threat to order. Fearing the return of Jews under protection of U.S. citizenship, it denied them visas. A new series of pogroms early in the century posed a more serious problem. As many as three hundred pogroms took place in the years 1903 through 1906, one of the worst at Kishinev, the capital of Bessarabia, where in April 1903, forty-seven Jews were killed, hundreds wounded, and thousands left homeless.[41]

American Jews vigorously protested. By this time, they comprised a populous and well-organized group and controlled several major New York banking houses. They represented a crucial voting bloc in major cities. Already angry over Russian travel restrictions, they expressed outrage at the pogroms. They conducted mass protests in New York and Chicago that drew support from human rights advocates such as social worker Jane Addams and journalist Carl Schurz. They flooded the government with petitions demanding action.[42]

The Roosevelt administration responded cautiously. The president and Hay to some degree shared the anti-Semitism that pervaded old-stock America and viewed the Jewish protest as an unwelcome intrusion from a minority group promoting narrow interests. They believed that protest was futile. On the other hand, they had little use for the tsar, shared Jewish anger at these "fiendish cruelties," and feared that the pogroms might provoke flight to the United States of "hordes of Jews…in unabsorbable numbers," something to "rank with the exodus from Egypt," Hay warned. With an election a year away, they recognized the value of doing something. They passed on to the Russian government a petition drafted by the protestors. To secure maximum political advantage, they released it to the press.

41. Norman E. Saul, *Concord and Conflict: The United States and Russia, 1867–1914* (Lawrence, Kans., 1996), 474–77.
42. Ibid.; Stuart E. Knee, "The Diplomacy of Neutrality: Theodore Roosevelt and the Russian Pogroms of 1903–1906," *Presidential Studies Quarterly* 19 (Winter 1989), 71–73.

This marked the first official U.S. protest against Russian anti-Semitism in a case where the nation's interests were not directly involved.[43]

Hay congratulated himself that the administration had at least laid the issue before the world, but the protest had little practical effect. The Russian government naturally bristled at U.S. intrusion and refused to accept the petition. Ambassador Artur Cassini pointedly retorted that the lynching of African Americans and beating of Chinese in the United States made it "unbecoming for Americans to criticize" Russia. A new wave of pogroms accompanied the outbreak of revolution in Russia in 1905, with an estimated 3,100 Jews killed in that year alone.[44]

"What inept asses they are, these Kalmucks!" Hay privately fumed, but the administration refused to do more, and Jewish protest mounted and took new forms. The powerful financier Jacob Schiff called for military intervention, and fifty thousand Jews marched in New York City. Schiff and other Jewish bankers blocked U.S. and European loans to Russia for its war with Japan and helped the Japanese secure funds, hoping that a Russian military defeat might provoke revolution and ultimately improve conditions for Jews. In 1906, the protestors formed the American Jewish Committee to orchestrate their actions. Increasingly, they focused on abrogation of the Russian-American commercial treaty of 1832, pointing out that it called for equal treatment for citizens of all countries and should be either honored or scrapped. Upon succeeding Roosevelt, Taft tried to head off congressional action by negotiating an agreement with Russia for joint abrogation. The Russians stubbornly refused. In December 1911, responding to Jewish pressures, the House of Representatives passed 300 to 1 a resolution favoring abrogation. Bowing to the inevitable, a reluctant Taft gave the required year's notice for termination of the treaty.[45]

American Jewish leaders hailed abrogation as a "great victory for human rights," but it was considerably less. It did little to help Russian Jews; by provoking an anti-American backlash, it may have worsened their condition.[46] Russia raised tariffs on U.S. imports and imposed boycotts on some items, leading some Americans to protest that minority groups were exercising mischievous influence on U.S. foreign policy. The affair was of more than passing importance. The United States alone among the great powers spoke out against Russian treatment of Jews. The protest made

43. Knee, "Neutrality," 73–74; Gould, *Roosevelt*, 89–90; John Lewis Gaddis, *Russia, the Soviet Union, and the United States: An Interpretive History* (2nd ed., New York, 1990), 42–43.
44. Knee, "Neutrality," 72–73.
45. Gaddis, *Russia*, 43–46; Saul, *Concord and Conflict*, 523–37, 567.
46. Alexander DeConde, *Ethnicity, Race and American Foreign Policy* (Boston, 1992), 71.

clear the growing importance of ethnic groups in foreign policy. It brought into being one of the most powerful lobbies in twentieth-century America.

While American Jews protested human rights abuses in Russia, violations of human rights in the United States set off loud protests in China and Japan. The Chinese had ample reason for anger. After extended debate, Congress in 1904 bowed to exclusionist pressure and made permanent late nineteenth-century restrictions imposed on Chinese immigration. In the meantime, the Bureau of Immigration interpreted exclusionist laws in an arbitrary and intimidating manner.[47] Bureau officials interrogated, harassed, and humiliated Chinese seeking admission to the United States and used the most whimsical reasons to keep them out. State and local laws blatantly discriminated against the ninety thousand Chinese already in the United States, reducing them to the "status of dogs," one Chinese American complained. The Bureau of Immigration seemed intent on driving them all from the country.[48] Even Chinese exhibitors at the 1904 Louisiana Purchase Exposition in St. Louis were subjected to discriminatory regulations and restrictions.[49]

Mounting Chinese anger exploded in 1905 in a boycott of U.S. goods. Centered in the treaty ports, the boycott was one of the first visible signs of an emerging nationalist sentiment among a proud people subjected to foreign domination and insult. Chinese Americans helped instigate the boycott and supported it with contributions of money. Inspired by Japan's war against Russia, gentry, students, women, and intellectuals struck out in whatever ways seemed most available. They singled out the United States because of its gross abuses of human rights and because it appeared least likely to exact harsh retribution. They displayed anti-American posters and sang anti-American songs. They destroyed American property, even such prized personal possessions as record players. A Cantonese student denied access to the United States took his own life on the steps of the U.S. consulate. "My chair coolies are hooted in the street and I would not be surprised if my servants left me," a beleaguered U.S. consul whined. The Chinese government did not officially support the protestors, but it acquiesced in and approved what they did. The Open Door constituency begged the government to do something.[50]

47. Michael H. Hunt, *The Making of a Special Relationship: The United States and China to 1914* (New York, 1983), 228.
48. Delber McKee, "The Chinese Boycott of 1905–1906 Reconsidered: The Role of Chinese-Americans," *Pacific Historical Review* 55 (May 1986), 171.
49. Hunt, *Special Relationship*, 228–34.
50. Delber McKee, "The Boxer Indemnity Remission: A Damage Control Device," *Society for Historians of American Foreign Relations Newsletter* 23 (March 1992), 10.

Roosevelt handled the boycott with political acumen and dexterity. A person who admired strength in people and nations, he deplored Chinese weakness—one of his major terms of opprobrium was "Chinaman." In the 1890s, he had backed exclusion on racial and economic grounds. He sensed the new winds blowing in China, however, and he recognized the blatant injustice in U.S. policies. To quiet U.S. China hands and the Chinese, he vaguely called for changes in the law on the grounds that "we cannot expect to receive equity unless we do equity." He also promised to implement existing laws more equitably and pressed the immigration bureau to mend its ways. But he would not take risks to ensure equity, and he recognized that his power to sway Congress and the states was limited. He assured exclusionists that he would continue to oppose the admission of Chinese laborers: "We have one race problem on our hands and we don't want another." When the boycott spread and five Americans were killed in an unrelated incident, he demanded an end to the protest and beefed up U.S. military forces in and around China.[51]

The incident faded without tangible result. The boycott fizzled from its own weakness rather than Roosevelt's threats. The boycotters disagreed on what they were trying to do and overestimated the capacity of economic pressure to influence U.S. policies. The boycott was mainly important as an early manifestation of the rising nationalism that would soon erupt in revolution. In the United States, little changed. Exclusionists continued to control the Congress. The bureau temporarily softened its methods and ended its efforts to drive Chinese from the United States. Americans continued to treat Chinese badly. In its death throes, the Chinese government could do little more than feebly protest.

The United States sought to appease the Chinese by remitting the indemnity imposed after the Boxer Rebellion. Often viewed as an act of generosity, remission was in fact an act of calculated self-interest. For Roosevelt, it provided a substitute for Congress's refusal to modify the exclusion laws. For those merchants and missionaries who sought to extend U.S. influence and trade in China, it offered a means to palliate the justifiably righteous indignation of the Chinese. It could also be "used to make China do some of the things we want," State Department official Huntington Wilson observed. Alarmed at the number of Chinese going to Japan to study, diplomats also saw remission as a "cultural investment." "The Chinese who acquires his education in this country," diplomat Charles Denby observed, "goes back predisposed toward America and American goods." The United States thus forbade the funds from being

---

51. Hunt, *Special Relationship*, 243.

used for economic development, insisting rather upon the establishment of an American school in China and creation of a program to send Chinese to study in the United States.[52]

A similar conflict with Japan provoked in 1907 a sustained war scare. Ironically, the restrictions placed on Chinese immigration and a continued demand for cheap labor led to a dramatic influx of Japanese workers, mostly from Hawaii. This sudden appearance of "hordes" of immigrants from a nation that had just thrashed a European power provoked working-class resentment against those who would "labor for less than a white man can live on" and wild fears of the "Orientalization of the Pacific Coast." Ostensibly to solve a shortage of school space caused by the recent catastrophic earthquake, in fact to avoid racial "contamination," the San Francisco School Board in October 1906 placed Chinese, Korean, and Japanese children in segregated schools.[53]

This ill-considered order provoked conflict with a nation that could do more than boycott U.S. goods. The Japanese government was not inclined to go to war over a relatively minor issue, but it could not but view the order as an insult and felt compelled to respond to the protests of its own people. Tokyo underestimated the depth of Californians' fears. Viewing U.S. politics through the prism of its own political culture, it also overestimated Washington's ability to control state and local governments. The Japanese thus sharply protested the segregation order.[54]

Roosevelt badly mishandled this issue. He shared to some degree the racial prejudices of the Californians, although he greatly respected what the Japanese had accomplished and admired their discipline and patriotism. He recognized, too, the threat they posed to the Philippines and Hawaii. He also at first underestimated the depth of anti-Japanese sentiment in California. Privately, he raged at the "idiots" who had proclaimed the order and employed racist terms to denounce racist actions—as "foolish as if conceived by the mind of a Hottentot," he declaimed. Publicly, he denounced the segregation order as a "wicked absurdity." But he could not persuade the Californians to rescind it. "Not even the big stick is enough to compel the people of California to do a thing which they have a fixed determination not to do," the *Sacramento Union* thundered.[55] He compounded his problems with a hasty and ill-conceived

52. McKee, "Indemnity," 13: Hunt, *Special Relationship*, 270.
53. Walter LaFeber, *The Clash: U.S. Japanese Relations Through History* (New York, 1997), 88.
54. Charles E. Neu, *The Troubled Encounter: The United States and Japan* (New York, 1975), 48–49.
55. Gould, *Roosevelt*, 258.

effort to charm the Japanese into accepting a treaty providing for the mutual exclusion of laborers. They naturally took offense at the obviously one-sided nature of the treaty and the patronizing manner in which it was presented.[56]

Having won over neither Californians nor Japanese, a chastened Roosevelt set out to cobble together a settlement. He secured from Congress legislation banning immigration from Hawaii, Canada, and Mexico, thus stopping the major source of Japanese immigration without singling them out by name. He used the leverage thus gained to prevent the California legislature from passing discriminatory legislation and to persuade the San Franciscans to revoke their obnoxious order. As part of what came to be known as the "Gentleman's Agreement," Japan agreed to restrict the emigration of laborers to the United States.

In the short run, the crisis persisted. Japanese immigration actually increased following the Gentleman's Agreement, fanning tensions on the West Coast. Anti-Japanese riots in California further provoked Japan. Hotheads in both countries warned ominously of "yellow perils" and "white perils." Some commentators compared the warlike atmosphere to 1898. Roosevelt seems to have overestimated at this stage Tokyo's inclination toward war. He also exploited the crisis to promote his beloved navy and to indulge his boylike zest for playing war. He persuaded Congress to authorize four new battleships and pressed the navy to develop War Plan Orange, the first time Japan had officially been declared a potential enemy. His master stroke, as he saw it, was to send the fleet on a world cruise that included a stop in Japan. He hoped through this blatant show of force to publicize the importance of the navy, build political capital in California, and give pause to the Japanese.

Fortunately for Roosevelt, what could have resulted in disaster ended without incident. The Japanese cut the flow of laborers, fulfilling their part of the Gentleman's Agreement and taking the steam out of the agitation in California. The world cruise exposed the deficiencies of the Great White Fleet more than its power, but the Japanese warmly received the sailors. Crowds sang "The Star-Spangled Banner" in English and waved American flags. United States sailors played baseball against Japanese teams. Although agitators in both countries continued to talk of war and the immigration issue would not go away, Roosevelt left office without further crisis.[57]

---

56. Neu, *Troubled Encounter*, 51.
57. James R. Reckner, *Teddy Roosevelt's Great White Fleet* (Annapolis, Md., 1982).

IV

In the first decade of the twentieth century, Americans took an active role in promoting world peace. The American peace movement was part of a larger Western phenomenon. One hundred and thirty new nongovernmental organizations dedicated to various international causes sprouted up in the early 1900s, many of which would play an important role in years to come. Like their European counterparts, U.S. peace advocates believed that a shrinking world, frightening advances in military technology, and the escalating costs of weapons gave a special urgency to their cause. Optimistic about humankind and confident of progress, they hoped that the growth of capitalism and democracy would make war less likely. They also worried about rising tensions in Europe and sought to take steps to reduce the chances of conflict. Conservative in politics, these "practical" peace reformers equated peace with order and respect for the law. They believed the United States must work closely with other "civilized" nations, especially Great Britain, and that their cause could best be furthered by the extension of Anglo-Saxon principles, especially the codification of international law and arbitration. They saw no contradiction between working for peace and maintaining military strength.[58]

The organized peace movement flourished in the United States early in the century. Some groups sponsored international friendship and understanding among schoolchildren and college students. The World Peace Foundation focused on research and education. Solid citizens such as Root and steelmaker Carnegie gave the movement respectability and resources. Like others of his era, Carnegie believed that the wealthy must assume responsibility for making a better world. Peace became one of his passions. His Endowment built up the international relations sections of Carnegie-funded libraries. It promoted peaceful resolution of disputes. Its charter reflected the optimism of the era. Once war had been eliminated, it declared, the Endowment could move on to the "next most degrading remaining evil or evils."[59]

Firm internationalists, the peace seekers believed that understanding and cooperation among nations were essential for world peace. They were also firmly ethnocentric. In their view, the world could best be regenerated by the spread of American values, principles, and institutions. They worked within precisely defined limits. Certain that their nation's security was not threatened by war in Asia or Europe, they did not consider

58. Charles DeBenedetti, *The Peace Reform in American History* (Bloomington, Ind., 1984), 65–68, 79–83.
59. Curti, *Philanthropy*, 198.

breaking with tradition by joining alliances or involving the United States in world politics. Acting as "enlightened bystanders," they had no sense that achievement of their goal might require drastic measures.

They fastened rather on cautious, legalistic means such as arbitration. Arbitration was a natural for U.S. peace advocates. The U.S. practice of submitting disputes to arbitration dated to the 1794 Jay Treaty with England. Arbitration fitted within the Anglo-American tradition of extending legal concepts to international relations. It perfectly suited those peace advocates who desired to take practical steps without compromising U.S. freedom of action.

The peace advocates won the ear of policymakers, but they never determined how to take effective steps without compromising national sovereignty. With Roosevelt's blessing, Hay negotiated in 1904–5 with all the major European nations and Japan eleven bilateral treaties providing arbitration of all disputes that did not involve questions of national honor or vital interests—glaring exceptions. Already embroiled with the activist TR over numerous issues, a contentious Senate insisted that it must approve each case in which the United States went to arbitration. Dismissing the amended treaties as a "sham," Roosevelt refused to sign them.[60] A more accommodating and cautious Root tried to pick up the pieces, conciliating the Senate and then negotiating twenty-four bilateral arbitration treaties with all the major powers except Russia and Germany. The Root treaties were easily approved and won their author a Nobel Peace Prize. They were so restrictive as to be of dubious value.[61]

American peace advocates and policymakers also supported the idea of regular great-power meetings to discuss matters of war and peace. Such efforts had the advantage of being multilateral rather than bilateral. They could deal with a broad spectrum of issues. The tsar had proposed the first "peace" conference, which met at The Hague in May 1899. Befitting its new world status, the United States took an active role. Male and female peace enthusiasts from across the world also flocked to The Hague, where they held "fringe" meetings and, in the words of the U.S. delegate, submitted "queer letters and crankish proposals." The Quakers were "out in full force," he complained. Military figures such as Mahan and British admiral Sir John Fisher attended as delegates. The conference has been aptly characterized as a noble undertaking with limited results. It did "outlaw" several weapons, took steps to ensure better treatment of

60. Gould, *Roosevelt*, 149.
61. Hilderbrand, *Power and the People*, 86–87; Richard W. Leopold, *The Growth of American Foreign Policy: A History* (New York, 1962), 284–90.

prisoners of war, thus seeking to render war more humane if not eliminating it, and agreed on a multilateral arbitration treaty. But it accomplished nothing in disarmament beyond an innocuous statement that the reduction of military budgets was "extremely desirable for the increase of the material and moral welfare of mankind." It did not even approve a U.S. proposal for a court of neutral nations to arbitrate disputes.[62]

Roosevelt proposed a second Hague conference to push for arbitration and reductions in armaments, but he politely allowed the tsar to issue formal invitations. Forty-four nations gathered in the summer of 1907. The conferees did not address such crucial issues as neutral rights and accomplished nothing in arms reduction. Finley Peter Dunne's fictional newspaper humorist, Mr. Dooley, acidly observed that they spent most of the time discussing "how future wars should be conducted in th' best inthrests iv peace."[63] The delegates also rejected Root's proposal for a permanent world court. They initiated the practice of attaching reservations to their signatures, a method already used by U.S. senators. The main result was acceptance of Carnegie's proposal for the construction of a "peace palace" at The Hague.[64]

Ironically, it was the warmonger of 1898 and hero of San Juan Hill who gave practical expression to the burgeoning peace sentiment by helping to end the Russo-Japanese War and prevent war between France and Germany. Much has been made of Roosevelt's realpolitik, and power politics undoubtedly entered into his unprecedented intrusions in world affairs. Other factors were more important. Like the peace advocates, he felt that the United States must work actively to promote peace. "We have become a great nation...and we must behave as beseems a people with such responsibilities."[65] As one of the "civilized" nations, the United States had a moral duty to preserve peace.[66] TR also loved to be at the center of things, and such interventions gave him a bigger stage to perform on. As much as he complained about the pretensions of foreign heads of states and the intractability of diplomacy, he reveled in the intrigue and secrecy and the manipulation of people and nations. He also believed that his intercession could further vital U.S. interests.

The outbreak of war between Russia and Japan in 1904 provided the first opportunity for the onetime warrior to play the role of peacemaker.

62. Saul, Concord, 440–44; Geoffrey Best, "Peace Conferences and the Century of Total War," International Affairs 75, no. 3 (1999), 623, 631.
63. Leopold, American Foreign Policy, 292.
64. Saul, Concord, 522.
65. Gould, Roosevelt, 173.
66. Ninkovich, "Roosevelt," 241.

Since Japan's rise to world power, the two nations had competed for influence and markets in northeast Asia. Rivalry erupted into military conflict in February when Japan suddenly terminated six months of negotiations and launched a surprise attack on the Russian fleet at Port Arthur in southern Manchuria.

Roosevelt moved slowly toward mediation. At first, he and Root cheered Japanese successes—and even the way they began the war! TR feared Russian advances in East Asia; he profoundly disliked their autocratic form of government and branded the tsar "a preposterous little creature."[67] Although he shared the racism of his contemporaries, he respected Japanese economic and military prowess, even conceding that they would be a "desirable addition" to "our civilized society." He hoped to thwart a possible threat to the Philippines and Hawaii by deflecting Japan's expansion toward the Asian mainland. The Japanese, he crowed, were "playing our game." As they drove from victory to victory over shockingly inept Russian forces, however, he began to fear they might get the "big head." It would be best if the two nations fought to a draw, exhausting each other in the process. At the outset, he concentrated on preventing the war from becoming another occasion for plundering China. Later, he decided that it must be stopped before Japan could gain too great an edge and offered his good offices.[68]

With difficulty, he got the combatants to the conference table. Each Russian military disaster seemed to render the tsar less amenable to compromise. Surprised with the ease of their success, the Japanese began to push for total victory. Roosevelt privately railed at the stubbornness and delusions of each. The Russians were capable of "literally fathomless mendacity"; Japan was an "oriental nation, and the individual standard of truthfulness is low."[69] His persistence paid off. Japan's destruction of the Russian fleet at Tsushima in May 1905 forced the tsar to negotiate. Japan's military success came at the cost of financial ruin; its leaders also found reason to talk. In the summer of 1905, the two nations agreed to attend a peace conference.

The meeting opened at the navy yard in Portsmouth, New Hampshire, August 9, 1905. Its location in the United States was without precedent. Roosevelt played a major role. He did not attend, but he watched closely from his Long Island home and exerted influence through tennis cabinet

67. Gould, *Roosevelt*, 182.
68. Howard K. Beale, *Theodore Roosevelt and the Rise of America to World Power* (New York, 1962), 236–39.
69. H. W. Brands, *TR: The Last Romantic* (New York, 1997), 534.

intermediaries such as von Sternburg and Jusserand, and even Kaiser Wilhelm II. In a preconference gathering at his Oyster Bay estate, he displayed diplomatic finesse by ordering a stand-up buffet dinner to avoid touchy protocol questions of seating and by delivering an admirably tactful toast. Privately, he vented his frustration: the Russians were "soddenly stupid, corrupt, treacherous, and incompetent," the Japanese "entirely selfish." It was difficult to be patient, he told friends, when "what I really want to do is to give utterance to whoops of rage and jump up and knock their heads together."[70] To free itself of financial dependence on U.S. bankers, Japan sought a large indemnity and the retention of Manchurian territory it had taken. Despite its enormous losses, Russia refused concessions—"not an inch of ground, not a kopek of compensation."[71] "The Japanese ask too much," Roosevelt complained, "but the Russians are ten times worse than the Japs because they are so stupid." Russian stubbornness paid off. Chief negotiator Count Sergei Witte made peace possible by ignoring the tsar's objections to ceding half of Sakhalin. Recognizing that their financial plight prevented them from resuming the war, the Japanese agreed to Roosevelt's pleas for compromise. The September 1905 Treaty of Portsmouth provided no indemnity. Japan secured Port Arthur, southern Sakhalin, and Russian recognition of its sphere of influence in Korea. Manchuria was left open to both powers.[72]

Roosevelt quickly discovered the curses as well as blessings that befall the peacemakers. Americans cheered this new evidence of their nation's benign influence in the world and exulted that their president's big stick could be used to impose peace. TR won the 1906 Nobel Peace Prize, the first American to be so honored. As with most such compromises, neither of the signatories was happy. Russians denounced Witte as "Count Half-Sakhalin." Russian-American relations, already strained over the Jewish issue, were further poisoned. Unable to grasp why their smashing military victories had not won a bigger diplomatic payoff, Japanese found in the United States a handy scapegoat. Mourning crepe was hung from government buildings. In September 1905, during anti-peace riots, mobs surrounded the U.S. legation in Tokyo.[73]

Even before the Portsmouth conference, Roosevelt had begun to shore up the U.S. position in the Philippines. While inspiring Asians, Japan's

70. Beale, *Rise to World Power*, 265.

71. Saul, *Concord*, 504.

72. Eugene Trani, *The Treaty of Portsmouth: An Adventure in American Diplomacy* (Lexington, Ky., 1969).

73. Saul, *Concord*, 505; LaFeber, *Clash*, 84.

stunning military success worried some Americans. United States officials, Roosevelt included, increasingly recognized that its naval prowess
threatened the Philippines and even Hawaii, where the Japanese population continued to grow. Now painfully aware of the vulnerability of islands
once touted as the nation's outer defenses, Roosevelt in July 1905 dispatched to Tokyo his protégé and favorite troubleshooter, Taft. The president's flamboyant and outspoken daughter Alice also went along and
dominated the headlines. Meanwhile, Taft held secret discussions with
Prime Minister Taro Katsura. In the resulting agreement, the United
States gave Japan a free hand in Korea, violating the U.S.-Korea treaty of
1882; Katsura disavowed any Japanese aspirations toward the Philippines
or Hawaii. Approved by the president, the so-called Taft-Katsura agreement remained secret until unearthed in his papers nearly two decades
later. When Korea in November 1905 called upon the United States to
live up to its treaty obligations, TR demurred, privately commenting that
the Koreans could do nothing to defend themselves.[74]

The rise in tensions following the Treaty of Portsmouth, the concurrent
crisis over Japanese immigration, fueled by reckless talk of yellow and
white perils, and the growing possibility of conflict over Manchuria created pressures for further initiatives. In late November 1908, Root and
Japanese ambassador Takahira Kogoro negotiated another secret agreement pledging respect for the status quo in the Pacific region, thus tacitly
conceding Japan's preeminent interests in southern Manchuria. When
Root proposed that the Senate might at least be informed of the understanding, Roosevelt, now a lame duck, responded curtly: "Why invite the
expression of views with which we may not agree?"[75]

Roosevelt's role in averting war between France and Germany was less
direct but still important. French efforts to create an exclusive sphere of
influence in Morocco threatened existing German interests. Germany
naturally objected and by threatening war hoped to drive a wedge between France and its new ally, Great Britain. Engaging in a histrionic
display so typical of the era, the kaiser made a dramatic, saber-rattling
speech aboard a warship at Tangier, at the same time calling for an international conference to discuss the issue. Privately, he appealed to the
United States to intercede.

Roosevelt moved cautiously. Some "civilized" nation should uphold
order in Morocco, he reasoned, and France seemed a logical candidate.
He did not want to alienate France or Britain, with whom he sympathized

74. Gould, *Roosevelt*, 185.
75. LaFeber, *Clash*, 92.

and sought to maintain close ties. "We have other fish to fry," he also noted, "no real interests in Morocco." Ultimately, the threat of a "world conflagration" drove him to act. In doing so, he broke precedent even more sharply than in the Russo-Japanese War, implicitly altering the Monroe Doctrine by asserting the right of the United States to intervene in European matters that affected its security.[76] He nudged both sides toward the peace table. He helped resolve haggling over the agenda by persuading France and Germany to go "with no program." Largely through a major gaffe on the part of von Sternburg, he extracted a crucial German promise to accept the settlement he might work out.

The conference opened in January 1906 in Algeciras, Spain. Roosevelt played a less conspicuous role than at Portsmouth, but he exerted important and at times decisive influence. As before, he closely watched the proceedings and worked through trusted personal intermediaries. He took a consistently pro-French position while effusively flattering the kaiser. When Wilhelm backed himself into a corner from which there appeared no face-saving exit, TR threatened to publish Germany's inadvertent pledge to compromise. Faced with this dismal prospect, the kaiser gave in and then had to swallow Roosevelt's fulsome praise for his "epoch-making political success" and "masterly policy." France got most of what it wanted; the kaiser got Roosevelt's praise. War was averted, achieving the president's short-term aim; Germany was isolated and angry.[77]

V

During the first years of the new century, U.S. officials devoted much effort to managing the empire taken from Spain in 1898. They brought to the task a keen sensitivity to their new world role and the importance of what they were doing. They imparted to their work the zeal for social engineering that marked the Progressive Era. Forms of governance and relationships with the United States varied markedly in the new possessions. In all cases, Americans believed in their exceptionalism. They were doing the "world's work," Roosevelt boasted, bringing to their new wards the blessings of civilization rather than exploiting them. Whatever the intentions, of course, U.S. policies were exploitative. It was not simply a matter of Americans taking advantage of helpless victims. Local elites, often Creoles who shared the racist assumptions of their new colonial masters,

---

76. Serge Ricard, "Theodore Roosevelt: Principles and Practices of a Foreign Policy," *Theodore Roosevelt Association Journal* 28 (Fall/Winter 1992), 4.

77. Beale, *Rise to World Power*, 331.

collaborated with the imperial power to advance their personal interests and maintain their privileged position.

At first overlooked in imperial calculations, Puerto Rico came to assume exaggerated importance in American eyes. It would provide bases to guard the canal. It could serve as a transit point for the growth of U.S. trade and investment in Latin America. The expansion of sugar production would reduce dependence on Europe for a vital consumer product. As Americans optimistically set out to educate Puerto Ricans to "our way of looking at things," they reasoned that if they did their job well they could "win the hearts" of other Latin Americans and "weld together" the civilizations of the two continents.[78]

The United States carved out a unique status for its new Caribbean possession. Racist attitudes toward Puerto Ricans made incorporation and self-government equally unthinkable. The island's dense population made colonization by Americans impractical. The Foraker Act of 1900 established Puerto Rico as an unincorporated territory, a possession of the United States but not part of it, the United States' first legally established overseas colonial government. The Supreme Court in the 1901 Insular Cases ruled that the United States could govern the island without the consent of the people for an unspecified period. The Constitution "follows the flag," Root declared sardonically, "but doesn't quite catch up with it."[79] The United States also kept Puerto Rico at a distance economically, imposing a tariff on most of its imports. The new scheme of governance—what Root called "patrician tutelage"—took away much of the autonomy Spain had conceded in 1897. The vote was limited to literate male property owners, disfranchising 75 percent of the male population. An executive council composed of five Americans appointed by the president worked closely with local elites and wielded such power that Puerto Ricans compared it to the "Olympian Jupiter."[80]

The occupation government and colonial administration set out to Americanize the island, hoping in the process to create a model of order and stability.[81] They built roads to attract investment and facilitate economic development. They implemented sanitation and public health programs to ensure a healthy workforce and permit "white American officials" to "escape death in doing their duty." They rewrote the legal code.

78. Cabán, *Colonial People*, 124.
79. Ibid., 90–91.
80. Gervasio Luis García, " 'I Am the Other': Puerto Rico in the Eyes of North Americans, 1898," *Journal of American History* 87 (June 2000), 40–41.
81. Cabán, *Colonial People*, 105.

United States officials viewed Puerto Ricans as morally deficient and lazy— "where a man can lie in a hammock, pick a banana with one hand, and dig a sweet potato with one foot," Gov. Charles Allen explained, "the incentive to idleness is easy to yield to." Viewing the local population as "plastic" and capable of being molded, they reconstructed the educational system to instill into Puerto Ricans that "indomitable thrift and industry which have always marked the pathway of the Anglo-Saxon."[82] English replaced Spanish as the language of instruction. Classes promoted such values as honesty, hard work, and equality before the law. In the mode of Tuskegee Institute, Puerto Ricans were taught manual and technical skills to make them productive workers. Through high tariffs and incentives, the island was integrated into the U.S. economic system, transforming a reasonably diverse agricultural economy into one based on large-scale sugar production. Experts like Jacob H. Hollander of Johns Hopkins University reformed the tax code and made tax collection more efficient. United States officials even sought to Anglicize the name of the island by changing the spelling to "Porto Rico," a move *National Geographic* magazine adamantly rejected.[83]

The new name never quite caught on, and proconsuls could not undo centuries of Spanish rule and remake the United States' new colonial subjects into North Americans. The roads and public health programs improved the quality of life and laid a basis for economic expansion. Educational programs were at best a qualified success. Efforts to force-feed the English language hindered instruction in other areas. Puerto Ricans clung to Spanish; illiteracy rates remained high. Despite vigorous efforts to Americanize the islanders, nationalist sentiment remained alive. Puerto Ricans challenged government dictates and agitated for greater self-government.

Even more than in Puerto Rico, the United States in the Philippines set out with missionary zeal to replicate its institutions. Idealistic young Americans went forth to educate the "natives." Colonial officials built roads and railroads, modernized port facilities at Manila, and through public health programs contained the deadly diseases of malaria and cholera. Experts stabilized the Philippine currency and reformed the legal system. Through what was called reciprocal free trade, the United

82. Wolfgang Binder, "The Tropical Garden and the Mahanesque Resting Place in the Caribbean: Remarks on the Early Incorporation of Puerto Rico by the United States of America," in Serge Ricard, ed., *An American Empire: Expansionist Cultures and Policies, 1881–1917* (Aix-en-Provence, 1990), 100.
83. García, "Puerto Rico," 49–50.

States sought to foster a mutually beneficial economic development. Beginning with reforms at the local levels, U.S. officials instructed their new wards in democratic politics as a basis for eventual self-government. "We are doing God's work here," Governor General Taft exulted.[84]

As in Puerto Rico, the results were no better than mixed. To its credit, the United States avoided the worst exploitation of European imperialism. Congress imposed restrictions that prevented Americans from taking over huge chunks of land. Literacy and life expectancy levels rose markedly; an honest judiciary and efficient tax system were put into place. The use of English gave scattered islanders with a bewildering diversity of dialects a lingua franca, even if an alien one. Upper-class Filipinos aped American manners. The masses took to baseball and Sousa marches. As journalist Stanley Karnow has observed, however, the "Filipinos became Americanized without becoming Americans."[85] Racism further tainted an already unequal and distant relationship between master and subject. Suffrage was limited to property owners, and no more than 3 percent of the population voted. Behind the facade of democracy, an oligarchy of wealthy Filipino collaborators dominated politics and society and exploited their own people. Reciprocal free trade tied the two economies together, making the Philippines vulnerable to the booms and busts of the U.S. business cycle, stimulating uneven economic growth, and widening an already huge gap between rich and poor. Whatever the United States' intentions, the result was a colonial relationship.[86]

In terms of long-term ties, the United States set the Philippines on a very different course from Puerto Rico. From the outset, U.S. rule had been rationalized in terms of noble intentions. The Schurmann Commission of 1899 recommended eventual independence for the islands, and the United States could not easily scrap promises to prepare them for self-government. Some Filipinos were ambivalent. Those who benefited from the colonial relationship recognized the economic perils that might accompany independence and feared Japan. The elite nevertheless ritualistically clamored for independence, finding eager listeners among traditionally anti-imperialist Democrats in the United States. When the Democrats won the presidency in 1912, the Wilson administration introduced a program of "Filipinization," giving Filipinos more seats on the governing executive council and larger roles in the bureaucracy. In 1916,

84. Stanley Karnow, *In Our Image: America's Empire in the Philippines* (New York, 1989), 228.
85. Ibid., 204–9.
86. Ibid., 209.

Congress passed the Jones Act, committing the United States to independence as soon as the Filipinos could establish a "stable government." The pledge was vaguely worded, to be sure, but it was still unprecedented. No imperial nation to this point had promised independence or even autonomy.[87]

By the time TR took office, the United States was poised to fulfill the dream of a canal across the Central American isthmus. In late 1901, after extensive deliberation, a private commission recommended that it be built across Nicaragua, which was closer to the United States, had a more favorable climate, and posed fewer engineering challenges than the rival site in Panama. Within six months, the United States had shifted to Panama. Fearing the loss of its sizeable investment, the French company that had failed to build a canal across Panama and its redoubtable agent Philippe Bunau-Varilla reduced the price for its concession and mounted a frantic lobbying campaign. Its chief agent, the unscrupulous and powerful New York lawyer William Nelson Cromwell, spent lavishly and may have bribed key congressmen. The lobbyists even placed on the desks of senators as a warning against that route stamps portraying a Nicaraguan volcano belching forth tons of lava. Meanwhile, an engineering firm concluded that Panama's technical problems could be managed. Congress in June 1903 voted overwhelmingly for that route.[88]

Only Colombia now stood in the way. Although separated from Panama by a stretch of impenetrable jungle, Colombia had withstood countless revolutions to maintain its precarious hold over the isthmus. Having just suffered a long civil war, it desperately needed money and was sensitive to questions of its sovereignty. When Hay negotiated a treaty giving Colombia $10 million with annual payments of $250,000 and the United States a one-hundred-year lease over a six-mile strip of land, Colombian politicians understandably balked. They did not want to lose the treaty, but they feared giving away so much for so little. For reasons noble and petty, they hoped by holding out to get a better deal.

Colombian rejection of the treaty set in motion powerful forces. Panamanians eager for independence and U.S. largesse plotted yet another revolt. They were encouraged by the indefatigable Bunau-Varilla, who feared going home empty-handed and sought to manipulate the political situation to salvage his clients' investment. Outraged at Colombia's "obstruction," Roosevelt and Hay made no effort to understand its

87. Ibid, 247.
88. Walter LaFeber, *The Panama Canal: The Crisis in Historical Perspective* (New York, 1979), 19–28.

legitimate concerns or to exploit its continuing interest. They were not to be deterred by a pipsqueak nation. Roosevelt privately denounced the Colombians as "contemptible little creatures," "jack rabbits," and "homicidal corruptionists." He did not instigate the rebellion—he knew he did not have to. He and Hay dealt with Bunau-Varilla discreetly. But they made clear they would not obstruct a revolt, and their timely dispatch of warships to the isthmus prevented Colombia from landing troops to suppress the uprising. A stray jackass and a "Chinaman" were the lone casualties in a relatively bloodless revolution. The United States recognized the new government with unseemly haste.[89]

Having contrived to secure appointment as envoy to the United States, the opportunistic Bunau-Varilla moved swiftly to consummate the deal. Even before the revolution, he had drafted a declaration of independence and constitution for Panama. His wife had designed a flag (later rejected because it too closely resembled Old Glory). Determined to complete the transaction before real Panamanians could get to Washington, he negotiated a treaty drafted by Hay with his assistance and far more favorable to the United States than the one Colombia had rejected. The United States got complete sovereignty in perpetuity over a zone ten miles wide. Panama gained the same payment promised Colombia. More important for the short run, it got a U.S. promise of protection for its newly won independence. Bunau-Varilla signed the treaty a mere four hours before the Panamanians stepped from the train in Washington. Nervous about its future and dependent on the United States, Panama approved the treaty without seeing it.[90]

Colombia, obviously, was the big loser. Panama got nominal independence and a modest stipend, but at the cost of a sizeable chunk of its territory, its most precious national asset, and the mixed blessings of a U.S. protectorate. Panamanian gratitude soon turned to resentment against a deal Hay conceded was "vastly advantageous" for the United States, "not so advantageous" for Panama. TR vigorously defended his actions, and some scholars have exonerated him.[91] Even by the low standards of his day, his insensitive and impulsive behavior toward Colombia is hard to defend. Root summed it up best. Following an impassioned Rooseveltian defense before the cabinet, the secretary of war retorted in the sexual allusions he seemed to favor: "You have shown that you have been accused

89. Gould, *Roosevelt*, 95–97.
90. John Major, "Who Wrote the Hay–Bunau-Varilla Convention?" *Diplomatic History* 8 (Spring 1984), 115–23.
91. Collin, "Symbiosis Versus Hegemony," 477–79.

of seduction and you have conclusively proven that you were guilty of rape."[92] Although journalists criticized the president and Congress investigated, Americans generally agreed that the noble ends justified the dubious means. Even before completion of the project in 1914, the canal became a symbol of national pride. The United States succeeded where Europe had failed. It wiped out yellow fever and surmounted enormous engineering challenges. The canal symbolized for Americans their ingenuity and resourcefulness rather than imperialism; "the greatest engineering wonder of the ages," it was hailed, "a distinctively American triumph." Its symbolic importance in turn gave them a special attachment to it that make subsequent adjustments difficult.[93]

"The inevitable result of our building the canal," Root observed in 1905, "must be to require us to police the surrounding premises." In fact, the United States had long claimed the Caribbean as its exclusive preserve. In 1892, Harrison and Blaine arranged with U.S. bankers to get the Dominican Republic's debts out of the hands of European creditors. The Platt Amendment had imposed a protectorate on Cuba. Before the first dirt was shoveled in Panama, breakdown of the Harrison-Blaine deal and the threat of foreign intervention in the Dominican Republic led to the assertion through the so-called Roosevelt Corollary to the Monroe Doctrine of broad U.S. police powers in the hemisphere.[94]

The corollary developed out of a prolonged crisis in Venezuela that for nervous U.S. officials highlighted the threat of European and especially German intervention. Since independence, Latin American nations had contracted sizeable foreign debts, and private citizens of the Western nations mounted growing claims against Latin governments. Some claims were legitimate, some spurious, most inflated, but in the heyday of gunboat diplomacy governments were not disposed to discriminate and often backed their citizens with force. Latin Americans sought to turn European concepts of international law to their favor. The so-called Calvo Doctrine asserted that investors and creditors were entitled to no special rights just because they were foreigners. The Drago Doctrine boldly claimed that the forcible recovery of loans violated the principle of sovereign equality among nations. Neither the Europeans nor the United States recognized

92. Howard Jones, *The Course of American Diplomacy* (New York, 1985), 248.
93. J. Michael Hogan, "Theodore Roosevelt and the Heroes of Panama," *Presidential Studies Quarterly* 19 (Winter 1989), 79, 86, 89.
94. LaFeber, *Panama Canal*, 53–54; Cyrus Veeser, "Inventing Dollar Diplomacy: The Gilded Age Origins of the Roosevelt Corollary to the Monroe Doctrine," *Diplomatic History* 27 (June 2003), 301–26.

such heretical notions. "We do not guarantee any state against punishment if it misconducts itself," Roosevelt proclaimed.[95]

Venezuelan indebtedness provoked a crisis in 1902. Falling back on the Calvo and Drago doctrines, the feisty and defiant dictator Cipriano Castro defaulted on loans held by British creditors and insisted that claimants must seek justice through Venezuelan courts. The great powers informed the United States in late 1902 that they would collect the debts—by force if necessary. Roosevelt gave them a green light, although he did warn, in view of the melon carving in China, that punishment must not "take the form of the acquisition of territory by any non-American power." The Europeans demanded that Venezuela pay. When Castro refused, they seized the dilapidated vessels that constituted his "navy," blockaded Venezuela's ports, and even bombarded Puerto Cabello. Other claimants—including the United States—now lined up to profit from Anglo-German aggressiveness.[96]

Roosevelt later claimed that by issuing a stern ultimatum he had forced the Germans to arbitrate, but resolution of the crisis appears to have been more complicated. Castro originally proposed U.S. arbitration, a shrewd ploy to exploit growing U.S. concern with European intervention. Roosevelt *was* increasingly troubled by German belligerence. The United States *did* have a strong naval force in the area, including Adm. George Dewey's flagship. But no evidence has ever been discovered of a presidential ultimatum. Recent research concludes, on the contrary, that although the Germans behaved with their usual heavy-handedness, in general they followed Britain's lead. The British, in turn, went out of their way to avoid undermining their relations with the United States.[97] Both nations accepted arbitration to extricate themselves from an untenable situation and stay on good terms with the United States.

The Venezuelan episode persuaded administration officials to take steps to head off future European interventions. Britain and Germany encouraged the United States to take the lead in policing its hemisphere. In May 1904—ironically, or perhaps appropriately, at a dinner celebrating the anniversary of Cuba's "independence"—Root delivered the statement that would become the Roosevelt Corollary to the Monroe Doctrine. "Any country whose people conduct themselves well can count on our

95. Lars Schoultz, *Beneath the United States: A History of U.S. Policy Toward Latin America* (Cambridge, Mass., 1998), 180.

96. Nancy Mitchell, "The Height of the German Challenge: The Venezuela Blockade, 1902–1903," *Diplomatic History* 20 (Spring 1996), 190.

97. Ibid., 200.

hearty friendliness," he pledged. But "brutal wrongdoing, or an impotence which results in a general loosening of the ties of civilized society, may finally require intervention by some civilized society, and in the Western Hemisphere the United States cannot ignore this duty."[98] Roosevelt's corollary thus upheld the original intent of the Monroe Doctrine by reversing one of its key provisions and explicitly giving the United States the right of intervention. It cleared up any ambiguity as to who controlled the region.

The administration first applied the corollary in the Dominican Republic. Even before Root's May 1904 statement, that beleaguered Caribbean nation had begun to come apart. A massive influx of U.S. investments and the conversion to an export economy had hopelessly destabilized Dominican life. The nation was deeply in debt to European and U.S. creditors, the victim of an incredibly complex set of sordid deals between its own often unscrupulous leaders and foreign loan sharks. It could not pay. It verged on anarchy, the result of bitter conflicts among groups an American with typical disdain dismissed as "political brigands...little better than savages."[99] Dictator Carlos Morales flirted with saving himself from internal foes and external creditors by inviting a long-term U.S. protectorate. Dominican default on a stopgap debt arrangement and the Hague Court's award to Britain and Germany, seemingly rewarding their aggressiveness in Venezuela, threatened by late 1904 another European intervention in the Caribbean. Safely reelected, Roosevelt decided to act.[100]

The United States developed for the Dominican Republic what has aptly been called a "neo-colonial substitute."[101] Roosevelt had no interest in annexation or even the protectorate proposed by Morales. He sought less drastic means that would help stabilize the Dominican Republic economically and politically and give the United States some control without formal responsibility. With two warships providing a "powerful moral effect on the rash and ignorant elements," a U.S. diplomat with a naval officer at his side negotiated a treaty (first proposed by Morales) giving the United States control of the customs house and providing that 45 percent of the receipts should go to domestic needs, the rest to foreign creditors.

98. Gould, *Roosevelt*, 175; the corollary itself is in *Congressional Record* 39 (December 6, 1904), part 1, 19.
99. Schoultz, *Beneath the United States*, 183, 188.
100. Collin, "Symbiosis Versus Hegemony," 488–89.
101. Emily S. Rosenberg and Norman L. Rosenberg, "From Colonialism to Professionalism: The Public Private Dynamic in United States Financial Advising, 1898–1929," *Journal of American History* 74 (June 1987), 61.

When a now thoroughly contentious Senate refused to consider the treaty, Roosevelt used the threat of foreign intervention to proceed with an informal arrangement under an executive agreement. In 1907, the Senate approved a modified treaty.[102]

The Dominican experiment brought together diplomats, financial experts, and bankers in best Progressive Era fashion to employ "scientific" methods to promote stability and modernization. The U.S. government served as midwife, bringing in economist Hollander, who had already revamped Puerto Rico's finances, to scale back the Dominican debt, improve tax collection, and limit expenditures. Through government intercession, U.S. bankers offered Dominican bonds at high prices. To get the loan, the Dominican Republic accepted a receivership. The key was U.S. control of the customs houses, which would ensure regular payments to foreign creditors and the availability of funds for domestic needs. By removing the major prize and the means for competing factions to buy arms, it would also reduce the likelihood of revolution. Stabilization of the economy would encourage U.S. investment, which in turn would promote economic development.[103] The arrangement brought dramatic short-term improvement and became the model for de facto protectorates elsewhere in the Caribbean and Central America and even in Africa.

William Howard Taft and his secretary of state, Philander Knox, formalized TR's ad hoc arrangements into policy. The enormous Taft and the diminutive (5' 5" tall) Knox, a corporate lawyer with the sobriquet "Little Phil," made an odd couple in appearance. Taft had a very hard presidential act to follow. It did not help that the onetime friends became bitter enemies before he took office. A capable diplomatic troubleshooter, Taft, by his own admission, had an "indisposition to labor as hard as I might" and a "disposition to procrastinate."[104] He lacked Roosevelt's gift for public relations. Relations with Congress, already bad when Roosevelt left office, deteriorated sharply under his successor. Knox was cold, aloof, and impeccably dressed, a socialite and an avid golfer—he once affirmed that he would not let "anything so unimportant as China" interfere with his golf game. He worked short hours and took long Palm Beach vacations. While setting the broad contours of policy, he left the details to his

102. Schoultz, *Beneath the United States*, 185–188.
103. Rosenberg and Rosenberg, "Colonialism to Professionalism," 62–63; Emily S. Rosenberg, "Revisiting Dollar Diplomacy: Narratives of Money and Manliness," *Diplomatic History* 22 (Spring 1998), 159–68.
104. Hilderbrand, *Power and the People*, 76.

subordinates, mainly his abrasive and short-tempered assistant secretary of state, Francis Huntington Wilson.[105]

Taft and Knox adopted the Dominican model to develop a policy called "dollar diplomacy," which they applied mainly in Central America. They sought to eliminate European political and economic influence and through U.S. advisers promote political stability, fiscal responsibility, and economic development in a strategically important area, the "substitution of dollars for bullets," in Wilson's words.[106] United States bankers would float loans to be used to pay off European creditors. The loans in turn would provide the leverage for U.S. experts to modernize the backward economies left over from Spanish rule by imposing the gold standard based on the dollar, updating the tax structure and improving tax collection, efficiently and fairly managing the customs houses, and reforming budgets and tariffs. Taft and Knox first sought to implement dollar diplomacy by treaty. When the Senate balked and some Central American countries said no, they turned to what has been called "colonialism by contract," agreements worked out between private U.S. interests and foreign governments under the watchful eye of the State Department.[107] Knox called the policy "benevolent supervision." One U.S. official insisted that the region must be made safe for investment and trade so that economic development could be "carried out without annoyance or molestation from the natives."[108]

These ambitious efforts to implement dollar diplomacy in Central America produced few agreements, little stability, and numerous military interventions. Part of the problem was attitude. Knox and Wilson had little regard for Central Americans—"rotten little countries," the latter called them.[109] They provoked staunch nationalist opposition. Guatemala and Costa Rica flatly rejected U.S. proposals, the latter turning to Europe to refinance its debt. Honduras's finance minister took flight rather than sign an agreement; its congress, under death threat from nationalist mobs, refused to make the country an "administrative dependency of the United States."[110] When diplomacy failed, private interests took over. "Sam the

105. Walter Scholes, "Philander Knox, 1909–1913," in Norman A. Graebner, ed., *An Uncertain Tradition: American Secretaries of State in the Twentieth Century* (New York, 1961), 59–60.
106. Schoultz, *Beneath the United States*, 208.
107. Rosenberg and Rosenberg, "Colonialism to Professionalism," 65–67; Rosenberg, "Dollar Diplomacy," 166–168.
108. Cabán, *Colonial People*, 103–4.
109. Schoultz, *Beneath the United States*, 209.
110. Ibid., 214.

Banana Man" Zemurray, the legendary entrepreneur who had already begun converting Honduras into a "banana republic," helped finance a rebellion led by an African American soldier of fortune and supported by a U.S. warship. Upon taking power, a pro-U.S. government showed its gratitude by granting favors to Zemurray, who in turn negotiated a loan to help the new president pay off his debts.[111] In the Dominican Republic itself, the much ballyhooed 1907 agreement broke down five years later amidst political upheaval. When rebels seized control of several customs houses, Taft sent in the Marines to put down the revolution, force out the president, and hold a new election. The U.S. military intervention of 1912 was the prelude to a much larger and longer intervention four years later.

Efforts to "stabilize" Nicaragua through dollar diplomacy also required U.S. military power. The independent and highly nationalist dictator José Santos Zelaya demonstrated his displeasure with the U.S. selection of Panama as the canal site by hinting that he might negotiate with a European nation. He also aspired to dominate Central America. When Zelaya threatened to invade El Salvador in 1909, the United States expressed strong disapproval, and U.S. investors encouraged a rebellion. When two Americans assisting the rebels were captured and executed, the United States broke relations and vowed to apprehend and prosecute Zelaya. The dictator fled to Mexico. After another change of government, the United States negotiated a Dominican-like treaty with Adolfo Díaz, formerly a bookkeeper with a U.S. mining company. By this time, the U.S. Senate was in full rebellion. The treaty never got out of the Foreign Relations Committee.

More deals and another revolution led to military intervention. Once it was clear the Senate would not approve the treaty, Taft, emulating TR, oversaw the negotiation of a private arrangement by which U.S. bankers gave the Díaz government cash in return for control of the National Bank of Nicaragua and 51 percent ownership of its railroads, initiatives that tied Nicaragua firmly to the U.S. economy and gave a huge boost to trade.[112] The United States sent 2,700 marines to put down a 1912 rebellion. It left a "legation guard" of several hundred marines to symbolize its presence. In a treaty negotiated just before Taft left office, it gave Nicaragua $3 million for a naval base and canal rights. The treaty was not ratified until 1916.

111. Walter LaFeber, *Inevitable Revolutions: The United States in Central America* (New York, 1984), 44; Lester D. Langley, *The Banana Wars: An Inner History of American Empire, 1900–1934* (Lexington, Ky., 1983), 133–34.
112. Schoultz, *Beneath the United States*, 217.

The Taft administration also tried dollar diplomacy in Liberia. By 1908, this West African nation founded in the nineteenth century by colonization societies and freed slaves was deeply in debt to British creditors, torn by internal rebellion, and embroiled in border disputes with neighboring British and French colonies. A U.S. commission warned that failure to solve Liberia's problems could result in its being colonized by Europeans and "speedily disappear[ing] from the map." It recommended use of the Dominican model with a U.S. Army officer assuming responsibility for building a military force to protect its frontiers. Taft approved the proposal to help America's "ward." A loan was arranged and a warship sent to contain the rebellion. When Congress blocked the Nicaraguan treaty, the administration worked out a private contract for Liberia under State Department supervision. The arrangement did not succeed. The U.S. receiver general and the Frontier Force were "unpopular and inept." The loss of trade from World War I plunged Liberia into deeper economic doldrums.[113]

In applying dollar diplomacy in East Asia, the Taft administration broke sharply with its predecessor. Roosevelt had little sympathy for China and no use for the Open Door policy. His major concern was protecting a vulnerable Philippines against Japan. Egged on by Willard Straight, a former consul general at Mukden and staunch partisan of China, Taft and Knox came to see China and especially Manchuria as a ripe field for U.S. trade and investment and an independent and friendly China as important to the United States. Deeply suspicious of Japan—"a Jap is first of all a Jap," Taft once proclaimed, "and would be glad to aggrandize himself at the expense of anybody"—they sought to use private U.S. capital to thwart Japanese expansion and bolster the independence of China.[114] They found eager accomplices in Beijing and among Chinese officials in Manchuria who saw the United States as a useful counterweight against Russia and Japan.

A bold move to promote American investments in Chinese railroads proved counterproductive. United States officials correctly recognized that control of the railroads was the key to political and economic power. Taft personally interceded with the Chinese to secure for the United States an equal share of an international loan to fund the construction of a railroad in southern China. Chinese officials went along but refused to push other nations to agree. The powers eventually accepted U.S.

113. Emily S. Rosenberg, "The Invisible Protectorate: The United States in Liberia, 1909–1940," *Diplomatic History* 9 (Summer 1985), 191–99.
114. Hunt, *Special Relationship*, 210.

participation, but the arrangement was never completed. At about the same time, the embattled Chinese governor general of Manchuria, with the support of Beijing, devised a plan to secure U.S. funding for a trans-Manchurian railroad to counter the growing power of Russia and Japan. Knox eagerly agreed and took the scheme a giant step further by proposing the internationalization of all railroads in Manchuria, a quite unprecedented venture and an obvious attempt to check Japanese influence.[115] As naive as it was ambitious, the scheme totally misfired. Hoping to divide Russia and Japan, Knox and Taft drove them together. In a July 1910 pact, they divided Manchuria into spheres of influence and agreed to cooperate to maintain the status quo. Knox's scheme depended on support from the other powers, but Britain refused to offend its new Asian ally, Japan, and France would not antagonize its ally Russia.

Undaunted, the dollar diplomats launched one last effort in East Asia. Claiming it their "moral duty" to help China, Knox finally persuaded hardheaded U.S. bankers to put up $2 million as part of an international consortium to promote economic development. He then elbowed his way into the consortium. Before the deal was consummated, revolution broke out in China. The new Chinese government sought better terms. Wary of the revolution, the great powers and indeed the United States delayed recognition for months. U.S. bankers left out of the consortium screamed in protest. By the time the deal was finally concluded in early 1913, the Taft administration was on its way out.[116]

FILLED WITH GOOD INTENTIONS, Americans took a much more active role in the world after 1901. Even in the implementation of colonial policies, they saw themselves charting a new course. Theodore Roosevelt embodied the American spirit of his era. He served in a time of peace when the United States was not threatened and there was no major crisis. He exemplified the best and worst of his country's tradition. Recognizing that the nation's new position brought responsibilities as well as benefits and that international involvement served its interests, Roosevelt took unprecedented initiatives, in the process demonstrating the president's capacity to be a world leader. He began to modernize the instruments of U.S. power. He recognized that the combination of "practical efficiency" and idealism was both necessary and rare.[117] His practical idealism helped end a war in East Asia and prevent war in Europe, each of which served

---

115. LaFeber, *Clash*, 95.
116. Robert D. Schulzinger, *U.S. Diplomacy Since 1900* (5th ed., New York, 2002), 42–43.
117. Gould, *Roosevelt*, 298.

U.S. needs. Recognizing limited U.S. interests in China and Korea and the vulnerability of the Philippines and even Hawaii, he was the consummate pragmatist in East Asia, refusing to take on commitments he could not uphold.

In Central America and the Caribbean, on the other hand, Roosevelt and Taft displayed the narrowness of vision and disdain for other peoples that had afflicted U.S. foreign policy from the birth of the republic. To be sure, Roosevelt launched what his predecessors had long dreamed of, the construction of an isthmian canal, by any standard a huge achievement. And some measure of U.S. influence in the region was inevitable. But the arrogant way he dealt with Colombia and its offspring Panama and the heavy-handed interventions under the Roosevelt Corollary and dollar diplomacy changed forever the way the United States was viewed in its own hemisphere. As implemented by Roosevelt and Taft, "benevolent supervision" was not benevolent for those supervised. The attempt to impose American ideas, institutions, and values upon different cultures was arrogant and offensive—and did not work. Rampant U.S. economic intervention destabilized a region where Americans professedly sought order. The almost reflexive military interventions further damaged U.S. long-term interests and left an enduring and understandable legacy of suspicion among Latin Americans of the "Colossus of the North." "A wealthy country," Latin poet Rubén Darío put it, "joining the cult of Mammon to the cult of Hercules; while Liberty, lighting the path to easy conquest, raises her torch in New York."[118]

Revolutions in China, Mexico, and Russia and the outbreak of war in Europe would pose even sterner challenges for Woodrow Wilson and the foreign policy of the new world power.

---

118. Rubén Darío, "To Roosevelt," in Dennis Merrill and Thomas G. Paterson, eds., *Major Problems in American Foreign Relations*, vol. 1, *To 1920* (6th ed., Boston, 2005), 405.

10

"A New Age"

Wilson, the Great War, and the Quest for a New World Order, 1913–1921

It was called the Great War, and its costs were horrific, its consequences profound. Between August 1914 and November 1918, the European powers fought it out across a blood-soaked continent. Harnessing modern technology to the ancient art of war, they created a ruthlessly efficient killing machine that left as many as ten million soldiers and civilians dead, countless others wounded and disfigured. The war inflicted huge economic and psychological damage on people and societies; it shattered once mighty empires. It coincided with and in important ways shaped the outbreak of revolutionary challenges to the established economic and political order. Together, the forces of war and revolution unleashed during the second decade of the twentieth century set off an era of conflict that would last nearly until the century's end.

Woodrow Wilson once declared that it would be an "irony of fate" if his presidency focused on foreign policy.[1] Indeed, it seems more than a twist of fate if not quite predestination that placed him in the White House during this tumultuous era. He brought to the office an especially keen sense of his own calling to lead the nation and of America's destiny to reshape a war-torn world. From his first days as chief executive, he confronted revolutions in Mexico, China, and later Russia. Initially content to follow the traditional path of U.S. neutrality in Europe's wars, in the face of Germany's U-boat attacks he eventually—and reluctantly— concluded that intervention was necessary to defend his nation's rights and honor and assure for himself and the United States a voice in the peacemaking. Once at war, he gave urgent and eloquent expression to a liberal peace program that fully reflected American ideals dating to the beginning of the republic. He enjoined Americans to assume a leadership position in world affairs. Committing himself and his nation to little short of revolutionizing the international system, he learned through bitter experience that the world was less malleable than he had assumed. He met frustration abroad and bitter defeat at home, a failure that took the form of

---

1. Arthur S. Link, *Woodrow Wilson and the Progressive Era, 1910–1917* (New York, 1954), 81.

grand tragedy when a new and even more destructive war broke out less than two decades hence. Yet the ideas he set forth have continued to influence U.S. foreign policy throughout the twentieth century and beyond.

I

Wilson towers above the landscape of modern American foreign policy like no other individual, the dominant personality, the seminal figure. Born in the South shortly before the Civil War, the son of a Presbyterian minister, from his youth he assiduously prepared himself for leadership— "I have a passion of interpreting great thoughts to the world," he wrote even as a young man.[2] After studying law, he earned a doctorate in history and political science at Johns Hopkins University. He became a "public intellectual" before the phrase was coined, establishing a national reputation through his writing and speeches as a keen student of U.S. history and government. Drawn to the world of action, he shifted to university administration and then to politics, as president of Princeton University and subsequently governor of New Jersey demonstrating brilliant leadership in implementing sweeping reform programs against entrenched opposition. Much has been made of his moralism. Like many of his contemporaries, he was a deeply religious man. Religion gave a special fervor to his sense of personal and national destiny. He was also a practical person who quickly grasped the workings of complex institutions and learned how to use them to achieve his goals. Somewhat forbidding of countenance, with high cheekbones, a firm jaw, and stern eyes, he was a shy and private man who could come across as cold and arrogant. Yet among friends he was capable of great warmth; among those he loved, great passion. He was an accomplished and entertaining mimic. His practiced eloquence with the written and spoken word gave him a capacity to sway people matched by few U.S. leaders. Those who worked with him sometimes complained that his absorption in a single matter limited his capacity to deal with other issues. His greatest flaws were his difficulty working with strong people and, once his mind was made up, a reluctance to hear dissenting views.[3]

Wilson prevailed in 1912 mainly because Republicans were split between party regulars who supported Taft and progressives who backed the increasingly radical Bull Moose candidate Theodore Roosevelt. Socialist Eugene V. Debs won 6 percent of the vote in this most radical election in

2. Thomas J. Knock, *To End All Wars: Woodrow Wilson and the Quest for a New World Order* (New York, 1992), 13.
3. Kendrick A. Clements, *The Presidency of Woodrow Wilson* (Lawrence, Kans., 1992), 1–14.

U.S. history. Wilson came to power fully committed to his New Freedom reform program that sought to restore equality of opportunity and democracy through tariff and banking reform and curbing the power of big business.[4]

He also brought to the presidency firm convictions about America's role in the world. He fervently believed that foreign policy should serve broad human concerns rather than narrow selfish interests. He recognized business's need for new markets and investments abroad, but he saw no inherent conflict between America's ideals and its pursuit of self-interest, believing, in biographer Kendrick Clements's phrase, that the United States "would do well by doing good."[5] He shared in full measure and indeed found religious justification for the traditional American belief that providence had singled out his nation to show other peoples "how they shall walk in the paths of liberty."[6] He had watched with fascination his nation's emergence as a world power, and he perceived that this new status put it in a position to promote its ideals. He shared the optimism and goals of the organized peace movement. At first opposed to taking the Philippines, he went along on grounds that nations like the United States and Britain that were "organically" disposed toward democracy should educate other peoples for self-government.[7] An admirer of conservative British political philosopher Edmund Burke, he feared disorder and violent change. As at home, he viewed powerful economic interests as obstacles to equal opportunity and democratic progress in other countries.[8]

Wilson's views were influenced by Col. Edward M. House (the title was honorific), a wealthy Texas politico who without official position remained his alter ego and closest adviser until the last years of his presidency. Small of stature, quiet and self-effacing, House was a shrewd judge of people and a skilled behind-the-scenes operator. His aspirations were revealed in his anonymously published novel, *Philip Dru: Administrator*, the tale of a Kentuckian and West Point graduate who after corralling the special interests at home launched a crusade with Britain against Germany and Japan for disarmament and the removal of trade barriers.[9]

4. H. W. Brands, "Woodrow Wilson and the Irony of Fate," *Diplomatic History* 28 (September 2004), 503–12.
5. Clements, *Wilson Presidency*, 93.
6. Knock, *End All Wars*, 11.
7. Woodrow Wilson, "A Political Essay," October 1, 1900, in Arthur S. Link, ed., *The Papers of Woodrow Wilson* (69 vols., 1966–94), 12:17–18.
8. Knock, *End All Wars*, 7–8.
9. Lloyd C. Gardner, *Safe for Democracy: The Anglo-American Response to Revolution, 1913–1923* (New York, 1987), 43–44.

Wilson's genuine and deeply felt aspirations to build a better world suffered from a certain culture-blindness. He lacked experience in diplomacy and hence an appreciation of its limits. He had not traveled widely outside the United States and knew little of other peoples and cultures beyond Britain, which he greatly admired. Especially in his first years in office, he had difficulty seeing that well-intended efforts to spread U.S. values might be viewed as interference at best, coercion at worst. His vision was further narrowed by the terrible burden of racism, common among the elite of his generation, which limited his capacity to understand and respect people of different colors. Above all, he was blinded by his certainty of America's goodness and destiny. "A new age has come which no man may forecast," he wrote in 1901. "But the past is the key to it; and the past of America lies at the center of modern history."[10]

As a scholar, Wilson had written that the power of the president in foreign policy was "very absolute," and he practiced what he had preached, expanding presidential authority even beyond TR's precedents. He was fascinated by the challenge of leading a great nation in tumultuous times. Early in his presidency, he wrote excitedly to a friend about the "thick bundle of despatches" he confronted each afternoon, a "miscellany of just about every sort of problem that can arise in the foreign affairs of a nation in a time of general questioning and difficulty." He distrusted and even had contempt for the State Department, complaining on one occasion that dispatches written there were not in "good and understandable English." Like the professor he had been, he corrected and returned them for resubmission. He composed much diplomatic correspondence on his own typewriter and handled some major issues without consulting either the State Department or his cabinet.[11]

Wilson's early forays into the world of diplomacy suggest much about the ideas and ideals he brought to office. His naming of William Jennings Bryan as secretary of state was politic in light of the Great Commoner's stature in the Democratic Party and crucial role in the 1912 campaign. It followed a long tradition of appointing the party leader to that important post. Bryan had traveled widely, including an around-the-world jaunt in 1906. In this respect, at least, he was better qualified than Wilson to shape U.S. foreign policy. Even more than Wilson, Bryan believed that Christian principles should animate foreign policy. A longtime temperance advocate,

10. Knock, *End All Wars*, 14.
11. Frederick S. Calhoun, *Power and Principle: Armed Intervention in Wilson's Foreign Policy* (Kent, Ohio, 1986), 13, 17; House Diary, December 18, 1914, *Wilson Papers* 27:415; Wilson to Mary Ellen Hulbert, April 4, 1915, ibid. 32:476.

he set the diplomatic community abuzz by refusing to serve alcohol at official functions (the Russian ambassador claimed not to have tasted water for years and to have survived one event only by loading up on claret before he arrived).[12] Wilson and Bryan negotiated a treaty with Colombia apologizing and offering monetary compensation for the U.S. role in the Panamanian revolution. This well-intentioned and truly remarkable move quite naturally provoked cries of rage from the Rough Rider, Theodore Roosevelt, and sufficient opposition in the Senate that it was not ratified. It won warm applause in Latin America. In a major speech at Mobile, Alabama, in October 1913, Wilson explicitly disavowed U.S. economic imperialism and gunboat diplomacy in Latin America, linking the exploitative interests that victimized other peoples to the bankers and corporate interests he was fighting at home and promising to replace those old "degrading policies" with a new policy of "sympathy and friendship."[13]

As war enveloped Europe, Wilson and Bryan sought to implement ideas long advocated by the peace movement. Bryan's agreement to serve had been conditioned on freedom to pursue "cooling off treaties." During 1913–14, ironically as Europe was rushing headlong toward war, he negotiated with twenty nations—Britain and France included—treaties designed to prevent such crises from escalating to military conflict. When diplomacy failed, nations would submit their disputes for study by an international commission and refrain from war until its work was completed. Dismissed by critics then and since as useless or worse, the treaties were indeed shot through with exceptions and qualifications. Bryan nevertheless considered them the crowning achievement of his career. Wilson took them more seriously after the Great War began, even concluding that they might have prevented it. The Bryan treaties marked Wilson's initial move toward an internationalist foreign policy.[14]

The quest for a Pan-American Pact reveals in microcosm Wilson's larger designs and the obstacles they encountered abroad. Originally proposed by Bryan in late 1913, the idea was embraced by the president after the outbreak of war in Europe. Viewing it as a means to preserve peace following the war, he rewrote it on his own typewriter. It called for mutual guarantees among hemispheric nations of political independence and territorial integrity "under republican government" and for member governments to take control of the production and distribution of arms and

12. Michael Kazin, A Godly Hero: The Life of William Jennings Bryan (New York, 2006), 216–19.
13. Mobile Speech, October 27, 1913, Wilson Papers 28:448–52.
14. Knock, End All Wars, 22.

munitions. He later linked the pact with U.S. efforts to expand trade in Latin America. Presented first to Argentina, Brazil, and Chile, it drew suspicion. Chile especially feared that its consent would affect its ongoing border dispute with Peru. More important, politicians were alarmed by the huge expansion of U.S. trade and feared that, despite his soothing words, Wilson no less than his predecessors wished to dominate the hemisphere economically and might use the provision calling for republican government to impose U.S. values. Chilean objections delayed consideration of the treaty; U.S. military intervention in Mexico doomed it. It became the basis of Wilson's later proposals for a League of Nations[15]

II

From the outset, Wilson grappled with the complex issues raised by revolution. These early twentieth-century upheavals erupted first in East Asia and Latin America. Although they shared the aim of overthrowing established orders, they were as diverse as the nations in which they occurred. In China, reformers inspired by Japan and the West sought to replace a monarchical, feudal order with a modern nation-state. In Mexico, middle- and lower-class revolutionaries challenged the power of entrenched economic and political interests and the Catholic Church. In each case, nationalists sought to eliminate or at least curb the power of foreign interests that had undermined their country's sovereignty and economic independence.

Wilson's response to these revolutions revealed his good intentions and the difficulties of their implementation. Traditionally, the United States had sympathized with revolutions at least in principle, but when they turned violent or radical or threatened U.S. interests, it had called for order or sought to channel them in moderate directions.[16] With China and Mexico, Wilson plainly sympathized with the forces of revolution. He understood better than most Americans the way in which they expressed the desire of people for economic and political progress. Even in Central America, he hoped to seize the opportunity to improve the lot of the peoples involved. Wilson's "ethnocentric humanitarianism" failed to recognize that in seeking to direct the future of these nations he limited their ability to work out their own destiny. His presumptuous interference overlooked their own national pride and aspirations.[17]

After a decade of agitation, nationalist reformers in late 1911 overthrew the moribund Qing regime. Upon taking office, Wilson responded

---

15. Ibid., 39–45, 83–84.
16. Michael H. Hunt, *Ideology and U.S. Foreign Policy* (New Haven, Conn., 1987), 106–8.
17. Calhoun, *Power and Principle*, 23–24.

enthusiastically and optimistically to the Chinese Revolution. True to his reformist instincts and taking his cues mainly from missionaries, he concluded that China was "plastic" in the hands of "strong and capable Westerners." He and Bryan believed that the United States should serve as a "friend and exemplar" in moving China toward Christianity and democracy. They also agreed that "men of pronounced Christian character" should be sent there.[18] Wilson took bold steps to help China. In March 1913, without consulting the State Department, he withdrew the United States from the international bankers' consortium formed by Taft and Knox to underwrite loans to China. Certain that the Europeans preferred a weak and divided China, a week later and without consulting them he recognized strongman Yüan Shih-k'ai's Republic of China. The open door, he proclaimed, was a "door of friendship and mutual advantage . . . the only door we care to enter."[19]

Wilson's gestures did nothing to alter the harsh realities in China. In its early stages, the revolution brought little substantive change. The masses were not involved. Leaders sought to advance their own power rather than build a modern state. Reformers fought with each other; Yüan's government was shaky at best. The powers sought to exploit China's weakness to expand their influence. Continued U.S. involvement in the consortium might have helped check Japanese and European ambitions. Wilson's well-intentioned withdrawal thus did as much harm as good. He subsequently rejected China's request for loans, making clear the limits of American support.

The outbreak of war in Europe exposed even more starkly the limits of U.S. helpfulness. "When there is a fire in a jeweler's shop the neighbours cannot be expected to refrain from helping themselves," a Japanese diplomat candidly admitted.[20] Japan immediately joined the Allies and took advantage of Europe's preoccupation to drive the Germans from Shandong province. In early 1915, Tokyo presented the embattled Chinese government with its Twenty-One Demands, which sought mainly to legitimize gains made at Germany's expense and expand Japanese influence in Manchuria and along the coast. Even more intrusively, Tokyo demanded that China accept Japanese "advisers" and share responsibility for maintaining order in key areas.

The Chinese sought U.S. support in resisting Japan. Some nationalists saw the United States as little different than other imperial powers;

18. Michael H. Hunt, *The Making of a Special Relationship: The United States and China to 1914* (New York, 1983), 218–19.
19. Wilson statement, March 18, 1913, *Wilson Papers* 27:194.
20. Clements, *Wilson Presidency*, 108.

others admired and hoped to emulate it. Still others viewed it as the least menacing of the powers and hoped to use it to counter more aggressive nations. Yüan hired an American to promote his cause and used missionaries and diplomats to gain support from Washington. Working through the U.S. minister, he appealed to the United States to hold off Japanese pressures.

Although deeply concerned with Japanese actions, Wilson and his advisers were not inclined to intercede. State Department counselor Robert Lansing concluded that it would be "quixotic in the extreme to allow the question of China's territorial integrity to entangle the United States in international difficulties."[21] True to his pacifist principles, Bryan gave higher priority to avoiding war with Japan than to upholding the independence of China. He made clear the United States would do nothing. Preoccupied with the European war and the death of his beloved wife, Ellen, Wilson at first did not dissent. He continued to sympathize with China, however, informing Bryan that "we should be as active as the circumstances permit" in championing its "sovereign rights."[22] Wilson's firmer stance combined with British protests and divisions within the Tokyo government led Japan to moderate its demands.

Wilson continued to take limited measures to help China. In 1916, he encouraged private bankers to extend loans, both to preserve U.S. economic interests and to counter Japanese influence. Soon after, he retreated from his 1913 position by authorizing a new international consortium of bankers to provide loans, even agreeing to help them collect if the Chinese defaulted. Alarmed by America's more assertive stance, Japan sent a special emissary to Washington in the summer of 1917. Kikujiro Ishii's discussions with Lansing, who was by this time secretary of state, revealed major differences, but the two nations eventually got around them by agreeing that Japan's geographical propinquity gave it special but not paramount interests in China. In a secret protocol, the United States again pushed for the open door. The two nations agreed not to exploit the war to gain exclusive privileges. Wilson's position revealed his continuing concern for the Chinese Revolution and Japanese intrusion but made clear to both nations his unwillingness to act.[23]

Closer to home, the United States had no such compunctions. In Central America and the Caribbean, revolution was an established part of

21. Warren I. Cohen, *America's Response to China: An Interpretative History of Sino-American Relations* (New York, 1971), 92.
22. Wilson to Bryan, April 14, 1915, *Wilson Papers* 32:521.
23. Cohen, *Response to China*, 96.

the political process, its aims, at least in U.S. eyes, less about democracy and progress than power and spoils. The growing U.S. economic and diplomatic presence had further destabilized an already volatile region while the opening of the Panama Canal and the outbreak of war in Europe heightened U.S. anxiety about the area. The United States had vital interests there. It also had the power and was willing to use it to contain revolutions and maintain hegemony over small, weak states whose people were deemed inferior. "We are, in spite of ourselves, the guardians of order and justice and decency on this Continent," a Wilson confidant wrote in 1913. "[We] are providentially, naturally, and inescapably, charged with maintenance of humanity's interest here."[24]

During the campaign and the early days of his presidency, Wilson had denounced Taft's dollar diplomacy and military interventionism and spoken eloquently of treating Latin American nations "on terms of equality and honor."[25] He and Bryan genuinely hoped to guide these peoples — "our political children," Bryan called them — to democracy and freedom. They sought to understand their interests even when they conflicted with those of the United States. However they packaged it, the two men ended up behaving much like their predecessors. Wilson deemed it "reprehensible" to permit foreign nations to secure financial control of "these weak and unfortunate republics." But he endorsed a form of dollar diplomacy to control their finances.[26] He and Bryan looked upon them with the same sort of paternalism with which they regarded African Americans at home. They assumed that U.S. help would be welcomed. When it was not, they fell back on diplomatic pressure and military force.[27]

The result was a period of military interventionism exceeding that of Roosevelt and Taft. During its two terms in office, the administration sent troops to Cuba once, Panama twice, and Honduras five times. Wilson and Bryan added Nicaragua to an already long list of protectorates. Despite his anti-imperialist record, Bryan sought to end a long period of instability there with a treaty like the Platt Amendment that would have given the United States the right to intervene. When the Senate rejected this provision, the administration negotiated a treaty giving the United States exclusive rights to the Nicaraguan canal route, a preemptive move depriving Nicaragua of a vital bargaining lever, and providing for a Dominican-type

24. William Bayard Hale to Wilson, July 9, 1913, Wilson Papers 28:33.
25. Mobile Speech, October 27, 1913, ibid. 28:448–52.
26. House Diary, October 30, 1913, ibid. 28:476.
27. Kazin, Godly Hero, 228–30.

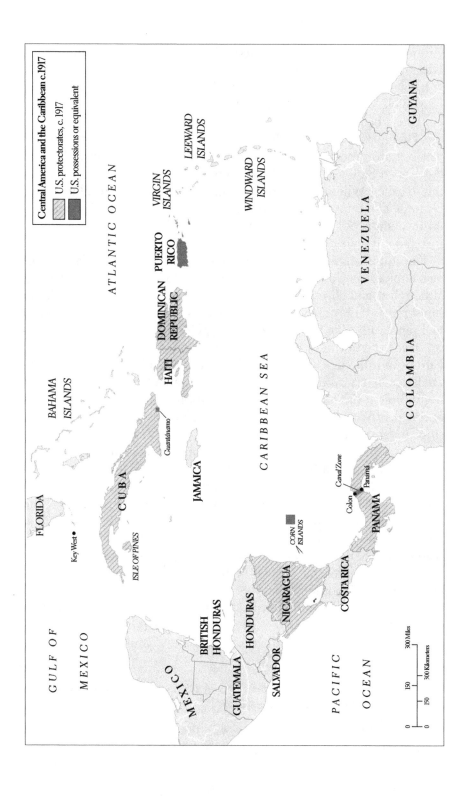

Central America and the Caribbean c.1917

■ U.S. protectorates, c. 1917
■ U.S. possessions or equivalent

ATLANTIC OCEAN

GULF OF
MEXICO

FLORIDA
Key West

BAHAMA
ISLANDS

CUBA
ISLE OF PINES
Guantánamo

JAMAICA

HAITI
DOMINICAN
REPUBLIC

PUERTO
RICO

VIRGIN
ISLANDS

LEEWARD
ISLANDS

CARIBBEAN SEA

WINDWARD
ISLANDS

MEXICO

GUATEMALA
BRITISH
HONDURAS
SALVADOR
HONDURAS
NICARAGUA
CORN
ISLANDS
COSTA RICA

PACIFIC
OCEAN

PANAMA
Colon
Canal Zone
Panamá

COLOMBIA

VENEZUELA

GUYANA

0   150   300 Miles
0   150   300 Kilometers

customs receivership that facilitated U.S. economic control and reduced Nicaragua to protectorate status.[28]

Because of its position astride the Windward Passage, the island of Hispaniola was considered especially important. Dollar diplomat Jacob Hollander boasted in 1914 that the U.S. protectorate had accomplished in the Dominican Republic "little short of a revolution...in the arts of peace, industry and civilization."[29] It had not produced stability. Efforts by the United States in 1913 to impose order through supervised elections, the so-called Wilson Plan, provoked the threat of a new revolution and civil war. Dominicans ignored Bryan's subsequent order for a moratorium on revolution. All else failing, Wilson ordered military intervention in 1915 and full-scale military occupation the next year.[30]

The administration also sent troops to neighboring Haiti. Partly by its own choice, the United States traditionally had little influence in Haiti, although it had coveted the Môle St. Nicolas, one of the Caribbean's finest ports. Historically, the black republic had been most influenced by France; after the turn of the century, German merchants and bankers secured growing power over its economy. Wilson viewed rising European influence as "sinister." United States officials ascribed more credence than warranted to rumors of German establishment of a coaling station at the mole and to the even more bizarre report—*after* the outbreak of World War I—of a joint French-German customs receivership. Bryan set aside his anti-imperialist views long enough to try to take the mole "out of the market" with a preemptive purchase. He subsequently attempted to head off any European initiative by imposing on Haiti a Dominican-type customs arrangement. Haiti defiantly resisted U.S. overtures, but an especially brutal revolution in which the government massacred some 167 citizens and the president was killed and his dismembered body dragged through the streets provided ample reason for U.S. intervention. In July 1915, allegedly as a strategic measure and to restore order, the United States placed Haiti under military occupation. Wilson admitted that U.S. actions in that "dusky little republic" were "highhanded," but he insisted that in the "unprecedented" circumstances the "necessity for exercising control there is immediate, urgent, imperative." The better elements of the country would understand, he

28. Lars Schoultz, *Beneath the United States: A History of U.S. Policy Toward Latin America* (Cambridge, Mass., 1998), 224–29.

29. Ibid., 229.

30. Bruce J. Calder, *The Impact of Intervention: The Dominican Republic During the United States Occupation of 1916–1924* (Austin, Tex., 1984), 6–19.

hoped, that the United States was there to help, not subordinate, the people.[31]

Whatever Wilson's intentions, the military occupations on Hispaniola represent major blots on the U.S. record. The United States imposed at the point of a gun the stability it so desperately sought, but at great cost to the local peoples and to its own ideals. In the Dominican Republic, the U.S. Marines fought a nasty five-year war against stubborn guerrillas in the eastern part of the country, often applying brutal methods against those they contemptuously labeled "spigs." Using models developed in Puerto Rico and the Philippines, U.S. proconsuls implemented technocratic progressive reforms, building roads and developing public health and sanitation programs. The reforms benefited mainly elites and foreigners. Little changed as a result, and when the marines withdrew in 1924, life quickly reverted to normal. The Americans bequeathed to Dominicans a keen interest in baseball. The domineering presence of outsiders certain of their superiority also created a nascent sense of Dominican nationalism. Perhaps the main result of the occupation, an unintended consequence, was that the Guardia Nacional established to assist in upholding order would become the means by which Rafael Trujillo maintained a brutal dictatorship for thirty-one years.[32]

In Haiti, the marines also encountered stubborn resistance, making it impossible for Wilson to remove them when he was so inclined in 1919. The United States systematically eliminated German economic interests and gained even tighter control over Haiti's finances and customs than it had of the Dominican Republic's. But it could not attract much investment capital, and the country remained impoverished. There was no pretense of democracy: Secretary of the Navy Josephus Daniels was jokingly called "Josephus the First—King of Haiti." The U.S. financial adviser employed the threat of not paying the salaries of Haitian officials to gain veto power over legislation. The racism of occupying forces was even more acute where the people were stereotyped like African Americans—"the same happy, idle, irresponsible people we know," as a marine colonel put it. United States officials imposed the Jim Crow style of segregation already in place in the American South. They promoted a Tuskegee-type educational system emphasizing technical education and manual labor. Once the marines left, as in the Dominican Republic, the roads (built with forced labor) fell into disrepair and public health programs languished.

31. Wilson to Edith Bolling Galt, August 15, 1915, *Wilson Papers* 34:209; Hans Schmidt, *The United States Occupation of Haiti, 1915–1934* (New Brunswick, N.J., 1985), 12–63.
32. Calder, *Impact of Intervention*, 238–47.

The blatant racism of the occupation forces pushed a local elite in search of its identity to look back to its African roots.[33]

Wilson's problems in Central America paled compared to the challenges posed by Mexico. The most profound social movement in Latin American history, the Mexican Revolution was extremely complex, a rebellion of middle and lower classes against a deeply entrenched old order and the foreigners who dominated the nation's economy followed by an extended civil war. It would be six years before the situation stabilized. The ongoing struggle created major difficulties for Wilson. His well-intentioned if misguided meddling produced two military interventions in three years and nearly caused an unnecessary and possibly disastrous war. The best that can be said is that he kept the interventions under tight control and learned from his Mexican misadventures something of the limits of America's appeal to other nations and its power to effect change there.

For thirty-one years, Porfirio Díaz had maintained an open door for foreign investors. Under his welcoming policies, outsiders came to own three-fourths of all corporations and vast tracts of land—newspaper mogul William Randolph Hearst alone held some seven million hectares in northern Mexico. United States bankers held Mexican bonds. British and U.S. corporations controlled 90 percent of Mexico's mineral wealth and all its railroads and dominated its oil industry. Díaz hoped to promote modernization and economic development, but the progress came at enormous cost. Centralization of political control at the expense of local autonomy caused widespread unrest, especially in the northern provinces, provoking growing anger toward the regime and its foreign backers. Foreigners used Mexican lands to produce cash crops for export, disrupting the traditional economy and village culture and leaving many peasants landless. Mexican critics warned of a "peaceful invasion." Díaz's policies, they charged, made their nation a "mother to foreigners and a stepmother to her own children."[34] Mexico's economy was at the mercy of external forces, and a major recession in the United States helped trigger revolution. In 1910, middle and lower classes under the leadership of

33. Schmidt, *Haiti*, 74, 174–88; Emily S. Rosenberg, *Financial Missionaries to the World: The Politics and Culture of Dollar Diplomacy, 1900–1930* (Durham, N.C., 2003), 82–84.

34. Yves-Charles Grandjeat, "Capital Ventures and Dime Novels: U.S.-Mexican Relations during the Porifiriano," in Serge Richard, ed., *An American Empire: Expansionist Cultures and Policies, 1881–1917* (Aix-en-Provence, 1990), 137–49; William Schell Jr., "American Investment in Tropical Mexico: Rubber Plantations, Fraud, and Dollar Diplomacy," *Business History Review* 64 (Summer 1990), 219.

Francisco Madero rose up against the regime. In May 1911, they overthrew Díaz.

Counterrevolutions quickly followed. Madero instituted a parliamentary democracy but maintained the status quo economically, disappointing many of his backers. Díaz's supporters plotted to regain power. In his last years in office, Díaz had balanced rising U.S. power in Mexico by encouraging European and especially British economic and political influence. When Madero sustained this policy, U.S. businessmen who at first welcomed the revolution turned against him. They gained active support from Ambassador Henry Lane Wilson, a conservative career diplomat friendly to U.S. business interests and skeptical of the revolution. A heavy drinker, something of a loose cannon, and meddlesome in the worst tradition of Joel Poinsett and Anthony Butler, Wilson sought to undermine official support for Madero and sympathized with plots to get rid of him.General Victoriana Huerta overthrew the government in February 1913 and brutally murdered Madero and his vice president. Out of negligence and indifference, Ambassador Wilson bore some responsibility for this gruesome outcome. Madero's corpse was scarcely in the grave when his supporters launched a civil war against Huerta.[35]

In one of his first ventures in diplomacy, President Wilson set a new subjective standard for recognizing revolutionary governments. Responding to the French Revolution, Thomas Jefferson had established the precedent of recognizing any government formed by the will of the nation. The United States traditionally had recognized governments based simply on whether they held power and fulfilled their international obligations. With Mexico, Wilson introduced a moral and political test. Huerta was indeed a despicable character, crude, corrupt, cruel, "an ape-like man" who "may be said almost to subsist on alcohol," a presidential confidant reported.[36] Wilson was appalled by the murder of Madero and indignantly vowed that he would not "recognize a government of butchers." He also suspected Huerta's ties to U.S. and especially foreign businessmen. In view of the importance of the Panama Canal, he told the British ambassador, it was vital for Central American nations to have "fairly decent rulers." He "wanted to teach those countries a lesson by insisting on the removal of Huerta."[37] He hoped, in his own pretentious and oft-quoted words, to teach U.S. neighbors to "elect good men." Aware that

35. Karl M. Schmitt, *Mexico and the United States, 1821–1973: Conflict and Co-existence* (New York, 1974), 116–26.
36. William Bayard Hale report, July 9, 1913, *Wilson Papers* 28:31.
37. British Embassy in Washington to Sir Edward Grey, October 14, 1913, ibid., 543.

recognition might cripple the opposition, he withheld it in hopes of bringing to power a more respectable government. In so doing, he created yet another instrument to influence the internal politics of Latin American nations.[38]

Wilson also dispatched two trusted personal emissaries to Mexico to push for a change of government. Neither was up to the task. William Bayard Hale was a journalist and close friend; John Lind, a Minnesota politician. Neither spoke Spanish or knew anything about Mexico; Lind indeed considered Mexicans "more like children than men" and claimed they had "no standards politically."[39] Their mission—to counsel Mexico "for her own good," in Wilson's patronizing words—was a fool's errand. They were to persuade Huerta to hold elections in which he would not run and all parties would abide by the result. The president authorized Lind to threaten the stick of military intervention and dangle the carrot of loans before those Mexican leaders who went along.

Predictably, the ploy failed. The crafty Huerta dodged, feinted, and parried. At first flatly rejecting proposals he deemed "hardly admissible even in a treaty of peace after a victory," he then appeared to acquiesce, promising to give up the presidency and hold elections in late October.[40] After a series of military defeats, however, he arrested most of the congress and in what amounted to a coup d'état established a dictatorship. Huerta's opposition responded no more positively to U.S. interference. Constitutionalist "First Chief" Venustiano Carranza expressed resentment at Wilson's intrusion and angrily insisted that he would not participate in a U.S.-sponsored election.

Admitting to a "sneaking admiration" for Huerta's "indomitable, dogged determination," Wilson stepped up the pressure.[41] He blamed the British for Huerta's intransigence and combined stern public warnings with soothing private explanations of U.S. policy. He seriously considered a blockade and declaration of war, again claiming it to be his "duty to force Huerta's retirement, peaceably if possible but forcibly if necessary."[42] Ultimately, he contented himself with measures short of war, warning the Europeans to stay out, sending a squadron of warships to Mexico's east coast, and lifting an arms embargo to help Carranza militarily.

38. Peter V. N. Henderson, "Woodrow Wilson, Victoriano Huerta, and the Recognition Issue in Mexico," *Americas* 41 (October 1984), 154, 173.
39. Schoultz, *Beneath the United States*, 243; Wilson to Bryan, September 19, 1913, *Wilson Papers* 28:293.
40. Schoultz, *Beneath the United States*, 243.
41. Wilson to Mary Ellen Hulbert, February 2, 1914, *Wilson Papers* 29:211.
42. Ibid., 245.

If Wilson was looking for a pretext for military intervention, he got it at Tampico in April 1914 when local officials mistakenly arrested and briefly detained a contingent of U.S. sailors who had gone ashore for provisions. The officials quickly released the captives and expressed regret, but the imperious U.S. admiral on the scene demanded a formal apology and a twenty-one-gun salute. A Gilbert and Sullivan incident escalated into full-scale crisis. Undoubtedly seeking to gain diplomatic leverage, Wilson fully backed his admiral. Huerta at first rejected U.S. demands. Sensing an opportunity for gainful mischief, he then cleverly proposed a simultaneous salute and next a reciprocal one. Wilson rejected both; Huerta rebuffed America's "unconditional demands."[43]

Seizing what he called a "psychological moment," Wilson ordered a military intervention at Veracruz to promote his broader goal of getting rid of Huerta.[44] He pitched his actions on grounds of defending national honor. He easily secured congressional authorization to use military forces, although some hotheads, including his future archenemy, Republican senator Henry Cabot Lodge of Massachusetts, preferred all-out war, military occupation of Mexico, and even a protectorate. To demonstrate his good intentions, the president recruited veterans from Philippine nation-building to show the Mexicans and others through the U.S. occupation the values of progressive government. "If Mexico understood that our motives were unselfish," Colonel House affirmed, "she should not object to our helping adjust her unruly household."[45]

It was a very big "if," of course. For the short term, at least, the intervention failed on all counts. Instead of welcoming the North Americans as liberators, Mexicans of varied political persuasions rallied to the banner of nationalism. In Veracruz, civilians, prisoners quickly released from jails, and soldiers acting on their own fiercely resisted the invasion. It took two days to subdue the city. More than two hundred Mexicans were killed, nineteen Americans. Across Mexico, newspapers cried out for "Vengeance! Vengeance! Vengeance!" against the "pigs of Yanquilandia." In several cities, angry mobs attacked U.S. consulates. Even Carranza demanded U.S. withdrawal.[46]

United States forces took control of the city in early May, remained there for seven months, and performed numerous good works—with phemeral results. The military government implemented progressive

43. Link, *Progressive Era*, 122–23.
44. Clements, *Wilson Presidency*, 99.
45. Robert E. Quirk, *An Affair of Honor: Woodrow Wilson and the Occupation of Vera Cruz* (New York, 1962), 77.
46. Ibid., 107.

reforms to show Mexicans by "daily example" that the United States had come "not to conquer them, but to help restore peace and order." Occupation troops built roads and drainage ditches; provided electric lighting for streets and public buildings; reopened schools; cracked down on youth crime, gambling, and prostitution; made tax and customs collection more equitable, efficient, and lucrative for the government; and developed sanitation and public health programs to transform a beautiful but filthy city into "the cleanest town in the Republic of Mexico." As in the Dominican Republic and Haiti, within weeks after the marines left it was hard to tell that Americans had been in Veracruz.[47]

The intervention contributed only indirectly to the removal of Huerta. At first, the dictator used the U.S. presence to rally nationalist support. Shaken by Mexican resistance, saddened by the loss of life, and increasingly fearful of a Mexican quagmire, Wilson as a face-saving gesture accepted in July a proposal from Argentina, Brazil, and Chile to mediate. While Wilson and Huerta's representatives quickly deadlocked in the surreal and inconclusive talks at Niagara Falls, New York, the civil war intensified. Now able to secure arms, Carranza's forces steadily gained ground and in mid-1914 forced Huerta to capitulate. Chastened by the experience, Wilson confided to his secretary of war that there were "no conceivable circumstances which would make it right for us to direct by force or by threat of force the internal processes of a revolution as profound as that which occurred in France."[48] In November 1914, with Carranza firmly in power, the president removed the occupation forces.

A year of relative quiet followed. In Mexico itself, the civil war raged on, rival factions under populist leaders Emiliano Zapata in the south and Francisco "Pancho" Villa in the north challenging Carranza's fragile government. To promote order and perhaps a government he could influence, Wilson tried to mediate among the warring factions, issuing at least a veiled threat of military intervention if they refused. Carranza and Zapata flatly rejected the overture. Villa's fortunes were obviously declining, and he appeared receptive, opening a brief—and fateful—flirtation with the United States. Carranza continued to gain ground militarily, however. Increasingly preoccupied with the European war, having just weathered the first U-boat crisis with Germany, and fearful of growing German intrigue in Mexico, Wilson did an abrupt about-face. Even though he considered Carranza a "fool" and never established the sort of

47. Ibid., 171; Jodi Pettazonni, "The Occupation of Veracruz, Mexico" (M.A. thesis, University of Kentucky, 2000), 57–79.
48. Wilson to Lindley M. Garrison, August 8, 1914, *Wilson Papers* 30:362.

paternalistic relationship he sought, he reluctantly recognized the first chief's government. He even permitted Carranza's troops to cross U.S. territory to attack the Villistas.[49]

Villa quickly responded. To the end of 1915, he had seemed among various Mexican leaders the most amenable to U.S. influence. A sharecropper and cattle rustler before becoming a rebel, the colorful leader was a strange mixture of rebel and caudillo.[50] At first viewed by Wilson and other Americans as a dedicated social reformer, a kind of Robin Hood, he sought to secure arms and money by showing restraint toward U.S. interests in areas he controlled. He refused even to protest the occupation of Veracruz. As his military and financial position worsened, however, he began to tax U.S. companies more heavily. Several major military defeats in late 1915 and Wilson's seeming betrayal caused him to suspect—incorrectly—that Carranza had made a sordid deal with Wilson to stay in power in return for making Mexico an American protectorate.[51]

Denouncing the "sale of our country by the traitor Carranza" and claiming that Mexicans had become "vassals of an evangelizing professor," Villa struck back.[52] He began to confiscate U.S. property, including Hearst's ranch. In January 1916, his troops stopped a train in northern Mexico and executed seventeen American engineers. Even more boldly, he decided to attack the Americans "in their own den" to let them know, he informed Zapata, that Mexico was a "tomb for thrones, crowns, and traitors."[53] On March 9, 1916, to shouts of *"Viva Villa"* and *"Viva México,"* five hundred of his troops attacked the border town of Columbus, New Mexico. They were driven back by U.S. Army forces after a six-hour fight in which seventeen Americans and a hundred Mexicans were killed. Villa hoped to put Carranza in a bind. If the first chief permitted the Americans to retaliate by invading Mexico, he would be exposed as a U.S. stooge. Conflict between Carranza and the United States, on the other hand, might permit Villa, by defending the independence of his country, to promote his own political ambitions.[54]

Wilson had little choice but to respond forcibly. He may have feared that Villa's actions would have a domino effect throughout Central America in a time of rising international tension. In the United States,

49. Memorandum by Thomas Beaumont Hohler, October 21, 1915, ibid. 35:98.
50. Friedrich Katz, *The Secret War in Mexico* (Chicago, 1981), 145.
51. Friedrich Katz, "Pancho Villa and the Attack on Columbus, New Mexico," *American Historical Review* 83 (February 1978), 112–17.
52. Katz, *Secret War*, 307.
53. Ibid.
54. Katz, "Attack on Columbus," 101.

hotheads who had demanded all-out intervention since 1914, including oilmen, Hearst, and Roman Catholic leaders, grew louder. This first attack on U.S. soil since 1814 provoked angry cries for revenge that took on greater significance in an election year. Wilson may also have seen a firm response to Villa's raid as a means to promote his plans for reasonable military preparedness and strengthen his hand in dealing with European belligerents. He quickly put together a "punitive expedition" of more than 5,800 men (eventually increased to more than 10,000), under the command of Gen. John J. Pershing, to invade Mexico, capture Villa, and destroy his forces. United States troops crossed the border on March 15.[55]

The expedition brought two close, yet distant, neighbors to the brink of an unwanted and potentially disastrous war. Pershing's forces eventually drove 350 miles into Mexico. Even with such modern equipment as reconnaissance aircraft and Harley-Davidson motorcycles, they never caught a glimpse of the elusive Villa or engaged his troops in battle. Complaining that he was looking for a "needle in a haystack," a frustrated Pershing urged occupation of part or all of Mexico. All the while Villa's army, now estimated at more than ten thousand men, used hit-and-run guerrilla tactics to harass U.S. forces and seize northern Mexican cities. On one occasion, Villa reentered the United States, striking the Texas town of Glen Springs.[56]

Although Wilson had promised "scrupulous respect" for Mexican sovereignty, as Pershing drove south tensions with Carranza's government inevitably increased. Mexican and U.S. forces first clashed at Parral. On June 20, a U.S. patrol engaged Mexican troops at Carrizal. Americans at first viewed the incident as an unprovoked attack and demanded war. Wilson responded by drafting a message for Congress requesting authority to occupy all Mexico. Now embroiled in yet another dangerous submarine crisis with Germany, he also mobilized the National Guard and dispatched thirty thousand troops to the Mexican border, the largest deployment of U.S. military forces since the Civil War.

Cooler heads ultimately prevailed. Peace organizations in the United States, including the Women's Peace Party, pushed Wilson for restraint, and when they publicized evidence that Americans had fired first at Carrizal, he hesitated. Carranza's freeing of U.S. prisoners helped ease tensions. Wilson admitted shame over America's first conflict with Mexico

55. Schoultz, *Beneath the United States*, 249; Linda Hall and Don Coerver, "Woodrow Wilson, Public Opinion, and the Punitive Expedition: A Re-assessment," *New Mexico Historical Review* 72 (April 1997), 171–94.

56. Calhoun, *Power and Principle*, 57.

in 1846 and had no desire for another "predatory war." He suspected that it would take more than five hundred thousand troops to "pacify" Mexico. He did not want one hand tied behind his back when war with Germany seemed possible if not indeed likely.[57] "My heart is for peace," he told activist Jane Addams. In a speech on June 30, 1916, he eloquently asked: "Do you think that any act of violence by a powerful nation like this against a weak and distracted neighbor would reflect distinction upon the annals of the United States?" The audience resoundingly answered "No!"[58] After six months of tortuous negotiations with Mexico, the punitive expedition withdrew in January 1917, just as Germany announced the resumption of U-boat warfare.

Wilson's firm but measured response helped get military preparedness legislation through Congress in 1916, strengthened his hand with Germany during yet another U-boat crisis, and aided his reelection in November. Mobilization of the National Guard and the training received by the army facilitated U.S. preparations for war the following year.[59] On the other hand, the failed effort to capture Villa left a deep residue of ill will in Mexico. Only recently dismissed as a loser, the elusive rebel joined the pantheon of national heroes as the "man who attacked the United States and got away with it."[60] Carranza moved closer to Germany, encouraging Berlin to explore with Mexico the possibility of an anti-American alliance.

Wilson's Mexican policy has been harshly and rightly criticized. More than most Americans, he accepted the legitimacy and grasped the dynamics of the Mexican Revolution. He deeply sympathized with the "submerged eighty-five percent of the people...who are struggling towards liberty."[61] At times, he seemed to comprehend the limits of U.S. military power to reshape Mexico in its own image and the necessity for Mexicans to solve their own problems. But he could not entirely shed his conviction that the American way was the right way and he could assist Mexico to find it. He could never fully understand that those Mexicans who shared his goals would consider unacceptable even modest U.S. efforts to influence their revolution. Conceding Wilson's good intentions, his actions were often counterproductive. He averted greater disaster mainly because in 1914 and again in 1916 he resisted demands

57. Wilson conversation with Newton Baker, May 12, 1916, *Wilson Papers* 37:36.
58. Knock, *End All Wars*, 82–83.
59. Hall and Coerver, "Punitive Expedition," 192–94.
60. Katz, "Attack on Columbus," 130.
61. Interview, April 27, 1914, *Wilson Papers* 29:516.

for occupation, even the establishment of a protectorate, and declined to prolong fruitless interventions.[62]

III

If Mexico, by Wilson's admission, was a thorn in his side, the Great War was far more, dominating his presidency and eventually destroying him, politically and even physically. On the surface, Europe seemed peaceful in the summer of 1914. In fact, a century of relative harmony was about to end. For years, the great powers felt increasingly threatened by each other, their fears and suspicions manifested in a complex and rigid system of alliances, an arms race intended to gain security through military and naval superiority, and war plans designed to secure an early advantage. Unstable domestic political environments in Germany and Russia cleared the path to war. When a Serbian nationalist assassinated the Austrian Archduke Franz Ferdinand and his wife, Sophie, in Sarajevo in June, what might have remained an isolated incident escalated to war. Its honor affronted, Austria-Hungary gained German support and set out to punish Serbia. Russia responded by mobilizing behind its Serbian ally, an act designed to deter Germany that instead provoked a declaration of war. Britain joined Russia's ally France in war against Germany. None of the great powers claimed to want war, but their actions produced that result. Expecting a short and decisive conflict, Europeans responded with relief and even celebration. Young men marched off to cheering crowds with no idea of the horrors that awaited them.[63]

The conflict that began in August 1914 defied all expectations. Technological advances in artillery and machine guns and an alliance system that encouraged nations facing defeat to hang on in expectation of outside support ensured that the war would *not* be short and decisive. The industrial revolution and the capacity of the modern nation-state to mobilize vast human and material resources produced unprecedented destructiveness and cost. Striking quickly, Germany drove to within thirty miles of Paris, reviving memories of its easy victory in 1870–71. This time French lines held. An Allied counteroffensive pushed the Germans back to France's eastern boundary, where they dug into heavily fortified entrenchments. By November 1914, opposing armies faced each other along a 475-mile front from the North Sea to the Swiss border. The combatants had already incurred staggering costs—France's battle deaths alone exceeded three

---

62. Clements, *Wilson Presidency*, 103.
63. John Keegan, *The First World War* (New York, 2000), 48–74; Michael Howard, *The First World War* (London, 2003), 18–31.

hundred thousand, and its losses from dead, wounded, or missing surpassed nine hundred thousand. Despite huge casualties on both sides, the lines would not move significantly until March 1917. These first months destroyed any illusions of a quick end and introduced the grim realities of modern combat.[64]

Conditioned by more than a century of non-involvement in Europe's quarrels, Americans were shocked by the guns of August. The outbreak of war "came to most of us as lightning out of a clear sky," one thoughtful commentator wrote. They also expressed relief to be remote from the conflict. "Again and ever I thank God for the Atlantic Ocean," the U.S. ambassador in Great Britain exclaimed.[65] Americans were not without their prejudices. More than one-third of the nation's citizens were foreign born or had one parent who was born abroad. A majority, including much of the elite, favored the Allies because of cultural ties and a belief that Britain and France stood for the right principles. German Americans, on the other hand, naturally supported the Central Powers, as did Irish Americans who despised Britain, and Jewish and Scandinavian Americans who hated Russia. "We have to be neutral," Wilson observed in 1914, "since otherwise our mixed populations would wage war on each other."[66]

Whatever their preferences, the great majority of Americans saw no direct stake in the struggle and applauded Wilson's proclamation that their country be "neutral in fact as well as in name..., impartial in thought as well as in action." Indeed, in terms of the nation's long tradition of noninvolvement in Europe's wars, the seeming remoteness of the conflict, and the advantages of trading with both sides, neutrality appeared the obvious course. The president even wrote a brief message to be displayed in movie theaters urging audiences "in the interest of neutrality" not to express approval or disapproval when war scenes appeared on the screen. From the outset, Wilson also saw in the war a God-given opportunity for U.S. leadership toward a new world order. "Providence has deeper plans than we could possibly have laid ourselves," he wrote House in August 1914.[67]

As a neutral, the United States could provide relief assistance to wartorn areas, and its people responded generously. The American Red Cross shipped supplies worth $1.5 million to needy civilians; its hospital units

64. Keegan, *First World War*, 133.
65. Link, *Progressive Era*, 145; Ross Gregory, *The Origins of American Intervention in the First World War* (New York, 1971), 3.
66. Melvin Small, *Democracy and Diplomacy: The Impact of Domestic Politics on U.S. Foreign Policy, 1789–1994* (Baltimore, Md., 1996), 43.
67. Wilson to House, August 13, 1914, *Wilson Papers* 30:336.

cared for the wounded.[68] Belgian relief was one of the great humanitarian success stories of the war. Headed by mining engineer and humanitarian Herbert Hoover, the program found ingenious ways to get around the German occupation and the British blockade to save the people of Belgium. Admiringly called a "piratical state organized for benevolence," Hoover's Commission for Belgian Relief had its own flag and cut deals with belligerents to facilitate its work. It raised funds from citizens and governments across the world, $6 million from Americans in cash, more than $28 million in kind. The commission bought food from many countries, arranged for its shipment, and, with the help of forty thousand Belgian volunteers, got it distributed. It spent close to $1 billion, fed more than nine million people a day, and kept a nation from starving. Known as the "Napoleon of mercy" for his organizational and leadership skills, Hoover became an international celebrity.[69]

The implementation of neutrality policy posed much greater challenges. It had been very difficult a century earlier for a much weaker United States to remain disentangled from the Napoleonic wars. America's emergence as a major power made it all the more problematical. Emotional and cultural ties to the belligerents limited impartiality of thought. Wilson and most of his top advisers, except for Bryan, favored the Allies. The United States' latent military power made it a possibly decisive factor in the conflict. Most important, its close economic ties with Europe and especially the Allies severely restricted its ability to remain uninvolved. At the outbreak of war, exports to Europe totaled $900 million and funded the annual debt to European creditors. Some Americans saw war orders opening a further expansion of foreign trade. At the very least, maintaining existing levels was an essential national interest. That this might be incompatible with strict neutrality was not evident at the beginning of the war. It would become one of the great dilemmas of the U.S. response.

In reality, trade was so important to Europe and the United States itself that whatever Americans did or did not do would have an important impact on the war and the domestic economy. Attempts to trade with one set of belligerents could provoke reprisals from the other; trading with both, as in Jefferson and Madison's day, might result in retaliation from each. A willingness to abandon trade with Europe might have ensured U.S. neutrality, but it would also have entailed unacceptable

68. Merle Curti, *American Philanthropy Abroad* (New Brunswick, N.J., 1963), 230–31.
69. George H. Nash, "An American Epic: Herbert Hoover and Belgian Relief in World War I," *Prologue* (Spring 1989), 57–86.

sacrifices to a nation still reeling from an economic downturn. The United States could not remain unaffected, nor could it maintain an absolute, impartial neutrality.

Although legally and technically correct, Wilson's neutrality policy favored the Allies. Seeking to establish the "true spirit" of neutrality, Bryan, while the president was absent from Washington mourning the death of his wife, imposed a ban on loans to belligerents on the grounds that money was the worst kind of contraband. The consequences quickly became obvious. The Allies desperately needed to purchase supplies in the United States and soon ran out of cash. Bryan's strict neutrality thus threatened the Allied cause and U.S. commerce. Drawing a sharp distinction between public loans, by which U.S. citizens would finance the war with their savings, and credits that would permit Allied purchases and avoid "the clumsy and impractical method of cash payments," Wilson modified the ruling in October 1914.[70] In the next six months, U.S. bankers extended $80 million in credits to the Allies. A year later, the president lifted the ban on loans entirely. Wilson correctly argued that loans to belligerents had never been considered a violation of neutrality. The result, House candidly admitted in the spring of 1915, was that the United States was "bound up more or less" in Allied success.[71]

Far more difficult to explain, Wilson also acquiesced in Britain's blockade of northern Europe. Employing sea power in a manner sanctioned by its gloried naval tradition, Britain set out to strangle the enemy economically, seeking to keep neutral shipping from entering north European ports and threatening to seize contraband. British officials used precedents set by the Union in the Civil War. Sensitive to history, they also applied the blockade in ways that minimized friction with the United States. In marked contrast to Jefferson and Madison, Wilson acquiesced, an "astonishing concession" of neutral rights, in the words of a sympathetic biographer.[72] His position may have reflected his pro-Allied sympathies. More likely, he perceived that, in part because of the British blockade, U.S. trade with Germany was not important enough to make a fuss over. His acquiescence reflected a pragmatic response to a situation he realized the United States could not change. A historian himself, at the start of the war he appears mostly to have feared drifting into conflict with England over neutral rights like his fellow "Princeton man" James Madison a century

70. Robert Lansing memorandum, October 23, 1914, *Wilson Papers* 31:219.
71. House to Wilson, May 25, 1915, ibid. 33:254.
72. Clements, *Wilson Presidency*, 120–21.

before.[73] He worried that getting drawn into the war might compromise his role as a potential peacemaker. He informed Bryan in March 1915 that arguing with Britain over the blockade would be a "waste of time." The United States should simply assert its position on neutral rights and in "friendly language" inform London that it would be held responsible for violations.[74] Acceptance of the blockade tied the United States closer to the Allied cause. It also encouraged British infringements on U.S. neutral rights, leading to major problems in 1916.

By contrast, Wilson took a firm stand against the U-boat, Germany's answer to the British blockade. In February 1915, Berlin launched a submarine campaign around the British Isles and warned that neutral shipping might be affected. Wilson responded firmly but vaguely by holding the Germans to "strict accountability" for any damage done to Americans. A hint of future crises came in March 1915 when a U.S. citizen was killed in the sinking of the British freighter *Falaba*, an incident Wilson privately denounced as an "unquestionable violation of the just rules of international law with regard to unarmed vessels at sea."[75]

On May 7, 1915, a U-boat lurking off the southern coast of Ireland sent to the bottom in eighteen minutes the British luxury liner *Lusitania*, taking the lives of twelve hundred civilians, ninety-four of them children (including thirty-five babies), from injuries, hypothermia, and drowning. Bodies of victims floated up on the Irish coast for weeks. One hundred and twenty-eight U.S. citizens died. The sinking of the *Lusitania* had an enormous impact in the United States, becoming one of those signal moments about which people later remember where they were and what they were doing. It stunned the United States out of its complacency and brought the Great War home to its people for the first time. It propelled foreign policy to the forefront of American attention.[76] Some U.S. citizens expressed great moral outrage at this "murder on the high seas." Ex-president Theodore Roosevelt condemned German "piracy" and demanded war. After days of hesitation and a careful weighing of the alternatives, Wilson dispatched to Berlin a firm note reasserting the right of Americans to travel on passenger ships, condemning submarine warfare in the name of the "sacred principles of justice and humanity," and warning that further sinkings would be regarded as "deliberately unfriendly."[77]

73. House Diary, September 30, 1914, *Wilson Papers* 31:109.
74. Wilson to Bryan, March 25, 1915, ibid. 32:432–33.
75. Wilson to Bryan, April 3, 1915, ibid. 32:469.
76. John Milton Cooper Jr., "The Shock of Recognition: The Impact of World War I on America," *Virginia Quarterly Review* 76 (Autumn 2000), 557.
77. Gregory, *Origins of Intervention*, 63–64.

Wilson's strong stand derived from a rising fear of Germany and especially from concern for his own and his nation's credibility. Suspicion of Germany had grown steadily in the United States since the turn of the century, especially with regard to its hostile intentions in the Western Hemisphere. German atrocities in neutral Belgium, exaggerated by British propaganda, their crude and shocking efforts to bomb civilians from the air, and rumors, sometimes fed by top Berlin officials, of plans to foment rebellion within the United States provoked fear and anger among Americans, the president included. U-boat warfare further called into question basic German decency. The submarine had not been used extensively or effectively in warfare prior to 1915. This new and seemingly horrible weapon violated traditional rules of naval warfare that spared civilians. It killed innocent people—even neutrals—without warning. Britain could compensate U.S. merchants for property seized or destroyed, but lives taken by submarines could not be restored. Most Americans held to what Wilson called a "double wish." They did not want war, but neither did they want to remain silent in the face of such a brutal assault on human life. Republicans appeared ready to exploit the sinking of the *Lusitania* if the president did not uphold the nation's rights and honor. Wilson also did not want war, but he recognized that to do nothing would sacrifice principles he held dear and seriously damage his stature at home and abroad.[78]

Wilson's tough line on the *Lusitania* provoked crises in Washington and Berlin. Still committed to a strict neutrality, no matter the cost, Bryan insisted that Americans must be warned against traveling on belligerent ships. Protests against U-boat warfare must be matched by equally firm remonstrances against British violations of U.S. neutral rights. When Wilson rejected his arguments, the secretary resigned as an act of conscience, removing an important dissenting voice from the cabinet. The Germans also claimed that equity required U.S. protests against a blockade that starved European children. They insisted, correctly as it turned out, that the *Lusitania* had been carrying munitions. Chancellor Theobald von Bethmann-Hollweg nevertheless recognized that it was more important to keep the United States out of the war than to use submarines without restriction. When a U-boat sank the British ship *Arabic* in August, killing forty-four, two Americans included, Wilson extracted from Berlin a public pledge to refrain from attacks without warning on passenger vessels and a commitment to arbitrate the *Lusitania* and *Arabic* cases.

78. Ibid., 60–63. The "double wish" is noted in John A. Thompson, *Woodrow Wilson* (London, 2002), 112.

The president weathered his first crisis with Germany, but only because of decisions made in Berlin. He perceived that at some future date Germany could force on him a painful choice between upholding U.S. honor and going to war.[79]

After a respite of nearly a year, Wilson in the spring and summer of 1916 faced neutrality crises with both Germany and Britain. On March 24, 1916, a U-boat torpedoed the British channel packet *Sussex*, killing eighty passengers and injuring four Americans. Following a month's delay, the president and Robert Lansing, Bryan's successor as secretary of state, sternly responded that Germany must stop submarine warfare or the United States would break diplomatic relations, a step generally recognized as preliminary to war. After a brief debate, Berlin again found it expedient to accommodate the United States. Bethmann-Hollweg's *Sussex* pledge of early May promised no further surprise attacks on passenger liners. Wilson won a great victory, but in doing so he further narrowed his choices. Should German leaders decide that use of the U-boat was more important than keeping the United States out of war, he would face the grim choice of submission or breaking relations and possibly war. The United States' neutrality hung on a slender thread.[80]

In the meantime, tensions with Britain increased sharply. A crisis had been averted the previous year when London after declaring cotton contraband bought enough of the U.S. crop to sustain prices at an acceptable level. Britain's brutal suppression of the Irish Easter Rebellion in the spring of 1916 and especially the execution of its leaders inflamed American opinion, even among many people normally sympathetic to the Allies. In the summer of 1916, the Allies tightened restrictions against neutral ships and seized and opened mail on the high seas. In July, London blacklisted more than eighty U.S. businesses charged with trading with the Central Powers, thereby preventing Allied firms from dealing with them. Wilson privately fumed about Britain's "altogether indefensible" actions, threatened to take as firm a position with London as with Berlin, and denounced the blacklist as the "last straw." Meanwhile, U.S. bankers financed Britain at a level of about $10 million a day. Britain bought more than $83 million of U.S. goods per week, leaving the nation more closely than ever tied to the Allied cause.[81]

79. Ernest R. May, *The World War and American Isolation, 1914–1917* (Chicago, 1959), 225–27; Thompson, *Wilson*, 114–17.
80. Gregory, *Origins of Intervention*, 94–96; Thompson, *Wilson*, 121–22.
81. Wilson to House, May 16, 1916, *Wilson Papers* 37:57–58; July 24, 1916, ibid., 467.

The neutrality crises provoked sweeping reassessments of the most basic principles of U.S. defense and foreign policies. In 1915–16, Americans heatedly debated the adequacy of their military preparedness, the first time since the 1790s that national security concerns had assumed such prominence in U.S. political discourse.[82] Preparedness advocates, many of them eastern Republicans representing the great financial and industrial interests, insisted that America's defenses were inadequate for a new and dangerous age. Claiming that military training would also Americanize new immigrants and toughen the nation's youth, they pushed for expansion of the army and navy. They promoted their cause with parades, books, and scare films such as *Battle Cry for Peace*, which portrayed in the most graphic fashion an invasion of New York City by enemy troops unnamed but easily identifiable as German by their spiked helmets.

On the other side, pacifists, social reformers, and southern and midwestern agrarians denounced preparedness as a scheme to fatten the pockets of big business and fasten militarism on the nation. They professed to favor "real defense against real dangers, but not a preposterous 'preparedness' against hypothetical dangers." They warned that the programs being considered would be a giant step toward war.[83] Popular songs such as "I Didn't Raise My Boy to Be a Soldier" expressed their sentiments. The divisions were reflected in Congress, where by early 1916 Wilson's proposals for "reasonable" increases in the armed services were mired in controversy.

Fearful that America might be drawn into war and facing reelection, Wilson in 1916 belatedly assumed leadership of a cause he had previously spurned, breaking one of the most difficult legislative logjams of his first term. To build support for his program, he went on a speaking tour of the Northeast and Middle West, seeking to educate the nation to the dangers posed by a world at war. To thunderous ovations, he called for increased military expenditures—even at one point for "incomparably the greatest navy in the world." Returning to Washington, he skillfully steered legislation through a divided Congress. "No man ought to say to any legislative body 'You must take my plan or none at all,'" he proclaimed on one occasion, a striking statement given the stand he would take on the League of Nations in 1919. The National Defense Act of June 1916 increased the regular army to 223,000 over a five-year period. It strengthened the National Guard to 450,000 men and tightened federal controls. A Naval Expansion Act established a three-year construction program including

82. Knock, *End All Wars*, 58.
83. Jane Addams et al to Wilson, October 29, 1915, *Wilson Papers* 35:134.

four dreadnought battleships and eight cruisers the first year. Ardent preparedness advocates such as Theodore Roosevelt dismissed Wilson's program as "flintlock legislation," measures more appropriate for the eighteenth century than for the twentieth. "The United States today becomes
the most militaristic naval nation on earth," critics screamed from the
other extreme. In fact, Wilson's compromise perfectly suited the national
mood and significantly expanded U.S. military power. A remarkably progressive revenue act appeased leftist critics by shifting almost the entire
burden to the wealthy with a surtax and estate tax.[84]

The Great War also sparked a debate over basic foreign policy principles that would rage until World War II and persist in modified form
thereafter. Breaking with hallowed tradition, those who came to be called
internationalists insisted that the American way of life could be preserved
only through active, permanent involvement in world politics. Conservative internationalists such as former president William Howard Taft
and senior statesman Elihu Root, mostly Republicans and upper-class
men of influence, had long promoted international law and arbitration.
In response to the war, they embraced still vague notions of collective security. Generally pro-Allied, they saw defeat of Germany as an essential
first step toward a new world order. In June 1915, during the *Lusitania*
crisis, Taft announced formation of a League to Enforce Peace to promote the creation of a world parliament, of which the United States
would be a member, that would modify international law and use arbitration to resolve disputes. The conservatives also supported a buildup of
U.S. military power and its use to protect the nation's vital interests.
Progressive internationalists, on the other hand, fervently insisted that
peace was essential to ensure advancement of domestic reforms they
held dear: better working conditions for labor; social justice legislation;
women's rights. Liberal reformers such as social worker Jane Addams
and journalist Oswald Garrison Villard vigorously pushed for ending the
Great War by negotiation, eliminating the arms race and economic causes
of war, compulsory arbitration, the use of sanctions to deter and punish
aggression, and establishing a "concert of nations" to replace the balance
of power.[85]

In response to the new internationalism, a self-conscious isolationism
began to take form, and the word *isolationism* became firmly implanted
in the nation's political vocabulary. Previously, non-involvement in

84. Knock, *End All Wars*, 90; George C. Herring Jr., "James Hay and the Preparedness
    Controversy," *Journal of Southern History* 30 (November 1964), 383–404.
85. Knock, *End All Wars*, 50–58.

European politics and wars had been a given. But the threat posed by the Great War and the emergence of internationalist sentiment gave rise to an ideology of isolationism, promoted most fervently by Bryan, to preserve America's long-standing tradition of non-involvement as a way of safeguarding the nation's way of life.[86]

While Democratic Party zealots during the election campaign of 1916 vigorously pushed the slogan "He Kept Us Out of War," Wilson began to articulate an internationalist position and also the revolutionary concept that the United States should assume a leadership position in world affairs. In a June 1916 speech Colonel House described as a "land mark in history," he vowed U.S. willingness to "become a partner in any feasible association of nations" to maintain the peace.[87] "We are part of the world," he proclaimed in Omaha in early October; "nothing that concerns the whole world can be indifferent to us." The "great catastrophe" brought about by the war, he added later in the day, compelled Americans to recognize that they lived in a "new age" and must therefore operate "not according to the traditions of the past, but according to the necessities of the present and the prophecies of the future." The United States could no longer refuse to play the "great part in the world which was providentially cut out for her. ... We have got to serve the world."[88]

Shortly after his narrow reelection victory over Republican Charles Evans Hughes, a gloomy Wilson, fearing that the United States might be dragged into war, redoubled his efforts to end the European struggle. Twice previously, he had sent House—"my second personality"—on peace missions to Europe. His hands strengthened by reelection, he began to promote a general peace agreement including a major role for the United States. In December 1916, he invited both sides to state their war aims and accept U.S. good offices in negotiating a settlement.

In a dramatic January 22, 1917, address to the Senate, Wilson sketched out his revolutionary ideas for a just peace and a new world order. To the belligerents, he eloquently appealed for a "peace without victory," the only way to ensure that the loser's quest for revenge did not spark another war. In terms of the postwar world, a "community of power" must replace the balance of power, the old order of militarism, and power politics. The equality of nations great and small must be recognized. No nation should impose its authority on another. A new world order must guarantee freedom of the seas, limit armaments, and ensure the right of all peoples to

86. Cooper, "Shock of Recognition," 579–81.
87. Knock, *End All Wars*, 77.
88. Wilson speeches, October 5, 1916, *Wilson Papers* 38:337–38, 347.

form their own government. Most important, Wilson advocated a "covenant" for an international organization to ensure that "no such catastrophe shall ever overwhelm us again." Speaking to his domestic audience, the president advanced the notion, still heretical to most Americans, that their nation must play a key role in making and sustaining the postwar settlement. Without its participation, he averred, no "covenant of cooperative peace" could "keep the future safe without war." He also stressed to his domestic audience that his proposals accorded with American traditions. The principles of "President Monroe" would become the "doctrine of the world." "These are American principles, American policies…," he concluded in ringing phrases. "They are the principles of mankind and must prevail."[89]

Wilson's speech was "at once breathtaking in the audacity of its vision of a new world order," historian Robert Zieger has written, "and curiously detached from the bitter realities of Europe's battlefields."[90] His efforts to promote negotiations failed. His equating of Allied war aims with those of Germany outraged London and Paris. When the blatantly pro-Allied Lansing sought to repair the damage with an unauthorized public statement, he infuriated Wilson and aroused German suspicions. In any event, by early 1917, none of the belligerents would accept U.S. mediation or a compromise peace. Both sides had suffered horribly in the ratinfested, disease-ridden trenches of Europe — "this vast gruesome contest of systematized destruction," Wilson called it.[91] The battles of attrition of 1916 were especially appalling. Britain suffered four hundred thousand casualties in the Somme offensive, sixty thousand in a single day, with no change in its tactical position. Germans called the five-month struggle for Verdun "the sausage grinder"; the French labeled it "the furnace." It cost both sides nearly a million casualties. German and French killed at Verdun together exceeded the total dead for the American Civil War.[92] By the end of the year, both sides were exhausted.

As investments of blood and treasure mounted, attitudes hardened. In December 1916, David Lloyd George, who had vowed to fight to a "knockout," assumed leadership of a coalition government in Britain and responded to Wilson's overture with a list of conditions unacceptable to the Central Powers. The Germans made clear they would state their war aims only at

89. "Peace Without Victory" speech, January 22, 1917, ibid. 40:533–39.
90. Robert H. Zieger, *America's Great War: World War I and the American Experience* (Lanham, Md., 2000), 48.
91. Knock, *End All Wars*, 107.
92. My thanks to Thomas Knock for sharing this information with me.

a general conference to which Wilson would not be invited. In the meantime, more ominously, German leaders finally acceded to the navy's argument that with one hundred U-boats now available an all-out submarine campaign could win the war before U.S. intervention had any effect. On January 31, Berlin announced the beginning of unrestricted submarine warfare.[93]

Wilson faced an awful dilemma. Stunned by these developments, he privately labeled Germany a "madman that should be curbed." But he was loath to go to war. He still believed that a compromise peace through which neither side emerged triumphant would be best calculated to promote a stable postwar world. It would be a "crime," he observed, for the United States to "involve itself in the war to such an extent as to make it impossible to save Europe afterward." In view of his earlier threats, he had no choice but to break relations with Germany, and he did so on February 3. Despite the urging of House and Lansing, he still refused to ask for a declaration of war. He continued to insist that he could have greater influence as a neutral mediator than as a belligerent. He recognized that his nation remained deeply divided and that many Americans opposed going to war. As late as February 25 he charged the war hawks in his cabinet with operating on the outdated principles of the "Code Duello."[94]

Events drove him to the fateful decision. The infamous Zimmermann Telegram, leaked to the United States by Britain in late February, revealed that Germany had offered Mexico an alliance in return for which it might "reconquer its former territories in Texas, New Mexico, and Arizona." The document fanned anti-German sentiment in America and increased Wilson's already pronounced distrust of Berlin.[95] In mid-March, U-boats sank three U.S. merchant vessels with the loss of fifteen American lives. For all practical purposes, Germany was at war with the United States. Reluctantly and most painfully, Wilson concluded that war could not be avoided. The Germans had repeatedly and brutally violated American rights on the high seas. A failure to respond after his previous threats would undermine his position abroad and open him to political attack at home. Wilson had long since concluded that the United States must play a central role in the peacemaking. Surrender on the U-boat issue would demonstrate its unworthiness for that role. Germany's own repeated violation of its promises and its intrigues as evidenced in the Zimmermann Telegram made clear to Wilson that it could not be trusted. Only through

93. May, *World War*, 404–15.
94. Franklin Lane to W. Lane, February 5, 1917, *Wilson Papers* 41:282.
95. Katz, *Secret War*, 350–78.

active intervention, he now rationalized, could U.S. influence be used to establish a just postwar order. War was unpalatable, but at least it would give the United States a voice at the peace table. Otherwise, he told Addams, he could only "call through a crack in the door."[96] Moving slowly to allow public opinion to coalesce behind him, Wilson concluded by late March that he must intervene in the war.

On April 2, 1917, the president appeared before packed chambers of Congress to ask for a declaration of war against Germany. In a thirty-six-minute speech, he condemned Germany's "cruel and unmanly" violation of American rights and branded its "wanton and wholesale destruction of the lives of non-combatants" as "warfare against mankind." The United States could not "choose the path of submission," he observed. It must accept the state of war that had "been thrust upon it." He concluded with soaring rhetoric that would echo through the ages. "It is a fearful thing to lead this great peaceful people into war," he conceded. But "the right is more precious than peace, and we shall fight for the things which we have always carried dearest to our hearts, for democracy, for the right of those who submit to authority to have a voice in their own Governments, for the rights and liberties of small nations, for a universal dominion of right by such a concert of free people as shall bring peace and safety to all nations and make the world itself at last free." As critics have repeatedly emphasized, Wilson set goals beyond the ability of any person or nation to achieve. Perhaps he felt such lofty aims were necessary to rally a still-divided nation to take action unprecedented in its history. He may have aimed so high to justify in his own mind the horrors he knew a war would bring. In any event, he set for himself and his nation an impossible task that would bring great disillusionment.[97]

IV

Germany's gamble to win the war before the United States intervened in force nearly succeeded. Adhering to the nation's long-standing tradition of non-entanglement and in order to retain maximum diplomatic freedom of action, Wilson and General Pershing insisted that Americans fight separately under their own command rather than being integrated into Allied armies. It took months to raise, equip, and train a U.S. army and then transport it to Europe. A token force of "doughboys" paraded in Paris on July 4, 1917, but it would be more than a year before the United States could throw even minimal weight into the fray. In the meantime, buoyed

96. Knock, *End All Wars*, 120.
97. "Wilson War Message," April 2, 1917, *Wilson Papers* 41:519–27.

by promises of future U.S. help, France and Britain launched disastrous summer 1917 offensives. French defeats provoked mutinies that sapped the army's will to fight. Allied setbacks in the west combined with the Bolshevik seizure of power in late 1917 and Russia's subsequent withdrawal from the war gave the Central Powers a momentary edge. Facing serious morale problems at home from the Allied blockade, Germany mounted an end-the-war offensive in the spring of 1918.

It was a transformative moment in the war.[98] The German army again drove close to Paris, but it could not break through Allied lines and suffered irreplaceable losses. The addition of 850,000 fresh U.S. troops made possible an Allied summer counteroffensive. More important, as the German high command conceded, huge numbers of Americans arriving at the front produced foreboding of defeat.[99]

Long before the fighting ended, Wilson had begun to fashion a liberal peace program to reshape the postwar world. The ideas he advanced were not original with him. Even before the founding of the nation, Americans believed they had a special destiny to redeem the world. Prior to 1914, European, British, and American thinkers had dreamed of reforming international politics, a task made urgent by the horrors of the Great War. But Wilson promoted these ideas with a special fervor and eloquence and made himself their leading spokesman. In the process, he formulated and articulated a set of principles that would bear his name—Wilsonianism—and would influence U.S. foreign policy and world politics for years to come.

In Wilson's view, the war provided that opportunity for world leadership for which Americans had been preparing themselves since the birth of the nation. The death and destruction visited upon Europe made clear the bankruptcy of the old order. Scientific and technological advances created the means to uplift the human race. The United States must therefore take the lead in building a better world. "We are participants, whether we would or not, in the life of the world," Wilson affirmed in 1916. Replacing traditional American unilateralism with a universalist view, he insisted that "the interests of all nations are our own also. We are partners with the rest. What affects mankind is inevitably our affair."[100]

Wilson insisted that a just and lasting peace must be constructed along American lines. He assumed the superiority of Western civilization and the continued dominance of the West. But he believed that European

98. Keegan, *World War I*, 373.
99. Ibid., 410–11.
100. "Peace Without Victory" speech, January 27, 1917, *Wilson Papers* 40:539.

imperialism had exploited helpless peoples and generated explosive tensions among the great powers. Old World diplomacy had produced only "aggression, egotism, and war." Economic nationalism, with its tariff wars and exclusive, monopolistic trading arrangements, had exacerbated international conflict. Wilson found equally abhorrent the radical notions of Bolshevik leader Vladimir Lenin, who had seized power in Russia in late 1917, that the international system could be freed of war only by a worldwide revolution that eliminated capitalism. He firmly believed in American exceptionalism. Only a world reformed along liberal-capitalist lines would serve the United States and the broader interests of mankind. Economic nationalism must give way to a commercial internationalism in which all nations had equal access to the markets and raw materials of the world, tariff barriers were eliminated, and freedom of the seas guaranteed. Colonial empires should eventually be dissolved and all peoples given the right to determine their own destiny. Power politics must be replaced by a new world order maintained by an organization of like-minded nations joined to resolve disputes and prevent aggression—"not a balance of power but a community of power."[101]

In a series of public statements, most notably in his Fourteen Points address of January 8, 1918, Wilson molded these broad principles into a peace program. Called by the *New York Herald* "one of the great documents in American history," the speech responded to Lenin's revelations of the Allied secret treaties dividing the spoils of war and his calls for an end to imperialism as well as a speech by Lloyd George setting out broad peace terms. Wilson sought to regain the initiative for the United States and rally Americans and Allied peoples behind his peace program. He called for "open covenants of peace, openly arrived at." He reiterated his commitment to arms limitations, freedom of the seas, and reduction of trade barriers. On colonial issues, to avoid alienating the Allies, he sought a middle ground between the old-style imperialism of the secret treaties and Lenin's call for an end to empire. He did not use the word *self-determination*, but he did insist that in dealing with colonial claims the "interests" of colonial peoples should be taken into account, a marked departure from the status quo. He also set forth broad principles for European territorial settlements—a sharp break from the U.S. tradition of non-involvement in European affairs. The peoples of the Austro-Hungarian and Ottoman empires should be assured "an absolutely unmolested opportunity of autonomous development." Belgium must be evacuated, territory

---

101. N. Gordon Levin Jr., *Woodrow Wilson and World Politics: America's Response to War and Revolution* (New York, 1968), 61–64.

formerly belonging to France restored. A "general association of nations" must be established to preserve the peace.[102]

Germany was the key, and here Wilson had to balance his desire for an early end to the war against the need to keep the alliance together and palliate the Allies and Republican war hawks at home. As a belligerent, he abandoned of necessity his "peace without victory" stance of 1917. He came to blame Germany more for the origins of the war and view German autocracy and militarism as threats to the peace. While continuing to seek "impartial justice," he concluded that Germany must be defeated and its government purged of autocratic and expansionist elements. A reformed Germany could be reintegrated into the community of nations.[103]

From the time the United States entered the war, Wilson worked tirelessly to achieve a peace along these lines. Recognizing their mutual dependence and hoping to establish a solid basis for postwar collaboration, he actively promoted cooperation with the Allies, pushing his military leaders to work closely with the British and French and agreeing to a unified command. American and Allied scientists shared information and collaborated in solving problems such as the U-boat, chemical warfare, camouflage, and signals.[104] Aware, on the other hand, of the Allied secret treaties and deferring to America's unilateralist tradition, he carefully maintained his freedom of action, making clear that his nation was fighting for its own reasons, refusing to join a formal alliance, and even referring to the United States as an "Associated" rather than "Allied" power. In the best tradition of the 1776 Model Treaty, he declined to appoint a *political* representative to the Allied Supreme War Council.[105]

The administration in late 1917 mounted a major overseas propaganda program, the first such effort in U.S. history.[106] Under the leadership of the zealous journalist George Creel, a Committee on Public Information (CPI) had already begun drumming up support for the war at home.

---

102. Fourteen Points address, January 8, 1918, *Wilson Papers* 40:534–39; Knock, *End All Wars*, 142–47.
103. Arthur S. Link, *Woodrow Wilson: Revolution, War and Peace* (Arlington Heights, Ill., 1979), 85; Thompson, *Wilson*, 157–60.
104. Calhoun, *Power and Principle*, 167–74; Roy MacLeod, "Secrets Among Friends: The Research Information Service and the Special Relationship in Allied Scientific Information and Intelligence," *Minerva: A Review of Science, Learning, and Policy* 37 (Autumn 1999), 201–33.
105. Link, *Revolution, War, and Peace*, 76–77; Calhoun, *Power and Principle*, 178–79.
106. Gregg Wolper, "Wilsonian Public Diplomacy: The Committee on Public Information in Spain," *Diplomatic History* 17 (Winter 1993), 17.

Wilson soon extended the program abroad to counter German propaganda and educate world opinion about his peace principles. In the major cities of Europe and Latin America and in revolutionary Russia and China, hastily established CPI offices translated stories from the U.S. press for placement in local newspapers, distributed photographs and war posters, and in some areas showed films such as *America's Answer*, a depiction of the arrival of U.S. troops in France and their movement to the western front. Wilson's speeches were translated and widely distributed in books and pamphlets.[107] The CPI campaign won some support for the Allied cause and for Wilson's peace aims. It also raised hopes among peoples throughout the world. Abroad as at home, Wilson conceded to Creel, U.S. propaganda had "unconsciously spun a net for me from which there is no escape," high expectations that could lead to a "tragedy of disappointment."[108]

Wilson also had to contend with a Russia torn by war and revolution. He cheered the overthrow of the tsarist regime in March 1917, declaring the newly formed and moderate Provisional Government a "fit partner" for a "league of honor" and quickly recognizing it. He also sought to boost its prestige by sending to Petrograd a mission headed by Elihu Root. With characteristic American optimism and abysmal misunderstanding of what was happening, Root reported that the government could survive and even continue the war with limited U.S. assistance. Wilson promised $450 million in aid (of which $188 million was actually transferred) and dispatched transportation experts to keep the railroads going, a YMCA mission to boost army morale, and a Red Cross team to provide relief and, on the side, encourage the people to back the government and continue the war. Such well-intentioned gestures had little impact on a complex and fluid situation. Lenin's Bolsheviks overthrew the shaky Provisional Government in November, sparking a prolonged civil war. The new rulers in March 1918 negotiated a separate peace, allowing Germany to shift forces to the western front.[109]

After six months of relentless pressure from the Allies and much "sweating blood" on his part, Wilson in July 1918 reluctantly agreed to interventions

107. Ibid., 17–34; James D. Stratt, "American Propaganda in Britain During World War I," *Prologue* 28 (Spring 1996), 17–33; Kazuyuki Matsuo, "American Propaganda in China: The U.S. Committee on Public Information, 1918–1919," *Journal of American-Canadian Studies* 14 (1996), 19–42.

108. Matsuo, "Propaganda," 21.

109. John Lewis Gaddis, *Russia, the Soviet Union, and the United States: An Interpretive History* (2nd ed., New York, 1990), 61–63.

in Siberia and North Russia.[110] The operations occurred under very con-fused circumstances; the motives behind them and Wilson's support for them remain elusive. In early 1918, the Allies began to advocate interven-tion in Siberia to keep the eastern port of Vladivostok open and vital sup-plies out of German hands. Subsequently, they pushed for intervention at the northern ports of Murmansk and Archangel and urged support for a seventy-thousand-man Czech Legion committed to fighting the Central Powers—and also the Bolsheviks. Stunned and outraged by Lenin's sepa-rate peace, Allied leaders desperately sought to sustain some kind of east-ern front against Germany.

Wilson sympathized on this point. As much as he understood Bolshevism, moreover, he despised it. He never felt Lenin's regime represented the Russian people. He refused to recognize it. Following the November Revolution, the administration continued to channel funds and supplies to anti-Bolshevik forces through the Provisional Government embassy in Washington and reimbursed the British for their aid. But Wilson was keenly aware from his own travails in Mexico the limits of military force in solving complex political problems. He feared that interference in Russia, as in Mexico, might actually solidify Bolshevik control. In June 1918, precisely when German forces advanced to within artillery range of Paris, he acceded to Allied pressure. Wilson wanted to demonstrate that he was a "good ally," thus establishing a basis for postwar cooperation.[111] He also hoped that the twenty thousand U.S. troops he sent to Siberia would help thwart any Japanese ambitions in that region. When the Czech Legion reached Vladivostok in June, threw out the Bolshevik gov-ernment, and vowed to fight with the Allies, he saw the "shadow of a plan" for a viable eastern front and felt a moral obligation to aid the Czechs. If Russians rallied around their "slavic kinsmen" against the Bolsheviks, so much the better, although he placed strict limits on the number of U.S. troops and the ways they could be used. He convinced himself that lim-ited and indirect Allied aid might inspire representatives of the "Real Russia" to rally against the Bolsheviks and would thus be an act of libera-tion rather than interference.[112] The United States did not intervene suffi-ciently to influence events in Russia. Its intervention did feed the myth among Soviet propagandists and some revisionist historians that Wilson had sought to overthrow the Bolshevik government.

---

110. Knock, *End All Wars*, 156.
111. Calhoun, *Power and Principle*, 199–200.
112. David S. Fogelsong, *America's Secret War Against Bolshevism: U.S. Intervention in the Russian Civil War* (Chapel Hill, N.C., 1996), 190–91.

The autumn of 1918, in historian Arthur Walworth's apt phrase, was "America's moment."[113] By the summer, the United States had more than a million troops in Europe, with another three million in training. At Château-Thierry in June, U.S. forces helped blunt the German drive toward Paris. In the late summer and early fall, the doughboys played a key role in the Allied counteroffensive that forced the Germans back to the Hindenburg Line. The mere presence of huge numbers of fresh U.S. troops had a hugely demoralizing effect on an exhausted German army.[114] The United States thus determined the outcome of the war. And under Wilson's leadership, it was poised to shape the peace. Inspired by the president's vision of their nation's new role and by the chance for leadership and constructive achievement, Americans excitedly took up the challenge. As early as January 1918, preparing for the Fourteen Points address, House boasted of "remaking the map of the world" in two hours. A "remarkably productive morning!" he added.[115] Lansing's nephew Allen Dulles waxed eloquent about "pulchritudinous [American] youth" taking up the "greatest obligation and opportunity that a nation ever had....We are called to put the world in order again."[116] The Americans would soon learn that huge expectations and intractable problems were an integral part of their new world role.

Negotiations for an armistice with Germany revealed the challenges that lay ahead and the conflict between Wilson's hopes for an enduring peace and his appeals for a crusade against German autocracy. Seeking to divide the Allies and salvage some semblance of victory, a dispirited Germany in early October approached Wilson directly for an armistice based on the Fourteen Points. A new parliamentary government sought to avoid the punitive terms favored by Britain and France and was prepared to make concessions.

Wilson's position was extremely delicate. He still believed that a fair peace was the best way to end the war. At home, however, he faced congressional elections that would affect his ability to negotiate a settlement and sell a League of Nations to his own people. His Republican foes vigorously pressed for a hard line against Germany. Wilson also recognized that the Allies wanted a victor's peace, sought territorial gains at Germany's expense, and preferred to leave the armistice to the military to ensure that

113. Arthur Walworth, *America's Moment, 1918: American Diplomacy at the End of World War I* (New York, 1977).
114. Keegan, *First World War*, 410–14.
115. Knock, *End All Wars*, 142.
116. Peter Grose, *Gentleman Spy: The Life of Allen Dulles* (Boston, 1994), 35, 45.

Germany could not use a cease-fire to prepare for resumption of the war. He proceeded with great caution, exploring Germany's commitment to the Fourteen Points and its willingness to evacuate territory then held. He told a skeptical Democratic senator that he was thinking of "a hundred years hence." When advised that if he was too conciliatory he might be destroyed politically, he retorted that "I am willing if I can serve my country to go into a cellar and read poetry for the remainder of my life."[117] Under pressure from the Allies and critics at home and eager to gain control of the peace process, he gradually toughened his stance, at one point even acceding to Allied occupation of German territory and insisting that Germany's "military masters and the monarchical autocrats" must go.[118] He sent House to deal with the Allies, instructing him only that he would know what to do.

The armistice emerging from these confused triangular discussions ended the fighting but also set the tone for what would follow. House confronted vengeful Allies who feigned ignorance of the Fourteen Points. After difficult negotiations, he secured their agreement in principle, but Britain reserved the right to interpret freedom of the seas, and France insisted that Germany must compensate the Allies for civilian and property losses. The military was to handle the armistice, opening the way for occupation of German territory. House claimed a "great diplomatic victory." Under the circumstances, he may have got as much as could be expected. But it was not what Wilson had envisioned, and it opened the way for more serious problems. The fundamental contradiction between Wilson's desire to join with the Allies in defeating Germany and mediate between the two sides made it difficult if not impossible for him to achieve his lofty goals.[119]

Greater challenges awaited in Paris, where the peace conference opened on January 12, 1919. In heading the U.S. delegation himself, Wilson broke precedent, becoming the first president to go to Europe while in office and personally to conduct major negotiations. He remained abroad for more than six months, with only a two-week interlude in the United States, suggesting the extent to which foreign relations now dominated his agenda. The president has often been criticized for this initial venture in summit diplomacy. To be sure, his deep personal involvement deprived

117. Thompson, *Wilson*, 175–76.
118. Ibid., 177.
119. Klaus Schwabe, "U.S. Secret War Diplomacy, Intelligence, and the Coming of the German Revolution in 1918: The Role of Vice Consul James McNally," *Diplomatic History* 16 (Spring 1992), 200.

him of the detachment that can be invaluable in negotiations and severely strained his already frail constitution. Given the urgency of the negotiations, his personality and leadership style, and the fact that British and French heads of government were leading their delegations, it is impossible to envision him acting any other way.[120]

The peacemakers confronted monumental problems. Europe lay devastated, "a laboratory resting on a vast cemetery," Czech leader Thomas Masaryk observed.[121] Old boundaries were torn asunder, leaving intractable territorial problems. The German, Austro-Hungarian, and Ottoman empires lay in ruins, raising hopes of nationhood for peoples throughout Central Europe, the Balkans, and the Middle East and leaving a powder keg of conflicting nationalist and ethnic aspirations. Anarchy prevailed in many areas. The threat of revolution hung like a storm cloud over Germany and Central Europe. A truly daunting agenda included disarming the losers, reviving European economies, confronting the Bolshevik challenge, and creating new states in Europe and the Middle East.

The passions set loose by four years of fighting further complicated the peacemaking. Excluded from the conference, the defeated Germans nervously awaited their fate, while among the victors a spirit of revenge prevailed. France had lost two million men, the most of any belligerent, suffered massive destruction to its territory, and was intent upon avenging its losses. Prime Minister Georges Clemenceau embodied his nation's spirit. "I had a wife, she abandoned me," he once snarled; "I had children, they turned against me; I had friends, they betrayed me. I have only my claws, and I use them."[122] The seventy-seven-year-old "Tiger" survived an assassin's bullet during the conference. He expressed open cynicism for the Fourteen Points. Britain too had suffered enormous losses, and although its government and its prime minister, the charming, shrewd, and hard-bitten Welshman David Lloyd George, supported much of Wilson's program, they could not go too far toward conciliating Germany without risking domestic political backlash. The Allies had sweeping imperial goals. On the other side, the war and Wilson's rhetoric raised hopes of freedom among nationalities and oppressed peoples across the world. Representatives of many different peoples—African Americans included—came to Paris in search of guarantees of racial equality. Chinese nationalists looked to the peace conference to end great-power domination of their country. The young Vietnamese patriot Nguyen Tat Than

120. Thompson, *Wilson*, 212.
121. Walworth, *America's Moment*, 1.
122. Quoted in "Fighting Men," *National Interest* 69 (Fall 2002), 129.

(later to adopt the sobriquet Ho Chi Minh) rented a tuxedo to present a petition to the conference for his country's independence. Spokespersons for Haiti and the Dominican Republic appealed to Wilson in Paris for self-determination.[123]

In dealing with these formidable problems, Wilson was hampered by an inadequate advisory system and his own leadership style. He had never liked or trusted Lansing; during the long stay in Europe, his relationship with Colonel House suffered an irreparable break. The peace commission he chose to accompany him was not a distinguished group — ex-president Taft called them a "bunch of cheapskates" — and did not play a major role. At the president's direction, House in the fall of 1917 assembled a group of scholars to analyze postwar problems, a significant and innovative effort to bring scholarly expertise to bear on foreign policy issues. The so-called Inquiry employed 150 people and produced more than three thousand papers and reports. Its Red and Black Books were extensively used in resolving numerous specific issues, especially the territorial settlements that recast the maps of Europe and the Middle East. As Wilson relied even less on the State Department, the Inquiry's importance grew.[124]

Ultimately, as was his custom, Wilson depended mainly on himself. Especially after he broke with House, he was largely on his own. Most decisions were made in small groups, the Council of Four and the Council of Ten. The so-called Big Four met 140 times between January and May. The negotiations were arduous and tension-ridden, with frequent threats from various quarters, Wilson included, to bolt the conference. On one occasion, Clemenceau and Lloyd George came close to fisticuffs. After his February trip to the United States, Wilson also recognized that he would face stern opposition from Senate Republicans. He was sixty-three years old, in poor health, and the strain told on him. He became seriously ill in March, largely because he had pushed himself beyond normal limits. His illness may have affected his ability to function in the last stages of the conference. At times, he displayed odd behavior. He took a more hostile position than previously toward Germany; once, oddly, when Lloyd George sought to soften the Allied stand on a particular issue, he sided with Clemenceau.[125]

123. Erez Manela, *The Wilsonian Moment: Self-Determination and the International Origins of Anticolonial Nationalism* (New York, 2007), 1–51.
124. Jonathan M. Nielson, "The Scholar as Diplomat: American Historians at the Paris Peace Conference of 1919," *International History Review* 14 (May 1992), 228–51.
125. Thompson, *Wilson*, 212, minimizes the effects of Wilson's illness on the actual negotiations.

Wilson's triumphant arrival in Europe could not but have led him to overestimate the leverage he would have in dealing with his Allied counterparts. His ship, the *George Washington* (a captured and renamed German luxury liner), docked at Brest on December 13, 1918—the president considered thirteen his lucky number. Banners welcomed the "Champion of the Rights of Man," the "Founder of the Society of Nations." The moaning sounds of bagpipes resounded amidst shouts of "*Vive l'Amérique! Vive Wilson!*" According to one observer, the president's reception in Paris, where crowds lined the Place de Concorde and the Champs-Elysées to view him, was "the most remarkable demonstration of enthusiasm and affection...that I have ever heard of, let alone seen."[126] This scene was replicated in London and Manchester, Rome, Genoa, Milan, and Turin. Hailed across the Continent almost as a messiah, Wilson, according to British economist and future critic John Maynard Keynes, "enjoyed a prestige and moral influence throughout the world unequaled in history."[127] The exuberant greeting misled him to believe that Allied peoples supported his aims regardless of where their leaders stood.

Wilson in other ways seems to have exaggerated his bargaining power. Early in the war, he had confidently predicted that the Allies would be "financially in our hands" and thus could be brought around "to our way of thinking." The Allies in fact owed more than $10 billion to the U.S. government and private bankers, but such leverage worked both ways. The U.S. economy came to depend on war orders from Britain and France. European debts provided useable leverage only if the United States was willing to forgive them, which was never an option.[128] At times, Wilson seemed to believe that the threat of a separate peace with Germany might force the Allies to go along with his proposals, but once the armistice had been arranged this weapon lost its potency. Wilson's negotiating position had been compromised before he arrived in Europe. Responding to pleas from fellow Democrats and seeking to build support for his peace plans, he made a blatantly partisan appeal for the election of a Democratic Congress. Republican victories in the 1918 elections weakened him in dealing with European leaders. His commitment above all to a League of Nations and his insistence on including its charter in the treaty gave his adversaries precious leverage over him. The United States emerged from

126. Margaret Macmillan, *Paris 1919: Six Months That Changed the World* (New York, 2003), 15–16.
127. Manela, *Wilsonian Moment*, 45.
128. Clements, *Wilson Presidency*, 174; Thompson, *Wilson*, 191–93. 129.

the war relatively much stronger, but it was not powerful enough to impose its will on other nations. The Allies were in a position to ignore him when they so chose.[129]

Amidst these difficulties, Wilson sought to negotiate a lasting peace. Germany was the most difficult problem, and the terms eventually settled upon represented a compromise between France's quest for vengeance and future security and Wilson's pleas for a just peace. Clemenceau ultimately yielded his demands for dismemberment of Germany and permanent occupation of parts of it. But the Allies agreed to fixed limits on German military power, temporary occupation of the Rhineland and the Saar Basin, and an Anglo-American pledge (quite unprecedented for the United States) to aid France in the event of German attack. Wilson refused Allied demands that Germany pay the entire cost of the war. Under enormous pressure from France and Britain, however, and in his anti-German phase, he went along with the notorious "war guilt clause," drafted by another Lansing nephew, future U.S. secretary of state John Foster Dulles, which placed responsibility on Germany for all the damages caused by the war. He reluctantly agreed that Germany should pay extensive reparations, the figure to be fixed by a separate commission. He made such concessions mainly because Clemenceau and Lloyd George repeatedly insisted that their people demanded them. He also needed to give them something to secure their support for changes Americans such as Taft insisted must be made in the League of Nations. When Lloyd George belatedly tried to soften the terms, Wilson stood firmly with Clemenceau, indicating his belief that Germany had earned a "hard peace."[130]

In disposing of the German and Ottoman empires, Wilson confronted stiff resistance from the Allies, who had made secret commitments to each other and Japan. To avert the seemingly inevitable land grab, he proposed that the former German and Ottoman colonies should be governed through "mandates," by which advanced nations operating under the aegis of the League of Nations would serve as trustees to prepare the colonial areas for independence. The European allies and Japan at first adamantly resisted but eventually went along, perhaps confident that mandates could be used to advance their aims. In the Middle East and Africa, the Allies snapped up former enemy colonies. The mandate system proved little more than annexation in disguise.

129. Macmillan, *Paris 1919*, xxx; Thompson, *Wilson*, 191–93.
130. Thompson, *Wilson*, 210; Macmillan, *Paris*, *1919*, 459–83; Clements, *Wilson Presidency*, 179–82, 186.

Wilson's most damaging concession politically was on the Chinese province of Shandong, which Japan had seized from Germany in 1914. Chinese nationalists demanded restoration of the birthplace of Confucius, "the cradle of Chinese civilization," they called it, a "dagger pointed at the heart of China."[131] Throughout the world, Shandong became an emotionally charged symbol of Wilson's failure to honor self-determination. Already angry that the Big Four had rejected their proposal for a clause on racial equality, the Japanese threatened to leave the conference and stay out of the League if they were not permitted to "carry out their obligations to China."[132] To secure their endorsement of the treaty, Wilson accepted their verbal assurances that Chinese sovereignty would be restored by 1922. It was the "best that could be accomplished out of a 'dirty past,'" he told his physician.[133] On the other hand, the president resisted Italy's demands for Fiume on the Adriatic and appealed to the Italian people over the heads of their leaders, provoking anti-American demonstrations across Italy and Prime Minister Vittorio Orlando's departure from Paris.

Redrawing the maps of Central Europe and the Balkans posed special problems. The term *self-determination* had never been defined with any clarity, and its practical application in regions of mixed nationalities and ethnic groups proved nightmarish. Wilson admitted that he had no idea what demons the concept would unleash. The peacemakers established a number of new independent nations, including Poland, to which Wilson was deeply committed, Yugoslavia, and Czechoslovakia, not only to satisfy nationalist aspirations but also to create buffers between Germany and Russia. They attempted to draw boundary lines on the basis of ethnic considerations and collaborated in containing a Communist revolution in Hungary. But large numbers of Germans still lived in some of the new states; some also included ethnic groups that despised each other. The settlements left old problems unresolved and created new ones, setting off conflicts that would vex international relations into the next century.[134]

Although it was not on the agenda, the Russian problem, in delegate Herbert Hoover's words, was "the Banquo's ghost sitting at every conference

131. Macmillan, *Paris 1919*, 334; Stephen G. Craft, "John Bassett Moore, Robert Lansing, and the Shandong Question," *Pacific Historical Review* 66 (May 1997), 239.

132. Noriko Kawamura, "Wilsonian Idealism and Japanese Claims at the Paris Peace Conference," *Pacific Historical Review* 66 (November 1997), 524.

133. Knock, *End All Wars*, 250.

134. Macmillan, *Paris 1919*, 109–42, 207–70; Betty Miller Unterberger, "The United States and National Self-Determination: A Wilsonian Perspective," *Presidential Studies Quarterly* 26 (Fall 1996), 926–41.

table."[135] Preoccupied with other issues, the Allies never developed a consistent policy toward revolutionary Russia. Efforts to arrange meetings with Bolshevik leaders failed, in part because of Big Four absorption in matters deemed more pressing. Russia's exclusion from the conference seriously weakened the settlement. The end of the war eliminated much of the rationale for the military interventions. Confronted with rising political opposition at home and declining morale and even the threat of mutiny among the troops, Wilson withdrew U.S. forces from North Russia in June 1919. Americans remained in Siberia for almost another year.

Wilson could never quite make up his mind what to do with Bolshevik Russia. He had learned from Mexico the limits of military intervention. He stubbornly rejected various Allied proposals, including one by British cabinet officer Winston Churchill, to eliminate the Bolshevik government through a full-fledged military effort—"trying to stop a revolutionary movement by troops in the field is like using a broom to hold back a great ocean," he snapped.[136] He distrusted opposition leader Adm. Alexander Kolchak and feared a return to traditional Russian autocracy. Yet, as in Mexico, he continued to delude himself that limited intervention was not intervention at all. He may have hoped that the Bolshevik government would collapse of its own weight. He persisted in sending clandestine military aid to opposition forces through the still-functioning Washington embassy of the Provisional Government. Persuaded that food was "the real thing" to combat Bolshevism, he also authorized the American Red Cross and Hoover's American Relief Administration to distribute food and other relief supplies to anti-Bolshevik forces in the Baltic region. The United States did just enough to anger the Bolsheviks but not nearly enough to achieve the aim of a non-Communist Russia.[137]

Committed above all to establishing a workable League of Nations, Wilson justified concessions on other issues to attain that goal. He also hoped that a strong League in time would modify the harsh terms of the treaty and resolve issues left unsettled. In designing an international organization, the president had to struggle with people like Lansing, who opposed any commitments, and with the French, who preferred to maintain the wartime alliance. He finally secured Allied agreement to a League composed of an Assembly of all nations and a Council made up of the five victorious powers and four other nations elected by the Assembly. It would be empowered to supervise the mandated territories, encourage peaceful

135. Gaddis, *Russia, the Soviet Union, and the United States*, 78.
136. Link, *Revolution, War, and Peace*, 96.
137. Fogelsong, *Secret War*, 187.

resolution of disputes through arbitration and adjudication—the key peacekeeping provisions, in Wilson's mind—and employ economic and military sanctions against aggressors. The most controversial provision was a collective security mechanism that Wilson hoped would "disentangle all the alliances in the world." Article X provided that member nations would "respect and preserve as against external aggression the political integrity and existing political independence of all Members of the League." Although painfully aware of the treaty's shortcomings, Wilson was pleased with his accomplishment. The League was a "living thing...," he said, "a definite guarantee of peace...against the things which have just come near bringing the whole structure of civilization into ruin."[138]

The peace settlement evoked cries of protest from many quarters. Having never seen Allied armies or experienced occupation, most Germans deluded themselves that they had not been defeated. They viewed the treaty as vengeful and punitive and claimed to have been betrayed. Flags flew at half mast. Germans angrily protested a "shameful treaty," "the worst act of world piracy under the flag of hypocrisy."[139] Liberals across the world expressed shock and bitterness at Wilson's seeming abandonment of the Fourteen Points. Disillusioned American progressives shared dismay at the terms of the treaty. Bolting the conference, Wilson's young, idealistic adviser William Bullitt told reporters he was going to the Riviera to lie on the beach and watch the world go to hell.[140]

Disappointment was especially keen among colonial peoples. The peacemakers in Paris focused mainly on European issues. Wilson gave little attention to the application of self-determination elsewhere. Recognizing the explosive potential of the issue, he refused to take it up with the Allies. Although sharply qualified, his rhetoric of self-determination, disseminated across the world by modern communications techniques, inspired among peoples under colonial rule hopes for freedom. Nationalists adopted his words to legitimize their cry for independence. The struggle for independence became internationalized and Wilson its unwitting champion. Oppressed people across the world looked to Paris for realization of their aspirations. Failure of the peacemakers even to acknowledge their demands naturally sparked widespread disillusion and anger. Mass protests erupted in India, Egypt, Korea, and China, among other places. "So much for national self-determination," a young library assistant, Mao Zedong, protested. "I think it is really shameless!" Across the world, an

138. Thompson, *Wilson*, 201; Link, *Revolution, War, and Peace*, 99.
139. Macmillan, *Paris 1919*, 463–65, 474.
140. Ibid., 80.

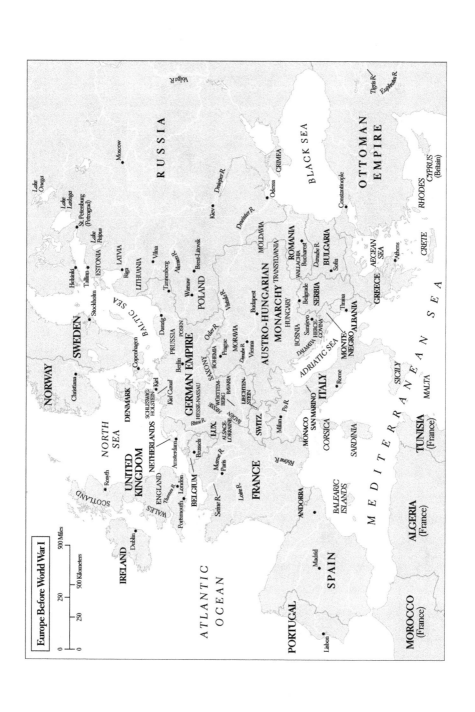

Europe Before World War I

0   250   500 Miles
0   250   500 Kilometers

ATLANTIC OCEAN

IRELAND
Dublin

SCOTLAND
Rosyth

UNITED KINGDOM
ENGLAND
WALES
Portsmouth
London
Thames R.

NORTH SEA

NORWAY
Christiana

SWEDEN
Stockholm

Lake Ladoga
Lake Onega

St. Petersburg (Petrograd)

Helsinki
Tallinn
ESTONIA
Lake Peipus

LATVIA
Riga

LITHUANIA
Vilna

RUSSIA

Moscow

Volga R.

BALTIC SEA

DENMARK
Copenhagen
SCHLESWIG-HOLSTEIN
Kiel Canal

NETHERLANDS
Amsterdam
Brussels
BELGIUM
LUX.

GERMAN EMPIRE
Berlin
PRUSSIA
POSEN
Danzig
Tannenberg
Warsaw
POLAND
Brest-Litovsk
Niemen R.

Vistula R.

Oder R.
SAXONY
BOHEMIA
Prague
MORAVIA
Vienna
Danube R.

HESSE-NASSAU
WÜRTTEM-BERG
BAVARIA
LIECHTEN-STEIN
BADEN
Rhine R.

Dnieper R.

Kiev

Dniester R.

MOLDAVIA
ROMANIA
Bucharest
WALLACHIA
Danube R.

Odessa

CRIMEA

BLACK SEA

Constantinople

OTTOMAN EMPIRE

AUSTRO-HUNGARIAN MONARCHY
TRANSYLVANIA
HUNGARY
Budapest
Belgrade
SERBIA
BOSNIA
HERCE-GOVINA
Sarajevo
DALMATIA
MONTE-NEGRO
ALBANIA
Tirana

BULGARIA
Sofia

GREECE
Athens
AEGEAN SEA

CRETE

FRANCE
Paris
Seine R.
Marne R.
Loire R.
Rhône R.

ALSACE-LORRAINE

SWITZ.

ITALY
Rome
Milan
Po R.

SAN MARINO
MONACO
CORSICA
SARDINIA

ADRIATIC SEA

SICILY
MALTA

MEDITERRANEAN SEA

TUNISIA (France)

ALGERIA (France)

MOROCCO (France)

SPAIN
Madrid

PORTUGAL
Lisbon

ANDORRA

BALEARIC ISLANDS

RHODES
CYPRUS (Britain)

Tigris R.
Euphrates R.

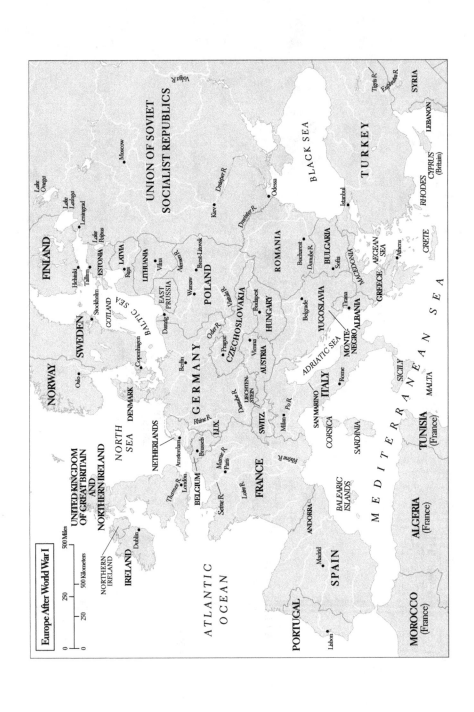

Europe After World War I

ATLANTIC
OCEAN

UNITED KINGDOM
OF GREAT BRITAIN
AND
NORTHERN IRELAND

NORTHERN
IRELAND

IRELAND
• Dublin

NORTH
SEA

NETHERLANDS

Amsterdam •
Brussels •
BELGIUM
LUX.

London •
Thames R.

Seine R.
Marne R.
Paris •
Loire R.

FRANCE

Rhône R.

ANDORRA

SPAIN
Madrid •

BALEARIC
ISLANDS

PORTUGAL
Lisbon •

MOROCCO
(France)

ALGERIA
(France)

MEDITERRANEAN   SEA

TUNISIA
(France)

CORSICA

SARDINIA

SAN MARINO

ITALY
Rome •

Milan •
Po R.

LIECHTEN-
STEIN

SWITZ.

Rhine R.
Danube R.

GERMANY
Berlin •

DENMARK

NORWAY
Oslo •

SWEDEN
Stockholm •

GOTLAND

BALTIC SEA

Copenhagen •

FINLAND
Helsinki •
Tallinn •
ESTONIA

Lake
Peipus

Lake
Onega

Lake
Ladoga
Leningrad •

UNION OF SOVIET
SOCIALIST REPUBLICS

Moscow •

Volga R.

LATVIA
Riga •

LITHUANIA
Vilna •

EAST
PRUSSIA
Danzig •

Warsaw •
POLAND

Memel R.

Brest-Litovsk •

Kiev •

Dnieper R.

Dniester R.

Odessa •

BLACK   SEA

Oder R.

Prague •
CZECHOSLOVAKIA

Vistula R.

Vienna •
AUSTRIA

Budapest •
HUNGARY

ROMANIA
Bucharest •

Danube R.

YUGOSLAVIA
Belgrade •

Tirana •
ALBANIA
MONTE-
NEGRO

ADRIATIC SEA

BULGARIA
Sofia •

MACEDONIA

GREECE
Athens •

AEGEAN
SEA

TURKEY

Istanbul •

Tigris R.
Euphrates R.

SYRIA

LEBANON

CYPRUS
(Britain)

RHODES

CRETE

SICILY

MALTA

SARDINIA

0   250   500 Miles
0   250   500 Kilometers

anti-colonial movement began to form that in time would achieve what Wilson had spoken of.[141]

Wilson recognized the limits of his handiwork, but he felt, probably correctly, that it was the best that he could accomplish given the formidable obstacles he faced and the limits of his power. He hoped that a League in operation could remedy the treaty's defects. He signed the document in the ornate Hall of Mirrors of the palace at Versailles, the very symbol of the old order he sought to displace, on June 28, 1919, the anniversary of the assassination in Sarajevo that had sparked the conflagration. Exhausted from his labors, still not recovered from a debilitating illness, he hastened home to secure ratification of the treaty. Speaking before Congress on July 10, he issued a ringing challenge: "Dare we reject it and break the heart of the world?"[142]

V

For the next eight months, the nation engaged in yet another great debate over its role in the world. The carnage of the war gave a special urgency to the discussions. They took place in a politically supercharged environment, against the backdrop of strikes and labor violence, race riots, and the notorious Red Scare, with a presidential election just a year away.

The struggle contained many interlocking elements. Wilson had stretched executive powers before and during the war. At one level, it represented a clash between competing branches of government. It was also an intensely personal feud between two men who despised each other. Senator Henry Cabot Lodge had disliked Wilson from the start. By 1915, he called the president, except for James Buchanan, "the most dangerous man that ever sat in the White House" and confided in Roosevelt that he "never expected to hate anyone in politics with the hatred I feel towards Wilson."[143] Lodge set out to defeat and humiliate his archenemy over the League issue. The president was determined not to let his foe thwart his great cause.

It was a fiercely partisan battle. There was no tradition in U.S. politics of bipartisanship on major foreign policy issues. On the contrary, since the Jay Treaty in 1794, parties had fought bitterly over such matters. Raised in the South during the Civil War and Reconstruction, Wilson was a

141. Cohen, *Response to China*, 97, 101; Manela, *Wilsonian Moment*, 194–95, 215–25.
142. John Milton Cooper Jr., *Breaking the Heart of the World: Woodrow Wilson and the Fight for the League of Nations* (New York, 2001), 8–9.
143. William C. Widenor, *Henry Cabot Lodge and the Search for an American Foreign Policy* (Berkeley, Calif., 1983), 173, 208.

dyed-in-the-wool Democrat. Republicans resented his success and were out to get him. They launched fierce partisan attacks on his international-ist proposals even before he went to Paris. The president's own actions helped to ensure greater opposition. He had done little during the war to build a bipartisan coalition behind his proposals. His appeal for the elec-tion of a Democratic Congress in 1918 gave them an opening they readily exploited. He had not taken a leading Republican with him to Paris or consulted closely with the opposition in formulating his peace proposals.

The battle centered around what part the United States should play in the postwar world. It was not primarily a debate between isolationists and internationalists, as it has often been portrayed, although inflated rhetoric on both sides sometimes made it appear so. Rather, it focused on the ex-tent and nature of the commitments the United States should assume. "Internationalism has come," Democratic Senate leader Gilbert Hitchcock observed, "and we must choose what form the internationalism is to take." The debate marked a "great historical moment," historian John Milton Cooper Jr. has concluded, and "elicited a breadth and depth of discus-sion" of fundamental foreign policy issues "that had not risen before and that remained unmatched since."[144]

By the time Wilson returned home, the lines had formed. Polls of news-paper editors and resolutions from state legislatures, the only measures of public opinion at the time, indicated strong support for the president's proposals, but opposition had developed. Progressive internationalists, Wilson's key allies in 1916, were profoundly disillusioned by his wartime acquiescence in the suppression of civil liberties. They were also angered by the "madness at Versailles," Wilson's seeming abandonment of the Fourteen Points and his support for a League that seemed better designed to uphold rather than reform the old order of world politics. Their ranks included some of the nation's leading intellectuals, who provided highly articulate arguments that other opponents used with devastating effect.[145] Ethnic groups poured out resentment against the treatment of their home-lands: German Americans castigated the punitive treaty and the "League of Damnations"; Italian Americans denounced Wilson's opposition to Italy's territorial claims; Irish Americans attacked him for failing even to consider freedom for their homeland and warned that Article X would be

---

144. Cooper, *Breaking the Heart of the World*, 1, 4. The Hitchcock quote is from Thomas Knock, " 'Playing for a Hundred Years Hence': Woodrow Wilson's Internationalism and His Would-be Heirs," paper in possession of author. My thanks to Professor Knock for bringing this quote to my attention.

145. Knock, *End All Wars*, 242–43, 252–59.

used to suppress legitimate nationalist movements and keep U.S. money from being sent to Ireland.[146] Their passions still aflame from the fervor of the Great Crusade against autocratic Germany, nationalists warned in overblown rhetoric that Wilson's League would surrender U.S. sovereignty to a world body.

The issue would be decided in the Senate, where a particularly complex array of forces was at work. The Republicans had a majority of only two. While most of them accepted involvement in some form of international organization—indeed, their party had pioneered such efforts—they were not disposed to accept Wilson's proposals uncritically or hand him a major victory on the eve of a presidential election. Many Republicans resented Wilson's aloofness and arrogance and distrusted what progressive senator George Norris branded his "anxiety for power."[147]

Most important, Republicans differed with the president on key substantive questions. Fourteen Republican senators, the so-called Irreconcilables, opposed entry into the League in any form. They represented different geographical regions and political philosophies and opposed Wilson for various reasons. Some, like Norris, felt the United States should use its influence to promote disarmament and help oppressed peoples. The Nebraskan had originally supported Wilson's peace efforts, but he became disillusioned by the terms of the treaty, particularly Shandong, which he condemned as the "disgraceful rape of an innocent people."[148] He feared the league would perpetuate the status quo and bind the United States to the reactionary great powers. Conservative nationalists like former secretary of state Philander Knox viewed the League as hopelessly utopian and argued that U.S. interests could best be protected by using military power in cooperation with friendly states. Staunch unilateralists like senators Hiram Johnson of California and William Borah of Idaho expressed horror at the thought of surrendering U.S. freedom of action to a world organization. "What we want," Borah asserted, "is . . . a free, untrammeled Nation, imbued again with the national spirit; not isolation but freedom to do as our own people think wise and just."[149]

Most Republicans accepted a League in some form. A group of mild reservationists, mostly from the Middle West and moderate in view and

146. Elizabeth McKillen, "The Corporatist Model, World War I, and the Public Debate over the League of Nations," *Diplomatic History* 15 (Spring 1991), 177–79.
147. Richard W. Lowitt, *George W. Norris: The Persistence of a Progressive, 1913–1933* (Urbana, Ill., 1971), 109.
148. Ibid., 116.
149. Ralph Stone, *The Irreconcilables: The Fight Against the League of Nations* (Lexington, Ky., 1970), 57.

demeanor, sought only minor changes that would protect U.S. sovereignty and clarify and limit obligations under Article X. These Republicans provided the basis for a compromise, but they could not go too far for fear of undercutting their party's interests. A larger group of strong reservationists headed by Lodge raised searching questions about the League. Some doubted it would work: Nation-states could not be expected to transfer sovereignty to an untested international organization and would not send troops to implement Article X unless their vital interests were threatened. Others warned that the League would involve the United States in disputes that were not its concern, undermine its preeminence in the Western Hemisphere, threaten control of domestic issues such as immigration and tariff policy, and take from Congress the power to declare war. While willing to endorse U.S. participation in a League, they wanted stronger reservations to protect its sovereignty and weaken obligations under Article X, which they viewed as an unacceptable departure from U.S. tradition.[150]

The opposition seized the initiative before Wilson returned from Paris. Amply financed by millionaire industrialists Henry Clay Frick and Andrew Mellon, the Irreconcilables launched a nationwide campaign, sending out thousands of pamphlets denouncing the "Evil Thing with a Holy Name" and making hundreds of speeches, many of them appealing to the racial and nationalist prejudices of Americans. Senator Joseph Medill McCormick of Illinois warned that Wilson's superstate would lead to "efficient and economical Japanese operating our street railways...Hindoo janitors in our offices and apartments...Chinese craftsmen driving rivets, joining timbers, laying bricks in the construction of our buildings." Borah claimed that through the League the United States would "give back to George V what it took away from George III."[151]

In the meantime, Foreign Relations Committee chairman Lodge stacked his committee with anti-League Republicans, including six Irreconcilables. His strategy was to stall, allowing opposition to build, and then secure defeat of the treaty or its approval with major reservations. Lodge consumed six weeks reading the massive document aloud to his committee. He invited large numbers of witnesses to testify, most of them hostile, including Lansing, who had broken with Wilson in Paris, and representatives of disgruntled ethnic groups.

150. Link, *Revolution, War, and Peace*, 109–12; Cooper, *Breaking the Heart of the World*, 129–31.
151. Stone, *Irreconcilables*, 82.

Wilson was not uncompromising at the start of the fight. During his trip back from Europe in February, he had met with members of the foreign affairs committees of both houses of Congress, explained his proposals for a League of Nations, and attempted to address objections. While responding firmly to hard-core foes like Lodge, he sought to palliate moderates like Taft. Indeed, he had taken back to Paris for discussion with his counterparts proposals set forth by the former president. But there were limits beyond which he would not go, most notably the obligations under Article X. And at times he breathed defiance to his critics. In a dramatic meeting on August 19, the only time a congressional committee has ever subjected a president to direct questioning, the Foreign Relations Committee met with Wilson at the White House for three hours. The tone was civil, although some senators sought to extract from the president information that could be used against him. But the meeting changed no minds and produced no movement toward compromise.[152]

Facing possible defeat and persuaded—mistakenly—that an outpouring of popular support might move the recalcitrant senators, an already feeble Wilson, against the advice of his wife, Edith (whom he had married in 1915), and his personal physician, decided to take the fight to the nation. McKinley had done the same thing in 1898 to gain backing for the Treaty of Paris. In 1916, Wilson had used a similar trip to secure preparedness legislation. In September, at Columbus, Ohio, he launched a ten-thousand-mile swing through the West. He delivered forty-two speeches in twenty-one days, all without benefit of microphone, and made numerous other public appearances. Speaking to large and generally enthusiastic crowds, he passionately defended the League of Nations—"the only possible guarantee against war," he called it. The alternative, he warned, would be more foreign wars and a national security state that might threaten American democracy. He sought to ease fears about Article X, noting on one occasion that U.S. troops would not be sent to the Balkans or Central Europe—"If you want to put out a fire in Utah, you don't send to Oklahoma for the fire engine." Often, he touched the emotions of his listeners, singling out in the audience mothers of young men killed in battle. He appealed to Americans to accept the responsibilities of world leadership.[153]

By the time the president reached Pueblo, Colorado, on September 25, he was exhausted and suffering from severe headaches. After what turned out to be the last speech of the tour, he collapsed. Reluctantly admitting

152. Thompson, *Wilson*, 223–24.
153. Thompson, *Wilson*, 227–32; Cooper, *Breaking the Heart of the World*, 158–197.

that he could not go on—"I just feel as if I am going to pieces"—he looked out the window of his train and began to weep. A week later, back in Washington, he suffered a massive stroke that left him partially blind and paralyzed on the left side.[154]

During the next two months, the treaty went down to defeat. The speaking tour had been a personal success in many ways, but it changed nothing in the Senate. Wilson could barely function. Although his wife and his physician shielded him from problems and hid from the government and the nation the extent of his incapacity, he could not provide leadership during the most critical stage of one of the most important political struggles in U.S. history. His illness may have made him less disposed to compromise.[155]

Ironically, although an overwhelming majority of senators favored a League in some form, friend and foe combined to keep the United States out. While Wilson was on tour, the Foreign Relations Committee submitted a majority report proposing forty-five amendments and four reservations. Democrats and mild reservationists defeated the amendments, but the votes were close, suggesting the difficulties ahead. In October, Lodge reported the treaty with fourteen reservations—the number was not coincidental! Ratification would depend on acceptance by three of the four Allied powers. The most significant reservations excluded the Monroe Doctrine and domestic issues from League jurisdiction, allowed member nations to withdraw, and severely restricted U.S. obligations under Article X. The United States would accept no obligation to defend the territorial integrity or political independence of any country. United States naval or military forces could not be deployed without the explicit approval of Congress. The reservation effectively gutted the key collective security provision. It exceeded what the mild reservationists wanted, but they went along rather than bolt the party on a crucial issue.[156]

The threat of defeat raised the possibility of some sort of compromise, but Wilson refused to go along. Hitchcock approached him on the eve of the vote and found him unmoveable. He insisted that Article X—what he had called the "king pin of the whole structure"—was essential to the concept of collective security. Without it, there would be no new world order, only a reversion to old-style power politics. He vowed that if the treaty passed with reservations, he would kill it by pocket veto. He seemed almost to welcome defeat. The onus would be squarely on Lodge and the

154. Cooper, *Breaking the Heart of the World*, 189.
155. Ibid., 199–208.
156. Thompson, *Wilson*, 234–35.

Republicans. Believing that the public still supported him, Wilson speculated that the 1920 election could then be made a "great and solemn referendum" on a noble cause. At times during these weeks, he even toyed with running for a third term. He seemed to have lost touch with the political mood of the nation, even with reality.[157]

Wilson's adamancy sealed the fate of the treaty. Before packed chambers, on November 18 and 19, among the most dramatic days in the Senate's storied history, thirty-four Republicans and four Democrats voted for the treaty *with* reservations. The remaining Democrats combined with the Irreconcilables for fifty-five votes against. In a second roll call shortly after, the Irreconcilables joined with the strong reservationists to defeat the treaty as Wilson had presented it, 38 for, 53 against.[158]

The shock of outright defeat generated pressures in Congress and the country for compromise, but they came to nothing. Wilson had begun to recover from the stroke, but his improvement did not bring a return to full leadership or a willingness to compromise. He saw his opponents as seeking to destroy his internationalist program. The qualified commitment they proposed was completely unacceptable to him. A young and healthy Wilson might have salvaged something of his brainchild, but the first stages of recuperation seem to have heightened his defiance. Denouncing the opposition as "nullifiers," he vowed he would "make no compromise or concession of any kind," leaving with Republicans "undivided responsibility" for the fate of the treaty. In a letter to Hitchcock released to the press on March 8, he insisted that any reservation that weakened Article X "cuts at the very heart and life of the Covenant itself," that any agreement that did not guarantee the independence of members was a "futile scrap of paper."[159] The mild reservationists pressed Lodge to compromise, but the Irreconcilables threatened to leave the party and the Massachusetts senator held firm. Some Democrats eventually broke with Wilson, preferring a modified treaty to none at all, but it was not enough. When the final vote was taken on March 19, 1920, the eight dissident Democrats and reservationist Republicans failed by a mere seven votes to get the two-thirds majority needed to pass the treaty with Lodge's reservations.[160]

At the time and since, blame has been variously cast for the outcome of 1919–20. Lodge and other Republicans have been charged with rabid partisanship and a deep-seated personal animus that fueled a determination

157. Ibid., 239–40.
158. Cooper, *Breaking the Heart of the World*, 234.
159. Ibid., 346.
160. Ibid., 362–70.

to embarrass Wilson. It can be argued, on the other hand, that they were simply doing the job the political system assigned to the "loyal" opposition and that the Lodge reservations were necessary to protect national sovereignty. The Democrats have been criticized for standing firmly—and foolishly—with their ailing leader, instead of working with Republicans to gain a modified commitment to the League of Nations. Wilson himself has been accused of the "supreme infanticide," slaying his own brainchild through his stubborn refusal to deal with the opposition. There is much truth here also, although as his defenders have pointed out, he passionately believed that the treaty as he had crafted it was the only way to mend a broken world. There has also been much speculation about the way his mental and physical health influenced his actions of 1919–20, even a psychoanalytic study by no less than Sigmund Freud. The ultimate reason appears much more fundamental. Throughout his career and especially in the Great War, Wilson acted with rare boldness in seeking to reshape a war-torn world and educate Americans to a new leadership role. His aspirations are understandable given the gruesome destruction caused by the war. What he sought may indeed have been necessary to avert the disaster that lay ahead. Still, it is difficult to avoid the conclusion that he aimed too high. In Paris, his European counterparts took the Fourteen Points apart. Americans were simply not ready to undertake the huge break from tradition and assume the sort of commitments he asked of them.[161]

The defeat of Wilson's handiwork leaves haunting if ultimately unanswerable questions. The Wilson of 1919–20 believed that vital principles were at stake in the struggle with Lodge and that compromise would render the League of Nations all but useless. Would a more robust and healthy Wilson—the artful politician of his first term—have built more solid support for his proposals or found a middle ground that would have made possible Senate approval of the treaty and U.S. entry into the League of Nations? Could a modified League with U.S. participation have changed the history of the next two decades?

Whatever the answers to these questions, it is strikingly clear that the Great War and Woodrow Wilson transformed U.S. foreign policy

161. Thomas A. Bailey, *Woodrow Wilson and the Great Betrayal* (Chicago, 1977), 277, coins the phrase "supreme act of infanticide." Thomas Knock's "'Playing for a Hundred Years Hence'" emphasizes Wilson's commitment to principles and the importance of those principles. Sigmund Freud and William C. Bullitt coauthored a vindictive psychobiography entitled *Thomas Woodrow Wilson, Twenty-eighth President of the United States: A Psychological Study* (Boston, 1967). Thompson, *Wilson*, 241–42, offers a broader and more persuasive conclusion.

dramatically. As a result of the war, the United States became a major player in world politics and economics. The more Europe indulged in self-destruction, the greater America's relative power. Americans still did not see themselves as threatened by events beyond their shores and hence remained unwilling to take on the sort of commitments Wilson asked of them. But they began to recognize their changing position in the international system. In trying to establish for his nation a leadership role, Wilson articulated a set of principles that in various forms would guide U.S. foreign policy for years to come. The venerable Elihu Root observed in 1922 that Americans had "learned more about international relations within the past eight years than they had learned in the preceding eighty years." And they were "only at the beginning of the task."[162]

Root spoke with characteristic wisdom and foresight of America's past and future. During its tumultuous first century and a half, the United States had achieved remarkable success in its foreign policy and diplomacy. As a small, vulnerable new nation surrounded by great powers, it used skillful diplomacy and more than a bit of good luck to win its independence, fend off external threats, and acquire a vast expanse of territory. It survived a bloody civil war—and indeed emerged much stronger. And in ensuing decades, it built the world's leading industrial economy and acquired an overseas empire. U.S. intervention in 1917 helped decide the outcome of the Great War. Even in the darkest days of their revolution, American leaders believed it their destiny, in Tom Paine's words, to "begin the world over again." Using ideas first outlined by the Founders, Wilson at the 1919 peace conference sought to construct a new world order based on American principles. In Paris, he butted up against the conflicting interests of allies, at home, the buzz saw of partisan politics, foreshadowing difficulties that lay ahead. The American Century would pose even more formidable challenges.

---

162. Selig Adler, *The Isolationist Impulse: Its Twentieth-Century Reaction* (New York, 1957), 112.

Bibliographical Essay

The literature on the history of U.S. foreign relations is enormous, and I am including in this brief and highly selective listing only those works most valuable to me and most likely to be useful to nonspecialists. The indispensable bibliography is Robert L. Beisner, ed., *American Foreign Relations Since 1600* (2nd ed., 2 vols., Santa Barbara, Calif., 2003). Jerald A. Combs discusses trends in historical writing in *American Diplomatic History: Two Centuries of Changing Interpretations* (Berkeley, Calif., 1983). Michael J. Hogan, ed., *America in the World: The Historiography of American Foreign Relations Since 1941* (New York, 1995) covers recent historiography. Bruce W. Jentleson and Thomas G. Paterson, eds., *Encyclopedia of U.S. Foreign Relations* (4 vols., New York, 1997) is a valuable reference work. The State Department's *Foreign Relations of the United States* series, now publishing on the Nixon years, is an indispensable and splendidly edited collection of documents.

Numerous books set forth broad interpretations. George F. Kennan, *American Diplomacy, 1900–1950* (New York, 1951) outlines this scholar/ diplomat's realist critique of U.S. foreign policy. William Appleman Williams, *The Tragedy of American Diplomacy* (3rd ed., New York, 1972) elaborates the highly influential interpretation of Open Door imperialism. Robert Dallek, *The American Style of Foreign Policy: Cultural Politics and Foreign Affairs* (New York, 1983) stresses domestic politics, and Michael H. Hunt, *Ideology and U.S. Foreign Policy* (New Haven, Conn., 1987) ideology. Walter A. McDougall, *Promised Land, Crusader State: The American Encounter with the World Since 1776* (New York, 1997) is a readable neorealist interpretation. In *Special Providence: American Foreign Policy and How It Changed the World* (New York, 2001), Walter Russell Mead uses key figures to elaborate different approaches to U.S.

foreign policy. Paul Kennedy's *Rise and Fall of the Great Powers* (New York, 1987) places the U.S. ascension to great-power status in the larger context of world politics and especially economics. Surveys of specific topics include Melvin Small, *Democracy and Diplomacy: The Impact of Domestic Politics on U.S. Foreign Policy* (Baltimore, Md., 1996), Ralph B. Levering, *The Public and American Foreign Policy, 1918–1978* (New York, 1978), Ole Holsti, *American Opinion and American Foreign Policy* (Ann Arbor, Mich., 1996), Alexander DeConde, *Ethnicity, Race, and American Foreign Policy* (Boston, 1992), and Alfred E. Eckes, *Opening America's Market: U.S. Foreign Trade Policy Since 1776* (Chapel Hill, N.C., 1995).

There are countless books analyzing U.S. relations with individual countries and regions. Some of the most useful for this study were Warren I. Cohen, *America's Response to China: An Interpretative History of Sino-American Relations* (4th ed., New York, 2000), Charles E. Neu, *The Troubled Encounter: The United States and Japan* (New York, 1975), Walter LaFeber, *The Clash: A History of U.S.-Japan Relations* (New York, 1997), Robert J. McMahon, *The Limits of Empire: The United States and Southeast Asia Since World War II* (New York, 1999), John Lewis Gaddis, *Russia, the Soviet Union, and the United States: An Interpretive History* (rev. ed., New York, 1990), David Schoenbaum, *The United States and the State of Israel* (New York, 1993), Howard F. Cline, *The United States and Mexico* (rev. ed., Boston, 1963), Karl M. Schmitt, *Mexico and the United States, 1821–1973: Conflict and Coexistence* (New York, 1974), Lars Schoultz, *Beneath the United States: A History of U.S. Policy Toward Latin America* (Cambridge, Mass., 1998), Mark T. Gilderhus, *The Second Century: U.S.–Latin American Relations Since 1889* (Wilmington, Del., 2000), Kyle Longley, *In the Eagle's Shadow: The United States and Latin America* (Wheeling, Ill., 2002), Douglas Little, *American Orientalism: The United States and the Middle East Since 1945* (Chapel Hill, N.C., 2002), and Michael B. Oren, *Power, Faith, and Fantasy: America in the Middle East, 1776 to the Present* (New York, 2007).

1776–1815: Max Savelle's *The Origins of American Diplomacy: The International History of Anglo-America, 1492–1763* (New York, 1967) is still valuable for the colonial background. Fred Anderson, *The War That Made America* (New York, 2005) is superb on the French and Indian War. Bradford Perkins, *The Creation of a Republican Empire, 1776–1865* (New York, 1993) and William Earl Weeks, *Building the Continental Empire: American Expansion from the Revolution to the Civil War* (Chicago, 1996) are excellent surveys of the beginnings of U.S. foreign policy.

Books that put Revolutionary War diplomacy in an international setting are Samuel Flagg Bemis, *The Diplomacy of the American Revolution* (rev. ed., Bloomington, Ind., 1957), Richard Van Alstyne, *Empire and Independence: The International History of the American Revolution* (New York, 1965), and Jonathan R. Dull, *A Diplomatic History of the American Revolution* (New Haven, Conn., 1985). Felix Gilbert, *The Beginnings of American Foreign Policy: To the Farewell Address* (New York, 1965) offers stimulating insights not only for the Revolutionary period but also for subsequent U.S. policies. Robert Middlekauff, *The Glorious Cause: The American Revolution, 1763–1789* (rev. ed., New York, 2005) is a richly detailed, readable account of the period. Major studies of key figures include James H. Hutson, *John Adams and the Diplomacy of the American Revolution* (Lexington, Ky., 1980) and Richard B. Morris, *The Peacemakers: The Great Powers and American Independence* (New York, 1965), which highlights John Jay's role. Gordon S. Wood, *The Americanization of Benjamin Franklin* (New York, 2004), Edmund S. Morgan, *Benjamin Franklin* (New Haven, Conn., 2002), and Stacy Schiff, *A Great Improvisation: Franklin, France, and the Birth of America* (New York, 2005) chronicle Franklin's major role. William Stinchcombe, *The American Revolution and the French Alliance* (Syracuse, N.Y., 1969) is a valuable monograph. James M. Merrell, "Declarations of Independence: Indian-White Relations in the New Nation," in Jack P. Greene, ed., *The American Revolution: Its Character and Limits* (New York, 1987) covers a much neglected dimension of the Revolution.

There is no up-to-date study of diplomacy during the Confederation period. The older surveys by Merrill Jensen, *The New Nation: A History of the United States During the Confederation, 1781–1789* (New York, 1950) and Richard B. Morris, *The Forging of the Union, 1781–1789* (New York, 1987), are still useful. Jack N. Rakove, *The Beginnings of National Politics: An Interpretive History of the Continental Congress* (New York, 1997) has much to say about foreign policy. Charles R. Ritcheson, *Aftermath of Revolution: British Policy Toward the United States, 1783–1795* (New York, 1971) provides a British perspective, and Frederick W. Marks III, *Independence on Trial: Foreign Affairs and the Making of the Constitution* (2nd ed., Wilmington, Del., 1986) stresses the importance of foreign policy in the making of the Constitution. David C. Hendrickson, *Peace Pact: The Lost World of the American Founding* (Lawrence, Kans., 2003) puts a new "internationalist" twist on the origins of the Constitution.

Stanley Elkins and Eric McKitrick's *The Age of Federalism: The Early American Republic, 1788–1800* (New York, 1993) provides a richly detailed and eminently readable introduction to the period. Lawrence S. Kaplan analyzes the roles of two key figures in *Alexander Hamilton: Ambivalent Anglophile* (Wilmington, Del., 2002) and *Thomas Jefferson: Westward the*

Course of Empire (Wilmington, Del., 1999). For Hamilton, see also John Lamberton Harper, *Alexander Hamilton and the Origins of American Foreign Policy* (Cambridge, Eng., 2004). Richard H. Kohn, *Eagle and Sword: The Beginnings of the Military Establishment in America* (New York, 1984) is excellent on military policy. Drew R. McCoy, *The Elusive Republic: Political Economy in Jeffersonian America* (Chapel Hill, N.C., 1980) illuminates the connection between landed and commercial expansion in republican ideology. Harry Ammon, *The Genet Mission* (New York, 1973) is the standard account. With somewhat different emphases, Samuel Flagg Bemis, *Jay's Treaty: A Study in Commerce and Diplomacy* (rev. ed., New Haven, Conn., 1962) and Jerald A. Combs, *The Jay Treaty: Political Battleground of the Founding Fathers* (Berkeley, Calif., 1970) analyze that controversial accord. For Anglo-American relations subsequent to the treaty, see Bradford Perkins, *The First Rapprochement: England and the United States, 1795–1805* (Berkeley, Calif., 1967). Samuel Flagg Bemis, *Pinckney's Treaty: America's Advantage from Europe's Distress, 1783–1800* (rev. ed., New Haven, Conn., 1960), remains the best account. The crisis with France is studied in Alexander DeConde, *Entangling Alliance: Politics and Diplomacy Under George Washington* (Durham, N.C., 1958) and *The Quasi-War: The Politics and Diplomacy of the Undeclared War with France, 1797–1801* (New York, 1966), and William Stinchcombe, *The XYZ Affair* (Westport, Conn., 1981).

Jefferson's leadership is evaluated critically in Forrest McDonald, *The Presidency of Thomas Jefferson* (Lawrence, Kans., 1976) and more favorably in Merrill Peterson, *Thomas Jefferson and the New Nation* (New York, 1970), still the best one-volume biography. Robert W. Tucker and David C. Hendrickson, *Empire of Liberty: The Statecraft of Thomas Jefferson* (New York, 1990) is a provocative realist critique. Robert J. Allison, *The Crescent Obscured: The United States and the Muslim World, 1776–1815* (New York, 1995) treats the Barbary wars in the context of American attitudes toward Islam. Peter S. Onuf, *Jefferson's Empire: The Language of American Nationhood* (Charlottesville, Va., 2000) is a stimulating analysis of Jefferson's expansionist vision. Alexander DeConde, *This Affair of Louisiana* (New York, 1976) is the standard study, but see also Sanford Levison and Bartholomew Sparrow, *The Louisiana Purchase and American Expansion, 1803–1898* (Lanham, Md., 2006) and Frank L. Owsley Jr. and Gene A. Smith, *Filibusters and Expansionists: Jeffersonian Manifest Destiny* (Tuscaloosa, Ala., 1997). Steven E. Ambrose, *Undaunted Courage: Meriwether Lewis, Thomas Jefferson, and the Opening of the American West* (New York, 1996) provides a stirring account of that exciting and enormously significant venture. The importance of the Haitian revolution, which cannot be overestimated, is analyzed in David Geggus, *The Impact of the Haitian Revolution in the Atlantic World* (Columbia, S.C., 2001). The origins of the War of 1812 have been one of the more controversial topics in early U.S. diplomatic history. Bradford Perkins, *Prologue to War: England and the United States* (Berkeley, Calif., 1961) is critical of Jefferson and Madison. Roger H. Brown, *The Republic in Peril: 1812* (New York, 1971) stresses party politics, while Reginald Horsman, *The Causes of the War of 1812* (1962) emphasizes sectional issues. The best recent analysis is J.C.A. Stagg, *Mr. Madison's War: Politics, Diplomacy, and Warfare in the Early Republic, 1783–1830* (Princeton, N.J., 1983). Steven Watts, *The Republic Reborn: War and the Making of Liberal America, 1790–1820* (Baltimore, Md., 1987) highlights generational anxieties. Burton I. Spivak, *Jefferson's English Crisis: Commerce, Embargo, and the Republican Revolution* (Charlottesville, Va., 1979) is good on the embargo. Clifford L. Egan, *Neither Peace nor War: Franco-American Relations, 1803–1812* (Baton Rouge, 1983) and Peter P. Hill, *Napoleon's Troublesome Americans: Franco-American Relations, 1804–1815* (Washington, 2005) deal with that sometimes neglected aspect of the larger crisis. The Indian "problem" is discussed from the Indian perspective in R. David Edmunds, *The Shawnee Prophet* (Lincoln, Neb., 1983), and *Tecumseh and the Quest for Indian Leadership* (New York, 1984). Donald R. Hickey, *The War of 1812: A Forgotten Conflict* (Urbana, Ill., 1989) is the best scholarly study. Robert Allen Rutland, *The Presidency of James Madison* (Lawrence, Kans., 1990) provides a balanced analysis of that president's much criticized war leadership. The military aspects are analyzed from a British/ Canadian perspective in George F. G. Stanley, *The War of 1812: Land Operations* (Ottawa, 1983).

1815–1861: Charles Sellers, *The Market Revolution: Jacksonian America, 1815–1846* (New York, 1991) and Daniel Walker Howe, *What Hath God Wrought: The Transformation of America, 1815–1848* (New York, 2007) provide detailed and lively accounts of the period with sharply divergent interpretations. Paul A. Varg, *United States Foreign Relations, 1820–1860* (East Lansing, Mich., 1979) is still useful. Noble Cunningham Jr., *The Presidency of James Monroe* (Lawrence, Kans., 1996), Mary Wilma Hargreaves, *The Presidency of John Quincy Adams* (Lawrence, Kans., 1985) and Donald R. Cole, *The Presidency of Andrew Jackson* (Lawrence, Kans., 1993) are scholarly analyses of these administrations. The activities of Adams, the most important figure in foreign policy, are discussed in the still-valuable Samuel Flagg Bemis, *John Quincy Adams and the Foundations of American Foreign Policy* (rev. ed., New York, 1973) and the more critical William Earl Weeks, *John Quincy Adams and American*

Global Empire (Lexington, Ky., 1992) and James E. Lewis Jr., *John Quincy Adams: Policymaker for the Union* (Wilmington, Del., 2001). Robert V. Remini's *Henry Clay: Statesman for the Union* (New York, 1991) and *The Life of Andrew Jackson* (New York, 2001) are scholarly, highly readable biographies of two key leaders. Bradford Perkins discusses the budding Anglo-American accord in *Adams and Castlereagh: England and the United States, 1812–1823* (Berkeley, Calif., 1964). The Monroe Doctrine not surprisingly has inspired a sizeable literature. The background in terms of Russia can be found in the excellent Norman E. Saul, *Distant Friends: The United States and Russia, 1763–1867* (Lawrence, Kans., 1991) and in terms of Greece and Turkey in James A. Field Jr., *America and the Mediterranean World, 1776–1882* (Princeton, N.J., 1969). Arthur P. Whitaker, *The United States and the Independence of Latin America, 1800–1830* (New York, 1964) remains the standard work. Dexter Perkins's extensive writing on the subject is conveniently summarized in *A History of the Monroe Doctrine* (Boston, 1963). William W. Kaufman, *British Policy and Latin America, 1800–1830* (New Haven, Conn., 1951) is still useful. Ernest R. May, *The Making of the Monroe Doctrine* (Cambridge, Mass., 1976) stresses domestic politics. John M. Belohlavek, *"Let the Eagle Soar!" The Foreign Policy of Andrew Jackson* (Lincoln, Neb., 1985) is an excellent "revisionist" study. John H. Schroeder, *Shaping A Maritime Empire: The Commercial and Diplomatic Role of the American Navy, 1829–1861* (Westport, Conn., 1985) appraises the role of the Navy in nineteenth-century expansion. Theda Perdue and Michael D. Green, *The Cherokee Removal: A Brief History with Documents* (Boston, 1995) compile varied perspectives on this tragic episode.

Administrations from 1841 to 1861 are covered in Norma Lois Peterson, *The Presidencies of William Henry Harrison and John Tyler* (Lawrence, Kans., 1989), Paul H. Bergeron, *The Presidency of James K. Polk* (Lawrence, Kans., 1987), Elbert B. Smith, *The Presidencies of Zachary Taylor and Millard Fillmore* (Lawrence, Kans., 1988), Larry Gara, *The Presidency of Franklin Pierce* (Lawrence, Kans., 1991), and Elbert B. Smith, *The Presidency of James Buchanan* (Lawrence, Kans., 1975). Edward P. Crapol, *John Tyler: The Accidental President* (Chapel Hill, N.C., 2006) is an excellent recent biography of a neglected figure. The classic analysis of Manifest Destiny remains Albert K. Weinberg, *Manifest Destiny: A Study of Nationalist Expansionism in American History* (Baltimore, Md., 1935). Other major works include Frederick Merk, *Manifest Destiny and Mission in American History: A Reinterpretation* (New York, 1966), Thomas Hietala, *Manifest Design: Anxious Aggrandizement in Jacksonian America* (Ithaca, N.Y., 1985), and Anders Stephanson, *Manifest Destiny–American*

Expansion and the Empire of Right (New York, 1995). Reginald Horsman, *Race and Manifest Destiny* (Cambridge, Mass., 1981) is indispensable. For Anglo-American relations in the 1840s, see Reginald Stuart, *United States Expansionism and British North America, 1775–1871* (Chapel Hill, N.C., 1988), Howard Jones and Donald Rakestraw, *Prologue to Manifest Destiny: Anglo-American Relations in the 1840s* (Wilmington, Del., 1997), and Howard Jones, *To the Webster-Ashburton Treaty: A Study in Anglo-American Relations, 1783–1843* (Chapel Hill, N.C., 1977). The crises with Britain over Oregon and Texas are expertly covered in Norman A. Graebner, *Empire on the Pacific: A Study in American Continental Expansion* (rev. ed., Claremont, Calif., 1989) and David M. Pletcher, *The Diplomacy of Annexation: Texas, Oregon and the Mexican War* (Columbia, Mo., 1973). Thomas M. Leonard, *James K. Polk: A Clear and Unquestionable Destiny* (Wilmington, Del., 2001) is an up-to-date study of that leading expansionist. Mexico's perspective can be gleaned from Enrique Krauze, *Mexico: Biography of a Nation-A History of Modern Mexico* (New York, 1997), Gene Brack, *Mexico Views Manifest Destiny, 1821–1846: An Essay on the Origins of the Mexican War* (Albuquerque, N.M., 1975), and William Depalo, *The Mexican National Army, 1822–1852* (College Station, Tex., 1997). K. Jack Bauer, *The Mexican War, 1846–1848* (New York, 1974) is a good military history. John M. Schroeder, *Mr. Polk's War: American Opposition and Dissent, 1846–1848* (Madison, Wisc., 1973) analyzes domestic opposition. Robert W. Johannsen, *To the Halls of the Montezumas: The Mexican War in the American Imagination* (New York, 1987) looks at literature, art, music, and the popular press to show the excitement and expansive vision aroused by the war. The most recent study of the Great United States Exploring Expedition is Nathaniel Philbrick, *Sea of Glory: America's Voyage of Discovery, the U.S. Exploring Expedition, 1838–1842* (New York, 2003). Arthur Power Dudden, *The American Pacific: From the Old China Trade to the Present* (New York, 1992) offers a readable overview of U.S. expansion into the Pacific region. Michael H. Hunt, *The Making of a Special Relationship: The United States and China to 1914* (New York, 1983) provides a good introduction to involvement in China. Jack L. Hammersmith, *Spoilsmen in a "Flowery Fairyland": The Development of the U.S. Legation in Japan, 1859–1906* (Kent, Ohio, 1998) is valuable for the Harris mission and its successors. For filibustering in South and Central America and the demise of Manifest Destiny, see Michael A. Morrison, *Slavery and the American West: The Eclipse of Manifest Destiny and the Coming of the Civil War* (Chapel Hill, N.C., 1997), Joseph A. Stout, *Schemers and Dreamers—Filibustering in Mexico, 1848–1921* (Fort Worth, Tex., 2002), Robert E. May, *Manifest Destiny's Underworld:*

Filibustering in Antebellum America (Chapel Hill, N.C., 2002), and Joseph A. Fry, *Dixie Looks Abroad: The South and U.S. Foreign Relations, 1789–1973* (Baton Rouge, La., 2002).

1861–1901: James M. McPherson, *Battle Cry of Freedom: The Civil War Era* (New York, 1988) is a splendid survey of that epic struggle, Charles P. Roland, *An American Iliad: The Story of the Civil War* (Lexington, Ky., 1991) an excellent shorter study. Robert E. May, ed., *The Union, the Confederacy and the Atlantic Rim* (Lafayette, Ind., 1995) includes essays by leading scholars on the international dimensions of the conflict. The best foreign policy survey is D. P. Crook, *Diplomacy During the American Civil War* (New York, 1975), a shorter version of *The North, the South, and the Great Powers, 1861–1865* (New York, 1974). The Union presidencies are covered in Philip S. Paludan, *The Presidency of Abraham Lincoln* (Lawrence, Kans., 1994) and Albert Castel, *The Presidency of Andrew Johnson* (Lawrence, Kans., 1979). Emory M. Thomas, *The Confederate Nation, 1861–1865* (New York, 1979) and Charles P. Roland, *The Confederacy* (Chicago, 1960) provide insights into southern diplomacy. Charles M. Hubbard, *The Burden of Confederate Diplomacy* (Knoxville, Tenn., 1998) is an up-to-date survey. Frank L. Owsley and Harriet C. Owsley, *King Cotton Diplomacy: Foreign Relations of the Confederate States of America* (2nd ed., Chicago, 1959) is the standard account. Howard Jones's *Union in Peril: The Crisis over British Intervention in the Civil War* (Chapel Hill, N.C., 1992) and *Abraham Lincoln and a New Birth of Freedom: The Union and Slavery in the Diplomacy of the Civil War* (Lincoln, Neb., 1999) are excellent, the latter especially on Lincoln's vision of a slavery-free Union. Doris Kearns Goodwin, *Team of Rivals: The Political Genius of Abraham Lincoln* (New York, 2005) highlights the extraordinary working relationship between the president and his secretary of state. R.J.M. Blackett, *Divided Hearts: Britain and the American Civil War* (Baton Rouge, La., 2001) is very good on British public opinion, which, he argues, was important in determining policy. Saul's *Distant Friends* is excellent on the Russo-American relationship. Martin B. Duberman, *Charles Francis Adams, 1807–1886* (Boston, 1961) and Joseph A. Fry, *Henry S. Sanford: Diplomacy and Business in Nineteenth Century America* (Reno, Nev., 1982) are fine biographies of two key Union diplomats. Post–Civil War expansion is treated in Ernest N. Paolino, *The Foundations of American Expansionism: William Henry Seward and U.S. Foreign Policy* (Ithaca, N.Y., 1973), Ronald J. Jensen, *The Alaska Purchase and Russian-American Relations* (Seattle, Wash., 1975), and Paul Holbo, *Tarnished Expansion: The Alaska Scandal, the Press, and Congress, 1867–1877* (Knoxville, Tenn., 1983).

Not surprisingly, the Gilded Age has drawn only modest attention from historians of U.S. foreign relations. Good surveys are John A. Garraty, *The New Commonwealth, 1877–1890* (New York, 1968) and Mark Wahlgren Summers, *The Gilded Age, or, The Hazard of New Functions* (New York, 1997). Broad studies of U.S. foreign policy, all emphasizing expansionist tendencies, are David Healy, *U.S. Expansionism: The Imperialist Surge in the 1890s* (Madison, Wisc., 1970), Charles C. Campbell, *The Transformation of American Foreign Relations, 1865–1900* (New York, 1976) and Milton Plesur, *America's Outward Thrust: Approaches to Foreign Affairs, 1865–1900* (DeKalb, Ill., 1971). Robert L. Beisner, *From the Old Diplomacy to the New, 1865–1900* (2nd ed., Arlington Heights, Ill., 1986) develops an interesting interpretation of what he calls "old paradigm diplomacy." Walter LaFeber's *The New Empire: An Interpretation of American Expansion, 1860–1898* (Ithaca, N.Y., 1963) and *The American Search for Opportunity, 1865–1913* (New York, 1993) emphasize economic forces, while David M. Pletcher, *The Diplomacy of Trade and Investment: American Economic Expansion in the Hemisphere, 1865–1900* (Columbia, Mo., 1998) questions the existence of a systematic policy of economic expansion. Eric T. L. Love, *Race over Empire: Racism and American Imperialism, 1865–1900* (Chapel Hill, N.C., 2004) is excellent. Ari Hoogenboom, *The Presidency of Rutherford B. Hayes* (Lawrence, Kans., 1988), Justus D. Doenecke, *The Presidencies of James A. Garfield and Chester A. Arthur* (Lawrence, Kans., 1981), Richard E. Welch Jr., *The Presidencies of Grover Cleveland* (Lawrence, Kans., 1988), and Homer E. Socolofsky and Allan B. Spetter, *The Presidency of Benjamin Harrison* (Lawrence, Kans., 1987) cover the administrations. David M. Pletcher, *The Awkward Years: American Foreign Relations Under Garfield and Arthur* (Columbia, Mo., 1962) is a valuable monograph. Edward P. Crapol, *James G. Blaine: Architect of Empire* (Wilmington, Del., 2000) is a fine biography of the period's most colorful and dynamic figure; David F. Healy, *James G. Blaine and Latin America* (Columbia, Mo., 2001) is also useful. Joseph A. Fry, *John Tyler Morgan and the Search for Southern Autonomy* (Knoxville, Tenn., 1992) skillfully covers the career of a southern expansionist. Norman E. Saul, *Concord and Conflict: The United States and Russia, 1867–1914* (Lawrence, Kans., 1996), is excellent on U.S. business activities in Russia. David L. Anderson, *Imperialism and Idealism: American Diplomats in China, 1861–1898* (Bloomington, Ind., 1985) is good on China policy, Stuart Creighton Miller, *The Unwelcome Immigrant: The American Image of the Chinese, 1785–1882* (Berkeley, Calif., 1969) on Chinese in the United States. The missionary movement took off during the Gilded Age. Among the best studies are Jane Hunter, *The Gospel of Gentility: American Women Missionaries in Turn-of-the-Century China* (New Haven, Conn., 1984), Patricia R. Hill, *The World Their Household: The American Women's Foreign Mission Movement and Cultural Transformation, 1870–1920* (Ann Arbor, Mich., 1985), and Sylvia M. Jacobs, ed., *Black Americans and the Missionary Movement in Africa* (Westport, Conn., 1982). Wayne Flynt and Gerald Berkeley, *Taking Christianity to China: Alabama Missionaries in the Middle Kingdom, 1850–1950* (Tuscaloosa, Ala., 1997) emphasizes the missionaries' selling of their work at home.

Eighteen nineties expansionism has drawn a great deal of attention. A readable recent survey of the period by a specialist in U.S. foreign relations is H. W. Brands, *The Reckless Decade: America in the 1890s* (New York, 1998). Interpretive studies include Julius W. Pratt, *Expansionists of 1898: The Acquisition of Hawaii and the Spanish* Islands (Baltimore, Md., 1936), Ernest R. May, *Imperial Democracy: The Emergence of America as a Great Power* (New York, 1961) and *American Imperialism: A Speculative Essay* (New York, 1968), LaFeber, *New Empire* and *Search for Opportunity*, Beisner, *Old Diplomacy to the New*, and Thomas Schoonover, *Uncle Sam's War of 1898 and the Origins of Globalization* (Lexington, Ky., 2003). Emily S. Rosenberg, *Spreading the American Dream: American Economic and Cultural Expansion, 1890–1945* (New York, 1982) covers a broader period and looks at cultural as well as economic and landed expansion. The once lampooned William McKinley has emerged as a key figure, the first modern president. Important works include H. Wayne Morgan, *William McKinley and His America* (Syracuse, N.Y., 1963) and especially Lewis L. Gould, *The Presidency of William McKinley* (Lawrence, Kans., 1980). Robert C. Hilderbrand, *Power and the People: Executive Management of Public Opinion in Foreign Affairs, 1877–1921* (Chapel Hill, N.C., 1981) is excellent on McKinley's innovations in management of the press.

The War of 1898 and the acquisition of overseas empire are analyzed from the perspective of gender in Kristin Hoganson, *Fighting for American Manhood: How Gender Politics Provoked the Spanish-American and Philippine-American Wars* (New Haven, Conn., 1998) and from a more traditional point of view in John L. Offner, *An Unwanted War: The Diplomacy of the United States and Spain over Cuba, 1895–1898* (Chapel Hill, N.C., 1992). *The Crisis of 1898: Colonial Redistribution and Nationalist Mobilization*, edited by Angel Smith and Emma Dávila-Cox (New York, 1998), contains valuable essays on numerous topics. Louis A. Pérez has challenged long-standing ideas about the war and its aftermath in *Cuba Between Empires, 1878–1902* (Pittsburgh, 1983), *Cuba and the*

United States: Ties of Singular Intimacy (2nd ed., Athens, Ga., 1997), *On Becoming Cuban: Identity, Nationality, and Culture* (Chapel Hill, N.C., 1999), and the especially insightful *The War of 1898: The United States and Cuba in History and Historiography* (Chapel Hill, N.C., 1998). David F. Trask, *The War with Spain in 1898* (2nd ed., Lincoln, Neb., 1996) is a good military history, Gerald F. Linderman, *The Mirror of War: American Society and the Spanish-American War* (Ann Arbor, Mich., 1974) a valuable social history. Robert Beisner, *Twelve Against Empire: The Anti-Imperialists, 1898–1900* (2nd ed., Chicago, 1985) is excellent on the debate over imperialism. The United States' involvement in the Philippines is broadly treated in H. W. Brands, *Bound to Empire: The United States and the Philippines* (New York, 1992) and Stanley Karnow, *In Our Image: America's Empire in the Philippines* (New York, 1989). The Philippines War is handled quite critically in Stuart Creighton Miller, *"Benevolent Assimilation": The American Conquest of the Philippines, 1899–1903* (New Haven, Conn., 1982) and more sympathetically in John M. Gates, *Schoolbooks and Krags: The United States Army in the Philippines, 1898–1902* (Westport, Conn., 1973) and Brian McAllister Linn, *The Philippine War, 1899–1902* (Lawrence, Kans., 2000), the most up-to-date and comprehensive study. Glenn Anthony May, *Battle for Batangas: A Philippine Province at War* (New Haven, Conn., 1991), an important local study, raises new questions and offers new interpretations. Richard E. Welch, *Response to Imperialism: The United States and the Philippine-American War, 1898–1902* (Chapel Hill, N.C., 1978) is good on the domestic reaction. Paul A. Kramer, *The Blood of Government: Race, Empire, the United States and the Philippines* (Chapel Hill, N.C., 2006) is an important new study. Thomas J. McCormick, *China Market: America's Quest for Informal Empire, 1893–1901* (Chicago, 1967) and Paul A. Varg, *The Making of a Myth: The United States and China, 1897–1912* (East Lansing, Mich., 1968) debate the role of economic interests in the Open Door policy and the importance of the policy itself.

1901–1921: Judy Crichton, *America 1900: The Turning Point* (New York, 1998) provides an interesting glimpse at turn-of-the-century America. A good recent biography of the major figure is H. W. Brands, *T. R.: The Last Romantic* (New York, 1997). Studies of Roosevelt's foreign policy include Howard K. Beale, *Theodore Roosevelt and the Rise of America to World Power* (New York, 1962), Raymond Esthus, *Theodore Roosevelt and the International Rivalries* (Waltham, Mass., 1970), Frederick Marks, *Velvet on Iron: The Diplomacy of Theodore Roosevelt* (Lincoln, Neb., 1979), Richard H. Collin, *Theodore Roosevelt: Culture, Diplomacy, and Expansionism: A New View of American Imperialism* (Baton Rouge, La.,

1985), and Lewis L. Gould, *The Presidency of Theodore Roosevelt* (Lawrence, Kans., 1991). Surprisingly, there is no good biography of Root, one of the more important figures of twentieth-century America. Richard W. Leopold, *Elihu Root and the Conservative Tradition* (New York, 1954) is useful. Kenton J. Clymer, *John Hay: The Gentleman as Diplomat* (Ann Arbor, Mich., 1975) is good on another important and especially colorful person. The beginning of the modern foreign service is analyzed in Warren Frederick Ilchman, *Professional Diplomacy in the United States, 1779–1939* (Chicago, 1961) and Richard Hume Werking, *The Master Architects: Building the United States Foreign Service, 1890–1913* (Lexington, Ky., 1977). Studies of the peace movement include Charles DeBenedetti, *The Peace Reform in American History* (Bloomington, Ind., 1984), John W. Chambers, ed., *The American Peace Movement and United States Foreign Policy, 1900–1922* (Syracuse, N.Y., 1991), C. Roland Marchand, *The American Peace Movement, 1898–1918* (Princeton, N.J., 1973), and David S. Patterson, *Toward a Warless World: The Travail of the American Peace Movement, 1887–1914* (Bloomington, Ind., 1976). For relations with Britain, see Bradford Perkins, *The Great Rapprochement: England and the United States, 1895–1914* (Berkeley, Calif., 1968) and William N. Tilchin, *Theodore Roosevelt and the British Empire: A Study in Presidential Statecraft* (New York, 1997). For China, see Hunt, *Making of a Special Relationship*, and Delber L. McKee, *Chinese Exclusion Versus the Open Door Policy, 1900–1906* (Detroit, Mich., 1977). Saul's *Concord and Conflict* is good on the conflicts over Jewish immigration and trade, as is Gary Dean Best, *To Free a People: American Jewish Leaders and the Jewish Problem in Eastern Europe, 1890–1914* (Westport, Conn., 1982). Roosevelt's role in the Russo-Japanese War is covered in Raymond A. Esthus, *Double Eagle and Rising Sun: The Russians and Japanese at Portsmouth in 1905* (Durham, N.C., 1988) and Eugene P. Trani, *The Treaty of Portsmouth: An Adventure in American Diplomacy* (Lexington, Ky., 1969). For the expanding U.S. role in the Caribbean, see David F. Healy, *Drive to Hegemony: The United States in the Caribbean, 1898–1917* (Madison, Wisc., 1988) and Richard H. Collin, *Theodore Roosevelt's Caribbean: The Panama Canal, the Monroe Doctrine, and the Latin American Context* (Baton Rouge, La., 1990). International rivalries are covered in Nancy Mitchell, *The Danger of Dreams: German and American Imperialism in Latin America* (Chapel Hill, N.C., 1999) and Thomas D. Schoonover, *Germany in Central America: Competing Imperialism, 1821–1929* (Tuscaloosa, Ala., 1998). Walter LaFeber's *Search for Opportunity* and *The Panama Canal: The Crisis in Historical Perspective* (New York, 1979) are excellent. For U.S. colonial administration, see Pedro A. Cabán,

Constructing a Colonial People: Puerto Rico and the United States, 1898–1932 (Boulder, Colo., 1999) and Glenn Anthony May, *Social Engineering in the Philippines: The Aims, Execution, and Impact of American Colonial Policy, 1900–1913* (Westport, Conn., 1980), which finds little lasting impact from U.S. activities. Emily S. Rosenberg, *Financial Missionaries to the World: The Politics and Culture of Dollar Diplomacy, 1900–1930* (Durham, N.C., 2003) breaks new ground by analyzing the role of the ubiquitous U.S. financial advisers. Cyrus Veeser, *A World Safe for Capitalism: Dollar Diplomacy and America's Rise to World Power* (New York, 2002) is good on that topic.

Two excellent recent studies of the Great War by distinguished military historians are John Keegan, *The First World War* (New York, 2000) and Michael Howard, *The First World War* (London, 2003). The United States during the war period is covered in Robert H. Ferrell, *Woodrow Wilson and World War I, 1917–1921* (New York, 1985), Ellis W. Hawley, *The Great War and the Search for a Modern Order: A History of the American People and Their Institutions, 1917–1933* (2nd ed., New York, 1992), and Robert H. Zieger, *America's Great War* (Lanham, Md., 2000). David M. Kennedy, *Over Here: The First World War and American Society* (New York, 1980; rev. ed., 2004) focuses on the home front. Studies of Woodrow Wilson abound. Arthur Link was his authoritative biographer, and his *Woodrow Wilson: Revolution, War, and Peace* (Arlington Heights, Ill., 1979) summarizes his major arguments on Wilson's foreign policy. Other valuable studies include Kendrick Clements, *Woodrow Wilson, World Statesman* (Boston, 1987) and *The Presidency of Woodrow Wilson* (Lawrence, Kans., 1992), Lloyd E. Ambrosius, *Wilsonian Statecraft: Theory and Practice of Liberal Internationalism During World War I* (Wilmington, Del., 1991), a neo-realist critique, Frederick Calhoun, *Power and Principle: Armed Intervention in Wilson's Foreign Policy* (Kent, Ohio, 1986), which focuses on Wilson's military interventions, Thomas J. Knock, *To End All Wars: Woodrow Wilson and the Quest for a New World Order* (New York, 1992), which provides numerous insights into his ideas and foreign policy, Lloyd C. Gardner, *Safe for Democracy: The Anglo-American Response to Revolution, 1913–1923* (New York, 1987), and John A. Thompson, *Woodrow Wilson* (London, 2002), a balanced and thoughtful survey. Biographies of other key figures include William C. Widenor, *Henry Cabot Lodge and the Search for an American Foreign Policy* (Berkeley, Calif., 1980), Godfrey Hodgson, *Woodrow Wilson's Right Hand: The Life of Colonel Edward M. House* (New Haven, Conn., 2006), and Michael Kazin, *A Godly Hero: The Life of William Jennings Bryan* (New York, 2006), a needed revision of a much maligned secretary of state. Wilson's interventions in Central

America and the Caribbean are critically analyzed in Bruce J. Calder, *The Impact of Intervention: The Dominican Republic During the United States Occupation of 1916–1926* (Austin, Tex., 1984), Hans Schmidt, *The United States Occupation of Haiti, 1915–1934* (New Brunswick, N.J., 1985), Mary A. Renda, *Taking Haiti: Military Occupation and the Culture of U.S. Imperialism* (Chapel Hill, N.C., 2001), Brenda Gayle Plummer, *Haiti and the United States: The Psychological Moment* (Athens, Ga., 1992), and Michael Gobat, *Confronting an American Dream: Nicaragua Under U.S. Imperial Rule* (Durham, N.C., 2005). Wilson's involvement with Mexico is broadly covered in Mark T. Gilderhus, *Diplomacy and Revolution: U.S.-Mexican Relations Under Wilson and Carranza* (Tucson, Ariz., 1977). Robert E. Quirk, *An Affair of Honor: Woodrow Wilson and the Occupation of Veracruz* (Lexington, Ky., 1962) is readable and still useful. Friedrich Katz, *The Life and Times of Pancho Villa* (Stanford, Calif., 1998) is authoritative and much broader in coverage than might appear. John Mason Hart, *Empire and Revolution: The Americans in Mexico Since the Civil War* (Berkeley, Calif., 2002) is a first-rate study by a leading scholar of the Mexican revolution. The United States' entry into World War I was controversial from the outset. Ernest R. May, *The World War and American Isolation, 1914–1917* (Chicago, 1959), based on multi-archival research, and Ross Gregory, *The Origins of American Intervention in the First World War* (New York, 1971) are still valuable on U.S. involvement in the war. John W. Coogan, *The End of Neutrality: The United States, Britain, and Maritime Rights, 1899–1915* (Ithaca, N.Y., 1981) takes a broader approach to neutral rights issues and is more critical of U.S. policy. Anti-war opposition is analyzed in Frances H. Early, *A World Without War: How U.S. Feminists and Pacifists Resisted World War I* (Syracuse, N.Y., 1997).The armistice is covered in Bullitt Lowry, *Armistice 1918* (Kent, Ohio, 1997) and Klaus Schwabe, *Woodrow Wilson, Revolutionary Germany, and Peacemaking, 1918–1919: Missionary Diplomacy and the Realities of Power*, translated by Rita and Robert Kimber (Chapel Hill, N.C., 1985). A readable recent study of the Versailles peacemaking is Margaret Macmillan, *Paris 1919: Six Months That Changed the World* (New York, 2001). Arno J. Mayer, *Politics and Diplomacy at Peacemaking: Containment and Counterrevolution at Versailles, 1918–1919* (New York, 1967) is sweeping in scope and bold in interpretation. Erez Manela, *The Wilsonian Moment: Self-Determination and the International Origins of Anticolonial Nationalism* (New York, 2007) skillfully analyzes the reactions of oppressed people worldwide to Wilson's diplomacy. The problem of Bolshevik Russia at the peace conference is discussed in N. Gordon Levin Jr., *Woodrow Wilson and World Politics: America's Response to War and*

Revolution (New York, 1968). The interventions in North Russia and Siberia are covered in Betty Miller Unterberger, *America's Siberian Expedition: A Study of National Policy* (Durham, N.C., 1959) and David Fogelsong, *America's Secret War Against Bolshevism: U.S. Intervention in the Russian Civil War* (Chapel Hill, N.C., 1996). David W. McFadden, *Alternative Paths: Soviets and Americans, 1917–1920* (New York, 1992) deals with official and informal contacts during these years. Unterberger's *The United States, Revolutionary Russia, and the Rise of Czechoslovakia* (Chapel Hill, N.C., 1989) provides a valuable case study of the application of self-determination. Wilson's 1919–20 defeat is analyzed from various perspectives in Ralph Stone, *The Irreconcilables: The Fight Against the League of Nations* (Lexington, Ky., 1970), Lloyd E. Ambrosius, *Woodrow Wilson and the American Diplomatic Tradition: The Treaty Fight in Perspective* (New York, 1987), and Herbert F. Marguiles, *The Mild Reservationists and the League of Nations Controversy in the Senate* (Columbia, Mo., 1989). An authoritative recent study is John M. Cooper Jr., *Breaking the Heart of the World: Woodrow Wilson and the Fight for the League of Nations* (New York, 2001).

Index

Note: Page numbers in *italics* refer to illustrations.